Multidimensional Perspectives on Principal Leadership Effectiveness

Kadir Beycioglu
Dokuz Eylul University, Turkey

Petros Pashiardis
Open University of Cyprus, Cyprus

A volume in the Advances in Educational
Marketing, Administration, and Leadership
(AEMAL) Book Series

Information Science
REFERENCE
An Imprint of IGI Global

Managing Director:	Lindsay Johnston
Managing Editor:	Austin DeMarco
Director of Intellectual Property & Contracts:	Jan Travers
Acquisitions Editor:	Kayla Wolfe
Production Editor:	Christina Henning
Development Editor:	Erin O'Dea
Typesetter:	Michael Brehm
Cover Design:	Jason Mull

Published in the United States of America by
Information Science Reference (an imprint of IGI Global)
701 E. Chocolate Avenue
Hershey PA, USA 17033
Tel: 717-533-8845
Fax: 717-533-8661
E-mail: cust@igi-global.com
Web site: http://www.igi-global.com

Library of Congress Cataloging-in-Publication Data

Beycioglu, Kadir, 1968-
  Multidimensional perspectives on principal leadership effectiveness / Kadir Beycioglu and Petros Pashiardis, editor.
    pages cm
  Includes bibliographical references and index.
  Summary: "This book combines best practices and the latest approaches in school administration and management by exploring the challenges faced by principals, as well as the impact of new managerial tactics being employed"-- Provided by publisher.
  ISBN 978-1-4666-6591-0 (hardcover) -- ISBN 978-1-4666-6592-7 (ebook) -- ISBN 978-1-4666-6594-1 (print & perpetual access) 1. School principals--United States. 2. Educational leadership--United States. 3. School management and organization--United States. I. Title.
  LB2831.92.B49 2014
  371.2'012--dc23
                                    2014029330

This book is published in the IGI Global book series Advances in Educational Marketing, Administration, and Leadership (AEMAL) (ISSN: 2326-9022; eISSN: 2326-9030)

British Cataloguing in Publication Data
A Cataloguing in Publication record for this book is available from the British Library.

All work contributed to this book is new, previously-unpublished material. The views expressed in this book are those of the authors, but not necessarily of the publisher.

For electronic access to this publication, please contact: eresources@igi-global.com.

Advances in Educational Marketing, Administration, and Leadership (AEMAL) Book Series

Siran Mukerji
IGNOU, India

Purnendu Tripathi
IGNOU, India

ISSN: 2326-9022
EISSN: 2326-9030

MISSION

With more educational institutions entering into public, higher, and professional education, the educational environment has grown increasingly competitive. With this increase in competitiveness has come the need for a greater focus on leadership within the institutions, on administrative handling of educational matters, and on the marketing of the services offered.

The **Advances in Educational Marketing, Administration, & Leadership (AEMAL) Book Series** strives to provide publications that address all these areas and present trending, current research to assist professionals, administrators, and others involved in the education sector in making their decisions.

COVERAGE

- Academic Pricing
- Consumer Behavior
- Technologies and Educational Marketing
- Educational Marketing Campaigns
- Direct Marketing of Educational Programs
- Enrollment Management
- Educational Leadership
- Students as Consumers
- Academic Administration
- Governance in P-12 and Higher Education

IGI Global is currently accepting manuscripts for publication within this series. To submit a proposal for a volume in this series, please contact our Acquisition Editors at Acquisitions@igi-global.com or visit: http://www.igi-global.com/publish/.

Titles in this Series

For a list of additional titles in this series, please visit: www.igi-global.com

Multidimensional Perspectives on Principal Leadership Effectiveness
Kadir Beycioglu (Dokuz Eylul University, Turkey) and Petros Pashiardis (Open University of Cyprus, Cyprus)
Information Science Reference • copyright 2015 • 434pp • H/C (ISBN: 9781466665910) • US $205.00 (our price)

Marketing the Green School Form, Function, and the Future
Tak C. Chan (Kennessaw State University, USA) Evan G. Mense (Southeastern Louisiana University, USA) Kenneth E. Lane (Southeastern Louisiana University, USA) and Michael D. Richardson (Columbus State University, USA)
Information Science Reference • copyright 2015 • 400pp • H/C (ISBN: 9781466663121) • US $205.00 (our price)

Handbook of Research on Teaching and Learning in K-20 Education
Victor C.X. Wang (Florida Atlantic University, USA)
Information Science Reference • copyright 2013 • 1180pp • H/C (ISBN: 9781466642492) • US $525.00 (our price)

Strategic Role of Tertiary Education and Technologies for Sustainable Competitive Advantage
Patricia Ordóñez de Pablos (Universidad de Oviedo, Spain) and Robert D. Tennyson (University of Minnesota, USA)
Information Science Reference • copyright 2013 • 369pp • H/C (ISBN: 9781466642331) • US $175.00 (our price)

Academic Entrepreneurship and Technological Innovation A Business Management Perspective
Anna Szopa (Jagiellonian University, Poland) Waldemar Karwowski (University of Central Florida, USA) and Patricia Ordóñez de Pablos (Universidad de Oviedo, Spain)
Information Science Reference • copyright 2013 • 423pp • H/C (ISBN: 9781466621169) • US $175.00 (our price)

Transnational Distance Learning and Building New Markets for Universities
Robert Hogan (University of the South Pacific, Fiji)
Information Science Reference • copyright 2012 • 332pp • H/C (ISBN: 9781466602069) • US $175.00 (our price)

Cases on Innovations in Educational Marketing Transnational and Technological Strategies
Purnendu Tripathi (IGNOU, India) and Siran Mukerji (IGNOU, India)
Information Science Reference • copyright 2011 • 392pp • H/C (ISBN: 9781609605995) • US $180.00 (our price)

Student Satisfaction and Learning Outcomes in E-Learning An Introduction to Empirical Research
Sean B. Eom (Southeast Missouri State University, USA) and J. B. Arbaugh (University of Wisconsin Oshkosh, USA)
Information Science Reference • copyright 2011 • 472pp • H/C (ISBN: 9781609606152) • US $180.00 (our price)

DISSEMINATOR OF KNOWLEDGE

www.igi-global.com

701 E. Chocolate Ave., Hershey, PA 17033
Order online at www.igi-global.com or call 717-533-8845 x100
To place a standing order for titles released in this series, contact: cust@igi-global.com
Mon-Fri 8:00 am - 5:00 pm (est) or fax 24 hours a day 717-533-8661

Editorial Advisory Board

Table of Contents

Section 1
Understanding the Principalship and Principal Preparation: Management Tasks of
Principals/Time Management for School Principals

Section 2
Understanding School and Teacher Leadership: Theoretical and Organizational
Foundations

Section 3
School Leadership Effects and Student Achievement

Detailed Table of Contents

Section 1
Understanding the Principalship and Principal Preparation: Management Tasks of Principals/Time Management for School Principals

This chapter reports quantitative and qualitative survey data from Turkey as part of a larger International Study of Principal Preparation (ISPP) that examines the utility of principal preparation programs for novice principals in 13 contexts to find out what lessons can be learnt from each context. Conducted in 2010, this study sought responses from 123 principals in their first three years of appointment to identify the challenges they faced and the extent to which they perceived they were adequately prepared to face these challenges. The findings indicated that, although the participants perceived early years of principalship as challenging work, they felt that they were ready for these challenges, despite the emphasis on theory over practice in their preparation programs. Interestingly, principals who reported having greater than 10 years as assistant principals felt less adequately prepared than did their colleagues who had spent fewer than 10 years as assistant principals.

Educational reforms are challenging and difficult with high-stakes political, economic, and societal consequences. A few years ago, the State of Illinois changed its specifications for principal preparation programs so as to better equip its school leaders to meet the contemporary learning needs of children in Illinois. In this chapter, the authors describe and analyze how the revision took place. They look for evidence of constructs presented in theories of change in complex organizations. The findings show that the complexity lens—with a focus on structures, interactions, relationships, and connectedness—contributes to an enriched appreciation of change in complex organizations like universities.

Chapter 3

Georgeta Ion, Universitat Autònoma de Barcelona, Spain
Marina Tomàs, Universitat Autònoma de Barcelona, Spain
Diego Castro, Universitat Autònoma de Barcelona, Spain
Esther Salat, Universitat Autònoma de Barcelona, Spain

School principals have important jobs. To achieve a better understanding of their working lives, this chapter uses the professional diary and timetabling data of all the secondary School Principals, from schools in the Sant Cugat area of Catalonia, Spain. It begins by describing the context of the Catalonian educational system, its leadership and managerial model from a double perspective: on the one hand, the normative requirements; and on the other, the "day-to-day" tasks. The authors adopt a qualitative methodology. The analysis of the school principals' diaries and timetables was conducted over the course of one month (November 2013). The results permit us to relate the day-to-day tasks of the school principal to those tasks identified in the local and national school regulations and in the Education Law. This examination will lead to a better understanding of how the distribution of their activities and their time management is related to these requirements.

Chapter 4

Joaquín Gairín, Universitat Autònoma de Barcelona, Spain
Miren Fernández-de-Álava, Universitat Autònoma de Barcelona, Spain
Aleix Barrera-Corominas, Universitat Autònoma de Barcelona, Spain

Management has an ever-greater need to surpass its mere organisational function. This chapter reviews the current situation in the competency-based training of 10 Latin American countries with two objectives: a) to understand the legislative situations and perspectives of the school management and b) to analyse the activity of the management from the perspective of competencies. This study identifies competencies as personal characteristics linked to successful activity in the workplace. School principals must display personal and procedural competencies, as well as the achievement of actions, objectives, and results. The results allow us to identify the persistence of bureaucratic and administrative model of management, and the emerging roles and competencies that would lead us to a model more focused on people and the community. School principals, as agents of change, would fit into this last perspective, which links us with the most current focus of school management.

Chapter 5

Michael H. Romanowski, Qatar University, Qatar

Launched in 2004, Qatar's massive educational reform, Education for a New Era, has introduced numerous changes to the K-12 educational system forcing school leaders to face challenges and issues in their role of leading and managing the school community. This chapter reports the results of a qualitative research study that examines the critical issues K-12 principals face as they implement educational reform. Using semi-structured interviews, the voices of 20 principals are presented centering on the critical issues that have evolved during the reform and the skills and leadership styles necessary to address these issues that have shaped the Qatari educational reform. Discussion and recommendations are provided to assist educational leaders in similar contexts.

This chapter explores the journey of one Australian primary school that participated in an internationally renowned school revitalization project, where the nature and quality of leadership and results of change are able to achieve and sustain pedagogical reform and improve and enhance student achievement. It illuminates the nature of school change and examines its impact on pedagogy and learning. Through mapping a school's journey and a focus on research, changes in practices such as use of frameworks and protocols, teacher professional learning, and the compilation and use of assessment data are explored, as are the vital roles of both teachers and students in achieving change. The inclusion of students in the process, combined with leadership in school-wide pedagogy, is shown to have contributed to building students' capacity for learning besides that of teachers to implement a school-wide approach to pedagogy.

Chapter 7

Becoming a principal is not an easy feat. Principals are the custodians of a nation's education future and development. As such, they should represent the "best" of the stock of experience, skills, and capacities that exist within a school. Whereas this chapter does not consider the quality of principals in post, it spotlights the perceptions of discrimination in the appointments and promotions process of principals in both Jamaica and England. Drawing on data from a small-scale two-phase exploratory study, the chapter compares the process of appointing principals whilst contrasting the perceived discriminatory practices in getting an appointment as a school principal. The chapter calls for further detailed research of the issues identified and for changes to process for promoting and/or appointing a principal so that actors in the system, teachers especially, can feel confident of putting themselves forward for suitable positions where these may be available.

Section 2
Understanding School and Teacher Leadership: Theoretical and Organizational
Foundations

Chapter 8

Principals' responsibilities for quality in schools and preschools have, during recent years, been accentuated in Sweden. The Swedish Education Act of 2010 can be interpreted as an attempt to improve the orientation and effectiveness of teaching in schools, as it states that education should be based mainly on research and proven experience. The purpose of this chapter is to illuminate how principals understand and relate to the Education Act of 2010. The empirical foundation of the chapter consists of examining policy documents and two surveys sent to principals and heads of preschools. The findings reveal that the principals show different understandings of the term research basis. Three significant areas of manifestations emerged from the data: keeping up to date with new knowledge, building a scientific culture, and practicing research-based knowledge. However, a challenge for principals is to foster a critical evaluative approach to research.

Chapter 9

Anna Kanape-Willingshofer, Linz University, Austria
Sabine Bergner, Graz University, Austria

The chapter discusses the relevance of individual differences in personality traits for the study of school leadership, especially with regard to leadership success. Findings from psychological leadership research have shown that, amongst others, personality, cognitive and emotional intelligence, as well as creativity predict leadership outcome variables. The authors investigate how far these traits have been able to predict leadership success across different occupations and also across different situational and methodological conditions. In addition, studies on the relationship of individual trait differences and school principals' effectiveness are discussed. The chapter shows that individual differences research holds potential for educational leadership, but further studies are needed to draw conclusions about the potential cognitive ability, personality traits, emotional intelligence, as well as creativity hold for predicting leadership success of school principals.

Chapter 10

Savvas Trichas, Open University of Cyprus, Cyprus

The aim of this chapter is to add to our knowledge of the contribution of facial expression to educational leadership perception. Although there is a considerable amount of studies investigating leaders' emotional displays, the majority of this research does not use the sophisticated facial expression coding methods available in other psychological settings. However, research using such sophisticated methods shows that even subtle facial actions can result in significantly different impressions, indicating that credibility of facial expression interpretation might depend on the accuracy of facial expression description (see Rosenberg, 2005). In this chapter, the few leadership studies that have used sophisticated facial expression coding methods are reviewed. On the basis of these studies, it is recommended that educational organizations should be aware of the added value of these methods in order increase research credibility and provide educational leaders with specialized knowledge and skills that could eventually increase their effectiveness.

Chapter 11

Nikoletta Taliadorou, Open University of Cyprus, Cyprus
Petros Pashiardis, Open University of Cyprus, Cyprus

In this chapter, the authors investigate the social skills that school principals ought to exhibit in order to be more effective in the complex environment that characterizes modern schools. Thus, the main aim of this chapter is to provide an in-depth exploration of those social skills that are needed in order for school principals to become more flexible to external and internal requirements and to balance the need for change with stability. Therefore, an attempt is made to investigate the linkages between school leadership, emotional intelligence, political skill, and teachers' job satisfaction, as well as to examine the correlation of emotional and political skills of principals with the job satisfaction of their teachers.

This chapter focuses on teacher leadership, an important variable in the classroom and school improvement literature. The concept of teacher leadership has attracted increased attention in the past two decades. Teachers are assuming more responsibility for leadership roles and functions within schools. Despite the considerable amount of scholarly effort and time spent on investigating the teacher leadership concept, less is known about how it flourishes in the school context and how it relates to classroom and school improvement. Therefore, this chapter tries to shed some light on the teacher leadership concept and discusses its meaning, teacher leadership roles, factors influencing teacher leadership, the relationship between teacher leadership and classroom and school improvement, and future research areas on teacher leadership. Offering a framework for teacher leadership, this chapter is expected to contribute well to the guidance of further research on teacher leadership.

The increasing expectations of the principalship and the intensification of the challenges facing schools today have resulted in the emergence of distributive forms of leadership in schools worldwide. These developments prompted research in schools in South Africa, more specifically in the Soweto region, to inquire if distributed leadership had manifested. Soweto is a township in the Gauteng province of South Africa that is associated with the historic struggle against the apartheid government (pre-1994). A qualitative approach executed by means of focus group interviews was employed at three schools to explore the views of teachers who did not hold formal leadership positions. It was found that distributive leadership had not transpired in the schools that are largely rooted in classical leadership practices. This chapter provides an account of the study while elucidating the concept of distributive leadership and examines the role of formal leaders within a distributive leadership framework.

Chapter 14

This chapter elaborates on the conceptual and empirical bases of continuous change, a newly developing perspective of organizational change, and brings this new perspective of organizational change to the attention of change scholars and practitioners in educational organizations. Rather than conceptualizing change as a macro-level discrete set of actions, continuous change suggests that change is a micro-level process embedded in daily practices of organizational members. However, continuous change and planned change should not be considered as alternatives to each other in the practice of change, since the former represents the informal, unstructured, and emergent side, and the latter represents the formal, structured, and intentional side of change in organizational context. This chapter argues that the success of change largely depends on the artful interplay between continuous change and planned change rather than focusing on the superiority of one perspective over another.

Section 3
School Leadership Effects and Student Achievement

Chapter 15

Jasmin-Olga Sarafidou, University of Thessaly, Greece
Efstathios Xafakos, University of Thessaly, Greece

This chapter presents an empirical investigation on aspects of leadership that may predict a school climate promoting research and innovativeness in Greek primary schools. Specifically, the authors examine principals' innovativeness and dimensions of transformational leadership as possible predictors of innovative school climate and teachers' attitudes towards research. Self-administered questionnaires were completed by 190 primary school teachers. The questionnaire included inventories measuring a) principals' innovativeness, b) three dimensions of transformational leadership style (vision building, individual consideration, intellectual stimulation), c) innovative school climate, and d) different aspects of teachers' attitudes towards educational research. Results demonstrate that principals' innovativeness tends to coexist with a leadership style that is transformational. Moreover, an innovative school climate is very likely to be established if the school principal not only provides stimulation and personalized care for teachers but also s/he acts as a model of innovativeness in school. Nevertheless, principals' innovativeness and a transformative leadership does not also ensure a research orientation in school.

Chapter 16

Andreas Kythreotis, Cyprus International Institute of Management, Cyprus
Panayiotis Antoniou, University of Cambridge, UK

The chapter aims to explore the various models proposed in the literature related with the impact of school leadership on student academic achievement. In doing so, and drawing mainly from the mediate and indirect models, the chapter also discusses the role of various intermediate/moderate variables that facilitate the impact of principal leadership on student-learning outcomes. Results from a qualitative exploratory study that took place in Cyprus are also presented. This study developed a framework of school principals' actions and strategies that teachers considered as effective in relation to improving their quality of teaching and student outcomes. Some of the problems related with measuring the impact of school leadership on student achievement, such as issues of conceptual and operational definitions of school leadership and methodological issues in research design are also elaborated. Finally, implications for policy and practice on school leadership are discussed and suggestions for future research are provided.

The mandated approach to school leadership in South Africa has not produced any significant improvement in learner achievement during the last decade. A new approach to leadership with greater emphasis on the ideographic dimension of school leadership is necessary. This chapter investigates how principals' can utilize emotional competence and instructional leadership to influence learner achievement. The structures of emotional competence and instructional leadership are investigated using factor analysis and Structural Equation Modeling. These constructs are linked to learner achievement data. Intrapersonal emotional competence impacted directly on interpersonal emotional competence, which in turn, impacted directly and indirectly on all the components of instructional leadership. The postulated pathways in the model were statistically significant and substantively meaningful. The model suggested by this research indicates that learner achievement can be influenced in a collaborative way by school leaders via utilization of emotional competence and the four components of instructional leadership.

Preface

AN OVERVIEW OF THE SUBJECT MATTER

School leadership is a key factor in school settings. Principals are expected to lead and manage schools effectively in the face of multiple and varied competing pressures. Thus, they are, out of traditional ways of thinking and working, in search of new ways of managing their schools. While the traditional role of principals and the nature of work are changing, principals sometimes look into new ways to administer a school effectively. This book discusses and addresses the new approaches and challenges that principals are being faced with in managing schools. The authors try to explore issues that address different aspects of school administration and leadership and to examine the impact of new and critical ways of school management and leadership on the principalship. Through the contents of this book, school leadership is once again coming into the forefront under a comparative and multi-perspective lens.

A DESCRIPTION OF WHERE YOUR TOPIC FITS IN THE WORLD TODAY

International or comparative perspectives in Educational Leadership are very much in demand nowadays as the world is becoming more globalized. School principals are increasingly turning towards comparative approaches to leading and managing people in education, expecting to learn from best practice elsewhere. Over the past years, the ideas and the language of theory and practice in Educational Leadership have become increasingly debated and explored in an international and comparative context because of the similarities in the issues we are faced with. More and more we can observe policy borrowing and lending in order to learn from best practices. This book is trying to show how international practices can contribute to improvements in Educational Leadership and to lessons learnt about different cultural and social perspectives with regards to leadership theorizing and its practice. The authors of the various chapters do not only present a synthesis of literature on this topic from their own cultural/contextual perspective but also present different strategies that have been used in their respective countries/areas. This feature makes this book an ideal companion to today's exploration of issues on school leadership worldwide.

A DESCRIPTION OF THE TARGET AUDIENCE

The audience for the book would consist of six primary constituencies: (1) academics who will use the book in their teaching, research, program development, and course improvement; (2) professional development providers who will use the book in their professional development activities; (3) practitioners who serve in primary and secondary education settings who would use the book to inform their practice; (4) policymakers who participate in the accreditation, program approval, licensure/certification, and development of preparation systems; (5) other administrators in different organizational settings, such as state agencies, ministries of education, international organizations, and other agencies may also find this book useful; finally, (6) graduate students will find this book extremely helpful during the course of their studies.

A DESCRIPTION OF THE IMPORTANCE OF EACH OF THE CHAPTERS

In Section 1, "Understanding the Principalship and Principal Preparation: Management Tasks of Principals/Time Management for School Principals," the various chapters tackle with issues of principal preparation and our general understanding of the principalship as it has evolved during our era. Moreover, the various chapters deal with the tasks that school leaders perform within their various contexts from an international and multifaceted perspective.

More specifically, the chapter by Kadir Beycioglu and Helen Wildy, titled "Principal Preparation: The Case of Novice Principals in Turkey," reports quantitative and qualitative survey data from Turkey as part of a larger International Study of Principal Preparation (ISPP) that examines the utility of principal preparation programs for novice principals in 13 contexts to find out what lessons can be learnt from each context. Conducted in 2010, this study sought responses from 123 principals in their first three years of appointment to identify the challenges they faced and the extent to which they perceived they were adequately prepared to face these challenges. The findings indicated that, although the participants perceived early years of principalship as challenging work, they felt that they were ready for these challenges, despite the emphasis on theory over practice in their preparation programs. Interestingly, principals who reported having greater than 10 years as assistant principals felt less adequately prepared than did their colleagues who had spent fewer than 10 years as assistant principals.

In the chapter titled, "Reinventing Principal Preparation in Illinois: A Case Study of Policy Change in a Complex Organization," Angeliki Lazaridou discusses a major piece of reform that took place in the state of Illinois in the USA. As she informs us, some years ago the State of Illinois changed its specifications for principal preparation programs. Following this change, institutes of higher education were asked to reconstruct their programs to reflect the new mandates. Thus, this chapter provides an eloquent description and an in-depth analysis of the changes that took place at the state level. In her analysis, the author looks for evidence of the principles of complexity theory, which she utilizes as her main guiding framework and examines the case of Illinois results through this lens – with a focus on structures, interactions, relationships, connectedness, and strong leadership in an effort to contribute to an enriched appreciation and understanding of how chaos and complexity theories can be used when we try to comprehend the process of change in complex organizations, which deal with principalship preparation programs.

The next chapter is written by Georgeta Ion, Marina Tomàs, Diego Castro, and Esther Salat. Its title is "Analysis of the Tasks of School Principals in Secondary Education in Catalonia: A Case Study." As the authors inform us, in order to achieve a better understanding of school principals' working lives, this study utilized the agendas and timetabling data of all secondary school principals from the schools in the Sant Cugat area in Catalonia, Spain. More concretely, the authors examined the relationship between the time principals spend on different types of activities and the participative model of management. In order to examine this association, they used the context of the Catalonian educational system, its leadership and managerial model from a double perspective: on the one hand, the normative requirements that the system has on its principals, and on the other, the "day-to-day" tasks, as actually executed by these same principals. As the authors conclude, the sample of the 10 centers of secondary education which were examined are representative of the typology of the existing centers in the Sant Cugat region in that these schools are different as regards their way of management which is reflected in the diversity of tasks, timetabling slots, and the time dedicated to the different management tasks. The distribution of these tasks throughout a day (i.e., according to the timetabling slot [morning, evening, or night]) is also very diverse, and, in a sense, the authors cannot determine differences with respect to the ownership but rather to the type of responsibilities which the school principal has in one or another center.

Joaquín Gairín, Miren Fernández-de-Álava, and Aleix Barrera-Corominas wrote the chapter on "Considering Latin American School Management from a Skills-Based Perspective." The authors begin their chapter by reminding us that there is an ever-greater need for management, as a system of encouragement, support, and guidance to pedagogical and institutional activity in order to help schools operate as educational institutions and not merely as organizations. With this in mind, they present the situation of 10 Latin American countries bearing in mind two objectives: a) to understand the situation and perspectives of school management in the countries included in their descriptions; and b) to analyses the practice of these schools' leadership and management through the lenses of competencies seen as personal characteristics linked to successful activity in the workplace. As the authors claim, a school principal must display, in a coordinated manner and according to the professional situation at hand, cognitive, strategic, management, personal, and procedural competencies in order to achieve objectives and results. However, the results of this study provide evidence towards the existence of a bureaucratic and administrative model of management in the various countries explored.

The next chapter deals with a country that is not often in the international literature and provides an in-depth description of "Qatar's Educational Reform: Critical Issues Facing Principals." Written by Michael Romanovski, the chapter begins with Qatar's massive educational reform, Education for a New Era, which was launched in 2004. The reform has introduced numerous changes to the K-12 educational system forcing school leaders to face challenges and issues in their role of leading and managing the school community. Thus, in this chapter, the author reports the results of a qualitative research study that examines the critical issues K-12 principals face as they implement the current educational reform. Using semi-structured interviews, the voices of 20 principals are presented as they describe and analyze the critical issues that have evolved during the reform and the skills and leadership styles necessary to address these issues that have shaped the Qatari educational reform. In closing, the author stresses the fact that educational reform and change take time. He further discusses the knowledge and skills needed to effectively address the critical issues facing principals during educational reform, such as the need for complex understanding of change and resistance, good communication skills, the ability to change one's leadership style by delegating to others, and the importance of having a solid knowledge base about education that can be used to make informed decisions.

The chapter by Shirley O'Neill, titled, "School Leadership and Pedagogical Reform: Building Student Capacity," explores the journey of one Australian primary school that participated in an internationally renowned school revitalization project, where the nature and quality of leadership and results of change are able to achieve and sustain pedagogical reform, and improve and enhance student achievement. The author further illuminates the nature of school change and examines its impact on pedagogy and learning. Through mapping a school's journey and a focus on research, changes in practices, such as use of frameworks and protocols, teacher professional learning, and the compilation and use of assessment data are explored, as are the vital roles of both teachers and students in achieving change. Moreover, the inclusion of students in the process, combined with leadership in school wide pedagogy, is shown to have contributed to building students' capacity for learning besides that of teachers to implement a school-wide approach to pedagogy.

In the chapter titled "Becoming a Principal: Exploring Perceived Discriminatory Practices in the Selection of Principals in Jamaica and England," Paul Miller compares the actual process for appointing principals and contrasts the perceptions of discriminatory practices in both countries. In addition, the researcher questions the effectiveness of principals appointed through perceived discriminatory means. Mapping the organization of schooling in Jamaica and England, the author gives detailed information about the process of appointing a principal. From the data collected for this qualitative exploratory study, the author explores how religious affiliation, political affiliation, and government policies, school and ministry level interference, and social connections have influences on principal appointment. The researcher calls for more research to be done to investigate and unpack the explicit and implicit factors and "issues" involved in the promotion and/or appointment process of school principals in Jamaica and England.

In Section 2, "Understanding School and Teacher Leadership: Theoretical and Organizational Foundations," the authors of the chapters focus on the concept of school leadership and its theoretical roots. They also discuss current issues of leadership in school such as distributive and teacher leadership.

In the chapter titled "Principals' Understanding of Education Based on Research: A Swedish Perspective," Maj-Lis Hörnqvist aims to illuminate how principals understand and relate to the Swedish Education Act of 2010 that can be interpreted as an attempt to improve the orientation and effectiveness of teaching in schools, as it states that education should be based mainly on research and proven experience. From the data gathered through surveys, the author claims that three significant areas of manifestations emerged: keeping up to date with new knowledge, building a scientific culture, and practicing research-based knowledge. The researcher explores the fact that the principals in the study seemed to strive to direct their schoolwork toward research-based activities, primarily by keeping themselves up to date and facilitating discussions among teachers; at the same time, the author stresses that fostering a critical and evaluative approach to research is a challenge for principals. The author discusses that more collaboration between teachers, principals, and researchers could be helpful in integrating scientific knowledge and experience-based knowledge.

Anna Kanape-Willingshofer and Sabine Bergner, in their chapter, titled "Individual Differences and Educational Leadership," discuss the relevance of individual differences in personality traits for the study of school leadership, especially with regard to leadership success, and they investigate how far these traits have been able to predict leadership success across different occupations and also across different situational and methodological conditions. They especially try to understand the relationship between leadership and individual differences, leadership, personality and leadership, cognitive ability and leadership, emotional intelligence and leadership, and creativity and leadership; then, they reflect these concepts into educational leadership. The chapter shows that individual differences research holds potential for educational leadership, but further studies are needed to draw conclusions about the potential cognitive ability, personality traits, emotional intelligence, as well as creativity hold for predicting leadership success of school principals. The chapter also shows that individual differences research holds potential for educational leadership. Moreover, the authors claim that further studies are needed to draw conclusions about the potential cognitive ability, personality traits, emotional intelligence, as well as creativity hold for predicting leadership success of school principals.

The next chapter by Savvas Trichas sheds light on a relatively new research area in educational administration. In the chapter titled "New Methods Exploring Facial Expressions in the Context of Leadership Perception: Implications for Educational Leaders," the author submits that there is a considerable amount of studies investigating leaders' emotional displays; however, the majority of this research does not use the sophisticated facial expression coding methods available in other psychological settings. In the chapter, the author aims to add to our knowledge of the contribution of facial expression to educational leadership perception by reviewing the few leadership studies that have used sophisticated facial expression coding methods and recommends that educational organizations should be aware of the added value of these methods in order to increase research credibility and provide educational leaders with specialized knowledge and skills that could eventually increase their effectiveness.

In the chapter titled "Emotional Intelligence and Political Skill Really Matter in Educational Leadership," Nikoletta Taliadorou and Petros Pashiardis investigate the social skills that school principals ought to exhibit in order to be effective in the complex environment that characterizes modern schools. They discuss that there has been little empirical research examining the linkages between school leadership, emotional intelligence, political skill, and teachers' job satisfaction, and their chapter attempts to investigate the extent to which the emotional and political skills of principals correlate to their leadership styles; further, an attempt is made to examine the correlation of emotional and political skills of principals with the job satisfaction of their teachers. Thus, the first section of this chapter attempts to answer whether emotional intelligence and political skill really matter in educational leadership and notes the need for further research on these areas. In addition, they examine whether emotional intelligence and political skill are two distinct constructs. The second section of the chapter refers to suggestions for educational policy and practice in dealing with the issues arising. The third section deals with the main study conclusions. At the end of the chapter, they suggest that emotional and political skills can be included in the range of characteristics of effective Cypriot principals of primary schools. Such a relationship highlights the social skills of principals as an important area for further research, and in the future, it would be possible to design experimental or interventional procedures for further examination of this field. They also indicate that there is the need for developing appropriate training and development programs for principals, and leadership programs could take into consideration the importance of the "Emotional-Political Capacity" in leadership and thus give future leaders the tools to navigate effectively through both the personal and the structural/political challenges of leadership. They finally conclude that two relatively new concepts in school leadership, emotional intelligence and political skill of the principal, should be subjects of further study, as they have emerged as two very important variables that have direct impact on the leadership radius of the principal and on the job satisfaction of teachers.

Servet Özdemir and Ali Çağatay Kılınç's chapter titled "Teacher Leadership: A Conceptual Analysis" tries to shed some light on the teacher leadership concept and discusses its meaning, teacher leadership roles, factors influencing teacher leadership, the relationship between teacher leadership and classroom and school improvement, and future research areas on teacher leadership. The chapter aims to reveal teacher leadership, teacher leadership roles, factors influencing teacher leadership, the relationship between teacher leadership and classroom improvement, and leadership and school improvement. The authors suggest that various factors, such as organizational culture, time, and the support of the school principal are influential to the development of teacher leadership. Then, they argue that a literature review on teacher leadership shows that it is an important factor influential on student learning and school improvement, and they call for more empirical studies on teacher leadership.

In the chapter titled "Exploring Distributive Leadership in South African Public Primary Schools in the Soweto Region," by Raj Mestry and Suraiya Naicker, the authors employ a qualitative approach executed by means of focus group interviews to explore the experiences and perceptions of teachers at three schools in Soweto, a township in the Gauteng province of South Africa, which is prominent for its association with the historic struggle against the apartheid government. In the chapter, the authors try to portray the historical background of distributive leadership and teacher leadership. They also try to illustrate who the principal is as a facilitator of distributive leadership. Then they elicit teachers' views regarding how leadership is enacted at their schools as well as their perspective of a distributed approach to leadership. The findings indicate that distributive leadership had not transpired in the schools that are largely rooted in classical leadership practices. Hierarchical structures, autocratic leadership styles, and non-participative decision-making hinder distributive leadership practice. Moreover, their study indicates that leadership in the three primary schools investigated is rooted in classical leadership practices and that a shift from autocratic styles of leadership, hierarchical structures, and non-participative decision-making is needed if distributive leadership is to develop. In order to facilitate this shift towards more collegial and collaborative leadership styles, they recommend that the Department of Education provide professional development training programs and workshops for principals and teachers focusing on distributive leadership, which promotes teacher leadership and their role in school transformation. They suggest that principals need to learn that they can, and how to, share power and decision-making with others.

In "Continuous Change in Educational Organizations," the last chapter of this section, Yasar Kondakci, Merve Zayim, and Kadir Beycioglu intend to document criticisms for dominant change understanding and practice both in educational administration and attempt to capture the dynamics of continuous change in educational organizations. Reviewing the criticisms advanced on the theory and practice of the dominant change perspective, the conceptual and empirical studies on alternating change paradigms in a comparative manner, this chapter aims to bring continuous change to the attention of change scholars and practitioners in educational organizations. The chapter depicts basic premises of continuous change, dynamics of continuous change, and leadership in continuous change. Then, the authors try to characterize what continuous change in educational organizations means, ways of achieving continuous change in educational organizations, and continuous change leadership in schools. This chapter suggests that the success of change is largely based on the artful interplay between continuous change and planned change rather than focusing on the superiority of one perspective over another.

The chapters included in the last section of the book, "School Leadership Effects and Student Achievement," examine the ever-present and interesting question of the effects of school leadership, direct or indirect, on student achievement. This area of research is increasingly gaining more importance in our days, especially due to very recent research that shows that indeed school leadership matters.

The chapter on "Transformational Leadership and Principals' Innovativeness: Are They the 'Keys' for the Research and Innovation Oriented School?," by Jasmin-Olga Sarafidou and Efstathios Xafakos, presents an empirical investigation on aspects of leadership that may predict a school climate that helps promote research and innovativeness at the school site. Specifically, the authors examined principals' innovativeness and dimensions of transformational leadership as possible predictors of innovative school climate and teachers' attitudes towards research. As the authors inform us, self-administered questionnaires were completed by 190 primary school teachers representing a convenience sample of school leaders in Greece. The questionnaire included inventories measuring a) principals' innovativeness, b) three dimensions of transformational leadership style (vision building, individual consideration, intellectual stimulation), c) innovative school climate, and d) different aspects of teachers' attitudes towards educational research. The authors claim that an innovative school climate is very likely to be established if the school principal not only provides stimulation and personalized care for teachers but also if s/he acts as a role model of innovativeness in school.

The next chapter is titled "Exploring the Impact of School Leadership on Student Learning Outcomes: Constraints and Perspectives" and is written by Andreas Kythreotis and Panayiotis Antoniou. As the authors explain, the chapter aims to explore the various models proposed in the literature related with the impact of school leadership on student academic achievement. In doing so, and drawing mainly from the mediate and indirect models, the authors discuss the role of various intermediate/moderate variables that facilitate the impact of principal leadership on student learning outcomes. Primarily, the two authors present results from a qualitative exploratory study that took place in Cyprus. As we are informed, this study developed a framework of school principals' actions and strategies that teachers considered effective in relation to improving their quality of teaching and student outcomes. In the remaining of the chapter, some of the problems related with measuring the impact of school leadership on student achievement, such as issues of conceptual and operational definitions of school leadership, and methodological issues in research design are also discussed.

The last chapter in this section was written by Bennie Grobler and is titled "The Relationship between Emotional Competence and Instructional Leadership and their Association with Learner Achievement." The author claims that the mandated approach to school leadership in South Africa has not produced any significant improvement in learner achievement during the last decade. He goes on to make the argument that a new approach to leadership with greater emphasis on the ideographic dimension of school leadership is necessary. Thus, through this chapter, the author investigates how principals can utilize emotional competence and instructional leadership in order to influence learner achievement. These two constructs were linked to learner achievement data. As the author concludes, one of the main findings is that the intrapersonal emotional competence impacted directly on interpersonal emotional competence and on modeling effective teaching while having an indirect influence on all the other components of instructional leadership.

HOW THE BOOK IMPACTS THE FIELD AND CONTRIBUTES TO THE SUBJECT MATTER

Political, economic, cultural, and managerial effects of globalization in organizations have resulted in leaders seeking new and creative ways of thinking and leading styles in schools in order to manage organizations effectively. We emphasized that international or comparative perspectives in educational leadership are very much in demand nowadays as the world is becoming more globalized. People are increasingly turning towards comparative approaches to leading and managing people in education, expecting to learn from best practice elsewhere. Leaders and/or managers in education are encouraged to think of themselves "in an international context, to look to what is happening elsewhere in the world and to learn from each other" (Foskett & Lumby, 2003, p. x). This book, then, aims to explore a range of new approaches and challenges that principals have faced and they have to cope with while managing their schools. Favoring a cross-cultural perspective, the book provides an overview of the current issues that address different aspects of school administration and leadership, and it aims to explore the impact of new and critical ways of school management and principal leadership. The authors of the book are, in a sense, portraying a wide range of issues and approaches in educational administration and leadership from their diverse context, and they are trying to map a global landscape of educational management. The book brings together a wide range of perspectives and examples from educational researchers working in different educational settings in the world. This is the uniqueness of the book that could impact the field, contribute to the subject matter, and make this book project go beyond the dominant and/or orthodox Western thinking in educational management.

Kadir Beycioglu
Dokuz Eylul University, Turkey

Petros Pashiardis
Open University of Cyprus, Cyprus

REFERENCES

Foskett, N., & Lumby, J. (2003). *Leading and managing education: International dimensions*. London: Sage.

Acknowledgment

The editors would like to acknowledge the help of all the people involved in this project and, more specifically, the authors and reviewers who took part in the review process. Without their support, this book would not have become a reality.

First, the editors would like to thank each one of the authors for their contributions. Our sincere gratitude goes to the chapter authors who contributed their time and expertise to this book.

Second, the editors wish to acknowledge the valuable contributions of the reviewers regarding the improvement of quality, coherence, and content presentation of chapters. Most of the authors also served as referees; we highly appreciate their double task.

Kadir Beycioglu
Dokuz Eylul University, Turkey

Petros Pashiardis
Open University of Cyprus, Cyprus

Section 1

Understanding the Principalship and Principal Preparation:
Management Tasks of Principals/Time Management for School Principals

Chapter 1
Principal Preparation:
The Case of Novice Principals in Turkey

Kadir Beycioglu
Dokuz Eylul University, Turkey

Helen Wildy
University of Western Australia, Australia

ABSTRACT

This chapter reports quantitative and qualitative survey data from Turkey as part of a larger International Study of Principal Preparation (ISPP) that examines the utility of principal preparation programs for novice principals in 13 contexts to find out what lessons can be learnt from each context. Conducted in 2010, this study sought responses from 123 principals in their first three years of appointment to identify the challenges they faced and the extent to which they perceived they were adequately prepared to face these challenges. The findings indicated that, although the participants perceived early years of principalship as challenging work, they felt that they were ready for these challenges, despite the emphasis on theory over practice in their preparation programs. Interestingly, principals who reported having greater than 10 years as assistant principals felt less adequately prepared than did their colleagues who had spent fewer than 10 years as assistant principals.

INTRODUCTION

Principal leadership has long been accepted as a key factor in school improvement. Not only are principals expected to manage their schools efficiently in the face of multiple, varied and competing and changing pressures (Thomson, 2009; Wildy & Louden, 2000), they are also required to improve the learning outcomes for students (DiPaola, 2003). The challenges are exacerbated for novice principals, when their previous training has prepared them to be classroom teachers. In some instances principals enter their role without further preparation than being an effective teacher. For novices the challenges are great: for example, understanding what it means to manage the school; what it means to lead the school; and what is to be changed to bring about improvement (Daresh & Arrowsmith, 2003).

This paper presents findings from the International Study of Principal Preparation (ISPP), a collaboration of researchers spanning 13 countries,

DOI: 10.4018/978-1-4666-6591-0.ch001

seeking to identify how principals are prepared, what challenges they face in the beginning of their career as principals, and how adequately they feel prepared to face these challenges. The research reported in this paper was conducted in Turkey in 2010, using an instrument that was generated collaboratively by members of the ISPP (Wildy & Clarke, 2009). We now describe three contexts: a summary of what is known in the literature about the preparation of principals; the historical background of principal preparation in Turkey; and lastly, the ISPP study design and outcomes to date.

Research on Principal Preparation

We then proceed to examine the research literature and provide a summary of what is known about the preparation of principals from a range of educational settings. There is no doubt among educational researchers that context counts. Nowhere is this more evident than in principal preparation. What principals can do depends on what they may do and this in turn is shaped by the authority delegated to them by the educational system in which they work (Middlewood, 2010). Notwithstanding the influence of the local context, there is evidence of cross cultural and cross context benefits accruing from the study of principal preparation (Huber & West, 2002; Lumby et al., 2009; McCarthy, 1999; Smylie & Bennett, 2005).

Two issues are well recognized in the literature: one is the central role of the principal in bringing about improvement in students' learning (second to the role of the teacher); the other is that the work of the principal is changing and becoming increasingly complex and demanding. For example, Hallinger (2005) lists the array of roles for the principal, including setting the vision for improvement; actively engaging in curricular pro-grams; developing staff as both teachers and leaders; modeling not only leading but also learning; and being accountable for students' performance.

Although there is agreement about the difficulty of the job of the principal, the need for preparation prior to appointment and support while in the job (Caldwell, Calnin & Cahill, 2003), there is less agreement about what constitutes appropriate preparation that develops the skills and knowledge to do the job (Blase & Blase, 2004; Bush, 2010; Bush & Jackson, 2002; Foskett & Lumby, 2003; Hallinger & Snidvongs, 2008; Lumby, Walker, Bryant, Bush, & Björk, 2009; McCarthy, 2002). For example, Daresh and Male (2000) are critical of the blend between theory and practice. The importance of internship and mentoring and coaching have been examined by Ackerman, Ventimiglia and Juchniewicz (2002), Browne-Ferrigno and Muth (2004) and Sherman (2008). The role of standards, knowledge, skills and dispositions associated with successful practice in the principalship has been researched by Bellamy et al., (2003), English (2003) as well as Hackman, Walker and Wanat (2006). Others have questioned the usefulness of principal preparation programs (Bush & Oduro, 2006; Gonzaléz, Glassman & Glassman, 2002; Oplatka & Waite, 2010).

Research has reported that novice principals experienced difficulty in some areas of school administration such as leading and managing staff, professional knowledge, use of resources, self-efficacy, school-community relations, issues related to the system they act in, leading learning processes in school, etc. Some research on leadership and preparation of school leaders has also revealed that new principals felt that they were not well prepared for the role of headship and felt that there had been a lack of preparation for the demands of school leadership posts (Caldwell, Calnin & Cahill, 2003).

Context

Principal Preparation in Turkey

Principal preparation has been a feature of the educational landscape in Turkey for more than 40 years. When the Turkish Republic was established in 1923, the country's newly founded parliament undertook significant educational reforms. John Dewey who was invited by the founder of the Turkish Republic, Mustafa Kemal Atatürk, to review educational reform in the country emphasized the importance of programs to prepare principals (Sisman & Turan, 2004). Historically, teaching experience had been the basic requirement for principalship and learning to be a principal was done on the job. It was not until the 1950s that universities in Turkey took up Dewey's advice and set up educational administration departments. By 1965 universities were offering a Bachelor level degree in educational administration for those who had at least five years teaching experience (Isik, 2003a). By 1997, with the decision of the Higher Education Council of Turkey, the departments discontinued accepting students for Bachelor's degrees and have since provided educational administration programs at the postgraduate level.

Turkey's Ministry for National Education (MoNE) has complemented the university-based degree programs with in-service training programs since 1999 (Şimşek, 2004). Despite the collaborative efforts of Turkish universities and the MoNE to provide for the preparation and continuing support of principals, the programs are criticized for being overly reliant on theory (Isik, 2003a), focusing on management at the expense of leadership and failing to address change for improved student learning (Cemaloglu, 2005). The topics covered in the educational administration programs to prepare principals look familiar: public administration; educational administration; school management; democracy and human rights; organizational change and innovation; team work; school-environment relations; social interaction and communication; personnel management; total quality management; teaching and instruction; and school laws and regulations. However, according to the review conducted by Cemaloglu (2005), the programs do not address the need for changes in school management following centrally initiated reforms nor do they highlight the importance of school leadership.

The lack of attention to leadership in principal preparation and support programs is not surprising. Education in Turkey is delivered through a highly centralized system with a heavy reliance on management. The vision for education is provided by the MoNE (Aslan, Beycioglu & Konan, 2008) aligned with the Turkish public administration structure. Private and public schools are hierarchically affiliated to 81 province directorates and 850 district national education directorates. The directorates implement the MoNE's centrally imposed policies and carry out its functions at the local level. However, restructuring of the education system is on the agenda. The 8th Five Year Development Plan and the 15th National Education Council both recommended changes to the MoNE services, such as transferring some authority to the provincial units and local administrations (Wildy et al. 2010).

Not only is restructuring on the agenda, but also the status of university programs in educational administration is being debated (Beycioglu & Donmez, 2007; Şimşek, 2004; Turan, 2004). When selecting principals for positions their university qualification in educational administration is not regarded (Akbaba-Altun, 2007). Teachers without such qualifications are as likely to receive an appointment as those with a qualification. There is media speculation that these appointments result from party political affiliation. More worrying is the recent regulation changing the number of years of experience before being eligible for the assistant principalship from 5 years to 1 year of teaching experience. From there to the principalship is a short step: passing an exam to become a school principal and one year as an assistant principal.

In such a context, there is neither time for principal preparation nor support from employers to provide motivation to those who are interested in a career as a leader to undertake principal preparation at tertiary level. Despite its 40 years of principal preparation provision, Turkey appears to be in the position in which principals learn on the job, through an apprenticeship model of preparation. The limited research on novice principals in Turkey indicates that the early years are difficult times for newly appointed principals. They are challenged by managing the school budget, personnel services, building positive relationships with staff, achieving work/life balance, student services, and supporting the teaching and learning program (Çukadar, 2003; Wildy et al., 2010). Learning on the job does not appear to equip novice principals for the challenges they face. This study is designed to identify what is needed to provide preparation and support for their work as school leaders.

The ISPP

Throughout the last decade's research on principal preparation, and leadership development in general, a number of international studies have emerged. One of these is the International Study of Principal Preparation (ISPP) and it is to this that we now turn to provide a brief summary of its aims, processes and outcomes, since being established in 2004. ISPP involves researchers from Australia, Canada, China, England, Germany, Jamaica, Mexico, New Zealand, Scotland, South Africa, Tanzania, Turkey, and the United States. The study aims to examine the usefulness of principal preparation programs for novice principals in different contexts, for the purpose of identifying lessons that can be learnt from each context (Cowie & Crawford, 2007). The assumption is that preparation programs would be expected to have positive outcomes for those who undertake them. In the ISPP novice principals' views were sought, partly because they were considered most vulnerable to the pressures of the job and partly because the effect of initial preparation fades as principals gain on-the-job experience (Fuller, Young & Baker, 2011).

The ISPP is conceived as a three stage study with an initial mapping of provision in each context, followed by in-depth case studies of novice principals, and concluding with a cross-cultural survey. The mapping is designed to explicate the nature and extent of principal preparation programs in each country. The case studies are designed to elucidate the range and nature of challenges faced by early career principals. The survey is structured to generate data on the extent to which novice principals experience these challenges in different contexts and to the extent to which they feel they are prepared to deal with the challenges they face (Wildy & Clarke 2008; Wildy, Clarke & Slater 2007). It is the ISPP survey that is used as the source of data reported in this paper.

Since 2004, a large number of papers have been published, for example, by Clarke, Wildy and Pepper (2007); Cowie and Crawford (2008); Karstanje and Webber (2008); Nelson, de la Colina and Boone (2008); Slater and colleagues (2007); Slater, Garcia and Gorosave (2008); Onguko, Abdallaa and Webber (2008); Thody, Papanaoum, Johansson and Pashiardis (2007); Webber and Sherman (2008); Webber and Scott (2010); Wildy and Clarke 2008; Wildy and colleagues (2010). Our paper focuses on the principalship in Turkey. In particular the paper examines the challenges faced by novice principals in Turkey and the extent to which novice principals in Turkey feel prepared to deal with these challenges. The findings of this study, like the previous studies, are expected to make a contribution to knowledge base on principal preparation in Turkey and elsewhere.

METHOD

Instrument

Data were gathered using the ISPP survey (Wildy & Clarke, 2009). The survey has four sections. The first section of the survey comprises 10 items on biographical details about the respondents, including the number of years as assistant principals, and information about their schools. There are 21 items in the second section that includes four key categories of challenges facing the novice principals: Dealing with Place; Dealing with People; Dealing with System; and Dealing with Self. The respondents gave two ratings according to a five point Likert scale: first, an evaluation of the extent to which the aspect of principals' work represented by the item was problematic in the first three years of appointment; and second, the extent to which the respondent felt adequately prepared before appointment for this aspect of principals' work (Wildy et al., 2010).

The scale's Turkish adaptation study was conducted by Beycioglu and Ozer (2010). For that earlier study factor analysis revealed that the items clustered according to the design of the survey into four subscales: Dealing with Self (the items were o*rganizing my time; adjusting to the isolation of the position; feeling confident as the school's leader; coping with public visibility in my day-to-day work;* and *achieving a work/life balance*); Dealing with System (the items were *managing paperwork; getting access to system personnel; balancing system imperatives with local needs;* and *acquiring appropriate resources);* Dealing with Place (the items were *understanding the cultures of the community in which my school is located; developing relationships within the community in which my school is located*; and *initiating school improvement)*; and Dealing with People (the items were *dealing with poorly performing staff, building positive relationships with staff,* and *enhancing capacity of staff)*.

The third section of the survey seeks to identify, on 10 bipolar continua, characteristics of the learning experiences of respondents prior to taking up their current principal position. The fourth section contains three open-ended questions about the nature of the preparation received prior to appointment as a principal and the usefulness of that preparation (Wildy & Clarke, 2009).

Participants

In this study purposive sampling was used. The sample consisted of 123 principals appointed within three years of the study – between 2007 and 2010 – who were employed in elementary schools in five different cities in eastern Turkey. Data were collected by June 2010.

Data Analysis

This study aimed to examine the extent to which the novice principals perceived their work challenging and were adequately prepared for these challenges. It was also aimed to find if there were any differences in principals' opinions in terms of vice-principalship experience.

Two types of analyses were used for this paper. One was to compare the means for each of the four sets of items (Dealing with Place; Dealing with People; Dealing with Self; and Dealing with System). The other was thematic analysis of the qualitative responses to the open-ended questions:

1. What other aspects of the principalship were you not well prepared to handle?
2. How useful was the preparation for the principalship that you did experience?
3. Any other comments?

RESULTS

Responses to Clusters of Items

The overall mean of the 123 participants' responses to the items using the 4 point Likert rating scale for the extent to which they found the items problematic was 2.85. The overall mean of the 123 responses to the items using the 4 point Likert rating scale for the extent to which they felt adequately prepared for these aspects of their work, before they were appointed, was 2.90. The congruence of these means suggest that they felt the aspects of their work were as problematic as they felt they were adequately prepared to deal with them.

The variation between responses to the clusters of items was consistent in terms of the problematic nature of the aspects of the job and the extent to which they felt prepared for those aspects. For example, Dealing with People was the most challenging ($\bar{x} = 3.00$) but also the cluster for which they felt best prepared ($\bar{x} = 2.99$). Dealing with Self was the second most challenging cluster ($\bar{x} = 2.91$) and the cluster for which they felt less well prepared ($\bar{x} = 2.86$). The least problematic cluster was Dealing with Place ($\bar{x} = 2.75$).

The aspects of their work for which these novice principals felt they were less well prepared than perceived them challenging appear to relate to interpersonal relationships. Among these were *developing relationships within the community in which my school is located*; *initiating school improvement*; *building positive relationships with staff*; *enhancing capacity of staff*; *feeling confident as the school's leader*; and *coping with public visibility in my day-to-day work*. As a group, these aspects of the principal's work pertain to the principal's leadership, rather than to management or administration.

Differences in Principals' Opinions in Terms of Vice-Principalship Experience

We explored the survey responses from the assistant principal perspective because the assistant principal position is not only a stepping stone to the principalship, but it is also a prerequisite for the principalship. Recent controversy in Turkey surrounds the reduction in from 5 years to 1 year before a teacher is eligible to take up the assistant principal role. Length of experience as an assistant principal was classified as fewer than 9 years and more than 10 years. These results are now presented.

Table 1 shows the means and standard deviations of principals' responses according to their length of time as an assistant principal for the extent to which they found the clusters of aspects of their work problematic: Dealing with Self; Dealing with System; Dealing with Place; and Dealing with People. In relation to Dealing with System and Dealing with Place, novice principals who had fewer than 9 years' experience as assistant principals perceived their work more challenging than principals who had 10 years or more experience.

Table 2 shows the means and standard deviations of principals' responses according to their length of time as an assistant principal for the extent to which they felt they were adequately prepared to deal with the clusters of aspects of their work: Dealing with Self; Dealing with System; Dealing with Place; and Dealing with People. Quite a different picture emerges for the extent to which these novice principals felt adequately prepared when they took up their principal positions. Novice principals who had 10 years or more experience as assistant principals felt that they were less ready for these challenges than principals who had fewer

Table 1. Differences, in terms of assistant principalship experience, from the principals' perceptions regarding the problematic nature of their work

Sub-Scale	Assistant Principalship Experience	N	Mean	SD	F	p	Post-Hoc (LSD)
Dealing with Self	1. Below 9 years	78	15,01	5,36	1,795	,17	
	2. 10-19 years	25	14,84	5,05			
	3. 20 years +	20	12,65	3,29			
	Total	123	14,59	5,06			
Dealing with System	1. Below 9 years	78	11,64	4,16	5,290	,01	1>3
	2. 10-19 years	25	10,48	4,09			
	3. 20 years +	20	8,45	2,89			
	Total	123	10,88	4,11			
Dealing with Place	1. Below 9 years	78	8,79	3,19	4,353	,01	1>3
	2. 10-19 years	25	7,88	2,75			
	3. 20 years +	20	6,65	2,34			
	Total	123	8,26	3,06			
Dealing with People	1. Below 9 years	78	9,44	3,25	1,883	,15	
	2. 10-19 years	25	8,16	3,57			
	3. 20 years +	20	8,35	3,31			
	Total	123	9,00	3,35			

Table 2. Differences, in terms of assistant principalship experience, in principals' beliefs of the adequacy of their preparation the challenges

Sub-Scale	Assistant Principalship Experience	N	Mean	SD	F	p	Post-Hoc (LSD)
Dealing with Self	1. Below 9 years	78	15,87	5,41	7,626	,00	1>2
	2. 10-19 years	25	11,64	6,02			1>3
	3. 20 years +	20	11,90	5,99			
	Total	123	14,36	5,93			
Dealing with System	1. Below 9 years	78	12,73	4,22	4,274	,02	1>2
	2. 10-19 years	25	10,56	4,34			1>3
	3. 20 years +	20	10,20	4,42			
	Total	123	11,87	4,39			
Dealing with Place	1. Below 9 years	78	9,00	3,33	5,458	,01	1>2
	2. 10-19 years	25	6,68	3,41			
	3. 20 years +	20	7,40	3,10			
	Total	123	8,26	3,43			
Dealing with People	1. Below 9 years	78	9,24	3,49	,717	,49	
	2. 10-19 years	25	8,28	3,66			
	3. 20 years +	20	8,90	3,44			
	Total	123	8,99	3,51			

than 9 years' experience as assistant principals for aspects of their work relating to Dealing with Self, Dealing with System, and Dealing with Place.

What Other Aspects of the Principalship Were You Not Well Prepared to Handle?

Now we turn to the second analysis reported in this paper: the qualitative data from responses to each of the three open-ended questions. The first question was: What other aspects of the principalship were you not well prepared to handle? Of the 123 principals who responded to the survey, 56 principals answered this question. The responses were grouped thematically into;

- Difficulty in mastering school law and regulation issues;
- Inadequate resources such as staff and materials;
- Beginning the principalship in a big school;
- Personnel issues;
- Difficulty in coping with changes in technology;
- Difficulty in monitoring the budget of the school; and
- Inadequate graduate education for the principalship.

While some of the responses were not surprising, others were surprising. For example, that novice principals stated that they struggled to master the laws and regulations within which they were required to act is not surprising, given the highly centralized and bureaucratized nature of the education system in which they work. Knowing the laws, policies and regulations is a basic requirement of the principal role in Turkey.

One of the respondents stated:

As the principals, we are supposed to do what the Ministry wants from us. That is why principals in Turkey have to know and be aware of lots of school laws and regulations. A principal should always consult the school laws. This is our responsibility. When I organize, for example, a school-family meeting, there stands the related regulation that I must comply with, or, another example, I should prepare routine school ceremonies in line with the laws.

Similarly, it is not surprising that novice principals responding to the survey identified as problematic *Inadequate resources such as staff and materials.* Schools in Turkey expect families to raise funds to pay for school resources such as photocopying, paper, chalk, markers, school cleaning services. Novice principals are therefore expected to work with their community to acquire some of the basic resources to run their school. For example, one principal expressed:

I do not have full freedom to buy anything for my school because of the centralized budgeting system. Although ministers always declare publicly that families do not have to donate for schools, in schools managers and teachers have to find financial support from families for school expenses.

Nor is it surprising that principals who begin their careers in large schools view smaller, less complex schools as a better context in which to hone their leadership and management schools. Another area that does not seem surprising for novice principals to find difficult is dealing with personnel issue. There is evidence that schools in Turkey experience shortage of staffing especially subject teachers, and guidance services, and that teachers experience low levels of job satisfaction and motivation (Çınkır, 2010), as well as remuneration. Finally, that novice principals in Turkey are challenged by changes in technology is not a surprise. The rapid development of ICT in education settings, the mandatory use of technology to provide information to families coupled with the lack of adequate training programs are factors which exacerbate the challenges for these beginning principals.

That these novice principals expressed difficulty in monitoring the school is surprising, however, given that allocation of at least three quarters of the school's budget is decided centrally (Aytaç, 2004). Perhaps the difficulty principals are experiencing lies in their having no control over the school's budget. It is also surprising that novice principals do not feel they are well prepared for the reality of school life, given that they can avail themselves of both academic qualifications and in-service provided by the MoNE. However, the theory-based programs that are offered do not appear to be meeting the needs of these novice principals.

How Useful Was the Preparation for the Principalship That You Did Experience?

We move now to the second of the open-ended questions in the ISPP survey: *How useful was the preparation for the principalship that you did experience?* Of the 123 survey respondents, 62 principals gave written responses to this question. Of these respondents, 28 stated that the preparation they experienced was not useful for them and 34 stated that the preparation was useful for them. These respondents interpreted 'preparation' broadly, to include both their roles as assistant principals, and their on-the-job training in general. For example, one respondent stated:

I worked as an assistant principal for two years. The formal and informal knowledge and skills that I had gathered from my experience were really useful for my job when I started to work as a principal.

Another respondent stated:

It was my principal's mentorship during my assistant-principalship years that helped me

when I first came into my office as a principal in my new school. Then I thought that a successful leader is the one who does not find the old experience as the only guide for him, but she/he is the one who saves her/his experiences and adds new ones. So, she/he can be helpful, innovative and effective in school.

Those who responded to this question indicated that their on-the-job experience was the most useful preparation for them as a principal.

Any Other Comments?

Finally, the open-ended question: *Any other comments?* was designed to provide an opportunity for respondents to give feedback on any relevant topic. Among the topics mentioned, such as in-service training, graduate courses on school leadership, and collaborative district-wide work with principals, the two most frequently mentioned topics were mentoring; and the theory-practice nexus. For example one principal lamented:

I wish I had taken advantage of my principals before I became a principal. They might have taught me more than I speculated when I was thinking of being a principal. It may be more helpful than anything...

Another principal commented:

There is a big gap between what you learn in graduate courses and what you experience in schools. I mean you learn it [how to administer the school], when you are in it [the school]

In summary, the qualitative data from the open-ended questions show some important disjunctions between formal training and leadership in practice. Novice principals believe they derive more benefit from practice-based informal training such as mentorship than from the theory-based formal programs. Their responses suggest that their experience of the gap between theory and practice is unhelpful in preparing them for their work as principals.

DISCUSSION AND CONCLUSION

This study examined the extent to which the novice principals perceived their work challenging and were adequately prepared for these challenges. Despite contextual differences among ISPP sites, this study revealed parallel findings. For example, aspect of the principals' work such as finance management, dealing with ineffective staff, dealing with law and regulation, dealing with technology were found to present challenges in Mexico, Europe, Australia and China (Slater et al., 2007; Thody et al., 2007; Wildy & Clarke, 2008, 2009; Yan & Enrich, 2009). This study indicated that the participants perceived the early years of principalship to be challenging work, and yet most of the participants affirmed they felt that they were ready for these challenges. However, a number of participants felt that they were not adequately prepared for the challenges. Given the theory-based academic programs and the in-service support provided through a traditional centralized bureaucracy, this finding is not surprising.

This study raises questions about the type of experience that novice principals value as preparation for their role. It appears that the transition from teaching to any role of management is a significant step. Huber refers to the 'practice shock' of this transition (2005, p. 278). Adequate preparation enables aspiring principals to develop a new perspective, one that will reduce the practice shock, according to Huber. However, the step from assistant principal to principal may also represent another significant step. There is evidence (Daresh & Male, 2000), at least in the UK context, which experience in the head of department/deputy head/assistant head role itself can bridge this transition. While all the novice principals in the study have had experience as assistant principals - indeed about one sixth of them had had more than 20 years' experience - this experience did not appear to prepare them for the challenges they faced when newly appointed to the principalship.

There is a second reason for the surprising nature of the finding of this study that assistant principals who had previously spent greater than 10 years in the role felt less prepared than those who had more years in the role. The assistant principal role is as close to the principal role as any role. In some cases the assistant principal deputizes for the principal. In other cases the assistant principal and the principal work as a team. The work of the principal is not only visible to the assistant, close-up, but it is also sometime done by the assistant principal. The role of the assistant principal can be viewed as a dress rehearsal for the role of the principal. Incumbents can be seen to be having a lengthy and intensive practice-based preparation for the principalship. We see from the data in this study that 20 such incumbents have more than 20 years of practice-based experience, as preparation for the principalship. Yet they felt less prepared than those with shorter periods as assistant principals. This is indeed surprising, particularly when most research points to the shortcomings of the highly theory-based, academic postgraduate degrees as preparation for the principalship over the positive effects of on-the-job experience (Daresh & Male, 2000; Kelley & Peterson, 2007; Orr & Orphanos, 2011).

It is likely that, as the years pass, the experience of being an assistant principal merges with life's experiences and become less distinguishable as a source of preparation for novice principals, particularly for those 20 novice principals who had more than 20 years as assistant principals before taking up the principal position.

The irony is that the longer the experience as assistant principal, the less well prepared novice principals feel, and yet it is hard to imagine a more practice-based experience than being an assistant principal, as a preparation for the principalship.

Perhaps the complexity of the challenges are no longer challenging for principals who have had a long 'internship' as an assistant. However, the level of responsibility and accountability for the principal is dramatically increased from that of the assistant principal, and it is possibly this change that the novice principals are responding to when they report feeling inadequately prepared for the principalship. Alternatively, professional fatigue may leave newly appointed principals feeling under-prepared, particularly those who have already spent 20 or more years in the assistant principal role.

We can infer that these highly experienced assistant principals were exhausted when they finally attained the principalship, and they were disappointed by what they found when they finally achieved their goal. It may also be concluded that the heightened responsibility and accountability of the job was more burdensome than they antici- pated (Young & Brewer, 2008). Perhaps, given the highly centralized and bureaucratized nature of the Turkish education system, they were not permitted the discretion or authority to exert the influence they might have wished to exert (Beycioglu & Aslan, 2010). Their leadership aspirations might have outstripped their authority to lead, or their capacity to do so. Perhaps they imagined adopting the 'heroic model of leadership' that does not fit the realities of the contemporary workplace (Bush, 2010). We do not know the reasons for the views of the novice principals who had a long apprentice- ship as assistant principals. The data available from the written responses to open-ended questions of the survey do not provide the reasons for these unexpected findings. Further research is needed using face-to-face interviews to probe principals' experiences and attitudes, especially those who have already spent more than 20 years as assistant principals prior to taking up the principalship.

From the findings of this study it can be inferred that the Ministry and/or the senior personnel in MoNE should rethink the principal preparation policy in Turkey, and put necessary reforms into practice to make the principals able to address the demand of changing schools in a changing context. Those with responsibility for bringing about change in the Turkish educational landscape might consider, in the light of the findings of this study, the importance of leadership development for principals. They might reflect on incorporat- ing the kind of development to improve novice principals' effectiveness via induction programs or mentoring – both prior to appointment and during appointment – that support principals to deal with difficult and underperforming teachers, building the capacity of their staff both as teachers and as leaders, and most importantly, focusing on the ways in which principals, as leaders, can work closely with teachers to improve the learning outcomes of their students.

REFERENCES

Ackerman, R., Ventimiglia, L., & Juchniewicz, M. (2002). The meaning of mentoring: Notes on a context for learning. In K. Leithwood & P. Hallinger (Eds.), Second International handbook of educational leadership and administration (pp. 1133-1161). Dordrecht, The Netherlands: Kluwer Academic.

Akbaba-Altun, S. (2007). Harmonious texture of cultural values and democracy: Patterns of success. In S. Donahoo & R. C. Hunters (Eds.), *Advances in Educational Administration Teaching Leaders to Lead Teachers: Educational Administration in the Era of Constant Crisis* (pp. 77–97). Amsterdam: Elsevier. doi:10.1016/S1479-3660(07)10005-6

Aslan, M., Beycioglu, K. & Konan, N. (2008). Principals' openness to change in Malatya, Turkey. *International Electronic Journal for Leadership in Learning, 12*(8).

Aytaç, T. (2004). School-based budgeting. *Milli Eğitim Dergisi, 162*. Available at http://yayim. meb.gov.tr/dergiler/162/aytac.htm

Bellamy, G. T., Fulmer, C., Murphy, M., & Muth, R. (2003). A Framework for school leadership accomplishments: Perspectives on knowledge, practice, and preparation for principals. *Leadership and Policy in Schools, 2*(4), 241–261. doi:10.1076/lpos.2.4.241.17892

Beycioglu, K., & Aslan, B. (2010). Teacher Leadership Scale: A validity and reliability study. *Elementary Education Online, 9*(2), 764–775.

Beycioglu, K., & Dönmez, B. (2006). Issues in theory development and practice in the field of educational administration. *Educational Administration: Theory and Practice, 12*(47), 317–342.

Beycioglu, K., & Ozer, N. (2010). *Investigating the aspects of principals' work perceived to be most challenging in the early years: Turkish adaptation of a scale.* Paper presented at EYEDDER. Antalya, Turkey.

Blase, J., & Blase, J. (2004). The dark side of school leadership: Implications for administer preparation. *Leadership and Policy in Schools, 3*(4), 245–273. doi:10.1080/15700760490503733

Browne-Ferrigno, T., & Muth, R. (2004). Leadership mentoring in clinical practice: Role socialization, professional development, and capacity building. *Educational Administration Quarterly, 40*(4), 468–494. doi:10.1177/0013161X04267113

Bush, T. (2010). Leadership development. In T. Bush, L. Bell, & D. Middlewood (Eds.), *The principles of educational leadership and management* (2nd ed., pp. 112–132). London: Sage.

Bush, T., & Jackson, D. (2002). A preparation for school leadership: International perspectives. *Educational Management Administration & Leadership, 30*(4), 417–429. doi:10.1177/0263211X020304004

Bush, T., & Oduro, G. K. T. (2006). New principals in Africa: Preparation, induction and practice. *Journal of Educational Administration, 44*(4), 359–375. doi:10.1108/09578230610676587

Caldwell, B., Calnin, G., & Cahill, W. (2003). Mission impossible? An international analysis of headteacher/principal training. In N. Bennett, M. Crawford, & M. Cartwright (Eds.), *Effective educational leadership* (pp. 111–130). London: Paul Chapman Publishing.

Cemaloglu, N. (2005). The Training of school principals and their employment in Turkey: Current situation, possible developments in the future and problems. *Journal of Gazi Educational Faculty, 25*(2), 249–274.

Çınkır, Ş. (2010). Problems of primary school headteachers: Problem sources and support strategies. *Elementary Education Online, 9*(3), 1027–1036.

Clarke, S., Wildy, H., & Pepper, C. (2007). Connecting preparation with reality: Primary principals' experiences of their first year out in Western Australia. *Leading and Managing, 13*(1), 81–90.

Cowie, M., & Crawford, M. (2007). Principal preparation – still an act of faith? *School Leadership & Management, 27*(2), 129–146. doi:10.1080/13632430701237198

Cowie, M., & Crawford, M. (2008). Being a new principal in Scotland. *Journal of Educational Administration, 46*(6), 676–689. doi:10.1108/09578230810908271

Çukadar, C. (2003). *Managerial problems faced by basic education school principals who are appointed according to regulation No 23472.* (M.A. Thesis). Ankara Unv. YOK document center (No. 126487).

Daresh, J., & Male, T. (2000). Crossing the border into leadership: Experiences of newly appointed British head teachers and American principals. *Educational Management Administration & Leadership, 28*(1), 89–101. doi:10.1177/0263211X000281013

Daresh, J. C., & Arrowsmith, T. (2003). *A practical guide for new school leaders*. London: Paul Chapman Publishing.

DiPaola, M. F. (2003). Conflict and change: Daily challenges for school leaders. In N. Bennett, M. Crawford, & M. Cartwright (Eds.), *Effective Educational Leadership* (pp. 143–158). London: Paul Chapman Publishing.

English, F. W. (2003). Cookie-cutter leaders for cookie-cutter schools: The teleology of standardization and the de-legitimization of the university in educational leadership preparation. *Leadership and Policy in Schools, 2*(1), 27–46. doi:10.1076/lpos.2.1.27.15254

Foskett, N., & Lumby, J. (2003). *Leading and managing education: International dimensions*. London: Sage.

Fuller, E., Young, M., & Baker, B. D. (2011). Do principal preparation programs influence student achievement through the building of teacher-team qualifications by the principal? An exploratory analysis. *Educational Administration Quarterly, 47*(1), 173–216. doi:10.1177/0011000010378613

Gonzalez, M., Glassman, N. S., & Glassman, L. D. (2002). Daring to link principal preparation programs to student achievement in schools. *Leadership and Policy in Schools, 1*(3), 265–283. doi:10.1076/lpos.1.3.265.7889

Hackman, D. G., Walker, J. M., & Wanat, C. L. (2006). A professional learning community at work: Developing a standards-based principal preparation program. *Journal of Cases in Educational Leadership, 9*(3), 39–53. doi:10.1177/1555458906289777

Hallinger, P. (2005). The emergence of school leadership development in an era of globalization: 1980-2002. In P. Hallinger (Ed.), Reshaping the landscape of school leadership development (pp. 3-22). Lisse: Swets & Zeitlinger.

Hallinger, P., & Snidvongs, K. (2008). Educating leaders: Is there anything to learn from business management. *Educational Management Administration & Leadership, 36*(1), 9–31. doi:10.1177/1741143207084058

Huber, S. G. (2005). School leader development: Current trends from a global perpective. In P. Hallinger (Ed.), Reshaping the landscape of school leadership development (pp. 273-288). Lisse: Swets & Zeitlinger.

Huber, S. G., & West, M. (2002). Developing school leaders: A critical review of current practices, approaches and issues, and some directions for the future. In K. Leithwood & P. Hallinger (Eds.), Second International handbook of educational leadership and administration (pp. 1071-1102). Dordrecht, The Netherlands: Kluwer Academic. doi:10.1007/978-94-010-0375-9_37

Isik, H. (2003a). A new model for training the school administrators. *Hacettepe Üniversitesi Eğitim Fakültesi Dergisi, 24*, 206–211.

Isik, H. (2003b). From policy into practice: The effects of principalship preparation programs on principal behavior. *International Journal of Educational Reform, 12*(4), 260–274.

Karstanje, P., & Webber, C. F. (2008). Programs for school principal preparation in East Europe. *Journal of Educational Administration, 46*(6), 739–751. doi:10.1108/09578230810908325

Kelley, C., & Peterson, K. D. (2007). The work of principals and their preparation: Addressing critical needs for the twenty-first century. In Jossey-Bass Reader on Educational leadership (pp. 351-402). San Francisco: Wiley and Sons.

Lumby, J., Walker, A., Bryant, M., Bush, T., & Björk, L. G. (2009). Research on leadership preparation in a global context. In M. D. Young, G. M. Crow, J. Murphy & R. T. Ogawa (Eds.), Handbook of research on the education of school leaders (pp. 157-194). New York: Routledge.

McCarthy, M. M. (1999). The evolution of educational leadership preparation programs. In J. Murphy & S.K. Louis (Eds.), Handbook of research on educational administration (pp. 119-140). San Francisco: Jossey-Bass Inc.

McCarthy, M. M. (2002). Educational leadership preparation programs: A glance at the past with an eye toward the future. *Leadership and Policy in Schools, 1*(3), 201–221. doi:10.1076/lpos.1.3.201.7890

Middlewood, D. (2010). Managing people and performance. In T. Bush, L. Bell, & D. Middlewood (Eds.), *The principles of educational leadership and management* (2nd ed., pp. 135–150). London: Sage.

Nelson, S. W., de la Colina, M. G., & Boone, M. D. (2008). Lifeworld or systems world: WShat guides novice principals? *Journal of Educational Administration, 46*(6), 690–701. doi:10.1108/09578230810908280

Onguko, B. B., Abdalla, M., & Webber, C. F. (2008). Mapping principal preparation in Kenya and Tanzania. *Journal of Educational Administration, 46*(6), 715–726. doi:10.1108/09578230810908307

Oplatka, I., & Waite, D. (2010). The new principal preparation program model in Israel: Ponderings about practice-oriented principal training. In A. H. Mormore (Ed.), Global Perspectives on Educational Leadership Reform: The Development and Preparation of Leaders of Learning and Learners of Leadership (pp. 1071-1102). Bingley, UK: Emerald Group Publishing.

Orr, M. T., & Orphanos, S. (2011). How graduate-level preparation influences the effectiveness of school leaders: A comparison of the outcomes of exemplary and conventional leadership preparation programs for principals. *Educational Administration Quarterly, 47*(1), 18–70. doi:10.1177/0011000010378610

Sherman, A. (2008). Using case studies to visualize success with first year principals. *Journal of Educational Administration, 46*(6), 752–761. doi:10.1108/09578230810908334

Şimşek, H. (2004). *Training educational administrators: Comparative cases and implications for Turkey*. Available at: http://www.hasansimsek.net/files/EĞİTİM%20YÖNETİCİLERİNİN%20YETİŞTİRİLMESİ.doc

Sisman, M., & Turan, S. (2004). Education and school management. In Y. Özden (Ed.). Handbook of education and school management (pp. 99-146). Ankara: Pegem A.

Slater, C. L., Boone, M., Nelson, S., De La Colina, M., Garcia, E., & Grimaldo, L. et al. (2007). *El Escalafón y el Doble Turno*: An International Perspective on School Director Preparation. *Journal of Educational Research & Policy Studies, 6*(2), 60–90.

Slater, C. L., Garcia, J. M., & Gorosave, G. L. (2008). Challenges of a successful first-year principal in Mexico. *Journal of Educational Administration, 46*(6), 702–714. doi:10.1108/09578230810908299

Smylie, M. A., & Bennett, A. (2005). What do we know about developing school leaders? A look at existing research and next steps for new study. In W. A. Firestone & C. Riehl (Eds.), *A new agenda for research in educational leadership* (pp. 138–155). New York: Teachers College Press.

Thody, A., Papanaoum, Z., Johansson, O., & Pashiardis, P. (2007). School principal preparation in Europe. *International Journal of Educational Management, 21*(1), 37–53. doi:10.1108/09513540710716812

Thomson, P. (2009). *School leadership: Heads on the block?* London: Routledge.

Turan, S. (2004). Educational administration as a balancing discipline in the human sciences between modernity and post-modernity. *Akdeniz University Journal of Faculty of Education, 1*(1), 1–8.

Webber, C. F., & Scott, S. (2010). Mapping principal preparation in Alberta, Canada. *Journal of Education and Humanities: Theory and Practice, 1,* 75–96.

Webber, C. F., & Sherman, A. (2008). Researching leadership preparation from the inside: A Canadian perspective. In P. Sikes & A. Potts (Eds.), *Researching education from the inside: Investigations from within* (pp. 64–79). Oxon, UK: Routledge.

Wildy, H., & Clarke, S. (2008). Charting an arid landscape: The preparation of novice principals in Western Australia. *School Leadership & Management, 28*(5), 469–487. doi:10.1080/13632430802500106

Wildy, H., & Clarke, S. (2009). Using cognitive interviews to pilot an international survey of principal preparation: A Western Australian perspective. *Educational Assessment, Evaluation and Accountability, 21*(2), 105–117. doi:10.1007/s11092-009-9073-3

Wildy, H., Clarke, S., Styles, I., & Beycioglu, K. (2010). Preparing novice principals in Australia and Turkey: How similar are their needs? *Educational Assessment, Evaluation and Accountability, 22*(4), 307–326. doi:10.1007/s11092-010-9106-y

Wildy, H., Clarke, S. R. P., & Slater, C. (2007). International perspectives of principal preparation: How does Australia fare? Leading and Managing Special Edition, 13(2), 1-14.

Wildy, H., & Louden, W. (2000). School restructuring and the dilemmas of principals' work. *Educational Management and Administration, 28*(3), 173–184. doi:10.1177/0263211X000282006

Yan, W., & Enrich, L. C. (2009). Principal preparation and training: A look at China and its issues. *International Journal of Educational Management, 23*(1), 51–64. doi:10.1108/09513540910926420

Young, M. D., & Brewer, C. (2008). Fear and the preparation of school leaders: The role of ambiguity, anxiety, and power in meaning making. *Educational Policy, 22*(1), 106–129. doi:10.1177/0895904807311299

ADDITIONAL READING

Anderson, M., Kleinhenz, E., Mulford, B., & Gurr, D. (2008). Professional Learning of School Leaders in Australia. In *J. Lumby, J. Crow & P. Pashiardis, International Handbook on the Preparation and Development of School Leaders* (pp. 435–451). London: Routledge.

Barnett, B. G., & O'Mahony, G. R. (2008). Mentoring and coaching programs for the professional development of school leaders. In J. Lumby, G. Crow, & P. Pashiardis (Eds.), *Preparation and Development of School Leaders*. New York: Routledge.

Brundrett, M., Fitzgerald, T., & Sommefeldt, D. (2006). The creation of national programmes of school leadership development in England and New Zealand: A comparative study. *International Studies in Educational Administration, 34,* 89–105.

Bush, T. (2010). Leadership Development. In *T. Bush, L. Bell & D. Middlewood, The Principles of Educational Leadership and Management*. London: Sage.

Bush, T., & Oduro, G. (2006). New principals in Africa: Preparation, induction and practice. *Journal of Educational Administration, 44*(4), 359–375. doi:10.1108/09578230610676587

Crow, G., Lumby, J., & Pashiardis, P. (2008). Introduction: Why an international handbook on the preparation and development of school leaders? In J. Lumby, G. Crow, & P. Pashiardis (Eds.), *Preparation and Development of School Leaders*. New York: Routledge.

Darling-Hammond, L., Meyerson, D., LaPointe, M., Orr, M., & Barber, M. (2010). *Preparing principals for a changing world: Lessons from effective school leadership programs*. New York: John Wiley & Sons.

Fullan, M. (2009). Leadership development: The larger context. *Educational Leadership, 6*(2), 45–48.

Hallinger, P. (2005). The emergence of school leadership development in an era of globalization: 1980-2002. In P. Hallinger (Ed.). Reshaping the landscape of school leadership development. (3-22). Lisse: Swets & Zeitlinger.

Huber, S. (2004). *Preparing School Leaders for the 21st Century: An International Comparison of Development Programs in 15 Countries*. London: Routledge.

Kitavi, M., & Van der Westhuizen, P. C. (1997). Problems facing beginning principals in developing countries: A study of beginning principals in Kenya. *International Journal of Educational Development, 17*(3), 251–263. doi:10.1016/S0738-0593(96)00050-8

Lumby, J., Crow, G., & Pashiardis, P. (2008). *Preparation and Development of School Leaders*. New York: Routledge.

Murphy, J., Young, M. D., Crow, G. M., & Ogawa, R. (2009). *Introduction:Exploring the broad terrain of leadership preparation in education*. New York: Routledge.

Nelson, S. W., De la Colina, M. G., & Boone, M. D. (2008). Lifeworld or systems world: What guides novice principals? *Journal of Educational Administration, 46*(6), 690–701. doi:10.1108/09578230810908280

Orr, M., & Orphanos, S. (2010). How Graduate-Level Preparation Influences the Effectiveness of School Leaders: A Comparison of the Outcomes of Exemplary and Conventional Leadership Preparation Programs for Principals Educational Administration Quarterly, 47 (1), 18-70.

Ribbins, P. (2008). A Life and Career Based Framework for the Study of Leaders in Education. In *J. Lumby, G. Crow & P. Pashiardis, International Handbook on the Preparation and Development of School Leaders* (pp. 61–80). London: Routledge.

Simkins, T., Coldwell, M., Close, P., & Morgan, A. (2009). Outcomes of in-school leadership development work: A study of three NCSL Programmes. *Educational Management Administration & Leadership, 37*(1), 29–50. doi:10.1177/1741143208098163

Wildy, H., & Clarke, S. (2008). Principals on L-plates: Rear view mirror reflections. *Journal of Educational Administration, 46*(6), 727–738. doi:10.1108/09578230810908316

KEY TERMS AND DEFINITIONS

Assistant Principals: Vice principals who are expected to enter school principalship.

Novice Principals: Principals who are in early years of their principalship career.

Principal: Head administrator of a school.

Principal Preparation: Developmental programs/processes that prepare educators for principalship career and that ought to include considerable attention to managing schools effectively. It can also be defined as a process that develops the skills and knowledge to do the job.

The International Study of Principal Preparation (ISPP): ISPP involves researchers from Australia, Canada, China, England, Germany, Jamaica, Mexico, New Zealand, Scotland, South Africa, Tanzania, Turkey, and the United States. The study aims to examine the usefulness of principal preparation programs for novice principals in different contexts, for the purpose of identifying lessons that can be learnt from each context.

The ISPP Survey: is an instrument that is structured to generate data on the extent to which novice principals experience these challenges in different contexts and to the extent to which they feel they are prepared to deal with the challenges they face.

Chapter 2
Reinventing Principal Preparation in Illinois:
A Case Study of Policy Change in a Complex Organization

Angeliki Lazaridou
University of Thessaly, Greece

ABSTRACT

Educational reforms are challenging and difficult with high-stakes political, economic, and societal consequences. A few years ago, the State of Illinois changed its specifications for principal preparation programs so as to better equip its school leaders to meet the contemporary learning needs of children in Illinois. In this chapter, the authors describe and analyze how the revision took place. They look for evidence of constructs presented in theories of change in complex organizations. The findings show that the complexity lens—with a focus on structures, interactions, relationships, and connectedness—contributes to an enriched appreciation of change in complex organizations like universities.

INTRODUCTION

Contemporary institutions of higher education are under great pressure to change how they operate. These pressures come from such vectors as increasing globalization, government initiatives, fiscal retrenchments and reforms, and critiques of the quality of students' learning experience (e.g., Clark, 2004; Meister-Scheytt & Scheytt, 2005). However, effecting change in universities is difficult, particularly because of their complexity: they are professional service organizations that have complex governance structures, high workloads, and no single center responsible for implementing organization wide change initiatives (Clark, 2004; De la Harpe & Thomas, 2009; Eckel & Keza, 2003 Meister-Scheytt & Scheytt, 2005;). Moreover, the professionals within them vary in their training, interests, and methods of working; hence faculties and programs of study operate in various ways and the differences between groups within the university are likely to be significant. Stacey (2000, p. 42) put it this way:

DOI: 10.4018/978-1-4666-6591-0.ch002

[A university is] a complex and adaptive system [that] consists of a large number of agents, each of which behaves according to its own principles of local interaction. No individual agent (e.g., teacher or administrator), or group of agents (e.g., teaching team or department) determines the patterns of behavior that the system as a whole displays or how these patterns evolve, and neither does anything outside the system.

Managing such diversity is a complex business (Clark, 2004; Meister-Scheytt & Scheytt, 2005) and effecting change is even more challenging. To compound the challenge, attempts to change universities must often be undertaken at times of budget cuts and with unclear objectives (Meister-Scheytt & Scheytt, 2005; Shattock, 2005).

The literature about change points to the conclusion that administrators in complex settings cannot expect to control change; at best they can guide it (Fullan, 2007). In addition, if change is to be effective and lasting it should involve all stakeholders, and it requires willingness on the part of stakeholders to accept the need for change and to change the way they do things (de la Harpe & Radloff, 2008). Further, recent developments in leadership theory point to the importance of dispersed leadership in complex situations – where problems, goals, and means are ambiguous.

A Study: Focus, Purpose, Methodology, and Method

A few years ago the State of Illinois initiated a complex process for reforming its principal preparation programs (PPPs) with the collaboration and cooperation of all interested parties. By studying the change process with complexity theory, we may gain new insights about how major reforms take place, the challenges that surface during the change process, and how they are best resolved.

The research reported here was directed at this general objective, to be attained through the pursuit of two general purposes. The first was to describe how the State of Illinois changed its prescriptions for principal preparation programs (PPPs). The second was to analyze the change process through the lenses of complexity and change theories, with the aim of determining to what extent the case evidenced constructs from the relevant theoretical literature.

In service to the first objective I elected to develop an ethnographic case study. Ethnographers look for patterns, describe local relationships (formal and informal), understandings and meanings (tacit and explicit), and try to make sense of a place and a case in relation to the entire social setting and all social relationships (Stake, 2000; Yin, 2009). The ethnographer is socially and physically immersed in the case to accumulate local knowledge. Yet, in doing so, the ethnographer must be constantly self-critical and reflexive to ensure an authentic analytical description and interpretation of the case. For my study I spent four months in Illinois as a Fulbright Scholar, engaged in formal and informal meetings with state officials while housed in the Department of Educational Administration and Foundations at Illinois State University in Bloomington/Normal. The data used for this chapter derived from semi-structured interviews with key informants who were involved in designing and implementing the new protocols, observations of meetings, and analysis of relevant documentation.

In connection with my second objective I elected to use complexity theory, a relatively new way of studying organizations. Complexity theory depicts organizations as complex adaptive systems that have the capacity to learn new behaviors (Lawrimore, 2005). Complexity theory provides insights into the dynamics of human organizations, focusing on processes rather than structures. Especially when it comes to changing parts of an organization, focusing on flexible, open, and more fluid processes and structures helps the organization adapt more quickly and increases the probability of success. As universities around the world face increasing demands to restructure their programs, processes, and their ways of operating, understanding the dynamics of change through complexity theory is significant for policy-makers as well as individuals in the organizations who are currently faced with change challenges or who will likely deal with major changes in the future.

The rest of this chapter comprises three sections. The first contextualizes my case study, providing information about Illinois' education system; the processes used to arrive at new prescriptions for PPPs and to disseminate them throughout the State; and the prescriptions themselves. The second presents my analysis of the State's change initiative using concepts from complexity and change theories; hence it begins with highlights of said theories. In the third section I discuss the utility of the complexity perspective in analyzing change in a university setting and the implications of my findings for current understandings about the improvement of principal preparation.

CONTEXT

The Education System of Illinois

Illinois is the fifth most populated state in Midwestern United States (with over 12 million people) and it is the 25th most extensive. With Chicago in the northeast, small industrial cities and great agricultural productivity in central and northern Illinois, and natural resources like coal, timber, and petroleum in the south, Illinois has a diverse economic base and is a major transportation hub. It is often noted as a microcosm of the entire country (Illinois, nd).

Illinois' education is a three-tier system, with both public and private schools. It is structured as shown in Table 1.

Nearly half of the two million students enrolled in Illinois public schools are racially and ethnically diverse. Almost half of students enrolled in K-12 (49%) are low-income. About one in ten is identified as an English-language learner – meaning they have not yet passed an English-competency exam. And 14% of Illinois students enrolled in kindergarten through high school are identified as having special learning needs (Advance Illinois, n.d.).

The Illinois School Board of Education (ISBE) administers public education in the state. ISBE is autonomous of the governor and the state legislature. Local municipalities and their respective school districts operate individual public schools. The ISBE also makes recommendations to state leaders concerning education spending and policies.

Illinois has eleven National Universities and more than twenty additional accredited four-year universities, both public and private, and dozens of small liberal arts colleges. Additionally, Illinois supports 49 public community colleges. Under the

Table 1. Structure of education system in Illinois state

Early Childhood Education	Kindergarten-Grade 12	Postsecondary Education
Preschool for all (0-4) State funded	Ages 5-17 (Funded locally, by the State, and Federally)	Ages 18-24
Head start programs Federally funded	Public	Public 2 years (Community Colleges)
Home visits State funded Federally funded	Public Charter	Public 4 years (Universities)
Private	Private	Private not-for-profit
		Private for-profit

newly mandated law for PPPs, not only public and private universities, but also not-for-profit entities approved by the State Board of Education may offer principal preparation programs. This has had the effect of increasing the pool of organizations that are involved in the new principal preparation programs.

The Illinois Board of Higher Education (IBHE) coordinates Illinois' system of colleges and universities. Board members are appointed by the Governor, with the advice and consent of the Senate.

Preparation of Principals in the US: Alarm and Response in Illinois

The literature on school leadership postulates that effective schools depend to a large extent upon the skills, knowledge, and dispositions of well-prepared, competent principals (Seashore Louis, Leithwood, Wahlstrom, & Anderson, 2010). For example, we have Leithwood, Louis, Anderson and Wahlstrom (2004, p. 5) stating: "Leadership is second only to classroom instruction among all school-related factors that contribute to what students learn at school". While teachers have a direct impact on student learning through classroom practice, the principal serves as the lever for scaffolding quality-teaching school wide, which includes selecting and retaining the highest quality teachers.

Nonetheless, it is widely agreed, principal preparation programs have been unimaginative, overly theoretical, impervious to reform, and insensitive to the tacit knowledge of practitioners (Archer, 2005; Creighton and Jones, 2001; Daresh, 2001; Doud & Keller, 1998; Fenwick, 2000; Ferrandino, 2001; Lashway, 2003). Such problems, moreover, are exacerbated by a failure to acknowledge that school principals now need to be skilled in offering leadership that is more participative, open, and unguarded than the traditional patriarchal or "heroic" form (Lazaridou, 2009) as well as facilitating school improvement efforts (Elmore, 2000; Farcas, Johnson, Duffett, Foleno, and Foley, 2001; Ferrandino, 2001; Farkas, Johnson, and Duffett, 2003; Levine, 2005; Hess & Kelly, 2006).

In 2005 an alarming report published by Levine became the catalyst for a nation-wide reform movement in the USA to improve school leader preparation programs. Levine's study *Educating School Leaders* examined programs for preparing school principals and superintendents across the United States. The study was based on surveys of deans, faculty, alumni of America's schools of education, principals in school systems, and case studies of individual schools. The research revealed a number of issues and gaps in how principals were being prepared to lead American schools: a lack of definition of what good leadership is, use of irrelevant curriculum, inadequate clinical instruction, low admission and graduation standards, and poor quality of candidates. Levine concluded that school leader preparation program were "in curricular disarray, disconnected from what is needed to run a school or school system" (Levine, 2005, p.61). He ended his report with recommendations that included redesigning curricula to make them more relevant to the needs of prospective principals; adoption of high standards for recruitment, selection, and admission to principal preparation programs; and closing of inadequate programs. This and similar reports on the quality of school leader preparation (e.g., Darling-Hammond et al, 2007; Darling-Hammond et al, 2009; Murphy, 2001) pushed the State of Illinois to mandate that all its principal preparation programs be redesigned.

Accordingly, in 2005 the Illinois Board of Higher Education (hereafter IBHE), responsible for all higher education programs across Illinois, took up the challenge. For this purpose it established a *Commission on School Leader Preparation in Illinois Colleges and Universities*. The role of the commission was to evaluate the findings and recommendations of the Levine report, to examine how school leaders were being prepared in Illinois, and to propose strategies for improving school leader preparation throughout Illinois. This commission comprised leaders from K-12 schools, colleges, universities, business and professional education organizations, the Illinois State Board of Education (ISBE), and the Illinois Board of Higher Education (IBHE).

A year later a report called *School leader preparation: A blueprint for change* (2006) was presented to IBHE by the Commission. Subsequently, in 2007 ISBE, ISHE, and the Office of the Governor jointly appointed the *Illinois School Leader Task Force*. The task force consisted of 28 people, including legislators, deans, higher education faculty, practicing principals and superintendents. The job of this task force was to develop a plan – based on, but not limited by, the commission's report – that would guide further statewide initiatives to improve school leader preparations in Illinois. In 2008 the task force released its report, recommending three primary instruments for improving leadership: (a) state policies that set high standards for school leadership certification, (b) formal partnerships between school districts, institutions of higher education, and other qualified partners to support principal preparation and development, and (c) refocused principal preparation programs committed to developing in aspiring principals the capacities that are more likely to improve student learning in PreK-12 schools.

Within one year the task force, ISBE, and IBHE invited faculty and deans from 33 education administration programs in the State to form a redesign group to discuss the task force's report and to plan the next steps. The representatives of two of the existing programs declined to participate and their education administration certification programs have since lapsed. The redesign group established a web site and created five redesign teams: New Structure for Leadership Certification and Endorsements; School/University Partnerships and Candidate Selection Process; School Leadership Standards; Residencies & Internships; and Assessments of Candidates and Graduates.

A total of 50 representatives of public and private institutions of higher education, regional offices of education, school districts, and professional organizations (including the Illinois Principals' Association and the Illinois Federation of Teachers), along with representatives from the two boards (ISBE and IBHE) participated in these five redesign teams whose job was to research and make recommendations for the newly designed principal preparation programs. At the same time, invited representatives of parents, special education, early childhood education, and English Language Learners from around Illinois attended the meetings of the redesign teams and provided feedback and input.

After eight regional meetings to gather feedback, on 1 June 2010 Governor Quinn signed Public Act 96-0903 (General Assembly of Illinois, 2010) creating a new principal endorsement. In the months that followed, ISBE and IBHE worked together to roll out the newly defined principal preparation requirements across the State by holding meetings with institutions of higher education, school districts, regional offices of education, and legislators and by providing assistance to higher education institutes as they began working on developing new programs and/or phasing out the old.

Ultimately, in the academic year 2011-12, eight new principal preparation programs were approved under the new law. In the academic year 2012-13, 18 more were approved, bringing the total to 26 newly designed PPPs across the State. Three additional institutions were in the process of submitting applications for approval while I was compiling this report, and an evaluation process for assessing the effectiveness of new PPPs was being put into place. Under the new rules, all programs for the preparation of principals in the State of Illinois were to be approved by June 1st 2014.

Policy for PPPs Adopted by the State of Illinois

In its report to the Illinois General Assembly, the School Leader Preparation Task Force stated the following: "Improvement of student learning in Illinois schools requires high quality leadership that establishes in every school a culture of high expectations and collaboration among all partners in support of student learning" (2008, p. 4). It went on to say that principal preparation programs ought to reflect this philosophy and, in particular, should reflect the following principles.

1. The reform will not involve the redesigning of old programs to meet the requirements of the new. Rather, it is to be a process to redefine school leadership and to create new principal endorsement programs that focus on instructional leadership at all school levels, from pre-school to grade 12.
2. New *Teacher Leader Programs* will be made available to those who do not aspire to become school principals but they still want a degree in school administration.
3. The new programs are to be grounded in the motto "district as consumer", which requires joint establishment and maintenance of partnerships between institutions of higher education and PK-12 education. Through an agreement called "memorandum of understanding" (MOU), institutions must demonstrate that their programs are developed, maintained, and evaluated in partnership with a PK-12 school or district.
4. For the first time, alongside public and private institutions, not-for-profit entities approved by the State's Board of Higher Education will be permitted to offer principal preparation programs.
5. Program curricula should enhance principals' ability to address student learning and school improvement for all students in preschool through grade 12, with particular attention to students with special needs and English Language Learners.
6. Prospective candidates must have a minimum of 4 years of teaching experience before they are eligible for admission to the program.
7. The new programs must include specific requirements for selection and assessment of candidates, training in the evaluation of staff, an internship, and a partnership with one or more school districts or state-recognized non-public schools.
8. The change process should be outcome oriented. The primary questions that should drive the discussions and the decisions are "What is it we want to accomplish with this change?" and "Whose interests are we here to protect – those of the candidates or those of our children?"

THE ILLINOIS CASE THROUGH THE LENSES OF CHANGE AND COMPLEXITY THEORIES

In preparation for my analysis of the development and dissemination of the new PPP policy for the State of Illinois, I present next highlights from change theory and complexity theory.

Change Theory

Fundamentals of Change

The literature on change in higher education specifies three fundamental steps for success: understanding the change process, understanding the rationale for change, and implementing change (Eckel, Green, Hill, & Mallon, 1999). The first step is essentially preparatory. Individuals in organizations need time to prepare themselves; they need to work with the emotions that come with it, such as fear, anxiety, and resistance. The second step, understanding the "why" of change, is critical. Some of the questions that must be addressed concern where the change comes from, what the pressures for it are, and how to best proceed. With step three the actual change takes place: individuals in the organization assume certain roles, resources (including technology) are marshaled and brought to bear, and the first signs of change begin to appear.

In higher education, changing a program is daunting and challenging, and requires the engagement, active involvement, and open communication among all stakeholders in order to be successful (de la Harpe & Radloff, 2000). In addition, the change effort should provide opportunities for debate, discussions, and resolutions of concerns; should include measures to ensure that tasks are completed on time by those responsible for them; and should provide for support systems to monitor and promote the change.

Brownlee (2000) identified seven requisites to successful change implementation: outlining the rationale for change, having a vision and an implementation plan, communicating plans, acquiring resources, aligning structures to assist change, recognizing resistance and where it may surface, and providing supportive feedback. In similar fashion Kotter (1996) advanced a nine-step generic change model that has been used widely by higher education institutes: (1) establishing a sense of urgency; (2) creating a guiding team; (3) developing a vision and strategy; (4) communicating the change vision; (5) empowering broad-based action; (6) generating short-term wins; (7) consolidating gains and producing more change; (8) anchoring new approaches in the culture and (9) managing emotions (cited in de la Harpe and Radloff, 2008).

The literature on change also emphasizes the importance of communication, interactions, and leadership (Eckel & Keza, 2003; Keup, Walker, Astin, & Lindholm, 2001). Especially in higher education contexts, the way change process is communicated, leadership exercised, and interac-

tions transpire, is instrumental for the success of the change. Keup and colleagues (2001) add that the development of trust among members of the organization is essential, and that the development of trust is highly dependent on open communication and transparent decision-making.

Obstacles to Change

There is no change without resistance to it. Especially in academia, resistance is reinforced by the various subcultures that exist in universities, the tradition of academic freedom, and tenure. Usually, senior academics with tenure, power, and prestige are the ones who don't want to change while new members strive for acceptance, change, and new ways of working (Arnold & Civian, 1997). According to Brownlee (2000), resistance to change can be the result of: (a) a top-down mandate for the change; (b) a lack of knowledge about the change and its processes; (c) implementing organization-wide initiatives without taking into account individual differences of schools, departments, and programs of study; (d) structures that promote individualism and competition versus collaboration and cooperative resolution of issues: (e) too much change at once; and (f) insufficient resources to support the change.

An important factor for the successful implementation of change in universities is the development of specific management structures and governance systems that on the one hand will curb the resistance and inertia of individuals, and on the other will provide opportunities for people to be involved in the change process to ensure a successful outcome (Pearson, Honeywood, & O'Toole, 2004).

Complexity Theory

Complexity theory focuses on *structures* and *behaviors* that emerge as a result of a dynamic network of interactions. In general such behaviors are seen as self-generative and not the result of direct leadership intervention (Marion & Uhl-Bien, 2002). The characteristics of such behaviors include nonlinearity, autopoiesis, emergence, and co-evolution.

Complexity Theory *vis-a-vis* Open Systems and Chaos Theory

Intensive and sustained study of complexity theory was initiated in the 1980s at the Santa Fe Institute in the United States (Santa Fe Institute, n.d.) in an attempt "to explain how open systems operate, as seen through holistic spectacles" (Lucas, 2000, p. 3). Complexity theory is an extension of chaos theory. While chaos theory highlights the unpredictability of the future, the importance of nonlinear systems, and systems' sensitivity to initial conditions (Morrison, 2002; Stacey, 2000), it appears to build on the premises of open system theory insofar as the outcomes of a process are seen as constituting the inputs for a subsequent phase of the system (Gleick, 1987; Stacey, 2000). Complexity theory, on the other hand, incorporates the premises of chaos theory but adds the propositions that unpredictable and non-average behavior are prerequisites of change and innovation, and development takes place through self-organization (Morrison, 2002). This self-organization is the result of dynamic interactions among the elements that comprise the system. Where chaos theory allows little room for spontaneous change, for creativity and innovation, complexity theory posits that spontaneous reorganization of the interacting elements of the system contributes to the emergence of new forms of the system.

Characteristics of Complex Systems

According to Cilliers (2001) the essential general characteristics of complex systems are as follows.

1. Complex systems consist of a large number of elements.

2. The elements of complex systems interact with themselves by exchanging energy or information. These interactions are dynamic and they affect everything in the system.

3. Complex systems are non-linear.

4. They are characterized by many direct and indirect feedback loops.

5. Complex systems are open systems constantly in interaction with their environments.

6. Complex systems have memory that permeates the whole system. The memory is in the system's history and it affects the behavior of the elements of the system.

7. The behavior of complex systems is the result of the interactions that take place within the system. Since these interactions are dynamic, non-linear, and fed-back, the behavior of the system in its totality cannot be predicted from the examination of each component separately. This is the notion of "emergence", a property of complex systems that is antithetical to notions of determinism, causality, and predictability.

8. Complex systems are adaptive. They organize themselves from within.

Suffice to say, complex systems do not display all the above characteristics to the same degree. Some characteristics are more prominent than others, thus they account for the variations that exist among systems. Social organizations share these properties of complex systems to various degrees based on the nature of the organization.

Complexity Theory and Organizations

Theorists and researchers of organizations have been using complexity theory to analyze and describe social organizations for some time (Allen, 2001; Richardson, 2005), and it has been found that it provides a powerful general framework for understanding complex organizations. However, this framework or "lens" should not be viewed as the ultimate perspective; to expect that uncovering the secrets of complex systems will show THE way to run organizations is futile and unrealistic. Nevertheless, complexity theory can add significantly to understandings of the structures and dynamics in social organizations.

What social organizations have in common with other complex systems is presented hereafter:

9. Like complex systems, social organizations are comprised of many dynamically interacting elements (i.e., employees, units, subunits, and departments).

10. The larger an organization, the greater its complexity.

11. Interactions in social organizations, as in other complex systems, are nonlinear and result in emergent behaviors.

12. Social organizations are open systems, just as complex systems are open systems, and have many direct and indirect feedback loops. Their survival depends on maintaining "fit" with the environment, which ultimately affects the directions organizations take.

13. Small events can have huge impacts on an organization; reciprocally, big changes may have little or no effect. Thus, cause-and-effect relationships cannot be predicted or become fully known.

14. Self-organization is a key property of complex systems. Social organizations, like other complex systems, can be self-organizing. Historically, social organizations have been hierarchical, control-oriented, and reliant on stable structures; but contemporary social organizations are often fluid, networked, team-based, and process-oriented (Veliyath & Sathian, 2005).

Until recently complexity theory has not been used extensively for understanding educational organizations and can be used to gain insights that complement traditional, reductionist ways of looking at organizations – adding insights that are organic, holistic, non-linear (Santonus, 1998). In complexity theory "relations within interconnected networks are the order of the day" (Youngblood, 1997, p. 27). The key components of complexity theory as applied to analysis of social organizations are: connectedness, emergence, distributed control, feedback and recursion, relationships, self-organized criticality, self-organization, communication, organizational learning, networks, nonlinearity, and structures (Morrison, 2002). Each of these will be elaborated when appropriate in my analysis of Illinois' revision of its prescriptions for principal preparation programs.

Case Analysis

In 2005 the State of Illinois faced up to a major challenge: principal preparation programs across the State did not adequately prepare effective school leaders. The State had two options: to closely examine each of the many existing programs to judge whether it should be revised or closed down, or to revise pertinent policies and require all institutions that wished to offer principal preparation programs to align their programs appropriately. The first option would have been easier and less time consuming, but the resistance and the political costs were thought to be a big impediment to achieving change, so the second and more difficult option was seen to be the only viable solution. According to members of the Illinois State Board of Education this presented an opportunity "to *redefine*, not just redesign our leadership programs across the State" (personal communication).

This change required the coordinated effort and interaction of multiple groups of individuals at several levels, and the resultant scenario was complex and richly textured. Due to space constraints I can only sketch its features in point form:

15. A large number of participants. In total about 1,400 individuals participated in redefining and redesigning the new PPP policy.

16. A large number of groups was involved, each with its unique agenda, specialist knowledge, interests, concerns, values, priorities, and sphere of influence.
17. An incredible number of highly varied, often-incompatible ideas were proffered by members of the different groups.
18. The huge number of tasks that individuals and groups had to undertake in order to design the new PPP prescriptions.
19. Considerable potential for different interpretations among team players.
20. A critical need to use legislative processes judiciously and effectively.
21. Considerable differences in the power-capital of the various groups.
22. A need for co-evolution, dictated by the dependence of participants on each other.
23. The challenges of achieving consensus through synergy (Wallace & Pocklington, 1998).
24. The dispersal or diffusion (rather than distribution) of control and leadership amongst the groups involved in the change.
25. The State's emphasis on inclusion – all interested parties had to be included in the change and in the process of co-evolution.

In terms of behaviors, the State's initiative was based on long deliberations among the five design teams that were established (School leadership Standards, New Structure for Leadership Certification & Endorsements, School/University Partnerships & Selection Process, Internship/Residency, and Assessments of Candidates & Graduates). Those deliberations required a flow of interaction and cross-level communication between and among the team members. Team members were engaged in long discussions, reflections, and accessing multiple sources of information over a long period in order to come up with their recommendations for the new PPP policy. It is noteworthy, and of great import, that the motto adopted during the early phases of the enterprise was "Working together to prepare Illinois school leaders". This supported non-linear behavior in the designing teams – allowed emergence of new understandings among team members, autopoiesis (new learning to occur), and co-evolution to take place as each team player influenced the behavior and development of others (Kauffman, 1995) in what McDaniel (2007) calls "a constant dance of change."

Wallace and Pocklington (1998) suggest that to understand change in complex systems it is better to think of the complexity of change as a network like the neural networks of the brain, with different players being the nodes, and extensive inter- and intra-communication taking place (Morrison, 2002). A network operates in such a way that a single player represents a node with connections to all others and "the reorganization process unfolds without any of the people who make up the parts being able to see the process in its entirety" (Wallace & Pocklington, 1998, p. 17). The five School Leadership Redesign Teams were assigned different tasks, each relating to one aspect of the new policy to be crafted. Although teams worked independently, they met regularly to report progress, to exchange and receive feedback, and to further discuss, clarify, and refine the proposed changes. Thus leadership was diffused to all levels and exercised by all participants. In keeping with this philosophy of decentralization, representatives of the State were involved actively in the change process but facilitated the work of the teams as opposed to imposing a command-and-control style of leadership. This is in line with one of complexity theorists' arguments that creativity, productivity, and innovation are bottom-up processes and take place when people are provided opportunities to innovate and network (McKelvey, 2002; Stacey, 2000).

Critical Issues: Bifurcation Points

A key feature of a complex adaptive system is its propensity to create order through self-organization of interacting elements and "constant self-readjustment of the system" (Coveney & Highfield, 1995, p. 85). This self-organization takes place at bifurcation points that signify the unstable condition of a system and its potential to develop in several new ways that cannot be predicted (Capra, 1997). There were several bifurcation points in the initiative to change Illinois State's policy for principal preparation programs.

The first bifurcation point in this case was Levine's report that principal preparation programs across the United States were not preparing school leaders who could effect improvement in the nation's schools, who could provide school leadership for the demands of the 21st century. The inadequacies in principal preparation programs (see summary above) were undeniable and intolerable. The State of Illinois was compelled to re-organize its principal preparation programs. The ability an organization or a system to develop, replace, adapt, reconstruct, or change its internal structures so that they become responsive to their environment is a key feature of complex adaptive systems (Morrison, 2002) and Illinois is an excellent example of how systems can reconfigure themselves to achieve better states. Evidence of it is Illinois' attempt to redefine what principal preparation means, not just revise existing programs. This process parallels what happens in the natural world: when organisms are threatened by environmental hazards, they reconfigure and metamorphose in order to survive. Complex adaptive systems follow the same procedure – it is a "bottom-up" process, one that involves interactions, communications, adaptability, feedback, and learning at all levels. This is the essence of self-organization. From a complexity point of view, things do not happen in isolation but during interactions (Cilliers, 2001). The State of Illinois allowed this "bottom-up" process to become the driving force behind its initiative to change its policy for PPPs. Although the two state boards of education (the Illinois State Board of Education and the Illinois Board of Higher Education) were

behind this process, the decisions – and ultimately the metamorphosis of the system – came from the numerous stakeholders who participated in the various committees and teams that worked diligently to create the new PPP policy.

The second bifurcation point was the emergence of a new partnership between the State Board of Education and the State Board of Higher Education. This partnership "set the tone" for the continuation and the success of the reform. Historically, the two boards had been functioning independently of one another. The Illinois Board of Higher Education (IBHE) is responsible for the planning and coordination of Illinois' system of colleges and universities, whereas the Illinois State Board of Education (ISBE) sets educational policies and guidelines for public and private schools, preschool through grade 12, as well as vocational education. Little interaction had existed between the two boards in the past. For the first time the two entities came together as equal partners to help design the new PPP. As one board member said, "This was not *us* and *them*, this was US [emphasis added] working together." In the complexity perspective this first-time partnership can be understood as "an emergent set of relations that constitute a system in terms of meaningful communications" (Medd, 2005). These communications led to new codes of interaction among the partners, ones that did not exist before. At the same time, the partnership created new ways of thinking and operating among the partners; hence it created a new form of complexity.

A third bifurcation point that influenced the direction of the change involved a shift in thinking. Development of the new prescriptions for PPPs was grounded in a "district as consumer" approach, which meant that emphasis was on children's learning rather than other objectives. As one board member said, "We were working for the good of the children, not the candidates."

The fourth bifurcation point was in the discussion that took place in the advisory committee meetings. These discussions were influenced significantly by the comments, facial expressions, and expression of views from groups that hitherto had not been allowed to participate in the process – such as parents' representatives, preschool specialists, and special education specialists. The flow of communication added by these constituents provided a better appreciation of how different people saw the change differently, and where there were "loopholes."

To conclude this analysis, Table 2 summarizes the key complexity elements in the State's reform initiative.

Overall, then, effecting changes in Illinois' principal preparation program involved a complex, dynamic process which was grounded thoroughly in a wide distribution of control and leadership, and the nurturing of a web of relationships among all interested stakeholders that supported free-

Table 2. Summary of the key complexity elements in the State's reform initiative

Adaptation to environmental conditions	State of Illinois adapted its policy, procedures, and programs for principal preparation in response to the changing demands from the environment. This adaptation was carried out internally with the synergy of several parts of the systems, through their extensive, dynamic, challenging, and unpredictable interactions.
Emergence	a) One outcome of the partnership between the two boards (ISBE & IBHE) b) Paradigm shift (district as consume) - a result of interactions among the elements of the system (i.e., the various constituencies) c) Internships came to be based upon competencies instead of being defined solely by time requirements.
Connectedness (through communication)	a) The partnership between the two boards (ISBE & IBHE) b) Joint establishment and maintenance of partnerships between higher education institutions and PK-12 education. c) Growing support from key stakeholders from early childhood to teacher unions to legislators (1,400 individuals were involved actively in the process).
Distributed control and leadership	Control distributed widely, mainly through the various groups and committees: School Leaders Task Force, Commission on School Leadership, the 5 design teams, and many informal groups.
Feedback and recursion	a) Advisory meetings b) 1st conference to discuss the Task Force report c) 2nd conference to develop school leader redesign teams d) 3rd conference for feedback and input to the recommending changes of the redesign teams e) Feedback from special interest representatives (i.e. parents, special education, early childhood education, English language) d) Further clarification, discussion and refinement of changes by the School Leaders Advisory Council.
Relationships	a) The unprecedented collaboration of the two boards (ISBE & IBHE). b) The partnerships between higher education and PK-12 institutions. c) 1,400 stakeholders
Self-organized criticality (A system's spontaneous evolution through diversity and deviance)	Advisory group meetings.
Self-organization	a) Emergence of new State policy for PPP. b) Formal partnerships c) Refocused principal preparation
Communication	a) Review of research on leadership and best practices in PPPs. b) Formal meetings with teams, professional organizations, school districts, Regional Offices of Education, and legislators. c) Reports d) Feedback session, documents, and other forms of communication. e) Collaboration of ISBE and IBHE to make available the newly defined policy for PPPs across the State of Illinois.

continued on following page

Table 2. Continued

Organizational learning (the ability to learn from the internal and external environment)	a) Scanning of the environment to identify problems in existing PPPs across the State. b) Cultivation of relationships among all stakeholders through open communication, dynamic interactions among the constituencies, exchange of information and knowledge. c) Use of technology to facilitate communication among constituents. d) Participative decision making to form the new PPP policy. e) Forming learning alliances with districts and ROEs.
Networks	a) Commission group b) Task Force c) Design teams d) Professional organizations & associations e) Advisory committees d) Districts and ROEs e) Government bodies f) Legislators
Non-linearity	a) The result of many networks and complex interactions among constituents to effect change. b) Paying attention to nuances and other seemingly insignificant events during interactions that could potentially change the course of things.
Structures	Open, fluid, non-hierarchical, dispersed throughout the system, multi-level.

flow communications between and among the constituencies. Indeed, the success of the whole initiative was the result of the many networks and complex interactions that allowed for emergence and new knowledge to develop, and the use of non-hierarchical multi-level structures.

DISCUSSION AND IMPLICATIONS

So far in this chapter I have described and analyzed how a State changed entirely its principal preparation programs. I framed my analysis primarily to investigate how the lens of complexity theory might contribute to better understandings of change. But I was also interested in how the approach taken by the State of Illinois compared with what is advocated in the literature about improving programs for principal preparation. In this section I turn to these two matters.

Utility of the Complexity Lens

Heifetz and Linsky (2002) distinguish between technical and adaptive change. The former deals

with problems and challenges for which answers are available. The latter involves transformation of a system because "it requires new experiments, new discoveries, and adjustments from numerous places in the organization or the system" (p. 27). What took place in the State of Illinois was a massive adaptive change that did not just alter principal preparation programs across the State, but it *redefined* the notion of school leadership. This could not have been achieved without abandoning old ways of operating and introducing new ways of learning, without changing attitudes, values, and behaviors. And the State of Illinois did indeed succeed in transforming people's ways of thinking about the preparation of school principals. It was not an easy task as the transformation required changes at not only the bottom of the pyramid but also at the top. For example, the two boards of education (ISBE and IHBE) for the first time had to set aside their traditionally different roles and responsibilities and agree to collaborate to promote the change. New ways of operating had to be learned in both associations. The collaboration and success they achieved showed that in large-scale reforms "the top matters," yet mandated change is known to bring fear, resistance, and even passive dependency (Fullan, cited in Heifetz & Linsky, 2002).

Complexity theory suggests that the negatives of top-down mandated change could be offset with measures that promote inclusion, ownership, and creativity. In the State of Illinois case, these requisites were achieved by including all interested parties in the change process and building strong relationships at all levels allowing co-evolution and novelty to flourish, dispersing control, spawning flexible structures that propelled the advancement of change, and making effective use of the new laws and legislation.

However, adaptive change is not without its costs. Because of its transformative nature, adaptive change challenges people to adjust their values, beliefs, and philosophical systems. Indeed, as Heifetz and Linsky (2002) point out, adaptive change requires that people "question and perhaps refine aspects of their identity, take a loss, experience uncertainty, and also challenge their sense of competence." All such costs were in evidence during the implementation of the new PPP in Illinois. Established principal preparation programs were judged as inadequate (with some closing down as a result of the reform); and this, in turn, resulted in considerable revenue and personnel losses at the institution level. Yet, despite the negatives and the resistance, the change was in the end successful because it was seen to serve a higher moral goal: the betterment of children's learning in Illinois.

Effecting Whole-System Change

In the literature there are now numerous analyses of "what works" when it comes to improving educational programs (e.g., Campbell, 2013; Fullan, 2005). Among these, an article by Levin and Fullan (2008) is particularly useful here, for it focuses on lessons learned about effective change from international experience with large-scale reform in about twenty countries. Although the reforms examined by these authors were directed at school systems, to a large degree the article is about system renewals through changes to central government policies – renewals that parallel the change for tertiary education undertaken by the State of Illinois.

Levin and Fullan (2008) extracted seven premises for successful reform, and my analysis revealed that the Illinois initiative satisfied these criteria. This is summarized in Table 3.

Finally in this regard, the most important "lesson" is that improvement in principal preparation requires focused and *sustained* effort by all parts of the system and its stakeholders (emphasis added; Levin & Fullan, 2008, p. 291). In the case of Illinois' push to improve its programs for principal preparation, this was indeed the case: many, many individuals and agencies worked hard for a long time to generate the new PPP policies. Moreover, this eighth "lesson" served as mantra for all stakeholders as they labored to *implement* the new policy for PPPs – but an account of that phase of the change initiative is beyond the scope of this article and will have to be reported elsewhere.

CONCLUSION

The following statements provide a summary of the main outcomes of the research presented in this chapter in regard to change and complexity theory.

Change

- Successful large-scale reforms are initiated at the top, but they are advanced from the bottom. They feature a dynamic process that involves excellent communication, strong relationships, and distribution of control.
- In order for a change to be successful, learning has to take place at all levels in a complex adaptive system.

Table 3. Foundations of successful change initiatives

Levin & Fullan Criteria	Illinois State Reform
A small number of ambitious yet achievable goals, publicly stated.	Unrelenting focus on one high priority objective. The selected objective was fundamental to success in school improvement..
A positive stance.	Although the reform effort was precipitated by negative messages about PPPs, which could have been demotivating, the reform strategies was promoted and implemented in a way that engaged the idealism and professional commitments of stakeholders.
Multi-level engagement, strong leadership by "guiding coalitions."	The reform efforts were supported by politically credible groups external to the university faculties responsible for providing PPPs. Key political and administrative leaders at various levels understood and supported the reform in similar ways.
Emphasis on capacity building with a focus on results	Help to develop individual and collective knowledge and competencies – providing opportunities and resources for learning in context, ensuring that accountability pressure was fair and reasonable. New organizational structures,
Keeping the focus on key strategies by managing competing interests.	Strong political leadership to manage competing agendas and continuous public communication to sustain support for the main objective.
Effective use of resources.	Some additional resources brought to bear but the most powerful strategy was the way existing resources (particularly personnel) were (re) deployed to support the change effort.
Constant transparency	Frequent, honest, communication among all participants and stakeholders about successes and challenges, setbacks, and accomplishments.

- Change with a moral purpose is the glue that ties together systems that promote change.
- Conflict, resistance, and diversity are parts of the change process and they should be embraced and resolved rather than fought.
- Change of a complex adaptive system is the outcome of a long, dynamic learning process that asks participants to operate at the edge of chaos.
- Change takes time, and sufficient time should be made available to all participants.

Complexity Theory

- Critical issues (bifurcation points) in a system are potential attractors for change.
- Complexity theory at the macro level focuses mainly on structures and behaviors.
- Emergence in complex adaptive systems leads to the production of new knowledge,

new dynamics, and a paradigm shift, which is the result of the intense and focused interactions of individuals in the system.

Research

- A final lesson from this investigation is that a multi-perspective approach to analyzing an organizational case is recommended as it provides a richer depiction of reality in complex systems such as institutes of higher education.

REFERENCES

Advance Illinois. (n.d.). *Profile of Illinois' education system*. Retrieved from http://www. advanceillinois.org/profile-of-our-education-system-pages-264.php

Allen, C. (2001). What is complexity science? Knowledge of the limits of knowledge. *Emergence: A Journal of Complexity Issues in Organizations and Management, 3*(1), 24-44.

Archer, J. (2005). Leadership training seen to fall short. *Education Week, 24*(38), 9.

Arnold, G., & Civian, J. T. (1997). The ecology of general education reform. *Change, 29*(4), 18–23. doi:10.1080/00091389709602323

Brownlee, P. P. (2000). Effecting transformational institutional change. *National Academy Newsletter, 1*(3). Retrieved at http://www.thenationalacademy.org/readings/effecting.html

Campbell, C. (2013). *Whole system change*. Paper presented at the Annual Conference of the British Educational Leadership and Management Association (BELMAS). Edinburg, UK.

Capra, F. (1997). *The web of life: A new understanding of living systems*. New York: Doubleday.

Cilliers, P. (2001). Boundaries, hierarchies, and networks in complex systems. *International Journal of Innovation Management, 5*(2), 135–147. doi:10.1142/S1363919601000312

Clark, B. R. (2004). *Sustaining change in universities: Continuities in case studies and concepts*. New York: Open University Press.

Commission on School Leader Preparation in Illinois Colleges and Universities. (2006). School leader preparation: A blueprint for change. *Education*.

Coveney, P., & Highfield, R. (1995). *Frontiers of complexity*. New York: Fawcett Columbine.

Creighton, T. B., & Jones, G. D. (2001). *Selection or self-selection? How rigorous are our selection criteria for education administration preparation programs?* Paper presented at the annual conference of the National Council of Professors of Educational Administration. Houston, TX.

Daresh, J. C. (2001). *Beginning the principalship* (2nd ed.). Thousand Oaks, CA: Corwin Press.

Darling-Hammond, L., LaPointe, M., Meyerson, D., Orr, M. T., & Cohen, C. (2007). *Preparing school leaders for a changing world: Lessons from exemplary leadership development programs*. Stanford, CA: Stanford Educational Leadership Institute.

Darling-Hammond, L., Meyerson, D., LaPointe, M. M., & Orr, M. T. (2009). *Preparing principals for a changing world*. San Francisco, CA: Jossey-Bass. doi:10.1002/9781118269329

de la Harpe, B., & Radloff, A. (2008). Developing graduate attributes for lifelong learning - How far have we gone? In *Proceedings of the Lifelong Learning Conference*. Central Queensland University.

de la Harpe, B., & Thomas, I. (2009). Curriculum change in universities: Conditions that facilitate education for sustainable development. *Journal of Education for Sustainable Development, 3*(1), 75–85. doi:10.1177/097340820900300115

Doud, J., & Keller, E. (1998). *A ten-year study: The K-8 principal in 1998*. Alexandria, VA: National Association of Elementary School Principals.

Eckel, P., Green, M., Hill, B., & Mallon, W. (1999). Taking charge of change: A primer for colleges and universities. *Change*, III.

Eckel, P. D., & Keza, A. J. (2003). *Taking the reins: Transformation in higher education*. Traverse City, MI: American Council on Education and Praeger Publishers.

Elmore, R. F. (2000). Building a new structure for school leadership. Washington, DC: The Albert Shanker Institute. Retrieved at http://www.shankerinstitute.org/Downloads/building.pdf

Farkas, S., Johnson, J., & Duffett, A. (2003). *Rolling up their sleeves: Superintendents and principals talk about what's needed to fix public schools*. New York: Public Agenda.

Farkas, S., Johnson, J., Duffett, A., Foleno, T., & Foley, P. (2001). *Trying to stay ahead of the game: Superintendents and principals talk about school leadership*. Washington, DC: Public Agenda.

Fenwick, L. T. (2000). *The principal shortage: Who will lead?* Cambridge, MA: Harvard Graduate School of Education.

Ferrandino, V. L. (2001). Challenges for 21st century elementary school principals. Phi Delta Kappan, 82(6), 440-442.

Fullan, M. (2007). *Leading in a culture of change*. San Francisco, CA: Jossey-Bass.

Fullan, M. (2005). Leadership and sustainability: Systems thinkers in action. Thousand Oaks, CA: Corwin Press.

General Assembly of Illinois. (2010). *Public Act 96-0903*. Retrieved at http://www.ilga.gov/legislation/publicacts/fulltext.asp?Name=096-0903

Gleick, J. (1987). *Chaos: Making a new science*. London: Abacus.

Heifetz, R. A., & Linsky, M. L. (2002). *Leadership on the line: Staying alive through the dangers of leading*. Boston, MA: Harvard Business Publishing.

Hess, F. M., & Kelly, A. P. (2002). Learning to lead: What gets taught in principal preparation programs? Washington, DC: American Enterprise Institute. Retrieved from http://www.ksg.harvard.edu/pepg/PDF/Papers/Hess_Kelly_Learning_to_Lead_PEPG05.02.pd

Illinois. (n.d.). In *Wikipedia, the free encyclopedia*. Retrieved at http://en.wikipedia.org/wiki/Illinois

Illinois School Leader Task Force. (2008). *Illinois School Leader Preparation Task Force recommendations*. Springfield, IL: Author.

Kauffman, S. A. (1995). *At home in the universe: The search for the laws of self-organization and complexity*. New York: Oxford University Press.

Keup, J. R., Walker, A. A., Astin, H. S., & Lindholm, J. A. (2001). *Organizational culture and institutional transformation (ERIC Digest ED464521)*. ERIC Clearinghouse on Higher Education.

Kotter, J. P. (1996). *Leading change*. Boston, MA: Harvard Business School Publishing.

Lashway, L. (2003). Transforming principal preparation. *ERIC Digest 165*. Retrieved at cepm.uoregon.edu/publications/digests/digest165.html

Lawrimore, B. (2005). From excellence to emergence: The evolution of management thinking and the influence of complexity. In K. A. Richardson (Ed.), *Managing organizational complexity: Philosophy, theory, and application* (pp. 115–132). Greenwich, CT: Information Age Publishing.

Lazaridou, A. (2009). The kinds of knowledge principals use. *International Journal of Education Policy & Leadership*, *4*(10).

Leithwood, K., Louis, K. S., Anderson, S., & Wahlstrom, K. (2004). *How leadership influences student learning: A review of research for the Learning from Leadership Project*. New York: The Wallace Foundation.

Levin, B., & Fullan, M. (2008). Learning about system renewal. *Educational Management Administration & Leadership*, *36*(2), 289–303. doi:10.1177/1741143207087778

Levine, A. (2005). *Educating school leaders*. Washington, DC: The Education School Project.

Lucas, C. (2000). *Self-organizing systems FAQ*. Retrieved at http://www.calresco.org/sos/sosfaq.htm

Marion, R., & Uhl-Bien, M. (2002). Leadership in complex organizations. *The Leadership Quarterly, 12*(4), 389–418. doi:10.1016/S1048-9843(01)00092-3

Mc Daniel, R. R. Jnr. (2007). Management strategies for complex adaptive systems: Sensemaking, learning, and improvisation. *Performance Improvement Quarterly, 2*(2), 21–41.

McKelvey, B. (2002). Microstrategy from microleadership: Distributed intelligence via new science. In A. Y. Lewin & H. Volberda (Eds.), *Mobilizing the self-renewing organization*. Thousand Oaks, CA: Sage.

Medd, W. P. (2005). Imagining complex partnerships. In K. A. Richardson (Ed.), Managing organizational complexity: Philosophy, theory, and application (pp. 301-311). Greenwich, CT: Information Ager Publishing.

Meister-Scheytt, C., & Scheytt, T. (2005). The complexity of change in universities. *Higher Education Quarterly, 59*(1), 76–99. doi:10.1111/j.1468-2273.2005.00282.x

Morrison, K. R. B. (2002). *School Leadership and Complexity Theory*. London: Routledge-Falmer.

Murphy, J. (2001). *Re-Culturing the profession of educational leadership: New blueprints*. Paper commissioned for the first meeting of the National Commission for the Advancement of Educational Leadership Preparation. Racine, WI. Retrieved at ED 464 380.

Pearson, S. S., Honeywood, S., & O'Toole, M. (2004). Not learning for sustainability: The challenge of environmental education in a university. *International Research in Geographical and Environmental Education, 14*(3), 173–186. doi:10.1080/10382040508668349

Richardson, K. A. (2005). To be or not to be? That is [not] the question: Complexity theory and the need for critical thinking. In K. A. Richardson (Ed.), Managing organizational complexity: Philosophy, theory, and application, (pp. 21-46). Greenwich, CT: Information Age Publishing.

Santa Fe Institute. (n.d.). Retrieved at http://en.wikipedia.org/wiki/Santa_Fe_Institute

Santonus, M. (1998). *Simple: Yet complex*. Retrieved at http://www.cio.com/archive/enterprise/041598_qanda_content.html

Seashore, K., Leithwood, K., Wahlstrom, K., & Anderson, S. (2010). *Learning from leadership: Investigating the links to improved student learning*. New York: WallaceFoundation.

Shattock, M. (2005). European universities for entrepreneurship: Their role in the Europe of knowledge. The theoretical context. *Higher Educational Management and Policy, 17*(3), 13–26. doi:10.1787/hemp-v17-art16-en

Stacey, R. (2000). *Strategic management and organisational dynamics* (3rd ed.). Essex, UK: Pearson Education Ltd.

Stake, R. E. (2000). Case studies. In N. K. Denzin & Y. S. Lincoln (Eds.), *A handbook of qualitative research* (p. 437). Thousand Oaks, CA: Sage.

Veliyath, R., & Sathian, K. (2005). Dealing with complexity in organizational control processes: Drawing lessons from the human brain. In K. A. Richardson (Ed.), Managing organizational complexity: Philosophy, theory, and application, (pp. 201-216). Greenwich, CT: Information Age Publishing.

Wallace, M., & Pocklington, F. (1998). *Managing complex change: Large scale reorganisation of schools*. Paper presented at the Annual Meeting of the American Educational Research Association. San Diego, CA.

Yin, R. K. (2009). *Case study research: Design and methods* (4th ed.). Thousand Oaks, CA: Sage.

Youngblood, M. (1997). *Life at the edge of chaos.* Dallas, TX: Perceval Publishing.

ADDITIONAL READING

Albert, S., Ashforth, B., & Dutton, J. (2000). Organizational identity and identification: Charting new waters and building new bridges. *Academy of Management Review, 25*(1), 13–17. doi:10.5465/AMR.2000.2791600

Albert, S., & Whetten, D. A. (1985). Organizational identity. *Research in Organizational Behavior, 7,* 263–295.

Allen, C. (2001). What is complexity science? Knowledge of the limits of knowledge. *Emergence: A Journal of Complexity Issues in Organizations and Management, 3*(1), 24-44.

Amis, J., Slack, T., & Hinings, C. R. (2004). The pace, sequence, and linearity of radical change. *Academy of Management Journal, 47*(1), 15–39. doi:10.2307/20159558

Andriani, P., & Passiante, G. (2004). Complexity theory and the management of networks. In P. Assiante & G. Passiante (Eds.), *Complexity Theory and the Management of Networks* (pp. 3–19). London: Imperial College Press. doi:10.1142/9781860947339_0001

Ashkenas, R., Ulrich, D., Jick, T., & Kerr, S. (1998). *The boundaryless organization: Breaking the chains of organizational structure.* San Francisco, CA: Jossey Bass.

Bak, P. (1996). *How nature works: The science of self-organized criticality.* New York: Copernicus. doi:10.1007/978-1-4757-5426-1

Baraba'si, A. L. (2002). *Linked: The new science of networks.* Cambridge, MA: Perseus.

Barling, J., Slater, F., & Kelloway, E. K. (2000). Transformational leadership and emotional intelligence: An exploratory study. *Leadership and Organization Development Journal, 21*(3), 157–161. doi:10.1108/01437730010325040

Battram, A. (1999). *Navigating complexity.* London: The Industrial Society.

Black, J. A. (2000). Fermenting change: Capitalizing on the inherent change found in dynamic non-linear (or complex) systems. *Journal of Organizational Change Management, 13*(6), 520–525. doi:10.1108/09534810010378551

Brodbeck, P. W. (2002). Complexity theory and organization procedure design. *Business Process Management, 8*(4), 377–402. doi:10.1108/14637150210435026

Brooke-Smith, R. (2003). *Leading learners, leading schools.* London: Routledge Falmer.

Brown, S. L., & Eisenhardt, K. M. (1998). *Competing on the edge: Strategy as structured chaos.* Boston, MA: Harvard Business School Press.

Buchanan, M. (2002). *Nexus: Small worlds and the groundbreaking theory of networks.* New York: W.W. Norton.

Burnes, B. (2005). Complexity theories and organizational change. *International Journal of Management Reviews, 7*(2), 73–90. doi:10.1111/j.1468-2370.2005.00107.x

Cilliers, P. (2001). Boundaries, hierarchies, and networks in complex systems. *International Journal of Innovation Management, 5*(2), 135–147. doi:10.1142/S1363919601000312

Davis, B., & Sumara, D. J. (2005). Challenging images of knowing: Complexity science and educational research. *International Journal of Qualitative Studies in Education, 18*(3), 305–321. doi:10.1080/09518390500082293

Davis, B., & Sumara, D. J. (2006). *Complexity and education*. Upper Saddle River, NJ: Lawrence Erlbaum Associates.

Diaz, C. J. D. (2007). Complexity and environmental education. In F. Capra, A. Juarerro, P. Sotolongo, & J. van Uden (Eds.), *Reframing complexity: Perspectives from North and South* (pp. 47–58). Mansfield, MA: ISCE Publishing.

Espinosa, A., Harnden, R., & Walker, J. (2007). Beyond hierarchy: A complexity management perspective. *Kybernetes*, *36*(3/4), 333–347. doi:10.1108/03684920710746995

Fitzgerald, L. A., & Van Eijnatten, F. M. (2002). Reflections: Chaos in organizational change. *Journal of Organizational Change Management*, *15*(4), 402–411. doi:10.1108/09534810210433700

Galal, H., & Nolan, R. (1995). *Toward an understanding of organizational boundaries*. Boston, MA: Harvard Graduate School of Business Administration, Working Paper 95-057.

Gioia, D., Schultz, M., & Corley, K. (2000). Organizational identity, image, and adaptive instability. *Academy of Management Review*, *25*(1), 63–81.

Goodwin, B. (2000). Out of control into participation. *Emergence*, *2*(4), 40–49. doi:10.1207/S15327000EM0204_06

Greene, B. (1999). *The elegant universe: Superstrings, hidden dimensions, and the quest for the ultimate theory*. New York: W. W. Norton.

Jervis, J. (1998). *Exploring the modern*. Oxford, UK: Blackwell.

Lissack, M., & Roos, J. (1999). *The next common sense*. London: Nicholas Brealey.

Richardson, K. A. (2001). *On the status of natural boundaries and the limits to knowledge: A complex systems perspective*. Paper presented at workshop on Living with Limits to Knowledge, Central European University, Budapest.

Richardson, K. A., & Cilliers, P. (2001). What is complexity science? A view from different directions. *Emergence*, *3*(1), 5–22. doi:10.1207/S15327000EM0301_02

Richardson, K. A., Cilliers, P., & Lissack, M. R. (2001). Complexity science: A 'gray' science for the 'stuff in between.'. *Emergence*, *3*(2), 6–18. doi:10.1207/S15327000EM0302_02

Scott, R. (1992). *Organizations: Rational, natural, and open systems*. Upper Saddle River, NJ: Prentice Hall.

Sommerer, J. C., & Ott, E. (1993). A physical system with qualitatively uncertain dynamics. *Nature*, *365*(6442), 138–140. doi:10.1038/365138a0

Yan, A., & Louis, M. R. (1999). Migration of organizational functions to the work unit level: Buffering, spanning, and bringing up boundaries. *Human Relations*, *52*(1), 96–120. doi:10.1177/001872679905200103

KEY TERMS AND DEFINITIONS

Change: The process of transforming something into a new form.

Complexity Theory: A theory that studies complex systems and explains how order, structure, pattern, and reorganization emerges from the interaction of the elements of systems.

Distributed Leadership: An approach to leadership that mobilizes, engages, and actively involves individuals at all levels in an organization for the attainment of common goals.

Higher Education Institute: A public, private, or not-for profit organization that offers degree programs to students beyond the age of compulsory school attendance.

Leadership: A process of social influence for the achievement of a common goal in which one or multiple persons can solicit the assistance and support of others in order to succeed.

Open Systems: Systems that continually interact with their external environments, exchanging energy, information, resources, and materials that are conducive to their survival.

Principal Preparation Programs: Officially accredited training programs for prospective school principals that are offered by public, private, and not-for-profit higher education institutes.

Chapter 3
Analysis of the Tasks of School Principals in Secondary Education in Catalonia:
Case Study

Georgeta Ion
Universitat Autònoma de Barcelona, Spain

Diego Castro
Universitat Autònoma de Barcelona, Spain

Marina Tomàs
Universitat Autònoma de Barcelona, Spain

Esther Salat
Universitat Autònoma de Barcelona, Spain

ABSTRACT

School principals have important jobs. To achieve a better understanding of their working lives, this chapter uses the professional diary and timetabling data of all the secondary School Principals, from schools in the Sant Cugat area of Catalonia, Spain. It begins by describing the context of the Catalonian educational system, its leadership and managerial model from a double perspective: on the one hand, the normative requirements; and on the other, the "day-to-day" tasks. The authors adopt a qualitative methodology. The analysis of the school principals' diaries and timetables was conducted over the course of one month (November 2013). The results permit us to relate the day-to-day tasks of the school principal to those tasks identified in the local and national school regulations and in the Education Law. This examination will lead to a better understanding of how the distribution of their activities and their time management is related to these requirements.

INTRODUCTION

In the current school environment, School Principals have a very complex job dealing with various internal and external challenges, which make their role one of the most important for the functioning of a school, in supporting change and providing quality educational (Brauckmann and Pashiardis, 2011). In this study we start by presenting different approaches to the principals' tasks in secondary schools. We situate our study in the context of the Catalan education system, and finally we analyze the tasks performed by school principals using as a point of reference two classificatory approaches:

DOI: 10.4018/978-1-4666-6591-0.ch003

a theoretical approach, and an approach based on Catalan educational law, which specifies and regulates the functions of principals. Finally we discuss our findings in the light of the current prevailing model of management found in Catalonia.

The school principal's role has been analysed in terms of the different aspects of the main activities: managerial tasks and responsibilities, motivating staff and students, monitoring and assessing the educational aspects of the school, among others. Authors such as Goldring et al (2009) emphasise knowledge and skills, personal characteristics, and values and beliefs as the underpinning of the sort of leadership exhibited by individuals and teams when fulfilling their leadership role. The authors identify the core components and key processes associated with effective principal-ship. The key processes are, according to the authors: planning; implementing; supporting; advocating; communicating; monitoring and setting high standards for student learning; rigorous curriculum (content); quality pedagogy; culture of learning and professional behaviour; connections to external communities; and systemic performance accountability. In a similar vein Pashiardis (1998) identifies the main characteristics that are needed in order to perform effectively as a principal. These are: having great love and ambition for their profession which they regard as a sacred and holy duty; being deep thinkers and constant learners; having the deep conviction that they can have greater influence from a position of leadership such as the principal-ship than from any other position in the school system; being risk-takers and not being afraid to "express their inner thoughts freely": they should be self-confident and know that they are doing a good job and, therefore, are not afraid to be compared with others; being honest and lovers of the truth; finding innovative ways to reward both their teachers and their students; being ambitious and having the drive for constant improvement and advancement to positions of authority and influence for both personal and professional reasons; being focussed on creating and maintaining good school-parent relations; believing in trait-leadership theory whilst acknowledging that they should familiarise themselves with theoretical approaches to leadership in order to improve their management style.

Both the effectiveness of the school principal and the impact of their work have been analysed in the literature. The differences between leaders must in any case be measured according to their outcomes: performance, achievement of objectives, growth and individual development. Pont, Nusche and Moorman (2008) summarise this by outlining three reasons for the importance of school leadership:

- It plays its part in helping students to learn better. The conditions in which one learns and teaches have an effect upon learning, and ultimately leadership helps to determine these conditions. The research into the relationship between leadership and learning establishes that there is an indirect correlation given that the leader generally works outside the classroom and their impact on the student is mediated by the teachers, the classroom environment, practices in the classroom, etc. The consequences of the actions of leaders must be sought in the motivation, capacity and working conditions of the teachers, who work directly with the students. The four tasks of leadership that have a direct relationship with learning are: supporting and developing teaching quality, defining aims and measuring progress, allocating strategic resources and collaborating with other schools.

- It builds a bridge between educational policy and practice. School principals have an important role in the application of educational reform within schools, in that they exercise the vital role of mediator between those who must implement reforms or innovation in the classroom and those who have designed or authorised them. They represent a link between bottom-up and top-down strategies.

- It links the school to its environment. The task of principals in connecting the school with the outside environment has been shown to have a cumulative impact, as the effect they have on their environment has important knock-on effects on students. Schools must adapt to the needs of the outside world and redefine their tasks in response to a changing world (Stoll and Fink, 1999).

Leithwood, Harris and Hopkins (2008) summarise the key findings what they refer to as "strong claims" about successful school leadership:

1. School leadership is second only to classroom teaching as an influence on pupil learning.
2. Almost all successful leaders draw on the same repertoire of basic leadership practices.
3. The ways in which leaders apply these basic leadership practices – not the practices themselves - demonstrate responsiveness to, rather than dictation by, the contexts in which they work.
4. School leaders improve teaching and learning indirectly and most powerfully through their influence on staff motivation, commitment and working conditions.
5. School leadership has a greater influence on schools and students when it is widely distributed.
6. Some patterns of distribution are more effective than others.
7. A small handful of personal traits explains a high proportion of the variation in leadership effectiveness.

Because of increased pressure for educational improvement, school principals have assumed new roles and responsibilities within the school administration. Thus, principals have to prioritize

their tasks and allocate their time accordingly. Several studies investigate the importance school principals attach to their various job responsibilities and the proportion of time they devote to carrying them out (Chan and Pool, 2002).

Principals have a critical influence on school development and effectiveness. There have been several analyses of the relationship between school principal-ship and student performance (Branch, Hanushek and Rivkin, 2009, Hallinger and Heck, 1998; Cotton, 2003; Waters, Marzano and McNulty, 2003; Witziers, Bosker and Kruger, 2003; Leithwood, Louis, Anderson and Wahlstrom, 2004; Levacic, 2005; Nettles and Herrington, 2007).

Studies have been conducted analyzing principals' influence on school dynamics, such as motivating teachers and students, identifying the goals to be achieved, managing resources (materials and human) and developing organizational structures which support the attainment of the educational goals of the school (teaching, learning and evaluation processes) (Knapp et al, 2003 and Leithwood, Louis, Anderson, Wahlstrom, 2004 among others). Staff management represents another of the principals' tasks which has received wide attention (Harris at al, 2010).

If we want to improve schools is necessary to optimize the work of managers. And for that, it is essential firstly to know what they do and then to determine which of their actions have a positive impact on school performance; especially as they perform a dual role, as managers or administrators, and as educational leaders (Viñao, 2005 and Coronel, 2008). The importance of the principal for improving school performance is widely acknowledged and highlights the importance of knowing the day to day activities of school principals, their schedule and how their time is distributed between tasks and how this may vary as a result of the school profile and context.

School principals can play critical roles in the development of high-quality schools (see Darling-Hammond, LaPointe, Meyerson, Orr and Cohen,

2007, among others). While some of the research into leadership links school principals directly to student achievement (e.g. Branch, Hanushek and Rivkin, 2009), there is another strand of research into the topic which relates school management models to school principals' tasks and duties. In addition, some researchers have attempted to quantify the contribution of principals in these areas, so, for example, Waters, Marzano and McNulty (2003) state that student performance can be increased by 0.25 standard deviations, and Leithwood and Riehl (2005) argue that 20% of the school 's contribution to student achievement is due to the work of school leader.

The tasks that School Principals should undertake constitute a very widely debated subject in the scientific literature. There are different approaches to defining their role in schools and debates about the main priorities they should have. The research into school principals' tasks divides into two approaches. On the one hand, the most important areas and tasks are related to the curricular field (programs, teaching, curriculum), management (external and internal administration) and interpersonal relationships (teachers, students, parents). On the other hand, there is a debate about the role of the school principal in solving conflicts, and in establishing a good culture and climate within the organization.

Finally, there are the aspects related to the low interest shown by school principals in tasks such as external administration, student behavior or teachers' professional development, and their high interest in tasks such as curricular planning, staff management and internal administration. A much larger research base documents school principals' effects on school activities, through motivating teachers and students, identifying and articulating a clear vision and goals, developing high performance expectations, fostering communication, allocating resources, and developing organizational structures to support teaching and learning (Knapp, Copland, Plecki and Portin, 2006; Leithwood, Louis, Anderson and Wahlstrom, 2004, among others).

Principals also affect the quality of education within schools through the recruitment, development, and retention of teachers (Harris, Stacey, Ingle and Thompson, 2010). Leithwood, (2005) has demonstrated that the tasks corresponding to these dimensions has a significant impact on the teaching staff, itself a key element for student learning. A direct relationship has been shown to obtain in the following areas: individual teaching effectiveness; collective teaching effectiveness; job satisfaction; organizational commitment; stress/collapse; encouragement and commitment to the school or the profession.

The actions of the principal are determined by the type of leadership employed, the specific style, as well as the legal educational framework. Therefore, different styles of leadership will place more emphasis on some types of tasks than on others, and similarly, there will be some variation in the way the tasks are carried out. A thorough analysis of the tasks of leadership would need to take this into account.

A degree of agreement exists within the various studies on leadership which points to various broad categories, which can be further subdivided into tasks. These, according to Leithwood (2005), are as follows. The first consists in establishing approaches, aims or direction. This category refers to a series of practices in which the principal aim is to develop a shared commitment and understanding regarding the organization, its aims and activities. The main objective is to ensure that staff feel that they are carrying out their work in line with a specific purpose or vision. This category is associated with the adoption of specific leadership practices such as: identifying and articulating a vision, fostering group acceptance of objectives and aims in line with the fulfilment of that vision and the creation of high expectations. The second task is related to developing people, and refers to the ability of the principal to strengthen those capacities and skills of the staff which are essential to the fulfilment of the common aims. The specific practices include providing individual support to teachers, ensuring that they have an intellectually stimulating working environment, and modelling the attitudes and behavior that are consistent with achieving that vision and those aims. The third task involves time devoted to redesigning the organization.

The contribution that the schools make towards student learning depends on the motivation and capacities of the teaching staff. However, organizational conditions can impose limits upon the use of effective practices and undermine the good intentions of the educators. Redesigning the organization means establishing working conditions which permit the staff to develop their motivation and capabilities to the maximum. Some of the specific associated practices include: strengthening the professional culture of the school, modifying the organizational structure, fostering productive relations with the family and the community and taking the best possible advantage of external support from outside actors, irrespective of whether they are educational authorities or not. Finally school principals have to manage the study programme: the last category of key practices linked to successful principal leadership relates to curriculum management. Some of them, such as those of staffing levels (selection of teachers, decisions made inside the school with respect to its professional staff), the provision of technical and material support to teachers (e.g. drawing up the curriculum, material resources), and the supervision of the teachers, are part of the official responsibilities of each school principal and their technical team.

More recently studies carried out by Lai Horng, Klasik and Loeb (2009) collected time-use data from 41 high school principals, with 12 elementary and 12 middle school principals used for purposes of comparison. Analyses the principals' tasks be-

gan with a description of how principals spend their time during the school day. The study identifies the distribution of principals' time across six task categories: administration, teaching programmes, organization management, internal relations, external relations, day-to-day teaching. On average, principals spent the most time on administrative activities to keep the school running smoothly, such as managing student discipline and fulfilling compliance requirements, which accounted for about thirty percent of the school day. They spent just over a fifth of the day on management tasks, such as managing budgets and staff and hiring personnel. On average, they spent 15 percent of their time on internal relations, such as developing relationships with students and interacting socially with staff; and five percent on the external relations, such as fund raising. Principals appear to devote the least amount of time to education related activities including day-to-day teaching tasks (six percent) and more general educational responsibilities (seven percent). Day-to-day education includes activities such as conducting classroom visits and informally coaching teachers; while general educational activities include activities such as evaluating the curriculum and planning professional development. Approximately a fifth of activities did not fit into any of these six broad task categories. These included the principal taking "personal time" (e.g., eating lunch, using the bathroom), interacting with the researcher, or in transition between activities.

Gimeno and others (1995: 151-153), in the context of Spanish education, following a study carried out among school principals in Spain, propose the following categorization of functions and of tasks corresponding to each function: The first function is related to assessment. This category includes such tasks as: giving suggestions on subject content or on a particular topic or area, suggesting changes in the methodology employed by each teacher in order to improve teaching, assessing teachers, showing an interest in how teachers evaluate their students, pointing out to teachers the necessity of supporting students with difficulties at school, analyzing examination failure and providing teachers with advice on how to deal with their students.

The second function is co-ordination and includes such tasks as: suggesting common aspects not related with any particular area or subject (study habits, fostering reading, etc.) which need to be taken into account by the teachers, stimulating cooperation and coordination between the teachers, monitoring to ensure that all teachers set similar standards of performance, preventing teachers from overloading some students more than others with homework, ensuring that exams do not coincide or pile up on the same day, fostering the carrying out of cultural and extra-curricular activities, proposing and taking measures to facilitate the acclimatization of students when they attend the school for the first time.

The third function consists in facilitating a social climate. This category includes: intervening as a mediator when there are conflicts between the teacher and his/her students, encouraging a good working environment and good relations between teachers, helping teachers with personal problems if requested by them, helping teachers in problems of a professional character, encouraging and having meetings with students, taking steps to ensure the effective integration of boys and girls, or of students from another country or culture etc., maintaining good relations with parents and encouraging the participation and the commitment of the students in the school.

A further category is the control function, which comprises such tasks as: being vigilant in ensuring that the school aims for high academic performance from its students, ensuring and keeping an eye on discipline in the places of common use: corridors, school yards, taking care that each teacher fulfils their duties: attendance in class, timetables, controlling student absenteeism, reminding about pending tasks to be done,

ensuring agreements are fulfilled, and developing an evaluation procedure for the school's activities, results, etc.

The next category relates to the dissemination of information. Principals need to ensure that each teacher receives all the pertinent information about the school: provisions, laws, etc; to inform and suggest strategies for improvement: courses, books, and relevant journals; and transmitting information about meetings with parents: their concerns, wishes, protests, etc.

In the category of management, principals take responsibility for economic management, are concerned to ensure that the institution is up-to date with documentation, secretarial tasks, devise strategies for obtaining resources, apart from those allocated by the Public Administration, meet the needs of teachers for resources and materials for the optimal functioning of their classes and concern themselves with the upkeep of the school: the building, decoration, etc.

The last category consists of representation. In this group the author includes tasks in which principals work on representing the school to the outside world, ensuring the recruitment of students for the school where they work, ensuring that contacts with the Administration (Inspection, Provincial departments, etc.) are maintained, maintaining relations with other school of a similar nature or of a different type, endeavoring to make sure that the school has its own image and that it stands out from the rest, and maintaining good relations with Teachers' school.

While Gimeno and others (1995), emphasize the way of carrying out tasks and Leithwood (2005) refers to generic functions, there is a broad correspondence between the two analyses.

The academic study of how managers of schools allocate their time has provided valuable data in the area of leadership and international studies and has helped to improve the performance of school directors. There have been many studies that have looked at this issue (eg: Burke, 1980; Selman, 1991, Gorman, 1993; Helps, 1994, Chan and Pool, 2002; Larry, 2003, Rayfield and Diamond, 2004; Taylor, 2007; Walker, 2009, Murillo and Román, 2013). These studies, in addition to establishing what tasks school leaders dedicated their time to, have analyzed how variations in way time is distributed depend upon variables such as gender, age, experience, and the size and characteristics of the school, as well as looking at the differences between the actual distribution of time and the ideal, in the opinion of their protagonists, and the impact of this distribution on the performance of students and upon school dynamics.

Comparing the different approaches to the principals' tasks we can see that there are similarities between them. In every approach the principals are seen to engage in: management activities, staff oriented activities, educational activities and tasks related to the school environment. The Leithwood model, for instance, offers a global approach towards the principal's functions, based on a political and strategic perspective. The Spanish approaches are based on the public school model, highlighting the tasks related to the educational dimension. The principal's tasks cover all of a school's activities from a curricular and pedagogical perspective (Gimeno, 1995).

1. THE CONTEXT OF STUDY

Catalonia is one of 20 autonomous regions of Spain established by the democratic constitution of 1978. Since the 1980s a process of decentralisation has increasingly taken place, devolving power to the various autonomous communities in ways which, despite similarities, also show significant differences. With a population of seven million, Catalonia is a region with a long history, a language of its own and distinct traditions, many of which date back to the medieval period. Today it enjoys very wide powers in many administrative areas, including its schools. In practice, this means that although certain general areas come under state control, the specific regulations and administrative management of Catalan schools are the responsibility of the regional government, in this case the Generalitat de Catalunya (Catalan Autonomous Government). Power over school management was transferred to the autonomous communities by the Spanish central government in 1983.

1.1. The Catalan Educational System

The educational system in Catalonia tends to be a decentralised model. Hence, the political control of education is distributed between the different administrations: the Government of Spain, the Autonomous Communities (Regions) and local and municipal authorities. Our study is confined to Catalonia; a Region which in 1981 received a degree of authority, the means and the resources to assume responsibility for education. Despite this, the centralising tendency of the State means that, for instance, 55% of the school calendar must conform to the requirements of the state government, on the grounds of ensuring a degree of uniformity in the curriculum and of ensuring that qualifications achieved a common standard.

The State devises the structures that ensure the homogeneity and the unity of the educational system and which guarantee the integrity of the system (the issuing of certificates, basic structure of the system, general legislation, general inspection, etc.). The Autonomous Communities (Regions) have the authority to develop their own rules and to regulate the non-basic elements of the educational system, as well as determining the administrative-executive limits of the management of the system in their own territory. The local authorities can cooperate with other administrations, however they are not considered to be education administrations and as such, they will normally engage in aspects such as the creation, construction and maintenance of publicly-funded schools, the management of activities or complementary services, the design of projects within the revitalisation of municipal education and the planning of specific teaching programmes (pre-primary 0-3 years, teaching of music, compensatory education for adults, etc.).

The structure of the educational system in Catalonia is characterised by the fact that it is divided into stages, cycles and courses. The stages regulate the psycho-pedagogical processes based on cognitive development and comprise Pre-Primary School (0-6 years), Primary Education (6-12 years), Lower Secondary Education (compulsory, from 12 to 16 years) Upper Secondary Education (from 16 to 18 years) and university. Compulsory education is composed of 10 courses which are taught between the ages of 6 and (6 at Primary level and 4 at Secondary level). Cycles correspond to syllabus design criteria within each of the stages and determine pedagogical aspects such as evaluation, the sequencing of content, tutorial activities, etc. Finally, courses are the more concrete units of

the system and integrated into the socio-cultural context; the academic course is offered between the months of September and June.

The system is also differentiated, in relation to the centres, 'schools' which offer Pre-School and Primary education and 'schools' that offer Secondary education (compulsory or not). Depending on their nature, educational centres can be state-run (financed and managed by the Public Administration), publicly funded private schools (where the financial and organisational unit is shared between the private sector and the public sector) and those that are exclusively private where the ownership, management and financing depend on a private body. According to data from 2010-11, 65% of the centres are state-owned, 30% are publicly-funded private schools and 5% are private. Figure 1 illustrates the Spanish education system.

1.2. The Management of Secondary Schools

The model of management in Catalonia was established by the Catalan Education Act (LEC, 2009). This established the governing bodies in Second-

Figure 1. The Spanish educational system

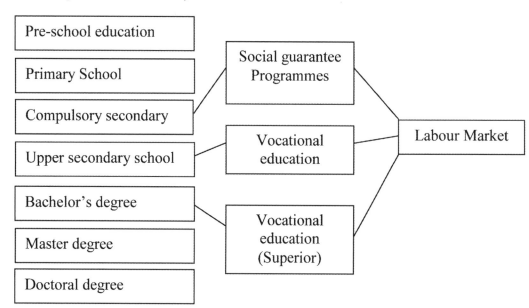

ary Schools (compulsory and non-compulsory education) and the functions each body must develop (Table1). The managerial model used in Catalan schools and regulated by the LEC is known as the participatory model, and its main element is the involvement of everyone in education in the decision making process (students, parents, teachers).

This in turn defines the functions of management in schools that are publicly-funded or publicly-funded private schools.

Differences between the management of publicly-funded schools and publicly-funded private schools as regards their management. The fundamental difference, in terms of the legislation governing the management and running of the schools between publicly-funded private schools and publicly-funded public ones is that: Publicly-funded centres have to have a management team and the publicly-funded private centres do not. Publicly-funded centres must in addition specify the criteria for recruitment to the post of school principal (management project, years of experience, etc.), whereas it is only the functions of the school principal that are specified for the publicly-funded private schools. Publicly-funded private schools are subjected to fewer regulations, they have greater autonomy and there is considerable variation between the schools. Publicly-funded schools are, however, more homogeneous since they are obliged to follow the same legal requirements which specify in precise terms how the centres must be administered.

2. THE STUDY

2.1. Purpose

The objective of our research is to describe and analyse the tasks school principals carry out in their day to day activity, and to compare these with the tasks as defined by the local legislation. We will examine the theoretical principles of the participative management model and management practice in secondary schools through the analysis of the principal's day-to-day tasks in order to compare those with the legislation. The final aim of the study is to classify the principal's tasks.

2.2. Context

Sant Cugat del Vallés, the town where this study was carried out, faces challenges of guaranteeing development and innovation and strengthening social cohesion. The town of Sant Cugat del Val-

Table 1. The school principal's tasks and functions, according to the Catalan Education Act

Government Bodies and the Functions they Perform	Publicly-Funded Schools (Chapter I, Article 139)	Publicly-Funded Private Schools (Chapter II, Article 49)
Government bodies and coordination	• The School Principal • The faculty • The management team • The school board	• The School Principal • The faculty • The school board
Functions of the School Principal	Responsible for the organisation, functioning and the administration of the centre and also for educational management and is responsible for all the staff. To represent the educational establishment, to fulfill an educational role, provide leadership, and serve as head of the school board, management, etc.	Responsible for educational management in the centre Leadership role
Appointed by	The selection of the School Principal is carried out by competitive examination, with the involvement of the School Board and the Educational Administration.	The educational community of the centre participates in the appointment of the School Principal via the School Board.

lés stands out from an educational point of view in that it forms part of what are called, at the European level, "learning cities", a status which derives from UNESCO in the report on education for the 21st century. This report establishes the fundamental pillars of education: learning how to do, learning how to be, learning how to learn and learning how to live together and this provided the framework upon which the educational project of Sant Cugat de Vallés was constructed. It is a town located in the metropolitan area of Barcelona, with a population of 87,000 inhabitants (25% of whom are less than 18 years old) and which stands out because of the quality of its educational centres and the educational policies that they implement.

The educational environment of Sant Cugat can be regarded as a microcosm, in that it is distinct from the other municipalities that surround it. In particular, three features create the special situation of Sant Cugat, and have particular significance for education: Sant Cugat was the site of the Education Science Faculty of the Autonomous University of Barcelona: the standard profile of families with a high level of education presupposes a high awareness of the importance of their children obtaining a good education and of offering them more access to educational resources, and at the same time, greater involvement in the school; and last but not least, the significant degree of involvement and support from the local administration in the development of educational policies.

As already suggested in this study, school leadership has a key role in connecting the school with its environment, and for this reason the case study was carried out in Sant Cugat, as due to its status as a "learning city" it has a long-standing track record of working together with other local educational centres and agencies, motivated by the idea that the town must be integrated into the school and the school must be integrated into the town. In this way, the 23 primary and secondary educational schools, which are diverse in terms

of ownership and educational projects, form an integrated group and work in unison when it comes to benefiting the town.

When UNICEF declared Sant Cugat to be a 'Child Friendly City', in November 2011, the selection committee specifically recognised the way in which the town was integrated in all the educational entities of the municipality and its ability to create networks and synergies using the distinct resources available. This is undoubtedly one of the greatest assets of this town.

2.3. Method

According to Lai Horng, Klasik, and Loeb (2009), previous research on the way prinicpals use their time can be grouped into two broad categories – ethnographic studies and self-report studies – each with their own benefits and limitations.

The first category, ethnographic studies allow for depth and detailed analysis, but generally include observations covering only a few principals and are consequently one cannot necessarily generalize to a larger population of schools, nor do they allow one to draw empirically based conclusions linking a principal's time-use to school outcomes (Morris, Crowson, Porter-Gehrie and Hurwitz, 1984, among others).

The second category, self-report research, usually conducted with surveys, allows for large samples but often sacrifices depth, and perhaps accuracy. These studies are likely to be susceptible to self-reporting and memory biases (e.g. Brewer, 1993; Martinko and Gardner, 1990).

Recent advances in self-report data collection methods, such as end-of-the-day logs and experience sampling methods (ESM), have reduced some of these potential biases (Goldring, Jason, Henry, and Camburn, 2008). For example, Spillane, Camburn and Pareja (2007) employ ESM by paging Principals up to 15 times a day on portable handheld devices on six consecutive days. Each time they were paged, Principals filled out a short survey about what they were doing, who they were with, and where they were. The real-time nature of this method eliminates the possibility that Principals forget or misremember their daily activities. The method, however, still suffers from the potential biases inherent in self-reporting. An additional drawback of ESM is that the surveys take time to complete and are thus inevitably limited in their scope so as not to overly disrupt the principal's working day.

The study we present in this chapter has the advantages of the last approach. Similar to self-report data, the data for this study covers the activities and locations of a sample of principals. The principals were asked for their work diaries and schedules which were analysed by the research team.

Specifically, 10 Principals in the Sant Cugat municipality offered their own diaries to the research team. The sample included all the schools in the region. There are publicly-funded state schools, publicly-funded private schools and completely private schools (private management and funding).

The diaries were very different in format and type. They were written by hand or using IT tools (i.e., excel, word, tables in word system) and written by the Principals themselves. Figure 2 shows a sample of a diary page.

The principals were contacted directly through the education delegate in Sant Cugat. A reminder was sent one week after the first call.

We analysed the principals' tasks, grouping them around different topics. Firstly, the tasks in the agendas were codified according to the following variables:

- Gender, to identify if the School Principal is male or female.
- Ownership of school, which could be public, publicly-funded private or completely private.
- Time slot, to which the activity is assigned in the diary: morning (0800 to 1300), evening (1300 to 1800) or night (from 1800 onwards).
- Time spent, that is the number of minutes required to carry out the task from start to finish.

Secondly, each task was assigned to a category according to the two models: the LEC model and the theoretical model based on Leithwood (2005). These two frameworks were used because they serve to complement each other. According to the participative managerial model of the LEC, the principal's task are divided into 4 categories:

Figure 2. Sample of a principal's diary

	Dilluns	**Dimarts**	**Dimecres**	**Dijous**	**Divendres**
9-10	Reunió coordinació primària			Reunió coordinació pedagògica	
10-11	Classe	Classe	Classe	Atenció Professors	Classe
11-12	Atenció Professors	Atenció Professors	Classe	Atenció Professors	
12-13	Atenció Professors	Classe	Classe		Atenció Professors
13-14	Classe	Classe	Atenció Professors		Atenció Professors
14-15					
15-16					
16-17	Visites de 17,15 a 19,15 h				Visites de 17,15 a 19,15 h

Del 7 al 15 de novembre, exposició de treballs de recerca de BAT.

Els dies 21, 25, 26 i 27 de novembre juntes d'avaluació.

representation, pedagogical, community oriented and management oriented. to complement this classification we chose the Leithwood (2005) model based on the following categories: objectives, people, organization and instruction.

The school principals' tasks were analysed using the Leithwood (2005) classification due to its international recognition, and the classification used in the local legislation which regulates the functions and principal tasks. The categories used are described below.

2.4. Participants

The participants of the study were principals from the schools in Sant Cugat. Out of a total of 10 participants, 8 were men and 2 were women and their experience in their positions varied from 1 to 27 years. Table 2 summarizes the principals' characteristics:

Of the 10 centres analysed, 2 are managed by women and 8 by men. As regards the ownership of the 10 centres, 3 are public (IES), 3 publicly-funded private (CC) and 4 private (CP).

3. RESULTS

3.1. Analysis of Agendas: Inductive Categories

803 tasks were analysed resulting in a total number of 1,242 hours in all 10 diaries of the School Principals in the region of Sant Cugat. The results were analysed using two complementary perspectives: one inductive in character, based on the records of the tasks which appeared in the diaries and a second one, deductive in character using the functions of management teams identified by Leithwood (2005) and the functions laid out in the Catalan Education Law (LEC).

From the inductive perspective, all the tasks were codified and classified into four different categories:

- Tasks that are related to the *organisational* aspects of the school centres like the control of the teachers, tasks related to the planning and the administration of the centre, ensuring the availability of personnel

Table 2. Participants profile

Nr.	School (Coded)	Type of School	Gender	Age	Years in the School	Years in the Leading Position
1	IES 1	Public	Male	52	12	1
2	IES 2	Public	Male	40	13	8
3	IES 3	Public	Male	57	13	9
4	CC1	Publicly-funded private	Male	52		4
5	CC2	Publicly-funded private	Female	41	0,5	7
6	CC4	Publicly-funded private	Female	44	10	10
7	CP2	Private	Male	48	9	3
8	CP5	Private	Male	41	3,5	3
9	CP3	Private	Male	68	13	2
10	CP4	Private	Male	54	1	21

and material resources on a daily basis, the functioning, organisation and running of meetings, faculty of teachers, etc.

- Tasks which are related to the *pedagogical* aspects of the centre, which include: teaching, helping in the preparation of the classes of other teachers, scientific conferences outside the centre, coordination and discussion of curricular matters, etc.

- Tasks related to *interpersonal relations:* encounters with families and students, meetings with former students, lunches with parents of new students or with parents of former students, interviews with the centre's teaching staff, meetings with inspectors and with the community, etc.

- Tasks related with the *internal coordination* of the centre: collaborative work with different commissions, coordination of the school year, coordination of leisure activities, interviews with the coordinators of the different activities and institutional projects, etc.

3.2. Deductive Perspective

From the deductive perspective, the variables which determine the typology of management functions according to Leithwood (2005) and which are established in the Catalan Education Law (LEC) are:

- The functions according to Leithwood make reference to four different types of typology: related to institutional goals and objectives, related to the management of the people, reorganisation functions, and those related to instructive processes.

- The functions according to the LEC make reference to the function of representation, to pedagogical leadership, to the community and to management.

Finally, we have assigned other functions which due to their characterisation and context are not set out in previous taxonomies and are teaching functions (teaching classes and attending to students receiving tutoring) and development activities and training for school principals.

The time assigned by each school principal varied between schools. Time allotted by principals in their diaries to the various tasks varied from 99 hours to 164 hours a week. It should be noted that this working time includes the teaching hours which the school principals must undertake, and this differs depending on the ownership of the centre (undertaking teaching tasks was higher in public centres and was non-existent in private ones). The use of time by school principals is analysed in Figure 3.

The categorisation of the tasks of school principals according to Leithwood's typology shows that the tasks related to leadership of people are the most frequent, followed by instruction tasks, then those of reorganisation and, lastly, those tasks related to the setting of goals and objectives.

The categorisation of the tasks of School Principals according to the typology laid out by the LEC shows that management tasks are the most numerous, followed by pedagogical ones, then those relating to the different elements of the community (fathers and mothers, teaching staff and pupils) and, lastly, the least frequent are of institutional representation. Figure 4 illustrates this distribution.

The distribution of time according to the type of task is shown in the Table 3.

We have observed that according to the typology of Leithwood, the largest amount of time is allocated to tasks oriented towards people, followed by those related to organisation, then to instruction and finally, to goals. According to the typology of the LEC, the school principals devote more time to management tasks, followed by pedagogical ones, then the community and finally to representation.

Figure 3. Time used by school principals in management tasks (in minutes)

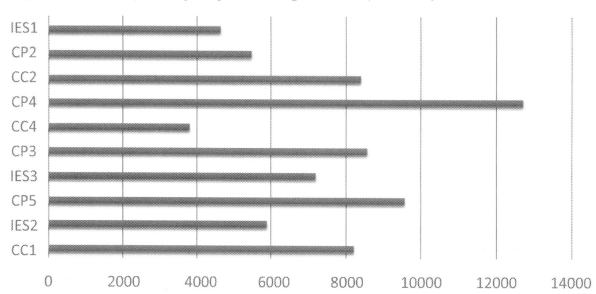

Figure 4. Distribution of tasks in function of their types

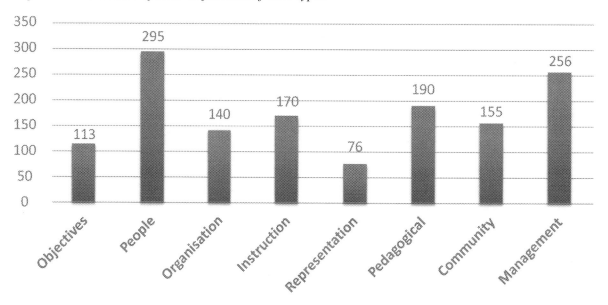

The distribution of the tasks in terms of time slots show that the largest number of activities are concentrated in time slot 1 (morning) with a total 439 tasks according to the Leithwood classification and 402 acoording to the LEC classification; in time slot 2 (evening) there are 234 tasks according to the Leithwood classification and 235 according to the LEC classification and finally in time slot 3 (night) 45 and 50 tasks respectively. The results for the distribution of the tasks in terms of timetabling slots, are shown in the following tables (Table 5 and 6) although it is important to take note that some of the tasks have been coded two or three times within the same typology. This entails that the total of recorded tasks in Table 4 does not coincide with those in Table 4 and Table 5.

Table 3. Distribution of tasks by hours

Typology	Tasks	Hours
Leithwood	Objectives	213
	People	428
	Organisation	218
	Instruction	216
LEC	Representation	163
	Pedagogical	246
	Community	221
	Management	403

Table 4. Distribution of tasks by time slots according to the Leithwood classification

Time Slot	Tasks Oriented to Goals	Tasks Oriented to People	Tasks Oriented to Organisation	Instruction Tasks	Total
1	69	157	100	113	439
2	36	110	36	52	234
3	8	28	4	5	45

Table 5. Distribution of tasks by time slots according to the LEC classification

Time Slot	Representation Tasks	Pedagogical Tasks	Community Tasks	Management Tasks	Total
1	37	126	74	165	402
2	39	57	60	79	235
3	10	7	21	12	50

Table 6. Distribution of tasks per days of the week

Task	Monday	Tuesday	Wednesday	Thursday	Friday
Goals	31	13	21	20	27
People	54	34	66	53	86
Organisation	38	23	37	22	20
Instruction	39	36	35	31	29
Representation	12	10	13	14	27
Pedagogical	38	36	48	32	36
Community	23	22	28	31	51
Management	53	71	39	53	40
Total	288	245	287	256	*316*

The data shows that school principals dedicate most of their time to activities in time slot 1 (morning), to tasks oriented to people, followed by tasks in instruction (according to the Leithwood classification) and to management and pedagogical tasks (according to the LEC classification). In time slot 2 (evening), the largest number of activities are oriented to people, followed by those of instruction (according to the classification of Leithwood) and to tasks of management followed by community, pedagogical and those of representation (according to the LEC classification). In time slot 3 (night), the School Principals principally dedicate their time to tasks oriented to people, followed by tasks towards goals, instruction and management. According to the LEC classification, school principals, dedicate their time at night to tasks related to the community, to management, to representation, and occasionally to pedagogical ones. In terms of days of the week, the distribution of the tasks is arranged in the following way (Table 6).

From the data, it can be seen that Friday is the day in which most of the tasks are concentrated, particularly those related to people and the community. Most of the management tasks are concentrated on Mondays with tasks related to attention to people being the second highest task. Tuesday is allocated mostly to management, Wednesday to pedagogical tasks and to attention to people and Thursday to people and management functions.

In terms of tasks (according to Leithwood), one can assume that tasks directed towards goals are carried out mostly on Monday, those directed towards people on Friday, those related to organisation and instruction tasks are done on Monday. The tasks (according to the LEC) are distributed in the following way: those of representation are carried out on Friday, pedagogical ones on Wednesday, those of the community on Friday and those of management on Tuesday.

The different taxonomies include functions which correspond to differentiated models of management. According to our analysis, three models can be identified according to the type of tasks and functions that school principals carry out. The first model corresponds to the participatory one which includes the functions of attention to people, attention to the community and the tasks of coordination and to the relational system; the second model is more oriented to instructive aspects and pedagogical functions; and thirdly, the more technological model focused on administrative and management tasks.

The results of our study indicate that the tasks that the School Principals carry out most frequently are linked to the participatory model, and this observation is born out by our analysis of the three categories.

Firstly, using the functional taxonomy of Leithwood (2005), we could identify the participatory model with those tasks associated with the management of people. Secondly, the functions of attention to the community which derive from the LEC policy framework could be associated with the participatory model. Finally, on the basis of the inductive, the taxonomy allows us to associate the functions of coordination and the relational system with the participatory model.

The functions can be grouped under each of the classifications as pedagogical or training functions. In this regard, using the taxonomy of Leithwood (2005), 170 tasks were categorised as being of an instructive nature; using the LEC (2009), there were 190 tasks with a pedagogical goal and using the inductive coding, 220 tasks would be assigned to this category.

In the third group, we find the tasks associated with a technological model of management and organisational processes. According to the taxonomy of Leithwood (2005), these tasks are linked to reorganisation and the redefinition of goals, and there were 253 such tasks; using the LEC (2009), 256 management tasks were identified and finally, using inductive coding, we have identified organisational 230 tasks. This grouping would show us that most of the tasks carried out by the school principal correspond to tasks typical of a participatory model of management, followed by a pedagogical model and to a lesser extent to a technocratic model.

4. DISCUSSION

The tasks and functions of management are diverse and complex and require the mastery of specific competencies. For public schools, there is no guarantee that principals will possess these competencies, since the system of professional recruitment and promotion does not demand these competencies. In the case of publicly-funded private schools and private schools, these competences are found more frequently, since these schools rely upon the principals' possessing these competencies in order to function effectively and to continue to attract pupils.

This type of analysis of the tasks carried out could be useful for school principals in that it permits them to reflect on whether what they are doing confirms to the model, whether that model is identified with the legislative process or defined institutionally. This in turn could be of interest to policy makers when formulating policies and guidelines on training, selection, promotion and the evaluation of school principals.

Our results are in line with results obtained by previous studies examining time usage by principals' functions as an indicator of their effectiveness (Murillo and Román, 2013). Principals in the Catalan schools spend more time on tasks related to the people (students, staff, parents), a finding which stands in contrast to studies such as Lai Horng, Klasik and Loeb (2009) where the major part of principals' time is dedicated to management activities.

The analysis of the principals' diaries provides rich data about their day to day activities. However further work is required in order to establish what the effects are or how these activities impact on school success. The models used provided information on how principals distribute their tasks during the working day, but further work needs to be done to identify how these activities can be evaluated and how principals implement courses of action in order to improve their performance and enhance school effectiveness.

We consider that the training of public school principals needs to be improved and also that public schools need a greater degree of autonomy in order to provide a quality service to the community.

5. CONCLUSION

The sample of 10 schools of secondary education are representative of the existing schools in the Catalan system. The schools analysed showed considerable diversity with regards to their approaches to management, which was reflected in the diversity of tasks, timetabling slots and the time dedicated to the different tasks. The size of the school and the range of educational stages which each centre teaches also influences this diversity of management models.

The distribution of these tasks throughout a day, i.e., according to the timetabling slot (morning, evening or night), varied from school to school but these differences did not appear to be related to the type of ownership but rather to the type of responsibilities which the school principal had in different schools.

With respect to the day of the week, there appeared to be a tendency to begin on Monday with organisational tasks and finish on Friday with more relational ones. Tasks related to the involvement of the various agents from within the educational community took up a great part of the school principal's time, followed by management tasks (bureaucratic and routine) and then by pedagogical tasks.

The tasks carried out clearly show a management model but the coding of each task by the researcher may involve a slight level of bias. Furthermore, a degree of stipulation is involved when identifying a task as exclusively pedagogical or as being devoted to the management of people, since tasks can share both features.

Finally, we would like to point out that the study was conducted in the month of November and while the sample of schools is representative, we cannot affirm the same degree of certainty that the tasks of the School Principal will be invariant throughout the school year. Thus a degree of caution needs to be exercised and our conclusions should be regarded as evidencing tendencies rather than offering conclusive results.

ACKNOWLEDGMENT

We would like to acknowledge our gratitude to all those School Principals who offered their work diaries for the purposes of this study.

REFERENCES

Branch, G. F., Hanushek, E., & Rivkin, S. (2008). *Principal Turnover and Effectiveness*. Paper presented at the annual meeting of the American Economics Association. San Francisco, CA.

Brauckmann, S., & Pashiardis, P. (2011). A validation study of the leadership styles of a holistic leadership theoretical framework. *International Journal of Educational Management*, *25*(1), 11–32. doi:10.1108/09513541111100099

Brewer, D. (1993). Principals and Student Outcomes: Evidence from U.S. High Schools. *Economics of Education Review*, *12*(4), 281–292. doi:10.1016/0272-7757(93)90062-L

Burke, J. R. (1980). *A study of similarities and differences in elementary principals' perceived allocation and ideal allocation of time.* (Doctoral thesis). Florida State University, Tallahassee, FL.

Catalan Education Act (LEC). (2009) *Generalitat de Catalunya*. Available at: http://portaldogc.gencat.cat/utilsEADOP/PDF/5422/950599.pdf

Chan, T., & Pool, H. (2002). *Principals' priorities versus their realities: Reducing the gap.* Paper presented at the annual meeting of the American Educational Research Association. New Orleans, LA.

Coronel, J. M. (2008). El liderazgo pedagógico: un reto y una posibilidad para la mejora educativa. In A. Villa (Ed.), *Innovación y cambio en las organizaciones educativas* (pp. 337–360). Bilbao: ICE de la Universidad de Deusto.

Cotton, K. (2003). *Principals and student achievement: What the research says.* Alexandria, VA: Association for Supervision and Curriculum Development.

Darling-Hammond, L., LaPointe, M., Meyerson, D., Terry Orr, M., & Cohen, C. (2007). Preparing School Leaders for a Changing World: Lessons from Exemplary Leadership Development Programs. In Stanford Educational Leadership Institute. Stanford University.

Gimeno, J., Beltrán, F., Salinas, B., & San Martín, A. (1995). *La dirección de centros: análisis de tareas.* Madrid: MEC-CIDE.

Goldring, E., Jason, H., Henry, M., & Camburn, E. (2008). School Context and Individual Characteristics: What Influences Principal Practice? *Journal of Educational Administration*, *46*(3), 332–352. doi:10.1108/09578230810869275

Goldring, E., Porter, A., Murphy, J., Elliott, S. N., & Cravens, X. (2009). Assessing learning-centered leadership: Connections to research, professional standards, and current practices. *Leadership and Policy in Schools*, *8*(1), 1–36. doi:10.1080/15700760802014951

Gorman, M. R. (1993). *Time management strategies and the implications for instructional leadership of high school principals: A case study analysis.* (PhD thesis). Widener University, Chester, PA.

Hallinger, P., & Heck, R. H. (1998). Exploring the principal's contribution to school effectiveness: 1980-1995. *School Effectiveness and School Improvement*, *9*(2), 157–191. doi:10.1080/0924345980090203

Harris, D. N., Stacey, R., Ingle, C., & Thompson, C. (2010). Mix and Match: What Principals Really Look for When Hiring Teachers. *Education Finance and Policy*, *5*(2), 228–246. doi:10.1162/edfp.2010.5.2.5205

Helps, R. (1994). The allocation of non-contact time to deputy head teachers in primary schools. *School Organization*, *14*(3), 243–246. doi:10.1080/0260136940140301

Knapp, M. S., Copland, M., Ford, B., Markholt, A., McLaughlin, M., Milliken, M., & Talbert, E. J. (2003). Leading for Learning Sourcebook: Concepts and Examples. Center for the Study of Teaching and Policy, University of Washington.

Lai Horng, E., Klasik, D., & Loeb, S. (2009). *Principal Time-Use and School Effectiveness*. Institute for Research on Education Policy and Practice, Stanford University.

Larry, C. D. (2003). *A study of time management use and preferred time management practices of middle and secondary school principals in selected southern states*. (PhD thesis). University of Alabama, Tuscaloosa, AL.

Leithwood, K. (2005). La dimensión emocional del mejoramiento escolar: una perspectiva desde el liderazgo. In Y. Townsend (Ed.), *International handbook of school effectiveness and school improvement* (pp. 615–634). Dordrecht, The Netherlands: Springer.

Leithwood, K., Harris, A., & Hopkins, D. (2008). Seven strong claims about succeeful school leadership. *School Leadership and Management: Formerly School Organization*, *28*(1), 27–42. doi:10.1080/13632430701800060

Leithwood, K., Louis, K., Anderson, S., & Wahlstrom, K. (2004). *How Leadership Influences Student Learning. Learning from Leadership Project*. Center for Applied Research and Educational Improvement, Ontario Institute for Studies in Education.

Leithwood, K. A., & Riehl, C. (2005). What we know about successful school leadership. In W. Firestone & C. Riehl (Eds.), *A new agenda for research on educational leadership* (pp. 12–27). New York: Teachers College Press.

Levacic, R. (2005). Educational leadership as a causal factor. *Educational Management Administration & Leadership*, *33*(2), 197–210. doi:10.1177/1741143205051053

Martinko, M. J., & Gardner, W. L. (1990). Structured Observation of Managerial Work: A Replication and Synthesis. *Journal of Management Studies*, *27*(3), 329–357. doi:10.1111/j.1467-6486.1990.tb00250.x

Morris, V. C., Crowson, R., Porter-Gehrie, C., & Hurwitz, E., Jr. (1984). Principals in action: The reality of managing schools. Columbus, OH: Charles E. Merrill Publishing Company.

Murillo, J., & Román, M. (2013). La distribución del tiempo de los directores y las directoras de escuelas de Educación Primaria en América Latina y su incidencia en el desempeño de los estudiantes. *Revista de Educación, 361*.

Nettles, S. M., & Herrington, C. (2007). Revisiting the importance of the direct effects of school leadership on student achievement: The implications for school improvement policy. *Peabody Journal of Education*, *82*(4), 724–736. doi:10.1080/01619560701603239

Pashiardis, P. (1998). Researching the Characteristics of Effective Primary School Principals in Cyprus. *Educational Management Administration & Leadership*, *26*(2), 117–130. doi:10.1177/0263211X98262002

Pont, B., Nushe, D., & Moorman, H. (2008). *Mejorar el liderazgo escolar*. Paris: OECD.

Rayfield, R., & Diamantes, T. (2004). Task analysis of the duties performed in Secondary School administration. *Education, 124*(4), 709–713.

Selman, J. W. (1991). *An analysis of time-on-task perceptions of public and private college administrators*. Unpublished research paper. University of Auburn, Auburn, Alabama.

Spillane, J. P., Camburn, E. M., & Pareja, A. S. (2007). Taking a Distributed Perspective to the School Principal's Workday. *Leadership and Policy in Schools, 6*(1), 103–125. doi:10.1080/15700760601091200

Stoll, L., & Fink, D. (1999). *Para cambiar nuestras escuelas. Reunir la eficacia y la mejora*. Barcelona: Ed. Octaedro.

Taylor, K. C. (2007). *A study of principal's perceptions regarding time management*. (PhD thesis). Kansas State University, Lawrence, KS.

Viñao, A. (2005). La dirección escolar: un análisis genealógico-cultural. In M. Fernández Enguita & M. Gutiérrez (Eds.), *Organización escolar, profesión docente y entorno comunitario* (pp. 35–81). Madrid: Akal.

Walker, J. (2009). *Reorganizing Leaders' Time: Does it Create Better Schools for Students?* Paper presented to the Annual Conference of the National Council of Professors of Educational Administration. San Antonio, TX.

Waters, T., Marzano, R. J., & McNulty, B. (2003). *Balanced leadership: What 30 years of research tells us about the effect of leadership on student achievement*. Aurora, CO: Mid-Continent Research for Education and Learning.

Witziers, B., Bosker, R. J., & Kruger, M. L. (2003). Educational leadership and student achievement: The elusive search for an association. *Educational Administration Quarterly, 39*(3), 398–425. doi:10.1177/0013161X03253411

KEY TERMS AND DEFINITIONS

Governing Bodies: Board of education of a school or administrative level.

Participatory Model: The practice of empowering employees to participate in organizational decision making.

Principal's Task Analysis: Process of identifying all the things that must be done to satisfactorily complete an activity.

Principals' Diary: Document provides independently collected data on hours and working patterns of principals in secondary schools.

School Effectiveness: Success in influencing people to strive willingly for group goals.

School Principal: School personal involved in planning, organizing, directing, and controlling human or material resources to accomplish predetermined goals.

Secondary School: Educational institutions at secondary level.

Chapter 4
Considering Latin American School Management from a Skills–Based Perspective

Joaquín Gairín
Universitat Autònoma de Barcelona, Spain

Miren Fernández-de-Álava
Universitat Autònoma de Barcelona, Spain

Aleix Barrera-Corominas
Universitat Autònoma de Barcelona, Spain

ABSTRACT

Management has an ever-greater need to surpass its mere organisational function. This chapter reviews the current situation in the competency-based training of 10 Latin American countries with two objectives: a) to understand the legislative situations and perspectives of the school management and b) to analyse the activity of the management from the perspective of competencies. This study identifies competencies as personal characteristics linked to successful activity in the workplace. School principals must display personal and procedural competencies, as well as the achievement of actions, objectives, and results. The results allow us to identify the persistence of bureaucratic and administrative model of management, and the emerging roles and competencies that would lead us to a model more focused on people and the community. School principals, as agents of change, would fit into this last perspective, which links us with the most current focus of school management.

INTRODUCTION

School centres, school principals and teachers are currently facing situations that are new, distinct and complex as a result of a society undergoing constant change and of user awareness as regards the quality of the services that they require. This new reality shows that the following issues are of relevance (Gómez-Dacal, 2013; Malpica, 2013; Pont, Nusche, & Moorman, 2008; Silva, 2010): (1) educational responses need to take into account complex phenomena such as the swift generation

DOI: 10.4018/978-1-4666-6591-0.ch004

and transformation of cultural content; increased availability of schooling; student diversity; new demands created by a multicultural knowledge society; the contextualization of approaches to the curriculum or the assumption of teaching as a collective task; (2) teachers update themselves professionally and thereby improve in an on-going manner; and (3) the role taken by principals adopts personal as well as institutional change.

There are new approaches and with them the need for new training processes. Training is, in this regard, an imperative need and a basis for providing principals with the tools necessary for the required transformation (Hallinger, 2003; Gairín, 2012). It is not simply a matter of providing them with skills and abilities but making general transformation possible through the acquisition of new knowledge and competencies (Teixidó, 2010) and with a personal orientation that includes the transformation of attitudes, values, discourse and motivations (Begley, 2006; Gairín, 2011). Their role must go beyond their organisational function and promote energising positions that manage the necessary changes (Lorenzo, 2012). Initial or permanent training in competencies must help the intended transformation.

In short, the professional development of school principals is directly linked to the processes of organizational improvement, seeing this as (1) a requirement that makes it possible to achieve organizational objectives; (2) a tool pertaining to the organization itself that acts in accordance with that organization's needs; (3) part of the strategy that makes it possible to establish advantageous positions with respect to change; or (4) the essence that permits the organization to learn. In this sense, traditional and lineal action and training models have become obsolete, giving way to new training strategies based on competencies and 'management-action', combining aspects of technical, personal, professional and social development in the framework of the triangle of relationships established between professional development, institutional development and social development.

This chapter is a critical synthesis of the contributions of 45 specialists from 14 Latin American countries on the situation and activity of the competency-based focus, carried out in the framework of the Support Network for Educational Management (RedAGE, http://www.redage.org/): a non-profit scientific association promoted by the Autonomous University of Barcelona (UAB, Spain) and the ORT University (Uruguay). It should be considered that the different contributions are linked to the educational stages of compulsory education and of the education system, although many of the references are also considered in some countries for other educational stages and for the private education system.

The text presented here falls within the framework of this association, which obtained university co-operation grants, financed by the Spanish Agency for International Development Co-operation (D/012227/07, 2008; D/018124/08, 2009; D/023860/09, 2010 and D/030241/10, 2011), and complements other publications made on the management of schools in Latin America (Gairín, 2011; Gairín and Castro, 2011), which can be used to understand the political-administrative contexts of the different situations.

The description of the situation and perspectives of the school management in 10 Latin American countries and the analysis of the activity of the management from the perspective of competencies allow us to understand a current system which is very bureaucratic and must evolve towards roles for schools principles which are more focussed on people and the community. We should, therefore, go into greater depth on the changes that the activity of principals must make, beyond other reflections that can be made on other processes related with the improvement of management and the promotion of change in schools.

The study presented here is part of the framework of this association, which acquired grants for university co-operation financed by the International Development Co-operation Agency of Spain (D/012227/07, 2008; D/018124/08, 2009; D/023860/09, 2010 y D/030241/10, 2011). The study complements other publications on the management of schools in Latin America (Gairín, 2011; Gairín & Castro, 2011). The description of the situation and perspectives of the school management in 10 Latin American countries and the analysis of the practice of management from the perspective of competencies allows us to understand the current situation, which is heavily bureaucratised and must be developed to include roles for school principals which are more focussed on people and community.

COMPETENCIES FOR THE PRACTICE OF MANAGEMENT

Although the term competency has been, and is, widely used in the field of professional training, it is not currently strange to link it to the education system and continued training, where competency-based management has become an integrating and directing model of the different policies of human resources. In this text, we relate competencies with the personal characteristics linked to successful activity in the workplace. They are developed from experiences of learning that integrate knowledge, abilities and attitudes. They make reference, therefore, to the co-ordinated activation and application of said experiences to resolve concrete professional situations efficiently.

Table 1 is a synthesis of the competencies involved in the activity of school principals, as related by different authors. The classification by fields is carried out for didactic purposes, with full awareness of the fact that the resulting fields and specificities have a relationship of systemic dependence. Therefore, those identified as cognitive competencies will be a reality to the extent that they are applied to management situations and put in relation with others such as strategic competencies.

According to (Le Boterf, 2001), the capacity for reflection and introspection is considered helpful in developing abilities related to self-regulation and permanent improvement, as an expression of a positive attitude towards change. It is also true that the analysis of one's own practice is an important factor in improvement and a basis for professional development.

On the basis of the observations that have been made on competency-based training (Gairín, 2011b; García San Pedro, 2010; MacCelland, 1973; ILO, en Vargas, 2004; Tuning América Latina, 2007), it is important to emphasise that competence, as well as an addition of elements, is the result of the interaction of these elements.

Competence cannot be reduced to simple professional performance, nor to the mere apprehension of knowledge of how to do, but instead encompasses a whole set of capacities, which are developed through processes that lead a responsible person to be capable of performing multiple actions (social, cognitive, sentimental, professional, productive), through which they project and display their capacity to resolve a given problem within a specific and changing context (Tuning América Latina, 2007, p. 32).

In this way, competency-based management is becoming an integrating and directing model for different human resources policies. However, many current education reforms focus only on the work plane, disregarding, as a consequence, the training of personal competencies and competencies for social coexistence. Furthermore, there is too much practicality in the new directions of the study and training plans, which seem to avoid personal reflexive processes or disregard the general culture.

Table 1. Managerial skills grouped by ambit. Source: Compiled by authors, based on Cardona and Chinchilla (1999); Hoyle, English and Steffy (2002); Lorenzo (2004); Spencer and Spencer (1993); and Villa (2003)

Field	Managerial Skills
Cognitive skills	Prior experience: techniques (professional or managerial) Analytical thought Conceptual reasoning
Strategic skills	Resource administration/management Orientation towards families Network of relationships Problem resolution Visionary leadership (ability to perceive opportunities, threats and external forces)
Management skills	Communication and relation with the community People development or people-centered management People management Empathy Innovation and change Leadership Teamwork and cooperation Values and ethics
Personal skills	Self-control Self-confidence Control of one's ego Behavior when facing failure Personal development and performance Flexibility Proactivity Responsibility
Procedural skills	Life-long learning Communication and relation with the community Curriculum planning and development
Attainment of targets and action	Searching for information Initiative Achievement-oriented Concern for order, quality and precision
Results	Results-oriented Learning-oriented Productivity

In any case, nothing impedes the desire to develop personal competencies, or rather to break the separation of the personal and the social (in the case of intelligence and emotional control), nor does any one say that training for a profession should only develop technical competencies and leave aside competencies related to social commitment and processes of change (Gairín, 2011b, p. 6)

Some biases that the use of competencies as a referential framework can and does have are related to the internationalisation of education processes, in the way in which reforms are applied or in the way in which they are related to the improvement of the situation and to professional development. Internationalisation is framed in contexts of globalisation that intend to respond to the social needs and the imperatives of the labour market, emphasising accountability and quality standards.

Internationalisation promotes reform processes designed to adjust study plans and programmes based on the logic of competency development.

However, there is no reason for these developments to be at odds with the consideration and reinforcement of contextual situations and the situations of the various educational and management systems.

The manner of application should reinforce the philosophy of the proposal of competencies. There is no doubt that the manner in which the reality of the intervention is ordered (partially or globally and based on problems or cases), the way in which it is acted upon (considering a totality or looking for a summation of isolated actions), the assessment method (analysing only the results or also considering the effects and processes followed) and the link made with professional development (to the extent that reflection and improvement of professional practice are promoted), can either be aligned, or not, with the focus mentioned above.

Furthermore, we cannot forget that the model, at first glance rigid and behaviourist, allows us to address different dimensions: (a) the linking of training with professional practice; (b) the recovery, more so than in other models, of the prominence of the people who are in training and the consideration of the intangible dimensions of the curriculum such as distance learning activities, directed work, allotted time, feedback on decision taking, etc.; (c) the incorporation of "curricular flexibility" in order to deal with the changing needs of the environment and of the people in training; (d) the dimension of "curriculum internationalisation" that promotes a renovation of educational programmes and the mobility of the people in training; (e) the making explicit and application of quality standards required by the context; and (f) the incorporation of new ways of promoting training (work in networks, development of communities of practice and promotion of processes of organisational learning).

Any consideration of professional competencies should remember the now classic contribution of McClelland when in 1973 he identified the term with "that which truly causes better performance in work". This relation of professional competencies with the quality of the results

of professional activity was also adopted by the International Labour Organisation, which defines competence as "the ability to perform tasks or do work according to set standards" (ILO, in Vargas, 2004). This practical dimension of competence demands that we consider other elements that can also be linked to the workplace. As García San Pedro (2010, p.14) already noted, professional competencies do not only include qualification (ability to perform tasks and activities related to a work activity) but also performance in variable labour contexts.

COMPETENCIES FOR THE PRACTICE OF MANAGEMENT IN LATIN AMERICAN COUNTRIES

According to Teixidó (2007), a focus of school management that considers the nature of management and competencies enables the identification of factors inherent to the practice of the position that will be useful for (a) carrying out assessments and prognostics with the objective of selecting the most appropriate people for the practice of management; and (b) helping active and future school principals in the identification of needs for their professional development and establishing an improvement plan.

The revision of the situation in 10 Latin American countries[1] –Argentina, Bolivia, Chile, Mexico, Nicaragua, Panamá, Paraguay, Peru, the Dominican Republic and Uruguay– will reveal the common factors to us as well as the specific factors and those that can give us clues for new developments of the activity of our school principals. In each case we identify school principals as the people with the highest levels of authority and responsibility in the organisation and we focus on the school principals of non-university levels.

The existing regulation in many Latin American countries reduces management to an executive organ of education policies and, in this sense, leaves little room for personal and contextual initiatives. This circumstance explains why many of the descriptions that we find centre on the competencies indicated by the education administration and has few references (the works of Leiva, 2014; Quiroga, 2013; Silva, 2010; and Villarroel, 2014 are almost an exception) that link with the practical problems of principals and which we will mention in the final sections.

Moreover, we must contextualise the study in the defined objectives, noting that improvement and changes in schools do not only depend on the activity of the principals, though it may be important. On one hand, it is important to consider the constant studies on change and improvement (for example, Hargreaves and Fullan, 2012), identifying other variables linked to effective and permanent changes; on the other hand, we must understand how the current dynamic and complex contexts demonstrate the need for 'soft' competencies that can give contextualised responses in accordance with determinate situations (which allow us to speak of circumstantial management activity).

ARGENTINA (AR)

The conditions of access and upward mobility in the different teaching positions of ARG are stipulated in the Teachers' Statute (Statute number 14.473), passed in 1958. Beyond these regulations, no specific regulation has been promulgated to determine which are the specific functions that school principals must perform in order to take on the leadership and direction of educational institutions.

According to the Teachers' Statute, to gain access to a managerial position it is necessary to be a qualified teacher, have a minimum of 10 years experience as a teacher and pass the specific tests that the different provinces set (article 77 of chapter XXII). For the preparation of these tests specific training courses are designed for teachers in the national sphere as well as the provincial.

While the competencies to be developed are not detailed in the design of the tests, some of the content worked on in the designs sheds light on the school principal profile that is desired. Some of the content dealt with at a national level is specified in (Gairín and Castro, 2011, p. 20):

- Preschool Level Thematic Focuses:
  - The challenges of teaching in scenarios of inclusion.
  - The work of the school principal and the construction of common pedagogy in school life.
  - Curricular development policy in the school institution: current challenges of managerial team work in different teaching contexts; and school principals and their relation with teaching processes. Thematic workshops on daily school practices, intercultural education, the development of proposals focused on the matter at hand, the library as a space for research and creativity, the treatment of teaching initiatives focused on artistic education, co-ordination with the primary level.
- Primary Level Thematic Focuses:
  - The work of the school principal and children's right to education.
  - The work of the school principal and attention to the school careers of the children.
  - The work of the school principal as a driving force and generator of institutional conditions for teaching and learning: curricular management.
  - Thematic workshops (sex education in school, co-ordination with the preschool and secondary levels, intercultural education, construction of civic responsibility and comprehension and memory of the facts and events that condition the recent past of ARG,

treatment of teaching proposals with ICT support, pedagogical treatment of environmental education, development of co-cooperativeness).

- Secondary Level Thematic Focuses:
  ○ The work of the school principal and the right to education of adolescents and young people.
  ○ The work of the school principal and attention to the school careers of the adolescents and young people.
  ○ The work of the school principal in the generation of institutional conditions for teaching and learning: curricular management.
  ○ Thematic workshops (sex education in school, construction of civic responsibility and comprehension and memory of the facts and events that condition the recent past of ARG, treatment of teaching proposals with ICT support, the specificity of artistic education, pedagogical treatment of environmental education).

The content mentioned clearly demonstrates an orientation towards pedagogical leadership, the strengthening of the knowledge of curricular development of future school principals in aspects linked to attention to diversity, contact with the environment, teaching with ICT support, co-operative education, artistic education, the teaching of national history and environmental education.

BOLIVIA (BO)

Article 35 of chapter VIII of the Education Reform Law of 2004 establishes that the school principals of educational establishments and schools must be educators trained at university level, of proven ability and educational experience. Furthermore, it established that they shall be selected through a competence exam and designated by the senior authority, in accordance with regulations and agreements.

Article 17 of Supreme Decree 0813, of 2011, establishes that the roles of the school principals are the following:

- To direct and supervise the performance of the school principals of the educative units and the proper running of these units.
- To establish permanent co-ordination mechanisms between the school principals of the educative units that make up the school.
- To take the request for designation of teachers for the educative units to the district management.
- To take the projected annual budget of the school, approved by the school board, to the district management.
- To maintain a constant link with the school board, to address and process its proposals and requirements.
- To comply with, and ensure compliance with, the Education Reform Law and related regulations.

The management of schools is considered another hierarchy within the teaching career, not as having a different character to the rest of the academic staff. In this sense, training processes have been established to develop competencies for management, despite the fact that it has not been established at a legislative level which competencies these should be.

Bolivian policies gives great importance to the role of district principals, article 32 of chapter II of Ministerial Resolution 001/2014 establishes that they must develop monitoring, accompaniment and support processes for teaching and learning processes in the curricular implementation of the educative-socio-communal-productive model, as well as the following specific roles:

- Pedagogical direction of the education unit that they manage.
- Design, development and evaluation of socio-productive projects and of technical and technological training.
- Generation of spaces for socialisation and exchange of innovative pedagogical experiences.
- Identification of the needs, vocations and productive potential of the region.
- Promotion of self-assessment and communal assessment in the education unit.
- Management of agreements with social institutions and organisations according to the vocation and productive potential (service, industry and agriculture) of their region for the technical and technological practical learning of the students.

In conclusion, the functions assigned to school principals focus largely on administrative activities and activities related to the institutions in their area.

CHILE (CL)

The Chilean education system began to transform in the 1980s, with various changes in the conception of school principals, who moved from concentrating on purely administrative and bureaucratic tasks at the beginning of the 80s to being considered the key element for the development of education institutions (Garay and Uribe, 2006; MINEDUC, 2005). This change in the conception of the school principal did not occur by chance but was rather a response to the need to adapt the figure of the school principal to the new needs of an ever more decentralised education system.

The Chilean Ministry of Education published the Framework for Good Managerial Performance in 2005, which defines the criteria for professional development and for the assessment of the performance of school principals. It addresses four wide fields with the following headers:

- Leadership:
  - To exercise leadership and administer the interior change of the school.
  - To communicate his or her own points of view with clarity and understand the perspectives of the other people involved in the education system.
  - To ensure the existence of useful information for decision taking and for the achievement of education results.
  - To administer in conflicts and resolve problems.
  - To disseminate the education project and ensure the participation of the key members of the education community in its development.
- Curricular management:
  - To know the curricular frameworks of the different education levels, the framework of good teaching and the mechanisms for assessment of his or her own performance.
  - To efficiently organise time for curricular implementation in the classroom.
  - To establish mechanisms to ensure the quality of didactic strategies in the classroom.
  - To ensure the existence of mechanisms to monitor and assess curricular implementation and the results of learning in cohesion with the institutional educational project.
- Resource management:
  - To administer and organise the establishment's resources according to its

institutional educational project and the learning results of the students.

 ◦ To develop initiatives for the attainment of additional resources, both from the immediate environment and from other sources of financing, directed at the achievement of educational and institutional results.

 ◦ To motivate, support and administer the staff to increase the effectiveness of the school.

 ◦ To generate appropriate institutional conditions for the recruiting, selection, assessment and development of the staff of the school.

- Management of the organisational environment and co-existence:

 ◦ To promote institutional values and an environment of trust and collaboration in the school for the achievement of its objectives.

 ◦ To promote an environment of collaboration between the school, the students and the parents and guardians.

 ◦ To foster relations with institutions in the community to strengthen the institutional educational project and the results of the learning of the students, generating pertinent support networks.

 ◦ To keep the community informed and sustain the achievements and needs of the schools.

The development of a regulation that considers the above-mentioned activities for the management of Chilean schools is linked to a great extent to the process of decentralisation of the education system, which has generated an atomisation of the public sector and a classist development of the private sector. Therefore, there is great emphasis on schools generating adequate interrelations that,

in line with general policies, avoid a trend toward the socioeconomic segmentation of the students (Donoso and Arias, 2011).

The existing polarisation between the private and public sectors has strengthened, on the other hand, the promotion and development of management models of managerial cuts and accounts for the difficulties in understand the complexity of the educational phenomenon.

MEXICO (ME)

The role of school principals in Mexican schools are regulated in the Federal Law on Civil Servants (Ordinance number 45), regulated by section B of Constitutional Article 123, in the documents created by the Office of Public Education (for example, the Regulation of the Hierarchy of the Workers of the Office of Public Education) and in the agreements published in the Official Journal of the Federation (Barrales & Medrano, 2011).

According to Agreement 96 (DOF, 1982), which establishes the organisation and running of primary schools in MEX, the following are functions of the school principal (article 16, of chapter IV), among others:

- To guide the general running of the school under their responsibility, defining the goals, strategies and operation policy, within the legal, pedagogical, technical and administrative framework set out in current legislation.

- To organise, direct, co-ordinate, supervise and assess the administrative, pedagogical, civic, cultural, sporting, social and recreational activity of the school.

- To respect, disseminate and ensure compliance with the regulations and instructions of the Office of Public Education, issued through the appropriate authorities.

- To represent the school technically and administratively.
- To study and resolve the pedagogical and administrative problems that occur in the school, as well as to bring up with the appropriate authorities those problems that fall outside his or her remit.
- To create the annual work plan of the school and present it to the school inspector and other competent authorities within the first month of work.
- To review and approve, where appropriate, the annual work plan that the teaching staff create in order to develop the current primary education programme, ensuring that it conforms to the applicable pedagogical techniques.
- To inform the competent authorities of the needs of the school, with regards to the training of the teaching material, extension of the building, equipment and didactic materials;
- To apply the disciplinary measures to which this legislation makes reference.
- To live in the community in which they provide their services.

The specification of the National System of Continued Training and Professional Improvement of Teachers in Service created by the Office of Public Education (SEP by its Spanish acronym) in 2008 establishes the following competencies for school principals:

- To know the structure and running of the education system and identify the main educational challenges.
- To learn to communicate with the social environment and with the educational structure to guarantee the development of schools.
- To identify and manage attention to the continued training and improvement needs of the professionals of the education com-

munity, including academic advice for the teachers and collectives.
- To understand and handle different forms of leadership and collective work for the practice of the managerial role.
- To handle and resolve institutional work, socio-affective and academic conflicts through previously agreed dialogue strategies, based on regulations, respect and tolerance.
- To understand the micro-policy of the school and to recognise of the value of the diversity of goals, interests, objectives and relationships of power in the organisational context.
- To collaboratively construct and implement projects of school transformation and innovation.
- To command basic ICT, its use in educational processes and institutional management.
- To assess and direct the processes of school teaching and learning.
- To design and develop mechanisms of educational assessment and intervention.
- To master the codes in which the social information necessary for civil participation circulates; one of which is the command of a second language.

The annual training programmes of the Office of National Education (http://goo.gl/SNCBii) focus on aspects linked to communication, the management of co-existence, democratic management in the school, the definition of managerial strategies, teamwork and co-operative work and the development of pedagogical leadership.

NICARAGUA (NI)

Article 8 of Law 413 on Educational Participation, of 11 March 2002, specifies that school principals must: (1) exercise the administration of the school, subordinated to the appropriate Board of School Trustees; (2) comply and ensure compliance with the educational policies set out by the Ministry of Education, Culture and Sport; and (3) ensure fulfilment of the School Development Plan, as well as educational results and efficiency in the administrative and academic management of the centre.

The regulation developed by chapter VII of the Educational Participation Act (Decree 46-2002) specifies the roles of the management of schools that are, among others, the following:

- To exercise the administration of the school, subordinated to the Board of School Trustees.
- To comply and ensure compliance with the educational policies set out by the Ministry.
- To ensure fulfilment of the School Development Plan, as well as educational results;
- To guarantee efficiency in the administrative and academic management of the school.
- To oversee the integration and running of the Board of School Trustees, of the Teachers' Board, of the Association of Parents and of the Students' Union, with whom they shall co-ordinate the administrative and technical activities of each sector for the running of the school, respecting established procedures and regulations.
- To carry out informative activities on the administrative, financial and technical pedagogical aspects of the school with the different sectors of the education community, through assemblies; the appropriate monthly report, which must be approved by the Board of School Trustees, must be published in a visible place in the school.

The study on school principals carried out by the National Autonomous University of Nicaragua

(Gairín and Castro, 2011, p. 119) confirms that 92% of principals carry out activities related to technical-administrative aspects, 53% academic activities and 7% activities related to human relations, which allows us to identify the real role of principals. In short, the administrative evolution of the role of school principals in the Nicaraguan context is evident, as well as the need to promote activities directed at their systematic training.

PANAMA (PA)

The Latin American Report on the Continued Training of Teachers (OEI, n.d.) contains the proposal of the University of Panama carried out in 1998 with the goal that all teachers and school principals fulfil the same requisites, which are:

Knowing How to Be

- Establishing values and actions that contribute to human and social transformation and to the preservation of ecological diversity.
- A balanced, strong and healthy personality.
- Feeling and acting with purpose.
- Being:
  - A social being that acts not only for his or her own wellbeing but also for the group.
  - Educators of the people with whom they are faced, preserving personal, familial and cultural values before the demands of a complex and dynamic world.
  - Supportive and developing a strong sense of individual and social responsibility.
- Having:
  - High self-esteem.
  - Leadership ability.

○ Social awareness, responsibility and commitment to work, as well as a sense of justice and personal and professional integrity.

- Initiative and creativity to develop intellectual activities through investigation and study.

Knowing How to Do

- Contextualising the education process according to socioeconomic problems and cultural and ecological realities.
- Creating:
  ○ Necessary abilities and attitudes to understand and appreciate the human-culture relationship and the surrounding environment.
  ○ Experience, knowledge strategies and techniques that develop in others the ability to function as a transmitter or receiver with the greatest efficacy and efficiency possible.
- Motivating students to reflect on the authenticity of the values that they each have and to act in accordance with them.
- Putting into practice the techniques and methodologies of the teaching-learning process.
- Promoting the exchange and dissemination of information and research to build up and strengthen national, regional and global culture.

Knowing How to Learn

- Increasing their knowledge of the world through reading with the objective of developing values and critical capacity and the capability to transfer them.
- Developing a critical attitude towards themselves and the surrounding situation.

- Interacting using logical arguments, critical sense and limiting them to what has been solicited and developed.
- Having:
  ○ An integrative vision of the most significant products of humanity's thought and creativity.
  ○ An all-encompassing vision of the various aspects that come into play in language as an instrument of communication and knowledge.
- Aptitude for abstract thought and the formulation of reasoning that enables the expression of logically founded judgements and not simple opinions.

Knowing How to Live Together

- Acting as a promoter and catalyst for educational processes that respect cultural plurality and diversity.
- Fostering the strengthening of the civil society in order to construct a new civilisation, based on a holistic, sustainable and systematic conception, respecting biological and cultural diversity and human dignity.
- Valuing harmony between human beings and between human beings and their environment, co-operation, solidarity, fairness and justice for all individuals and institutions.

Law 34 of 1995 indicates that through a merit-based system –established by the Constitution of the Republic of Panama–, professional aptitude, professional efficacy, social projection, educational processes and academic improvement shall be assessed, along with teaching and educational research and the ethical, moral and professional aspects of all candidates of teaching or administrative careers (articles 276 and 277).

The Ministry of Education and magisterial associations and organisations use Executive Decrees 203 of 27 September 1996, 305 of 30 April 2004 and 86 of 4 April 2005 as references for assessment. In particular, the latter declares that the school principal must have personal, professional technical-pedagogical and sociocultural competencies, such as:

- Knowledge of administrative and legal processes for the management of schools.
- Capability in:
  - Planning, supervising and assessing the management of the school and the work performed by the teaching staff under his or her responsibility.
  - Appropriate direction of the curricular management carried out by the teaching staff.
  - Directing the processes of learning to learn, learning to be, learning to do, learning to undertake and learning to live together as the basic means for meaningful learning.
  - Effectively carrying out the management of the school's resources – human, financial, physical and material.
  - Appropriately and efficiently using resources.
- Ability to mediate in the conflicts inherent in schools.
- Leadership to formulate and conduct the strategic plan, programmes and projects of the school that aim at integral, effective, efficient and transparent administration.
- Appropriate handling of interpersonal relations with the entire education community.
- Confidence and security in his or herself and in the actions that he or she undertakes.

PARAGUAY (PY)

Article 138 of General Education Act 1.264 states that the school principal is the authority responsible for the direction and administration of an education institution. Among his or her roles linked to the education community, he or she must encourage the organisation of three associations based on educational and democratic criteria and practices: one for parents and students, another for the professional educators of the institution and another for the administrative and assistant staff (article 143, chapter II).

Chapter 2 of the Regulation on the "Public Exam for the Selection of Educators", through Ministerial Resolution 9135 of 12 October 2009, states that: the public exam is a selection process for educators who must demonstrate – through an assessment of documentation and competencies – the requirements established to occupy said position in public educational institutions (article 15).

This exam has 3 stages: (a) documentary certification, where previous academic experience, work experience and other merits are assessed; (b) assessment of general and specific competencies, through written and oral tests; and (c) announcement, where the name of the person who will occupy the position is made public. Stage (a) is based on 6 categories of qualification – gradings of occupation according to technicality, complexity, level of responsibility and autonomy – related to theoretical-practical training necessary to exercise the role of the school principal (see Table 2).

Stage (b) sets the required competencies for the various profiles of managers in institutions of: mid-level education, special schooling, professional training and permanent education, and basic and mi-level education for young people and adults:

Table 2. Categories of qualification and characteristics. Source: Regulation on the "Public Exam for the Selection of Educators" (p. 23)

Categories	Characteristics
CAT 1 Work Updating	Corresponds to knowledge and abilities acquired through various events (seminars, workshops, forums, conferences, symposiums, panels, internships, etc.). Final assessment strategies may eventually be incorporated and in general are officially recognised by means of documents called evidences or other documents of participation according to hours attended.
CAT 2 Professional Training	Includes, for example, degrees or diplomas (accompanied by their certificate of studies) and other, informal, courses of professional training, the product of training programmes supported by the Ministry of Education and Culture and/or legally recognised institutions.
CAT 3 Mid-level Specialists	Corresponds to the qualifications given as a result of training in one of the mid-level disciplines, which qualify the beneficiary for productive activity in specialities recognised by the Ministry of Education and Culture.
CAT 4 Technologists	Corresponds to the regulated training for a given profession. The competencies associated with this category require training in universities or institutes of higher learning that are formally recognised in the country. Initial training of teachers for all levels of education, non-university third level teaching specialisations, training of Upper-level Specialists and Technologists at a university or non-university level.
CAT 5 Graduate Professionals	Corresponds to higher education with a minimum duration of hours that shall be established by the competent authorities, on the basis of current legislation and the international treaties signed in the regional or global sphere. Includes regulated consistent training for a given profession in a course of post-secondary studies in a university or higher education institute that is legally recognised in the country.
CAT 5.1 Education Graduate Professionals	Corresponds to higher education training with a minimum duration of hours that shall be established by the competent authorities, on the basis of current legislation and the international treaties signed in the regional or global sphere.
CAT 6 Postgraduate Professionals	Corresponds to higher education training characterised by specialist knowledge that requires basic university education carried out in any of the recognised universities or higher education institutes. Some examples of qualifications in this category are postgraduate diplomas, specialisations, master's degrees, doctorates and post-doctoral studies.

- Knowledge of:
  - Pedagogical and administrative management.
  - Legislation of the education sphere.
  - Mechanisms for quality management in education.
  - Planning, organisation, supervision and assessment of training processes.
  - Education policies and organisational and functional structure of the national education system.
- Ability in:
  - Management, motivation, negotiation, partnership building, effective social bonding, informed decision taking and management control.
  - Teamwork.
  - Judgement and administration of conflicts.
- Others:
  - Openness to continued training in the position and to accountability of professional performance.

Taking these general and specific competencies as a reference, all candidates must take written and oral tests. In the former they must resolve a case aimed at the improvement of the education service. In the latter they must demonstrate, at least, effective communication in Spanish and Guarani, disciplinary, pedagogical and management knowledge, as well as knowledge of global and regional legislation. Finally, for stage (c), marks are divided in the following way: documentary certification – 40 points; assessment of general and specific competencies – 50 points; and oral test – 10 points.

PERU (PE)

General Education Act 28044 defines the school principal as the maximum authority and legal representative of an education institution. Therefore, a school principal must (article 55): (a) direct the institution in accordance with article 68 of General Education Act 28044; (b) preside over the school board, promote harmonious human relations, teamwork and the participation of all the members of the education community; (c) promote the assessment and self-assessment of his or her management and present the results to the education community and his or her superiors; (d) train for his or her position; and (e) commit to a public career when working in state institutions.

Therefore, while the work spheres of teachers are teaching, administration and research, those of the school principal or school principal assistant are administrative (article 59). Specifically, the functions of a school principal are (article 19):

- To approve, by Managerial Resolution, the management instruments of the Education Institution.
- To drive the creation, execution and assessment – in a participative way – of the Institutional Education Project, of the Annual Work Plan and the Internal Regulation.
- To co-ordinate with the Parents' Association the use of funds, in accordance with the General Regulation of the Parent's Association
- To delegate roles to the school principals and other members of the education community.
- To develop training activities for the staff.

- To design, execute and assess pedagogical innovation and education management, experimentation and research projects.
- To establish, in co-ordination with the Institutional School Board and before the start of the school year, the schedule for the school year, adapting it to the geographic, productive-economic and social characteristics of the area, keeping in account regional directions and guaranteeing the effective use of the teaching time, in the framework of the national directions and regulations set out by the Ministry of Education for the start of the school year.
- To stimulate good teaching performance, establishing practices and strategies of public recognition of successful education innovations and experiences in the education community.
- To plan, organise, direct, execute, supervise and assess the education service.
- To preside over the Assessment Committee for the entry, upward mobility and permanence of the teaching and administrative staff; and to preside over the Institutional School Board.
- To promote agreements, pacts and consensus with other institutions and organisations of the community and to ensure compliance with them.
- To ensure the maintenance and conservation of the furniture, equipment and infrastructure of the education institution, and to manage the acquisition and/or donation of furniture and equipment as well as the rehabilitation of the school infrastructure.
- Others assigned by specific regulations in the sector.

The naming of the school principal or school principal assistant position of education institutions and programmes is done by public selection upon assessment of the candidates. The selection is the responsibility of the Local Education Management Unit, is carried out according to the needs of the education service and is objective, transparent, impartial and reliable (article 17).

The "Regulations for the public exam for access to school principal or school principal assistant positions in public education institutions of basic regular education" (Ministerial Resolution 0262 and Directive 018-2013) regulate the personal and professional competencies required of candidates and consider, in reference to the Framework of Good Managerial Performance, the following 5 competencies:

- Curricular management. Planning, organising, executing and assessing each curriculum in order to ensure that the students learn appropriate and pertinent knowledge in a systematic fashion.
- Support for the performance of teaching. Giving pedagogical support to the teaching staff in order to encourage their responsibility in the students' learning process, promote reflexive, systematic and creative practice and stimulate good teaching performance.
- Resource management. Efficient management of resources –human, financial, material, temporary and informative– to achieve the set learning challenges, linked with institutional objectives.
- Institutional environment and teamwork. Promotion of teamwork and creation of an environment of dialogue, co-operation, development of people, good performance and committed participation of the members of the education community and of society.
- Professional development. Assessment of management performance, development of continued learning processes and dis-

cussion with the education community in order to meet the requirements of the education project and professional project and responsibility for the results.

DOMINICAN REPUBLIC (DO)

In 1994, the State Education Office created a Manual of Posts and Functions for Basic Level Schools in which it describes the school principal as fulfilling the following functions and capabilities (pp. 9-11):

- Assuming knowledge as the most valuable resource for achieving the efficiency and efficacy of processes, and with it, the greatest possible result.
- Designing a team-based supervision model through strategies of accompaniment, advice, systematic tracking and monitoring of educational processes.
- Developing training activities for the theoretical-methodological strengthening of the teachers and administrative staff.
- Progressive innovation of the School Education Project.
- Demonstrating theoretical-practical competencies in management and the development of the curriculum.
- Promoting respect for life, human rights, protection of the environment and the use and enjoyment of natural and cultural resources.
- Organising the organisational structure, financial, didactic and educational resources and the explicit and implicit knowledge of human capital with which he or she acts in the school and its environment.
- Promoting the development of sports, fine arts and the development of the community.

- Budgeting the resources necessary to guarantee the running of the activities and tasks of the school project.

Years later, articles 121 and 124 of General Education Act 66-97 stated that school management ensures compliance with legal regulations and the regulations of superior bodies, and complies with the decisions of the school board. Comprising the school manager, two representatives of the teaching staff, two representatives of the parent's association, an educator, two representatives of organised civil society and a representative of the student body, the school board is responsible for (article 123):

- Applying the school's development plans, in the framework of the policies set out by the National Education Board.
- Articulating school activity and enriching it with extracurricular activities.
- Managing the budgets assigned by the State Office of Education and Culture and other resources required.
- Seeking consensus on the educational policies of the school and on the expression of civil society.
- Considering concerns of general interest or ideas about the running of the school.
- Strengthening relations between school and community and support for one another.
- Promoting curricular development.
- Recommending the appointment of teachers in schools of more than 300 students.
- Supervising the progress of matters of educational, economic and general interest for the school, including especially the maintenance of the building and nutrition programmes.
- Ensuring the quality of education and fairness in the educational service.

Departmental Order 03-2012 contains regulations referring to the System of Public Exams for the Selection of School Principals. In addition to moral, ethical, attitude-related, intellectual and affective qualities, and knowledge and competencies required for the practice of management, the following are required (chapter V – On documents and aspects to assess): capability in public relations, positive leadership and creativity in the search for solutions to the problems of the position; good handling of interpersonal relationships; understanding, sincerity, tolerance and truthfulness; ability in oral and written communication; impartiality in decision taking; responsibility; the physical and mental health necessary to carry out the tasks of the position; critical sense.

On the basis of 100 points –professional profile, 25; written knowledge test, 40; case study, 20; oral test, 15 –, those who obtain the highest marks pass the exam and are declared school principals. Their functions and responsibilities are the following (Regulation 63903, article 74 of chapter I, heading XIII):

- Co-ordinating the creation, application and assessment of the school's educational development plan, and co-ordinating the School Board.
- Complying with the information procedures and regulations of the general managements to enable the monitoring, analysis and planning of the general plans of the institution.
- Guaranteeing the smooth running of the technical, pedagogical and administrative matters of the school.
- Promoting decentralisation.
- Promoting relationships of integration and co-existence between the school, its staff and the community.
- Giving the appropriate attention and care to the building(s), furniture and other technical and didactic resources belonging to the school under his or her responsibility, and to discipline, co-existence and other factors that affect the school environment.

- Performing other tasks assigned to his or her immediate superior in his or her area of competence.

URUGUAY (UY)

The management of an education institution comprises the school principal and school principal assistant, if there is one. The former position must always be occupied and, in the event of leave, must be assumed immediately by the school principal assistant or the preceding staff member in the hierarchy, classified according to grade, seniority or merit, among other factors. According to articles 22, 44 and 48 the following are managerial competencies:

- Setting for each teacher the groups in which he or she must teach, according to the weekly hours he or she is assigned.
- Issuing documents that containing the judgements of the civil servants of direct and indirect teaching, when they have practised for at least 3 months. Said documents must consider:
  ◦ Aptitude and preparation for the performance of their role.
  ◦ Contribution to the development of the education community.
  ◦ Diligence and punctuality.
  ◦ Collaboration in the contribution made by the school for publication in social media.
  ◦ Contribution to the training of future teachers.
  ◦ Willingness in work and collaboration with the institution.
  ◦ Initiative and concern for the improvement of the service.
  ◦ Integration of Examining Boards and Evaluation Meetings.
  ◦ Interest in, concern for and handling of the problems of the students.
  ◦ Human relations.
  ◦ Technical research or complementary educational works.

The marks given to these documents range between 1 and 100, the following being the marks and their respective evaluations (article 37): (a) from 1 to 30, grave difficulties; (b) from 31 to 50, observed; (c) from 51 to 70, acceptable; (d) from 71 to 80, good; (e) from 81 to 90, very good; and (f) from 91 to 100, excellent. School principals who practise indirect teaching are assessed on 9 aspects, giving greater importance to the ability to direct and manage (article 48):

- Institutional administration ability and work efficiency.
- Pedagogical-technical ability in their role.
- Creation of a work environment that stimulates and promotes their initiatives and those of the institution.
- Advanced classes, grants, pedagogical-technical committees, and research.
- Impartiality in the judgment of subordinates.
- Initiatives aimed at the improvement and technical improvement of the service.
- Permanence and dedication.
- Work with the community and publication of educational activity in media.
- Human relations.

Analysis of the practice of management in Latin American countries from the perspective of competencies

Tables 3, 4, 5, 6 and 7 analyses the different competencies required for the practice of management based on the legislative policies of the 10 countries described, using the 7 fields of competencies detailed herein (see Table 1) as a basis.

With regards to cognitive competencies, referring to the meta-competencies of the profession which include self-awareness, critical analysis and reflection, all the countries except NI require prin-

Table 3. Cognitive competencies checklist of the 10 countries analysed. Source: Compiled by authors

Field	Management Competency	ARG	BOL	CL	MEX	NI	PA	PY	PE	DO	UYY
Cognitive competencies	Prior experience: technical, professional or management-related	X	X	X	X		X	X	X	X	X
	Analytical thought	X		X				X		X	
	Conceptual reasoning									X	

Table 4. Strategic competencies checklist of the 10 countries analysed. Source: Compiled by authors

Field	Management Competency	ARG	BOL	CL	MEX	NI	PA	PY	PE	DO	UY
Strategic competencies	Resource administration and management	X	X		X	X	X		X	X	X
	Orientation toward families			X			X	X			
	Network of relations		X	X	X		X		X	X	X
	Problem resolution			X	X		X	X			X
	Visionary leadership		X	X			X	X		X	

Table 5. Management competencies checklist of the 10 countries analysed. Source: Compiled by authors

Field	Management Competency	ARG	BOL	CL	MEX	NI	PA	PY	PE	DO	UYY
Management competencies	Community communication and relations		X	X	X	X	X	X	X	X	X
	Development of people			X	X			X		X	X
	Direction of people		X	X				X	X		X
	Empathy			X						X	
	Innovation and change		X	X	X				X	X	X
	Leadership		X	X			X		X	X	X
	Teamwork and co-operation	X	X		X		X	X	X	X	X
	Values and ethics			X						X	

Table 6. Personal and procedural competencies checklist of the 10 countries analysed. Source: Compiled by authors

Field	Management Competency	ARG	BOL	CL	MEX	NI	PA	PY	PE	DO	UYY
Personal skills	Self-control		X	X							
	Proactiveness		X	X	X			X			
	Responsibility		X		X	X		X			
Procedural competencies	Continued learning							X	X	X	X
	Community communication and relations		X	X		X	X		X	X	X
	Curriculum planning and development	X	X	X	X	X	X	X	X	X	X

Table 7. Achievement of objectives and results competencies checklist of the 10 countries analysed. Source: Compiled by authors

Field	Management Competency	ARG	BOL	CL	MEX	NI	PA	PY	PE	DO	UYY
Achievement of objectives and action	Search for information			X							
	Initiative		X	X	X					X	X
	Orientation toward success		X				X				
	Concern for order, quality and precision		X		X	X	X		X		X
Results	Orientation toward results		X	X			X		X		X
	Orientation toward learning	X		X			X		X	X	X
	Productivity		X	X							X

cipals to have previously exercised said function (in school management positions) and to present technical, professional or management-related proof. If we consider the taxonomy presented by Huberman (1989), in which, in addition to prior experience, more ontogenetic and personal aspects of each subject are considered, only CL, PY and UY consider analytical thought as a basic competence and the Dominic Republic conceptual reasoning.

All the countries except Chile and Paraguay include strategic competencies as a requirement, considered key to transforming systems based on school administration towards education management (Pozner, 2000). Having said that, the management of relationships with families is only mentioned in CL, PA and PY; even when these relationships are important to understand the expectations and attributions regarding the results of the children, the direction of the learning environment in the home, family relationships, family methods and the involvement of the parents (Christenson, Round and Gorney, 1992), while the network of relationships is considered in CL and PA together with the rest of the countries except PY. The resolution of partial and general problems is taken into account by CL, ME, PA, PY and UY, and the strengthening of global visions of the complexity of the reality by BO, CL, Panama, PY and the DO.

All the countries except AR require specific management competencies in information and involvement with the community and all except CL and NI in teamwork and co-operation. The introduction of actions linked to the development of educators is valued by half of the countries studied, although some put more emphasis on the development of people and others on the direction of people. At the same time, CL and the DO consider empathy, values and ethics as specifics of management practice, and these two countries along with BO, ME, PE and UY want their school principals to promote processes of innovation and change.

At the level of personal competencies, or personal efficacy competencies, we differentiate between self-control, self-confidence, control of the ego, behaviour towards failures, personal development and updating, flexibility, proactiveness and responsibility. BO and CL consider self-control important as well as, together with ME and PY, proactiveness. No country makes reference to self-confidence, control of the ego, behaviour towards failures, personal development and updating or flexibility. Finally, BO, ME, NI and PY recognise responsibility in the practice of the profession as a merit.

Continued training is only a specific competency for 4 of the 10 countries studied. Nor are communication and involvement with the community unanimous. However, the way in which the curriculum is organised and developed is considered by all the countries and is surely related to the competency-based training designs and their continued development.

Regarding the field of achievement of objectives and action, the search for and acquisition of new information is only considered by CL, while the promotion of initiative is considered in BO, CL, ME, the DO and UY. The co-operation of the various education professionals to obtain long-lasting results is only considered by two countries, while the majority of them (6 of 10) demand order, quality and precision in candidates for managerial positions.

Orientation toward results –for continued improvement– is a specific competency required by five of the countries, it being worth highlighting that four of them consider a methodological model aimed at learning results verifiable by standards. Finally, only BO, CL and UY require productivity as a specific competency.

Beyond the specific considerations that can be made, the review carried out demonstrates the still strong consideration of competencies related to cognitive, managerial, strategic and procedural aspects for the exercise of management. They are thus aligned with the activities of planning and direction that constitute the basic nature of management (Antúnez, 2002, 2013). It should be highlighted, however, the lack of consideration for the concrete references, in the framework of the above-mentioned competencies, to analytical and conceptual thought, orientation towards families and continued learning, which suggests to us the existence of a management model which is very technocratic and focused, basically, on the application of knowledge for the management of the reality and not so much for the promotion of change and greater opening to families.

The strong presence of the above-mentioned management model is also made evident when one considers the lack of presence of personal competencies and competencies related to the fulfillment of objectives and results. It would seem, in this context that the concern of the education systems is more on principals performing their assigned task than on them achieving their own development and providing results to society. The personal competencies considered, of great importance for Antúnez (2004) and Quiroga (2013), are not cited in five countries and in four are only cited partially. Furthermore, there are references to quality and learning, but it is not generalised (as one would expect), and in few cases is an orientation towards achievement, results and productivity made explicit.

We cannot forget, in this context that the basic action of the principals is working with and for people, which requires attention to the presence and development of emotional intelligence, strongly linked to empathy, very rarely considered in the different countries.

SOLUTIONS AND RECOMMENDATIONS FOR IMPROVING LATIN AMERICAN SCHOOL MANAGEMENT

In the teaching field, it is necessary to create a new sphere of professions that encompass new meanings, revisions and conceptualisations (Bravslavsky, 2002). Teachers that become school principals must take into account the fact that their new position is different to teaching, has different requirements and demands different roles. In this respect, it is important to know and train in the new competencies that relate to a society in a process of change and schools that are ever more contextualised and focused on their users.

The results obtained in the analysis carried out allow us to specify three strategies to achieve professionalization of school management based on the current context:

- **Initial Training:** Although all the countries require prior experience in teaching or management (except Nicaragua) to access school management, the obligation for compulsory initial training to get the position is not often considered. This initial training should be a requirement for the position, focus on the knowledge of schools as organisations and on the assumption of the role and functions that management must fulfill. In this vein, it would be just as important to emphasise principals as agents of change (Gairín, 2011b) as to provide them with tools for the management of themselves and for the analysis of their professional practice.

- Permanent training must promote the exchange of experiences, through networks that allow the exchange of information, knowledge and experiences linked to function related to their professional practice The existence of few management staff in each school must be compensated by their participation in networks, if we do not want them to be affected by the loneliness of the position or the loss of perspective.

- Improving strategic and result-related strategies. In a changing society (of "liquid modernity" for Bauman, 2007) it is important for school principals to have tools and knowledge to plan the course of their schools with strategic and contingent vision that allows them to adapt to sudden new circumstances. The commitment must always be on the objectives and results determined by the community, achieving adequate processes pertinent to the human and social context.

- The development of managerial competencies includes care for people; in any case, if something is key it is not only its consideration as a key element of organisations but also a way to act that includes processes (empathy, development of people) aimed at integrating the diversity of personalities

and promoting an institutional environment favourable to change and innovation.

- Schools are organisations of and for society and, from this perspective, it seems necessary to redirect a large part of their activity toward the needs of the social environment and the families.

There are undoubtedly other options, but we defend those provided as they are transferable to many of the situations analysed and we consider them key to modern practice in school management.

FUTURE RESEARCH DIRECTIONS

Management in Latin American countries is largely based on bureaucratic and administrative models, consistent with very centralised and uniform education system models. This focus reduces the action of the management to an activity centred on the application of external regulations and the monitoring of compliance with these regulations.

The development of further studies on the nature of the work of school principals in the circumstances detailed will surely enable us to discover facets of their work, especially those related to their work with people and the processes of change. It better prepares the current school principals to be able to respond to the requirements of people, not just of the education system. To do so with a view to the future requires us, on one hand, to initiate studies on the competencies to promote, the means to do so and the systems of assessment of professional practice. It is also important to continue to advance in the analysis and specification of studies that enable the identification of the role of families and the community in relation to education institutions and, most importantly, the role that school principals must play in promoting greater involvement of and collaboration of those with communities in the day-to-day activity of their schools.

CONCLUSION

The analysis carried out highlights a role for school principals focused on administrative and monitoring tasks, such as those related to the administration of resources, the exercise of administrative leadership, relations with families, the planning and development of the curriculum, the orientation of the learning and concern for order, quality and precision, While the development of people and the system of internal and external relations are mentioned, the context of interpretation suggests that they are considered more as a resource to order than as the basis of the actions to carry out.

It is also certain that the education systems and their development have differences in Latin American, though trends cannot be identified by geographical area. Bolivia, Chile, the Dominican Republic and Uruguay are the countries that consider the most competencies analysed (beyond them developing them and requiring them in professional practice). Nicaragua and Argentina are the countries that have regulated the least in this respect and neither of the two makes reference to personal competencies and only mention one of the seven that refer to the achievement of objectives and results.

By contrast, the trend of current education systems to decentralisation and strengthening of institutional autonomy requires a management model which is more focused on the internal and surrounding context and more attentive to the needs of its users and society. A tendency toward the professionalization of principals stands out, in countries with greater decentralisation, where the action must be based on knowledge and be directed at the user of the education service (Wise, Bradshaw and Cartwright, 2012, p. 126). The improvement processes based on data (Bolívar, 2011; Gómez-Dacal, 2013) and linked to pedagogical leadership (Martínez, Badia and Jolonch, 2013; Pont, Nusche and Moorman, 2008) lead

us to some of the challenges proposed for school leaders (Bolívar, 2012; Pont, Nusche and Moorman, 2008; Tomás, 2013) and also linked to the new management trend (Smith, 2012).

We speak of principals who support people, are focused on the internal and external community and who act as managers of the necessary changes. Distributed leadership, leadership focussed on teaching, organisational ethics, process management, collective knowledge management, the school as a community, management teams, contingent planning, value-based management and the importance of emotional intelligence are, among others, reference points for management work. These issues, addressed in classic works from Bass and Avolio (1993) to Bolivar (2012), are those that should consider the regulatory and training processes that can be developed in the next few years in Latin America.

The development of more open and democratic management focus must give way to participative management models, where the principal is seen as a leader and facilitator of educational change, who works in collaboration with the community and with the professionals to achieve the results expected by society and required by the users of the education system.

The selection and training of the principals must consider, moreover, the new competencies that must be developed, promoting their strategic thought, driving their social, not only technical, leadership and promoting a permanent attitude to analyse, act and reflect on their practice, which can make them effective managers of the change that we must promote. In any case, the training orientation is that conceptualised on competency-based training, which puts emphasis on the multidimensional, interrelated and applied nature of competencies.

However, and above all, principals as professionals must act in accordance with changing contexts, analysing the effects of their actions and working accordingly. Many of the competencies reviewed and abilities that accompany them can lead to better professional practice but will be useless if applied mechanically and out of context. In this regard, the observation and analysis of one's own practice, reflexive dialogue, introspection and critical analysis are important identifiers of professional practice appropriate for a complex and constantly changing reality.

REFERENCES

Antúnez, S. (2002). La acción directiva en las instituciones escolares (2nd ed.). Barcelona: ICE-Horsori.

Antúnez, S. (2004). *Organización Escolar y Acción Directiva*. D. F., México: Secretaría de Educación Pública.

Antúnez, S. (2013). *La dirección escolar. Postgrado/Master en dirección de centros para la innovación educativa*. Barcelona: Universitat Autònoma de Barcelona.

Barrales, A., & Medrano, H. (2011). Realidad y perspectiva de las competencias para el ejercicio directivo en México. In J. Gairín & D. Castro (Eds.), Competencias para el Ejercicio de la Dirección de Instituciones Educativas: Reflexiones y experiencias en Iberoamérica (pp. 98-116). Santiago de Chile: Redage.

Bauman, Z. (2007). *Tiempos líquidos*. Barcelona: Tusquets editores.

Begley, P. T. (2006). Self-knowledge, capacity and sensitivity: Prerequisites to authentic leadership by school principals. *Journal of Educational Administration*, *44*(6), 570–589. doi:10.1108/09578230610704792

Bolívar, A. (2011). Procesos de mejora basados en datos. La mejora del sistema educativo como proceso derivado de los resultados de la evaluación. In *P. Badía & Mª Vietes (Eds.), Evaluación, resultados -Escolares y sistemas educativos* (pp. 17–30). Madrid: Wolters Kluwer.

Bolívar, A. (2012). *Políticas actuales de mejora y liderazgo educativo*. Málaga: Aljibe.

Bravslavsky, C. (2002). *Teacher education and the demands of curricular change*. New York: American Association of Colleges for Teacher Education.

Cardona, P., & Chinchilla, N. (1999). Evaluación y desarrollo de las competencias directivas. *Harvard Deusto Business Review*, *89*, 10–19.

Christenson, S. L., Rounds, T., & Gorney, D. (1992). Family factors and student achievement: An avenue to increase student's success. *School Psychology Quarterly*, *7*(3), 178–206. doi:10.1037/h0088259

Decree 46-2002 (Decreto número 46-2002 - Reglamento de la Ley de Participación Educativa). Retrieved February 16, 2014, from: http://goo.gl/aNFWwM

Departmental Order 03-2012 contains regulations referring to the System of Public Exams for the Selection of School Principals (Orden Departamental No. 03-2012 que reglamenta el Sistema de Concurso de Oposición para seleccionar Directores/as y Sub-Directores/as de los Niveles Básico y Medio, Orientadores/as y Maestras/os de Educación Inicial, Básica y Educación Física de los Centros Educativos públicos en el año 2012). Retrieved February 15, 2014, from: http://goo.gl/zmuRPP

DOF. (1982). *Acuerdo número 96, que establece la organización y funcionamiento de las escuelas primarias.* Retrieved February 16, 2014, from: http://goo.gl/JXI4uV

Donoso, S., & Arias, O. (2011). Diferencias de escala en los sistemas de educación pública en Chile. *Ensaio Avaliação e Políticas Públicas em Educação, 19*(71), 283–306. doi:10.1590/S0104-40362011000300004

Executive Decree 86 of 4 April 2005 (Decreto Ejecutivo 86 de 4 de abril de 2005, por el cual se establece el perfil para el cargo de Director(a) de Centro Educativo de Educación Media). Retrieved February 15, 2014, from: http://goo.gl/DbYwcb

Federal Law on Civil Servants. Ordinance number 45 (Ordenanza nº 45 del Estatuto del Funcionario Docente). Retrieved February 15, 2014, from: http://goo.gl/VKyxUl

Framework for Good Managerial Performance (Marco de Buen Desempeño del Directivo. Directivos construyendo escuela). Retrieved February 15, 2014, from: http://goo.gl/sXEib4

Gairín, J. (Ed.). (2011a). *La dirección de centros educativos en Iberoamérica: Reflexiones y experiencias.* Santiago de Chile: FIDECAP.

Gairín, J. (2011b). Introducción. In J. Gairín, & D. Castro (Eds.), Competencias para el ejercicio de la dirección de instituciones educativas: Reflexiones y experiencias en Iberoamérica (pp. 6-9). Santiago de Chile: FIDECAP.

Gairín, J. (2012). La formación permanente en organización escolar. In D. Lorenzo, & M. López (Eds.), Respuestas emergentes desde la organización de instituciones educativas (pp. 45-81). Granada: Editorial Universidad de Granada.

Gairín, J., & Castro, D. (Eds.). (2011). *Competencias para el ejercicio de la dirección de instituciones educativas: Reflexiones y experiencias en Iberoamérica.* Santiago de Chile: FIDECAP.

Garay, S., & Uribe, M. (2006). *Dirección escolar como factor de eficacia y cambio: situación de la dirección escolar en Chile.* Retrieved February 18, 2014, from: http://goo.gl/VHf79e

García San Pedro, M. ª J. (2010). *Diseño y validación de un modelo de evaluación por competencias en la universidad.* (Unpublished doctoral dissertation). Universitat Autònoma de Barcelona, Spain. General Education Act 66-97 (Ley 66-97 Ley General de Educación). Retrieved February 15, 2014, from: http://goo.gl/ErjNU

General Education Act 1.264 (Ley 1.264/68 General de Educación). Retrieved February 15, 2014, from: http://goo.gl/bGRa52

General Education Act 28044 (Ley General de Educación Nº 28044). Retrieved February 15, 2014, from: http://goo.gl/9mKe9f

Gómez-Dacal, G. (2013). *Claves para la excelencia educative: Organizaciones escolares únicas y excepcionales.* Madrid: Wolters Kluwer.

Hallinger, P. (2003). The emergence of school leadership development in an era of globalization: 1980-2002. In P. Hallinger (Ed.), *Reshaping the Landscape of School Leadership Development: A global perspective* (pp. 3–22). Lisse: Swets and Zeitlinger.

Hargreaves, A., & Fullan, M. (2012). *Professional capital: Transforming teaching in every school.* New York, NY: Teachers College Press.

Hoyle, J., English, F., & Steffy, B. (2002). *Actitudes del directivo de centros docentes.* Madrid: Editorial Centro de Estudios Ramón Areces.

Huberman, M. (1989). The professional Life Cicyle of Teachers. *Teachers College Record, 91*(1), 31–57.

Law 34 of 1995 (Ley 34 de 1995 por la cual se deroga, modifican, adicionan y subrogan artículos de la Ley 47 de 1946, Orgánica de Educación). Retrieved February 15, 2014, from: http://goo.gl/EESb7G

Law 413 on Educational Participation (Ley n° 413 de Participación Educativa). Retrieved February 16, 2014, from: http://goo.gl/V317EG

Le Boterf, G. (2001). *Construire les compétences individuelles et collectives*. Paris: Editions d'Organisation.

Leiva, V. (2014) (Ed.). Asesoramiento educativo. ¿Qué necesitan nuestras escuelas? Viña del Mar: Ediciones Altazor.

Lorenzo, M. (2004). La función de liderazgo de la dirección escolar: Una competencia transversal. Enseñanza & Teaching. *Revista Interuniversitaria de Didáctica, 22*, 193–211.

Lorenzo, M. (2012). Las comunidades de liderazgo de centros educativos. *Educar, 48*(1), 9-21.

MacClelland, D. C. (1973). Testing for Competence Rather Than for 'Intelligence'. *The American Psychologist, 28*(1), 1–14. doi:10.1037/h0034092 PMID:4684069

Malpica, F. (2013). *8 ideas clave. Calidad de la práctica educativa. Referentes, indicadores y condiciones para mejorar la enseñanza-aprendizaje*. Barcelona: Graó.

Martínez, M., Badía, J., & Jolonch, A. (2013). *Lideratge per a l'aprenentatge. Estudis de cas a Catalunya*. Barcelona: Fundación Jaume Bofill.

MINEDUC. (2005). *Marco para la Buena Dirección: Criterios para el Desarrollo Profesional y Evaluación de Desempeño*. Santiago de Chile: MINEDUC.

Ministerial Resolution 001/2014 (Resolución Ministerial 001/2014 Normas Generales para la Gestión Educativa 2014). Retrieved Februrary 14, 2014, from: http://goo.gl/Cxyrkb

OEI. (n.d.). *Informe Iberoamericano sobre Formación Continua de Docentes*. Retrieved February 15, 2014, from: http://goo.gl/nZNTLq

Pont, B., Nusche, D., & Moorman, H. (2008). *Mejorar el liderazgo escolar: Política y práctica*. París: OECD. Retrieved May 24, 2014, from: http://goo.gl/aAQZwC

Pozner, P. (2000). *Competencias para la profesionalización de la gestión educativa*. Buenos Aires: IIPE-UNESCO.

Quiroga, M. (Ed.). (2013). *Crónica directiva docente: Cambio y liderazgo desde la zona de incomodidad*. Valparaíso: U. Católica de Valparaíso. Regulation on the "Public Exam for the Selection of Educators" (Reglamento "Concurso Público de Oposición para la Selección de Educadores"). Retrieved February 15, 2014, from: http://goo.gl/DYSr8i

Regulation 63903 (Reglamento N° 63903 del Estatuto Docente). Retrieved February 15, 2014, from: http://goo.gl/bwFwLQ

SEP. (2008). *Sistema Nacional de Formación Continua y superación de maestros en servicio*. México: SEP.

Silva, J.M. (2010). *Líderes e lideranças em escolas portuguesas: Protagonistas, práticas e impactos*. Vila Nova de Gaia: Fundacçao Manuel Leão.

Smith, C. R. (Ed.). (2012). *El management del siglo XXI*. Madrid: BrandSmith.

Spencer, L. M., & Spencer, S. M. (1993). *Competence at work. Models for superior performance*. New York: John Wiley & Sons.

State Education Office. (1994). *Propuesta para un Manual de Puestos y Funciones para Escuelas del Nivel Básico*. Retrieved February 15, 2014, from: http://goo.gl/mGFipJ

Supreme Decree 0813, of March, 9, 2011 (Decreto Supremo 0813 de 9 de marzo de 2011). Retrieved February 14, 2014, from: http://goo.gl/JPFC17

Teachers' Statute. Act number 14.473 (Ley 14.473 de 1958, Estatuto del Docente). Retrieved February 14, 2014, from: http://goo.gl/YGLw2x

Teixidó, J. (2007). *Competencias para el ejercicio de la dirección escolar: Bases para un modelo de desarrollo profesional de directivos escolares basado en competencias*. Retrieved October 21, 2013, from: http://goo.gl/lwMC5

Teixidó, J. (2010). Hacia un cambio de modelo en la dirección escolar. Luces y sombras de un camino tortuoso. In *A. Manzanares (Ed.), Organizar y dirigir en la complejidad: Instituciones educativas en evolución* (pp. 81–118). Madrid: Wolters Kluwer.

Tomás, M. (2013). *El liderazgo educativo. Postgrado/Master en dirección de centros para la innovación educativa*. Barcelona: Universitat Autònoma de Barcelona.

Tuning América Latina. (2007). *Proyecto Tuning*. Retrieved February 15, 2014, from: http://goo.gl/pQl8Kd

Vargas, F. (2004). *40 preguntas sobre competencia laboral*. Montevideo: CINTERFOR/OIT.

Villa, A. (2003). *Elementos significativos de la LOCE con relación a las competencias directivas*. Retrieved October 21, 2013, from: http://goo.gl/Xrm6xC

Villarroel, D. (2014). *Competencias profesionales del Equipo Directivo del sector particular subvencionado chileno en contexto vulnerable*. (Unpublished doctoral dissertation). Universitat Autònoma de Barcelona, Barcelona, Spain.

Wise, C., Bradshaw, P., & Cartwright, M. (2012). *Leading Professional Practice in Education*. New York: Sage.

ADDITIONAL READING

Arias, A. R., & Cantón, I. (2005). *El liderazgo y la dirección de centros educativos*. Barcelona: Davinci Continental.

Bass, B. M., & Avolio, B. J. (1993). *Improving Organizational Effectiveness through Transformational Leadership*. Newbury Park, CA: Sage Publications.

Blase, J., & Kirby, P. C. (2000). *Bringing Out the Best in Teachers. What Effective Principals Do*. London: Sage Publications Ltd.

Blase, J., & Kirby, P. C. (2010). *Des stratégies pour une direction scolaire efficace. Motiver et inspirer les enseignants*. Paris: Chenelière Éducation.

Campo, A. (2009). *Herramientas para directivos escolares*. Madrid: Wolters Kluwer.

Condon, C., & Clifford, M. (2010). *Measuring Principal Perfomance: How Rigorous Are Commonly Used Principal Performance Assessment Instruments?* Chicago: Learning Point Associates.

Delors, J. (1996). *La educación encierrra un tesoro*. Madrid: Santillana, Ediciones UNESCO.

Fullan, M. (2002). The Change Leader. Beyond Instructional Leadership, 59(8), 16-21.

Fullan, M. (2007). *Leading in a Culture of Change*. San Francisco: Jossey-Bass.

Gairín, J. (2011). Formación de profesores basada en competencias. *Bordón, 63*(1), 93–108.

Gómez, G. (2006). *K sigma. Control de procesos para mejorar la calidad de la enseñanza*. Madrid: Wolters Kluwer.

Hallinger, P. (2003). Leading Educational Change: Reflections on the practice of instructional and transformational leadership. *Cambridge Journal of Education*, *33*(3), 329–351. doi:10.1080/0305764032000122005

Hallinger, P., & Heck, R. H. (2010). Collaborative leadership and school improvement: Understanding the impact on school capacity and student learning. *School Leadership & Management*, *30*(2), 95–110. doi:10.1080/13632431003663214

Mas, O., & Tejada, J. (2013). *Funciones y competencias en la docencia universitaria*. Madrid: Síntesis.

Montero, A. (2008). *Proyecto de dirección y ejercicio directivo*. Madrid: Wolters Kluwer.

Montero, A. (2012). *Selección y evaluación de directores de centros educativos*. Madrid: Wolters Kluwer.

Pérez, E., & Camejo, D. (2009). *Síntesis gráfica de supervisión educativa. Manual de apoyo a supervisores, directores escolares y docentes*. Madrid: Editorial La Muralla.

Perrenoud, P. (2004). *Diez nuevas competencias para enseñar*. Barcelona: Editorial Graó.

Scott, E. (2011). Leadership Strategies: Re-Conceptualising Strategy for Educational Leadership. *School Leadership & Management*, *31*(1), 35–46. doi:10.1080/13632434.2010.540559

Spillane, J. P., Halverson, R., & Diamond, J. B. (2004). Towards a theory of leadership practice: A distributed perspective. *Journal of Curriculum Studies*, *36*(1), 3–34. doi:10.1080/0022027032000106726

Townsend, T. (2011). School leadership in the twenty-first century: Different approaches to common problems? *School Leadership & Management*, *31*(2), 93–103. doi:10.1080/13632434.2011.572419

UNESCO. (2011). *Manual de Gestión para Directores de Instituciones Educativas*. Lima: Lance Gráfico.

Vázquez, R. (2013). *La dirección de centros: gestión, ética y política*. Madrid: Ediciones Morata.

Vera, J. Mª., Mora, V., & Lapeña, A. (2006). Dirección y gestión de centros docentes. Guía práctica para el trabajo diario del equipo directivo. Barcelona: Editorial Graó.

Villarroel, D., & Gairín, J. (2012). Elaboración del perfil de las competencias del director escolar en contextos vulnerables. In *J. Gairín (Coord.), Gestión del conocimiento y desarrollo organizativo: formación y formación corporativa*. Madrid: Wolters Kluwer.

KEY TERMS AND DEFINITIONS

Competencies: Personal characteristics linked to successful performance in a job position. They refer to the co-ordinated activation and application of different types of elements to resolve certain professional situations.

Competency-Based Model: Proposal of competency-based design linked to the key tasks of a given profession, which may or may not be structured by domains or problematic nodes.

Continuous Training: Permanent training after initial training, aimed at increasing and perfecting professional competencies. The objective is for the professional to widen and improve his or her knowledge, abilities and attitudes in relation to the new tasks demanded by his or her professional practice.

Management Development: Set of actions linked to the promotion of a school principal that usually involves options for selection, training, promotion and assessment.

Management Team: Group of first-level school principals, normally the highest authorities of an institution and its academic, administrative and economic managers.

Manager of Change: Characteristic of the professionals who rather than working to maintain the status quo, focus on promoting and stimulating changes to respond to unsatisfactory situations.

School Management: Set of activities related to the person or people with the highest level of authority and responsibility in an organisation.

Schools: Place where teachers and the management team carry out their teaching and management activity.

ENDNOTES

[1] Selected based on accessibility to sources of information, representation of the territory and level of development of the management function.

Chapter 5
Qatar's Educational Reform:
Critical Issues Facing Principals

Michael H. Romanowski
Qatar University, Qatar

ABSTRACT

Launched in 2004, Qatar's massive educational reform, Education for a New Era, has introduced numerous changes to the K-12 educational system forcing school leaders to face challenges and issues in their role of leading and managing the school community. This chapter reports the results of a qualitative research study that examines the critical issues K-12 principals face as they implement educational reform. Using semi-structured interviews, the voices of 20 principals are presented centering on the critical issues that have evolved during the reform and the skills and leadership styles necessary to address these issues that have shaped the Qatari educational reform. Discussion and recommendations are provided to assist educational leaders in similar contexts.

INTRODUCTION

Educational reform is a demanding task. There is little doubt that the assessment of a nation's educational system and the development of recommendations for reform is challenging. However, most of that work is on the theoretical level. The real challenge lies in the implementation of an educational reform and the recommendations because this moves the reform from the theoretical to the practical level and where most stakeholders are directly impacted by the reform. For many, the implementation of reform directly and significantly impacts their career and daily lives. This is certainly the case with principals. This

chapter provides insights from principals who are in the midst of a massive educational reform in Qatar. The focus on the discussion centers on the critical issues principals face, the skills and leadership styles they believe are needed to specifically address important issues, how their particular context influences and or creates these issues followed by several recommendations that could be applied to similar reform contexts.

BACKGROUND

In 2001, the country of Qatar became alarmed that the K-12 education system was "not producing

DOI: 10.4018/978-1-4666-6591-0.ch005

high-quality outcomes and was rigid, outdated, and resistant to reform" (Brewer, et al., 2007, p. iii). Considering possible reform options prompted the government to approach RAND, a nonprofit research organization, that was assigned the task of conducting a comprehensive assessment of Qatar's educational system and provide recommendations for building "a world-class system that would meet the country's changing needs" (Brewer, et al., 2007, p. xvii). The conclusions of the assessment revealed a number of fundamental problems. First, the current system was highly centralized and had limited strategies for evaluation and monitoring of policies and processes. Second, there was a lack of communication and shared vision among educational stakeholders because of the rigid top-down decision-making policy process. Finally, it demonstrated that there was an over-emphasis on rote learning and little attention to the development of critical thinking.

Upon the completion of a comprehensive examination of the existing Qatari educational system, RAND presented three specific system-changing options to the Qatari leadership. These included:

(1) a Modified Centralized Model, which upgraded the existing, centrally controlled system by adding or improving the basic elements; (2) a Charter School Model, which decentralized governance and encouraged variety through a set of schools independent of the Ministry and that allowed parents to choose whether to send their children to these schools; and (3) a Voucher Model, which offered parents school vouchers so that they could send their children to private schools and which sought to expand high-quality private schooling in Qatar (Brewer, et al., 2007, p. xix).

The Qatari leadership decided to proceed with the Charter School Model that encourages parent choice, a partially decentralized governance and provided new school models. Under a new

name, the Independent School Model, the new educational structure embodies the following characteristics:

1. Government Funded Schools
2. School Decentralization
3. Increased Accountability in Schools
4. Independent Monitoring of Schools
5. Government Evaluation of the System (Brewer et al., 2007).

As a result of RAND's report, a systematic reform designed to convert Qatar's schools into a competitive educational system known as *Education for a New Era* (EFNE) was initiated and is recognized as central to the development of the Qatari economy. EFNE was based on four principles: 1) autonomy for schools, 2) accountability through a comprehensive assessment system, 3) variety in schooling alternatives, and 4) choice for parents, teachers, and school operators. These principles represent a two-pronged strategy to reform requiring the establishment of government-funded Independent schools over a multi-year period and the implementation of annual assessments to measure student learning and school performance (Supreme Education Council, 2012).

EFNE not only introduced Independent schools but also established the Supreme Education Council (SEC) in order to guide education reform. The SEC has two main branches that deal with Independent schools—the Education and Evaluation Institute. The Education Institute recommends necessary financial allocation to support schools; establishes and monitors schools licensing; provides support and guidance to schools; develop curriculum standards and identify the competencies required for achieving quality and; provides finance to Independent Schools within the limits of their approved budget (Supreme Education Council, 2013a). The Evaluation Institute provides innovative evaluation ensuring that decision makers have access to high-quality, objective information and is responsible for collecting, analyzing and disseminating data in order to inform schools, teachers and students about their performance, thus helping them reflect and improve upon it and provide information to parents, to other parts of the SEC, and to other decision-makers on the extent to which schools are fulfilling their roles (Supreme Education Council, 2013b). The first group of 12 Independent schools opened in 2004 and, currently, all government-founded schools in Qatar have acquired independent status. Independent schools are gender segregated and categorized as elementary (grades 1-6), preparatory (grades 7-9) and secondary schools (grades 10-12).

The curriculum in the Independent schools is prescribed by the SEC with Arabic as the language of instruction and English, Islamic studies, math, and science all compulsory subjects. From sparkling new buildings to new school evaluations and student assessments, education in Qatar is rapidly changing and is now propelled by international curricula and curriculum standards all imported to Qatar from Western sources. Qatar is now one of the most active importers of foreign education providers in the world (Becker, 2009). Thus, it is safe to say that the educational landscape in Qatar has drastically changed and with it the role of the principal.

PRINCIPALS AND EDUCATIONAL REFORM

Educational reformers and researchers in Western countries have argued that the role of the school principal as the key decision-maker, facilitator, problem-solver, and the agent of change at the school site (Clark, Lotto, & Astuto, 1984; Gamage, 1996; Barth, 1991; Sergiovanni, 1991; Caldwell, 1994; Cranston, 1996). Research is quite clear that principals play a significant role in successful educational reform. The majority of educational research recognizes that both in the primary and secondary levels, schools addressing reform demonstrate that, leadership is the key factor in

successful reform (Leithwood, Louis, Anderson & Wahlstrom, 2004; Kirk & Jones, 2004; Houston, 1998; Sammons, 1999). When schools engage in educational reform, those reforms that prove successful have strong supportive leadership, especially principals who motivate staff, parents and students to deal with and overcome uncertainty and embrace the change process (Matthews and Crow, 2003; Fullan; 2001; Leithwood, et. al, 2004; Kirk & Jones, 2004; Houston, 1998). Principals are the focal point for ensuring that change initiatives do not remain on paper but are implemented within the school. In addition, a principal's leadership does not only play a significant role in educational reform but also shapes the school climate regarding how reform is perceived by teachers, parents and students.

It is well recognized that school reform requires both restructuring and reculturing (Fullan 1999; Hargreaves, 1994.) Not only do schools change, but also the role of the principal is reshaped (Murphy & Louis, 1999). When educational reform is initiated, principals must reframe their roles and shift their orientations in order to successfully implement reform (Fullan 2001.) Because educational reform requires major changes, the type of change that involves transforming the system (Reardon, Reardon & Rowe, 1998), principals must drastically alter their role. The fundamental change lies in the fact that principals can no longer be managers of the status quo but rather they must become facilitators of reform (Frederick, 1992) requiring a variety of leadership skills that are often lacking. Noonan and Renihan (2006) argue that the role of the principal has changed significantly because of educational reform and "the sustained emphasis among governments throughout the world on school accountability for student achievement" (p. 1). They further argue that reform has resulted in a "shift in emphasis from the supervision of teaching to the supervision of learning" (p. 4). It is clear that educational reform is demanding and reform presents principals with new challenges and new roles that require new skills and attitudes (Newmann & Wehlage, 1995).

Leiberman (1995) states that the reform process is difficult and fraught with challenge and conflict. For principals, educational reform can often result in role ambiguity or overload and cause a loss of the sense of identity (Murphy, 1994). Furthermore with reform, principals often find themselves promoting the school image more, working closer with parents and external agents and this role can be uncomfortable for some principals (Murphy, 1994). In addition, it is often the case that principals must closely monitor teachers' implementation of the reform and this might not fit some principals' leadership style. More importantly, principals will certainly face teacher resistance. Finally, when principals face educational reform, their leadership might be obstructed by experiences, or education and even their lack of understanding the reform itself (Neufeld, 1995) presenting major challenges for their leadership. Challenges such as the use of new technology, new teaching strategies and accommodating reform policies and changes are more likely than not to surface as challenges for principals.

Educational reform often requires radically new approaches to leadership that may be new to many educators (Leiberman, 1995; Sergiovanni, 1992). Making this shift requires principals to acquire and develop new skills to handle the challenges and issues accompanying reform changes. This shift is essential for school reform to develop and endure but it is not an easy task, especially for principals. For example, principals often have to learn the skills of collaboration and shared leadership rather simply delegating (Murphy & Datnow, 2003). Also, principals embedded in reform must learn the skills necessary to manage and guide the process of change (Fullan, 2002). Educational reform can be threatening and disruptive because of the massive changes involved in reform. For many principals, they may lack the experience and skill to manage massive change.

With educational reform comes barriers and resistance. Schools are notably resistant to change (Siskin & Little, 1995) and this creates the need for principals to be armed with the skills to reduce and remove barriers and obstacles. Being able to effectively remove barriers, obstacles and resistance to innovation is a key leadership skill required for educational reform. This demands effective communication skills often applied to different context than usual.

With the above in mind, there is clearly a need to examine the effects of reform on principals and necessary to identify the critical issues that principals face in addition to skills and leadership styles needed to successfully address these issues. However, I understand the best sources of information regarding issues and challenges facing principals and the skills to overcome these challenges are those directly involved in school leadership and educational reform. The input from principals is invaluable in understanding the impact of educational reform and how these issues can be effectively addressed. Through interviews, these voices are heard and used to uncover the critical issues and the roots and reasons for these issues, identify the skills needed to directly resolve these issues, provide relevant examples from these educational leaders and offer several recommendations for educational leaders who are in the midst of reform. Although the geographical parameters implied in this study center on the Middle East, findings and educational initiatives could reach wider global interests.

RESEARCH APPROACH AND METHODS

The purpose of this study is to examine principals' perceptions of the implementation of Qatar's educational reform initiatives. Using a phenomenological approach characterized by an emphasis on describing, understanding, and explaining complex phenomena (Sofaer, 1999), this study interprets the experiences and insights of principals by listening to their individual experiences and stories as they describe their understandings of the critical issues they face as they implement Qatar's massive educational reform and the skills they believe are essential for effective educational reform.

Willis (2007) argues that qualitative research seeks to examine a particular phenomenon through the subjective eyes of the participants and the major source of data collection to gain the participants' perspectives is interviewing. Interviewing allows the researcher to gain access to the other's perspective and that is the target of a phenomenological study, to describe the meanings and central themes of the participants experiences based on what the participants say (Kvale, 1996). Patton (2002) states the purpose of interviewing is "to find out what is in and on someone else's mind" (p. 341). Therefore, semi-structured interviews were conducted to establish the principals' understandings of the implementation of Qatar's educational reform. An interview guide was developed to collect data that would center on the following research questions.

1. What are the critical issues that have evolved during the Qatari educational reform?
2. What skills and leadership styles necessary to address these critical issues?
3. What are possible recommendations that can be made to assist principals who are dealing with educational reform?

Sample

In qualitative inquiry, there are no set rules for sample size. Sample size depends on several issues such as what the researcher wants to know, the purpose of the inquiry, what will provide credibility, and what is possible with the available time and resources (Patton, 1990). Polkinghorne (1989) recommends that researchers interview from 5 to 25 individuals who have all experienced the phenomenon. This study conducted semi-structured interviews with 20 Independent school

principals because these are the individuals who have experienced the phenomenon, in this case educational reform. The sample of schools in this study was selected based on several criteria. The study required a fair balance of male and female schools. Also, the study demanded that elementary, preparatory and secondary schools be included. The sample includes six elementary school principals (three males and three females); five preparatory schools (three males and two females); and nine secondary schools (four males and five females) representing approximately 12% of the Independent school principals. Finally, the participants' experiences as principals in Independent Schools ranges from two to seven years.

Data Analysis

Bogdan and Biklen (2002) define qualitative data analysis as "working with data, organizing it, breaking it into manageable units, synthesizing it, searching for patterns, discovering what is important and what is to be learned, and deciding what you will tell others" (p. 145). The interview data were examined in the context of the three research questions and involved selecting, focusing, condensing, and transforming data guided by thinking about which data best answer the research questions. During the analysis, data were organized identifying themes, patterns, and connections (Denzin & Lincoln, 2007; Taylor-Powell & Renner 2003; Miles & Huberman, 1994). As several themes emerged, they were content analyzed and relevant quotes were integrated into various themes in order to support or refute particular findings. The rationale was to provide an accurate account of the principals' understanding of the issues involved in educational reform. In what follows, the themes that are emerging from these interviews are presented and developed following by discussion and recommendations.

CRITICAL ISSUES FACING PRINCIPALS

From conversations with these principals, it is quite obvious, that not all issues discussed are directly related to education reform. Rather, issues that these principals face are rooted in a variety of changes that are embedded in not only educational change, but also in a rapid changing culture. The following discussion centers on the principals' perspective of the critical issues they are currently facing and the skills they believe are needed for principals to make educational reform effective and successful.

Regarding the critical issues that these principals faced, it is evident that a common theme throughout the interviews centered on a movement away from *tradition*. Tradition in this sense is a way of thinking about education and educational practices that have been the norm for quite some time. This shift away from tradition is either directly or indirectly linked to educational reform. All principals interviewed agreed that their role as principal greatly changed because of the reform. Since the reform was based on the principles of autonomy and accountability, principals lacked understanding of how to work or "be a principal" under this new framework. This philosophical shift and other demands forced a change in the principal's role. Included in this shift is an increase in the involvement of others such as faculty and parents, a release of power, control and decision-making, more delegation and less micro managing. All of these changes often conflict with the traditional role of principals in Qatar. Keep in mind that prior to Rand's analysis, school administrators had little autonomy or authority. Principals, teachers and staff were assigned to schools and all equipment and curriculum was provided. Principals evaluated teachers but only aligned with the Ministry of Education (the governing body prior to the SEC).

Another critical issue centering on teachers and teaching and also is linked to a movement away from tradition is the shift from traditional methods of teaching to the use of a diverse collection of teaching methods. The movement is from teaching that was teacher-centered stressing memorization to student-centered methods that encouraged critical thinking and problem solving. In addition, teachers are required to integrate technology and best practices and this requires principals to, as one principal stated, "keep informed about new strategies and other aspects of teaching." Principals indicated that this is difficult and often rely on professional development and other teachers to focus on this aspect of the school.

There is an issue of quality and teaching. These principals argued that it has been difficult to locate and hire qualified teachers. This view is supported by the SEC who points out that more than 30% of teachers in Qatar are not qualified to teach and 31% of teachers in Qatar have no formal qualifications to teach (Tuomi, 2011). In addition to the lack of qualified teachers, is the absence of Qatari teachers in the educational system. Other reports cite that at present there is "a huge shortage of qualified educators, and the subsequent hiring of inexperienced teachers" (Doha News Staff, 2013, p. 5). According to the participants in this study, implementing the reform in areas such as professional teacher standards and curriculum standards is difficult with unqualified teachers. One principal wrote, "some teachers cannot develop good lessons so how could they understand and use the curriculum standards?"

Not only is there a lack of qualified and experienced teachers, but also the reform has placed an increased burden on teachers creating problems for experienced teachers and magnifying problems of those teachers who lack the qualifications. Principals argued that the reform required teachers to take on additional responsibilities, many of these nonteaching tasks resulting in increased pressures on teachers. The argument regarding the requirements of educational reform is that the paperwork, learning new systems, new policies that often seem repetitive, the need to meet additional requirements and the reform forces teachers to spend time on things such as additional paperwork distracting them from their teaching and work with students. This additional work and what teachers see as unrealistic requirements imposed on them and schools, plays a role in developing a negative attitude towards the reform and for many teachers, they engage in resistance.

Educational reform requires new ways of thinking and this can be difficult to introduce and for some to embrace. Successful educational reform requires all those involved to approach the process of education in very different ways. Several principals stated that teachers needed to work with both professional and curriculum standards and this demanded a new way of understanding teaching and curriculum. One principal stated, "trying to build new curriculum and align it to standards is a very exhausting process. Even after textbooks were introduced, working with curriculum standards was one of the greatest challenges faced . . . we all have to think differently." This thinking influences curriculum, planning of instruction, student assessment and evaluation of teachers. If there is limited or weak professional development, those implementing the reform suffer as does the students and the effectiveness of the reform.

The issue of resistance is a critical issue located within education reform, not only here in Qatar, but worldwide. There is little doubt that these principals face resistance from teachers and parents. Bennett deMarrais and LeCompte (1995) define resistance in the context of student that can easily be applied to education reform. They state that resistance is a "principled, conscious, ideological non-conformity that has its philosophical differences between the individual and the institution" (p. 118-119). Resistance represents a decision on the part of individual not to engage the reform in any meaningful way other than minimal participation for job security. Any time there is change there is resistance.

One of the consequences of teacher resistance is the lack of consistency in the implementation of the new skills and knowledge that teachers have gained. One principal describes the behavior of teachers who are resisters, they "put on a show for us or when the SEC visits but continue in their old ways after we are gone." These teachers pretend they are using the strategies, they without truly embracing the new pedagogical skills, so the quality of their work is weak. Principals pointed out that another behavior that surfaces with resistors is their beliefs and behaviors are inconsistent. Principals argued that some teachers who resist correctly talk "about teaching and learning and their desire to learn, but they always have an excuse for not implementing particular strategies or provide reasons why the particular strategy did not go well giving them reason not to try it again." For many teachers who engage in resistance, they generalize when they try something new, regardless of the quality, and fail, they judge it as not working at all. Principals agreed that resistive behavior undermines educational reform and change.

Finally, changes are inevitable during educational reform. However, these principals believed that the constant changes that were made by the SEC are problematic to the success of educational reform. The SEC and *Education for a New Era* provided changes that seemed continuous and sudden. For example, the issue of bilingualism is a major change that has hampered the reform. A principal pointed out that "the reform began with the teaching of math and science in English and this lasted several years. Then the SEC made a sudden shift to Arabic for these subjects. The shift was sudden, completely changes the school and impacted teacher and students." From talking to these principals, it seems that the SEC often rushes to get results lacking the needed patience to allow aspects of the reform to take place and develop. In addition to these SEC sudden changes, the SEC can make it difficult to accomplish goals. Although autonomy is a fundamental principle in Qatar's educational reform, these principals argue there are numerous bureaucratic hurdles that plague the effectiveness of schools and undermine school autonomy.

SKILLS AND LEADERSHIP STYLES NECESSARY

The first skill set needed to effectively address educational reform, not limited to this context but relevant to any reform, is the skill to deal with change. According to these principals, one of the fundamental skills needed for effective leadership and a smoother implementation of educational reform is the ability to lead in the midst of constant change. One principal stated, "the leadership style that can adjust and help its followers to adjust to the constant change is the most required during the educational reform." According to these principals, having knowledge about change theory, creating a culture of change and the skills and abilities to place that theory into practice will prove worthwhile in achieving long-term goals that is vital in educational reform.

During educational reform when all stakeholders are facing change, school leaders must be able to embrace and sell the benefits of the reform. This requires principals to be able to communicate to teachers the benefits reform. One principal summed up this idea with the following comment:

We [principals] should be able to tell teachers about the benefits of dealing with these issues [implications of education reform]; for instance, using technology and thinking about the impact of technology will attract the interests of the student and support their learning, in addition to saving teachers' time and achieving the outcomes.

Several of these principals agreed that it was their responsibility to provide the positives of the reform so teachers, parents and students could see the value in the sometimes-difficult changes and challenges that occur during educational reform. More importantly, principals were aware and acknowledged the difficulty in getting excited and supportive of policies that they believe are not effective or useful, or even work against the reform. One principal stated, "leaders should accept the existing challenges and cope with them, even when they disagree, they have to enlighten the school community with the rapid and massive changes in areas like technology and other changes that come with the reform."

Another skill that these principals deemed valuable was the ability to understand various viewpoints and compromise when necessary. One principal stated "school leaders should listen to the different points of view and try to manage change by converging these views to come up with a sort of compromise supporting learning outcomes meanwhile implementing the SEC instructions." This requires not only the ability to understand diverse points of view, but also principals need to possess a great deal of knowledge about a variety of issues. One principal argued that leaders need an "intelligence or awareness of the existence of problems in school but also a knowledge or being able to predict in advance when indicators emergence of new or upcoming issues." According to this individual, this knowledge is necessary to place others' points of view into perspective and to be able to make well-informed decisions. One principal argued that in the midst of change such as in educational reform, individuals are "pushing their own interests and can be very convincing about what should be done." Principals need to have the knowledge to decide if the ideas or individuals or groups are valid and useful for the school, faculty and students or an idea that serves a limited interest. Other principals echoed this concern citing the need for an understanding of technology, extensive understanding of planning, knowledge and application of financial and human resources and the need to keep updated on numerous educational issues.

Finally, several principals argued that the demands of the reform force them to change their leadership practice and delegate responsibilities to others. One principal stated:

I changed lots of my practices. For example, I had to train people in ways so they can make decisions . . . delegate responsibilities to people who are working with me and building trust with others. This requires that you discover other's abilities and potentials.

It seems that the reform has created a great deal of work and change and principals realize that they alone cannot complete what is needed so they must rely on others. One principal stated, "The reform requires lots of changes and delegation must be used to ensure that all the new work gets done and the school continues to move forward." Clearly these principals now rely on delegation as a part of their leadership and for some, their view of leadership has changed, evidenced by one principal who commented, "I changed my leadership. Leaders are mentors and motivators." One principal summed up the use of delegation, "delegating contributed to the development of the teams and networks that helped in facilitating the tasks. Delegation helps earn the trust of employees and invests capacities correctly."

RECOMMENDATIONS

What are possible recommendations that can be drawn from these findings? The critical issues that school leaders face during educational reform, are complicated and no one-size-fits all approach is likely to work in any educational context. Decision makers must keep this in mind not only on the large-scale level of educational reform, but also within individual schools impacted by reform. The centralized control of schools limits the scope for principals to exercise leadership. Instead, they become managers that carry out prescribed plans and instructions from educational policy makers. In this study, although autonomy was a basis for *Education for a New Era,* this was quickly lost and principals expressed the concern that this hampered their leadership abilities. Thus, the first recommendation is that principals should be allowed to make decisions about issues closely related to their school during educational reform. Principals need to have some degree of autonomy and power in order to meet some of the specific needs of their school. However, principals must have the necessary leadership skills, must be able to ensure accountability for student outcomes, with appropriate oversight from education authorities and must have the appropriate support and guidance regarding matters such as training, teacher standards and curriculum.

Second, it goes without saying but principals must be well-qualified and independent thinkers. There is no doubt that school leaders must have the abilities to lead schools especially during times of reform. In Qatar, all principals must be Qatari and at times, this can be problematic because some do not have the educational background and experiences to truly lead schools. If this is the case, schools will suffer under inadequate leadership. The principals in this study argued this is the case and that principals should study to improve their skills. I would argue that in this context and similar contexts where principals might lack needed experiences and skills, that during educational reform, there should be a requirement that all principals must have a graduate degree in educational leadership or a diploma that centers on school leadership. Educational authorities and schools should work in collaboration with colleges of education to develop context specific programs based on research and data to provide the skills needed for leaders. This will enable schools to improve and increase student academic achievement. Leithwood et al. (2004) estimates that roughly one quarter of the total schools' effects on student outcomes can be attributed (directly and indirectly) to school leadership.

Third from the principals' perspectives, it is vital for educational policy planners to make informed decisions that are well researched and thought especially with consideration given to the local context. Fullan (2001) argues the main reason that educational reforms never fully develop and endure is that reformers fail to understand the local school development. There is a need for collaboration between stakeholders and educational policy makers. Furthermore, decisions that are implemented need time to develop and play out before results are evaluated. Most importantly, decision makers must consider (when appropriate) the input from stakeholders such as principals, parents, students and teachers.

Fourth, educational leadership preparation programs must prepare educational leaders with complex understandings of what is involved in reform and policy change. This requires scholarly study on education policy analysis so leaders are better equipped to analyze policies regarding issues such as the purpose of education, the objectives that policies are designed to attain, the methods for attaining them and the tools for measuring their success or failure. Furthermore, as one principal in this study suggested during an interview, it would be wise for principals to become familiar with other countries' problems, challenges, and experiences with educational reform. This would aid in broadening principals' thinking to include an understanding that their experiences are not all that unique, and other educational reform experiences are similar. This would prove beneficial for principals as they navigate educational reform.

Finally, this particular context in Qatar requires that principals receive some consultation. There are situations in Qatar where independent school principals lack the needed significant educational experiences and background. Several of these principals argued that school leaders should have a consultant to help him or her by providing proper advice, guidance and to give informed consultation when needed. This is vital specifically to avoid any misconceptions or misunderstandings with SEC regulations and rules but could also prove useful in daily decision-making. Consultations could be used to "fill in the gaps" where principals might need assistance and would provide a long-term solution by teaching principals with a type of on the job education.

FUTURE RESEARCH DIRECTIONS

This chapter addresses principals' perspectives regarding what they see as the knowledge and skills essential for dealing with issues during educational reform. Although important, this discussion is limited to the leadership skills and in some sense beliefs of how principals should lead. Future research should move this discussion further by examining the personal epistemological beliefs, that is, a principals' fundamental beliefs about knowing and learning to determine if these are aligned with their leadership styles and skills. More importantly, do these epistemological beliefs influence their leadership and if so, to what degree? This type of research could provide insights into the decision-making processes of principals and how this shapes decisions and polices in turn, influence teachers and students.

Particularly in this study, it is important to keep in mind that when reading these findings the basis of this discussion is self-reported data. This is very valuable information, but one could argue these descriptions are from the leaders' perspective and may not reflect the thoughts of those that they lead. Although this is beyond the scope of this chapter, it would be worthwhile to further research educational reform by exploring the leadership skills needed from the teachers' perspectives. In addition, studying what principals state as important skills during educational reform and comparing and contrasting these findings with how the teachers in their building view the principals' leadership would be interesting and beneficial. This research would draw attention to if what is said by principals and how what is said manifests in school policies, leadership styles, and possible impact on teachers and student learning.

Finally, additional research is needed to understand what motivates teachers and leaders to invest in educational reform. What are the extrinsic and intrinsic incentives that motivate teachers? How can other teachers and educational leaders be helped to develop a continued commitment to reform? It is important to understand the incentives and disincentives in the educational system.

CONCLUSION

In closing, educational reform and change takes time. It is vital for not only educational leaders, but also all those involved in educational reform to consider that educational reform is a slow process that must be embedded in the context of the nation undergoing reform. This chapter discusses the knowledge and skills needed to effectively address the critical issues facing principals during educational reform. The voices of principals express the need for complex understanding of change and resistance, good communication skills, the ability to change one's leadership style by delegating to others, compromising skills and the importance of having a solid knowledge base about education that can be used to make informed decisions. Various suggestions are offered to aid principals during the reform based on these principals' experiences.

There are numerous factors that contribute to the success of the educational reform. Leadership is certainly high on the list of important factors required for successful educational reform. Principals must understand that to some degree education reform is context specific, but there are also elements of reform that cross boundaries and are common among a variety of contexts. Therefore, it is vital for school leaders to understand reform in the larger context. This means that educational leaders need to look outwards to others countries that are or have reformed their educational system in order to gain insight to others' challenges and then begin to use this insight in cultural relevant ways to effectively address the many challenges that accompany educational reform. The bottom line is that principals need to understand and address all the issues that affect educational reform, not just the easy ones in order for educational reform to be effective and successful.

REFERENCES

Barth, R. (1991). *Improving schools from within.* San Francisco: Jossey-Bass.

Becker, R. F. (2009). *International branch campuses: Markets and strategies.* London: Observatory for Higher Education.

Bennett deMarrais, K., & LeCompte, M. (1995). *The way schools work: A sociological analysis of education* (2nd ed.). White Plains, NY: Longman Publishers.

Bogdan, R. C., & Biklen, S. K. (2002). *Qualitative research for education: An introduction to theory and methods* (4th ed.). Needham Heights, MA: Allyn and Bacon.

Brewer, D. J., Augustine, C. H., Zellman, G. L., Ryan, G. W., Goldman, C. A., Stasz, C., & Constant, L. (2007). *Education for a new era: Design and implementation of K-12 education reform in Qatar.* Rand Corp. Retrieved December 13, 2013, from http://www.rand.org/pubs/monographs/MG548/

Caldwell, B. J. (1994). Leading the transformation of Australia's schools. *Management in Education, 22*(2), 76–84.

Clark, D., Lotto, L., & Astuto, T. (1984). Effective schools and school improvement: A comparative analysis of two lines of inquiry. *Educational Administration Quarterly, 20*(3), 41–68. doi:10.1177/0013161X84020003004

Cranston, N. (1996). An investigation of the skills, knowledge and attitudes of principals. *Practising Administrator*, *18*(3), 4–7.

Denzin, N. L., & Lincoln, Y. (2007). *The Landscape of Qualitative Research* (3rd ed.). New York: Sage Publications.

Doha News Staff. (2013, March). *Are Qatar's independent schools broken? An in-depth report.* Retrieved December 13, 2013, from http://dohanews.co/are-qatars-independent-schools-broken-an-in-depth/

Frederick, J. (1992). Ongoing principal development: The route to restructuring urban schools. *Education and Urban Society*, *25*(1), 57–70. doi:10.1177/0013124592025001005

Fullan, M. (1999). *Change forces*. London: Falmer Press.

Fullan, M. (2001). *The new meaning of educational change* (3rd ed.). New York: Teachers College Press.

Fullan, M. (2002). *The change leader*. Retrieved December 13, 2013, from: http://www.cdl.org/resource-library/articles/change_ldr.php

Gamage, D. T. (1996). Institution of school-based management in New South Wales. In *D.T. Gamage (Ed.), School-based management: Theory, research and practice* (pp. 125–148). Colombo: Karunaratne & Sons.

Hargreaves, A. (1994). *Changing teachers, changing times*. New York: Teachers College Press.

Houston, P. D. (1998, June 3). The abc's of administrative shortages. *Education Week*.

Kirk, D. J. & Jones, T. C. (2004). *Effective schools*. Dallas, TX: Pearson Education. Retrieved December 9, 2013 from pearsoneducation.com

Kvale, S. (1996). *Interviews: An introduction to qualitative research interviewing*. Newbury Park, CA: Sage Publications.

Leiberman, A. (1995). Restructuring schools: The dynamics of changing practice, structure and culture. In A. Leiberman (Ed.), *The work of restructuring schools: Building from the ground up* (pp. 1–17). New York: Teachers College Press.

Leithwood, K., Louis, K. S., Anderson, S., & Wahlstrom, K. (2004). *Review of research: How leadership influences student learning*. New York: The Wallace Foundation.

Matthews, L. J., & Crow, G. M. (2003). *Being and becoming a principal: Role concepts for contemporary principals and assistant principals*. Boston, MA: Allyn and Bacon.

Miles, M. B., & Huberman, A. M. (1994). *Qualitative data analysis* (2nd ed.). Newbury Park, CA: Sage.

Murphy, J. (1994). Transformational change and the evolving role of the principal: Early empirical evidence. In J. Murphy & K. S. Louis (Eds.), *Reshaping the principalship: Insights from transformational reform efforts* (pp. 20–53). Thousand Oaks, CA: Corwin Press.

Murphy, J., & Datnow, A. (2003). *Leadership lessons from comprehensive school reform*. Thousand Oaks, CA: Corwin Press.

Murphy, J., & Lewis, K. S. (1999). Introduction: Framing the project. In J. Murphy & K. S. Lewis (Eds.), *Handbook of educational administration* (pp. xxi–xvii). San Francisco: Jossey-Bass.

Neufeld, B. (1995). *Teacher learning in the context of the SDP: What are the opportunities? What is the context?* Paper presented at the annual meeting of the American Educational Research Association. San Francisco, CA.

Newmann, F. M., & Wehlage, G. G. (1995). *Successful school restructuring: A report to the public and educators*. Madison, WI: Wisconsin Center for Education Research.

Noonan, B., & Renihan, P. (2006). Demystifying assessment leadership. *Canadian Journal of Educational Administration and Policy, 56*, 1–20.

Patton, M. Q. (1990). *Qualitative Evaluation and Research Methods* (2nd ed.). Newbury Park, CA: Sage.

Patton, M. Q. (2002). *Qualitative Evaluation and Research Methods* (3rd ed.). Newbury Park, CA: Sage.

Polkinghorne, D. E. (1989). Phenomenological research methods. In R. S. Valle & S. Halling (Eds.), *Existential-phenomenological perspectives in psychology* (pp. 41–60). New York: Plenum. doi:10.1007/978-1-4615-6989-3_3

Reardon, K. K., Reardon, K. J., & Rowe, A. J. (1998, Spring). Leadership styles for the five stages of radical change. *Acquisition Review Quarterly*, 129-146.

Sammons, P. (1999). *School effectiveness*. The Netherlands: Swetz and Zeitlinger.

Sergiovanni, T. (1992). *Moral leadership*. San Francisco: Jossey Bass.

Sergiovanni, T. J. (1991). *The principalship*. Boston: Allyn and Bacon.

Siskin, L., & Little, J. (1995). The subject department: Continuities and critiques. In L. Siskin & J. Little (Eds.), *The subjects in question* (pp. 1–22). New York: Teachers College Press.

Sofaer, S. (1999). Qualitative methods: What are they and why use them? *Health Services Research, 34*(5), 1101–1118. PMID:10591275

Supreme Education Council. (2011). *Above 30% teachers not qualified*. Retrieved December 18, 2013 from: http://thepeninsulaqatar.com/index.php/news/qatar/163929/above-30pc-teachers-not-qualified

Supreme Education Council. (2012). *Independent Schools*. Retrieved November 13, 2013, from http://www.sec.gov.qa/En/pages/Glossary.aspx

Supreme Education Council. (2013a). *Education Institute*. Retrieved November 13, 2013, from http://www.sec.gov.qa/En/SECInstitutes/EducationInstitute/Pages/home.aspx

Supreme Education Council. (2013b). *Evaluation Institute*. Retrieved November 13, 2013, from http://www.sec.gov.qa/En/SECInstitutes/EvaluationInstitute/Pages/home.aspx

Taylor-Powell, E., & Renner, M. (2003). *University of Wisconsin Extension, Program Development and Evaluation: Analyzing qualitative data*. Retrieved December 18, 2013 from website: http://learningstore.uwex.edu/assets/pdfs/g3658-12.pdf

Toumi, H. (2011). *Report: Around one third of teachers in Qatar lack proper qualification*. Doha, Qatar: Gulf. Retrieved November 13, 2013 from http://NewsDetailsTheTeachingProfession-07June2006currentsofreformoverturntraditionsonteachertrainingand careers/GulfNews.com

Willis, J. (2007). *Foundations of Qualitative Research: Interpretive and Critical Approaches*. Thousand Oaks, CA: Sage Publications.

ADDITIONAL READING

Bolman, L. G., & Deal, T. E. (2003). *Reframing organizations: Artistry, choice and leadership* (3rd ed.). San Francisco, CA: Jossey-Bass Publishers.

Dantley, M. E. (2005). Moral leadership: Shifting the management paradigm. In F. W. English (Ed.), *The Sage handbook of educational leadership: Advances in theory, research and practice* (pp. 35–46). Thousand Oak, CA: SAGE Publications.

Darling-Hammond, L., LaPointe, M., Meyerson, D., Orr, M. T., & Cohen, C. (2007). *Preparing school leaders for a changing world: lessons from exemplary leadership development programs.* Stanford, CA: Stanford University, Stanford Educational Leadership Institute.

Davis, S., Darling-Hammond, L., LaPointe, M., & Meyerson, D. (2005). Review of research developing successful principals school leadership study. Stanford, CA: Stanford Educational Leadership Institute (SELI).

DeVita, M. C., Colvin, R. L., Darling-Hammond, L., & Haycock, K. (2007). *Education Leadership: A Bridge to School Reform.* New York: The Wallace Foundation.

DuFour, R., & Mattos, M. (2013). How do principals really improve schools? *The Principalship, 70*(7), 34–40.

Fullan, M. (2000). The return of large-scale reform. *Journal of Educational Change, 1*(1), 5–27. doi:10.1023/A:1010068703786

Fullan, M. (2000, April). The three stories of education reform. *Phi Delta Kappan, 81*(8), 581–584.

Fullan, M. (2001). *Leading in a culture of change.* San Francisco: Jossey-Bass.

Geijsel, F., Sleegers, P., Leithwood, K., & Jantzi, D. (2003). Transformational leadership effects on teachers' commitment and effort toward school reform. *Journal of Educational Administration, 41*(3), 228–256. doi:10.1108/09578230310474403

Hallinger, P. (2003). Leading Educational Change: Reflections on the practice of instructional and transformational leadership. *Cambridge Journal of Education, 33*(3), 329–352. doi:10.1080/0305764032000122005

Hallinger, P. (2012). *School leadership that makes a difference: Lessons from 30 years of international research.* Rome, Italy: Ministry of Education.

Hargreaves, A., & Fink, D. (2004). The seven principles of sustainable leadership. *Educational Leadership, 61*(7), 8–13.

Jossey-Bass. (2006). *The Jossey-Bass reader on educational leadership.* San Francisco, CA: Jossey-Bass Publishers.

Kose, B. W. (2007). Principal leadership for social justice: Uncovering the content of teacher professional development. *Journal of School Leadership, 17*, 276–312.

Leithwood, K., & Jantzi, D. (2006). Transformational school leadership for large-scale reform: Effects on students, teachers, and their classroom practices. *School Effectiveness and School Improvement, 17*(2), 201–227. doi:10.1080/09243450600565829

Leithwood, K., & Jantzi, D. (2008). Linking leadership to student learning: The contributions of leader efficacy. *Educational Administration Quarterly, 44*(4), 496–528. doi:10.1177/0013161X08321501

Leithwood, K., Louis, K. S., Anderson, S., & Wahlstrom, K. (2004). *How leadership influences student learning: A review of research for the Learning from Leadership Project.* New York: The Wallace Foundation.

Leithwood, K. A., Aitken, R., & Jantzi, D. (2006). *Making schools smarter: Leading with evidence* (3rd ed.). Thousand Oaks, CA: Corwin Press.

Levin, B. (2000). Putting students at the centre in education reform. *Journal of Educational Change, 1*(2), 155–172. doi:10.1023/A:1010024225888

Marzano, R. J., Waters, T., & McNulty, B. A. (2005). *School leadership that works: From research to results.* Alexandria, VA: ASCD.

Murphy, J. F., & Datnow, A. (2002). *Leadership lessons from comprehensive school reforms.* Thousand Oaks, CA: Corwin Press.

Starratt, R. J. (2004). *Building an ethical school: A practical response to the moral crisis in schools*. London: Routledge.

Strike, K. A., Haller, E. J., & Soltis, J. F. (2005). *The ethics of school administration* (3rd ed.). New York: Teachers College Press.

Whitaker, T. (2002). *What great principals do differently: 15 things that matter most*. London: Routledge.

KEY TERMS AND DEFINITIONS

Critical Issues: Extremely important primary issues that have an impact on the principal's ability to implement elements of educational reform. Critical issues can be both external or internal and play a key role in the success or failure of educational reforms.

Education for a New Era: The name given to the massive Qatari national education reform based on four principles—autonomy, accountability, variety and choice.

Educational Reform: The name given to the demand for an improvement in the conditions of education. Reform moves beyond simple fine-tuning because reform demands fundamental change. Notions of educational reform can be wide ranged spreading across the spectrums of opinion, beliefs, values, experiences and educational philosophies and theories. Thus, the concept of educational reform has no agreed upon or universally accepted meaning.

Independent Schools: Government-funded school in Qatar that responsible to the Supreme Education Council's (SEC) directives but still have the freedom to define their individual educational vision, mission and goals and the liberty to appoint teachers and staff.

Phenomenological Study: A research study that centers on the descriptions of people's experiences of the world. Phenomenological inquiry is used to gain insight to the meanings and perspectives of research participants in an attempt to understand a phenomenon from the participants' perspectives. This requires that researchers gather information and perceptions through inductive qualitative research methods including interviews, discussions, focus groups and observations presenting the findings from the perspective of the research participants.

Resistance: In this content, resistance is when individuals oppose educational reform and policies based on a philosophical difference between what the individual believes and what the institution or policy demands. Resistance involves a lack of participation or minimal participation and often creates discomfort, tension and a lack of cooperation with the principal or individuals responsible for implement policies. For the resistor, it is a way of coping with change and disagreement.

Supreme Education Council (SEC): Formerly known as the Ministry of Education for Qatar, the SEC was established in November 2002 and is responsible for all Independent schools (publically funded schools) and the administration of higher education. The SEC plays a key role in the development and implementation of the country's massive educational reform. The SEC is composed of the Education Institute, the Evaluation Institute and the Higher Education Institute all having a unique role in the nation's education policy.

Chapter 6

School Leadership and Pedagogical Reform:
Building Student Capacity

Shirley O'Neill
University of Southern Queensland, Australia

ABSTRACT

This chapter explores the journey of one Australian primary school that participated in an internationally renowned school revitalization project, where the nature and quality of leadership and results of change are able to achieve and sustain pedagogical reform and improve and enhance student achievement. It illuminates the nature of school change and examines its impact on pedagogy and learning. Through mapping a school's journey and a focus on research, changes in practices such as use of frameworks and protocols, teacher professional learning, and the compilation and use of assessment data are explored, as are the vital roles of both teachers and students in achieving change. The inclusion of students in the process, combined with leadership in school-wide pedagogy, is shown to have contributed to building students' capacity for learning besides that of teachers to implement a school-wide approach to pedagogy.

INTRODUCTION

This chapter considers how one particular long-term school revitalization project known as IDEAS impacted on pedagogy and students' learning and engagement. It takes the view that a process such as that implemented in this project is necessary for a school community to successfully address an improvement agenda, achieve significant pedagogical improvement and ultimately improve student engagement and learning outcomes. The inclusion of students in the process of reform com-

bined with leadership in schoolwide pedagogy and practice is shown to have contributed to building students' capacity for learning as well as that of teachers, to implement a schoolwide pedagogical approach that assure consistency in practice. In this exploration an attempt is made to reconceptualise pedagogy to come to grips with the nature of a pedagogy that appeared central to the outcomes of this reform – 'GAMMA pedagogy'. It argues that for schools to develop students as independent lifelong learners, who are successful and have confidence and aspirations for their futures, there

DOI: 10.4018/978-1-4666-6591-0.ch006

needs to be a shift away from the traditional view of teachers as 'transmitters of information' and students whose task it is to remember what has been 'taught'. In contrast, 21st century students are seen as 'active learners' who can readily engage in the classroom dialogue and are able to discuss and justify why they are doing what they are doing in terms of their learning.

MAIN FOCUS OF THE CHAPTER

Through a focus on research the chapter moves beyond the typical description of a social constructivist approach to learning to one that is in keeping with that of Mayer (2012) who exemplifies a more in depth portrayal of the democratic classroom. The notion of third space is utilized to help illuminate the resultant construction of 'GAMMA pedagogy'. The objectives of the chapter are to describe the school's change process, show how it impacts on leadership and pedagogical reform, investigate the nature of students' learning and engagement, and synthesize emergent messages for reconceptualising pedagogy as a capacity building phenomenon. The chapter provides the essential background context of the research in terms of understanding the need for and kind of school reform in the context of Australia, and the nature of and role of the education system applicable to the school under study and the kind of leadership involved. It will conclude with a discussion of how the notion of GAMMA pedagogy is reflective of the kind of change in school practices that will more effectively equip students to embark on a lifelong learning journey. By elevating the discussion to hypothesise the notion of 'a third space' (Moje, Ciechanowski, Kramer, Ellis, Carrillo, & Collazo, 2004; Oldenburg, 1999; 2000) in which to reconceptualise pedagogy and learning for the 21st century, the nature of the change needed becomes clearer.

BACKGROUND

The Chapter View

The importance of leadership in education to enable school reform that can lead to improved student achievement is very well established, but there remains a question about what schools might do to successfully achieve this. The stance taken here is that in order to reform pedagogy and improve student learning and engagement the need for improvement should be acknowledged by all stakeholders in a positive light. School leadership needs to facilitate change through working with stakeholders, so that all are involved in collaboratively designing, owning and implementing their vision for the future. This includes teachers taking leadership of pedagogical reform and students developing the capacity to engage in and discuss their learning (Healy, 2008). Furthermore, it is argued that pedagogy for 21st century learners needs to be reconceptualised as a capacity building phenomenon for both teachers and students, where the language of learning and thinking, classroom dialogue, teacher-teacher dialogue (Isaacs & Smith, 1994), interactive tools, strategies and strategic use of resources to achieve explicit goals are mutually understood, and applied for students to continue learning and adapting to our dynamic, globalised world. School leadership in this sense is seen as a shared responsibility where leadership is distributed throughout the school according to various roles and responsibilities, such that teachers take leadership of the school's pedagogical approach to provide quality and consistency in practice and creativity in delivery. The principal is seen as a metastrategic leader (Behn, 1991; Crowther, Andrews, Morgan & O'Neill, 2012) who is able to facilitate change through incorporating transformative leadership practices that recognise the need to collectively build pedagogical knowledge (Schuh, 2003) in the context of a professional learning community. This view also recognizes that to develop and make the shift towards change from within the school there needs to be a fostering of school improvement initiatives, alignment of school's key organizational elements and provision of support from the system.

Contemporary Research into School Leadership and Pedagogical Reform

Although it is more than a decade into the 21st century, school reform remains high on the agenda. This is in spite of ongoing research (Hargreaves & Shirley, 2009; Harris, 2008; 2012; Fullan, 2006; Kamler & Comber, 2005; Newmann & Associates, 1996). However, according to Hopkins, Harris, Stoll and Mackay (2014) there has been less success in improving schools at the system level although Crowther, Andrews, Morgan and O'Neill (2012) present a case study of an exemplary system in Australia that has embedded and sustained an improvement philosophy and highly professional practice for many years. In the Australian context data on students' performance in literacy and numeracy is readily available and can be used for a variety of comparative purposes, including benchmarking between schools (ACARA, 2014; Adams, 2012). Governments are increasingly implementing such testing regimes that plot students' achievement at various points in time.

At the same time there is an increased focus on teachers and teaching to improve performance (Jensen & Reichl, 2011), which has seen the introduction of professional standards for teaching (AITSL, 2011). These standards apply to both in-service and pre-service teacher education and expand the debate to include the reform of teacher education. In this milieu the various stakeholder groups such as teachers, parents and principals and their associations, the various related unions and education sectors regularly give their views and advice. They represent a range of positions on what might be done and why, depending on whether one believes in government or systemwide edicts or working collaboratively from the ground up (Connell, 2012; Cullen, 2014; Fullan, 2005; 2012; Harris, Hadfield, Hopkins, Hargreaves & Chapman, 2003; Wrigley, 2006).

However, while there is, what may be argued as sufficient knowledge, based on research evidence, to guide school reform to provide quality education for today's diverse learners within the many different but equally challenging contexts, securing its implementation may be fraught with challenge. This section therefore seeks to address this challenge and illuminate the journey of school improvement to identify common issues and the way leadership and pedagogy may work to achieve a reconceptualised view to support it in current times.

What Is Known to Work?

It must be stressed that schools that seek to improve do not necessarily do this because of weak performance although much of the literature concentrates on the situation of lower performing schools. An improvement agenda is accepted as part of a schools raison d'être and in keeping with the moral imperative leaders should be committed to do their best for all students and schools. Research across the world is now showing commonality in findings on how schools manage to make changes and improve students' learning. For instance, most recently, Jensen and Sonnerman (2014, p. 1) stated that:

Some of Australia's most troubled schools are turning around their performance to achieve remarkable results. Formerly marked by behaviour problems, low expectations and poor staff morale, these schools are implementing reforms that make them models for all low-performing schools. These schools are thriving not just because their leaders are often inspirational, but also because they have followed the same path as turnaround schools around the world.

Jensen and Sonnerman (2014) identify five steps that they term 'turnaround schools' follow. These are (1) strong leadership that raises expectations, (2) effective teaching with teachers learning from each other, (3) development and measurement of students' learning, (4) development of a positive school culture and (5) engagement of parents and the community. However, they stress that merely following these five steps does not guarantee that change will follow, since effective change requires a "change in the behaviour and practices of leaders, teachers and students". Implementing a process to commit all stakeholders to change and building the capacity of school leaders and teachers to be able to change is seen as an essential first step.

Hopkins, Harris, Stoll and Mackay's (2014) "state of the art" review identify five phases for improvement for schools and system. These are: (1) understanding the organizational culture of the school, (2) action research and individual initiatives, (3) managing change and the emphasis on leadership, (4) building capacity for learning at the local level and (5) towards systemic improvement. Like Jensen and Sonnerman (2014) they highlight the challenge of changing the culture of the school and the need to build the community's capacity for learning. This is seen as gaining a major change in mindset from that of teaching to learning. In their identification of the key features of each phase they also note the importance of participants understanding the importance of leadership for change and the involvement of teachers in conducting their own research, and the school undertaking review. In the final phase they report how knowledge is then used to inform how approaches to school and system reform might be differentiated.

The importance of school communities initiating and leading their own change, with teachers leading pedagogical change is at the core of the Australian-based IDEAS Project (Crowther, 2011; Crowther, Ferguson & Hann, 2009). "IDEAS" is the acronym for Innovative Designs for Enhancing Achievement in Schools. Its underpinning philosophy and processes for school revitalization are clearly in keeping with the most recent findings as outlined above (Caldwell & Spinks, 2013; Hargreaves & Fullan, 2012; Hopkins, Harris, Stoll & Mackay, 2014; and Jensen & Sonnerman, 2014). Implementation of this project typically takes three to four years to move to the sustaining phase. By this time a school is deeply immersed in a new cultural paradigm created and owned by all stakeholders. They have grown out of the 'skin' of IDEAS such that any direct reference is usually replaced with the language, concepts and processes participants have constructed during development of their school's vision and values, and from their ensuing schoolwide pedagogy and related understandings and artifacts (Abawi, 2013a; Conway & Abawi, 2013). Through strong system-, principal- and teacher-leadership this project revitalises and embeds a culture of improvement, research and reflective practice, and teacher professional learning. It is applicable to all schools that seek to continuously improve. By employing a collaborative approach it aims to build social and intellectual capital (Hargreaves, 2001; Hopkins & Jackson, 2003) and in turn the capacity of all involved, redesigning their practice and sustaining improvement.

Building Leadership Capacity

Lambert (2000) clearly outlines how the role of principal as leader needs to change from that of the single authority and manager to a 'form of constructivist leadership'. She states:

What we wanted to do was bring learning and leading closer together, leading towards a form of 'constructivist leadership' — not the simpler style of leadership where you are 'in charge', but one marked by facilitation, and teacher-leaders asking themselves questions like 'How do I contribute to the learning of others?' and 'How do others contribute to my learning?' Reciprocity — co-learning, working collaboratively with each other — is invested in these questions (p. 3).

Taking a constructivist approach acknowledges adults have the capacity to learn as well as students. In this context it follows that the quality of relationships and dialogue between participants interacting in the school community and the development of skills exert an influence on the making of meaning/construction of knowledge and the leadership capacity required to both facilitate and sustain improvement. Lambert's (2000, p. 4) leadership capacity four-quadrant matrix identifies the ideal leader as demonstrating (1) broad-based, skilful participation in the work of leadership, (2) enquiry-based use of information to inform decisions and practice, (3) roles and responsibilities that reflect broad involvement and collaboration, (4) reflective practices and innovation as the norm, and outcomes that show high student achievement.

Contextualization

The context involves the study of schools that had, by choice, undertaken the long term school revitalization IDEAS Project that, along with a range of other professional learning and resourcing and support projects, was made available by their system as part of their ongoing improvement initiatives. Schools that undertake the IDEAS Project generally take three to four years to move through the phases of (1) individualising, (2) designing, (3) envisioning, (4) actioning to reach the sustaining phase (5) depending on their particular situation. The IDEAS Project has been implemented widely in Australia in government, independent and religious schools (Chesterton & Duignan, 2004; Crowther, Andrews, Morgan & O'Neill, 2012) and also internationally in Sicily and Singapore (Ng & Chew, 2008).

The schools at the focus of this chapter are part of a Catholic system that has a track record of improvement over several decades (Crowther, Andrews, Morgan & O'Neill, 2012). They generally represent a linguistically and culturally diverse student population typical in multicultural Australia. During the life of the project (four years),

the case study cohort of students, moving from Year Three through to Year Five, significantly improved in reading and numeracy on the national test (NAPLAN, 2011) compared with the system score and those of their 'like group' of schools. This revitalization process first involved the school community in collaboratively developing a school mission and vision, followed by a set of values (*Individualising*). From the ensuing values they collaboratively developed a set of pedagogical principles as a basis for a schoolwide approach to pedagogy – 'schoolwide pedagogy' (*Designing*). Schoolwide pedagogy (SWP) in this sense refers to the school's agreed upon view of what constitutes appropriate pedagogical approaches for the particular student population. It is in keeping with the school's values and is compatible with teachers' personal pedagogical beliefs, and is also justified through being rooted in authoritative pedagogical theory. The next phase involves teachers and students *Envisioning* what their SWP will look like in practice before *Actioning* it across the school. Following the actioning phase the school typically moves into the *Sustaining* phase where it is necessary to ensure the established SWP and new practices are able to be sustained regardless of changes in staffing and/or principal, curriculum or system demands and the like.

THE EDUCATIONAL SYSTEM

The System to Which This Research Refers

This research is based on research and evaluation of school improvement outcomes in the Catholic system in one Diocese in a state capital city of Australia. The Catholic Education Commission (CEC) is responsible for Catholic Education at the state level and provides leadership services to the various Diocese and Education Offices within the state. This Diocese' long term success in continuous improvement (Canavan, 2003; 2008), and facilitation of its schools' choice and uptake of a range of projects to improve is reported in Crowther, Andrews, Morgan and O'Neill (2012). All schools receive some Federal government funding according to a distribution formula through their State or Territory government. Australia has a recently instituted a national curriculum (ACARA, 2014) (previously each state/territory was responsible for its own) in order to facilitate national testing and comparison of literacy and numeracy outcomes. The system in focus has created a supportive, well resourced, professional learning community where goals are clear, implementation is focused, and system, school and classroom policy and accountability practices are strategically aligned, with systematic feedback being at the core of practice. Staff performance review is in place but it is integrated into the organizational structure and staff's work, such that in schools it is internalized in practice with a collaborative focus. In the project schools there is a collaborative approach to developing a schoolwide pedagogical framework, where teachers take leadership and become involved with deepening their understanding of how students learn and engage as opposed to taking a traditional focus on teaching.

The Australian Schooling System

The Australia's schooling system has its origins in the colonial era, where schools flourished under the banner of religion, and Mission schools were set up to convert the Indigenous peoples to Christianity (Schwarz & Dussart, 2010). However, in modern Australia the current national focus includes a move to quality standards for teachers and principals, national teacher registration, the collection of evidence to justify teachers' continued registration and a move to test graduate teachers' science, literacy and numeracy content and pedagogical knowledge, as well as related personal skills.

An increasing federal government focus on accountability has given rise to national full-population testing of children's literacy and numeracy at key development stages of schooling (Years 3, 5, 7 and 9, NAPLAN, 2011). The test places students on a single hierarchical performance scale of ten levels, where minimum performance for each cohort is set. This allows the tracking of students' performance over time and identifies students who require extra support because they have not performed at least at the minimum standard for their year. Variation in NAPLAN results between the different states (6) and territories (2) have led to concerns about the value and the validity of the test (Wu, 2009). Combined with a seemingly lowering of performance on the OECD initiated international test Programme for International Student Assessment (PISA) (Schleicher, 2014; Sellar & Lingard, 2013; Tovey & Patty, 2013) as well as TIMSS and PIRLS, managed by the International Association for the Evaluation of Education Achievement (IEA) (Thompson, Hillman, Wernert, Schmid, Buckley & Munene, 2012), particularly with regard to 15 year olds' reading, has contributed to the current conservative governments' decision to evaluate the relatively new national curriculum (ACARA, 2014) and argue for other reforms (Lingard & Sellar, 2013; Spiegelhalter, 2013). The curriculum has been criticized for being overcrowded (APPA, 2014) such that children may not be learning the essential skills. This adds to the pressure on schools, systems and tertiary providers to examine their practices and be prepared for change. This state of affairs is not new since over decades there has been the need to respond to changing governmental and political demands, while attempting to do justice to students' learning and prepare new teachers. In any case the teaching profession needs to demonstrate a high level of professionalism and confidence in their own practice and be proactive in providing a strong voice in the midst of continuous change.

As well, as more countries join in the international PISA test, Australia appears to be falling behind compared with, for instance, Shanghai and Hong Kong, in both reading and mathematics. By comparison, Australia has an increasingly linguistically and culturally diverse student population with large proportions who have English as an added language. This is a challenge as the population continues to grow in diversity in all education sectors as well as workplaces. It is therefore not surprising that the search for solutions that can significantly enhance literacy and numeracy outcomes in schools is vigorous.

Assuring School Improvement

In the light of current international research it is becoming very clear that there needs to be reform at both the system and the school level if improvement in student learning outcomes is to be achieved and sustained. It needs to be acknowledged that such reform is a long-term process that must be able to successfully change the cultural paradigm from the traditional view of schooling (Conway & Abawi, 2013; O'Neill, 2013; O'Neill, Geoghegan & Petersen, 2013) and ensure pedagogical reform that is inclusive (Abawi & Oliver, 2013). However, while there are strategies available that systems and schools may adopt, there are challenges to be faced along the way. These challenges relate firstly to the notion of change. Change may be seen as unnecessary, too time consuming or more work by some, or a threat to traditional values and practices. Related to this is the role of the principal and the style of leadership in facilitating change as this may also be controversial, particularly where the model of leadership has been the principal as the sole authority, as flag bearer leading the charge.

Secondly, and not unrelated, is the issue of change and pedagogy. For decades it has been very difficult for teachers to have the opportunity to observe other teachers teaching because to re-lease/replace a teacher during class teaching time is extremely expensive. It is also not possible to leave other teachers in charge of their own class as well as that of colleagues because of workplace health and safety issues. The initial challenge here then is to motivate and enable teachers to engage in discussions about pedagogy and learning. This needs to be in relation to their personal beliefs as well as the needs of their students. The third issue involves teachers gaining an understanding of the vital role of teacher-student-student dialogue used in the classroom in its capacity to make teaching and learning explicit.

An understanding of dialogic pedagogy is crucial to teachers being aware of how to best use language and make cognitive moves in their classroom talk that will most effectively scaffold students' learning (Geoghegan, O'Neill & Petersen, 2013; Mayer, 2012; Smith, Hardman, Wall & Mroz, 2004). However, this requires a different mindset from that of a traditional approach to teaching and a shift to appreciate a social constructivist paradigm where the classroom operates in more of a democratic context as opposed to authoritarian (Mayer, 2012). Thus, in turn it would be expected that the role of the student undergoes change and it is the nature of this change that is ultimately explored in this chapter. It is the thesis of this chapter that in order to reform pedagogy and improve student learning and engagement school leadership needs to be conceptualized under a distributed model where all stakeholders acknowledge the need for change and all are involved, collaboratively, in designing and implementing change. This includes teachers taking leadership of pedagogical reform and students having a voice in their own learning. Teaching and learning are made explicit and teachers and students alike acquire new skills within a generative pedagogical paradigm, where there is a mutuality in building teachers' and students' capacity for learning. These issues and challenges are discussed in the next section along with the way the IDEAS Project acts as a catalyst for change.

SCHOOL REFORM AND LEADERSHIP

Traditionally the school principal has been viewed as the person in charge of a school and in turn responsible for implementing the system policy. As the figure of authority, typically working within an equally authoritarian system s/he's role was more of an administrator than leader. This view harkens back to times when the principal's role and responsibilities were to ensure compliance with system/government policy, manage staff and implement programs to ensure students were prepared for examinations. In turn activity in classrooms reflected the same approach. Thus, in schools where staff, students, parents and the wider community are geared to this way of conceptualizing schooling, the idea of change and the need to understand the benefits of a more democratized practice may seem an anathema. The notion of the principal as a leader who is able to do more than management and administration would be the first challenge, while coming to grips with a pedagogical view that students need to be participants, besides have a voice, in their own learning. This not only relates to teachers but to parents and the local community. Conditions that would be supportive of such change would also need to be acceptable to the system within which a school was bound otherwise those who choose to lead change may find themselves in breach of their contracts and their community in uproar.

Embarking on the pathway of change in such circumstances requires a move away from what Avolio and Bass (1994) describe as a transactional leadership style to one of transformative. In practice the transactional leadership style is associated with ensuring compliance. One would expect to find a form of reward system in place to encourage compliance, although this may not be explicit and may be inadequate such that the leadership style may be described as laissez-faire.

On the other hand, the ideal of the transformative style is more demanding and time consuming for the principal to implement. It requires a different relationship with staff where there is trust and respect for the professional judgment of teachers and a valuing of their work, and of them as people. Avolio and Bass (1994) identify five components of this style that contribute to transformation of practice: (1) individualized consideration, (2) inspiration motivation, (3) intellectual stimulation, (4) idealized behaviour and (5) idealized attribute. Transformational leaders work with their staff as a team, creating more democratic, collaborative and creative workspaces that encourage reflective practice, new ideas and innovation. As a result, this leadership style is better able to facilitate the development of high quality interpersonal communication skills and create a mutual respect, trust, motivation and commitment among stakeholders. Transformational leaders consider their teachers' individualized needs (1), and stimulate them intellectually (3) besides model the idealized behaviour (5). They are typically more charismatic (4) and inspirational in their approach to the extent that they are able to motivate (2) staff to engage in a process of shared change practices. "This style of leadership is more able to overcome resistance to change by gaining the confidence and commitment of workers (Del Castillo, n.d., cited in Bass, 1998) [and] as Barnett, McCormick and Conners (2001) note, transformational leaders totally engage staff emotionally, intellectually and morally to encourage them to develop and perform beyond expectations" (cited in El Amouri & O'Neill, 2014, p. 3).

This depends more on being able to develop trusting relationships with staff, to motivate and engage so building their collective capital through well planned collaboration. As noted earlier Fullen (2010) sees this as the mobilizing of a major resource in being able to facilitate improvement. He "identifies 'collective capacity' built through planned collaboration as the 'hidden resource' that the U.S. school systems have neglected to cultivate" hence their failure to improve (cited in Nelson, 2012, p. 1). This also includes recognizing the skills of others and sharing the leadership among staff to harness their professional expertise in leading pedagogical change.

When schools embark on the IDEAS Project one of the first steps during the *discovering* stage is to administer a survey to teachers, students and parents. This is the Diagnostic Survey of School Alignment (DISA) that is designed to identify the extent to which there is internal alignment or consistency within the school's key organizational elements. The results are expressed in terms of indicators of social, organizational and intellectual capital (see DISA, 2014). Importantly,

in IDEAS, five organizational 'elements' are posited to be critically important to sustained school success. When the five characteristics are individually developed, and brought into 'alignment' with each other, a school's potential to enhance its outcomes has indeed been found to increase (Jeyaraj, 2011). The five elements are:

- *The school's strategic direction (i.e. vision and values);*
- *Stakeholder (i.e. parents, students, teachers) expectations of, and aspirations for, the school;*
- *The school's pedagogical framework;*
- *The school's infrastructural features (such as use of IT, curricula, time and space); and*
- *Teachers' professional learning strategies.*

(Crowther, Andrews, Morgan & O'Neill, 2012, p. 5)

The results of this survey provide a sound basis for any school to focus their attention on their situation and achievements through the evidence of the DISA diagnosis.

Pedagogical Approaches and Issues of Epistemology

Existing beliefs about how children learn and the way knowledge is constructed is also a major influence on being able to improve learning outcomes for students. This impacts on any need to change from traditional epistemology (Chandler, 2001) where there is a focus on teaching and transmission of information to learners, as opposed to seeing students as learners in accord with the contemporary constructivist view that draws upon Vygotsky's sociocultural theory (Mayer, 2012; Wells, 2010). There is a major conflict in their epistemologies as this requires a major cultural shift from the idea of teacher as sole authority and expert, where students are passive receivers of information, to one where students, as active learners, are cognizant of the way they learn, what they are supposed to learn and why. Edwards-Groves and Hoare (2012, p. 98) specify that classroom experiences need to be reconceptualised as 'learning-through-interaction' where pedagogy is seen as interactive practice. Thus, it is understandable that Mayer (2012), in her detailed examination of the kind of classroom discourse that illustrates the social constructivist approach (that emerges from a more democratic making of meaning), notes that this requires significant transformation of traditional teacher and student roles and associated interactive talk.

She specifies: "as with any socially established set of behaviours and guidelines, pedagogical discourse patterns must be learned, and new patterns can be challenging, perhaps even threatening to some, until classroom members have had a chance to become familiar with them" (p. 120). Table 1 outlines the contrastive features of the two kinds of learning environments. This is taken from Thirteen (2014) that is an interactive site, which presents an easily accessible and comprehensive description.

Table 1. Comparison of key features of the traditional and constructivist classrooms

Traditional Classrooms	Constructivist Classrooms
Curriculum begins with the parts of the whole. Emphasizes basic skills.	Pursuit of student questions and interests is valued.
Materials are primarily textbooks and workbooks	Materials include primary sources of material and manipulative materials.
Learning is based on repetition.	Learning is interactive, building on what the student already knows.
Teachers disseminate information to students; students are recipients of knowledge.	Teachers have a dialogue with students, helping students construct their own knowledge.
Teacher's role is directive, rooted in authority.	Teacher's role is interactive, rooted in negotiation.
Assessment is through testing, correct answers.	Assessment includes student works, observations, and points of view, as well as tests. Process is as important as product.
Knowledge is seen as inert.	Knowledge is seen as dynamic, ever changing with our experiences.
Students work primarily alone.	Students work primarily in groups.

Changes to pedagogy therefore, are also vital to improving student learning outcomes. As Hargreaves and Fullen (2012) point out good teaching involves wise judgment informed by evidence and experience and is a collective accomplishment and responsibility. They emphasize that improvement in students' learning is not merely because of the effect of an individual good teacher but rather the impact of "... how you maximize the cumulative effect of many many teachers over time for each and every student. Students do very well because they have a series of very good teachers–not by chance, but by design. In other words you have to transform the entire profession . . ." (pp. 15-16).

The need for professional collaboration to improve pedagogy and learning is discussed by Nelson (2012, p. 1). She cites Mourshed, Chijioke and Barber (2010) as identifying that in all successful systems around the world a common trait "is that teachers share and work on their practice together, 'becoming learners of their own teaching'." She reports several studies that link professional collaboration with student achievement (see Bryk, Sebring, Allensowrth, Luppesco, & Easton, 2010; Goddard, Goddard, & Tschannen-Moran, 2007; Louis & Marks, 1998; and Odden & Archibald, 2009). Good practices in introducing processes that can facilitate this change are evident in the IDEAS project during the *envisioning* phase. At this time, and based on the school's diagnostic data and the establishment of a stakeholder representative leadership team, processes are implemented to develop a shared vision of where they would like their school to be in the future. Their vision is then used to develop their values and in turn what these mean for the pedagogical approach needed to bring their vision into being. A key set of principles for change that identify the importance of teachers as leaders are listed in the IDEAS Project 'Teachers as leaders framework', which is summarized in Table 2 (as cited in Crowther, Andrews, Morgan & O'Neill, 2012, p. 7).

It is within this context of reform that teachers are seen as key players in leading pedagogical change. It ensures teachers' ownership of a preferred pedagogy that is well documented and justified, and importantly, better enables them to teach consistently across the school – hence the use of the term 'schoolwide pedagogy' (Abawi, 2013b; O'Neill, 2013). This goes a long way to addressing Hargreaves and Fullen's (2012) problem of the need for consistent good teaching and Nelson's (2012) emphasis on teachers sharing their practice and working together to learn from their teaching. This facilitates their reflective practice,

Table 2. Summary Teachers as leaders framework

Teacher Leaders . . .
■ Convey convictions about a better world by articulating a positive future for all students.
■ Facilitate communities of learning by encouraging a shared, schoolwide approach to core pedagogical processes.
■ Strive for pedagogical excellence by continuously developing personal teaching gifts and talents.
■ Confront barriers in the school's culture and structures by standing up for marginalised groups (and individuals) and encouraging student 'voice'.
■ Translate ideas into sustainable systems of action by managing projects that heighten school alignment.
■ Nurture a culture of success by emphasising high expectations and accomplishments.

(Adapted from Crowther, 2011, p. 178)

and focus on feedback and research, which can allow them to monitor students' progress, and improve and sustain.

Understanding the Nature of Change inside Classrooms

While there has been substantial research focus on school improvement, there remains a need to link it to actual changes at the classroom level to illuminate changes in the way students learn. This might be because research into classroom practice may be more difficult to achieve since teachers, schools, systems, students or parents may not welcome classroom obervations. It may also be partly due to the two different foci of the two fields of research. However, as shown by Smith, Hardman, Wall and Mroz's (2004) research, regardless of national reform strategies in the UK, that focused on 'interactive whole class teaching' to improve literacy and numeracy pedagogy, this did not engender significant change in students' achievement.

The main reason given for this was that teachers did not change their classroom dialogue. They were found to maintain a traditional pattern of teacher talk or sequence of cognitive moves (Bull & Anstey, 1996; Heap, 1985) of (1) initiate (e.g. ask a closed question), (2) choose a student to respond and (3) evaluate the response (e.g. acknowledge the correct answer or give a clue to finding a correct answer). This is in stark contrast to teachers in constructivist classrooms whose talk reflects

an understanding of explicit teaching (Louden et al., 2005; O'Neill, Geoghegan & Petersen, 2013; Rowe, 2005) where their various cognitive moves, use of metalanguage and strategies to scaffold students' learning through interactive talk are specifically designed to engage students in learning and are knowingly made apparent (Culican, 2005; Edwards-Groves & Hardy, 2013; Geoghegan, O'Neill & Petersen, 2013; Myhill, 2006; Rose, 2005a, 2005b; Walsh, 2006).

This research highlights the fact that any investigation of improvement of pedagogical practices and a search for evidence of their implementation, needs to recognise that every teacher needs to be aware of how his or her lesson discourse influences students' learning and learning opportunities. For example, the following excerpt cited in O'Neill, Geoghegan and Petersen (2013, p. 123) demonstrates how the teacher links the new learning with students' prior knowledge to motivate and engage the learner, as well as effectively identify the lesson focus on "adjectives". Here the constructivist, scaffolding interactional cycle's sequence of cognitive moves of (1) prepare, (2) identify, and (3) elaborate (Culican, 2005; Rose, 2005a), show how the teacher scaffolds and supports students' learning by affirming their responses and encouraging them to think about the meaning and acquire the metalanguage involved e.g. adjectives.

While this is a literacy example there is also much research into the importance of the pedagogical language applicable to learning in mathematics (Kyriacou & Issitt, 2008; Huinker

Excerpt 1.

Prepare: Teacher (T): If you were to go home and describe Harry Hippo to your parents, what sort of words are you going to be using to describe him, Harry Hippo.
Identify S1: Adjectives
Affirm . . . Prepare T: Adjectives. Who can tell me what an adjective is?
Identify S2: It's a describing word.
Affirm . . . Elaborate T: It's a describing word. Ok can you tell me, why do writers use adjectives in their writing? Why is it necessary to put adjectives in your writing?
Identify S3: To describe what they are talking about.
Affirm . . . Identify T: Yes. To describe what they are talking about. Any other reasons?
Elaborate S1: If you were to say it was a hippo you're not describing what it looks like.
Affirm . . . Prepare T: So you're not describing what it looks like. What is it that you are doing to the reader?
Identify S4: For example if the reader was blind (*Affirm T: Yes*) you have to say . . . for example the hippopotamus was light pink body and dark pink feet.
Affirm T: Ok, yes.
Elaborate S4: To convince him and to make sentences more interesting.
Affirm . . . Prepare T: Yes, to make sentences more interesting. But what else are you doing for the reader?
Identify S5: Giving them a picture.

& Freckmann, 2004; Marino, 2005; Pratt, 2006; SAD, 2011) and science (Alsop, Gould & Watts, 2002; Harris, Phillips & Penuel, 2011).

In addition, Van Es and Sherin (2002, p. 592) highlight how dialogic pedagogy allows one to differentiate between beginning teachers' understanding of their practice. The novice teacher typically describes what happens in classrooms in a literal sense compared with the expert teacher who is able to interpret the lesson events to discuss their pedagogical approach, metacognitive decisions and talk. They argue "reform requires that teachers develop new routines and attend to new aspects of practice in new ways". As pointed out by O'Neill and Geoghegan (2012, p. 99) "it follows that regardless of other strategies for improving pedagogy and learning without action at this level [the dialogic level] there would be a ceiling on the potential for improved learning outcomes."

In the context of the IDEAS Project, during the *actioning* phase, after conceptualizing their SWP, a school's major focus is to identify how it is translated into practice, and consider how it may be refined and enriched. This usually occurs through a process of critique, including a professional sharing of practices within the school and also with parties external to the school. It is typically consolidated in relation to the IDEAS Project's

notion of 3-dimensional pedagogy (3-DP), which recognizes the need to 'marry' one's personal pedagogy (personal philosophy and strengths) with authoritative pedagogy (recognized pedagogical approaches) and how these intersect with the school's SWP. This is necessary if teachers are to implement their SWP consistently across the school.

Recent research has not only shown the creativity involved in IDEAS Project school's construction of their visions and values and the high quality of their resultant pedagogical principles and schoolwide pedagogies (Abawi, 2013a; Crowther, Andrews & Conway, 2013)

but it has identified the emergence of a distinctive language for learning (Crowther, Andrews, Morgan & O'Neill, 2012; O'Neill, 2013). This language is described by O'Neill (2013, p. 115) as comprising "the language and concepts created through . . . [the school's] vision and pedagogical principles. It includes the language and metalanguage required for the explicit teaching of literacy and numeracy, and the language for critical thinking and reasoning in the implementation [of the school in question's] inquiry-based learning and personalized learning.

On the basis of this research . . . [the school's] language of learning may be defined as:

- Their system of communication and shared meaning-making created through the development and implementation of their . . . SWP
- Their SWP's concepts, language and meta-language used by teachers and students in the process of learning, teaching and assessment".

This research adds to the richness of knowledge on the school improvement process, and in doing so raises the issue of how students need to acquire the language of learning to active participants.

OVERVIEW OF ONE SCHOOL'S CHANGE PROCESS

This section provides a brief overview of one primary school's journey of improvement in the IDEAS Project. There were close to 450 students at this school who came from language backgrounds other than English, and were representative of over 30 nationalities. For the vast majority their home language did not make learning English easy since most came from Vietnam and others spoke Arabic, various African languages and languages stemming from the Indian subcontinent. Enrolments were on the increase and students needed to learn the English language when they started school. Initially, the principal decided to choose the IDEAS Project which was made available by the system to address this challenge.

Figure 1 provides a visual representation of the accumulative impact of the IDEAS processes over a period of four years on the right hand side and the school's actions and decisions on the left hand side during which the cohort of students who moved from Year 3 in 2008 to Year 5 in 2010 showed a statistically significant improvement in numeracy

Figure 1. Model of how IDEAS contributes to enhanced student outcomes

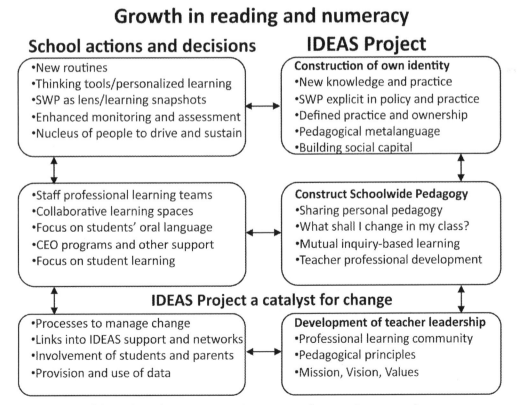

Growth in reading and numeracy

School actions and decisions

- New routines
- Thinking tools/personalized learning
- SWP as lens/learning snapshots
- Enhanced monitoring and assessment
- Nucleus of people to drive and sustain

- Staff professional learning teams
- Collaborative learning spaces
- Focus on students' oral language
- CEO programs and other support
- Focus on student learning

- Processes to manage change
- Links into IDEAS support and networks
- Involvement of students and parents
- Provision and use of data

IDEAS Project

Construction of own identity
- New knowledge and practice
- SWP explicit in policy and practice
- Defined practice and ownership
- Pedagogical metalanguage
- Building social capital

Construct Schoolwide Pedagogy
- Sharing personal pedagogy
- What shall I change in my class?
- Mutual inquiry-based learning
- Teacher professional development

IDEAS Project a catalyst for change

Development of teacher leadership
- Professional learning community
- Pedagogical principles
- Mission, Vision, Values

Principal leadership - Decision to take action to change

and reading on the national NAPLAN tests ($p <$ .05, one-sample t-test). This was compared with the system results, which were already higher than the state and national achievement, as displayed in Tables 3, and the 'like' schools comparative results (those with similar demographics) in Table 4 (as cited in O'Neill, 2013, p. 115). The figure also attempts to provide a model to show how the IDEAS Project processes contributed to the facilitation of enhanced student learning. It is important to note that the system set professional expectations to facilitate improvement initiatives and provided guidance through policy and strategic plans, and made available a range of resources and projects/professional learning programs in support. This included the IDEAS Project. The system also provided education consultants to work with all schools in their plans to improve. Principals saw this as a valuable strategy since their designated consultant had an understanding of the school and its needs. MacKillop school (pseudonym) was one of four selected for case study as part of the research and evaluation of the IDEAS Project (Crowther, Andrews, Morgan & O'Neill, 2012). Data were collected through interviews and focus groups with teachers (10), classroom observations (five classes), and interviews with students (10), interviews with the principal (1) and system school consultants (1), as well as this author's analyses of system performance on NAPLAN test results, and system support strategies (see O'Neill, 2013 and also Geoghegan, O'Neill & Petersen, 2013 for further details). This school was chosen for the focus of the chapter because of the author's in depth study of this school's success in the context of linguistic and cultural diversity, which as noted earlier is a growing phenomenon in Australian schools. It was also selected because of the data being available to exemplify how a school can build students' capacity to learn and the fact that the study of its changed practices, within the context of the IDEAS project research, has led to the proposed concept of GAMMA pedagogy, which is applicable to all schools that wish to improve. It is hoped this concept can be used by schools to interrogate their practice and indeed, continue the conversation on building students' capacity to learn in 21st. century times.

MacKillop school's vision was 'to ACT' – to **A**spire, **C**reate, **T**ogether, being derived from the

Table 3. MacKillop primary school's NAPLAN growth, compared with State and CEO growth, 2008-2010

		School Growth	State Growth	Difference	CEO Growth	Difference
MacKillop Primary school	Yr5 Reading	98.5% (*)	83.8%	**14.7%**	83.1%	**15.4%**
	Yr5 Numeracy	122.5% (*)	89.1%	**33.4%**	92.9%	**29.6%**

* significant at 0.05 level.
(As cited in O'Neill, 2013, p. 115)

Table 4. MacKillop primary school's NAPLAN growth, compared with Like School growth, 2008-2010

		School Growth	Like School Growth	Difference
MacKillop Primary school	Yr5 Reading	98.5% (*)	82.3%	**15.2%**
	Yr5 Numeracy	122.5% (*)	91.6%	**30.9%**

*significant at 0.05 level.
(As cited in O'Neill, 2013, p. 115)

motto for life: "Never see a need without doing something about it", of Mary MacKillop, the founder of the order of St Joseph of the Sacred Heart. This vision supported their commitment to serve their student community in keeping with the Josephite tradition to provide *active service to others, inclusion and bringing hope to all.* From this they constructed six pedagogical principles which gave rise to the acronym ACTIVE, **A**ctive commitment, **C**reativity, **T**eamwork, **I**ndividual and **E**mpathy, and led them to identify their SWP as 'active pedagogy' (O'Neill, 2013, p. 108).

This schoolwide pedagogy involves both teachers' and students' inquiry-based learning. While teachers began their exploration of their personal pedagogy by conducting action research projects to answer the question "What do I want to change in my classroom?", students were explicitly taught inquiry-based learning strategies.

The principal noted "the 'essence' of [our school] . . . can be captured in the pastoral nature – the lengths we go to help the kids". They reflect staff's valuing of collaboration and teamwork "to build a cohesive, inspiring and engaging learning environment" where teachers have opportunity to contribute and "share their professional gifts and talents"

Both teachers and students were found to be party to the newly constructed pedagogical dialogue that used the common language of the content and the language of learning, in terms of the school's metaphorical approach to SWP. Similarly, this dialogue involved the metalanguage and the thinking tools to support their inquiry-based learning. It was evident also in teacher-to-teacher professional conversations and the research interviews (Isaacs & Smith, 1994; O'Neill, Geoghegan & Petersen, 2013).

Collaborative processes, that included students in the schoolwide pedagogical design, contributed

to building the social capital of both teachers and students. During the IDEAS *actioning* phase they focused on:

- Linking their SWP with authoritative pedagogies and learning theories, school policies and the system's teaching and learning framework;
- Collaboratively writing a definition of each pedagogical principle to develop a shared understanding of its meaning; and
- Brainstorming how each principle should look in practice in each classroom and in the provision of special and ESL support needs (O'Neill, 2013).

There was strong teacher leadership throughout the IDEAS processes. Teachers described how this became "*a part of their schoolwide pedagogy's way of working*". Once their schoolwide pedagogy was well established the school continued to refine and deepen its practice, They developed additional documentation showing how it linked to policy and curriculum. They reported how their SWP became a major lens that assisted them to deal with any new requirements. It also facilitated the introduction of new routines and ways of working and ensured greater consistency of practice, including more systematic collection of formative assessment data. Teachers worked in professional teams and they opened their school for others to visit and view their SWP in action. As they entered the *sustaining* phase they continued to develop strategies in support that included ensuring prospective new staff were aware of their schoolwide pedagogical expectations, and new recruits received support. They also planned to repeat the Diagnostic Inventory of School Alignment (DISA, 2014) to provide comparative data on staff, students' and parents' views as a measure of the impact change.

EMERGENT MESSAGES AND THE RECONCEPTUALISING OF PEDAGOGY

Teachers as Expert Professionals

Teachers in IDEAS Project schools demonstrate a new level of sophisticated practice that they are able to describe and justify in terms of their school's vision and pedagogical principles, authoritative educational theories, their personal pedagogy and the schools' created *hallmark authoritative pedagogy*.

They are aware of and able to incorporate their professional gifts and talents into their pedagogy and engage in reflective practice to ensure their ongoing professional learning and active design of engaging learning experiences. As expert practitioners IDEAS teachers are connected into their school's implementation and sustaining of their SWP in practice in their daily work. This is particularly evident in their ongoing professional conversations with colleagues, and the way their interactive dialogues with students reflect the accompanying metalanguage and metacognitive processes that underpin their SWP and make their teaching explicit. They also recognize the need to gather, interpret and use data to inform pedagogical decision-making and diagnose students' learning needs. It is through the IDEAS processes and phases in which teachers connect and collaborate within their school community, with each other as well as students and parents, that they acquire a sense of their own expertise. This is facilitated through their engagement in helping to construct, and then working from within the framework of their SWP. Through this process and resultant sense of ownership of their SWP they better understand and/or strengthen their personal philosophy of practice and participate in ongoing generative practice. Ultimately, IDEAS Project teachers have acquired new knowledge and tools to not only achieve their school's vision through its SWP but to sustain, and their own professional practice and learning. The context of such SWP engages teachers as expert practitioners in the development of their school's hallmark pedagogy that one may argue has Generative practice, Active design, and Mutuality, and is Metaphorical and Authoritative, a pedagogy that is necessary for 21st century contexts for learning. These features are used to further illuminate the change discussed, and to offer a strategy to reconceptualise pedagogy and learning through the acronym of 'GAMMA'.

Generative Practice: Co-Construction of Pedagogical Knowledge

Through IDEAS processes and their catalytic effect teachers in IDEAS schools are connected into the collaborative development of their school's vision, mission and values. As a pedagogy that needs to be schoolwide and to ensure a shared understanding and consistency in practice, they collaboratively develop a set of principles that reflect the school's values to form the base. Teachers take leadership in developing a pedagogical framework that ultimately exemplifies their pedagogy and guides their decision-making. During this time they address the IDEAS Project six criteria for SWP (Crowther, 2011). Overall the SWP should be clear and concise, comprising a limited number of practical pedagogical principles (*Criterion One*) and should facilitate connectivity, reinforcement and consolidation in students' core learning experiences (*Criterion Two*). As well teachers come to grips with the need to honour the distinctive features and needs of their school's student community (*Criterion Three*) as central to their SWP. Through this intensive engagement and the supportive process the ensuing SWP framework is able to facilitate teachers' identification of their professional gifts and talents, and enable them to share and enrich their pedagogy (*Criterion Four*). They also become actively engaged in reflecting on their personal pedagogy and also authoritative educational theories and research (*Criterion Five*). This is a transformative time for teachers since through this process they gain confidence in their pedagogical knowledge, their ability to lead pedagogical development, contribute to its implementation and its sustainability (*Criterion Six*).

Through this transformation teachers as expert practitioners have acquired and internalized the feature of generative practice where they have the knowledge and skills to engage in continuous reflection and critical discussion with colleagues to develop, implement, improve and sustain high quality pedagogy in keeping with the needs of the particular student community and their school's vision.

Active Design through Professional Dialogue and Shared Pedagogical Language

The active design of pedagogy is a powerful process where in the IDEAS *actioning phase* it is take down to the level of classroom practice. Teachers reported that they address the question of "What will our SWP look like in the classroom?" Because they have been through the earlier IDEAS Project phases, at this point teachers are well equipped to answer. They have come to grips with their personal pedagogy and how it connects and compliments their SWP. They are able to justify their views and practice, and their SWP in relation to authoritative educational theories.

Additional professional learning is also facilitated through the IDEAS Project processes and becomes embedded in practice through teachers' engagement in professional conversations and action research. These are a vital part of the development, and the actioning and sustaining phases. It is through these that teachers apply the pedagogical language and concepts of their SWP. They are used in their collaborative active design of the learning experiences, and pedagogical decision-making. The expert teacher profes-

sional is able to use the pedagogical language and concepts that underpin their SWP to design authentic learning experiences that are valid for their hallmark pedagogy.

Mutuality: Teachers<->Students Shared Metalanguage and Pedagogical Transformation

Not only do teachers engage with each other in professional dialogue that reflects the pedagogical language and concepts of their SWP but they connect their students into their learning in this way too. This mutuality is a strong feature of practice. This is evident in the way teachers consciously engage students in learning experiences that are made explicit through the use of shared metalanguage, and are inquiry-based and incorporate critical reflection. Teachers are able to communicate how their pedagogy in practice relates to their school's vision, and their students are also able to engage in this conversation. In this IDEAS Project school, pedagogy is transformed through the building of social capital and the capacity of both students and teachers to engage in pedagogical dialogue, higher order thinking skills and learning. Students are supported in their ability to conceptualize and discuss their own learning, set goals and make choices according to their mutually defined needs. Teachers as expert practitioners are able to draw upon their SWP, their principal, and system in their mutual need to provide for their particular student community. This strong mutuality is evident in teachers' collaborative, active design of their SWP, and their strategic pedagogical-decision-making. It is a key feature of the way these schools and teachers ensure there is a mutually agreed upon view of what their SWP and classroom learning should look like in practice. It is synonymous with the oft-used comment made by teachers that as result of IDEAS and their SWP they are "*all on the same page*".

Metaphorical: Shift in Teacher Cognition through the Professional Learning of SWP

IDEAS processes engage teachers in a journey of personal professional learning. During this time they clarify their personal pedagogy in relation to authoritative educational theories and they collaborate with their school community. It is a journey of self-development that creates a cognitive shift to equip teachers with the cognitive, executive skills to conceptualize and implement their SWP in practice. The expert practitioner in IDEAS schools is able to draw upon metaphorical thinking to engage in their school's visioning processes, move between different cognitive domains in making pedagogical connections, and enriching and deepening their practice.

Through the use of metaphor teachers are able to make cognitive connections between vision, values and pedagogical theory and practice, and conceptualize what it means for students' learning. Through their change in pedagogical practice and their conscious use of metalanguage in their professional and teaching dialogue they display evidence of their metacognition and use of metaphor at work. They employ graphic organizers, mind mapping and other thinking tools in keeping with their SWP to support students in making connections and constructing knowledge, e.g. De Bono's six thinking hats (de Bono, 1995); Gardner's multiple intelligences (Gardner, 2006; Hatch & Gardner, 1993); and Habits of Mind (Costa & Kallick, 2000). They involve students in a new level of intellectual stimulation that facilitates their metacognitive engagement and acquisition of strategies to move them towards becoming independent in their learning, and articulate in being able to discuss it (Geoghegan, O'Neill & Petersen, 2013).

Authoritative: Creation of a School's Hallmark Pedagogy

Teachers understand their own personal pedagogy in relation to authoritative educational theories and their collaboratively developed SWP. They gain confidence and self-efficacy in their sense of ownership of their SWP as an authoritative practice that they have collaboratively designed to meet the needs of their student community. They have high aspirations and expectations of their students and themselves, and are able to take control of their ongoing professional learning. This is encouraged and supported by their principal, the Ideas School Management Team and colleagues, as well as their system. They are involved in leading pedagogical change that involves critical reflection and deepening of their knowledge and understanding of learning. To do this their role includes sharing their pedagogical practices, investigating how authoritative pedagogies may inform their SWP, defining their school's pedagogical principles, ensuring that their SWP is able to integrate curriculum and system requirements, and examining how their SWP can bring their school's vision to life. IDEAS Project concepts of parallel leadership and teacher leadership become part of their professional conversations, which are also enriched through their work with IDEAS Project external consultants, their system's school consultants (in this case) and the network of their system's schools. Thus, they are able to define their unique authoritative SWP to a level of a mutual understanding of its practice and outcomes. This was identifiable through analysis of classroom pedagogical dialogue and interviews with staff, and the way they used an inquiry-based approach, monitoring and evaluating their practice and outcomes.

THE TEACHER EXPERT PRACTITIONER AND 21ST CENTURY GAMMA PEDAGOGY

While each school's needs, journey and vision might be said to be different according to the distinctive features and needs of the school's student community and context, the similarities relate to the transformation of teachers in their capacity to show leadership in pedagogical matters, and demonstrate commitment to improving teaching and learning. The teachers as expert practitioners in IDEAS Project schools can be said to be engaged in SWP as *Generative practice*, that involves the *Active design* of a hallmark pedagogy to meet their students' needs and empower them as learners. Their practice reflects a strong *Mutuality* in the use of a common pedagogical metalanguage, critical reflective practice, consideration of interests and needs and provision of support. This applies to teachers in their professional learning and students' learning alike. There is use of *Metaphor* and metaphorical thinking embedded in practice and used as a tool to achieve a new level of intellectual stimulation, and adoption of strategies for engagement in learning thinking. Through their participation in the IDEAS project and their collaborative creation of their SWP, teachers learn and become expert practitioners where the pedagogy they have created is *Authoritative* in its own right and becomes the hallmark of their practice.

Students as Empowered Learners

The concept of GAMMA pedagogy does not see students as passive receivers of information who seek to please the teacher or learning as memorization and reproduction of information. Rather, GAMMA pedagogy provides a way of reconceptualising pedagogy to consider how it does build students' capacity to learn. Part of this capacity is to enable students to interpret and use the language of learning, and allow discussion of their learning and learning goals. It includes the capacity to use appropriate metalanguage, meta-cognitive processes and thinking tools in explicit ways to actively generate pedagogical responses, discussions and ideas. This requires teachers to be able to understand their own cognitive moves in maximizing the teaching moment, allowing students more time and more opportunities to respond and be authentic participants in learning, controlling dialogue to maximize the scaffolding of learning. In GAMMA pedagogy students and teachers are in a new third space so to speak, where pedagogical practices and cognitive resources operate in concert, in use in a mutually agreed and understood way, in keeping with the SWP in place. It is hypothesized that this capacity for learning provides an essential internalized generative disposition that has the potential to be the driver of lifelong learning. As students are actively engaged in their learning their capacity is self-regulating and provides an element of independence as opposed to conceptualizing their learning as completed when a task is done.

Future research might investigate this in the longer term to find out if students' continue to be able to be self-sustaining and resilient, and also to what extent this intersects with the notion of 'flow' in generating a sense of self-efficacy and accomplishment. In Csikszentimihalyi (1991) terms "flow may be described as a period of optimal performance that is both fulfilling and engaging. It most often occurs 'when a person's body and mind is stretched to its limits in a voluntary effort to accomplish something difficult and worthwhile' (p. 3). When one is *in the flow,* work can seem like play in that 'people are so involved in an activity that nothing else seems to matter; the experience itself is so enjoyable that people will do it at great cost, for the sheer sake of doing it (p. 4)" (cited in Huitt, 2007, p. 6).

SOLUTIONS AND RECOMMENDATIONS

This chapter has highlighted the complexity of school improvement and has outlined the key issues and challenges that impact on schools and systems in their attempts to improve schooling and student learning outcomes. It has shown that there is a strong body of research that provides critical advice on how schools and systems may approach the improvement agenda in ways that should be helpful and welcomed by those involved. It has provided insights into one very successful international improvement project's processes for change and proposes a reconceptualised, overarching pedagogy, 'GAMMA' pedagogy in an attempt to make more explicit the shift that is needed to enhance students' learning today. It takes this further in showing how through building the teachers' capacity to learn, critically reflect and construct their own SWP, in keeping with the constructivist paradigm, they can foster their students' capacity to learn.

It has raised the important issue of language and metacognitive processes in learning and how the nature of classroom dialogue is revealing with regards to scaffolding students' learning and thinking. Educators need to develop their understanding of dialogic pedagogy in this regard. Professional learning related to staff's perceived needs and the direction of their SWP needs to be incorporated. In addition, the area that often does not receive attention in the literature is the need to manage and monitor students' progress and the collection of performance data. If schools do not have systems in place to be able to understand their students' progress and needs, then learning programs will not be able to easily respond to and differentiate.

Those contemplating a change need to be aware that it is a long-term commitment, however, through working collaboratively in an informed way, that engages all stakeholders, the building of social capital and the gathering of data to promote the conversation is a sound first step.

Of course, it cannot be assumed that schools contemplating changes to improve have the support of their system or additional resources to assist. In such cases it is a matter of drawing upon the resources at hand, which are often the local community and perhaps the local university. On the other hand some schools link to their communities by assessing how they can assist. For example some schools offer English lessons to their multilingual community, which encourages participation where otherwise language might have been a barrier. Developing partnerships in this way can have multiple benefits for all involved.

FUTURE RESEARCH DIRECTIONS

It may seem that there is a long road to travel before a school's improvement agenda is able to reap the results of improved student learning outcomes. However, this does depend on the school and the stakeholders, and their starting point, as well as resource base. It is motivating that there are successful schools and importantly principals, teachers, students and parents who are willing to share their experiences. Schools and systems are in the fortunate situation today that international research on school improvement is generally in agreement in terms of the strategies that can enable positive change. The research into pedagogical change in school improvement may only be in its infancy and there remains some controversy as to whether learning will improve without the development of a SWP. This is because an effective SWP helps to ensure students receive consistency of learning experiences (Wright, Horn & Sanders, 1997), strategies and language of learning as they move through the year levels over time. The chapter focus on how the IDEAS Project improvement occurs and an outline of how a schoolwide pedagogy is constructed presents a valuable model for successful improvement that is supported by research in three states in Australia and two countries overseas. The proposed GAMMA pedagogy creates a third space to consider/critique how the way students' learning changed as a result of the improvement process' SWP. It is exploratory but it is supported by research into classroom observations, teachers' and administrators' views and outcomes data (Crowther, Andrews, Morgan & O'Neill, 2012; Geoghegan, O'Neill & Petersen, 2013; O'Neill, 2013). It is able to convey the more dynamic nature of the learning that takes place in the social constructivist classroom in keeping with Mayer's (2012) research into classroom discourse and democracy. There needs to be extensive research into the way language, thinking and pedagogy intersect to promote learning and to answer the question of knowledge creation which is often a learning objective yet difficult to exemplify. At the same time GAMMA pedagogy, as a new pedagogical paradigm, and an explanation for building students' capacity to learn needs to be further tested. It is only by exploring new pedagogical paradigms that the rhetoric that tends to surround such concepts as lifelong learning, constructivist pedagogy and independent learning can be more fully appreciated and addressed in the future.

CONCLUSION

In conclusion, this chapter reports on the school improvement literature from an international perspective in relation to leadership and pedagogical reform. It focuses on a particular Australian based school improvement initiative, the IDEAS Project that is in its second decade of implementation. It examines its research findings compared with the work of contemporary researchers. It shows how the underpinning philosophy and principles that guide its five phase, long-term process are in keeping with what is known to work in school reform, and examines the importance of building social capital, and its relationship to leadership capacity. The context for the research is described in relation to Australia, the education system of the research and the case study school at the centre of the discussion.

The chapter addresses the key controversies that impact on the research area in terms of traditional views of school leadership and pedagogy and how this may challenge reform. It includes discussion of traditional and constructivist classroom features and the importance of understanding the nature of change that needs to occur inside classrooms if students' learning outcomes are to improve. As these challenges are considered it explains how they are dealt with in the IDEAS Project. Central to the IDEAS Project's improvement phases is the school's creation of their vision for their school and their values that underpin their development of a schoolwide pedagogy. This major aspect is highlighted as central to engaging teachers in a distributed model of school leadership to take responsibility for the construction of their school's hallmark pedagogy.

Based on research the importance of students being familiar with the language for learning and being taught the metalanguage and associated metacognitive processes is emphasised. Similarly, the importance of teachers' classroom dialogue in scaffolding students' learning is highlighted. This discussion leads into the proposal for a reconceptualization of effective pedagogy as one that is able to build students' capacity to learn in keeping with a social constructivist view. This is described as GAMMA pedagogy that involves Generative practice in the construction of pedagogical knowledge and use of strategies and thinking; Active design through professional dialogue, shared pedagogical language and reflective practice; Mutuality in 'teachers<->students' shared metalanguage, mutual capacity building and pedagogical transformation; Metaphorical in facilitating creativity and Authoritative in the product of a school's hallmark pedagogy. The concept of GAMMA pedagogy recognizes the vital importance of building students' capacity to learn in 21st. century education and provides an important vehicle for those interested in improving pedagogy and students' learning, to interrogate their practice.

REFERENCES

Abawi, L. (2013a). School meaning systems: The symbiotic nature of culture and 'language-in-use'. *Improving Schools*, *16*(2), 89–106. doi:10.1177/1365480213492407

Abawi, L. (2013b). Metaphor: Powerful imagery bringing learning and teaching to life. *Improving Schools*, *16*(2), 130–147. doi:10.1177/1365480213492409

Abawi, L., & Oliver, M. (2013). Shared pedagogical understandings: Schoolwide inclusion practices supporting learner needs. *Improving Schools*, *16*(2), 159–174. doi:10.1177/1365480213493711

ACARA. (2014). *The Australian curriculum*. Canberra, Australia: Australian Curriculum, Assessment and Reporting Authority. Retrieved November 20, 2013, from http://www.australian-curriculum.edu.au

Adams, R. (2012). *NAPLAN reporting – Measures and models for reporting gain over time*. Retrieved August 10, 2012, from http://www.coagreform-council.gov.au/excellence/docs/improvement/CI_NAPLAN_reporting_2012.pdf

AITSL. (2011). *National professional standards for teachers, Australian Institute for Teaching and School Leadership (AITSL)*. Carlton South, Australia: Education Services Australia.

Alsop, S., Gould, G., & Watts, M. (2002). The role of pupils' questions in learning science. In S. Amos & R. Boohan (Ed.), Aspects of teaching secondary science: Perspectives on practice (pp. 39–48). London, UK: Routledge.

Anstey, M., & Bull, G. (1996). Re-examining pedagogical knowledge and classroom practice. In G. Bull & M. Anstey (Eds.), *The literacy labyrinth* (pp. 89–106). Sydney: Prentice-Hall.

APPA. (2014). *APPA submission to the Australian government review of the Australian curriculum*. Australian Primary Principals Association. Retrieved 20 March, 2014, from http://www.appa.asn.au/submissions/Review-of-Australian-curriculum.pdf

Avolio, B., & Bass, B. (1994). Transformational leadership and organizational culture. International Journal of Public Administration, 17(3-4), 541-554.

Barnett, K., McCormick, J., & Conners, R. (2001). Transformational leadership in schools-panacea, placebo or problem? *Journal of Educational Administration*, *39*(1), 24–46. doi:10.1108/09578230110366892

Bass, B. (1998). *Transformational leadership: Industrial, military, and educational impact*. Mahwah, NJ: Lawrence Erlbaum Associates.

Behn, R. D. (1991). *Leadership counts: Lessons for public managers from the Massachusetts welfare training and employment program*. Harvard University Press.

Bryk, A., Sebring, P., Allensowrth, E., Luppesco, S., & Easton, J. (2010). *Organizing schools for improvement: Lessons from Chicago*. Chicago: University of Chicago Press.

Caldwell, B. J., & Spinks, J. M. (2013). *The self-transforming school*. New York, NY: Routledge.

Canavan, K. (2003). The development of the Catholic Education Office and a system of schools in Sydney since 1965. Sydney, Australia: CEO Sydney.

Canavan, K. (2007). *School review and improvement*. Sydney, Australia: Catholic Education Office.

Canavan, K. (2008). *Building a leadership and learning culture across a school system.* Sydney, Australia: Catholic Education Office.

Chandler, D. (2001). *Semiotics: The Basics.* London: Routledge.

Chesterton, P., & Duignan, P. (2004). *Evaluation of a national trial of IDEAS Project: Report prepared for the Department of Education, Science and Training (DEST).* Canberra, Australia: DEST.

Connell, R. (2012). Ideology of the marketplace underpins school "reforms". *The Drum: Analysis and opinion on the issues of the day.* Retrieved December 16, 2013, from http://www.abc.net.au/unleashed/3892492.html

Conway, J. M., & Abawi, L. (2013). Creating enduring strength through commitment to schoolwide pedagogy. *Improving Schools, 16*(2), 175–185. doi:10.1177/1365480213493714

Costa, A. L., & Kallick, B. (Eds.). (2000). *Discovering and exploring Habits of Mind. Habits of Mind: A developmental series.* Alexandria, VA: Association for Supervision and Curriculum Development.

Crowther, F. (2011). *From school improvement to sustained capacity.* Thousand Oaks, CA: Corwin Press.

Crowther, F., Andrews, D., & Conway, J. M. (2013). *Schoolwide pedagogy: Vibrant new meaning for teachers and principals.* Melbourne, Australia: Hawker Brownlow Education.

Crowther, F., Andrews, D., Morgan, A., & O'Neill, S. (2012, Summer). Hitting the bull's eye of school improvement: The IDEAS arrow. *Leading and Managing*, 1-31.

Crowther, F., Ferguson, M., & Hann, L. (2009). Developing teacher leaders: How teacher leadership enhances school success (2nd. ed.). Thousand Oaks, CA: Corwin Press.

Culican, S. J. (2005). Troubling teacher talk: The challenge of changing classroom discourse patterns. Paper presented at the Annual Conference of the Australian Association for Research in Education. Sydney, Australia. Retrieved June 01, 2014, from http://www.aare.edu.au/data/publications/2005/cul05592.pdf

Cullen, S. (2014). *Teachers warn of 'culture wars' as Christopher Pyne announces back-to-basics curriculum review.* Australian Broadcasting Commission News. Retrieved February 15, 2014 from http://www.abc.net.au/news/2014-01-10/pyne-calls-for-national-curriculum-to-focus-on-benefits-of-west/5193804

de Bono, E. (1995). *Mind power: Discover the secrets of creative thinking.* Crows Nest, Australia: Allen & Unwin.

DISA. (2014). *The Diagnostic Survey of School Alignment (DISA).* Retrieved January 10, 2014 from http://www.acelleadership.org.au/diagnostic-inventory-school-alignment-disa

Edwards-Groves, C., & Hardy, I. (2013). "Well, that was an intellectual dialogue!" How a whole-school focus on improvement shifts the substantive nature of classroom talk. *English Teaching, 12*(2), 116–136.

Edwards-Groves, C. J., & Hoare, R. L. (2012). "Talking to learn": Focussing teacher education on dialogue as a core practice for teaching and learning. *Australian Journal of Teacher Education, 37*(8), 82–100. doi:10.14221/ajte.2012v37n8.8

El Amouri, S., & O'Neill, S. (in press). Leadership style and culturally competent care: Nurse leaders' views of their practice in the multicultural care settings of the United Arab Emirates. *Contemporary Nurse.* PMID:24950789

Fullan, M. (2005). *Leadership and sustainability.* Thousand Oaks, CA: Corwin Press.

Fullan, M. (2006). *Turnaround leadership*. San Francisco: Jossey-Bass.

Gardner, H. (2006). *Changing minds. The art and science of changing our own and other people's minds*. Boston, MA: Harvard Business School Press.

Geoghegan, D., O'Neill, S., & Petersen, S. (2013). Metalanguage: The 'teacher talk' of explicit literacy teaching in practice. *Improving Schools, 12*(2), 119–129. doi:10.1177/1365480213493707

Goddard, Y. L., Goddard, R. D., & Tschannen-Moran, M. (2007). A theoretical and empirical investigation of teacher collaboration for school improvement and student achievement in public elementary schools. *Teachers College Record, 109*(4), 877–896.

Hargreaves, A., & Fullen, M. (2012). *Professional capital: Transforming teaching in every school*. New York: Routledge.

Hargreaves, A., & Shirley, D. (2009). *The fourth way: A new vision for education reform*. Thousand Oaks, CA: Corwin Press.

Hargreaves, D. (2001). A capital theory of school effectiveness and improvement. *British Educational Research Journal, 27*(4), 487–503. doi:10.1080/01411920120071489

Harris, A. (2008). *Distributed school leadership: Developing tomorrow's leaders*. London: Routledge.

Harris, A. (2012). Leading system wide improvement. *International Journal of Leadership in Education, 15*(3), 395–401. doi:10.1080/13603124.2012.661879

Harris, A., Day, C., Hadfield, M., Hopkins, D., Hargreaves, A., & Chapman, C. (2003). *Effective leadership for school improvement*. London: Routledge Falmer.

Harris, C., Phillips, R., & Penuel, W. (2011). Examining teachers' instructional moves aimed at developing students' ideas and questions in learner-centered science classrooms. *Journal of Science Teacher Education*. doi:10.1007/s10972-011-9237-0

Hatch, T., & Gardner, H. (1993). Finding cognition in the classroom: an expanded view of human intelligence. In G. Salomon (Ed.), *Distributed cognitions: Psychological and educational considerations*. Cambridge, UK: Cambridge University Press.

Healy, A. (2008). Expanding student capacities. In A. Healy (Ed.), *Multiliteracies: Pedagogies for diverse learners* (pp. 2–29). Sydney: Oxford University Press.

Heap, J. L. (1985). Discourse in the production of classroom knowledge: Reading lessons. *Curriculum Inquiry, 15*(3), 245–279. doi:10.2307/1179585

Hopkins, D., Harris, A., Stoll, L., & Mackay, T. (2014). School and system Improvement: State of the art review. *School Effectiveness and School Improvement, 25*(2), 257–281. doi:10.1080/09243453.2014.885452

Hopkins, D., & Jackson, D. (2003). Building the capacity for leading and learning. In A. Harris, C. Day, D. Hopkins, M. Hadfield, A. Hargreaves, & C. Chapman (Eds.), *Effective leadership for school improvement* (pp. 84–104). New York: Routledge Falmer.

Huinker, D., & Freckmann, J. L. (2004). Focusing conversations to promote teacher thinking. *Teaching Children Mathematics, 10*(7), 352–357.

Huitt, W. (2007). *Success in the conceptual age: Another paradigm shift*. Paper delivered at the 32nd Annual Meeting of the Georgia Educational Research Association. Savannah, GA. Retrieved September 25, 2013, from http://www.edpsycinteractive.org/papers/conceptual-age.pdf

Isaacs, W., & Smith, B. (1994). Designing a dialogue session. In P. Senge, A. Kleiner, C. Roberts, R. B. Ross, & B. Smith (Eds.), The fifth discipline fieldbook: Strategies and tools for building a learning organization (pp. 374-381). London: Nicholas Brealey Publishing.

Jensen, B., & Reichl, J. (2011). *Better teacher appraisal and feedback: Improving performance.* Melbourne: Grattan Institute.

Jensen, B., & Sonnerman, J. (2014). *Turning around schools: It can be done, Grattan Institute Report No. 2014-1.* Retrieved March 22, 2013, from http://grattan.edu.au/static/files/assets/518f9688/805-turning-around-schools.pdf

Jeyaraj, S. (2011). *Organizational cognisance: Introducing a cognitive dimension to the concept of organizational alignment.* (Doctoral dissertation). Faculty of education, University of Southern Queensland. Retrieved March 02, 2014, from http://eprints.usq.edu.au/23412/

Kamler, B., & Comber, B. (2005). Turn-around pedagogies: Improving the education of at-risk students. *Improving Schools*, *8*(2), 121–131. doi:10.1177/1365480205057702

Kyriacou, C., & Issitt, J. (2008). What characterises effective teacher-initiated teacher-pupil dialogue to promote conceptual understanding in mathematics lessons in England in Key Stages 2 and 3: A systematic review. Report. In *Research Evidence in Education Library*. London: EPPI-Centre, Social Science Research Unit, Institute of Education, University of London.

Lambert, L. (2000). *Building leadership capacity in schools.* APC Monographs. Australian Principals Centre (APC). Retrieved November 4, 2013, from http://research.acer.edu.au/apc_monographs/2

Lingard, R., & Sellar, S. (2013). Looking east: Three national responses to Shanghai's performance in PISA 2009, School improvement. *Professional Voice, 9*(2), 10-19. Retrieved May 31, 2014, from http://www.aeuvic.asn.au/2504_pv_9_2_complete_lr.pdf

Louden, W., et al. (2005). *In teachers' hands: Effective literacy teaching practices in the early years of schooling.* Edith Cowan University. Retrieved July 29, 2013, from http://inteachershands.education.ecu.edu.au/index.php?page=43

Louis, K. S., & Marks, H. (1998). Does professional community affect the classroom? Teachers' work and student experience in restructured schools. *American Journal of Education, 106*(4), 532–575. doi:10.1086/444197

Marino, P. (2005). Dialogue in mathematics – is it important? *Mathematics in Schools, 34*(2), 26–28.

Mayer, S. J. (2012). *Classroom discourse and democracy: Making meanings together. Critical pedagogical perspectives.* New York: Peter Lang.

Moje, E. B., Ciechanowski, K. M., Kramer, K., Ellis, L., Carrillo, R., & Collazo, T. (2004). Working toward third space in content area literacy: An examination of everyday funds of knowledge and discourse. *Reading Research Quarterly, 39*(1), 38–70. doi:10.1598/RRQ.39.1.4

Mourshed, M., Chijioke, C., & Barber, M. (2010). *How the world's most improved school systems keep getting better.* McKinsey and Co. Consulting Report.

Myhill, D. (2006). Talk, talk, talk: Teaching and learning in whole class discourse. *Research Papers in Education, 21*(1), 19–41. doi:10.1080/02671520500445425

NAPLAN. (2011). *The national language conventions and numeracy report*. Canberra: MCEETYA.

Nelson, C. A. (2012). *Building capacity to improve literacy learning*. National Center for Literacy Education/National Council of Teachers of English. Retrieved August 12, 2013, from http://www.ncte.org/library/NCTEFiles/About/NCLE/NCLEshortlitreview.pdf

Newmann, F. M., & Associates. (1996). Authentic achievement: Restructuring schools for intellectual quality. San Francisco: Jossey-Bass Publishers.

Ng, D., & Chew, J. (2008). *Innovative designs for enhancing achievement in schools (IDEAS) in Singapore Report No. EP1/04KS*. Singapore: National Institute of Education, Nanyang Technological University.

O'Neill, S. (2013). Activating the *"language for learning"* through Schoolwide pedagogy: The case of MacKillop school. *Improving Schools*, *12*(2), 107–118. doi:10.1177/1365480213492408

O'Neill, S., & Geoghegan, D. (2012). Pre-service teachers' comparative analyses of teacher-/parent-child talk: Making literacy teaching explicit and children's literacy learning visible. *International Journal of Studies in English.*, *12*(1), 97–128. doi:10.1177/1365480213493709

O'Neill, S., Geoghegan, D., & Petersen, S. (2013). Raising the pedagogical bar: Teachers co-construction of explicit teaching. *Improving Schools*, *12*(2), 148–158. doi:10.1177/1365480213493709

Odden, A., & Archibald, S. (2009). *Doubling student performance ... and finding the resources to do it*. Thousand Oaks, CA: Corwin Press.

Oldenburg, R. (1999). *The great good place*. New York: Marlowe & Company.

Oldenburg, R. (2000). *Celebrating the third place: Inspiring stories about the "Great good places" at the heart of our communities*. New York: Marlowe & Company.

Pratt, N. (2006). 'Interactive' teaching in numeracy lessons: What do children have to say? *Cambridge Journal of Education*, *36*(2), 221–235. doi:10.1080/03057640600718612

Rose, D. (2005a). Democratising the classroom: A literacy pedagogy for the new generation. *Journal of Education*, *37*, 131–167.

Rose, D. (2005b). *Learning to read: Reading to learn: Submission to the National Inquiry into the Teaching of Literacy 2005*. Canberra: Department of Education, Science and Training. Retrieved September 12, 2013, from http://www.dest.gov.au/sectors/school_education/policy_initiatives_reviews/key_issues/literacy_numeracy/national_inquiry/documents/pdf2/sub_315_pdf.htm

Rowe, K. (2005). *Teaching reading: Report of the National Inquiry into the Teaching of Literacy*. Canberra: Department of Education, Science and Training. Retrieved June 16, 2013, from http://www.dest.gov.au/nitl/documents/report_recommendations.pdf

SAD. (2011), *Asking effective questions: Provoking student thinking/deepening conceptual understanding in the mathematics classroom*. Student Achievement Division (SAD), Ontario Schools, Special Edition 21: 1-8. Retrieved March 01, 2014, from http://www.edu.gov.on.ca/eng/literacynumeracy/inspire/research/CBS_AskingEffectiveQuestions.pdf

Schleicher, A. (2014). Attacks on PISA are entirely unjustified. *TES Magazine*. Retrieved April 30, 2014, from http://www.tes.co.uk/article.aspx?storycode=6345213

Schuh, K. L. (2003). Knowledge construction in the learner-centered classroom. *Journal of Educational Psychology*, *95*(2), 426–442. doi:10.1037/0022-0663.95.2.426

Schwarz, C., & Dussart, F. (2010). Christianity in Aboriginal Australia revisited. *The Australian Journal of Anthropology, 21*(1), 1–13. doi:10.1111/j.1757-6547.2010.00064.x

Sellar, S., & Lingard, R. (2013). Looking east: Shanghai, PISA 2009 and the reconstruction of reference societies in the global policy field. *Comparative Education, 49*(4), 464–485. doi:10.1080/03050068.2013.770943

Smith, F., Hardman, F., Wall, K., & Mroz, M. (2004). Interactive whole class teaching in the National Literacy and Numeracy Strategies. *British Educational Research Journal, 30*(3), 395–411. doi:10.1080/01411920410001689706

Spiegelhalter, D. (2013). The problems with PISA statistical methods. *Opinion, Stats Life, Royal Statistical Society.* Retrieved May 10, 2014, from http://www.statslife.org.uk/opinion/1074-the-problems-with-pisa-statistical-methods

Thirteen. (2014). *Workshop: Constructivism as a paradigm for teaching and learning.* Retrieved October, 08, 2013, from http://www.thirteen.org/edonline/concept2class/constructivism/index.html

Thompson, S., Hillman, K., Wernert, N., Schmid, M., Buckley, S., & Munene, A. (2012). *Highlights from TIMMS & PIRLS 2011 from Australia's perspective.* Melbourne, Australia: Australian Council for Education Research (ACER). Retrieved September 22, 2013, from http://www.acer.edu.au/documents/TIMSS-PIRLS_Australian-Highlights.pdf

Tovey, J., & Patty, A. (2013). OECD report finds Australian students falling behind. *The Sydney Morning Herald.* Retrieved February 20, 2014, from http://www.smh.com.au/national/education/oecd-report-finds-australian-students-falling-behind-20131203-2you0.html

Van Es, E. A., & Sherin, M. G. (2002). Learning to notice: Scaffolding new teachers' interpretations of classroom interactions. *Journal of Technology and Teacher Education, 10*(4), 571–596.

Walsh, S. (2006). Talking the talk of the TESOL classroom. *ELT Journal, 60*(2), 133–141. doi:10.1093/elt/cci100

Wells, G. (2010). Dialogue, inquiry and the construction of learning communities. In B. Lingard, J. Nixon, & S. Ranson (Eds.), *Transforming learning in schools and communities* (pp. 236–256). London: Continuum.

Wright, P., Horn, S., & Sanders, W. (1997). Teacher and classroom context effects on student achievement: Implications for teacher evaluation. *Journal of Personnel Evaluation in Education, 11*(1), 57–67. doi:10.1023/A:1007999204543

Wrigley, T. (2006). *Another school is possible.* New York, NY: Trentham Books.

Wu, M. (2009). *Interpreting NAPLAN results for the layperson.* Retrieved October 10, 2013, from http://www.edmeasurement.com.au/_publications/margaret/NAPLAN_for_lay_person.pdf

ADDITIONAL READING

Bandura, A. (1977). *Social learning theory.* Englewood Cliffs, NJ: Prentice-Hall. Bodrova, E.

Glasser, W. (1998). *The quality school.* New York: Harper Collins.

Goleman, D. (2005). *Emotional intelligence.* New York: Bantam Dell.

Goleman, D. (2006). *Social intelligence.* New York: Bantam Dell.

Gordon, M. (2009). Toward a pragmatic discourse of constructivism: Reflections on lessons from practice. *Educational Studies*, *45*(1), 39–58. doi:10.1080/00131940802546894

Haji Tarasat, H. S., & O'Neill, S. (2012). Changing traditional reading pedagogy: The importance of classroom interactive talk for year one Malay readers. [December. In Special Issue: Cross-cultural pedagogies: The interface between Islamic and Western pedagogies and epistemologies.]. *International Journal of Pedagogies and Learning*, *7*(3), 239–261. doi:10.5172/ijpl.2012.7.3.239

Hargreaves, A., & Shirley, D. (2007). *Raising achievement: Transforming learning*. Boston: Lynch School of Education.

Hargreaves, D. (2003). *Education epidemic: Transforming secondary schools through innovation networks*. London: Demos.

Hattie, J. (2003). Teachers Make a Difference: What is the research evidence? *Paper presented at the Australian Council of Educational Research Annual Conference on Building Teacher Quality, Melbourne*. Retrieved August 12, 2013, from: http://research.acer.edu.au/research_conference_2003/4

Hill, P., & Crevola, C. (1999). Key features of whole-school design approach to literacy teaching in schools. *Australian Journal of Learning Disabilities, 4*(3), 5–11. Hogan, M. (2008). Staying on top of things in a whitewater world. *Education Today: The Magazine for Educational Professionals, 8*. Retrieved March, 20, 2013, from: www.minniscomms.com.au/educationtoday/articles.php?articleid=36

Leong, D. J. (1996). *Tools of the mind: The Vygotskian approach to early childhood education*. Englewood Cliffs, NJ: Merrill/Prentice Hall.

Lodge, C. (2008). Engaging student voice to improve pedagogy and learning: An exploration of examples of innovative pedagogical approaches for school improvement. *International Journal of Pedagogies and Learning, 4*(5), 4–19. doi:10.5172/ijpl.4.5.4

Mercer, N. (1995). *The guided construction of knowledge: Talk amongst teachers and learners*. Clevedon: Multilingual Matters Ltd.

Mercer, N., & Sams, C. (2006). Teaching children how to use language to solve maths problems. *Language and Education, 20*(6), 507–528. doi:10.2167/le678.0

Nassaji, N., & Wells, G. (2000). 'What's the use of 'triadic dialogue'? An investigation of teacher-student interaction'. *Applied Linguistics, 21*(3), 376–406. doi:10.1093/applin/21.3.376

Newmann, F. M., King, B., & Youngs, P. (2000). *Professional development to build organizational capacity in low achieving schools: Promising strategies and future challenges*. Madison, WI: University of Wisconsin-Madison.

Newmann, F. M., & Wehlage, G. (1995). *Successful school restructuring: A report to the public and educators*. Madison, WI: University of Wisconsin-Madison.

Odden, A. (2009). *Ten strategies for doubling student performance*. Thousand Oaks: Corwin Press.

Robson, G., Lock, G., & Pilkington, K. (2009). *Evaluation of the innovative design for enhancing achievements in schools (IDEAS) program in 10 government secondary schools*. East Perth: W.A. Dept. of Education and Training.

Rowe, K. (2003). The importance of teacher quality as a key determinant of students' experiences and outcomes of schooling. In G. Masters (Ed.), *Building teacher quality: What does the research tell us?* (pp. 15–23). Camberwell, Australia: ACER.

Senge, P. (1990). *The fifth discipline: The art and practice of the learning organization*. New York, NY: Doubleday/Currency.

Stoll, L., & Seashore, L. K. (2007). Professional learning communities: Elaborating new approaches. In L. Stoll & K. L. Seashore (Eds.), *Professional learning communities: Divergence, depth, and dilemmas* (pp. 1–14). Berkshire, England: Open University Press.

Windschitl, M. (1999). The challenges of sustaining a constructivist classroom culture. *Phi Delta Kappan, 80,* 751–757.

Zabr, V., Marshall, G., & Power, P. (2007). *Better schools. Better teachers. Better results*. Melbourne: ACER Press.

KEY TERMS AND DEFINITIONS

Classroom Dialogue: The interactive talk that involves teachers and students during learning episodes.

Creating New Knowledge: The results of the process of school's development and actioning of their schoolwide pedagogy. It applies to the learning that occurs during this process and any resulting artifacts that contribute to its understanding.

Education Leadership: Those who seek to work with others to initiate and lead change with a view to improve student learning outcomes and life in schools. This may occur at the government, system, school, classroom and community level.

GAMMA Pedagogy: The features of a proposed pedagogy that build students' capacity to learn through generative practice, active design, mutuality, metaphorical and authoritative. When considered in terms of a third place it is an enabling device to help reconstruct and understand a new view of the learner.

Pedagogical Reform: The need to make changes to pedagogy to better enable students to learn.

Schoolwide Pedagogy: A school's agreed upon pedagogical approach for their school that is underpinned by the schools values and principles of pedagogy that relate to relevant theories of learning.

Student Capacity Building: The way schools and teachers design and implement their schoolwide pedagogy to facilitate students' ability to learn. This includes the teaching of concepts, meta-language, language for learning and accompanying thinking skills and tools that enable students to discuss how they learn and their learning goals.

Chapter 7

Becoming a Principal:
Exploring Perceived Discriminatory Practices in the Selection of Principals in Jamaica and England

Paul Miller
Brunel University London, UK

ABSTRACT

Becoming a principal is not an easy feat. Principals are the custodians of a nation's education future and development. As such, they should represent the "best" of the stock of experience, skills, and capacities that exist within a school. Whereas this chapter does not consider the quality of principals in post, it spotlights the perceptions of discrimination in the appointments and promotions process of principals in both Jamaica and England. Drawing on data from a small-scale two-phase exploratory study, the chapter compares the process of appointing principals whilst contrasting the perceived discriminatory practices in getting an appointment as a school principal. The chapter calls for further detailed research of the issues identified and for changes to process for promoting and/or appointing a principal so that actors in the system, teachers especially, can feel confident of putting themselves forward for suitable positions where these may be available.

INTRODUCTION AND CONTEXTUALISATION

Principals are the chief custodians on a nation's educational outcomes. They are, by virtue of their position, the guardians of a nation's future in the form of children and young people and their schools. That said, being appointed to the rank of a school Principal is not an easy feat; and nor should it be. It should not be easy, because schools and by extension the education system and society need to be assured that the most suitable person is given the job and therefore all appropriate steps have to be taken to recruit this person on board. However, a range of factors: legal, institutional, socio-cultural, task or role related, personality and experience related, and others *invisible*, have made an appointment to the rank of Principal not a straightforward enterprise.

DOI: 10.4018/978-1-4666-6591-0.ch007

There are approximately 23,330 state funded schools in England; 3,446 state funded secondary schools and 16,884 state primary schools. In Jamaica, there are just over 1,000 state funded schools; 206 state funded secondary schools or equivalent and 973 pre-primary, primary and equivalent types of schools. There are approximately 448,000 teachers in the state funded primary and secondary education sectors in England and approximately 25,000 teachers in state funded primary and secondary education sector in Jamaica, including approximately 23,000 principals in England and approximately 1,000 in Jamaica.

Effective leadership is arguably the most vital ingredient for a school's success, and given the amount of teachers compared with the number of posts available for Principals, there is a noticeable gap in terms of what is aspirational and what is realistic in terms of being appointed a principal. Similarly, well-motivated, experienced, highly skilled, and qualified teachers are needed in appropriate numbers, to support and lead school initiatives and programmes aimed at achieving the best possible educational outcomes for all students. Goal 6 of Education for All underpins these imperatives by highlighting the need for quality education. Quality education however, requires inputs in the form of human (strategic, technical, operational), and financial resources (including networks and physical material), and for these to be aligned to expected outcomes. In this regard, students at all levels of education, and in whichever country they live, need the best possible support so as to increase their life chances; and schools need the best available skills and talents, in the form of teachers and principals.

Educational policy reforms in England and Jamaica have intensified in recent years. For example, since the Coalition Government came to office in the United Kingdom in 2010, there have been changes to the design and delivery of teacher education, changes to the secondary curriculum and massive changes to the structure and organisation of schooling more noticeably through the

introduction of Academies and Free Schools. On the opposite side of the Atlantic, the then Jamaican government in 2004 launched the Education Sector Transformation Programme (ESTP) which led to the introduction of a National College for Educational Leadership, a National Education Inspectorate, a National Council on Education and the Jamaica Tertiary Education Commission. ESTP was followed, in 2010, by the launch of 'Vision 2030: National Development Plan Jamaica', an ambitious multifaceted programme of activities and initiatives aimed at scaffolding the country's ambitious goal of achieving "developed" country status by the year 2030. The Education Sector Plan of Vision 2030 identified the need for an excellent cadre of teachers and principals to be in place to realise many of the objectives of the National Development Plan (Planning Institute of Jamaica, 2010).

In England, the first and only comprehensive study to examine the selection process of principals was conducted by Morgan et al. (1983). Termed the *POST* project, the study's authors found several challenges associated with the appointments' process ranging from unclear job descriptions to unfair practices which led them to conclude, 'the selection of headteachers is carried out in an arbitrary and amateur way' (p145). Three decades later, Miller (2013) conducted pioneering work on principal appointments in Jamaica which led to the publication of a Research Report, *"The Politics of Progression: Primary teachers' perceived barriers to gaining a Principalship in Jamaica."* In this report, Miller concluded that the process for appointing of principals was flawed and did not always make use of the best talents available and was premised around an in-group and an out-group manifested in terms of various discriminatory practices. This chapter will explore the process that is involved in becoming a principal in both England and Jamaica, as is set out as follows: section one provides an introduction to the issue of appointment and promotion a leadership positions in schools; section two describes the requirement and process involved appointment a principal in Jamaica and England; section three considers, from the relevant literature, factors underpinning discriminatory practices in school leadership appointments; section four provides evidence of perceived discrimination in the appointments process in Jamaica and England; and, section five engages in a discussion of current practices, calling for changes to appointment processes, thereby building confidence and integrity in an education system and in those appointed as principals.

The Organisation of Schooling in Jamaica

Education in Jamaica is administered primarily by the Ministry of Education (MoE), through its head office and six regional offices. Formal education is provided mainly by the Government, solely or in partnerships with churches and trusts. Formal education also is provided by private schools. As stipulated in the 1980 Education Act (Government of Jamaica, 1981), the education system consists of four levels: Early Childhood; Primary; Secondary; and Tertiary.

The education system caters to circa 800,000 students in public institutions at the early childhood, primary and secondary (MoE, 2012). As set out in the Education Sector Plan: Vision 2030 (PIOJ, 2010, p. 6), Jamaica's education system is pursuing the following seven strategic objectives to:

1. Devise and support initiatives that are directed towards literacy for all, and in this way, extend personal opportunities and contribute to national development;
2. Secure teaching and learning opportunities that will optimise access, equity and relevance throughout the education system;
3. Support student achievement and improve institutional performance in order to ensure that national targets are met; and

4. Maximize opportunities within the Ministry's purview that promote cultural development, awareness and self-esteem for individuals, communities and the nation as a whole;
5. Devise and implement systems of accountability and performance management to improve performance and win public confidence and trust;
6. Optimize the effectiveness and efficiency of staff in all aspects of the service to ensure continuous improvement in performance; and
7. Enhance student learning by increasing the use of information and communication technology in preparation for life in the national and global communities. (p. 18)

Funding for education is provided primarily by the Government of Jamaica through allocations from the National Budget. In 2006, the Government began implementation of the recommendations of the National Education Task Force (Government of Jamaica, 2004) as well as introducing a number of programmes and projects aimed at improving quality, equity and access in the education system. It is widely debated that these reforms will lead to improvements in Jamaica's human capital, producing the skills necessary and thereby making it easier for Jamaicans to more effectively compete in the global economy.

The Organisation of Schooling in England

Education in England is overseen by the Department for Education and the Department for Business, Innovation, and Skills, supported by Local Authorities (LAs) which take responsibility for implementing policy for public education and state schools at the local level. The education system is divided into early years (ages 3–4), primary education (ages 4–11), secondary education (ages 11–18) and tertiary education (ages 18+) (The Independent, 2011).

Full-time education is compulsory for all children aged between 5 and 16. State-provided schooling and sixth form education is paid for by taxes. Since 1998 to the present, there have been six main types of maintained school in England:

- **Community Schools:** These are run by the local authority, which employs its own staff, owns the land and buildings the school is on, and decides on the admissions criteria.

- **Foundation and Trust Schools:** These are run by their own governing body, which employs the staff and sets the admissions criteria. Land and buildings are usually owned by the governing body or a charitable foundation. A trust school is a type of foundation school which forms a charitable trust with an outside partner – for example, a business or educational charity – aiming to raise standards and explore new ways of working. Before a decision to become a trust school is taken by the governing body, parents must be consulted.

- **Voluntary-Aided Schools:** These are mainly religious or 'faith' schools, although anyone can apply for a place. As with foundation schools, the governing body employs the staff and sets the admissions criteria. The buildings and land are normally owned by a charitable foundation, often a religious organisation although the governing body contributes to building and maintenance costs.

- **Voluntary-Controlled Schools:** These are similar to voluntary-aided schools, but are run by the local authority. As with community schools, the local authority employs the school's staff and sets the admissions criteria. School land and buildings are normally owned by a charity, often a religious organisation, which also appoints some of the members of the governing body.

- **Academies:** These were originally set up by the 1997-2010 New Labour Government to replace poorly-performing community schools in areas of high social and economic deprivation. Their start-up costs are typically funded by private means, such as entrepreneurs or NGOs, with running costs met by Central Government and, like Foundation schools, are administratively free from direct local authority control. The 2010 Conservative-Liberal Democrat coalition government expanded the role of Academies in the *Academy Programme*, in which a wide number of schools in non-deprived areas were also encouraged to become Academies, thereby essentially replacing the role of Foundation schools established by the previous Labour government. They are monitored directly by the Department for Education.

- **Free Schools:** Introduced by the Conservative-Liberal Democrat coalition following the 2010 general election, are newly established schools in England set up by parents, teachers, charities or businesses, where there is a perceived local need for more schools. They are funded by taxpayers, are academically non-selective and free to attend, and like Foundation schools and Academies, are not controlled by a local authority. They are ultimately accountable to the Secretary of State for Education. Free schools are an extension of the existing Academy Programme.

Schools in England are ether publicly or privately funded, and there are many different types (British Council, 2010). All children in England between the ages of five and 16 are entitled to a free place at a state school. Most go to state schools. Children normally start primary school at the age of four or five, but many schools now have a reception year for four-year-olds. Children normally leave primary school at the age of 11, moving on to secondary school. Most state schools admit both boys and girls, although some are single sex. The four main types of state schools all receive funding from local authorities. They all follow the National Curriculum and are regularly inspected by the Office for Standards in Education (Ofsted).

Appointing a Principal in Jamaica

The process and criteria for appointing a Principal in a public school in Jamaica is set out below. Regulation 43 (Schedule B) of the Education Act (1980) sets out the following process:

(a) The Board of Management of the public educational institution shall inform the Minister of the vacancy, which shall be advertised in the press;

(b) Applicants shall complete the prescribed application form and shall forward such form with any necessary or other specified requirements to the Board;

(c) The Board shall, subject to paragraph 2 (see below), and having regard to the criteria for the appointment of principals laid down by the Minister, submit to the Commission a list of all applicants together with details of their academic and professional qualification, teaching and other work experience and other particulars and stating the name of the applicant whom they consider to be acceptable for appointment; so, however, that if they consider each of a number of applicants to be acceptable, they shall set out the names of the first two or three in order of preference;

(d) After receiving such advice from the Commission may, if it thinks necessary, consult with the chairman of the Board of Management or with the Board of Management and make a recommendation to the Minister; and

(e) The Minister shall notify the Board of his decision. (para 1)

When the Board of Management of any public educational institution owned or administered by a religious denomination proposes to make a submission under sub-paragraph C of paragraph 1, they shall consult with the head or the proper authority of that denomination in Jamaica and shall indicate the name or names in order of preferences as required by that sub-paragraph and as approved by such head or proper authority (para 2).

The Education Act (1980) Regulation 43 (schedule B) provides:

For appointment as a principal, a teacher is required to be a registered trained teacher with at least three years of approved service as a trained teacher unless the requirements are varied in any particular case (para 3).

Appointing a Principal in England

The 2002 Education Act Sections 35(3) and 36(3) require every school to have a principal. The process involved in the appointment of a Principal in a state school that is not affiliated to the Catholic Church is as follows:

(a) The governing body must notify the local authority in writing of any vacancy for a principal post, and advertise the post in such manner as it considers appropriate, and then appoint a selection panel consisting of at least three of its members, other than the principal. The role of the selection panel is to notify the local authority, in writing, of the names of applicants selected for interview for the post of head teacher, interview the applicants selected, and recommend one of the applicants to the governing body for approval. The governing body's decisions should be fully documented, as it will need to demonstrate that it acted reasonably if challenged. The appointment process should be conducted in a fair manner that does not contravene any discrimination legislation and includes safer recruitment measures.

(b) The selection panel agrees with the local authority what additional information it needs in order to enable it to decide whether to make written representations about any of the candidates. If the local authority decides that a candidate chosen for interview is unsuitable for the post of head teacher, it must submit written representations to the selection panel within seven days. The selection panel must then consider the local authority's views before making a decision. If the selection panel decides to recommend an applicant for appointment about whom representations have been received, it must notify the local authority, in writing, of its reasons. If the selection panel makes no recommendation, the governing body does not approve the recommendation or the local authority declines to appoint the recommended candidate, or, in the case of foundation, voluntary aided and foundation special schools, the governing body declines to appoint the recommended candidate, the selection panel must carry out the process again, or recommend that an existing candidate identified as being suitable through the current selection process.

   (a) The local authority must appoint a person approved by the governing body of a community; voluntary controlled, community special or maintained nursery school, unless that person fails the relevant checks.

   (b) In foundation, foundation special or voluntary aided schools the governing body may appoint the person recom-

mended by the selection panel, unless that person fails the relevant checks (para 11) (DfE, 2012, p. 92).

However, in the case of an appointment to the rank of Principal in a state funded school affiliated to the Catholic Church, the following procedure applies:

(a) Regulation 34 of the School Staffing Regulations 2009 modifies the selection process for Schools of Roman Catholic Orders. The governing body must notify the local authority and the Major Superior of the vacancy in writing, interview those members of the Order who are proposed as candidates by the Major Superior, and appoint the successful applicant, unless they fail the relevant checks or it has other good reason not to make such an appointment. If, after interviewing the candidates proposed by the Major Superior of the Order, the governing body decides, for good reason, not to appoint any of them, the standard procedure for appointing a head teacher must be used to fill the post and this is set out in Chapter 5 of the Guidance on managing staff employment in schools (paras 5.10 to 5.20) (DCSF, n.d, p. 17).

Leadership, School Effectiveness, and Improvement

School improvement rests on appropriately qualified and experienced individuals who must provide quality teaching and leadership. Principals are tasked with establishing a collective vision for improvement and for leading innovation, student learning and achievement. Whether systemic or localised, improvements require multiple level investments in time, finance and human resources (Miller, 2014). For example, in Jamaica the National College for Educational Leadership (NCEL) and in England, the National College for Teaching & Leadership, through the provision of appropriate professional development programmes for school leaders, respective education departments are demonstrating an understanding of the critical role quality leadership plays in creating and sustaining school effectiveness. And in requiring current and prospective principals to undertake various professional qualification schemes, education departments are taking steps to secure and sustain improvements to the education system at local and national levels (Bubb & Earley, 2008).

Hutton (2013) provided that high-performing principals are crucial to improving an education system and to raising attainment of students. Quality education, according to UNESCO (2000), "nurtures human development and creativity, thereby contributing to the personal and professional growth of the individual person, as well as to contributing to the social, cultural, economic, political and environmental development of society as a whole" (p. 17). In both Jamaica and England, concerns have been raised through the Office for Standards in Education (OfSTED, 2012) and the National Education Inspectorate (NEI, 2010) about the quality of leadership in schools. The quality of principals has a direct impact on student attainments and efforts to harness and sustain school effectiveness and improvement agendas (Education International, 2011). For an education department or ministry, having adequate numbers of principals in post is an important goal. And, for an education department or ministry and a school, having principals in post who possess the best possible mix of qualifications, experience and skills is a key ingredient in building effective schools and an effective education system (Miller, 2014).

LITERATURE REVIEW

Organisational structures, institutional practices, societal assumptions and subscribed concepts impact significantly on an individual's career aspirations and progression and in educational and/or school leadership, there are no exceptions (Shah & Shaikh, 2010). The issue of teacher progression is highly subjective and teachers, School Boards and policy makers often have differing versions of what counts as the reality for a 'non-appointment'.

There is only limited data available on the criteria and process of selection for principal with one study completed in England (Morgan et al., 1983) and one in Jamaica (Miller, 2013) on this issue However, recent studies on career progression among certain groups of teachers have helped to shed some light on the problematic nature of teacher progression. Earley, Evans, Collarbone, Gold, and Halpin, (2002) and Early et al., (2012) highlighted the interplay between race/ethnicity and career progression as a barrier to career destinations as reflected in the small numbers of Black and Minority Ethnic (BME) teachers to be appointed to senior leadership posts in a school. This was also found to be the case by Bush, Glover and Sood (2006), and Lumby and Coleman (2007) in relation to race/ethnicity and the career progression of some Black and Minority Ethnic (BME) teachers.

Coleman (2007) also noted that the appointment of women principals in England is still problematic, commenting, "overall, women are more likely to become head teachers and are now less likely to be categorised into pastoral roles, but in some cases women still meet prejudice from governors and others in the wider community" (2007, p.389). Data from Moreau, Osgood, and Halsall (2007) and later from Bullock (2009) showed women are disproportionately represented in senior leadership posts. These observations were confirmed by Earley et al. (2012), underlining essentialist stereotypes and the glass ceiling. Shah and Shaikh (2010) pointed to religious and ethnic affiliation as a major contributing factor to teacher progression. Specifically, they found that being male and Muslim was problematic in the quest for a principal job. More generally, literature in England identified several barriers that limit teachers' progress to leadership positions in the forms of marginalisation and indirect racism (Powney, Wilson, & Hall, 2003): the subtle influence of informal networks that excludes some groups (Harris, Muijs, & Crawford, 2003). In a recent edited volume, *School Leadership in the Caribbean*, Miller (2013b) reported that in at least two Caribbean countries - Guyana and Trinidad, one's ethnicity can influence his/her career access and progression, more broadly and within education, depending on which ethnic group forms the government. Later, in his Seminal Paper, *Corruption as Redemption: Affiliation as a mark for progression among primary teachers in Jamaica*, Miller (2013c) provided four marks (national political affiliation, religious affiliation, social connections and ministry, and school level politicking), which satisfies an in-group, out-group typology and which are believed to be primary determinants of teachers' progression in the education system more broadly, and to the rank of a principal, specifically.

METHODOLOGY

Data collection for this qualitative exploratory study was conducted in two phases over 18 months, between September 2012 and February 2014. Phase One was conducted in Jamaica between September 2012 and May 2013 and included 13 participants: 11 females and two males. 11 teachers (nine females and two males) with ranks from classroom teacher to vice-principal were interviewed. Teachers were drawn from across seven of Jamaica's 14 parishes based on their willingness to participate in the study. Five teachers were interviewed via telephone; three were interviewed face-to-face and three completed and returned the interview questionnaire by email. One Education Officer from Region 6 was interviewed via telephone and the Chief Executive Officer of

the Jamaica Teaching Council (JTC) participated in an hour long face-to-face interview. All participants were interviewed using the semi-structured interview approach. Four sampling approaches were used. Deterministic sampling was used to include the Chief Executive Officer of the Jamaica teaching Council. Snowballing sampling was used to include five teachers and the Education Officer. Convenience sampling was used to include three teachers who were easily accessible to the researcher. Purposive sampling was used to include the remaining three teacher participants.

Phase Two data collection was completed in England between June 2013 and February 2014. The findings from the Jamaican leg of the study were summarised and presented to a total of eight teachers in England with job roles ranging from classroom teacher to principal. Participants were from both Primary and Secondary schools and from both in and outside London. They were asked to describe the promotion/appointment situation in England, using the four key themes from Phase One. All eight returned a response to the set of findings they had been presented. Their responses were analysed thematically to assess the perceived appointment/promotion situation in England based on the four themes previously identified. The sampling techniques used in Phase Two were snowballing and purposive.

FINDINGS

The findings from both phases of this study are presented below.

Religious Affiliation

Religious affiliation was a significant factor identified by participants in Jamaica and England that impacted their progression to a principal post. However, whereas in Jamaica the dominant church groups that operate church schools are Catholics,

Anglicans, Baptists and the United Church, in England, the Catholic Church is the dominant faith group recognised in law.

It's simple really; I am not Catholic and it's a Catholic school (Teacher 11, Jamaica).

Religion was a big factor. It was a Catholic school and many questions were asked about my role and involvement in the local church community (Teacher 1, Jamaica).

Although pointing to changing times and shifts in practice and attitudes, the teachers' views were well-supported by the Chief Executive Officer of the Jamaica Teaching Council:

Church schools prefer to have principals who share their values. If teachers can't adhere to these values then they should find work elsewhere- why not? If it's a Faith School the Church usually will have to endorse the person. They will want to know that the person's values are in sync with the particular religious community. Times are changing however and if someone not belonging to the said faith group is deemed to be highly skilled and has good references, the faith groups may take such a person. However, if another person from the faith group applies and is equally skilled then the person from the church group will usually get the edge from the School Board (CEO, Jamaica Teaching Council).

Teachers in England seemed more reluctant to apply for jobs in Catholic Schools on the basis that this would be a dead end, if they are not Catholics. One principal revealed,

Religious affiliation is a barrier here in England, but the criteria is very clear for Headship of Catholic School - 'you must be a practising catholic' - the person specification and job description are also very clear about this. I believe though that there are persons high in the ranks that are 100% in

favour of changing this practice and are lobbying for this to be done (Principal 1, England).

Citing a new wave of faith based schools impacting the educational and principal appointment landscape, another principal revealed,

The emergence of Muslim Schools also is an investing area of discussion and maintained schools in Moslem communities. I know of 'secular-orientated' high performing Principals who have lost their jobs because the hue of the Governing Body has shifted towards Islam (Principal 2, England).

Political Affiliation and Government Policies

In Jamaica, one's actual or perceived national political affiliation was thought to be a critical factor in gaining an appointment to the rank of a school principal.

The School Board does the selection of candidate. The Board Chairperson is usually a nominee of the sitting Member of Parliament (MP). That person [the Board Chair] can however be a recommendation from the principal but the MP would still have the last word. Political parties usually select political apologists. The Education Act does not specify that the MP must select the Chair of the Board but, over time, this has become the accepted practice..... (Education Officer, Jamaica).

Where candidates for posts were not directly linked to a political party, the influence of a political representative was considered no less poignant.

I have some friends who are kind of connected to politics. They keep telling me you can't keep saying you are qualified. That alone won't get you appointed as Principal. You have to join a [political] party. I tell them no because I believe in the integrity of system because I am qualified. But this has not worked for me. The Board Chair has the most important vote and he/she can find reasons not to give you the job. The outcome is usually set before the actual interview. Majority of points you earn, you do so before you get to the interview stage. If they want to weed you out they can weed you out and then put you against people who will outshine you. The entire process is a farce. You have to show your loyalty to a political party. You have to know the MP personally and you have to know his number (Teacher 8, Jamaica).

The Chief Executive Officer of the Jamaica Teaching Council, whilst not denying that there can be political influence at some levels of the appointment process, considers this to be a long shot, and not something that happens across the board.

The process for appointing a principal is rigorous so very little opportunity exists for cronyism to creep in. Subjective recruitment practice is more and more giving way to merit. Subjective recruitment is not the barrier it appears to be. People go through a process of short listing, interviews, selection, etc. It's not a walk over. There is a set process that is overseen by an Education Officer[B] ut only 1000 principals can be appointed out of 25,000 teachers at any one time and so persons who do not get the job "perceive" other factors to be at play (CEO, Jamaica Teaching Council)

The Education Officer was more direct in her characterisation of the influence politicians can have on the appointment process of a school Principal.

Politics does have a hand in the appointment process. But this is not as prevalent as it used to be. The Teacher Representative on the School Board in some cases may be a nominee of the MP and this can influence the outcome of a job interview. It does happen and this is the truth, although this is not as often these days (Education Officer, Jamaica).

In England, the political influence on an appointment as a principal was somewhat different. That is, whereas in Jamaica the issue was considered to be a teacher's alignment to a political, in England, the issue was directly connected to the educational policy being pursued by the incumbent government.

As you know, the education landscape is changing and fragmenting in many ways. Gove – love him or loathe him – has certainly changed things. Leadership succession and talent cultivation are high on the agenda and initiatives like Future Leaders and Teach First are attempts to get the 'best people' accelerated into leadership roles in schools. Although there is debate on what constitutes the 'best' – is it a high flying graduate, posh kid from a fancy school? Should these be the targeted group to get into school leadership? (Principal 3, England)

Government has made the priorities clear. The focus on teaching and learning and impacts a style of leader. Future Leaders and Teach First... Future Leaders now have the license to run training and development programmes for prospective school leaders. These are, in my view, extensions of Gove and other's 'Eton School / Oxbridge' ideologies. A bit like BBC prime time comedy... all the writers and their said material come from one place, one ideology... Oxbridge! (Principal 1, England)

School and Ministry Level Interference

Both in Jamaica and England, some teachers felt strongly that they were passed over for appointment due to some degree of interference that goes on at the school level (and in Jamaica, also at the regional offices of the Education Ministry).

I know I didn't get the job because the Education Officer (EO) and I have a challenging relationship.

I have been at this school for 29 years and have been Vice-Principal now for 15 years. I speak my mind and don't hold back and so I am not liked by many persons at the Regional Office. This, I believe, is responsible for me not getting the post of Principal (Teacher 3, Jamaica).

Politics at the Regional Office is definitely something that influences the outcome of the appointment process for a Principal. I know people who have been appointed because they have friends and family on the inside (Teacher 4, Jamaica).

Turning to school level politics:

A friend of mine got the job because she was a friend of the outgoing Principal. She was ''groomed' before. And this happens a lot with posts below the Principal- if you are friendly with the Principal you stand a chance (Teacher 4, Jamaica).

Two teachers and one principal in England offered some insights:

After two years I enquired about applying for threshold, the headteacher at the time said that she though the required time had passed for me to be considered. This was not true as I had done the research and knew the timelines involved and that I had met the criteria. Anyway, I did not persist with the request. The following year I resubmitted my application which was again not supported by the headteacher. I believe that it could have been school politics because someone in management didn't want it to be approved as I had only been at that school for two years (Teacher 1, England).

The process of getting an appointment as a headteacher, from my experience is a very strict one and so the issues of corruption, affiliation or similar tendencies may not easily influence such outcomes. However, from my experience, getting

an appointment as an Assistant Head teacher (AHT /Vice principal) is a different story. This, I believe, is a because of various influences such as networking and internal candidates being familiar with the roles, poached for the roles or using other means as gifts, lobbying etc. consciously or unconsciously. These are things that come into play. The selection process is meant to be open, transparent, fair and firm, but this is not really the case (Teacher 2, England).

'Who you know' is always going to be the case, but in England is it is no longer about the local government (Local Authorities) but it is becoming more and more about the Chains of Academies and 'families of schools' (Principal 2, England).

Social Connections

Social connection is seen as particularly problematic and was linked to social affluence outside the work environment. Social connections could include a church group, a political party or any other group or individual in a position to influence the outcome of the appointment process whether directly or indirectly. The main thrust here is: it is not about what a person knows, rather, who knew him/her and vice versa.

It's not about what you know it's about who know you, especially if you have connection at the Ministry of Education or with an MP (Teacher 10, Jamaica).

It's not the best person most that gets the job- it's who you know, sometimes who you are close to. With connections you don't even have to go to interviews. That happened to me for the job I am currently in (Teacher 7, Jamaica).

Whilst not dismissing the view expressed by the teachers, the Chief Executive Officer of the Jamaica Teaching Council reasons:

Connections are implicitly there. And you know they are there. Candidates come highly recommended, sometimes by persons connected to persons on the Board. However, if the person doesn't fit the bill, they will not be appointed. Connections alone in most cases can no longer guarantee a job (CEO, Jamaica Teaching Council).

Pointing to the situation in England, one principal and one teacher revealed:

The class system does still prevail in England. The university you went to still impacts and at secondary level, the subject you taught. These affect career progression and therefore progression to Principalship. There is also the element of some school leaders now no longer coming up through usual route of being a teacher first (Principal 2, England).

The jobs for some Assistant Head teachers (AHT) appear to be fixed, though the schools as expected by law have to go through the process. But I am unsure how the process is quality assured. Being socially connected will help. For instance colleagues have advised me to take advantage of networking outside the school. In fact I know of one colleague who got a job as an Assistant Headteacher (AHT) by recommendation from a Headteacher and was interviewed afterwards by the school, to formalise and legitimise the appointment process. I am also aware of colleagues who've gotten appointments as AHTs due to networking at external meetings. So the question is how much influence did their affiliation to the right people have on their appointment to these posts? (Teacher 2, England).

FUTURE RESEARCH DIRECTIONS

The findings presented in this chapter call for more research to be done to investigate and unpack the explicit and implicit factors and 'issues' involved in the promotion and/or appointment process of school principals in both Jamaica and England. More detailed research is also needed to ascertain the relationship between school effectiveness, school improvement and the factors identified in this study. It would also be useful to investigate, the extent to which, current principals feel their appointment and/or promotion was influenced by or related to the factors identified in this study.

DISCUSSION

Nevertheless, the findings should be not ignored. In two very different countries at very different stages of their development we find one common problem: perceptions of discrimination in the practice of appointments and/or promotion of teachers to the rank of principal. The law in both countries provide exclusions to some faith groups which operate publicly funded schools, most notably the Roman Catholic Church (GoJ, 1891; DfE, 2012). But, are these exclusions appropriate, given that in international law, education is regarded as a public good? Are teachers not public servants first and foremost, after which the matter of their religious and/or any other affiliation is considered? The law should protect the rights of all peoples equally and where minority groups (e.g.: the Maroons in Jamaica) exist, exclusions may be made to protect their interests, such as gaining access to education. To be clear, such exclusions should not apply in terms of the delivery of education, but rather in terms of educational access for persons belonging to a minority group. Could Jamaica's legal stance on this issue be a relic carried over from the period of British colonisation? Could it, however, be the result of something else? There are arguably many good reasons, as provided for in the findings above, for appointing subscribed members of a faith group to lead a faith based school. However, whatever, the reason, it appears that a law which simultaneously constructs and fragments the progression of suitably qualified and well experienced teachers to a principal post, on the basis of them not belonging to a particular faith group is flawed and needs rethinking. As the globalisation of education increases, and as the numbers of international schools increase, can recruitment practices that discriminate against some groups whilst simultaneously giving advantage to others be allowed to continue, especially in schools that are funded by tax payers of all race, colour, creed, sexual orientation, and beliefs systems? Should institutions of state, especially schools, where there exists naturally a plethora of difference and diversity, not be the standard bearer for society in terms of practices geared towards social cohesion and social justice?

On both sides of the Atlantic, teachers reported on cases of other teachers being appointed or promoted to jobs and afterwards being interviewed. These suggestions require further investigation. Nevertheless, how widespread are these practices? It is not inherently bad to have social connections, however, when these connections are used to advantage one person over another, and especially in the case of a school leadership appointment, this flouts meritocracy and ridicules the principles of hard work being taught by and in schools. As education is a public good, every individual, no matter his/her background, creed, colour, or any other special characteristics, should be free to participate in it without discrimination or fear of discrimination. Should this principle also not apply to the selection of principals? In other words, should all those who aspire to become principals not be encouraged and supported to do so, provided they satisfy the legal and practice based requirements such as relevant qualifications and work experience and provided there is a suitable vacancy? Could schools be missing out on their improvement and on achieving better due to the principal in post, and due to issues linked to his or her appointment? These are questions that require further investigations.

Lack of transparency weakens the democratic framework of any institution whether it is a publicly funded secular operated school or a publicly funded denominational operated school and whether practices are spontaneous or institutionalised (UNDP, 2004). An issue that has also emerged from this study is that Jamaica has a weaker framework for appointing principals compared with England. That is, in Jamaica, the potential for politicians to directly influence the principal selection process is real and can severely undermine the effectiveness of principals and the smooth running of schools more generally. How principals are appointed in Jamaica needs urgent re-examination particularly in relation to the role of and assembling of School Boards. The evidence also points to questionable practices to promoting teachers at a rank below a principal. Cronyism, jockeying and interference at the school level and ministry level in Jamaica (and in England, in terms of 'Families of Schools' or 'Chain of Academies') are believed to be invading the process and thereby excluding potentially well-qualified and experienced teachers.

The policy contexts also need urgent attention. What kinds of principals do schools need - business principals or educator principals? On both sides of the Atlantic, it was confirmed that an individual who is appointed as a principal has not always come from a teaching background and may not always possess the appropriate teaching qualifications and related work experience. And in England, this practice is much more widespread and appears to be growing stronger with what seems to be the massification of Academies and Free Schools (The Independent, 2011; Academies Commission, 2013). The legal and policy contexts in both countries needs an examination of the sort that considers the enduring nature of education and that acknowledges that only the best talents, skills, talents and experience can lead and sustain improvements and effectiveness in schools.

CONCLUSION

If the governments in both Jamaica and England do not wish to be accused of fostering corruption and discrimination, despite the rhetoric of equal opportunities, an urgent reconceptualisation of social justice, equity and fair play are all needed in the principal selection process in order to re-build and strengthen confidence among teachers who serve in the different systems. Both national educational systems are perceived by the teachers therein to foster corruption, favouritism, discrimination and cronyism. Neither country can afford to turn a blind eye to these perceptions and/or realities of unfair practices in their education systems. Nor can national political leaders, other leaders in education departments or ministries, from the policy-making to the operational levels, walk with their heads aloft as if the perceptions of participants in this study are unfounded. For corrective measure to be implemented it cannot be business as usual.

Education is a public good. The teaching profession needs to harness the best and brightest minds, possessing the finest skills, talents and experience available to it to lead schools and become principals in order for schools to become more effective at what they do. But this can only be done where selection to the rank of principal is not defined by affiliations and/or the prevailing governmental policy context, but rather by merit.

REFERENCES

Academies Commission. (2013). *Unleashing greatness: Getting the best from an academised system*. London: The Report of the Academies Commission.

British Council. (2010). *Secondary education: Opportunities in UK education at secondary level*. Retrieved from http://www.britishcouncil.org/macedonia-education-secondary-education.htm

Bubb, S., & Earley, P. (2008). *From self-evaluation to school improvement: The importance of effective staff development*. Reading, UK: CfBT Education Trust.

Bullock, K. (2009).*The impact of school leadership on pupil outcomes*. Research Report DCSF-RR108. London: Department for Children, Schools and Families (DCSF).

Bush, T., Glover, D., & Sood, K. (2006). Black and minority ethnic leaders in England: A portrait. *School Leadership & Management*, *26*(3), 289–305. doi:10.1080/13632430600737140

Coleman, M. (2007). Gender and educational leadership in England: A comparison of Secondary head teachers' views over time. *School Leadership & Management*, *27*(4), 383–399. doi:10.1080/13632430701562991

Department for Children, Schools and Families. (n.d.). Guidance on Managing staff employment in schools: Guidance for Governors, Headteachers, Local Authorities, London. *DCSF*.

Department for Education (2012). *Governor's Guide to the Law*. Nottingham, UK: DfE.

Earley, P., Evans, J., Collarbone, P., Gold, A., & Halpin, D. (2002). *Establishing the current state of school leadership in England. Department for Education & Skills research report RR336*. London: HMSO.

Earley, P., Higham, R., Allen, R., Allen, T., Howson, J., Nelson, R., & Sims, D. (2012). *Review of the school leadership landscape*. Nottingham, UK: National College for School Leadership.

Government of Jamaica. (1981). *The education act: The regulations 1980*. Kingston, Jamaica: Jamaica Gazette.

Government of Jamaica. (2004). *Task force on education reform Jamaica: A transformed education system*. Kingston, Jamaica: Government of Jamaica.

Great Britain. (2009). *The school staffing (England) regulations 2009: Elisabeth II, sections 15 & 34*. London: The Stationary Office. Retrieved from http://www.legislation.gov.uk/uksi/2009/2680/contents/made

Great Britain Education Act. (2002). *Great Britain education Act: Elizabeth II, sections 35 & 36*. London: The Stationary Office. Retrieved from http://www.legislation.gov.uk/ukpga/2002/32/contents

Harris, A., Muijs, D., & Crawford, M. (2003). *Deputy and assistant heads: Building leadership potential*. Nottingham, UK: NCSL.

Lumby, J., & Coleman, M. (2007). *Leadership and diversity: Challenging theory and practice in Education*. London: Sage.

Miller, P. (2013a). *The politics of progression: Primary teachers' perceived barriers to gaining a principalship in Jamaica. Research Report*. Kingston, Jamaica: University of Technology, Jamaica & the Institute for Educational Administration & Leadership – Jamaica.

Miller, P. (2013b). School leadership in the Caribbean: Perceptions, practices, paradigms, London: *Symposium Books*

Miller, P. (2013c). Corruption as redemption? Affiliation as a mark for leadership progression among primary school teachers in Jamaica. *Journal of Education & Practice, 24*(4), 170–180.

Miller, P. (2014). What is a Principal's Quality Mark? Issues and Challenges in Leadership Progression among Primary Teachers in Jamaica. *Research in Comparative International Education, 9*(1), 126–136. doi:10.2304/rcie.2014.9.1.126

Ministry of Education. (2012). *Education statistics 2011-1012: Annual statistical review of the education sector*. Kingston, Jamaica: Planning and Development Division, MoE.

Moreau, M. P., Osgood, J., & Halsall, A. (2007). Making sense of the glass ceiling in schools: An exploration of women teachers' discourses. *Gender and Education, 19*(2), 237–253. doi:10.1080/09540250601166092

Morgan, C., Hall, V., & Mackay, H. (1983). *The selection of secondary school headteachers*. Milton Keynes, UK: Open University Press.

National Education Inspectorate. (2010). *Chief Inspector's Report: Inspection Cycle, Round 2, November*. Kingston, Jamaica: Ministry of Education.

OfSTED. (2012). *Press release: The importance of leadership - The Annual Report of Her Majesty's Chief Inspector of Education, Children's Services and Skills 2011/12, Ref: NR2012-38*. Manchester, UK: Office for Standards in Education.

Planning Institute of Jamaica. (2010). *Vision 2030 national development plan: Education sector plan 2009-2030*. Kingston, Jamaica: PIOJ.

Powney, J., Wilson, V., & Hall, S. (2003). *Teachers' careers: The impact of age, disability, ethnicity, gender and sexual orientation*. London: Department for Education and Skills.

Shah, S., & Shaikh, J. (2010). Leadership progression of Muslim male teachers: Interplay of ethnicity, faith and visibility. *School Leadership & Management, 30*(1), 19–33. doi:10.1080/13632430903509733

Tallerico, M. (2000). Gaining access to the superintendency: Headhunting, gender and colour. *Educational Administration Quarterly, 36*(1), 18–43. doi:10.1177/00131610021968886

The Independent. (2011, September 10). *UK has too many types of school: As PM backs free schools, senior figures complain of 'liquorice allsorts' system*. Retrieved from http://www.independent.co.uk/news/education/education-news/experts-uk-has-too-many-types-of-school-2352191.html

United Nations Development Programme. (2004). *Anti-corruption: Practice note*. New York: United Nations Development Programme.

KEY TERMS AND DEFINITIONS

Affiliation: To receive into close connection or association.

Corrupt: Perversion of integrity; dishonest.

Discrimination: Treatment or consideration of, or making a distinction in favour of or against, a person or thing based on the group, class, or category to which that person or thing belongs rather than on individual merit.

England: The largest division of the United Kingdom, constituting, with Scotland and Wales, the island of Great Britain.

Jamaica: An island in the West Indies; a former British colony.

Leadership: The position or function of a leader, a person who guides or directs a group.

Principal: The head or director of a school or college.

Section 2
Understanding School and Teacher Leadership:
Theoretical and Organizational Foundations

Chapter 8
Principals' Understandings of Education Based on Research:
A Swedish Perspective

Maj-Lis Hörnqvist
Umeå University, Sweden

ABSTRACT

Principals' responsibilities for quality in schools and preschools have, during recent years, been accentuated in Sweden. The Swedish Education Act of 2010 can be interpreted as an attempt to improve the orientation and effectiveness of teaching in schools, as it states that education should be based mainly on research and proven experience. The purpose of this chapter is to illuminate how principals understand and relate to the Education Act of 2010. The empirical foundation of the chapter consists of examining policy documents and two surveys sent to principals and heads of preschools. The findings reveal that the principals show different understandings of the term research basis. Three significant areas of manifestations emerged from the data: keeping up to date with new knowledge, building a scientific culture, and practicing research-based knowledge. However, a challenge for principals is to foster a critical evaluative approach to research.

INTRODUCTION

The acquisition of knowledge is a topic that engages many people in various ways. Principals' responsibilities for the quality in schools and preschools have been accentuated during the last years in Sweden, where quality often is equated with measurable learning outcomes. The Swedish parliament declared in the Swedish Education Act (SFS, 2010:800) that education shall be based on research and on proven experiences. As such, what is understood by "based on research?" In the preparatory work for the Swedish Education Act of 2010, it had been highlighted that, in addition to knowledge and skills, basic education must give students the capacity for independent and critical assessment, the ability to solve problems, as well as the ability and interest to follow the development of knowledge, both nationally and internationally (Prop. 1992 / 93:1; Bet. 1992/93:UbU3). There is also a communicative aspect, as education should also develop the students' ability to exchange information in a scientific way.

DOI: 10.4018/978-1-4666-6591-0.ch008

The purpose of this chapter is to illuminate principals' understandings of an *education based on research* and what this will involve with regards to their readiness to lead educational work on that basis. In this text, the term *school* includes all educational institutions from preschools to upper-secondary school. The unit of analysis of this article will be principals and schools. The terms *principal, teacher*, and *student* will be used as general terms, denoting a person's occupation and/or role within the school setting.

As a leader, the principal's charge is now more clearly stated with regards to his/her responsibility for developing the school into a high-quality institution (made evident by the Swedish Education Act) and the national curricula. However, emphasis on educational development as well as developing and ensuring high quality within the institution is not new to the Swedish policy. As early as 1946, the School Commission Report highlighted the importance of the principal leading the educational work at his/her school as well as the importance of the principal's freedom to leave his or her mark on the school (see also SOU, 1948:27, p. 221). The Organisation for Economic Co-operation and Development (OECD) is an example of an agency that has great influence on policymakers (Moos, 2013). International studies, such as OECD's Programme for International Student Assessment (PISA), Trends in International Mathematics and Science Study (TIMSS), and Progress in International Reading Literacy Study (PIRLS), and national research, such as the Swedish Schools Inspectorate assessments, demonstrate results that are too low and not satisfying (Skolverket, 2013a). For example, the PISA 2012 results have shown a declining trend in mathematics, reading comprehension, and science since 2003 (OECD, 2013). The mean score declined to below OECD average in 2012, and Sweden ranked as number 38 among 65 participating countries, while the ranking in 2003 was number five. When compared with Swedish national subject tests (in mathematics, English, and Swedish), the trend

for the success rate is on the same level, with only small fluctuations since 2003 (Skolverket, 2013a). Since principals are responsible, they are held accountable by the government and society in general for the results presented after each report and inspection on international and national levels. This is one of the reasons that the leaders of the schools have increasingly come into the spotlight in recent years. As the focus in this chapter is on education based on research, I will not elaborate upon Swedish results further, just point out what Swedish principals have to deal with. In any case, the PISA results have to be taken seriously. As background, I will first briefly describe the Swedish context and educational system. Then I will provide a short, historical exposé of school management in Sweden and the current state of school leadership.

BACKGROUND: THE SWEDISH CONTEXT

Sweden is one of the world's northernmost countries and is sparsely populated. There are about 9.6 million inhabitants in a total area of 528,447 km², the third largest country in Western Europe. Most of the people live in three big cities: Stockholm, Gothenburg, and Malmö. The living standard in Sweden is above OECD average (OECD, 2014). Sweden is a constitutional monarchy with parliamentary democracy (see "Sweden in Brief", n.d.).

All education in Sweden is free for all and funded by public authorities by taxes (Ministry of Education & Research, 2008). Education is compulsory for all children aged 7 to 15/16 and is organized by the municipalities in Sweden. In 2011–2012, there were 3,850 municipal schools, 5 state Sami schools, and 761 independent schools at the compulsory school level. A majority, 87%, of compulsory school pupils attended municipal schools in 2011–2012 (see Skolverket, 2013b).

The Education Act of 2010 is valid within the whole educational system except for university studies. Regarding independent schools, they are likewise funded by public taxes, and their education follows the Education Act and the same national curricula as public schools (see "Facts about Sweden—Education", n.d.; Skolverket, 2013b).

For children ages 1–5, municipalities are obliged to offer voluntary preschool classes. The majority of children, 80%, attend preschool. There is a maximum fee for parents to pay for their preschool placement. The activities in preschool should be based on a holistic view of the child. At the age of 6, children attend a preschool class within the public school system. As many as 96% of all children were registered in preschool classes in 2011 (Skolverket, 2013b).

In compulsory education, there are national tests in year 3, 6, and 9. The subjects in year 3 are Swedish, Swedish as a foreign language, and mathematics. In year 6 and 9, there are national tests in English, mathematics, Swedish/Swedish as a foreign language, sciences, and social sciences (Skolverket, 2013b). Grades are set using a national grading scale of six grades. Grades awarded are A, B, C, D, E, and F—where A–E are passing grades and F a fail. The grade should express to what extent the pupil has met the knowledge requirements stated for each subject and course. Swedish students get their first grade in year 6.

The upper-secondary school is arranged by municipalities, local government federations, county councils, and private organizers. It is voluntary, but the majority of students continue on to upper-secondary school. There are 12 national programs and six higher education preparatory programs. The length of the upper-secondary schooling is three years (Skolverket, 2013b).

In Sweden, there are two national agencies focusing on school education. One is the Swedish National Agency for Education (Skolverket), whose main mission is to strengthen the quality in schools and preschools and work for attainment of the Education Act and curricula. The other agency is the Swedish School Inspectorate (Skolinspe-

ktionen), which monitors the compliance of the Education Act, quality issues, complaints from students or parents, and issues regarding independent schools ("Facts about Sweden—Education", n.d.).

A Historic Account of Leadership in Swedish Schools and Preschools

The importance of having someone to lead the activities of a school is demonstrated by the fact that schools have had leaders throughout a long period of time who have taken many different guises (Ullman, 1997). The Swedish term "rektor" (principal) can be traced back to the 1200s, which then referred to the person responsible for educating the priests at the cathedral schools. In 1865, regulations regarding the qualifications required to become a principal at a grammar school were introduced, meaning that up until 1953, a person needed a PhD to be a principal at a Swedish grammar school. There were also teachers who held PhDs, i.e., senior subject teachers in the faculty, and the principals had to be the first among peers, or "primus inter pares." Regarding the leadership of "Folkskolan," the first state elementary schools, there were no specific or written requirements when they were first introduced in Sweden in 1842. In a parliamentary resolution of 1859–1860, funds were reserved for the new leadership role: "folkskoleinspektörer" (school inspectors). Before this, the elementary school teachers had to lead themselves, according to Ullman (1997), despite the fact that the priests were officially responsible for the schools. Ullman describes how the use of the title "rektor" (principal) expanded at the beginning of the 1900s from having only been applied to grammar school leaders to now including the leaders of state middle schools and higher elementary schools. At the beginning of the 1940s, even the pattern for recruiting principals changed, and teachers with Master's degrees and an interest in administration began challenging teachers with PhDs for the title of principal.

Different academic backgrounds could then be found behind the principal's title, and at the end of the 1960s, the first state-run principal degree program was introduced.

In this historic account, an image emerges, not only of the necessity of both educational and administrative leadership of the school, but of the two different historical roots of today's principals: the head of the grammar school, who was required to have high academic qualifications, and the head of the elementary school, who wasn't required to have any formal qualifications. Where once there were high qualification requirements prior to employment, there is now training for this multifaceted group to carry out their roles once employed. The principal training program is mandatory for all principals employed after March 2010 and is the same for principals in elementary and grammar schools. In the same program, there are also heads of preschools, although the program is not mandatory for them.

The history of the preschool and its leadership is slightly different from that of the compulsory and grammar schools. One of the preschool's historical roots is in creches and another in kindergarten, two parts that today have more or less merged into one. The creches were developed in the middle of the 19th century and had a character of nursing, while the kindergartens were more focused on education. At the beginning of the 1930s, in connection with industrialization and the increasing number of women in gainful employment, the need for childcare increased (Martin Korpi, 2006). At the end of the 1990s, preschool became part of the general public education and was given its own curriculum, called Lpfö 98.

Regarding the leadership of institutions that worked with children who were too young to go to school, the "Fröbelseminariet" (The National Institute for Social Educators, Early Childhood, and Social Education) was set up in 1897 to be the first institution to educate daycare leaders. When

those headmistresses were appointed, their role was, according to Styf (2012), to lead and develop the educational and administrative work as a team leader. In the 1990s, the leadership role changed from being part of a team to being a superintendent. The educational program for preschools, which preceded the national curricula, did not regulate the responsibility of management, but only that "the institutions should be led by staff who are trained in preschool pedagogy" (SOU, 1997:157, p. 120). With the arrival of a national curricula for preschool, the preschool leader's title changed to *head of preschool* (Styf, 2012), and the head of preschool's responsibility was now regulated by the national curricula, in a similar way to that of principals. Today, the role and assignments of the head of a preschool can be equated with those of a principal of a school.

This brief historical account shows a need of administrative as well as pedagogical leadership for schools. It also makes clear that today's principals have two different historical roots: the grammar school headmaster with high academic standards and the elementary school principal without any demands of academic education. This pedagogy has developed from academic eligibility requirements for employment to the situation of today, where this multifaceted group of principals is educated *after* they are employed.

Today, requirements are being set as to who should be employed as principals or heads of preschools on state and local levels. On the state level, educational insight is a requirement for eligibility, and a minimum requirement is that principals must have completed specific, compulsory principal training programs or equivalents within four years from the date of entry (SFS, 2010:800). At a local level, the school superintendent or equivalent is one who employs and can set complementary requirements that are adapted to the operations that are going to be led.

Current State of School Leadership in Sweden

Despite that leadership for learning has long been established as the most important task of a principal, they are criticized for a lack of leadership with regard to leading the organization toward a higher rate of goal fulfillment. In several reports (Skolinspektionen, 2012; Skolverket, 2007, 2008, 2009, 2010b, 2011a), there has been serious criticism of the way in which educational work is led. A common opinion is that:

the principal's educational leadership, in connection to educational practice and what takes place in the classroom, needs to be strengthened. The principal provides active support, stimulation and inspiration to the teachers' own learning regarding what creates successful teaching [emphasis added]. (Skolinspektionen, 2012, p. 8)

The new preschool curriculum also provides preschools with a clear teaching assignment, stating that they must promote children's development and learning while laying the foundations for lifelong learning. In this new preschool curriculum, there are 22 goals under the heading of *Development and learning*. One example is that "the preschool should strive to ensure that each child . . . develop his/her ability to use mathematics to investigate, reflect over and test different solutions to problems raised by him/herself and others" (Skolverket, 2010a, p. 10). The head of a preschool has the overall responsibility and an expressed educational responsibility for the expertise of the staff and for ensuring that the design of the preschool's learning environment is supportive of the children's learning. It is leadership directed at the teachers and their work to promote the students' learning that is the most interesting factor in how the school leaders guide educational work.

EDUCATION BASED ON RESEARCH AND A SCIENTIFIC APPROACH

Educational work is, however, not completely independent. The Swedish Education Act (SFS, 2010:800), which covers both school and preschool, has introduced a requirement for all education to be based on research and proven experience. However, the notion that research knowledge should contribute to practice is not new (Levin, 2013). The issue of interplay between research and practice has been a concern of many researchers (Biesta, 2007; Brokkamp & van Hout-Walters, 2008; Hemsley-Brown & Sharp, 2003; Nutley, Jung, & Walters, 2008; Vandelinde & van Braak, 2010). Policies have strived to both make demands and support schools to use research results in educational practice. Researchers have studied the gap between educational research and educational practice and how to bridge this gap, which seems to be a challenge to both researchers and schools.

One attempt from policy level to strengthen quality in schools is the new Swedish Education Act (SFS, 2010:800), which is inspired by the Higher Education Act (Högskolelagen, 1992:1434). The Bill for the new Education Act (Prop. 2009/10:165) states that the term "based on research" is developed in the legislative history of the Higher Education Act. The main argument for introducing such a requirement in the Swedish Education Act is based on the teachers' freedom to choose content and methods in order to achieve educational goals. It says: "This requires a scientific approach in the sense of critically examining as well as testing and putting isolated factual knowledge into context" (Prop. 2009/10:165, p. 223). The reason for introducing it into the Swedish Education Act can be interpreted in two ways. One reason may be that part of society calls for a greater professionalization. One distinctive mark of a profession is "to embrace the potential of research to inform and help to improve practice" (Levin, 2010, p. 306). In addition to the requirement in the Education Act, the introduction of teachers' certification may also be understood as an ambition to contribute to a more scientific approach. This was introduced in 2011, and since December 2013, has been a requirement for being permanently appointed as a teacher or preschool teacher. The reason was to ensure that schools have qualified teachers. One part of the assessment criteria to become a qualified teacher or preschool teacher in Sweden is to take responsibility for one's own learning and professional development. This includes "keeping updated with current research and development work" (SKOLFS, 2011:37). It could also be viewed as an expression of distrust towards the teachers' knowledge and judgments when it comes to the basis for choosing content and methods, as is clarified by emphasizing that the teachers' knowledge must be based on research and proven experience. It is, however, not enough that research should be a base in teachers' knowledge. To improve students' outcomes, this research-based knowledge must also be used (Levin, 2010; Timperley, 2011). As traditions play an important role in teaching and learning, is educational research not yet a basis of educational practice (Norcini & Banda, 2011)?

In what way is the meaning of "research-based" expressed in policy? In the committee report regarding a new teacher training program (SOU, 2008:109), "research-based" is defined as research that is based on historical, systematic, or empirical evidence (p. 1) and understands that "The work in schools of choosing content and method and evaluating the results should therefore be characterized by a scientific approach and knowledge which is based on relevant research and proven experience" (Prop., 2009/10:165, p. 224). Which knowledge is this referring to? The discussion regarding what scientific knowledge is began as early as the 1600s and has alternated between two main schools of thought. Gustavsson (2000) describes how the

view of knowledge—the epistemology—has developed historically, from the 1600s when the development of scientific knowledge began as being based on the natural, scientific perspective of true, objective knowledge to the more multi-faceted approach toward scientific knowledge in the 1900s. The hermeneutical-phenomenological approach that was established in the 1900s viewed knowledge as a social construction within the human consciousness. It also means that humans interpret and understand things in light of their past experiences. Therefore, knowledge is subjective because it appears in our minds. It is, however, fair to assume that knowledge of scientific phenomena and knowledge regarding people and their circumstances are of different natures and must therefore be considered differently based upon their specific characteristics. How knowledge is regarded in teaching and learning in schools can be understood by the epistemological beliefs held by the educators.

Epistemological beliefs include beliefs about knowledge, learning, and teaching and influence teachers' and principals' instructional practices. According to Pashiardis, Kendeou, Michaelidou and Lytra (2014), the epistemological beliefs of principals have not been a focus of research. When we focus on teaching and learning, it is fair to equate principals with teachers since both are working to enhance student learning, teachers directly and principals indirectly via the teachers. Two main streams of epistemological beliefs are outlined by Pashiardis et al.: students as *passive receivers* of transmitted knowledge and students as *actively constructing* an understanding of the world. However, principals can admit a belief but for different reasons not be able to implement it in the daily work (see also Timperley, 2011). Pashiardis et al. explain this inconsistency as either an epistemological uncertainty or contextual constraint. As beliefs often are personally constructed, they might or might not agree with what research shows. This kind of disagreement could be sound, based on critical examination or on tradition. A scientific approach could then be helpful as a basis for decisions.

For a scientific approach, the abilities to think critically, do independent searching, and critically assess information are key abilities in the training of teachers. The Swedish Education Committee believes that an active and critical approach to knowledge is the best preparation for various kinds of professional activities. In the committee report ahead of the new teachers training program (SOU, 2008:109), requirements were set for students to demonstrate the ability to make independent and critical assessments and to independently identify, formulate, and solve problems. This may also come to apply to teachers currently working in primary and secondary schools. Two closely related terms are *proven experience* and *evidence*. Since the focus of this chapter is on the scientific basis, these will only be briefly discussed.

Proven Experience and Evidence

Proven experience is a term that has been introduced into the Swedish Education Act. How does this term compare to that of *experience* only, and how does it relate to the idea of a scientific basis? The Swedish National Agency for Education (Skolverket) refers to the Swedish National Agency for Higher Education (Högskoleverket), in accordance with the following:

Proven experience is something more than experience, even if it is long-term experience. It is tried and tested. This requires that it has been documented, in each case communicated in such a way as to allow it to be shared with others. It must also have been reviewed in a collegial context, based on criteria that are relevant to the operational content of the specific experience. It should also have been assessed based on ethical principles: not all experience is benign and thus worth following. It is possible in such an assess-

ment to come close to the academic approach, even if the content may be based on something other than research. (Skolverket, 2014, p. 12)

It is therefore important to note that according to Skolverket, proven experience is tested, communicated, examined, and generated by many people over a longer period of time. It is *not* narrow, personal, oral, or short-term. Proven experience is discussed in *Läkartidningen* (2007), a Swedish medical journal, where it emerges that even within the medical field, which has a long tradition of basing its operations on science and proven experience, problems in defining what "proven experience" really means are expressed. The term has never been explicitly defined. A sort of practice has developed, involving methods that have previously been found to be effective in practice within the field of medicine, but the methods need not be tested and examined in the same way, as the National Agency for Education states. Here, a difference in clarity between the interpretation of the Swedish National Agency for Education and the practices developed in the medical field is made visible.

A similar practice to the medical interpretation may also exist within schools and preschools. Proven experience is a common term, but even though it is common, it needs further clarification. It can be assumed that principals and pedagogues do not reflect on what the word "proven" means. This may lead to proven experience being equated with experience. SBU, the Swedish Council on Health Technology Assessment, concluded in 1997 that there is no good definition and that maybe everything that does not fit within the concept of science is placed within the "proven experiences" box (Levi, 1997). The concept is still unclear. Whose experiences are being referred to? How should they be tested? How extensive should the testing be? For how long should it be tested? How are the experiences communicated, and on what basis have they been reviewed, etc.?

Not all experience is necessarily good, and it can, in some cases, be counterproductive in relation to the mission of the school.

The other reoccurring concept is *evidence*, which is also borrowed from the medical field. The Swedish National Agency for Education (Skolverket, 2011b) claims, "there is a great lack of studies within the field of the Nordic languages that can be defined as evidence-based in accordance with current methods" (p. 5). This implies that context matters as well as that Swedish teachers and principals probably prefer to read studies written in their own language. Bohlin and Sager (2011) have studied this concept from different perspectives and argue that there are two main ways to consider evidence. One narrow definition can be considered the standard method and is mainly based and used in the medical field. It includes random clinical studies (cf. pharmaceutical drug testing), which are compiled into meta-studies that will ultimately lead to systematic reviews and guidelines. This is a clear but one-sided definition. The other point of view comes from the humanities and social sciences and has its roots in hermeneutics and phenomenology. Here, the point of departure is that results always depend on context. It is about qualitative and interpretative studies that are compiled in order to then critically analyze and evaluate the results in relation to one's own experiences, i.e., by taking a scientific approach.

Evidence will not be discussed further here, but it should be noted that it is problematic to import such a complex concept from an area that is so far divorced from the school. However, the Swedish National Agency for Education's interpretation of the Education Act greatly resembles that which is viewed here as a narrow, or at least semi-narrow, interpretation, a sort of evidence-based operation. In conclusion, there are different views on what can be understood as evidence, on what evidence involves, and whether it is even applicable or desirable in the school system.

WHEN POLICY MEETS PRACTICE

What happens then when this policy of research-based education meets practice? How is it understood and manifested? The empirical foundation of this study consists of policy documents and two surveys that are sent to principals and heads of preschools.

The first survey is quantitative and focuses on the relation between national policy and local implementation strategies. This national survey was answered by 4,000 principals from preschools, compulsory schools (ages 7 to 14/15), and upper-secondary schools. Three questions were chosen in order to describe perceptions within the group:

1. Which tasks do you consider to be most important in your current assignment?
2. What demands do you expect from the board in the following areas?
3. What demands do you expect from the state in the following areas?

Within each question, they had to consider nine areas. The principals answered by marking on a scale graded from 1 to 6, where 1 is not important and 6 is very important. The responses were compiled and constitute the basis of the second complementary survey.

The second complementary survey is qualitative, with open-ended responses, and focuses on the principals' interpretations of scientific basis as well as what it actually means to them and their capacity as leaders that education must rest on a scientific basis. A group of participants in the first and final semesters of the national principals' training program were invited to describe their interpretations of the term "scientific basis" with the help of an online qualitative survey containing three open-ended questions. The questions they were asked to answer were:

1. How do you interpret the concept *based on research*?
2. How should it be manifested in your school?
3. What does *based on research* concretely mean to you as a school leader? Please give some examples.

The respondents consisted of a total of 40 participants from compulsory and upper-secondary schools and heads of preschools. The majority of the respondents to both surveys were school principals. Preschool heads, responsible for preschool only, constituted about 20% of the respondents. The analysis of the open questions was inspired by a phenomenological-hermeneutic approach (Bengtsson, 1999; van Manen, 1997, 2007). This approach means close reading and re-reading of the texts. The texts were read several times by the researcher in order to capture significant aspects, according to the principals' understandings and manifestations of scientific basis. Thoughts and reflections were noted throughout the reading. First, preliminary themes were identified, which were altered during the readings until four aspects of understanding and three themes of concrete manifestations in practice emerged.

The Principals' Assessments of the Scientific Basis and Perceived Expectations

The descriptive documentation from the first survey showed that 85% of the respondents were of the opinion that "the teachers' pedagogical work must be based on research" is an important or very important duty in the work of a principal. It may seem that 85% is a high figure, but it is a low priority in relation to the duties that the principals were asked to consider. In the question in which the respondents were asked to state the relative importance of nine work duties, it was rated as number seven. They ranked the areas as follows:

1. Having a good ability to lead the pedagogical work in my school (97%)

2. That I develop the inner organization of my school to reach higher goal fulfilment (95%)
3. That students with special needs get relevant support (95%)
4. That I implement the revised curriculum (94%)
5. That I implement the new Education Act (92%)
6. That students that easily reach targets get support and guidance to go further in developing their knowledge (86%)
7. That the work of my teachers is based on research (85%)
8. To keep the budget (62%)
9. That the work in my school is characterized by interaction with the surrounding society (56%)

The comparison between the different types of schools did not show any differences. Accordingly, my interpretation is that the principals in this study appraised it as a comparatively unimportant work duty. However, on a scientific basis—how is it perceived? How principals understand the term "scientific basis" is supposed to influence how they lead their schools based on science.

Principals' Understandings of "Education Based on Research"

The most shallow and common understanding was described in general terms, as to *what research shows*. A similar attitude concerns overall activities in school, such as "We shall organize our activities according to what research shows." One more precise example is that "teaching should be based on research, and teaching methods and content knowledge in school should be supported by research."

It is also described as knowledge *evidenced* by research, that a scientific basis is research that constitutes the evidence for something, for example, "The methods we use in school should be proven by research." This understanding is similar to terms within the medical field, in which evidence-based knowledge is what should be practiced. Another example is that, "Changes should not be done just because they feel right." Others propose that both the content and way of working change the processes and organization that should be proven by research.

Many responses indicated that *education based on research* is not an unequivocal term. Moreover, it is remarkably common that in many descriptions, *no distinction was made between scientific basis and proven experience*. Many of the principals mentioned proven experience, when the question was about scientific basis: "Organize schools based on methods that are proven and have resulted in positive outcomes." There are also examples of a specific focus on teaching: "You should teach about things that are scientifically proven." One principal used the terms "evidence" and "proven experience" interchangeably and stated, "My school activities should be permeated by what is 'proven' by research and analyzed by earlier experiences." It is a vague use of significant terms. A few principals also mentioned scientific basis as an *approach* or, for example, having the ability to critically review and test different methods in various contexts.

The responses showed beliefs in research, and "scientific basis" seems to be a term that is understood slightly differently. A few principals showed an awareness of difficulties in using these terms. One of the principals stated, "We have to talk about the meaning of these concepts," which is new for many teachers and principals in schools and preschools. Another principal commented initially that "very little of the school's working practices have a scientific basis. The requirement is more an expression of ideology than science," and "The term 'scientific basis' is becoming too broad." However, it is perceived as important to have a common understanding of terms that are used. This indicates a need for further discussions to make it clearer. If scientific basis is as vague as it seems by the answers, there will probably be consequences in implementation.

Can scientific basis be free to interpret? Could it then be perceived as a non-binding expression, despite it being prescribed in the Education Act? Is it something that is to be noted but should not have too much energy devoted to it? Can this be because the significance is far too ambiguous? Or are the traditions far too strong? The principals' understandings of the statement that education must be based on research and proven experience, however, will influence their implementation and how their organizations will be led. A conclusion is that the principals in this study showed a strong belief in research, at least on a rhetorical level, but their displayed understanding seems vague.

Concrete Meanings and Manifestations in Practice

What are the consequences of *working from a scientific basis* for the principal? One principal writes, "If we are to take the wording of the Education Act that 'education must be based in research and proven experience' seriously, we must reasonably take heed of what research is saying and together use our collective and shared experience to develop the school and the educational programs." This principal draws upon both science and personal experience, but this experience is perhaps not yet proven in the sense implied by the Swedish National Agency for Education. To be proven in that sense it also has to be examined in a peer context and based on relevant criteria.

The analysis of open-ended survey responses about concrete meanings and expressions of scientific basis in practice resulted in three themes: *Keeping up to date, building a scientific culture, and practicing research-based knowledge.*

Keeping Up to Date

There was a common expression among the principals that education based on research means that they must expand their own knowledge and keep up to date with research primarily by reading research. It is described so that both principals and teachers need to stay updated and have good knowledge of what is indicated by research. This involves following the research in various fields; it also involves providing the staff with the conditions that allow them to assimilate the results of research. One example is: "I must keep myself up to date with research and make it possible for my educators to familiarize themselves with research." The image of a principal as a consumer of research results is striking. The principals read a lot, but what they read, they do not say. Whether they read first-hand sources, short abstracts, or other syntheses is not indicated.

Searching

Most of the principals mentioned that they have to be and are active in searching for new results from research. One principal said that it is difficult to sort out and prioritize among all the research published and that it would be beneficial to have a place in which all new research could be found. It is not only the principals who need to keep themselves up to date; teachers also must be up to date.

Sources

There were different kinds of support mentioned in respect to keeping up to date with research. The Web is a valuable source. One example of a source is the Swedish National Agency for Education, which publishes summaries of research in specific areas. Another source is teachers, who often are specialized and acquainted with actual research within their subjects. In some organizations, there are development divisions that support schools with research. Other important inputs mentioned are external influences, including participation in conferences, networks, and benchmarking.

Sharing

Another important aspect of keeping up to date is the distribution of knowledge. The principals,

as well as teachers, tell each other about the research they read, what has been learned from courses they have attended, and so on. In discussions about theories of why teaching is conducted in the way it is and similar topics, there is also a sharing of knowledge and a joint knowledge creation. The principals described their roles as being responsible for distributing and contributing to the understanding of research among their staff; this is done by initiating and driving discussions, based on the results of research. One principal wrote, "We have pages on our online platform where my staff and I collect links to and PDF files of relevant articles. We often discuss these in our group meetings." The types of discussions that take place and whether they involve a critical review of what has been read were not indicated. In the best case scenario, these are discussions that increase the understanding of what research shows and does not show. There were some examples of a critical attitude, in which the principal leads discussions about the results of research in relation to current working methods. One example is: "[We] continually reflect on the *why* and *how* of things and we document why we draw the conclusions we do; is what I see and say scientifically proven?" Another example is: "We have, for example, looked closely at Hattie's research and have further strengthened the areas that have been shown to have the greatest influence on goal fulfillment." It is clearly evident in the described examples of critical review that they are questioning their own activities. A critical evaluation of research was visible in some descriptions that showed how they reflect upon new research results in relation to how their work is done today. One example involved a couple of principals who have spaces in their calendars where certain research is evaluated in relation to current activities. One principal exemplified this with: "We regularly study the results of research and weigh up if and how they will be implemented in our activities."

Building a Scientific Culture

Many of the principals described in various ways how they try to develop a scientific culture in school and how they contribute to research-based knowledge in school in different ways.

Initiating and Facilitating

The principals in this study strived to stimulate teachers to adopt research by supporting an atmosphere of openness and cooperation. They showed a wish that teachers feel safe enough to have the courage to try new methods and not be afraid of failing. They also encouraged teachers to help each other to find new approaches to teaching, based on research findings, by creating spaces for cooperation. Some examples are in workplace meetings, pedagogical groups, and Facebook groups.

Resource allocation, time planning, and spaces for sharing, reflection, and discussion are tools that the principals use to encourage teachers to develop scientific knowledge. They also arrange book clubs related to scientific literature.

The Principal as a Role Model

Many of the principals wanted teachers to read research in an open and allowing atmosphere and reflect and discuss what they have read. The first step for the principal is to inform his/her staff about new research. Sometimes, there are big differences in the knowledge among the staff, so this kind of information is considered to be important to build a joint understanding as the basis in work. The principals hope that these efforts can make teachers interested in research. One of the principals wanted to provoke and challenge her staff and stated that she would "often take up questions that I know many have opinion[s] on, not always so scientifically based, and contrast it with what research say[s]." The current processes of teaching and learning at school are sometimes part of the starting point, which is then discussed and reflected upon in relation to theories.

Practicing Research-Based Knowledge

The school leaders in this study showed a strong reliance on research results. Organization as well as the methods of teaching and learning should be consistent with research findings.

Wishes and Thoughts

The principals wanted teachers to apply the findings from the research in their daily work with teaching, documentation, and action plans. They were well aware of the risks if teachers have their own homemade "theories" of how to organize the schoolwork, and they claimed that it is not good enough to read and be acquainted with research; it also has to be visible in practice. One of the principals wrote, "Principals, as well as teachers, have to study research results on a regular basis and consider if and how [they] can be implemented in school." This statement can exemplify a critical attitude and an awareness of the significance of the context.

Source for Justification

School leaders, as well as teachers, should be able to justify their actions by relating to research. One example is a principal who based arguments on research in order to explain and justify decisions and necessary changes. This principal stated, "[I] have become more scrupulous in using research in order to justify decision[s] and changes. This is received well by the staff. [It] gives an impression of seriousness and makes it easier to implement changes." These decisions may involve implementing successful teaching methods or organizing activities, based on what is shown by research. It is not indicated whether this has been preceded by comprehension or a critical review and evaluation of the research that is used as a justification.

In summary, the responses show that the most common methods for principals are to *read and keep themselves up to date* about the results of the research and that they create opportunities to discuss the research with their staff. This is done to *create understanding* and question current practices. There were relatively few examples of a culture in which there are *analytical and critical attitudes* toward the actual research results. There was only one example of research being *appraised* and relating to the respondents' own activities. The descriptions rarely included the way that the results of research are *applied* and are actually expressed in the groups of children and in the classrooms as well as how this affects the processes of teaching and learning. The focus was on the activities and how the principal thinks about the scientific basis for his/her own leadership; this appeared only in one case in which a principal wrote, "I want educational discussions and my own leadership to be permeated by science." This answer indicates a great confidence in research and a general invisibility of the critical attitude toward the actual research results. A general picture is that the results of the research are used as both theoretical and practical plans; this should be possible to do in a way that involves much more criticism and appraisal. However, one school leader demonstrated an awareness of that: "there is a lot of research that is contradictory . . . You have to decide by yourself what is relevant and reliable."

A Critical Attitude to Research Reviews

Internationally, there is a great deal of knowledge to be gained from research, albeit obtained in alternative culture contexts, which must be noted. There are also a great deal of conflicting results that should be considered (Hultman, 2012). Levin (2010) claims that educators rely mainly on intermediaries as their source of knowledge. Research reviews are an easily attainable source for teachers and principals. One book that has received much attention in recent years, and was also referred to by several of the principals, is John Hattie's *Visible Learning* (2009). Many have taken note of the

order of precedence he made when synthesizing over 800 meta-studies of student performance and taking them, more or less, as evidence of effectiveness. However, it would be appropriate to indicate that there are some pitfalls. Sjøberg (2012) and Snook, O'Neill, Clark, O'Neill, and Openshaw (2009) have conducted critical reviews of Hattie's book and have found that there are many uncertainties. The main feature of the criticism relates to quality and transferability. It is hard to assess the quality of the included studies, which have an impact on the results. It is also hard to compare different studies when the students' successes have been measured in different ways, and there are only quantitative studies of results that have been measured by exams or other tests. No comparison has been made for the students' ages, subjects, or similar areas. Moreover, all of the studies were conducted in English-speaking countries, primarily the United States and the United Kingdom. Nordic research results were not included. They maintain that Hattie provides a simplified picture, in which he ignores the complexity of the classroom, as he does for the historical, cultural, and social contexts in which learning takes place. There is a lack of results that indicate the significance of the students' attitudes toward learning, as well as their involvement, interests, and motivation. Considering that the governance documents differ in different countries, this aspect is also absent. Snook advises the reader to be critical of Hattie's order of precedence of good and bad and the belief that the results can be transferred to Norwegian (or Swedish) schools (see also Levin, 2013). The results of the research cannot automatically be transferred to one's own practice but must be critically reviewed and appraised against individual convictions, values, and experiences. However, it is important to both respect and appraise the results of the research, especially if they oppose one's own convictions. In their research review, Håkansson and Sundberg (2012) argue that the existence of knowledge transgresses contextual boundaries within the didactic fields they have studied. This means that they are translatable between different contexts. At the same time, the authors acknowledge that it has not been possible to assess the quality of the research that constitutes the basis of their review. Robinson (2008) is another researcher who has compiled international research about how two different types of leadership have been shown to affect the students' outcomes. Robinson has synthesized research showing how instructional and transformative leadership affect student results, both in terms of knowledge and other results. She describes in detail the choices she has made in order to make relevant and reliable comparisons. For example, she emphasizes the significance of, to the extent possible, comparing studies of a similar design.

Research reviews are an easy way to take large amounts of research within different areas, but the research needs to be critically reviewed and appraised. Both teachers and students are heterogeneous groups, and assuming that learning is context-bound, this makes generalizing the results of learning problematic. There is no method that applies to everyone, not even to all students in the same class. However, there may be general aspects that can be translated into individual practices.

Leading Educational Work Based on Research

The principals in this study seemed to strive to direct their school work toward research-based activities, primarily by keeping themselves up to date and facilitating discussions among teachers. To see oneself as a source of knowledge is in accordance with the findings of Timperley (2011). Leading the educational work, regardless of level, initially involves leading by *setting directions* (Leithwood, 2005). This is done by formulating and communicating a clear vision and goals. A challenge for these principals is to build a mutual understanding and create a scientific at-

titude in their educational programs. Leithwood emphasizes the significance of the goals that are collected and shared by all. Furthermore, in order to motivate colleagues, the goals must be challenging, convincing, and achievable. As the educational work will be based on research, it would have been interesting to capture the principals' perceptions of challenging, convincing, and achievable goals. For the question of how the text of the Education Act may be analyzed and how it affects leadership, there were many responses. For many principals, this involved leading their teachers toward relating to research that is not common in many schools. Like Hemsley-Brown and Sharp (2003) point out, the principals in this study were positive to research but showed a shallow understanding of education based on research. Many of the principals described in various ways how they steer in the direction of a basis in research. One example is the principal who writes, "It involves the organizational development that takes place on my unit being guided by the premise of a scientific basis. Projects must not be initiated or driven for other reasons, such as general opinions or gut feelings." This indicates that there is a clearly expressed ambition for the principals' leadership.

From the perspective of setting a direction, with a focus on the teachers, there are also examples of how principals

- Lead teachers to focus on the *content* of teaching having a scientific basis by using reliable literature,
- Lead the work of teachers to use *working practices* that are scientifically based (An example of this is the case in which Hattie's book is used as the basis for strengthening the areas that have been shown to greatly impact goal fulfillment.), and
- Lead teachers to assimilate scientific *attitudes* through questioning and critically reviewing their own activities and compar-

ing them with the results of research (This also involves leading discussions and initiating reflection about research.).

Another aspect of leadership is, according to Belchetz and Leithwood (2007), *understanding and developing people* (cf. Leithwood & Jantzi, 2005; Brauckmann & Pashiardis, 2011). In this case, it involves recognizing teachers' unique requirements and development potential, being a good listener, being aware of good performances, and treating teachers like professional colleagues. Moreover, this aspect also involves providing intellectual stimulation to the teachers and encouraging them to review their own practices in relation to what research shows in order to further develop the practices. Examples in this study show that the principals really strive to make teachers aware of the basis of teaching. With the teachers, the principals have conversations about how teaching can be developed from a scientific basis. To promote and participate in teacher learning and development is highlighted as a significant leadership dimension by Robinson, Lloyd and Rowe (2008) and Timperley (2011).

Leading and developing colleagues, according to Belchetz and Leithwood (2007), also involves being a role model with regards to behavior and attitude. One example is to be visible in the school and, with the teachers, show involvement by participating in the educational work and teachers' learning and development. This is corroborated by Robinson et al. (2008), who conducted a meta-analysis of a number of studies about the relationship between leadership and student performance. Their conclusion was that the greatest impact on student performance is the teacher's proximity to the core activities: learning and teaching (see also Timperley, 2011). For the principal, it is a matter of working strategically with visions and goals, as well as supporting and participating in the teachers' learning and development, in order to create an educational program that has a scientific basis. This involves both creating guidelines, while

also formally and informally being a source of knowledge, and offering good advice to teachers.

In this case, leadership means creating conditions for many different opportunities for teachers to learn and understand what types of research and scientific attitudes may be included in their own activities. This scientific attitude requires the knowledge and ability of both the teachers and the principals. According to Robinson (2008), the principal is an important source of both advice and support for the teachers, and it is thus important to have a clear direction and sound individual knowledge. To be a source of knowledge when promoting and participating in teachers' learning and development presupposes relevant knowledge. Drawing on the conclusions from Robinson et al. (2008), Timperley (2011), and Stein and Nelson (2003), relevant research for principals to read, evaluate, and spread is research on learning and teaching in specific subjects but also pedagogical content knowledge in general. Principals also need to know how to best assist teachers in their learning. To avoid distributing incompetence, the principals also need to develop a scientific attitude. This develops preferably when a teacher collaborates with other members of the staff and in collaboration with researchers.

Implementing a Scientific Approach/Culture

Knowledge and understanding are prerequisites for supporting education that is based on research. Since principals can be considered agents for change (Marks & Printy, 2003), the principals must introduce the idea of research-based education in their schools. However, there is a greater chance that the principals will succeed if they involve the teachers at an early stage. Formulating a vision and goals together with teachers can raise their consciousness (Leithwood & Jantzi, 2007) about the significance of research findings. However, a first step is *to find relevant research* that concerns different subjects, teaching methods, and ways of learning. The principals also have to decide on what is relevant. Levin (2013) and Vanderlinde and van Braak (2010) reported that one common barrier in using research results in educational practice was difficulties in finding relevant research. In this study, there were examples of how principals themselves have found research they consider to be relevant and also how their teachers contribute with the research they have obtained with activities that help them develop professionally. The next step is to *read, spread, and contribute to a mutual understanding* of the research. The principals in this study seemed to be aware of this and took the opportunity to use different arenas for discussions among staff. This is in accordance with Timperley (2011), who found that the primary dimension for principals' effectiveness in instructional leadership was to lead teachers' learning by participating in their learning activities. To progress, these discussions need individuals who can contribute to understand the meaning of the research they read. A *critical examination and evaluation of research* is the next step. Some concerns include: What questions should be asked about the text? How can we make an evaluation? Working with researchers can be one way to grasp a method to address scientific texts. At the same time, it may be necessary to scrutinize both principals' and teachers' own assumptions about knowledge, teaching, and learning (Marks & Printy, 2003) to find reasons for their approaches to education.

In summary, principals and teachers need to find, read, understand, adopt, and implement scientific attitudes to conduct research and examine their own activities. Principals and teachers also have to assess research in relation to their unique situations before they consider *applying the research results into practice*. Some questions that should be answered to show awareness of what will be implemented are: Why apply this research? When is the appropriate time? How should the implementation be conducted? By whom should it be conducted? When is the right time for evaluation?

I believe it is important to take the steps I suggested in order to successfully implement research-based education. However, a critical attitude can be applied as an overall approach but is especially important before applying research results into practice. Application of research results may create different forms of success and longevity, depending on when in the process it takes place. Being able to understand the results as well as critically review and appraise the results may be fundamental requirements to successfully select and apply the results to an individual context. Adopting a critical attitude should be viewed as particularly important for principals and teachers in connection to the results of various research projects that have been presented. Since not all results are worth pursuing, an analytical ability is important to critically review and compare results (Levin, 2013). Analysis is also important in appraising and assessing the results in order to form an attitude regarding their relevance in the actual local context.

Collaboration for an Improved Research-Based Practice in School

The idea that education should be based on research has been inspired by the world of higher education and the idea that teachers in higher-education institutions should conduct research in the subject in which they teach. Is it desirable and possible then to translate this to a school environment? McKinsey (2010) supports the idea that locally driven pedagogic development characterizes the world's most successful school systems. One principal wrote, "The universities and schools must view each other as resources and get closer to each other." This could be a way to support teachers and principals using and co-producing research in schools to bridge the gap between educational research and practice. However, researchers and teachers/principals often have different interests. Many researchers are, according to Vanderlinde and van Braak (2010), interested in finding new knowledge, while teachers are more practical-oriented and interested in finding solutions to educational problems. This can be solved by supporting praxis-oriented researchers and research-oriented teachers. Local collegial forms of cooperation contribute to the development of the teachers' pedagogic skills but are also ways of disseminating successful methods. The Japanese-influenced tradition of practicing collaborative studies of live classroom lessons is a tangible example of this.

Some examples of how a scientific approach can be implemented are:

- Conduct discussion groups within your own schools to share research. This can be initiated by the principal or by other educators (see Levin, 2010).
- Carry on research groups, which can be applied at several schools (see Holmstrand & Härnsten, 2003; Lahdenperä, 2011). The purpose is to get a deeper understanding by reading scientific literature and having discussions about their understanding of what they have read.
- Conduct practice-based research collaboration based on issues that the principal and other teachers address (see Alerby et al. 2010; Kroksmark, 2012; Nutley et al., 2008; SOU, 2009:94; Vanderlinde & van Braak, 2010). This is a way to integrate the different expertise held by researchers and teachers/principals (Biesta, 2007).
- Get involved in action research projects or ongoing evaluation, in which the research follows development projects that are initiated by the school (see, for example, Ahnberg et al., 2009; Levin, 2013; Vanderlinde & van Braak, 2010).

One advantage of cooperation between researchers and practitioners is that research results and individual experience-based knowledge can

interplay and lead to an increased understanding of what is happening in the activities of both researchers and teachers. In order for this to work, the principal needs to organize collegial exchanges and an organization that facilitates the development of scientific attitudes toward education. Otherwise, there can be a risk that teachers do not critically think about research and do not dare to try new ideas in the classrooms.

CONCLUSION

The implication that education should be based on research and proven experiences is still not clear and can therefore be difficult to realize in tangible practice. The Swedish National Agency for Education has several texts that attempt to explain what this means, but change takes time, presupposing that work continues. Two areas can be emphasized as being essential. These areas are: *the acquisition of scientific knowledge of and a scientific attitude toward teaching and learning* and *the significance of the principals' leadership ability to create visions and goals and to support and inspire the teachers.*

Most of the literature on the relation between educational research and practice has a top-down perspective, meaning a transmission of research findings to be implemented in practice. This is also valid in policy. It is important to develop knowledge and understanding of research and, at the same time, apply a scientific and critical attitude to the research. All research, not only contradictory results, needs a scientific approach, characterized by critical evaluation. In this study, there are only a few examples of ways to lead teachers to assimilate scientific attitudes through questioning and critically reviewing their own activities in comparison to research. In order to implement research-based education, research results and academic approaches should be considered. Levin (2013) states that people's interest in and use of research results depends on organizational setting and social relations. This is important for principals to take into account.

More collaboration between teachers, principals, and researchers could be helpful in integrating scientific knowledge and experience-based knowledge. This could help build a firm foundation for teaching and learning. This could also lead to a more analytical and critically scrutinizing approach to various research that applies to both teachers and principals. Compared with the academic backgrounds of the old grammar school heads, the principals of today find themselves in a different situation when it comes to understanding and conducting education with a sound scientific basis. It is not clear to what degree the principals in this study have acquired a scientific approach in their basic education. As no real difference has been found between principals in different types of schools, it is supposed that their different backgrounds do not matter. Since a majority of the principals have a background as teachers, this raises questions about the teacher education in Sweden and its training in research and a scientific approach. It could also be a question of strong traditions and culture in school settings.

The role of the principal to support, engage, and inspire teachers to change their views, knowledge, and practices seems important for successful education. The principals should show confidence in teachers, encourage them, and be good role models. These aspects will affect the success of the implementation of a research-based education. Leading the educational work also involves creating a systematic approach and continuity of the work in order to improve the quality of the work that is aimed at increasing the quality of education.

A worldwide trend is a turn toward a culture of measurable results that are compared to international studies. The focus on principals' leadership has had a tendency to obey authorities' demands, and much effort is spent on meeting those demands. There is a risk that principals do what others have told them to do without trusting their own knowledge and convictions, feeling safe with a scientific basis in regards to content, teaching methods, a critical scientific attitude, along with a leadership that includes a scientific basis. It can be assumed that it would be easier to control the development of a high-quality education in school. We need to know more about the links between scientific knowledge and its implementation in practices as well as how it influences student learning.

Concluding Remarks

Conducting these surveys and drawing conclusions from written answers generates some limitations in this study. How the principals interpret questions is one source of uncertainty common to all surveys. Their understanding of the questions affects what they choose to answer. Another limit is that they have to express themselves in written text, while they, on a daily basis, work in a much more oral environment. Despite these limitations, I would argue that the principals in this study showed an awareness of the importance of a scientific basis in education, although most of them have described it in general terms. Whether this is due to an uncertainty of what a research-based education really could mean or if it is difficult for them to express themselves in a concrete way, I cannot say. However, most of the principals might have been fostered in a school culture in which there are answers that are either right or wrong, which may have affected their ability to express themselves. If so, it could serve as a way of protecting themselves against "wrong" answers. One way that could be helpful to raise principals' and teachers' self-confidence within this field could be to acquire competence in searching for relevant research, along with a scientific attitude. It is also remarkable that these principals made such a relatively low estimation of the expectations from their employers for the principals to work toward a situation in which the work of their educational staff rests on research. It is well known that expectations play significant roles in how people prioritize and perform. However, the question is how significant expectations from the employer actually are perceived. The expectations did not seem to affect the principals' own ratings of important work tasks. One possible interpretation is that the principals' leadership has been in focus for a considerable time, whilst the demand for education to rest on a sound scientific basis is relatively new and has not been met with the same attention. For example, this has not (yet) been expressly examined by the Swedish National Agency for Education. Another interpretation is that working as a principal at an independent school is an active choice and might be experienced as a challenge in a new context; this can make the principals more inclined to try new directions. There are also many small, independent employers, which can indicate a closer relationship between the principal and the employer than in most public schools.

REFERENCES

Ahnberg, E., Lundgren, M., Messing, J. and von Schantz Lundgren, I. (2009). Följeforskning som företeelse och följeforskarrollen som konkret praktik. [The Phenomenon 'Research Followers']. *Arbetsmarknad och arbetsliv, 15*(1).

Alerby, E., Bergmark, U., Dahlén, G., Rosengren Larsson, I., Vikström, A., & Westman, S. (2010). Ömsesidig samverkan mellan pedagogisk forskning och pedagogisk praktik. [Mutual interaction between educational research and practise]. In Utbildning på veteneskaplig grund. Stockholm: Stiftelsen SAF i samarbete med Lärarförbundet.

Belchetz, D., & Leithwood, K. (2007). Successful school leadership: Does context matter and if so, how? In C. Day & K. Leithwood (Eds.), *Successful Principal Leadership in Times of Change* (pp. 117–137). Dordrecht, The Netherlands: Springer. doi:10.1007/1-4020-5516-1_8

Bengtsson, J. (1999). *En livsvärldsansats för pedagogisk forskning.* [A Lifeworld Approach for Educational Research]. Paper presented at NERA's Congress. Copenhagen, Denmark.

Bet. (1992/93:UbU3). *Utbildningsutskottets betänkande om ny Högskolelag.* [Committee Report on the New Education Act].

Biesta, G. (2007). Bridging the Gap between Educational Research and Educational Practice: The Need for Critical Distance. *Educational Research and Evaluation, 13*(3), 295–301. doi:10.1080/13803610701640227

Bohlin, I. and Sager, M. (2011). *Evidensens många ansikten.* [The Many Faces of Evidence]. Lund:Arkiv förlag.

Brauckmann, S., & Pashiardis, P. (2011). A validation study of the leadership styles of a holistic leadership theoretical framework. *International Journal of Educational Management, 25*(1), 11–32. doi:10.1108/09513541111100099

Broekkamp, H., & van Hout-Wolters, B. (2007). The Gap between Educational Research and Practice: A Literature Review, Symposium, and Questionnaire. *Educational Research and Evaluation, 13*(3), 203–220. doi:10.1080/13803610701626127

Facts about Sweden – Education. (n.d.). Retrieved from http://sweden.se/society/education-in-sweden/

Gustavsson, B. (2000). *Kunskapsfilosofi. Tre kunskapsformer i historisk belysning.* [The Philosophy of Knowledge. Three forms of Knowledge in a Historical Perspective]. Stockholm: Wahlström & Widstrand.

Håkansson, J. and Sundberg, D. (2012). *Undervisning på vetenskaplig grund.* [Teaching based on Research]. Stockholm: Natur och Kultur.

Hattie, J. (2009). *Visible learning.* London: Routledge.

Hemsley-Brown, J., & Sharp, C. (2003). The Use of Research to Improve Professional Practice: A systematic review of the literature. *Oxford Review of Education, 29*(4), 449–471. doi:10.1080/0305498032000153025

Högskolelagen (1992:1434). [The Higher Education Act].

Holmstrand, L., & Härnsten, G. (2003). *Förutsättningar för forskningscirklar i skolan.* [Prerequisites for Research Groups in School]. Stockholm: Skolverket.

Hultman, G. (2012). Ledarskapsforskning – Gamla sanningar och nya ambitioner. [Research on Leadership – Old Truths and New Ambitions]. *Leda & Styra,* (2), 1-22.

Kroksmark, T. (2012). *En modellskola på vetenskaplig grund.* [A School Model on a Scientific Basis][online]. Available: http://www.tomaskroksmark.se/modellskola_vet_grund.pdf

Lahdenperä, P. (2011). *Forskningscirkel - Arena för verksamhetsutvecking i mångfald.* [Reseach Circles, Arena for Development in Diversity]. Available: http://www.diva-portal.org/smash/get/diva2:511191/FULLTEXT01.pdf

Läkartidningen. (2007). Svårt att definiera beprövad erfarenhet. [Difficult to define proven experience]. *Läkartidningen, 104*(4), 198-199.

Leithwood, K. (2005). *Educational Leadership.* Toronto: Temple University Center for Research in Human Development and Education.

Leithwood, K., & Jantzi, D. (2007). A Review of Transformational School Leadership Research 1996-2005. *Leadership and Policy in Schools, 4*(3), 177–199. doi:10.1080/15700760500244769

Levi, R. (1997). *Vad menas med beprövad erfarenhet?* [What does proven experience mean?] [online]. Available: http://www.sbu.se/sv/Vetenskap--Praxis/Vetenskap-och-praxis/2095/

Levin, B. (2010). Leadership for Evidence-Informed Education. *School Leadership & Management, 30*(4), 303–315. doi:10.1080/13632434.2010.497483

Levin, B. (2013). To know is not enough: Research knowledge and its use. *Review of Education, 1*(1), 2–31. doi:10.1002/rev3.3001

Marks, H. M., & Printy, S. M. (2003). Principal Leadership and School Performance: An Integration of Transformational and Instructional Leadership. *Educational Administration Quarterly, 39*(3), 370–397. doi:10.1177/0013161X03253412

Martin Korpi, B. (2006). *Förskolan i politiken: om intentioner och beslut bakom den svenska förskolan framväxt.* [Preschool in politics: about intentions and decisions in the emergence of the Swedish preschool]. Stockholm:Utbildnings och kulturdepartementet, Regeringskansliet.

McKinsey. (2010). *How the world's most improved school systems keep getting better.* McKinsey & Company.

Ministry of Education and Research. (2008). *Funding of the Swedih school system.* Retrieved from http://www.regeringen.se/content/1/c6/10/15/00/14eaa35c.pdf

Moos, L. (2013). Comparing Educational Leadership Research. *Leadership and Policy in Schools, 12*(3), 282–299. doi:10.1080/15700763.2013.834060

Norcini, J., & Banda, S. (2011). Increasing the quality and capacity of education: The challenge for the 21st century. *Medical Education, 45*(1), 81–86. doi:10.1111/j.1365-2923.2010.03738.x PMID:21155871

Nutley, S., Jung, T., & Walter, I. (2008). The Many Forms of Research-Informed Practice: A Framework for Mapping Diversity. *Cambridge Journal of Education, 38*(1), 53–71. doi:10.1080/03057640801889980

OECD. (2013). *PISA 2012: Results in focus*. Available: http://www.oecd.org/pisa/keyfindings/pisa-2012-results-overview.pdf

OECD. (2014). *Society at a Glance 2014: OECD Social Indicators*. doi:10.1787/soc_glance-2014-en

Pashiardis, P., Kendeou, P., Michaelidou, A., & Lytra, E. (2014). Exploring a New Cocktail Mix in Cyprus: School Principals' Epistemological Beliefs and Leadership Styles. In P. Pashiardis (Ed.), *Modeling School Leadership across Europe - In Search of New Frontiers*. Dordrecht, The Netherlands: Springer. doi:10.1007/978-94-007-7290-8_8

Prop. 1992 / 93:1. Om universitet och högskolor – frihet för kvalitet. [About Universitys and University colleges – freedom for quality]

Prop. 2009/10:165. *Den nya skollagen - för kunskap valfrihet och trygghet*. [Govt. Bill, The New Education Act – for knowledge, freedom of choice, and safety].

Robinson, V., Lloyd, C., & Rowe, K. (2007). The Impact of Leadership on Student Outcomes: An Analysis of the Differential Effects of Leadership Types. *Educational Administration Quarterly, 44*(5), 635–674. doi:10.1177/0013161X08321509

SFS. (2010). *Skollag*. [Swedish Education Act 2010:800].

Sjøberg, S. (2012). Visible Learning - Ny giv for norsk skole. [Visible Learning – New deal for Norwegian Schools]. *Utdanning, 21*, 44–47.

SKOLFS. (2011:37). *Skolverkets föreskrifter om introduktionsperiod och kompetensprofiler för lärare och förskollärare*. [Regulations on introduction period and competency profiles for teachers and preschool teachers].

Skolinspektionen. (2012). *Rektors ledarskap*. [Principals' leadership]. Stockholm: Skolinspektionen.

Skolverket. (2007). *Skolverkets lägesbedömning 2007*. [Assessment 2007]. Stockholm: Skolverket.

Skolverket. (2008). *Skolverkets lägesbedömning 2008*. [Assessment 2008]. Stockholm: Skolverket.

Skolverket. (2009). *Skolverkets lägesbedömning 2009*. [Assment 2009]. Stockholm: Skolverket.

Skolverket. (2010a). *Curriculum for the Preschool, Lpfö 98 Revised 2010*. Stockholm: Skolverket.

Skolverket. (2010b). *Skolverkets lägesbedömning 2010*. [Assessment 2010]. Stockholm: Skolverket.

Skolverket. (2011a). *Skolverkets lägesbedömning 2011 Del 2 - Bedömningar och slutsatser*. [The Swedish Natonal Agency's assessment of the situation in 2011. Part 2 – Assessments and Conclusions]. Stockholm: Skolverket.

Skolverket. (2011b). *Promemoria om evidens på utbildningsområdet*. [Memorandum on evidence in the field of education]. Stockholm: Skolverket.

Skolverket. (2013a). *An assessment of the situation in the Swedish school system 2013 by the Swedish National Agency for Education*. Stockholm: Skolverket.

Skolverket. (2013b). *Facts and figures 2012*. Stockholm: Skolverket.

Skolverket. (2014). *Research for classrooms: Scientific knowledge and proven experienced in practise*. Stockholm: Skolverket. Retrieved from http://www.skolverket.se/om-skolverket/publikationer/visa-enskild-publikation?_xurl_=http%3A%2F%2Fwww5.skolverket.se%2Fwtpub%2Fws%2Fskolbok%2Fwpubext%2Ftrycksak%2FRecord%3Fk%3D3229

Skolverket. (n.d.). *An overview of the Swedish education system*. Retrieved from http://www.skolverket.se/om-skolverket/andra-sprak-och-lattlast/in-english/the-swedish-education-system/an-overview-of-the-swedish-education-system-1.72184

Snook, I., O'Neill, J., Clark, J., O'Neill, A.-M., & Openshaw, R. (2009). Invisible Learnings?: A Commentary on John Hattie's Book - Visible Learning: A Synthesis of Over 800 Meta-analyses Relating to Achievement''. *New Zealand Journal of Educational Studies, 44*(1), 93–106.

SOU. (1948). *1946 års skolkommissions betänkande med förslag till riktlinjer för det svenska skolväsendets utveckling* [The 1946 Education Commission report with proposed guidelines for the development of the Swedish school system]. Stockholm: Ecklesiastikdepartementet.

SOU. (1997). *Att erövra omvärlden.* [To conquer the external environment].

SOU. (2008) *En hållbar lärarutbildning.* [A sustainable teacher education program].

SOU. (2009). *Att nå ut och nå ända fram. Hur tillgången till policyinriktad utvärdering och forskningsresultat inom utbildningsområdet kan tillgodoses.* [Reaching out and reaching all the way. How the availability of policy-oriented evaluation and research results within the field of education can be met].

Styf, M. (2012). *Pedagogisk leding för en pedagogisk verksamhet - Om den kommunala förskolans ledningsstruktur.* [Pedagogical leadership for educational activities]. Umeå: Umeå University.

Sweden in brief. (n.d.). Retrieved from http://sweden.se/?s=sweden+in+brief

Timperley, H. (2011). Knowledge and the Leadership of Learning. *Leadership and Policy in Schools, 10*(2), 145–170. doi:10.1080/1570076 3.2011.557519

Ullman, A. (1997). *Rektorn. En studie av en titel och dess bärare.* (akad. avhandling) [A study of a title and its holders]. Stockholm: HLS förlag.

van Manen, M. (1997). *Researching lived experience* (2nd ed.). London, Canada: Althouse Press.

van Manen, M. (2007). Phenomenology of Practice. *Phenomenology & Practice, 1*(1), 11–30.

Vanderlinde, R., & van Braak, J. (2010). The Gap between Educational Research and Practice: Views of Teachers, School Leaders, Intermediaries and Researchers. *British Educational Research Journal, 36*(2), 299–316. doi:10.1080/01411920902919257

KEY TERMS AND DEFINITIONS

Critical Attitude: To view things from different perspectives and consider alternative interpretations.

Head of Preschool: The leader of a preschool.

Policy: Processes and documents used for governing schools.

Research Based Knowledge: Knowledge based on results from research.

Scientific Approach: An attitude characterized by questioning and analyzing.

Scientific Culture: A culture where teachers and principals are characterized by a critical approach.

Scientific Knowledge: Knowledge based on theory and/or research results.

Chapter 9
Individual Differences and Educational Leadership

Anna Kanape-Willingshofer
Linz University, Austria

Sabine Bergner
Graz University, Austria

ABSTRACT

The chapter discusses the relevance of individual differences in personality traits for the study of school leadership, especially with regard to leadership success. Findings from psychological leadership research have shown that, amongst others, personality, cognitive and emotional intelligence, as well as creativity predict leadership outcome variables. The authors investigate how far these traits have been able to predict leadership success across different occupations and also across different situational and methodological conditions. In addition, studies on the relationship of individual trait differences and school principals' effectiveness are discussed. The chapter shows that individual differences research holds potential for educational leadership, but further studies are needed to draw conclusions about the potential cognitive ability, personality traits, emotional intelligence, as well as creativity hold for predicting leadership success of school principals.

1. INTRODUCTION

Leaders make a difference. Same as any other individual's behavior, a leader's behavior is a function of personal traits and situational characteristics (Mischel, 1977). Interestingly, when we look at the school context, we find that there is "little research on leadership antecedents, particularly personal variables [as the research] regarding highly effective principals has primarily focused on effective approaches, functions, and activities

rather than on 'the characteristics that enable or increase the likelihood of a person performing those activities' (Boyatzis, 1982, p. 8)" (Williams, 2008, p. 39). This seems especially surprising as the study of personal variables in which people differ from one another is a promising field of psychology, particularly in the domain of leader selection and development.

This chapter discusses studies which were undertaken in the context of educational leadership by focusing on individual differences at the

DOI: 10.4018/978-1-4666-6591-0.ch009

trait level. At this point it is important to note that traits represent hypothetical, latent dispositions that need to be inferred from observable responses (e.g., behavior; Ajzen, 1987). There is wide agreement that traits are stable across situations as well as across the lifespan, because they are to a large extent rooted in biological differences and can usually only be altered or influenced to a certain degree (Chamorro-Premuzic, 2007). Although there is some debate among researchers what exactly constitutes a trait, there is also some agreement on its definition. In the present chapter we go with Antonakis' (2011) definition that traits "(a) are measureable, (b) vary across individuals, (c) exhibit temporal and situational stability, and (d) predict attitudes, decisions, or behaviors and consequently outcomes" (p. 270).

Commonly, individual traits are divided into cognitive and non-cognitive traits. The most comprehensive and best studied cognitive trait is intelligence, also referred to as cognitive ability. Whereas cognitive ability is usually measured by testing a person's performance on a number of objectively solvable problems (power tests), non-cognitive traits – also termed personality – are referred to subjective tendencies to behave in a specific manner (typical performance tests; see Cronbach, 1949). Regarding cognitive ability there are many different ways of conceptualization. Basically, flat models including a general factor of intelligence can be distinguished from hierarchical models that do not have a general factor. A large number of empirical studies demonstrated the importance of cognitive ability, especially general cognitive ability, for occupational performance (e.g., Judge, Colbert, & Ilies, 2004).

With respect to non-cognitive traits the most extensive recent attention has been directed at the Big Five model of personality that comprises the five broad and higher-order traits Openness, Conscientiousness, Extraversion, Agreeableness, and Emotional Stability. During the last three decades, a large body of literature provided compelling

evidence for the robustness of the five factors across different cultures, different instruments, and different rating-perspectives (Borkenau & Ostendorf, 1990; McCrae & Costa, 1987; Watson, 1989). Both, personality traits and intelligence are of theoretical and practical importance for leadership in general and educational leadership in particular. From a theoretical perspective, intelligence and personality are important because they provide an established and comprehensive frame of reference for the description of an individual's character. From an applied perspective, intelligence and personality are important in so far as they predict future behavior, for instance leadership performance (Judge, Bono, Ilies, & Gerhardt, 2002; Judge et al., 2004).

Within the context of educational leadership "personal variables" (i.e., traits) are underrepresented (Williams, 2008, p. 39). As noted by Hallinger (2008, p. 26) those antecedent variables that were mainly examined with respect to educational leadership were *group* differences (as opposed to *individual* differences) such as principal gender, years of experience as a principal, years of teaching experience prior to becoming a principal, age or ethnicity. The underrepresentation of research on trait differences in educational leadership is slightly puzzling since the trait approach has generally gained immense attention in leadership research and applied leadership settings.

As described in Judge and Long's (2012) comprehensive framework of leadership (see Figure 1), traits are distal antecedents of leadership performance (i.e., leadership emergence and leadership effectiveness). Distal antecedents are believed to affect performance indirectly through their influence on the proximal antecedents described in the model. The distal antecedents that have received the most research attention are cognitive ability and personality (van Iddekinge, Ferris, & Heffner, 2009). In contrast, proximal antecedents of leadership performance refer to situational characteristics that describe

Figure 1. Leadership model depicting relationships between individual differences and leadership criteria (adapted from Judge & Long, 2012, p. 187)

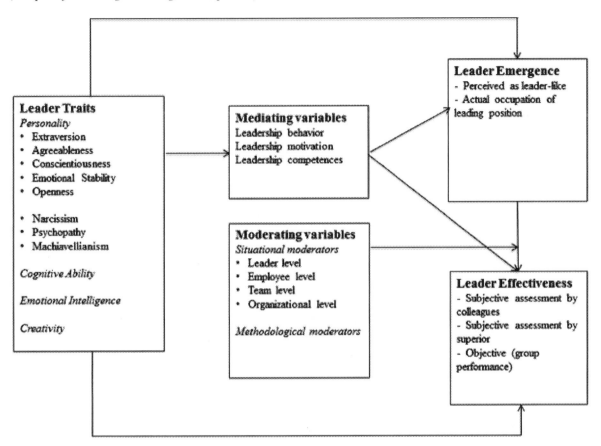

the 'where' and 'when' of leadership settings, as well as methodological issues of 'how' certain variables are operationalized.

According to Yukl (2011) situational variables, which leaders cannot modify quickly can include characteristics of the work (e.g., task structure, role interdependence), characteristics of subordinates (e.g., values, needs), characteristics of the leader (e.g.,expertise, interpersonal stress), and also characteristics of the leadership position (e.g.,leader authority, formal policies). In line with the so-called Contingency Theories it is argued in Figure 1 that these aspects of the leadership situation alter a leader's influence on

an individual or a work group (Yukl, 2011, p. 286). Thus, these aspects moderate or mediate the influence of relatively stable traits on leadership performance.

As stated at the beginning of this chapter, leaders make a difference. It is widely accepted that leadership behavior – as any other behavior – is a function of relatively stable traits and situational influences (Mischel, 1977). In the current chapter the focus is clearly set on the personality traits and how differences between individual leaders influence their behavior, or respectively performance. In accordance with Judge and Long (2012) empirical research on the distal antecedents that received the most attention in research and applied settings – cognitive ability and personality – is summarized.

The reason for focusing on cognitive ability and personality is twofold. First, cognitive ability and personality provide an established and comprehensive frame of reference for the description of an individual (Furnham & Chamorro-Premuzic, 2004). Second, as depicted in Figure 1 cognitive ability and personality are important because they can predict future leadership behavior and, thus, have direct implications for leader development and selection processes. With respect to the non-cognitive personality traits the focus will be on the Big Five model as it is currently the most widely accepted personality model and has received the most attention in research and applied settings (Salgado, Viswesvaran, & Ones, 2001).

In addition, the current review of empirical studies on personality traits is extended by two further traits, namely creativity and emotional intelligence. This extension appeared necessary as the tasks of (educational) leaders have been changing in the past decades and leadership tasks (as compared to mere administrative management ones) have become more important (cf. Huber, 2008). This, however, implies that future educational leaders have to fulfil tasks that are more interpersonal and creative, or respectively entrepreneurial in nature. Therefore, creativity and emotional intelligence are personality traits of tremendous importance for future leaders and must not be omitted in the current review (Vaccaro, Jansen, Van Den Bosch, & Volberda, 2012).

Although the traits we discuss in this chapter may influence principals in different educational systems in a similar way, we would like to provide some background information about school leaders in one specific educational system which provides the main basis for our discussion, i.e. the Austrian one. Austrian principals, in general, find themselves in often strongly regulated situations, which applies especially to the tasks and administrative aspects a school has to fulfill. How principals manage all the individual elements they are responsible for, is usually up to them. Austrian school leaders have recently seen an increase in governmental monitoring, which is a rebound of increased autonomy transferred to schools in the 1990s (Altrichter & Heinrich, 2007) allowing schools to operate somewhat independently from central governance structures. However, the PISA shock of 2003 quickly brought about a change of this decentralization and led to stronger monitoring in order to ensure comparable educational quality. This resulted ultimately in the recently introduced national education standards and – for the first time in Austria – to standardized national assessments of student achievement (cf. Altrichter & Kanape-Willingshofer, 2013, for a short summary in English).

This is only one of the many changes in the Austrian educational system which are very often the principal's responsibility to implement and supervise accordingly. Even with the introduction of objective outcome measures in form of national tests, the Austrian education system certainly has to be classified as a 'low-stake' accountability system. Students' results of the standardized national assessments have only feedback function and cannot be used for teacher or principal evaluations. The OECD's TALIS study has revealed that compared to other countries, actual as well as perceived autonomy of Austrian school leaders is still very limited. Within this generally limited freedom of decision Austrian school leaders report restrictions especially with regard to financial and personnel issues (cf. Suchan, Wallner-Paschon, & Bergmüller, 2009).

In addition to changes in principals' responsibilities due to profound educational reforms, also principal development has experienced a significant turn. In Austria only teachers with a certain teaching experience can apply for principalship, and each of the nine Austrian provinces has its own selection procedure (in addition, some schools are private and some public, which again leads to different selection procedures and criteria). Usually applicants should meet some additional criteria in order to improve their chances of successfully applying for a specific school principalship (e.g., taking part in or also teaching in post-graduate teacher education programs, writing publications, active role in teacher unions, receiving teaching awards). There is no uniform assessment center which candidates have to participate in and the composition of the committee depends on the (regional) school board. In 2013 the Austrian educational ministry introduced the first pre-service principal training on master's level, as principals usually have to participate in a compulsory training only after they were appointed as a school head. While some of the points we will raise in our chapter may be more fitting for educational systems similar to the Austrian one, most of the discussed aspects regarding individual differences and school leadership should be applicable to other countries too.

The chapter will highlight the importance of including individual differences when researching leadership in general, but more importantly also infer from studies in other contexts what implications these findings might have for school contexts. Initially, an overview of recent psychological research on leadership effectiveness from an individual differences angle, with special consideration of the four domains personality, cognitive and emotional intelligence and creativity is given. In a next step we try to identify research on individual differences of school leaders and will discuss the (potential) impact of these characteristics on leadership effectiveness in schools, investigating whether "a small handful of personal traits explains a high proportion of the variation in leadership effectiveness" (Leithwood, Day, Sammons, Harris, & Hopkins, 2006, p. 3) also in school settings. To conclude, we will indicate further research which is needed to shed light on the relations between abilities or personality traits and school outcome variables and discuss the

importance of two recently emerged psychological leadership research strands (i.e., neuroleadership and leadership succession) for educational leadership.

2. INDIVIDUAL DIFFERENCES AND LEADERSHIP

People as early as Plato remarked that only "some natures […] ought to […] be leaders in the State" (Republic, Book V; Jowett, 1871). The attempt to validly predict which people are those natures that Plato referred to, is based on specific psychological or biological characteristics which influence our behavior. In leadership literature this attempt is called the trait approach. The trait approach focuses on the question in how far individual differences in certain traits influence leadership behavior and leadership outcomes. This approach was one of the first attempts to systematically study leadership. Its history is split in half: Until the 1980s research failed to document consistent and stable relationships between latent traits and leadership (Mann, 1959; Stogdill, 1948). Thus, the trait approach was challenged by the universality of leadership relevant traits. In the second phase, the very same approach has gained steam since new research demonstrated meaningful and stable relations between latent traits and leadership (Antonakis, Day, & Schyns, 2012).

This upward trend was undoubtedly tied to two major advancements in research. The first advancement was the development of the meta-analytic research method that suddenly allowed quantitatively reviewing primary studies on the link between traits and leadership. With the introduction of meta-analytic research methods many sources of errors tied to primary studies could be controlled (e.g., sampling errors due to small samples) which in consequence lead to meaningful and stable correlates. The second advancement was a conceptual one that referred to the hierarchical organization of latent traits.

Theoretical considerations (primarily the lexical approach; Borkenau & Ostendorf, 1990) lead to a widely accepted taxonomy of personality traits – the Big Five taxonomy – that allowed classifying and systematizing the many non-cognitive traits. Therefore, personality traits received more clarity in their definition and hierarchical organization which had direct implications on their operationalization. As a consequence, research in this second phase of the trait approach was more aligned with regard to measurement, definition, and interpretation of personality traits. This alignment as well as the use of meta-analytic methods resulted in support for the trait approach (e.g., Judge et al., 2002).

As already mentioned ability and personality traits are commonly systematized in hierarchical models. Ability and the Big Five are considered as higher order or general traits that comprise a number of lower-order abilities or personality traits. These lower-order traits describe more specific dimensions (e.g., verbal intelligence, spatial intelligence or locus of control, self-esteem, sociability, dominance, achievement) and are also

related to leadership (Judge et al., 2002; Judge et al., 2004). While some individual differences researchers argue that general conceptions are too global to predict actual life criteria (e.g., Hough, 1992), others state that "broader and richer personality traits will have higher predictive validity than narrower traits" (Ones & Viswesvaran, 1996, p. 622).

Scheerens (2012) gives an overview of personality traits (both narrow and broad) and competencies which are regarded as relevant for leadership behavior and, subsequently, leader effectiveness in school settings (see Table 1). Although, we agree that lower-order personality traits can explain additional variance of leadership effectiveness and are certainly popular in (educational) research, it would be far too extensive to include also narrow personality traits and ability concepts in this chapter. Thus, we will provide a short overview of relevant empirical findings on the relationship between leadership and the higher order traits cognitive ability as well as personality. The subsequent review is divided into leadership findings in non-educational and educational settings.

Table 1. Overview on leadership traits, leadership styles, leadership behaviors, and potential intermediary variables (redrawn after Scheerens, 2012, p. 136)

Relevant Personality Traits and Competencies	Leadership Style	Leadership Behavior	Effectiveness Enhancing Factors
Extraversion Social appraisal skills	Task related →	External contacts Buffering	Enhanced teaching time
Intelligence Motivation Internal locus of control Doman specific knowledge Conscientiousness		Direction setting (goals, standards) Monitors curriculum and instruction (managing the instructional program)	Clear goals and standards Opportunity to learn Student monitoring & feedback Structured teaching Active teaching Active learning
Extraversion Social appraisal skills Self confidence	Person-related →	Human Resource Management & Development Coaches teachers Recruits teachers Builds consensus	Cohesion among teachers Professionalization Teacher competency Teacher's sense of self-efficacy
Basic human values General moral beliefs Role responsibility		Sets values Creates climate	Shared sense of purpose among teachers High expectations Disciplinary climate Supportive climate

Personality and Leadership

Meta-analytic research has clearly indicated that personality is related to leadership. When summarizing 73 primary studies, Judge et al. (2002) demonstrated that all Big Five factors explain 23% of the leadership performance variance. Undoubtedly, not every Big Five trait was equally strongly related to leadership. Extraversion was, in fact, the strongest correlate of leadership ($\rho = .31$), meaning that those who are assertive, outgoing, and energetic appear as strong and high performing leaders. Conscientiousness ($\rho = .28$) followed by Emotional Stability and Openness to Experience (both $\rho = .24$) also showed a substantive link to leadership. Solely Agreeableness displayed a relatively weak correlation with leadership ($\rho = .08$), indicating that modesty, tact, or sensitivity is not of high importance for leaders. Similar results not only apply to various cultures (e.g., China, Thailand; Silverthorne, 2001) but have also been reported in other meta-analyses (e.g., Barrick, Mount, & Judge, 2001).

With respect to variables moderating the link between personality and leadership, two major sets of moderators can be differentiated (Hoffman, Woehr, Maldagen-Youngjohn, & Lyons, 2011): 1) situational moderators describing variables that shape the working situation a leader is operating in and 2) methodological moderators relating to features that describe the research approach (cf. also Figure 1).

With regard to a leader's working situation Ng, Ang, and Chan (2008) reported that the degree of job autonomy positively impacts the relation between personality and leader effectiveness while work-related stress negatively influences the same relationship. Thus, it can be stated that extraverted, conscientious, or emotionally stable leaders are only performing well when there is freedom of decision and a low level of work-related stress. Mischel's (1977) Theory of Situational Constraint corroborates these findings. Pertaining to this theory the impact of personality is muted when the situation is strongly structured. Such situations are said to limit the expression of individual personalities, rendering them practically irrelevant. The opposite holds true for weakly structured, highly autonomous situations. In such situations individuals can be induced to act in many different ways and, thus, personality differences matter more.

Besides job autonomy and work-related stress there are further situational aspects that influence the importance of personality traits for leadership. Among these, organizational type as well as the duration leaders are working with their team, are the most influential ones. Hoffman et al. (2011) demonstrated, for instance, that the personality traits dominance and self-confidence were more strongly correlated with leader effectiveness in business compared to government organizations whereas the opposite held true for adjustment and interpersonal skills as the latter two were more strongly related to leader effectiveness in government compared to business organizations.

Cavazotte, Moreno, and Hickman (2012) argue that there are certain personality traits that lead to leadership success when the leader is rather unfamiliar with the team whereas the very same traits hamper success once the leader and the team know each other well. Extraversion, for instance, is one of these personality traits: While assertive, outgoing and extraverted behavior might be regarded as high performance when the team and the leader start working together or collaborate only in a short-term project. The very same behavior, however, might not be impressive anymore once the team gets to know the leader and the role of extraversion thus weakens.

Regarding the most important situational moderators it can be summed up that individual differences in personality traits are of particular importance for leadership when 1) leaders have a high level of autonomy in their job and 2) when they do not suffer from extreme stress. Moreover, there are certain personality traits that are more central in government compared to private organizations and some traits foster leadership at the beginning of a group dynamic process while they hamper performance once the team and the leader are familiar with one another.

In contrast to situational moderators methodological ones mainly refer to the way leadership outcomes and personality traits are operationalized. For example, personality traits operationalized by performance measures reveal the strongest correlation with leader effectiveness while personality traits assessed by paper-pencil-questionnaires and projective tests lead to lower trait-leadership correlations (Hoffman et al., 2011). Similarly, the operationalization of leadership outcomes clearly moderates the trait-leadership correlation. Personality traits were more strongly related to ratings of effectiveness ($r = .29$) than to objective indices of effectiveness ($r = .21$). Thus, personality traits seem to be better predictors of leadership effectiveness if effectiveness is rated by others.

Leadership is a process of influencing people to work towards the attainment of organizational goals, but for many years research tended to take a one-sided look at leadership: it concentrated on the positive aspects and more or less overlooked the dark side of leadership; leadership derailment. Recent failures and scandals as well as the economic crises in 2009 desensitized the topic of leadership derailment. Within the trait approach the question arose which traits lead to a leader's derailment? With regard to this question the Dark Triad is of particular interest. The Dark Triad is a term used to describe the three socially undesirable personality traits narcissism, psychopathy, and Machiavellianism (Paulhus & Williams, 2002). Psychopathy refers to a pattern of callous, remorseless manipulation and exploitation of others (Hare, 1991). Narcissism is characterized by dominance, exhibitionism, and exploitation as well as feelings of superiority and entitlement (Raskin & Terry, 1988) whereas Machiavellianism denotes individual differences in manipulativeness, insincerity, and callousness (Christie & Geis, 1970).

All three dark personality traits correlate positively with laissez-faire leadership, passive as well as abusive leadership and are negatively linked to transformational leadership (Felfe, Gatzka, Elprana, Stiehl, & Schyns, 2013; Westerlaken & Woods, 2013). Interestingly, it has been shown that these dark traits can also have a positive impact on leadership, particularly from a short-time view. Narcissists, for instance, had a higher chance of being promoted to a leading position because they were seen as self-confident and convincing, two socially desirable facets of narcissism (Brunell et al., 2008; see also Nevicka, De Hoogh, Van Vianen, Beersma, & McIlwain, 2011). On the long run this initial positive impression has been interpreted as arrogance and haughtiness, two socially undesirable facets of the very same trait (Benson & Campbell, 2007).

Furthermore, it appears as if the link between the dark triad and leadership can be described as non-linear. Benson and Campbell (2007) demonstrated an inverted u-shaped relationship between leadership behavior and the dark triad facets Ego-Centrism, Manipulation, Micro-Managing, Intimidation, and Passive Aggression. Those leaders who had medium high scores of these facets received better leadership ratings than those with extremely high or respectively low scores.

In summary, individual differences in personality clearly influence the emergence and performance of leaders. The relationship between personality traits and leadership outcomes is moderated by various situational and methodological variables and appears to be not only linear but also curvilinear in shape. Although there is ample evidence for the link between personality and leadership the question remains why this link exists. Besides the fact that personality could be per se relevant for being a successfully performing leader it might also be that personality is linked to leadership performance because it represents those traits that others implicitly expect leaders to have. Thus, it is also possible that empirical results partly provide support for Lord and colleagues' Implicit Theory of Leadership (e.g., Lord, de Vader, & Alliger, 1986). This, however, would mean that the summarized findings simply indicate a close correspondence between the way people's personalities are seen and the stereotypical conceptions of the characteristics of leaders. Therefore, it might be that, for instance, the link between extraversion and leadership performance partly exists because individuals implicitly expect leaders to be extraverted and not because extraversion contributes to better performance. Further research is certainly needed to study the reason why personality is related to leadership.

Cognitive Ability and Leadership

Undoubtedly cognitive ability (also called general mental ability or g) is one of the best predictors of work performance. Cognitive ability predicts both the occupational level attained by persons and their performance within the chosen occupation. It correlates about $\rho = .50$ with later occupational levels, performance in job training programs, and performance on the job (Hunter, Schmidt, & Le, 2006). Compared to other traits, particularly non-cognitive personality traits, the relationship between cognitive ability and work-related outcomes is much stronger. The importance of cognitive ability for the job even increases with the complexity of the job (Salgado, Anderson, Moscoso, Bertua, de Fruyt, & Rolland, 2003): The more complex a job, the more cognitive ability is needed to manage it successfully.

The fact that leadership tasks are of high complexity and that understanding complex issues is a core duty of leaders, suggests that cognitive ability is even more important for leaders compared to non-leaders. Interestingly, empirical research only partly supports this assumption. In general, the correlation between cognitive ability and job performance is weaker for individuals in supervisory compared to non-supervisory positions. In a meta-analysis with more than 40,000 leaders Judge

et al. (2004) reported a correlation of $\rho = .21$ ($\rho = .27$, corrected for range restriction) between cognitive ability and leadership. A similarly strong link between cognitive ability and leadership was described in a more recent meta-analysis by Hoffman, et al., (2011). Only weak links were found between cognitive ability and laissez-faire ($\rho = -.16$) as well as transformational ($\rho = .16$) leadership style (DeRue, Nahrgang, Wellman, & Humprey, 2011).

The impression might arise that the mental ability and capacity of a leader only marginally influences his/her performance. However, considering recent moderator analyses this impression is clearly one based on misinterpretation. Consecutively, a summary of the major results regarding moderator analyses as well as curvilinear and long-term effects of cognitive ability will be given.

Findings on moderator variables are split into methodological and situational ones (Hoffman et al., 2011). Regarding the latter it shall be recalled that leaders commonly fulfill their tasks under enormous pressure and with high risks. Cognitive Resource Theory, as one example of the initially discussed Contingency Theories, suggests that stressful situations nourish self-doubt, fear of failure, as well as evaluation anxiety. These emotions divert leaders' intellectual abilities from the task and may tie up his or her attentional resources that could otherwise be used for planning, problem solving and making judgments (Fiedler & Garcia, 1987). Thus, stressful situations impede the use of all intellectual abilities available and reduce the validity of cognitive ability. In line with Cognitive Resource Theory it was found that cognitive ability is of particular importance in relatively stress-free situations ($\rho = .32$; Judge et al., 2004).

Cognitive Resource Theory is also used to explain the finding that intelligent leaders who are directive, more likely lead effectively (Judge et al., 2004). The rationale behind this is that followers receive the benefit of the leader's cognitive ability (e.g., develops better strategies, makes better decisions) only if he or she clearly communicates what to do. In addition, it might be argued that directive leaders would rather focus on structuring tasks or developing strategies which are described as duties that demand high cognitive abilities. In contrast, those who prefer a more participating leadership style might place emphasis on people-oriented tasks that claim an elaborate set of non-cognitive traits for success.

The question of whether cognitive ability is of comparable importance for every industry sector was studied by Hoffman et al. (2011). The authors reported that the role of intelligence is far more important for being successful in private ($\rho = .23$) compared to governmental organizations ($\rho = .12$). One possible explanation might be that governmental organizations are commonly highly structured, reducing individual freedom for action and, thus, limiting the prognostic validity of individual differences (see Judge et al., 2002 for further information).

Regarding the most important situational moderators it can be summarized that cognitive ability makes a difference for leadership 1) when leaders operate in a relatively stress-free situation, 2) when they communicate rather directively with their followers, and 3) when they have a certain freedom of action to prove their cognitive abilities.

In addition to situational moderators, research on methodological moderators clearly displayed that it is important to consider how leadership outcomes are operationalized. For instance, Judge et al. (2004) stated that the intelligence-leadership link is stronger when leadership performance was measured using objective indices ($\rho = .25$) instead of subjective indices for leader emergence ($\rho = .19$) and leader effectiveness ($\rho = .15$).

With regard to the relation between cognitive ability and leadership it could also be argued that this relationship is a curvilinear one and linear approaches are simply not able to correctly characterize it. Several early studies around Ghiselli (1963) and Stogdill (1948) reported that individuals with either very high or very low IQ-scores had a higher

chance for career derailment. In fact, this inverted u-shaped correlation between cognitive ability and leadership might be due to the discrepancy between the leader's and the follower's cognitive ability. The more or respectively less intelligent a leader is the more his or her vocational objectives, communication strategies, interests, and behavioral patterns will diverge from those of the followers (cf. also Simonton, 1985).

In summary, individual differences in cognitive ability are related to the emergence and performance of leaders. The fact that the relationship is rather small and moderated by stress-level, directive communication and freedom of action suggests that effective leadership probably has less to do with solving complex problems but emphasizes more on getting the best out of people. One concept that concentrates not on cognitive, but socio-emotional abilities of leaders is discussed subsequently.

Emotional Intelligence and Leadership

Emotional intelligence (EI) is among the best studied alternative concepts of intelligence within the context of leadership. The importance of emotional intelligence for leadership is comparable with the importance of other non-cognitive traits (e.g., Conscientiousness or Emotional Stability) or, for some researchers it is even more important. Daniel Goleman (1998), one of the central researchers in emotional intelligence research even stated "that emotional intelligence is the sine qua non of leadership" (p. 2). Current research suggests that emotional intelligence explains 8% of leadership performance and 5% of transformational leadership behavior. However, in empirical studies EI could neither for leadership performance nor for transformational leadership provide incremental information above and beyond cognitive ability (Cavazotte et al., 2012). Since similar findings have been reported for jobs with no supervisory responsibilities it must be summarized, so far, EI does not contribute unique information to the topic of leadership.

Emotional Intelligence researchers debate heatedly how the concept could be operationalized and measured adequately. While Reuven Bar-On (2000) uses a self-assessment inventory, the EQ-I (Emotional-Quotient inventory), Salovey and colleagues (Mayer, Salovey, Caruso, & Sitarenios, 2003) developed the MSCEIT (Mayer-Salovey-Caruso Emotional Intelligence Test), an ability test, where one answer is more 'appropriate' than the other. A third approach is Goleman's ESCI (Emotional and Social Competence Inventory, Boyatzis, Goleman, & Rhee, 1999), which uses 360° evaluations to measure peoples' emotional intelligence. With regard to the last approach of operationalization it is important to note that the 360° evaluation uses the ratings of other people to measure a leader's emotional intelligence. This of course opens up the influence of implicit leadership theories as the relationship between leadership and emotional intelligence measured from an other person's perspective might easily occur solely because individuals implicitly expect leaders to be emotionally intelligent and not because the trait contributes to better leadership performance.

Two intelligence concepts related to emotional intelligence are also of high interest for leadership: Social Intelligence and Cultural Intelligence. While so far there are no empirical results on the relevance of social intelligence for leadership cultural intelligence is supposed to be a significant predictor for leader effectiveness in culturally diverse settings. The capability to manage culturally diverse settings is critical to leaders operating in international contexts. Rockstuhl, Seiler, Ang, van Dyne, and Annen (2011) demonstrated that emotional intelligence is a stronger predictor of domestic leadership effectiveness than cultural intelligence whereas cultural intelligence is a better predictor of cross-border leadership effectiveness than emotional intelligence. In summary, empirical

findings on alternative concepts of intelligence suggest that they are of similar importance to leadership as non-cognitive personality traits. However, there is no evidence that alternative concepts of intelligence offer information about leadership that is not already covered by cognitive ability (cf. discussion by Antonakis, Ashkanasy, & Dasborough, 2009).

Creativity and Leadership

The tasks of leaders have been changing in the past decades. Undoubtedly, there is a shift from management tasks to leadership and entrepreneurial tasks. In business it is commonly expected that leaders solve problems using new perspectives and innovative solutions. Moreover, leaders ought to support those employees that bring in creative business ideas. They should encourage their subordinates to try new ways of approaching well-known problems. All these expectations that should be fulfilled by leaders basically address their creative potential. Although creativity has often been proposed as an important component of effective leadership, its link is hardly understood. Recent meta-analytic findings show that leadership effectiveness is stronger related to creativity than to intelligence. Hoffman et al. (2011), for instance, reported a corrected creativity-effectiveness relationship for leaders of $\rho = .31$. So far, it cannot be ruled out that a part of this correlation is based on implicit leadership theories that build upon the assumption that it is necessary to be creative in order to be an effective leader. Thus, the rating of leadership effectiveness would include implicit judgments on a leader's creativity that bring forward the creativity-effectiveness relationship.

It is frequently argued that in order to obtain creativity in organizations it is necessary to bring in new leaders. Harris, Li, Boswell, Zhang, and Xie (2013) clearly demonstrated that empowering leadership positively predicts a newcomer's creativity. Empowering leadership seems to be a key aspect when fostering creativity. It primarily involves sharing power with a view towards enhancing followers' motivation and investment in their work. Empowering leadership positively influenced both, the employees' creative process engagement and their intrinsic motivation which directly led to higher employee creativity (Zhang & Bartol, 2010).

Next to leadership empowerment, leadership style appears to be of particular importance when fostering the creativity of employees. Among different leadership styles transformational leadership is certainly a promising approach when fostering creativity. Transformational leaders lead by identifying the needed change, creating a vision to guide the change through inspiration, and executing the change with the commitment of the team members. Employees' creativity seems to be particularly positively influenced by transformational and authentic leadership styles (Rego, Sousa, & Marques, 2012; Rosing, Frese, & Bausch, 2011). The inspiring and motivating nature of transformational leadership should enable employees to proactively bring in new ideas and thoughts and should further provide them with the confidence to perform beyond the expectations specified. Regarding meta-analytic results reported by Rosing et al. (2011) transformational leadership has a stronger correlation with innovation at the organizational level ($\rho = .37$) than at the team ($\rho = .25$) or individual level ($\rho = .17$).

Further research on the link between transformational leadership and creativity suggests that this relationship is moderated by many situational aspects. The relationship, for instance, gets stronger when employees receive a high degree of task and relational support from their leaders (Cheung & Wong, 2011). Moreover, Kearney and Gebert (2009) reported only a positive link for highly diverse working teams whereas Garcia-Morales, Matias-Reche, and Hurtado-Torres (2008) showed that transformational leadership is of particular importance for creativity when organizations focus more on organizational learning. Moreover, it seems as if transformational leadership creates

a basis that allows teams of cognitive diversity to inspire their team members to produce more creativity on an individual level (Shin, Kim, Lee, & Bian, 2012).

While transformational leadership positively relates to creativity, authoritarian and transactional leadership negatively influenced work group and, respectively, employee creativity (Pieterse, van Knippenberg, Schippers, & Stam, 2009; Zhang, Tsui, & Wang, 2011). In summary, present research has not yet arrived at a conclusion whether specific leadership styles foster or impede creativity on an individual, team, and organizational level. In addition, leadership is seldom studied in relation to creativity, compared to the other three individual traits discussed. One reason for this lack of attention might be the trouble of operationalizing creativity. Future advancement in the measurement of creativity is certainly needed to appropriately estimate the importance of creativity in the field of leadership.

3. INDIVIDUAL DIFFERENCES AND EDUCATIONAL LEADERSHIP

After discussing the relationships of selected leader traits on different leader outcomes in non-educational contexts, we will now review research on individual trait differences in relation to educational leadership. In addition we will draw implications from the findings in other organizational fields and examine in how far these variables could reveal similar results and impact school principals' effectiveness.

In educational leadership research many studies who claim to study individual differences at the trait level mainly include demographic variables such as age, gender, years of leadership experience etc. (e.g., Cox 2006; Ibukun, Oyewole, & Abe, 2011; cf. also a review by Hallinger, 2008). Therefore, Leithwood et al. (2006) state that "little research has focused on personality traits or intelligence" (p. 14) in connection with successful school leadership. Based on the empirical findings reviewed above it would seem advisable to include other than purely demographic variables as 'antecedent variables' influencing 'principal leadership' and 'outcomes' (cf. Hallinger, 2008). Including traits such as personality or intelligence in the research studies could provide additional information when predicting future leadership behavior. This information could then be used to select and develop leaders who work in the educational setting. The subsequent chapters summarize findings from studies on individual trait differences and educational leadership and also incorporate results from leadership studies in other occupational fields.

Personality and Educational Leadership

With regard to personality, most leadership research focuses on Costa and McCrae's (1992) factor analytical approach which identified the so-called *Big Five*: Neuroticism, Extraversion, Openness, Conscientiousness and Agreeableness (cf. Judge et al., 2002, for an overview of research on their relation to leadership). A recent study by Grunes, Gudmundsson, and Irmer (2014) examined 144 educational leaders with regard to their personality (i.e., Big Five Inventory; John, Donahue, & Kentle, 1991), cognitive ability (i.e., Wonderlic Personnel Test; Wonderlic, 2003) as well as emotional intelligence (i.e., MSCEIT; Mayer et al., 2003). The performance of the leaders was obtained through self, supervisor, colleague and staff ratings of leadership behavior and effectiveness.

Grunes et al. (2014) found significant correlations between transformational leadership behavior and openness ($r = .34$), neuroticism (i.e., the scale emotional stability reversed, $r = -.29$), and agreeableness ($r = .30$). Openness was also significantly related to all outcome variables (satisfaction, $r = .18$; effectiveness, $r =$

.24; extra effort; $r = .27$), while other personality traits only showed correlations with specific dependent variables (neuroticism*satisfaction, $r = -.22$; agreeableness*satisfaction, $r = .30$; conscientiousness*extra effort, $r = .20$). In multiple regression analyses, some personality traits could also significantly predict the criteria used in the study: Openness and neuroticism significantly predicted transformational leadership behavior ($\beta = .26$ and $\beta = -.25$, respectively) and effectiveness ($\beta = .20$ and $\beta = -.21$, respectively), while only openness (of all predictors) proved to be important for extra effort of followers ($\beta = .24$). The authors conclude that personality traits such as openness and emotional stability may be especially important in identifying transformational leaders, but also play a role for specific leadership outcomes (effectiveness, extra effort of followers).

What seems interesting is that the findings of Grunes et al. (2014) regarding the Big Five personality traits do not exactly reflect those of Judge et al. (2002) reported in section 2. Although both studies found personality traits to be significant predictors of leadership effectiveness, Judge and colleagues named extraversion and conscientiousness as strongest predictors whereas in the study with school leaders openness and emotional stability were the most important personality traits. Agreeableness predicted transformational leadership behavior in other organizational settings (Judge & Bono, 2000) as well as in school settings (Grunes et al., 2014). By conducting additional analyses with the data of school leaders presented by Grunes et al. (2014) significantly higher mean values were found in all personality traits but openness if compared to the mean described in the norm population (calculated using unpaired *t*-tests, norm values taken from Srivastava, John, Gosling, & Potter, 2003; Neuroticism was reversed into Emotional Stability). The descriptive statistics for agreeableness ($M=4.26$, $SD=.58$) and conscientiousness ($M = 4.47$, $SD = .52$) show that all principals seem to score strongly on these two traits (scales are from 1 = low to 5 = high value) with only small variability between individuals, which limits the predictive value of the independent variable.

The fact that most of the principals perceive themselves as very thorough, careful and vigilant—as could be inferred from Grunes et al. (2014)—could explain why conscientiousness does not indicate successful leader behavior in this particular organizational setting. Moreover, although replicated across different studies and cultures (Barrick et al., 2001; Judge et al., 2002; Silverthorne, 2002), it seems that for school leaders being extraverted is not predictive of being successful, but rather how open they are towards new ideas, cultures and experiences and how emotionally stable they are. This could also relate to Cavazotte et al.'s (2012) findings that leaders' extraversion plays a more important role for their success in short-lived encounters, which usually does not apply to school leaders who work with their team for longer periods of time (often, at least in Austria they have even worked with the same team as teachers before becoming principals in 'their' school). This aspect holds special importance if principal selection is strongly based on interviews in which extraverted individuals have shown to be more successful than others (Caldwell & Burger, 1998). This could mean that assessors better concentrate on other aspects than extraversion when interviewing school leadership candidates.

The Big Five model is certainly the most widely accepted personality model. However, when it comes to research in the organizational context a psychodynamic personality model based on Carl Gustav Jung's theory is also frequently employed. This personality model consists of the four bipolar dimensions Extraversion vs. Introversion (EI); Sensing vs. Intuition (SN); Judging vs. Perceiving (JP); Thinking vs. Feeling (TF) that show great overlap with the Big Five traits (see e.g., Furnham, 1996; Harvey, Murry, & Markham, 1995).

Two US dissertations (Holder, 2009; Mendiburu 2010) used this alternative personality model in an attempt to identify the relationship between principals' personality and school success. Holder (2009) found no relationship between the personality traits and student achievement as measured by Adequate Yearly Progress (AYP) on the math part of a national Georgia competency test. Mendiburu (2010) found individuals with high extroverted, intuitive, feeling, and judging scores (EIFJ) to be the prominent personality type among school leaders who were regarded as successful due to having continuously raised their school's Academic Performance Index (API) in the last three years. However, both studies have a mere descriptive approach and cannot be regarded as representative due to small sample sizes (N=39 and N=12, respectively).

Also Gardner and Martinko (1990) used the Myer-Briggs Type Indicator to identify personality types of 40 school leaders. Their dependent variables consisted of observed work behavior (principals were observed for several days by external assessors who coded their behavior) as well as of performance level which was obtained from a conglomeration of several indicators (student performance, supervisor ratings etc.). The authors found that 63% of the high performing principals were either ISTJs (introvert, sensing, thinking, judging) or ESTJs (extrovert, sensing, thinking, judging). Gardner and Martinko (1990) state that this result is in line with findings from lower and middle level managers in other occupational settings. Interestingly, however, none of the three studies using the MBTI found the same prevailing personality type amongst school leaders (Holder, 2009, identified ESFJ [extrovert, sensing, feeling, judging] as the most frequent type in her study). The fact that Gardner and Martinko (1990) found extraverted as well as introverted school leaders to be successful, corroborates the view that it does not matter whether school leaders score high or low on the trait Extraversion, as either can be effective if they work at a school for a longer period of time. At this point it is important to keep in mind that personal traits primarily seem to play a role in low stress situations, but lose their impact when – in this case – principals have to work under high pressure or strongly externally-determined circumstances, where the role of individual differences fades (Judge et al., 2002). Thus, it will depend on educational systems, school types but also on other situational aspects if principals find weakly structured, autonomous workplaces where their personality can actually matter.

The 'dark' side of personality has also found its way into educational research, however, focusing more strongly on, e.g., narcissism of children and youths (e.g., Twenge & Campbell, 2003) than on narcissism relating to principal leadership behavior. The only studies which could be found on narcissism of school leaders, do not relate the trait to leadership outcome variables (but to sources of stress and cognitive-decision making style, repetively; Carr, 1994; Maleki, 2013). The question whether narcissism, Machiavellianism and psychopathy are relevant for educators will hopefully fuel new research interests. This could be especially important as narcissists have been shown to have higher chances of obtaining a leading position, because they are very self-confident and convincing (Brunell et al., 2008). Moreover, a limited amount of manipulation, ego-centrism, micro-managing, intimidation and passive aggression were even perceived as positive for leaders (Benson & Campbell, 2007). However, strong 'dark' personality traits correlate with laissez-faire and abusive leadership (Felfe et al., 2013), which would not be desirable in any occupational setting, but especially not in schools were leaders not only influence their employees, but indirectly also pupil performance (e.g., Scheerens, 2012). With regard to these 'dark' traits it is suggested that they are taken into account when selecting principals at schools. This seems to be of specific importance as individuals scoring high on the 'dark' traits might have particularly strong faking

tendencies in selection settings. Maximum performance measures, such as cognitive intelligence are less affected by faking tendencies and will be discussed subsequently.

Cognitive Ability and Educational Leadership

An indicator of the underrepresentation of the concept of cognitive ability in educational research is the fact that the word 'cognitive ability' (or any synonyms thereof) does not even appear in the glossary of Kenneth Leithwood and Philip Hallinger's very extensive *Second International Handbook of Educational Leadership and Administration* (2002). What seems remarkable however, is that intelligence is frequently mentioned in articles on successful school principals as being an important characteristic. McEwan (2003) created a list of 37 – what she loosely called – traits and asked 108 principals, teachers, central office administrators and others to choose those 10 traits out of the 37 which are "essential to being a good principal" (p. xxiii). Nearly a quarter voted for 'intelligence' as a trait of highly effective principals.

The already discussed study by Grunes et al. (2014) also investigated the impact of cognitive ability on leadership behaviors and outcomes. Surprisingly, Grunes et al. (2014) found a significant negative relationship between cognitive ability and transformational leadership behavior ($r = -.26$) as well as extra effort of staff ($r = -.18$). Cognitive ability (together with the personality traits Neuroticism and Openness) also predicted transformational leadership behavior significantly in a regression analysis ($\beta = -.20$). The authors explain this finding on the one hand from a methodological perspective, namely that the negative relationship could be due to range restrictions in cognitive ability of the sample. On the other hand, Grunes et al. (2014) argue that principals with higher cognitive abilities might focus more on the instructional and teaching-related tasks of their job than on transformational leadership behaviors.

185

Keeping contingency theoretical approaches in mind, which strongly stress the importance of leadership styles appropriate to the specific setting in which a leader acts, high cognitive abilities could prove more important when instructional leadership is required. As Hallinger (2003) points out, this could more strongly be the case for 'schools at risk' which require setting clear and timely goals.

As research on the link between cognitive abilities and effective school leadership is rather scarce, we also have to look at results from other occupational settings. Even if it is by now well-established that cognitive ability is the single best predictor of work success and it also predicts leadership effectiveness substantially (Judge et al., 2004; Schmidt & Hunter, 1998), the question remains whether this is true in all occupational settings, especially that of a school leader. Overall, educational work is to be regarded as a job which involves tasks of high complexity, for which cognitive ability is more important than in jobs with lower complexity (Salgado et al., 2003). Depending on the country, a minimum cognitive ability level may be ensured by including cognitive ability-tests in selection procedures for students enrolling in teaching programs. In Austria, a new law determines that as of 2015 all applicants for teaching degrees must take an assessment test including a cognitive ability test, before they can start their teacher education program. Such selection procedures and the requirement of (in most educational systems) completing tertiary education programs to become a teacher, leads to the assumption that principals exhibit at least average cognitive ability. This is also shown in one of the most important studies regarding intelligence and job occupation (Harrell & Harrell, 1945) which revealed a mean intelligence quotient of 122.8 (SD=12.8) in teachers, which lies significantly over the population mean of 100. However, cognitive abilities are rarely used in principal selection procedures as an overview by Huber and Hiltmann (2010) shows.

The predictive value of cognitive ability for leadership success in schools might be restricted due to operationalization problems of the outcome variable, which, however, is common to all leadership research. It was found in non-educational settings that cognitive ability predicts objective leadership outcomes (e.g., salary or number of staff) better than subjective ones (e.g., 360° effectiveness evaluations; Judge et al., 2004). However, what is regarded as useful objective measurements in other organizational settings must clearly be re-evaluated for school leaders. In Austria as well as in other educational systems, the salaries of school leaders depend on school size as well as on working experience, and hold no relation to performance. Similarly, the number of staff (i.e., teachers, non-educational staff, and probably pupils) depends on school location and school type and does not necessarily reflect how effective a principal is (this might be different if pupils can choose which school to attend). One of the most frequently employed objective measures of school leadership effectiveness is students' achievement (cf. Scheerens, 2012). Whether such measures are more strongly linked to principals' cognitive ability than an assessment of his or her effectiveness by colleagues and supervisors, still needs to be examined.

The impact of intelligence on predicting leadership success also depends on situational aspects. Findings show that the impact of intelligence is higher in settings where leaders have more autonomy and, thus, their individual differences in cognitive ability play a more important role in their behavior. In situations (or also educational systems) which strongly limit the range of behaviors that people can demonstrate, individual traits become less important (cf. also Judge et al., 2004). To a certain extent this could also hold true for school leadership, especially in public schools which are strongly centralized. Hoffman et al. (2011) showed lower predictive validity of cognitive ability in governmental organizations compared to private ones. This finding nourishes the assumption that principals' intelligence has a stronger impact on their effectiveness in more autonomous, private schools as opposed to public ones.

Cognitive Resource Theory (Fiedler & Garcia, 1987) assumes that highly stressful situations tie leaders' intellectual abilities and, thus, reduce the validity of cognitive ability for predicting leadership outcomes. School leaders' work incorporates on the one hand many situations which are highly stressful and require rather immediate decisions or actions where they also carry strong responsibility for others. On the other hand, leading a school also includes situations where, e.g., long-term planning is required and principals can draw on their cognitive abilities more strongly due to low immediate stress. Therefore, it could well be that a more experienced school principal who has already provided a high quality solution to a specific stressful situation in the past (e.g., conflict with parents) can react more effectively in a stressful situation than an inexperienced but more intelligent leader (cf. Yukl, 2011).

For school leaders also the observed curvilinear relationships between cognitive ability and effectiveness (Ghiselli, 1963; Stogdill, 1948) could be an important issue. If, for instance, a school leader has very high cognitive ability this might also reflect in a rather sophisticated communicative style. As a consequence teachers, but also pupils and parents might not be able to relate to his or her ideas because they are simply communicated in a too complex manner to understand. This in consequence will lead to school outcomes that are not better than that of a school with a principal with average cognitive intelligence.

However, leaders' cognitive ability seems to have more impact if leaders explicitly share their ideas with their co-workers in a directive manner (Judge et al., 2004). Thus, for school leaders their higher intelligence could deem irrelevant if they only create brilliant school development plans, but do not tell their teachers and staff what to do and how to implement these developments. If the school leader does, in contrast, incorporate a more participative leadership style where decision-making processes are shared with the teachers, principals' cognitive ability would have less impact on the outcome and non-cognitive traits such as personality or emotional intelligence could gain greater importance.

Emotional Intelligence and Educational Leadership

With regard to emotional intelligence the research corpus in school leadership does not look as bleak as with cognitive ability as this seems to be a more popular concept in educational leadership research. Stone, Parker, and Wood (2005), e.g., examined whether self-assessed emotional intelligence is a significant predictor of successful school administration (assessed by superiors as well as colleagues). Four hundred principals and vice-principals filled in the Emotional Quotient Inventory (EQ-i; Bar-On (1997), while three staff members and their immediate supervisor were asked to fill in a questionnaire on task-oriented and relationship-oriented leadership performance.

Stone et al. (2005) found that participants with higher externally-assessed leadership abilities also had higher emotional intelligence scores in all four subscales (intrapersonal, interpersonal, adaptability and management) except for the general mood scale. In this study the problem of assessing leadership success by external raters became evident in rather low intercorrelations between staff members' and superiors' leadership ability assessments ($r = .20$ and $r = .21$ for relationship and task-oriented leadership, respectively). However, the intercorrelations with self-reported leadership abilities were even lower (between $r = .12$ and $r = .16$ for staff and supervisor rated leadership abilities, respectively). Moderate and significant correlations between leadership abilities and emotional intelligence scales were found if abilities were self-reported ($r = .51$), and low to non-significant relationships showed when leadership abilities were assessed by others (especially when assessed by superiors, $r = .11$, compared to staff, $r = .16$). Methodological moderators (i.e., which criterion was used and how this was measured) played an important role in determining which dimensions of emotional intelligence served as significant predictors. In general it was shown, that all of the five subscales from the EQ-i contributed significantly to predicting leadership abilities in one setting or another, although their predictive validity was not very high. The results also suggest that emotional intelligence as a predictor of leadership outcome variables is strongly influenced by various moderators, which discourages more generalized conclusions.

In a dissertation by Cook (2006), 143 elementary school principals in Montana, US, filled in a self-assessment instrument for leadership performance and a standardized emotional intelligence questionnaire based on Goleman's model (1998). He found that principals with very high self-ascribed emotional intelligence also differed significantly from those with high or improvable ratings with regard to their leadership performance. Cook (2006) interprets these findings as an indicator that emotional intelligence relates to successful school leadership performance, but also points to the problem of using self-assessments.

Bardach (2008) investigated the relationship between 50 principals' emotional intelligence (measured with the MSCEIT) and whether schools met the Annual Yearly Progress (AYP) targets which were set by the government in their state (Maryland, US). Using logistic regression, he found that an increase of 10 points in emotional intelligence of the school leader would increase the chances of the school to meet the AYP targets by 5.8%. From Bardach's (2008) results it could be concluded that there is a significant positive relationship between principals' emotional intelligence and school success, which can be seen as an objective indicator of leadership effectiveness.

Another dissertation in the US by Reynolds (2011) investigated the emotional intelligence of 34 principals of successful middle schools (designated Middle Schools to Watch, identified by a recognition program of highly effective schools). Reynolds could show that the principals of the highly successful schools displayed emotional intelligence scores, as determined by Goleman's ECI questionnaire, which were significantly higher than the norm population in all 18 facets. In line with Bardach (2008) she also concludes that there is a positive relationship between the emotional intelligence of a school leader and the school's success.

Williams (2008) used qualitative structured interviews which were then coded into quantitative data to determine whether outstanding principals can be distinguished from typical ones based on their emotional and social intelligence. The 20 principals (12 outstanding, 8 typical) of different school types were selected through a peer/supervisor/teacher nomination process. In the interview principals were prompted to vividly describe two situations where they felt effective and one situation where they felt ineffective in their job. Outstanding principals demonstrated significantly higher emotional intelligence scores in the following five competencies: self-confidence, self-control, conscientiousness, achievement orientation and initiative. In addition they scored higher in the following social competence factors: organizational awareness, developing others, leadership, influence, change catalyst, conflict management and teamwork. However, if we look at these clusters in detail, the question arises in how far the dependent variable of leadership behavior (average vs. outstanding) confounds with the independent variables (e.g. developing others, leadership or conflict management are core aspects of a leader's work and not necessarily antecedents) and thus findings may simply represent implicit leadership theories.

A very recent study (Grunes et al., 2014) on the relationship of emotional intelligence and perceived leadership outcomes, however, could not corroborate these significant relationships. Grunes et al. (2014) attempted to employ valid and reliable measures of both predictor and criterion and therefore used an ability test of emotional intelligence (MSCEIT), which has also been discussed by emotional intelligence researchers to be more useful than self-assessment questionnaires (cf. Antonakis et al., 2009). The authors could show divergent validity of emotional intelligence from cognitive ability and personality, although all dimensions also revealed significant correlations with cognitive ability (from $r = .19$ to $r = .26$). However, emotional intelligence did not significantly predict leadership behavior or leadership outcomes (satisfaction, effectiveness, extra effort). Grunes et al. (2014) conclude that the usefulness of emotional intelligence for predicting educational leadership outcomes will be limited and emotional intelligence does not have incremental validity over cognitive ability and personality, which is very much in line with what has been found in other occupational settings (Cavazotte et al., 2012).

Creativity and Educational Leadership

Creativity and 'creative leadership' has gained importance in the last decades, strongly influenced by Robert Sternberg's (2003) Triarchic Theory of Intelligence which adds creative and practical intelligence to traditional cognitive intelligence. While most people would agree that "the ability to produce work that is novel (original, unique), useful and generative" (Sternberg & Lubart, 1996, p. 677) is certainly very useful not only for school principals but in work settings in general, the major question is how this ability can be measured objectively, reliably and validly (cf. Mumford,

Hester, & Robledo, 2012). Traditional paper-pencil tests of creativity might at first sight not seem very adequate predictors of leadership success, but Hoffman et al. (2011) showed that these were more strongly related to leader effectiveness than performance measures of creativity. In addition, creativity proved to be a stronger predictor of leader effectiveness in government settings compared to business settings.

When we look at the present 'creative school leadership' research and discussions, they focus very often on the question how a leader can enable his staff to be more creative (e.g., Stoll & Temperley, 2009), but not on school leaders' own creativity. Also Leithwood, Jantzi, and Steinbach (1999) state that a core task of transformational leaders is to stimulate follower's efforts to be innovative and creative. Research on principals' creativity should receive more attention: Firstly, because according to Hoffman et al.'s (2011) findings creativity predicts leader success better than intelligence, especially in government settings and secondly, because leading a school is in most educational systems a job requiring many and frequent innovative and 'new' solutions and ideas.

4. SOLUTIONS AND RECOMMENDATIONS

It seems that researchers investigating the impact of individual differences on leadership, have not yet embarked on the journey of selecting, preparing and supporting leaders in the very specific occupational setting of schools. This task is especially important when we keep in mind that a high person-job-fit does not only contribute to fewer turnovers, but also to increased performance and job satisfaction (cf. a meta-analysis by Edwards, 1991). Thus, high accordance between a person's abilities or his or her personality traits and the demands of the job is central to positive work outcome. Although research has clearly demonstrated a link between leadership and cognitive as well as non-cognitive traits, this knowledge is, at least in the Austrian case of principal selection, not used when selecting or developing school leaders.

Using the trait approach to improve the person-job-fit of principal candidates or the person-environment-fit of a school leader and a school, is vital when we take into account the strong effects this one person has on various school outcomes (cf. Scheerens, 2012, for an overview). Considering the influence of situational moderator analyses, this also means that one applicant might be very well-suited for one (type of) school, while his or her abilities and personality traits would make a bad match for another one. Similarly to other occupational areas, where personnel development is already more strongly evolved, succession planning of school leaders in Austria could profit from using psychological assessments for teachers which involve feedback on their abilities and personality traits to increase self-awareness with regard to leadership-related abilities and traits.

Some of the (published) research we found is intentionally not reported in this chapter due to flawed application of statistical methods or other methodological weaknesses. Unpublished dissertational theses and other grey literature, however, often dealt with individual differences and educational leadership in an empirically very sound way and produced some of the results discussed in this chapter. This shows that there is a general interest in individual differences in educational leadership, but the field would profit from using psychometrically well-established measures of the independent variables, representative sample sizes and sound statistical applications. This also includes meta-analytical procedures, as we have seen from the history of the trait approach that results can remain inconclusive if they are not summarized accordingly.

In this sense, it would be desirable to conduct more studies on personality traits using Big Five measures, which can then be compared to results from other organizational settings. Psychological measures of personality have usually shown high

psychometric quality, but can also be intentionally distorted which limits their informative value in selection settings (Birkeland, Manson, Kisamore, Brannick, & Smith, 2006). They could, nevertheless, provide a highly useful feedback instrument in personnel development and career counselling settings. Although there have been studies on personality traits of school leaders, no conclusive findings could be obtained regarding which types show higher school leadership success than others. In addition, studies are needed which investigate whether the inconclusive relationships which have been found between certain personality traits and leadership effectiveness are mainly due to implicit assumptions of what a successful school principal should be like, as Implicit Leadership Theories suggest.

We have found that cognitive ability predicts leadership effectiveness significantly, but the correlation is influenced by situational and methodological moderating variables. We can only assume which results of other organizational settings will also play a role in school leadership, as we have found a very scarce research basis dealing with cognitive ability of school leaders. It could even be possible that more empirical research on intelligence and other individual differences of principals exists, but that leaders of schools may not explicitly be declared as such in the studies or datasets. In Austria, principals are usually also teachers and are often not labelled as leaders in studies which investigate traits of educational staff. This is – at least from the trait perspective – a shortcoming in this field of research which could easily be improved. It would also need further studies to detect whether situational aspects such as organizational structure and stress, which may relate to school characteristics, influence the impact of individual differences on the success of school principals. If cognitive abilities of school leaders can validly be shown to predict school outcomes is yet to be proven. In Austria, as of 2015 all students applying for teacher programs will undergo cognitive abilities' testing (and a personality assessment). This holds the potential of conducting longitudinal studies relating cognitive ability before teacher training to either leader emergence or even leader effectiveness in the distant future.

Most of the research we identified dealt with emotional intelligence of school leaders. As we have discussed and shown, this is an important trait, but so far it failed to show any incremental validity over cognitive ability and Big Five personality traits in educational as well as other occupational settings. Future studies need to control for these variables to determine whether it would make sense to include emotional intelligence tests in school leader assessment processes.

Creativity, in contrast to emotional intelligence, seems to have been completely neglected in empirical studies of educational leadership. With the number and speed of innovations and reforms presently taking place in many school systems (Austria is not to be excepted here), the ability to tackle problems from a different angle and find innovative solutions now seems more important than ever. It is, however, not only the leader's creativity which is necessary to improve school outcomes, but also his or her ability to foster creative thinking in employees, pupils and maybe even parents.

5. FUTURE RESEARCH DIRECTIONS

As we have shown in our chapter, educational leadership research in general and educational leadership in specific can profit from including cognitive and non-cognitive traits. However, the use of psychological measures of high psychometric quality is required, if we want to draw conclusions about whether well-replicated findings from other occupational fields and settings can be replicated in school leaders. We can only make use of the findings discussed in this chapter if future studies investigate whether leading schools can be compared to leading other organizations.

As an outlook on what is to come in future leadership research, we will discuss one emerging trend in psychological leadership research (i.e., neuroleadership) and one aspect which has already been prominent in other occupational fields for some time, but will gain increasing importance in school leadership research due to the present shortage of applicants (i.e., leader emergence and succession planning).

Neuroleadership

Even though the application of neuroscientific methods to gain insights into (efficient) leaders' perceptions, thinking processes and feelings, may still be relatively new, research in this field is increasing steadily. Recent advances in technology have helped neuroscience to become one of the most prominent research strands in psychology. For many social sciences, neuroscientific methods provide new opportunities to empirically consolidate theoretical constructs. In leadership research, neuroscience contributes to the clarification of whether and how successful leaders differ from less successful ones, how a leader's social influence impacts subordinates, and what the neurophysiological basis of leadership competences is (cf. Bergner & Rybnicek, 2015, for an overview in German).

Apart from research on genetic (e.g., on the heritability of taking over leadership roles; De Neve, Mikhaylov, Dawes, Christakis, & Fowler, 2013) and biological (e.g, the relationship between testosterone levels and leadership; Gray & Campbell, 2009) factors underlying leadership, neuroscientific studies also investigated whether successful and less successful leaders can be differentiated by measuring their brain activity during the completion of specifically designed cognitive tasks. Rule et al. (2011) could, e.g., show that participants' brains reacted differently to pictures of more vs. less successful managers (with stronger activation in the amygdala, a region which plays a crucial role in emotion processing, when successful managers were displayed). Such neurophysiological reactions of our brain show that decisions also have a biological correlate and may hint at the importance of emotional rather than cognitive aspects when making decisions about whether someone is a successful leader or not.

While neuroscientific leadership research is still in its infancy and is – due to highly artificial test settings – limited with regard to ecological validity, the term has also found entry in non-scientific areas, as can be seen from a number of trainings and books under the same name. Such coaching, consulting or training approaches, which aim to develop and improve peoples' leadership abilities by understanding how the human brain works (cf. e.g., the Neuroleadership Institute in Australia) have, however, only very remotely to do with the scientific investigation of neurobiological correlates of leadership. While we do agree that it is highly interesting and important to understand the workings of our brain, we are sceptical whether this form of 'Neuroleadership' is not largely Biological Psychology in new (and certainly better selling and more expensive) clothes. With the advancement of neuroscientific technologies and measurements in situations closer to the real life of (school) leaders, this field is likely to gain importance not only in leadership training, but also selection.

Leader Emergence and Succession

At the beginning of the 1990s Zaccaro et al. (1991) still observed that "trait explanations of leader emergence are generally regarded with little esteem by leadership theorists" (p. 308), but a decade later, Judge et al. (2002) could show that personality traits (if they are grouped into the Big Five) strongly predict leadership emergence (β = .53). This predictive value is especially strong in settings with weak external structure.

Many educational systems now encounter problems due to, firstly, principals being ill-prepared to fulfil all the various demands placed upon them by modern school systems and, secondly, due to a struggle to attract and retain qualified candidates for leadership positions in school (cf. Davis et al., 2005). A trait psychological approach could help to identify potential candidates, i.e. those which a generally strong motivation to lead others (Felfe et al., 2013) at an early stage (e.g., while they are still teachers). Subsequently these educators can be provided with trainings and leadership preparation programs which allow them to acquire and improve specific abilities which they would later need as principals.

One approach which uses (amongst other factors) psychological traits for school leader development is the Competence Profile School Management (CPSM) developed by Huber and colleagues (Huber & Hiltmann, 2011). In the CPSM inventory "the results of the self-assessment represent a person's self-image regarding personality aspects and a person's cognitive abilities" (Huber & Hiltmann, 2011, p. 69). The instrument serves as a feedback for teachers and principals as they are informed about their scores in comparison to other participants. Such a feedback enables potential candidates to reflect about the antecedents they bring with them and can also trigger the need to further engage with some aspects before applying for school leadership. In addition, such scores could also be used by personnel development planners to create individually required training possibilities and improve leadership succession planning. Here, trait personality can certainly contribute to school leadership in the long run, where succession planning and personnel development will play a more central role in the future.

6. CONCLUSION

The chapter investigated research from educational as well as non-educational leadership contexts with regard to personality traits that have been discussed to play a role in predicting how successful a leader is: personality, cognitive and emotional intelligence, as well as creativity. We have only found a larger body of research dealing with emotional intelligence and principals' success, but with often very small sample sizes. Compared to the many studies and especially meta-analyses in other occupational settings, we argue that educational leadership research certainly needs further investigations applying well-established individual differences measures to the field in order to find out whether results from, e.g., business settings can be transferred. Even so:

... [i]t is also important to remember that none of this research reveals any single characteristic that determines leadership. Rather it suggests there are groups or constellations of qualities that appear to correlate with leadership. Not all leaders have these traits, not even effective leaders have all of them. Many nonleaders have many of these characters, and still more have at least a few. Yet having many of these traits does appear to give one a better chance at leadership effectiveness. (Lashway, Mazzarella, & Grundy, 1996)

Psychological traits have reconquered leadership research after initial studies in the field brought inconclusive findings. The renaissance of individual differences is mainly due to improved conceptions of higher order personality traits, as well as meta-analyses summarizing results obtained from studies with different situational as well as methodological settings. This has allowed personality psychology to identify mediating and moderating variables which impact the predictive validity of traits on leadership outcome variables as has been shown in the framework by Judge and Long (2012; see Figure 1). When we adapt the initially presented framework to represent individual differences studies in educational leadership research, we can see in Figure 2 that the inclusion

of mediating and moderating variables is strongly needed in future research, as well as studies on creativity or dark personality traits.

Cognitive intelligence is a well-investigated trait which has continuously shown to predict leadership outcomes significantly across different occupational settings. Its influence, however, is greatest if leaders can operate in low-stress settings with a certain freedom to act as well as when leaders show a directive communication style. Interestingly, school leaders with high cognitive abilities showed less transformational leadership style. This is contrary to results from other occupational settings and it was proposed that principals with high cognitive ability focus more strongly on instructional leadership instead. Further research is necessary to examine the moderating influences on relationships between cognitive abilities and school leadership success, or also leader emergence.

Leaders who are extraverted, conscientious, open to new experiences and emotionally stable have usually been found to be the most effective leaders. Again, these characteristics can show most impact when leaders find themselves in a relatively stress-free situation with a certain amount of autonomy and when leadership effectiveness was rated by others rather than by objective indicators. Whether dark personality traits such as narcissism, psychopathy and Machiavellianism also influence leadership effectiveness of school principals will be another area for future research. What we know so far about effective school leaders' personality is not very conclusive. All studies showed that (effective) principals are very conscientious (Judging in the Myer-Briggs Type Indicator correlates with Conscientiousness in the Big Five; Furnham, 1996), but the predictive value of Openness and Neuroticism could not be found in studies using the MBTI (Sensing prevailed in the studies, but this correlates negatively to Openness, and Neuroticism is missing in the MBTI;

Figure 2. Model based on Judge and Long (2012, p. 187) depicting studies relating individual differences and educational leadership criteria. No studies were found investigating variables depicted in grey in relation to educational leadership. Superscripted numbers indicate studies as follows: (1) Grunes et al, 2004; (2) Stone et al., 2005; (3) Holder, 2009; (4) Mendiburu, 2010; (5) Gardner & Martinko, 1990; (6) McEwan, 2003; (7)Williams, 2008; (8) Cook, 2006; (9) Bardach, 2008; (10) Reynolds, 2011.

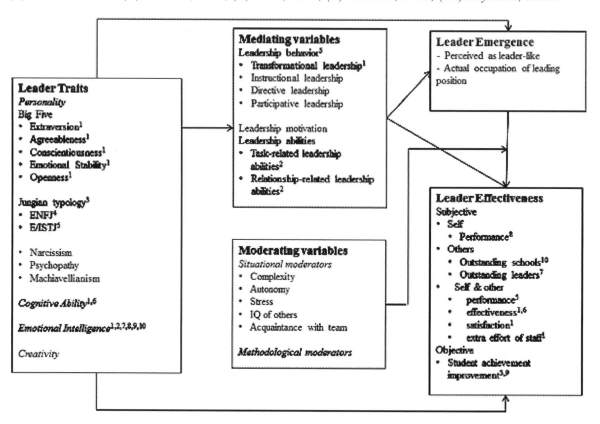

Furnham, 1996). To conclude, personality traits seem to play an important role also for successful school leadership, but further research using comparable operationalizations is needed to shed light on exactly which dimensions can predict educational leadership effectiveness.

Emotional intelligence and creativity have recently found entrance into psychological leadership research. Both concepts, however, led to discussions among psychologists regarding their independence from cognitive ability and the Big Five personality dimensions as well as to whether and in which form they can be validly operationalized as well as reliably and objectively measured. Although emotional intelligence correlates positively with leadership outcome variables in educational as well as non-educational settings, this relationship disappears once we control for cognitive ability and Big Five personality traits. Creativity has been found to relate strongly to transformational leadership and to play a more important role in governmental than business contexts.

We hope that future research schemes will revive trait approaches also in educational leadership as they have proven a valuable concept in other occupational settings and many high-quality measures have been developed in the last decades to assess such personal characteristics reliably. Further evidence is needed to determine whether findings from existing psychological leadership research can be transferred to educational leadership, or whether these settings are too different to generalize findings across. Still, it is time to change the fact that "*Leadership traits* and *leadership styles*, as more personality tied leadership dispositions, are hardly addressed in the [educational leadership] research literature" (Scheerens, 2012, p. 131).

REFERENCES

Ajzen, I. (1987). Attitudes, traits, and actions: Dispositional prediction of behavior in personality and social psychology. *Advances in Experimental Social Psychology*, *20*(1), 1–63. doi:10.1016/S0065-2601(08)60411-6

Altrichter, H., & Heinrich, M. (2007). Kategorien der Governance-Analyse und Transformationen der Systemsteuerung in Österreich. In H. Altrichter, T. Brüsemeister, & J. Wissinger (Eds.), *Educational Governance – Handlungskoordination und Steuerung im Bildungssystem* (pp. 55–103). Wiesbaden: Verlag für Sozialwissenschaften.

Altrichter, H., & Kanape-Willingshofer, A. (2013). Educational standards and external examination of pupils' competencies: Possible contributions of external measurements in attaining quality goals in schools. In B. Herzog-Punzenberger, M. Bruneforth, & L. Lassnigg (Eds.), *National Education Report Austria 2012: Indicators and Topics: An Overview*. Graz: Leykam. Retrieved, 20 February 2014, from https://www.bifie.at/system/files/dl/en_NBB_band3_web.pdf

Antonakis, J. (2011). Predictors of leadership: The usual suspects and the suspect traits. In A. Bryman, D. Collinson, K. Grint, B. Jackson, & M. Uhl-Bien (Eds.), *Sage Handbook of Leadership* (pp. 269–285). Thousand Oaks, CA: Sage Publications.

Antonakis, J., Ashkanasy, N. M., & Dasborough, M. (2009). Does leadership need emotional intelligence? *The Leadership Quarterly*, *20*(2), 247–261. doi:10.1016/j.leaqua.2009.01.006

Antonakis, J., Day, D. V., & Schyns, B. (2012). Leadership and individual differences: At the cusp of a renaissance. *The Leadership Quarterly*, *23*(4), 643–650. doi:10.1016/j.leaqua.2012.05.002

Bar-On, R. (2000). Emotional and social intelligence: Insights from the Emotional Quotient Inventory (EQ-i). In R. Bar-On & J. D. A. Parker (Eds.), *Handbook of Emotional Intelligence* (pp. 363–388). San Francisco, CA: Jossey-Bass.

Bardach, R. H. (2008). *Leading schools with emotional intelligence: A study of the degree of association between middle school principal emotional intelligence and school success*. (Unpublished Doctoral dissertation). Capella University, Minneapolis, MN.

Barrick, M., Mount, M., & Judge, T. (2001). Personality and performance at the beginning of the new millennium: What do we know and where do we go next? *International Journal of Selection and Assessment*, *9*(1/2), 9–30. doi:10.1111/1468-2389.00160

Benson, M. J., & Campbell, J. P. (2007). To Be, or Not to Be, Linear: An expanded representation of personality and its relationship to leadership performance. *International Journal of Selection and Assessment*, *15*(2), 232–249. doi:10.1111/j.1468-2389.2007.00384.x

Bergner, S., & Rybnicek, R. (2015). Führungsforschung aus neurowissenschaftlicher Sicht. In J. Felfe (Ed.), *Trends der psychologischen Führungsforschung – Neue Konzepte, Methoden und Erkenntnisse: (pp.543-566)*. Göttingen: Hogrefe Verlag.

Birkeland, S. A., Manson, T. M., Kisamore, J. L., Brannick, M. T., & Smith, M. A. (2006). A Meta-Analytic Investigation of Job Applicant Faking on Personality Measures. *International Journal of Selection and Assessment, 14*(4), 317–335. doi:10.1111/j.1468-2389.2006.00354.x

Borkenau, P., & Ostendorf, F. (1990). Comparing exploratory and confirmatory factor analysis: A study on the 5-factor model of personality. *Personality and Individual Differences, 11*(5), 515–524. doi:10.1016/0191-8869(90)90065-Y

Boyatzis, R. E. (1982). *The Competent Manager: A Model for Effective Performance.* New York, NY: John Wiley & Sons.

Boyatzis, R. E., Goleman, D., & Rhee, K. (2000). Clustering competence in emotional intelligence: Insights from the Emotional Competence Inventory (ECI). In R. Bar-On & J. D. A. Parker (Eds.), *Handbook of emotional intelligence* (pp. 343–362). San Francisco: Jossey-Bass.

Brunell, A. B., Gentry, W. A., Campbell, W. K., Hoffman, B. J., Kuhnert, K. W., & DeMarree, K. G. (2008). Leader Emergence: The Case of the Narcissistic Leader. *Personality and Social Psychology Bulletin, 34*(12), 1663–1676. doi:10.1177/0146167208324101 PMID:18794326

Caldwell, D. F., & Burger, J. M. (1998). Personality characteristics of job applicants and success in screening interviews. *Personnel Psychology, 51*(1), 119–136. doi:10.1111/j.1744-6570.1998.tb00718.x

Carr, A. (1994). 'For self or others? The Quest for narcissism and the ego-ideal in work organisations'. *Administrative Theory and Praxis, 16*(2), 208–222.

Cavazotte, F., Moreno, V., & Hickmann, M. (2012). Effects of leader intelligence, personality and emotional intelligence on transformational leadership and managerial performance. *The Leadership Quarterly, 23*(3), 443–455. doi:10.1016/j.leaqua.2011.10.003

Chamorro-Premuzic, T. (2007). *Personality and individual differences.* Malden, MA: BPS Blackwell.

Cheung, M. F., & Wong, C. S. (2011). Transformational leadership, leader support, and employee creativity. *Leadership and Organization Development Journal, 32*(7), 656–675. doi:10.1108/01437731111169988

Christie, R., & Geis, F. L. (1970). *Studies in Machiavellianism.* New York: Academic Press.

Cook, C. R. (2006). *Effects of emotional intelligence on principals' leadership performance.* (Unpublished dissertation). University of Montana. Retrieved, 21 February 2014, from http://scholarworks.montana.edu/xmlui/bitstream/handle/1/1099/CookC0506.pdf?sequence=1

Cooper, C. (2010). *Individual Differences and Personality* (3rd ed.). London: Routledge.

Costa, P. T. Jr, & McCrae, R. R. (1992). *NEO PI-R professional manual.* Odessa, FL: Psychological Assessment Resources, Inc.

Cowley, W. H. (1931). Three distinctions in the study of leaders. *Journal of Abnormal and Social Psychology, 26*, 304–313. doi:10.1037/h0074766

Cox, E. (2006). What Personality Inventories and Leadership Assessments Say About Aspiring Principals Conceptual Frame. *ERS Spectrum, 24*(4), 13–20.

Cronbach, L. (1949). *Essentials of Psychological Testing*. New York: Harper.

De Neve, J. E., Mikhaylov, S., Dawes, C. T., Christakis, N. A., & Fowler, J. H. (2013). Born to lead? A twin design and genetic association study of leadership role occupancy. *The Leadership Quarterly*, *24*(1), 45–60. doi:10.1016/j.leaqua.2012.08.001 PMID:23459689

DeRue, D. S., Nahrgang, J. D., Wellman, N., & Humphrey, S. E. (2011). Trait and behavioral theories of leadership: An integration and meta-analytic test of their relative validity. *Personnel Psychology*, *64*(1), 7–52. doi:10.1111/j.1744-6570.2010.01201.x

Edwards, J. R. (1991). Person-job fit: A conceptual integration, literature review, and methodological critique. In C. L. Cooper & I. T. Robertson (Eds.), *International review of industrial and organizational psychology* (Vol. 6, pp. 283–357). New York: Wiley.

Eysenck, H. J. (1983). The roots of creativity: Cognitive ability or personality trait? *Roeper Review*, *5*(4), 10–12. doi:10.1080/02783198309552714

Felfe, J., Gatzka, L., Elprana, G., Stiehl, S., & Schyns, B. (2013, May 22). *Further insights into the meaning of motivation to lead*. Paper presented at the European Association of Work and Organizational Psychology Conference 2013. Münster.

Fiedler, F. E., & Garcia, J. E. (1987). *New Approaches to Leadership, Cognitive Resources and Organizational Performance*. New York: John Wiley and Sons.

Furnham, A. (1996). The big five versus the big four: The relationship between the Myer-Briggs-Type Indicator (MBTI) and NEO-PI five factor model of personality. *Personality and Individual Differences*, *21*(2), 303–307. doi:10.1016/0191-8869(96)00033-5

Furnham, A., & Chamorro-Premuzic, T. (2004). Personality and intelligence as predictors of statistics examination grades. *Personality and Individual Differences*, *37*(5), 943–955. doi:10.1016/j.paid.2003.10.016

Garcia-Morales, V. J., Matias-Reche, F., & Hurtado-Torres, N. (2008). Influence of transformational leadership on organizational innovation and performance depending on the level of organizational learning in the pharmaceutical sector. *Journal of Organizational Change Management*, *21*(2), 188–212. doi:10.1108/09534810810856435

Gardner, W. L., & Martinko, M. J. (1990). The relationship between psychological type, managerial behavior, and managerial effectiveness: An empirical investigation. *Journal of Psychological Type*, *19*, 35–43.

Ghiselli, E. E. (1963). Intelligence and managerial success. *Psychological Reports*, *12*(3), 898. doi:10.2466/pr0.1963.12.3.898

Goldberg, L. R. (1990). An alternative „description of personality": The Big-Five factor structure. *Journal of Personality and Social Psychology*, *59*(6), 1216–1229. doi:10.1037/0022-3514.59.6.1216 PMID:2283588

Goleman, D. (1998). What makes a leader? *Harvard Business Review*, (Nov-Dec): 93–102. PMID:10187249

Goleman, D. (1995). *Emotional Intelligence: Why It Can Matter More Than IQ*. New York: Bantam Books.

Gray, P. B., & Campbell, B. C. (2009). Human male testosterone, pair-bonding, and fatherhood. In P. Gray & P. Ellison (Eds.), *Endocrinology of Social Relationships*. Cambridge, MA: Harvard University Press.

Grunes, P., Gudmundsson, A., & Irmer, B. (2014). To what extent is the Mayer & Salovey (1997) model of emotional intelligence a useful predictor of leadership style and perceived leadership outcomes in Australian educational institutions? *Educational Management Administration & Leadership*, *42*(1), 112–135. doi:10.1177/1741143213499255

Hallinger, P. (2003). Leading Educational Change: Reflections on the practice of instructional and transformational leadership. *Cambridge Journal of Education*, *33*(3), 329–351. doi:10.1080/0305764032000122005

Hallinger, P. (2008). *Methodologies for Studying School Leadership: A Review of 25 years of Research Using the PIMRS*. Paper prepared for presentation at the annual meeting of the American Educational Research Association. New York, NY. Retrieved, 15 February 2014, from: http://alex.state.al.us/leadership/Principals%20%20Files/RG-5,%20PIMRS_Methods_47.pdf

Hare, R. D. (1991). *The Hare Psychopathy Checklist - Revised*. North Tonawanda, NY: Multi-Health Systems.

Harris, T. B., Li, N., Boswell, W. R., Zhang, X. A., & Xie, Z. (2013). Getting What's New from Newcomers: Empowering Leadership, Creativity, and Adjustment in the Socialization Context. *Personnel Psychology*, n/a. doi:10.1111/peps.12053

Harvey, R. J., Murry, W. D., & Markham, S. E. (1995). *A "Big Five" Scoring System for the Myers-Briggs Type Indicator*. Paper presented at the Annual Conference of the Society for Industrial and Organizational Psychology. Orlando, FL. Retrieved, 3 January 2014, from: http://harvey.psyc.vt.edu/Documents/BIGFIVE.pdf

Hoffman, B. J., Woehr, D. J., Maldagen-Youngjohn, R., & Lyons, B. D. (2011). Great man or great myth? A quantitative review of the relationship between individual differences and leader effectiveness. *Journal of Occupational and Organizational Psychology*, *84*(2), 347–381. doi:10.1348/096317909X485207

Holder, S. C. (2009). *The relationship between dimensions of Principal Personality type and selected school characteristics*. (Unpublished Dissertation). Mercer University, Atlanta, GA.

Hough, L. M. (1992). The "big five" personality variables--construct confusion: Description versus prediction. *Human Performance*, *5*, 139–155.

Huber, S. G. (2008). Steuerungshandeln schulischer Führungskräfte aus Sicht der Schulleitungsforschung. In R. Langer (Ed.), *Warum tun die das?' Governanceanalysen zum Steuerungshandeln in der Schulentwicklung* (pp. 95–126). Wiesbaden: VS.

Huber, S. G., & Hiltmann, M. (2010). The recruitment and selection of school leaders – first findings of an international comparison. In S. G. Huber (Ed.), *School Leadership – International Perspectives* (pp. 303–330). Dordrecht: Springer. doi:10.1007/978-90-481-3501-1_16

Huber, S. G., & Hiltmann, M. (2011). Competence Profile School management (CPSM) – an inventory for the self-assessment of school leadership. *Educational Assessment, Evaluation and Accountability*, *23*(1), 65–88. doi:10.1007/s11092-010-9111-1

Hunter, J. E., Schmidt, F. L., & Le, H. (2006). Implications of Direct and Indirect Range Restriction for Meta-Analysis Methods and Findings. *The Journal of Applied Psychology*, *91*(3), 594–612. doi:10.1037/0021-9010.91.3.594 PMID:16737357

Ibukun, W. O., Oyewole, B. K., & Abe, T. O. (2011). Personality characteristics and principal leadership effectiveness in Ekiti State, Nigeria. *International Journal of Leadership Studies*, *6*(2), 246–262.

Jansen, P. G. W., & Vinkenburg, C. J. (2006). Predicting management career success from *assessment* center data: A longitudinal study. *Journal of Vocational Behavior*, *68*(2), 253–266. doi:10.1016/j.jvb.2005.07.004

John, O. P., Donahue, E. M., & Kentle, R. L. (1991). *The Big Five Inventory--Versions 4a and 54.* Berkeley, CA: University of California, Berkeley, Institute of Personality and Social Research.

Jowett, B. (Ed.). (1871). *Plato: The Republic.* Project Gutenberg. Retrieved, 15 February 2014, from: http://www.gutenberg.org/files/1497/1497-h/1497-h.htm

Judge, T. A., & Bono, J. E. (2000). Five-factor model of personality and transformational leadership. *The Journal of Applied Psychology*, *85*(5), 751–765. doi:10.1037/0021-9010.85.5.751 PMID:11055147

Judge, T. A., Bono, J. E., Ilies, R., & Gerhardt, M. W. (2002). Personality and leadership: A qualitative and quantitative review. *The Journal of Applied Psychology*, *87*(4), 765–780. doi:10.1037/0021-9010.87.4.765 PMID:12184579

Judge, T. A., Colbert, A. E., & Ilies, R. (2004). Intelligence and Leadership: A Quantitative Review and Test of Theoretical Propositions. *The Journal of Applied Psychology*, *89*(3), 542–552. doi:10.1037/0021-9010.89.3.542 PMID:15161411

Judge, T. A., & Long, D. M. (2012). Individual Differences in Leadership. In D. V. Day & J. Antonakis (Eds.), *The Nature of Leadership* (pp. 179–217). Los Angeles: Sage.

Kearney, E., & Gebert, D. (2009). Managing diversity and enhancing team outcomes: The promise of transformational leadership. *The Journal of Applied Psychology*, *94*(1), 77–101. doi:10.1037/a0013077 PMID:19186897

Lashway, L., Mazzarella, J., & Grundy, T. (1996). Portrait of a Leader. In S. C. Smith & P. K. Piele (Eds.), *School leadership handbook for excellence* (3rd ed., pp. 15–37). Clearinghouse on Educational Management.

Leithwood, K., Day, C., Sammons, P., Harris, A., & Hopkins, D. (2006). *Seven strong claims about successful school leadership*. Nottingham, UK: National College for School Leadership. Retrieved, 15 February 2014, from: http://www.aede-france.org/Seven-strong-claims.html

Leithwood, K., & Hallinger, P. (2002). *Second International Handbook of Educational Leadership and Administration* (Vols. 1-2). Boston: Kluwer Academic Publishers. doi:10.1007/978-94-010-0375-9

Leithwood, K. A., Jantzi, D., & Steinbach, R. (1999). *Changing leadership for changing times.* Buckingham, UK: Open University Press.

Locke, E. A., & Kirkpatrick, S. (1991). *The essence of leadership: The four keys to leading successfully.* New York: Lexington Books.

Lord, R. G., de Vader, C. L., & Alliger, G. M. (1986). A meta-analysis of the relation between personality traits and leadership perceptions: An application of validity generalization procedures. *The Journal of Applied Psychology*, *71*(3), 402–410. doi:10.1037/0021-9010.71.3.402

Maleki, M. (2013). Narcissism and Decision-Making Styles Principals. *Asian Journal of Research in Social Sciences and Humanities*, *10*(3), 359–370.

Mann, R. D. (1959). A review of the relationship between personality and performance in small groups. *Psychological Bulletin, 56*(4), 241–270. doi:10.1037/h0044587

Mayer, J. D., & Salovey, P. (1997). What is emotional intelligence? In P. Salovey & D. Sluyter (Eds.), *Emotional development and emotional intelligence: Implications for educators* (pp. 3–31). New York: Basic Books.

Mayer, J. D., Salovey, P., Caruso, D. R., & Sitarenios, G. (2001). Emotional intelligence as a standard intelligence. *Emotion (Washington, D.C.), 1*(3), 232–242. doi:10.1037/1528-3542.1.3.232 PMID:12934682

Mayer, J. D., Salovey, P., Caruso, D. R., & Sitarenios, G. (2003). Measuring emotional intelligence with the MSCEIT V2.0. *Emotion (Washington, D.C.), 3*(1), 97–105. doi:10.1037/1528-3542.3.1.97 PMID:12899321

McCrae, R. R., & Costa, P. T. (1987). Validation of the five-factor model of personality across instruments and observers. *Journal of Personality and Social Psychology, 52*(1), 81–90. doi:10.1037/0022-3514.52.1.81 PMID:3820081

McEwan, E. K. (2003). *Ten Traits of Highly Effective Principals: From Good to Great Performance.* Thousand Oaks, CA: Corwin.

Mendiburu, J. G. (2010). *Personality Typologies as a Predictor of Being a Successful Elementary School Principal.* (Unpublished Dissertation). University La Verne, La Verne, CA.

Mischel, W. (1977). The interaction of person and situation. In D. Magnusson & N. S. Endler (Eds.), *Personality at the crossroads: Current issues in interactional psychology* (pp. 333–357). Hillsdale, NJ: Lawrence, Erlbaum.

Mumford, M. D., Hester, K., & Robledo, I. (2012). Methods in Creativity Research: Multiple Approaches, Multiple Levels. In M. D. Mumford (Ed.), Handbook of Organizational Creativity (pp. 39-65). London: Waltham.

Neuroleadership Institute. (n.d.). *Neuroleadership Institute - Breaking new ground in our capacity to improve thinking and performance.* Retrieved, 21 February 2014, from: www.neuroleadership.org

Nevicka, B., De Hoogh, A. H. B., Van Vianen, A. E. M., Beersma, B., & McIlwain, D. (2011). All I need is a stage to shine: Narcissists' leader emergence and performance. *The Leadership Quarterly, 22*(5), 910–925. doi:10.1016/j.leaqua.2011.07.011

Ng, K.-Y., Ang, S., & Chan, K. Y. (2008). Personality and Leader Effectiveness: A Moderated Mediation Model of Leadership Self-Efficacy, Job Demands, and Job Autonomy. *The Journal of Applied Psychology, 43*(4), 733–743. doi:10.1037/0021-9010.93.4.733 PMID:18642980

Northouse, P. G. (2010). *Leadership: Theory and practice* (5th ed.). Los Angeles, CA: Sage Publications, Inc.

Ones, D. S., & Viswesvaran, C. (1996). Bandwidth-fidelity dilemma in personality measurement for personnel selection. *Journal of Organizational Behavior, 17*(6), 609–626. doi:10.1002/(SICI)1099-1379(199611)17:6<609::AID-JOB1828>3.0.CO;2-K

Paulhus, D. L., & Williams, K. M. (2002). The dark triad of personality: Narcissism, Machiavellianism, and Psychopathy. *Journal of Research in Personality, 36*(6), 556–563. doi:10.1016/S0092-6566(02)00505-6

Petrides, K. V. (2011). Ability and trait emotional intelligence. In T. Chamorro-Premuzic, A. Furnham, & S. von Stumm (Eds.), *The Blackwell-Wiley Handbook of Individual Differences*. New York: Wiley.

Pieterse, A. N., Van Knippenberg, D., Schippers, M., & Stam, D. (2009). Transformational and transactional leadership and innovative behavior: The moderating role of psychological empowerment. *Journal of Organizational Behavior, 31*(4), 609–623. doi:10.1002/job.650

Raskin, R., & Terry, H. (1988). A principal-components analysis of the Narcissistic Personality Inventory and further evidence of its construct validity. *Journal of Personality and Social Psychology, 54*(5), 890–902. doi:10.1037/0022-3514.54.5.890 PMID:3379585

Rego, A., Sousa, F., Marques, C., & Cunha, M. P. (2012). Authentic leadership promoting employees' psychological capital and creativity. *Journal of Business Research, 65*(3), 429–437. doi:10.1016/j.jbusres.2011.10.003

Reynolds, M. (2011). *An Investigation of the Emotional Intelligence Competencies of National Middle Schools to Watch Principals.* (Unpublished Dissertation). Eastern Kentucky University. Retrieved, 15 February 2014, from: http://encompass.eku.edu/cgi/viewcontent.cgi?article=1041&context=etd

Rockstuhl, Th., Seiler, S., Ang, S., Van Dyne, L., & Annen, H. (2011). Beyond General Intelligence (IQ) and Emotional Intelligence (EQ): The Role of Cultural Intelligence (CQ) on Cross-Border Leadership Effectiveness in a Globalized World. *The Journal of Social Issues, 67*(4), 825–840. doi:10.1111/j.1540-4560.2011.01730.x

Rosing, K., Frese, M., & Bausch, A. (2011). Explaining the heterogeneity of the leadership-innovation relationship: Ambidextrous leadership. *The Leadership Quarterly, 22*(5), 956–974. doi:10.1016/j.leaqua.2011.07.014

Rule, N. O., Freeman, J. B., Moran, J. M., Gabrieli, J. D. E., Adams, R. B., & Ambady, N. (2010). Voting behavior is reflected in amygdala response across cultures. *Social Cognitive and Affective Neuroscience, 5*(2-3), 349–355. doi:10.1093/scan/nsp046 PMID:19966327

Salgado, J. F., Anderson, N., Moscoso, S., Bertua, C., de Fruyt, F., & Rolland, J. P. (2003). A Meta-Analytic Study of General Mental Ability Validity for Different Occupations in the European Community. *The Journal of Applied Psychology, 88*(6), 1068–1081. doi:10.1037/0021-9010.88.6.1068 PMID:14640817

Salgado, J. F., Viswesvaran, C., & Ones, D. S. (2001). Predictors Used for Personnel Selection: An Overview of Constructs. In N. Anderson, D. Ones, H. Sinangil & C. Viswesvaran (Eds.), Handbook of Industrial, Work & Organizational Psychology: Personnel Psychology (vol. 1). Academic Press.

Salovey, P., & Mayer, J. D. (1990). Emotional intelligence. *Imagination, Cognition and Personality, 9*(3), 185–211. doi:10.2190/DUGG-P24E-52WK-6CDG

Scheerens, J. (2012). Summary and Conclusion: Instructional Leadership in Schools. In J. Scheerens (Ed.), School Leadership Effects Revisited: Review and Meta-Analysis of Empirical Studies (pp. 131-150). Dortrecht: Springer.

Schmidt, F. L., & Hunter, J. E. (1998). The validity and utility of selection methods in personnel psychology: Practical and theoretical implications of 85 years of research findings. *Psychological Bulletin, 124*(2), 262–274. doi:10.1037/0033-2909.124.2.262

Shin, S. J., Kim, T. Y., Lee, J. Y., & Bian, L. (2012). Cognitive team diversity and individual team member creativity: A cross-level interaction. *Academy of Management Journal, 55*(1), 197–212. doi:10.5465/amj.2010.0270

Silverthorne, C. (2001). Leadership effectiveness and personality: A cross-cultural study. *Personality and Individual Differences, 30*(2), 303–309. doi:10.1016/S0191-8869(00)00047-7

Simonton, D. K. (1985). Intelligence and personal influence in groups: Four nonlinear models. *Psychological Review, 92*(4), 532–547. doi:10.1037/0033-295X.92.4.532

Srivastava, S., John, O. P., Gosling, S. D., & Potter, J. (2003). Development of personality in early and middle adulthood: Set like plaster or persistent change? *Journal of Personality and Social Psychology, 84*(5), 1041–1053. doi:10.1037/0022-3514.84.5.1041 PMID:12757147

Sternberg, R. J. (2003). Giftedness According to the Theory of Successful Intelligence. In N. Colangelo & G. Davis (Eds.), Handbook of Gifted Education (pp. 88-99). Boston MA: Allyn and Bacon.

Sternberg, R. J. (2006). The Nature of Creativity. *Creativity Research Journal, 18*(1), 87–98. doi:10.1207/s15326934crj1801_10

Sternberg, R. J., & Lubart, T. I. (1996). Investing in creativity. *The American Psychologist, 51*(7), 677–688. doi:10.1037/0003-066X.51.7.677

Sternberg, R. J., & O'Hara, L. A. (1999). Creativity and intelligence. In R. J. Sternberg (Ed.), *Handbook of Creativity* (pp. 251–272). Cambridge University Press.

Stogdill, R. M. (1948). Personal factors associated with leadership: A survey of the literature. *The Journal of Psychology, 25*(1), 35–71. doi:10.1080/00223980.1948.9917362 PMID:18901913

Stoll, L., & Temperley, J. (2009). Creative leadership: A challenge of our times. *School Leadership & Management, 29*(1), 65–78. doi:10.1080/13632430802646404

Stone, H., Parker, J. D. A., & Wood, L. M. (2005). *Report on the Ontario Principals' Council leadership Study*. Consortium for Research on Emotional intelligence in Organizations. Retrieved, 15 February 2014, from: http://www.eiconsortium.org/pdf/opc_leadership_study_final_report.pdf

Suchan, B., Wallner-Paschon, C., & Bergmüller, S. (2009). Profil der Lehrkräfte und der Schulen in der Sekundarstufe I. In J. Schmich & C. Schreiner (Eds.), *TALIS 2008. Schule als Lernumfeld und Arbeitsplatz. Erste Ergebnisse des internationalen Vergleichs* (pp. 16–30). Graz: Leykam.

Twenge, J. M., & Campbell, W. K. (2003). "Isn't It Fun to Get the Respect That We're Going to Deserve?" Narcissism, Social Rejection, and Aggression. *Personality and Social Psychology Bulletin, 29*(2), 261–272. doi:10.1177/0146167202239051 PMID:15272953

Vaccaro, I. G., Jansen, J. J., Van Den Bosch, F. A., & Volberda, H. W. (2012). Management innovation and leadership: The moderating role of organizational size. *Journal of Management Studies, 49*(1), 28–51. doi:10.1111/j.1467-6486.2010.00976.x

Van Iddekinge, C. H., Ferris, G. R., & Heffner, T. S. (2009). Test of a multistage model of distal and proximal antecedents of leader performance. *Personnel Psychology, 62*(3), 463–495. doi:10.1111/j.1744-6570.2009.01145.x

Watson, D. (1989). Strangers' ratings of the five robust personality factors: Evidence of a surprising convergence with self-report. *Journal of Personality and Social Psychology, 57*(1), 120–128. doi:10.1037/0022-3514.57.1.120

Westerlaken, K. M., & Woods, P. R. (2013). The relationship between psychopathy and the Full Range Leadership Model. *Personality and Individual Differences, 54*(1), 41–46. doi:10.1016/j.paid.2012.08.026

Williams, H. W. (2008). Characteristics that distinguish outstanding urban principals: Emotional intelligence, social intelligence and environmental adaptation. *Journal of Management Development, 27*(1), 36–54. doi:10.1108/02621710810840758

Wonderlic, E. F. (2003). Wonderlic Personnel Quicktest (WPT-Q) User's Guide. Libertyville, IL: EF Wonderlic.

Yukl, G. (2011). Contingency theories of effective leadership. In A. Bryman, D. Collinson, K. Grint, B. Jackson, & M. Uhl-Bien (Eds.), *Sage Handbook of Leadership* (pp. 286-298). Thousand Oaks, CA: Sage Publications.

Zaccaro, S. J., Foti, R. J., & Kenny, D. A. (1991). Self-monitoring and trait-based variance in leadership: An investigation of leader flexibility across multiple group situations. *The Journal of Applied Psychology, 76*(2), 308–315. doi:10.1037/0021-9010.76.2.308

Zaccaro, S. J., Kemp, C., & Bader, P. (2004). Leader traits and attributes. In J. Antonakis, A. T. Cianciolo, & R. J. Sternberg (Eds.), *The Nature of Leadership* (pp. 101–124). Thousand Oaks, CA: Sage.

Zhang, A. Y., Tsui, A. S., & Wang, D. X. (2011). Leadership behaviors and group creativity in Chinese organizations: The role of group processes. *The Leadership Quarterly, 22*(5), 851–862. doi:10.1016/j.leaqua.2011.07.007

Zhang, X., & Bartol, K. M. (2010). Linking empowering leadership and employee creativity: The influence of psychological empowerment, intrinsic motivation, and creative process engagement. *Academy of Management Journal, 53*(1), 107–128. doi:10.5465/AMJ.2010.48037118

ADDITIONAL READING

Ames, D. R., & Flynn, F. J. (2007). What breaks a leader: The curvilinear relation between assertiveness and leadership. *Journal of Personality and Social Psychology, 92*(2), 307–324. doi:10.1037/0022-3514.92.2.307 PMID:17279851

Antonakis, J. Cianciolo, A. T. & Sternberg R. J. (Eds.). The nature of leadership. Thousand Oaks, CA: Sage.

Antonakis, J., Day, D. V., & Schyns, B. (2012). Leadership and individual differences: At the cusp of a renaissance. *The Leadership Quarterly, 23*(4), 643–650. doi:10.1016/j.leaqua.2012.05.002

Avolio, B. J., Walumbwa, F. O., & Weber, T. J. (2009). Leadership: Current theories, research, and future directions. *Annual Review of Psychology, 60*(1), 421–449. doi:10.1146/annurev.psych.60.110707.163621 PMID:18651820

Bar-On, R., & Parker, J. D. (Eds.). (2000). *Handbook on Emotional Intelligence*. San Francisco, CA: Jossey-Bass.

Bergner, S., Neubauer, A. C., & Kreuzthaler, A. (2010). Broad and Narrow Personality Measures for Predicting Managerial Success. *European Journal of Work and Organizational Psychology, 19*(2), 177–199. doi:10.1080/13594320902819728

Bertua, C., Anderson, N., & Salgado, J. F. (2005). The predicitve validity of cognitive ability tests: A UK meta-analysis. *Journal of Occupational and Organizational Psychology, 78*(3), 387–409. doi:10.1348/096317905X26994

Bono, J. E., & Judge, T. A. (2004). Personality and transformational and transactional leadership: A meta-analysis. *The Journal of Applied Psychology, 89*(5), 901–910. doi:10.1037/0021-9010.89.5.901 PMID:15506869

Boyatzis, R. E., Good, D., & Massa, R. (2012). Emotional, Social, and Cognitive Intelligence and Personality as Predictors of Sales Leadership Performance. *Journal of Leadership & Organizational Studies, 19*(2), 191–201. doi:10.1177/1548051811435793

Bryman, A., Collinson, D., Grint, K., Jackson, B., & Uhl-Bien, M. (Eds.). (2011). *Sage Handbook of Leadership*. Thousand Oaks: Sage Publications.

Chan, K. Y., & Drasgow, F. (2001). Toward a theory of individual differences and leadership: Understanding the motivation to lead. *The Journal of Applied Psychology, 86*(3), 481–498. doi:10.1037/0021-9010.86.3.481 PMID:11419808

Cherniss, C., & Goleman, D. (2001). *The emotionally intelligent workplace*. San Francisco: Jossey-Bass.

Deary, I. J. (2012). Intelligence. *Annual Review of Psychology, 63*(1), 453–482. doi:10.1146/annurev-psych-120710-100353 PMID:21943169

Dinh, J. E., & Lord, R. G. (2012). Implications of dispositional and process views of traits for individual difference research in leadership. *The Leadership Quarterly, 23*(4), 651–669. doi:10.1016/j.leaqua.2012.03.003

English, F. W. (Ed.). (2011). *The SAGE handbook of educational leadership* (2nd ed.). Thousand Oaks, CA: SAGE Publications. doi:10.4135/9781412980036

Ensari, N., Riggio, R. E., Christian, J., & Carslaw, G. (2011). Who emerges as a leader? Meta-analyses of individual differences as predictors of leadership emergence. *Personality and Individual Differences, 51*(4), 532–536. doi:10.1016/j.paid.2011.05.017

Goleman, D., & Boyatzis, R. (2008). Social intelligence and the biology of leadership. *Harvard Business Review, 86*(9), 74–81. PMID:18777666

Gottfredson, L. S. (1998). The General Intelligence Factor. *Scientific American Presents, 9*(4), 24–29.

Hülsheger, U. R., Maier, G. W., & Stumpp, T. (2007). Validity of General Mental Ability for the Prediction of Job Performance and Training Success in Germany: A meta-analysis. *International Journal of Selection and Assessment, 15*(1), 3–18. doi:10.1111/j.1468-2389.2007.00363.x

Hunter, J. E., Schmidt, F. L., & Le, H. (2006). Implications of Direct and Indirect Range Restriction for Meta-Analysis Methods and Findings. *The Journal of Applied Psychology, 91*(3), 594–612. doi:10.1037/0021-9010.91.3.594 PMID:16737357

John, O. P., Robins, R. W., & Pervin, L. A. (Eds.), *Handbook of personality: Theory and research*. New York, NY: Guilford Press.

Kristof-Brown, A. L., Zimmerman, R. D., & Johnson, E. C. (2005). Consequences of individuals' fit at work: A meta-analysis of person-job, person-organization, person-group, and person-supervisor fit. *Personnel Psychology*, *58*(2), 281–342. doi:10.1111/j.1744-6570.2005.00672.x

Lord, R. G., & Hall, R. J. (1992). Contemporary Views of Leadership and Individual Differences. *The Leadership Quarterly*, *3*(2), 137–157. doi:10.1016/1048-9843(92)90030-J

Mayer, J. D., Salovey, P., & Caruso, D. R. (2000). Models of emotional intelligence. In R. J. Sternberg (Ed.), *Handbook of Intelligence* (pp. 396–420). Cambridge, England: Cambridge University Press. doi:10.1017/CBO9780511807947.019

Mumford, M. D. (2011). Handbook of Organizational Creativity. London: Waltham.

Neisser, U., Boodoo, G., Bouchard, T. J., Boykin, A. W., Brody, N., & Ceci, S. et al. (1996). Intelligence: Knowns and unknowns. *The American Psychologist*, *51*(2), 77–101. doi:10.1037/0003-066X.51.2.77

Northouse, P. G. (2010). *Leadership: Theory and practice* (5th ed.). Los Angeles: Sage Publications, Inc.

Pendleton, D., & Furnham, A. (2012). *Leadership. All you need to know*. Basingstoke, England: Palgrave Macmillan.

Reichard, R. J., Riggio, R. E., Guerin, D. W., Oliver, P. H., Gottfried, A. W., & Gottfried, A. E. (2011). A longitudinal analysis of relationships between adolescent personality and intelligence with adult leader emergence and transformational leadership. *The Leadership Quarterly*, *22*(3), 471–481. doi:10.1016/j.leaqua.2011.04.005

Riggio, R. E., Murphy, S. E., & Pirozzolo, F. J. (Eds.). (2002). *Multiple intelligences and leadership. LEA's organization and management series*. Mahwah, NJ: Lawrence Erlbaum Associates Publishers.

Schmidt, F. L., & Hunter, J. E. (1998). The validity and utility of selection methods in personnel psychology: Practical and theoretical implications of 85 years of research findings. *Psychological Bulletin*, *124*(2), 262–274. doi:10.1037/0033-2909.124.2.262

Simonton, D. K. (1994). *Greatness: Who Makes history and Why*. New York: The Guilford Press.

Sternberg, R. J. (Ed.). (2000). *Handbook of Intelligence*. Cambridge, England: Cambridge University Press. doi:10.1017/CBO9780511807947

Tett, R., & Burnett, D. (2003). A personality trait-based interactionist model of job performance. *The Journal of Applied Psychology*, *88*(3), 500–517. doi:10.1037/0021-9010.88.3.500 PMID:12814298

Van Rooy, D. L., & Viswesvaran, C. (2004). Emotional intelligence: A meta-analytic investigation of predictive validity and nomological net. *Journal of Vocational Behavior*, *65*(1), 71–95. doi:10.1016/S0001-8791(03)00076-9

Yukl, G. (1998). *Leadership in organizations* (4th ed.). Englewood Cliffs, NJ: Prentice-Hall.

Zaccaro, S. J. (2012). Individual Differences and Leadership: Contributions to a Third Tipping Point. *The Leadership Quarterly*, *23*(4), 718–728. doi:10.1016/j.leaqua.2012.05.001

KEY TERMS AND DEFINITIONS

Cognitive Ability: The concept has numerous definitions. Common to most is the understanding of a very general mental capability that involves, e.g., the ability to reason, plan, solve problems, think abstractly, comprehend complex ideas, learn quickly and learn from experience. High cognitive ability also shows in being able to adapt quickly and adequately to new situations.

Creativity: The ability to generate ideas or products that are novel, but at the same time useful and appropriate to the circumstances.

Dark Triad of Personality: A group of the following three personality traits: Narcissism which is characterized by pride, egotism and lack of empathy; Machiavellianism which denotes strong tendencies to exploit and manipulate others; Psychopathy which shows in antisocial, impulsive and callous behavior.

Emotional Intelligence: The ability to perceive, appraise, and express emotions, to understand and analyze emotions, to use emotions to facilitate thinking, to use emotional knowledge effectively as well as to regulate one's own emotions for personal growth. It has been argued that Emotional Intelligence rather represents an ability than an intelligence.

Individual Differences: These describe why individuals behave differently in the same situation. They denote e.g. physical aspects in which people can differ, but also intelligence, memory, personality, self-esteem etc. and are the key element of personality psychology.

Neuroleadership: The application of neuroscientific methods and findings to leadership research OR a leadership training approach grounded in understanding neurobiological bases of behavior.

Personality: The unique emotional, attitudinal, and behavioral pattern which an individual shows across different situations and over time.

Trait: Enduring personal qualities or attributes that influence a person's behavior across situations. Traits are central to an individual's personality.

Chapter 10

New Methods Exploring Facial Expressions in the Context of Leadership Perception:
Implications for Educational Leaders

Savvas Trichas
Open University of Cyprus, Cyprus

ABSTRACT

The aim of this chapter is to add to our knowledge of the contribution of facial expression to educational leadership perception. Although there is a considerable amount of studies investigating leaders' emotional displays, the majority of this research does not use the sophisticated facial expression coding methods available in other psychological settings. However, research using such sophisticated methods shows that even subtle facial actions can result in significantly different impressions, indicating that credibility of facial expression interpretation might depend on the accuracy of facial expression description (see Rosenberg, 2005). In this chapter, the few leadership studies that have used sophisticated facial expression coding methods are reviewed. On the basis of these studies, it is recommended that educational organizations should be aware of the added value of these methods in order increase research credibility and provide educational leaders with specialized knowledge and skills that could eventually increase their effectiveness.

INTRODUCTION

Facial expressions appear to have a powerful influence on person perception, impressions, and image (Aguinis, Simonsen, & Pierce, 1998; Cohn & Ekman, 2008; Glaser & Salovey, 1998; Krumhuber, Manstead, & Kappas, 2006; McArthur & Baron, 1983; Zebrowitz & Montepare,

2008). Several professions such as such as flight attendants (Hochschild, 1983) or bill collectors (Rafaeli & Sutton, 1987) require the display of emotion as part of their organizational role. Leadership is also a role that expression of emotional display is considered important. Specifically, the significance of leaders' emotional expressions is underlined in studies on educational, business,

DOI: 10.4018/978-1-4666-6591-0.ch010

charismatic, transformational, political, and authentic leadership (Ashkanasy & Tse, 2000; Beatty, 2000; Bono & Ilies, 2006; Bucy, 2000; Goffee & Jones, 2005; Trichas, 2011). Nevertheless, our understanding regarding the impact of leaders' emotional displays is still narrow.

Even though, to the writer's knowledge, there is lack of research investigating facial expressions in the context of educational leadership, there is a considerable number of studies, which has contributed to an understanding of leaders' emotional displays, that explored leaders' emotional expressions in other contexts such as politics and business (e.g., Bucy, 2000; Bucy & Bradley, 2004; Bucy & Newhagen, 1999; Damen, Van Knippenberg, & Van Knippenberg, 2008; Gaddis, Connelly, & Mumford, 2004; Glomb & Hulin, 1997; Lewis, 2000; Masters & Sullivan, 1989; Medvedeff, 2008; Stewart, 2010; Sullivan & Masters, 1988). However, the majority of these studies do not use the sophisticated facial expression coding methods available in other psychological settings (e.g., Ekman, 1992; Ekman & Rosenberg, 1997; Hess, Blairy, & Kleck, 2000). Contemporary research using such sophisticated facial action coding analysis (see Ekman, Friesen, & Hager, 2002) shows that subtle facial actions can result in significantly different perceptions (e.g., Surakka & Hietanen, 1998). Consequently, incorporating detailed facial expression coding analysis in leadership studies might contribute to increasing research credibility (see Rosenberg, 2005).

The mission of the work presented here is to add to our knowledge of the contribution of facial expression to leadership perception. An additional aim of the current book chapter is to argue that the integration of sophisticated methods and principles of facial expression coding and decoding (e.g., Ekman, Friesen, & Hager, 2002) can provide educational leaders with knowledge and skills that could eventually increase their effectiveness.

In the following, after a general introduction to facial expressions perceptual concepts, the main literature on leaders' facial expressions is discussed. Additionally, an argument is constructed supporting that using sophisticated coding analysis of facial expression might be an approach to increasing credibility of educational leadership research designs. Furthermore, leadership studies that included such sophisticated facial expression techniques are presented. Finally, the general discussion and conclusions follow together with implications and recommendations for educational leadership research and practice.

BACKGROUND

Perceiving Facial Expressions

Facial expression is an area that receives a lot of research attention (e.g., Camras, 2000; Frijda & Tcherkassof, 1997; Scherer; 1992; Smith & Scott, 1997) and a reason for that might be that the face contains many of the sensor organs plus the brain in its region (Cohn & Ekman, 2008). In addition, people seem to begin realizing the communicative significance of facial expression from a very young age (Gladwell, 2005). Specifically, research shows that even newborns are able to perceive and react according to others' facial expressions (Field, Woodson, Greenberg, & Cohen, 1982; Tronick, 1989).

Facial expressions have also been demonstrated to influence person perception and impressions of trait characteristics (Aguinis, Simonsen, & Pierce, 1998; Cohn & Ekman, 2008; Glaser & Salovey, 1998; Hendriks & Vingerhoets, 2006; Krumhuber, Manstead, & Kappas, 2006). Darwin (1872/1965) stresses the critical importance of information received via facial expressions for the inferences people make regarding the underlying emotions of others. Furthermore, Van Kleef (2009) proposes a social model where emotional facial expressions influence observers' behavior through emotional procedures such as emotional contagion and/or inferential processes such as inferring that someone is happy because of the observation of a happiness facial expression. Scholars researching the human face often conceptualize reactions to facial displays through the idea of an approach, attack or avoidance three-fold (Madera & Smith, 2009; Monahan, 1998; Montepare & Dobish, 2003; Todorov, Said, Engell, & Oosterhof, 2008). In that sense, the perception of facial expression moves beyond assigning an emotional state to the transmitter (for example a facial expression of sadness which might serve as a sign of a person's negative mood) to the cause of existanse for that state (an avoidance behavior). Similarly, different inferential outcomes apply for different emotional facial expressions such as attack which can be signalled with the display of anger facial expressions and approach which can be conveyed with expressions of happiness (Hess, Blairy, & Kleck, 2000; Zebrowitz & Montepare, 2008). In other words, although people see the expression of an emotion, they use spontaneous causality to make speculations about the transmitter's intentions (Fiske & Taylor, 2008; McArthur & Baron, 1983; Montepare & Dobish, 2003; Montepare & Zebrowitz-McArthur, 1998; Todorov, Said, Engell, & Oosterhof, 2008; Zebrowitz & Montepare, 2008).

In terms of perception, even facial expressions exposed for a fraction of a second can have a significant perceptual impact (Winkielman & Berridge, 2004). Facial expressions that appear very briefly are defined as micro-expressions (Ekman 1992; Frank & Ekman 1997; 2004; Jenkins & Johnson, 1977). In other words, a person can be smiling, flash an anger facial expression, and return to smiling in less than a second. Although micro-expressions are so brief that most people cannot detect, they may unconsciously influence perception, and when showed in slow motion they have clear conscious emotional meaning (Ekman, 2003). Specifically, studies demonstrate that emotional facial displays such as anger, fear and happiness, can impact individuals' emotional responses without their awareness (Channouf

2000; Dimberg, Thunberg, & Elmehed, 2000; Marsh & Ambady 2007; Monahan & Zuckerman 1999; Wild, Erb, & Bartels, 2001; Winkielman, & Berridge, 2004; Winkielman, Berridge, & Wilbarger, 2005; Winkielman & Berridge 2003).

Facial expressions of emotion seem to give a basis for perceivers' theories of underlying emotions but respective perceptions could vary when put in a different context. Specifically, research revealed that the exact same facial expressions were interpreted differently when context information was manipulated (Carroll & Russell, 1996). Additionally, Trichas and Schyns (2012) found that context of communication not only determined whether positive or negative expression were going to be considered acceptable by participants, but also defined ranges of appropriate facial expressions which could explain how leader-like a person was perceived. Relevant to the above discussion is the concept of display rules (Ekman & Oster, 1979) or norms of expectations (Sutton & Rafaeli, 1988) which refer to appropriate expressions within the context. To be more specific, observers' interpretations of facial expressions are influenced by what they consider appropriate considering the context of communication. An example of violation of display rules might be laughing in a funeral. In a similar vein, emotional labor (Hochschild, 1983) refers to the emotional displays that are related with one's professional identity. Consequently, many people may consider crying an acceptable behavior in general but when they have to think about a military commander on duty they might consider the previous behavior unacceptable. Leadership is an organizational position that presupposes the use of specific facial expressions in several different contexts as part of their occupational role (Humphrey, Pollack, & Hawver, 2008). For example, in a context of school conflict, certain leader anger facial expressions may be considered more appropriate and acceptable than in a context of welcoming a parent.

MAIN FOCUS OF THE CHAPTER

Issues, Controversies, Problems: Traditional Research on Leaders Facial Expressions

Despite the recognition of the importance of nonverbal behavior in general and facial expression more specifically as a leader skill within educational leadership textbooks and manuscripts (e.g., Beatty, 2000; Brackett & Katulak, 2006; Hoy & Miskel, 2013; Johnson, 2003; Marzano & Marzano, 2003; Woodger, 2003), to the writer's knowledge, there is an overall lack of research regarding facial expression and perception of educational leadership. However, there is a considerable amount of studies that explored leaders' emotional displays in other leadership contexts. These have mainly focused on (1) political leaders' emotional expressions (e.g. Bucy & Bradley, 2004; Cherulnik, Donley, Wiewel, & Miller; 2001) (2) leaders' general emotional expressions (e.g. Gaddis, Connelly, & Mumford, 2004; Lewis, 2000) and (3) indirect investigation of leadership perception by exploring the effect of facial expression to leader relevant traits such as charisma, dominance, power, intelligence, likeability, status, and trustworthiness (e.g., Awamleh & Gardner, 1999; Keating, 2003).

Studies investigating emotional expressions of political leaders mainly used designs in which the participants had to observe and evaluate the emotional facial expressions in images or videos of USA presidents such as Bill Clinton or Ronald Reagan (e.g., Bucy & Newhagen, 1999; Sullivan & Masters, 1988). Sample results from Bucy and Newhagen (1999) reveal that observers considered negative and low intensity emotional expressions in speeches and other public appearances more appropriate than positive displays. In contrast, other studies reveal that viewers' emotional responses were positively influenced when political leaders' used happy and reassuring displays (Masters & Sullivan, 1989; Sullivan & Masters, 1988).

The second line of research that explored leaders' displays used mainly manipulations of leaders' general emotional expressions (e.g., Lewis, 2000; Damen, Van Knippenberg, & Van Knippenberg, 2008). For example, Lewis (2000) had men and women actors expressing sadness, anger, and neutrality finding a significant negative effect of negative emotional expressions on leadership effectiveness assessments. On the other hand, Damen et al. (2008) investigated the association between leaders' emotional displays and followers' positive affect. They used actor-leaders who conveyed anger or enthusiasm by displaying frowns or smiles and other, nonverbal, cues such as tone of voice and body language (e.g., body posture). Damen et al. (2008) found that leader emotional displays had more positive influence on followers if there was a strong congruency between followers' positive affect and the valence of leaders' emotion.

Finally, in the third line of research smiling, non-smiling displays and/or eyebrow movements were used as facial expression manipulations to examine effects on leader-specific trait characteristics (e.g., Dovidio, Heltman, Brown, Ellyson, & Keating, 1988; Keating, Mazur, & Segall, 1977; Lau, 1982; Mazur & Mueller, 1996). For instance, lowered eyebrows were found to increase perceptions dominance whereas raised eyebrows were found to decrease it (Keating, Mazur, & Segall, 1977). In addition, Lau (1982) presented still photos to the participants of people displaying a smiling or a non-smiling face. The results indicate that observers evaluated smiling comparing non-smiling individuals higher on likeability, intelligence and warmness.

Although the above studies contributed to an understanding of leaders' emotional displays, they did not utilized the added contribution that sophisticated facial expression coding could provide to the area of leadership perception. To illustrate that with an example, sample results show that participants preferred negative and low intensity emotional expressions of political leaders (Bucy

& Newhagen, 1999). However, an examination of the descriptors 'negative' and 'low intensity' with respect to detailed facial action coding reveals that the low-high and negative-positive dimensions could be displayed with several different levels of intensity and respective muscle movement (Ekman & Friesen, 1978). Figure 1 illustrates three different facial expressions which could be characterised as 'negative' and 'low intensity'.

The first display contains facial actions that are related with the emotion of anger, the second contains facial actions that are related with the emotion of distress and the third contains facial actions that are related with the emotion of disgust (Ekman, Friesen, & Hager, 2002). The fact that all of these quite different facial displays can be labelled as negative and low intensity implies that there might be a credibility issue with the latter description.

Taking the facial expression of anger as an example, even though it is universally recognised

(Matsumoto & Hee Yoo, 2005) it can be produced with 65 different facial muscle movement and intensity combinations (Ekman & Friesen, 1978). A few simple examples of such combinations, which are depicted in Figure 2, are anger expressions with teeth showing or with pressing the lips together (Ekman et al., 2002).

Additionally, contemporary research using modern facial action coding analysis demonstrates that subtle differences between facial expressions in terms of facial muscle movement and intensity can make a difference in terms of the perceptual impact (Ekman et al., 2002). Specifically, Snodgrass (1992) asked observers to describe photos with facial expressions from Ekman and Friesen's (1978) Facial Action Coding System (see description on Ekman and Friesen's, 1978, system later in this chapter). Her findings indicate that simple facial muscle movements alterations could differentiate the perceived emotional outcome of a facial expression. Additionally, Surakka and Hietanen

Figure 1. Negative and low intensity facial expressions

 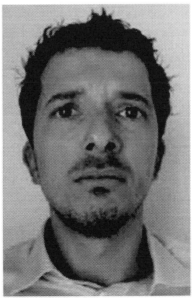 

Facial actions related with the emotion of anger

Facial actions related with the emotion of distress

Facial actions related with the emotion of disgust

Figure 2. Anger expressions of different facial muscle movement and intensity

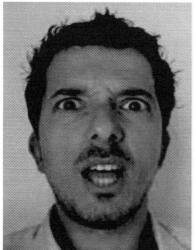

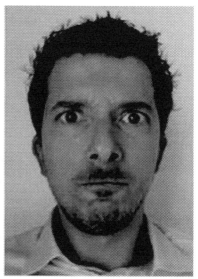

| Anger with teeth showing | Anger with pressing the lips together | Anger with pressing the lips together (higher intensity) |

(1998) discovered that participants reactions after observing smiles with eye muscle movement were much more positive from those observing smiles without the eye muscle movement. Consequently, the combination of facial actions involved in the facial expressions of Figure 2 might be categorized as the general emotion of anger, but the perceptual impact of each expression could be different because of the subtle differences in the muscle movement and intensity.

Similar issues appear in the research on facial expressions and the perception of leader related characteristics. Taking the example of assigning facial action descriptions such as 'eyebrow raise' (see Keating et al., 1977), sophisticated facial expression analysis based on facial anatomy (Ekman et al., 2002) maintains that there is much more to describing eyebrow upward movements than the simple notion of a raise. Specifically, three basic muscles are responsible for the eyebrow movements the combined activity of which can lead to quite different perceptual impacts. Figure

3 below demonstrates how an eyebrow raise can be involved in expressions with very different emotional impact.

Hence, depending on the combination of these muscles an 'eyebrow raise' can contribute to the perception of a completely different emotion such as fear, distress or surprise (Ekman et al., 2002; Surakka & Hietanen, 1998).

The latter studies emphasize the importance of describing facial expression in terms of exact facial muscle movement and intensity before interpretation of results. Consequently, the credibility of facial expression research designs might depend on the accuracy in facial expression description (see Rosenberg, 2005).

Solutions and Recommendations

In the following sections, one of the most popular sophisticated facial expression coding instruments, the Facial Action Coding System (Ekman et al., 2002), is going to be introduced together with

Figure 3. Eyebrow raise and different emotions

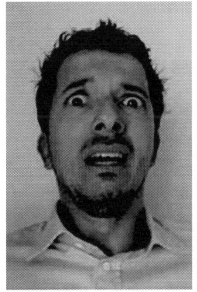
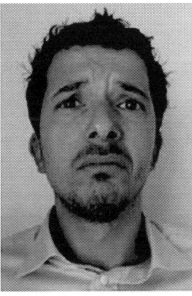

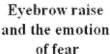

| Eyebrow raise and the emotion of fear | Eyebrow raise and the emotion of distress | Eyebrow raise and the emotion of surprise |

contemporary leadership research that used the specific method to address the credibility issues discussed above.

Accuracy in Describing Facial Expression Using Sophisticated Facial Expression Methods and the Facial Action Coding System

There are several systems developed for the coding of facial expressions (e.g. Affective expressions scoring system or AFFEX, Izard, Dougherty, & Hembree, 1983; Facial Action Coding System or FACS, Ekman, & Friesen, 1978; The Maximally Descriminative Facial Movement Coding System or MAX, Izard, 1983). These systems basically describe facial appearance changes in terms of facial actions using visual evidence such as still photo frames or videos. The FACS is perhaps the most widely used manual facial coding technique as it is considered to have high levels of validity (Cohn & Ekman, 2008) and reli-

ability (Sayette, Cohn, Wertz, Perrott, & Parrot, 2004). To be more specific, Ekman and Friesen (1976) integrated anatomy in an organized coding system to increase accuracy in facial action description. Particularly, they used the cause and effect rationale that facial movement originates from underlying muscle actions. They aimed to discover how muscle movement and intensity changes the appearance of the face so they could use these changes to infer which facial muscle has moved and with what intensity. Eventually, they combined facial anatomy and expression in constructing a sophisticated instrument for facial action coding (FACS, Ekman, & Friesen, 1978; Ekman et al., 2002). The FACS can objectively measure all visible facial movement with the use of 44 anatomically separate facial action units (Ekman & Rosenberg, 1997).

Consequently, the FACS provides the knowledge of what happens under the skin of the face (in terms of visible changes) to observers, to try to understand which muscle has moved, what was the movement, and when was the movement. The coding procedure requires slow-motion videotaped observation or comparison of photos with facial expressions with, at least, a frame (e.g. a photo) with the neutral face. Compared to the other systems mentioned earlier (e.g. MAX, Izard, 1983; AFFEX, Izard, Dougherty, & Hembree, 1983), an important advantage of FACS is that it is describes muscle movement without blending primary evaluation and emotion inferences. That reduces potential bias and allows consideration of a wider range of facial actions (Cohn, Zlochoher, Lien, & Kanade, 1999). Besides facial action, the intensity is coded in terms of how weak or strong the movement is (Cohn & Ekman, 2008). An example of such detailed muscle movement and intensity observation of a smile could involve descriptors like maximum intensity lip corners raised and angled up obliquely with high intensity activation of lid tightener, cheek raiser, and lid compressor (see Ekman et al., 2002). An important reason for the necessity of describing facial expressions accurately is that subtle differences between facial expressions can have different perceptual impacts (Snodgrass, 1992; Surakka & Hietanen, 1998). Consequently, identifying and interpreting such subtle movements could contribute to increasing the credibility of leadership research on facial expressions (see Rosenberg, 2005).

Research on Leaders Facial Expressions Using Sophisticated Facial Expression Methods

To the author's knowledge, there are only a few leadership studies that incorporate such sophisticated facial expression coding techniques to investigate leadership perception (Stewart & Dowe, 2013; Stewart, Waller, & Schubert, 2009; Trichas & Schyns, 2012). To begin with, Trichas and Schyns (2012) asked their respondents to observe and evaluate, in terms of business leadership first impressions, sequences of photos of facial expressions of different eyebrow movements

and smiles. In addition, these first impressions of leadership inferred from the observation of facial expressions were compared to the participants' Implicit Leadership Theories (context-specific cognitive schemas people have about leaders, see Dinh, Lord, Gardner, Meuser, Liden, & Hu, in press; Dinh, Lord, & Hoffman, in press; Epitropaki, Sy, Martin, Tram-Quon, & Topakas, 2013) dimensions inferred from facial expressions. The facial displays in Trichas and Schyns (2012) where coded in exact facial action movement and intensity with the use of FACS (Ekman et al., 2002). The results revealed that actors that displayed certain eyebrow raising and pulling together movements were perceived as less leader-like. Furthermore, Trichas and Schyns (2012) participants indicated an overall preference to smiling facial expressions but the extent of what type of smile was considered more appropriate each time, as regards FACS coding, was determined by the specific context. Particularly, when the participants were to be introduced to the actor-leader, they preferred low intensity smiles with no eye muscle activation but when they had to say goodbye after negotiating with the leader they proffered more intensity in smiling with eye muscle activation. In addition, the results showed that first impressions of leadership were higher when the facial expressions matched participants' ILTs. Furthermore, in a different line of research conducted by Stewart and Dowe (2013) also used sophisticated facial expression analysis to to discriminate between President Obama's emotional facial displays. Specifically their findings indicated that observers were influenced by marked but also by subtle differences displayed on the the president's face. Finally, Stewart et al. (2009) investigated the impact of micro-expressions using former US President George W. Bush's video footage. The previous scholars located smiling micro-expressions from the former US President's video and removed them from the original clip to examine the effect in leadership perceptions. Their results showed that removing these micro-momentary coded frames resulted in increased feelings of anger and threat by the participants. Consequently, observers' perceptions were influenced by emotional expressions exposed very briefly in former US President's face (Stewart et al., 2009).

IMPLICATIONS, CONTRIBUTIONS, AND FUTURE RESEARCH DIRECTIONS

Both traditional and contemporary research reviewed in the current chapter reveal that facial expressions have a strong influence on the perception of leadership. In addition, sophisticated facial expression coding in the area of leadership adds detail to our knowledge of leaders' facial expressions, thereby increasing the accuracy of the results and, at the same time, the depth of analysis. The Facial Action Coding System (FACS, Ekman et al., 2002) is one of the most widely used instruments of such sophisticated facial expression coding (Cohn & Ekman, 2008). The incorporation of the latter instrument in the leadership studies reviewed in this chapter uncovered findings which entail academic and practical value. Such findings include the influence of leaders' micro-expressions in observers' perceptions (Stewart et al., 2009) and the significant differences resulted in leadership perceptions when marked and subtle facial actions are altered (Stewart & Dowe, 2013; Trichas & Schyns, 2012).

Taken together, these findings allow drawing out recommendations for leaders' facial expression. To specify, educational organisations can benefit from the depth of such analysis by including basic facial expression workshops within school leadership preparation programs. In a primary level, these training programs may include facial action coding and decoding, instruction, and practice. On a more advanced level, they may also integrate important concepts such as the perceptual impact of facial expressions. For example these workshops may focus on the reproduction and explicit discrimination of the subtle facial actions that differentiate leadership perceptions (see Trichas & Schyns, 2012). This is important because taking into account that facial expression as a nonverbal channel is considered to be a vital communicational tool in educational administration (Hoy & Miskel, 2013), school leaders' awareness of the impact of subtle details in their facial expressions, can eventually help in improving accuracy in communication and shape perception. Furthermore, such advanced instruction can also include micro-expression training (see Stewart et al., 2009). Recent studies reveal that training improves recognition of micro-expressions (Hurley, 2010; Matsumoto, & Hwang, 2011; Porter, Juodis, ten Brinke, Klein, & Wilson, 2009). Additionally, research has found a positive correlation between peoples' skill to read micro-expressions and detection of deception (Frank & Ekman, 1997; Ekman, 2003). This could be useful, for example, in educational delinquencies or interview settings that require the skill of judgement of statement credibility to facilitate the decision making process (Kidwell, 2004; Wood, Schmidtke, & Decker, 2007). Overall, the outcomes of such training can eventually contribute to improving communication within educational organizations. Of course, in order for such training to be successful, further experimental investigations are needed within the educational context. Specifically, it would be interesting to investigate the relationship between the ability of educational leaders to detect and decode facial expressions of emotion and/or micro-expressions and leadership perceptions of subordinates, students and parents.

In addition to the above there is also a context specific contribution. Within the studies reviewed above, there is research that investigated leaders' facial expression influences in leadership perceptions using a Cypriot sample (Trichas & Schyns, 2012). To the author's knowledge, there is currently no other research involving facial expressions in leadership perception in Cyprus, so the study above introduces new contextual findings which, hopefully, might be considered in local educational leader development and preparation. The areas of perception and facial expression were not found to be highly developed in Cyprus in terms of research and professional training. The outcomes of giving more emphasis to the latter research areas could contribute to increasing the quality of educational leadership instruction and training in Cyprus. The general research approach and underlying philosophy of the research reviewed in the present chapter could potentially be used as a plan for similar leadership perception studies in educational contexts but also covering other areas (such as verbal communication, body posture, gestures, voice, proxemics, and touch) in a search for a more complete communication theory regarding leadership perception.

Apart from the interpretation of facial expression per se, another important outcome of research reviewed in the present chapter is that leadership perception of facial expressions is a complex situational process (e.g., Trichas & Schyns, 2012). Perceivers act as 'naive scientists': they take available stimuli, such as facial expresssions and combine them with stereotypical information when trying to make sense of what happens around them (Hassin, Bargh, & Uleman, 2002). Consequently, a fundamental rationale for penetrating the structures of leadership perception from facial expressions is to understand what is inside the perceiver's mind; to reveal leadership schemata (prototypes). A significant part of the leadership perception process comprises of a match between those schemata and the inferences the perceiver makes from facial expressions. Therefore, the weight of understanding observers' perceptions does not only fall on the facial expressions displayed, or even the intentions of the actor displaying the expression, but in how observers perceive these displays. This is important for academic knowledge because it reveals that a shift of the research focus from transmitter (leader) to perceiver (follower) can provide a different angle in the way leadership is viewed. Consequently, it is

recommended that leadership scholars need to be aware of followers' contribution to the leadership perceptual process (see Gray & Densten, 2007; Schyns, Felfe, & Blank, 2007). The complexity of perceivers preconceptions of leadership implies that any attempt to create rules from the findings of such research is extremely difficult, since there are too many variables to control. In that sense, leadership emergence is no longer a matter of searching for standard practices but strategically searching for an understanding of what is best under specific conditions (Meindl, 1995).

Calder (1977) proposes to try to make leaders "see" how people perceive them rather than trying to teach them how to act like leaders. The findings of research such as the one of Trichas and Schyns (2012) reinforce this notion. In other words leadership can also be approached as a socially constructed phenomenon emerging from perceivers (Meindl, 1995). Educational organizations could benefit from such a perspective by including leader preparation programs that focus on awareness of the beholders' perceptual processes. Specifically, Epitropaki and Martin (2004) suggest that management training programs should focus on making leaders aware of their followers ILTs. Educating managers regarding their subordinates' ILTs can help them diagnose their followers' needs. This may lead to a better quality of communication between leaders and followers. Consequently, such training may help to improve the quality of leader-member exchanges and, ultimately, attitudes in the workplace (Epitropaki & Martin, 2005). Going one step further, uncovering leader prototypes could help educational organizations in the selection of potential leaders who possess characteristics which are valued in the target population (Smith & Foti, 1998). Additional criteria for the evaluation of such selections could be the elements of facial expressivity which were found to exert a strong influence on leadership perceptions (e.g., Stewart et al., 2009). These could be especially useful for educational leadership where communicational competence and human relations might be more essential (see Hoy & Miskel, 2013). On the other hand, educational organisations can focus on "followers training" (see Schyns & Meindl, 2005, p. 16): Making people aware of their own perceptual procedures and potential biases may contribute to more realistic perceptions of leadership in the school context.

CONCLUSION

To conclude, the process of investigating structures of leadership perception in this chapter led to a number of contributions concerning academic knowledge and organisational practice. The first is that it extended the relevant literature by adding a perspective of increased credibility into the area of leadership perception with the use of sophisticated facial expression coding methods. The second is that the results from these studies highlight a number of areas in educational leadership development and preparation that can benefit from such instruction. The third is that certain research studying leadership perception via facial expressions (e.g., Trichas & Schyns, 2012) stressed the importance of viewing leadership as a socially constructed phenomenon emerging from perceivers (see Meindl, 1995). The perspective that emerged from the latter is facing leadership as a matter of understanding how people perceive leaders rather than trying to develop certain professional skills.

REFERENCES

Aguinis, H., Simonsen, M. M., & Pierce, C. A. (1998). Effects of Nonverbal Behaviour on Perceptions of Power Bases. *The Journal of Social Psychology, 138*(4), 455–469. doi:10.1080/00224549809600400 PMID:9664862

Ashkanasy, N. M., & Tse, B. (2000). Transformational leadership as management of emotion: A conceptual review. In N. M. Ashkanasy, C. E. Haertel, & W. Zerbe (Eds.), *Emotions in the workplace: Research, theory, and practice* (pp. 221–235). Westport, CT: Quorum Books/Greenwood.

Awamleh, R., & Gardner, W. L. (1999). Perceptions of Leader Charisma and Effectiveness: The Effects of Vision Content, Delivery, and Organizational Performance. *The Leadership Quarterly, 10*(3), 345–373. doi:10.1016/S1048-9843(99)00022-3

Beatty, B. (2001). The emotions of educational leadership: Breaking the silence. *International Journal of Leadership in Education, 4*, 331–357.

Bono, J. E., & Ilies, R. (2006). Charisma, positive emotions and mood contagion. *The Leadership Quarterly, 17*(4), 317–334. doi:10.1016/j.leaqua.2006.04.008

Brackett, M. A., & Katulak, N. A. (2006). Emotional intelligence in the classroom: Skill-based training for teachers and students. In J. Ciarrochi & J. D. Mayer (Eds.), *Applying emotional intelligence: A practitioner's guide* (pp. 1–27). New York: Psychology Press.

Bucy, E. P. (2000). Emotional and evaluative consequences of inappropriate leader displays. *Communication Research, 27*(2), 194–226. doi:10.1177/009365000027002004

Bucy, E. P., & Bradley, S. D. (2004). Presidential expressions and viewer emotion: Counter empathic responses to televised leader displays. *Social Sciences Information. Information Sur les Sciences Sociales, 43*(1), 59–94. doi:10.1177/05390184040689

Bucy, E. P., & Newhagen, J. E. (1999). The Emotional Appropriateness Heuristic: Processing Televised Presidential Reactions to the News. *Journal of Communication, 49*(4), 59–79. doi:10.1111/j.1460-2466.1999.tb02817.x

Calder, B. (1977). An attribution theory of leadership. In B. Staw & G. Salancik (Eds.), *New directions in organizational behavior* (pp. 179–204). Chicago: St. Claire Press.

Camras, L. A. (2000). Surprise!: Facial expressions can be coordinative motor structures. In M. D. Lewis & I. Granic (Eds.), *Emotion, development, and self-organization* (pp. 100–124). New York: Cambridge University Press. doi:10.1017/CBO9780511527883.006

Carroll, J. M., & Russell, J. A. (1996). Do Facial Expressions Signal Specific Emotions? Judging Emotion From the Face in Context. *Journal of Personality and Social Psychology, 70*(2), 205–218. doi:10.1037/0022-3514.70.2.205 PMID:8636880

Channouf, A. (2000). Subliminal exposure to facial expressions of emotion and evaluative judgments of advertising messages. *European Review of Applied Psychology, 50*, 19–23.

Cherulnik, P. D., Donley, K. A., Wiewel, T. S., & Miller, S. R. (2001). Charisma Is Contagious: The Effect of Leaders' Charisma on Observers' Affect. *Journal of Applied Social Psychology, 31*(10), 2149–2159. doi:10.1111/j.1559-1816.2001.tb00167.x

Cohn, J. F., & Ekman, P. (2008). Measuring Facial Action. In J. A. Harrigan, R. Rosenthal, & K. R. Scherer (Eds.), *The new handbook of Methods in Nonverbal Behavior Research* (pp. 9–64). New York: Oxford University Press. doi:10.1093/acprof:oso/9780198529620.003.0002

Cohn, J. F., Zlochoher, A. J., Lien, J., & Kanade, T. (1999). Automated face analysis by feature point tracking has high concurrent validity with manual FACS coding. *Psychophysiology, 36*(1), 35–43. doi:10.1017/S0048577299971184 PMID:10098378

Damen, F., VanKnippenberg, D., & VanKnippenberg, B. (2008). Leader Affective Displays and Attributions of Charisma: The Role of Arousal. *Journal of Applied Social Psychology, 38*(10), 2594–2614. doi:10.1111/j.1559-1816.2008.00405.x

Darwin, C. (1872/1965). The expression of the emotions in man and animals. Chicago: The University of Chicago Press. (Originally published, 1872.). doi:10.1037/10001-000

Dimberg, U., Thunberg, M., & Elmehed, K. (2000). Unconscious facial reactions to emotional facial Expressions. *Psychological Science, 11*(1), 86–89. doi:10.1111/1467-9280.00221 PMID:11228851

Dinh, J., Lord, R., Gardner, W., Meuser, J., Liden, R., & Hu, J. (in press). Leadership theory and research in the new millennium: Current theoretical trends and changing perspectives. *The Leadership Quarterly.*

Dinh, J. E., Lord, R. G., & Hoffman, E. (in press). Leadership perception and information processing: Influences of symbolic, connectionist, emotion, and embodied architectures. In D. Day (Ed.), *The Oxford Handbook of Leadership and Organizations*. New York: Oxford University Press.

Dovidio, J. F., Heltman, K., Brown, C. E., Ellyson, S. L., & Keating, C. E. (1988). Power Displays Between Women and Men in Discussions of Gender-Linked Tasks: A Multichannel Study. *Journal of Personality and Social Psychology, 55*(4), 580–587. doi:10.1037/0022-3514.55.4.580

Ekman, P. (1992). Facial expressions of emotion: New findings, new questions. *Psychological Science*, *3*(1), 34–38. doi:10.1111/j.1467-9280.1992.tb00253.x

Ekman, P. (2009). Lie catching and microexpressions. In C. Martin (Ed.), *The philosophy of deception* (pp. 118–142). New York, NY: Oxford University Press. doi:10.1093/acprof:oso/9780195327939.003.0008

Ekman, P., & Friesen, W. (1978). *Facial Action Coding System: A tecnhique for the Measurement of Facial Movement*. Palo Alto, CA: Consulting Psychologists Press.

Ekman, P., Friesen, W. V., & Hager, J. C. (2002). *Facial Action Coding System: The Manual*. Research Nexus division of Network Information Research Corporation.

Ekman, P., & Oster, H. (1979). Facial Expressions of Emotion. *Annual Review of Psychology*, *30*(1), 527–554. doi:10.1146/annurev.ps.30.020179.002523

Ekman, P., & Rosenberg, E. (1997). *What the face reveals: basic and applied studies of spontaneous expression*. New York: Oxford University Press.

Epitropaki, O., & Martin, R. (2004). Implicit Leadership Theories in Applied Settings: Factor Structure, Generalizability, and Stability Over Time. *The Journal of Applied Psychology*, *89*(2), 293–310. doi:10.1037/0021-9010.89.2.293 PMID:15065976

Epitropaki, O., & Martin, R. (2005). From Ideal to Real: A Longitudinal Study of the Role of Implicit Leadership Theories on Leader-Member Exchanges and Employee outcomes. *The Journal of Applied Psychology*, *90*(4), 659–676. doi:10.1037/0021-9010.90.4.659 PMID:16060785

Epitropaki, O., Sy, T., Martin, R., Tram-Quon, S., & Topakas, A. (2013). Implicit Leadership and Followership Theories "in the wild": Taking stock of information-processing approaches to leadership and followership in organizational settings. *The Leadership Quarterly*, *24*(6), 858–881. doi:10.1016/j.leaqua.2013.10.005

Field, T. M., Woodson, R., Greenberg, R., & Cohen, D. (1982). Discrimination and imitation of facial expressions by neonates. *Science*, *218*(4568), 179–181. doi:10.1126/science.7123230 PMID:7123230

Frank, M. G., & Ekman, P. (1997). The Ability to Detect Deceit Generalizes Across Different Types of High-Stake Lies. *Journal of Personality and Social Psychology*, *72*(6), 1429–1439. doi:10.1037/0022-3514.72.6.1429 PMID:9177024

Frijda, N. H., & Tcherkassof, A. (1997). Facial expressions as modes of action readiness. In *J. A. Russell, & J. M. Fernández-Dols (Eds.), The psychology of facial expression* (pp. 78–102). Cambridge, UK: Cambridge University Press. doi:10.1017/CBO9780511659911.006

Gaddis, B., Connelly, S., & Mumford, M. D. (2004). Failure feedback as an affective event: Influences of leader affect on subordinate attitudes and performance. *The Leadership Quarterly*, *15*(5), 663–686. doi:10.1016/j.leaqua.2004.05.011

Gladwell, M. (2005). *Blink: the power of thinking without thinking*. London: Penguin.

Glaser, J., & Salovey, P. (1998). Affect in Electoral Politics. *Personality and Social Psychology Review*, *2*(3), 156–172. doi:10.1207/s15327957pspr0203_1 PMID:15647152

Glomb, T. M., & Hulin, C. L. (1997). Anger and gender effects in observed supervisor-subordinate dyadic interactions. *Organizational Behavior and Human Decision Processes*, 72(3), 281–307. doi:10.1006/obhd.1997.2741 PMID:9606168

Goffee, R., & Jones, G. (2005). Managing authenticity. *Harvard Business Review*, 83, 86–94. PMID:16334584

Gray, J. H., & Densten, I. L. (2007). How Leaders Woo Followers in the Romance of Leadership. *Applied Psychology*, 56(4), 558–581. doi:10.1111/j.1464-0597.2007.00304.x

Harker, L. A., & Keltne, D. (2001). Expressions of Positive Emotion in Women's College Yearbook Pictures and Their Relationship to Personality and Life Outcomes Across Adulthood. *Journal of Personality and Social Psychology*, 80(1), 112–124. doi:10.1037/0022-3514.80.1.112 PMID:11195884

Hassin, R. R., Bargh, J. A., & Uleman, J. S. (2002). Spontaneous causal inferences. *Journal of Experimental Social Psychology*, 38(5), 515–522. doi:10.1016/S0022-1031(02)00016-1

Hendriks, M., & Vingerhoets, A. (2006). Social messages of crying faces: Their influence on anticipated person perception, emotion and behavioral responses. *Cognition and Emotion*, 20(6), 878–886. doi:10.1080/02699930500450218

Hess, U., Blairy, S., & Kleck, R. E. (2000). The Influence of Facial Emotion Displays, Gender, and Ethnicity on Judgments of Dominance and Affiliation. *Journal of Nonverbal Behavior*, 4(4), 265–283. doi:10.1023/A:1006623213355

Hochschild, A. R. (1983). *The managed heart: Commercialization of human feeling*. Berkeley, CA: University of California Press.

Hoy, W. K., & Miskel, C. G. (2013). *Educational administration: Theory, research and practice* (9th ed.). New York: McGraw Hill.

Humphrey, R. H., Pollack, J. M., & Hawver, T. (2008). Leading with emotional labour. *Journal of Managerial Psychology*, 23(2), 151–168. doi:10.1108/02683940810850790

Hurley, C. (2010). *The Effects of Motivation and Training Format on the Ability to Detect Hidden Emotions*. (Unpublished doctoral dissertation). New York: State University of New York at Buffalo.

Izard, C. (1983). *The maximally descriminative facial movement coding system*. Unpublished manuscript. University of Delaware.

Izard, C. E., Dougherty, L. M., & Hembree, E. A. (1983). *A system for identifying affect expressions by holistic judgments*. Unpublished manuscript. University of Delaware.

Jenkins, A. M., & Johnson, R. D. (1977). What The Information Analyst Should Know About Body Language. *Management Information Systems Quarterly*, 1(3), 33–47. doi:10.2307/248711

Johnson, P. E. (2003). Conflict and the School Leader: Expert or Novice. *Journal of Research for Educational Leaders*, 1, 28–45.

Keating, C. (2003). Messages from Face and Body: Women, Men, and the Silent Expression of Social Status. In D. S. Cobble, B. Hutchison, & A. B. Chaloupka (Eds.), Femininities, masculinities, and the politics of sexual difference(s) (pp. 65-70). Rutgers, the State University.

Keating, C. F., Mazur, A., & Segall, M. H. (1977). Facial Gestures Which Influence the Perception of Status. *Sociometry*, 40(4), 374–378. doi:10.2307/3033487

Kenny, D. A. (1994). *Interpersonal perception: A social relations analysis.* New York: Guilford.

Kidwell, R. E. Jr. (2004). "Small" Lies, Big Trouble: The Unfortunate Consequences of Résumé Padding, from Janet Cooke to George O'Leary. *Journal of Business Ethics, 51*(2), 175–184. doi:10.1023/B:BUSI.0000033611.50841.55

Krumhuber, E., Manstead, A., & Kappas, A. (2006). Temporal Aspects of Facial Displays in Person and Expression Perception: The Effects of Smile Dynamics, Head-tilt, and Gender. *Journal of Nonverbal Behavior, 31*(1), 39–56. doi:10.1007/s10919-006-0019-x

Lau, S. (1982). The effect of smiling on person perception. *The Journal of Social Psychology, 117*(1), 63–67. doi:10.1080/00224545.1982.9713408

Lewis, K. M. (2000). When leaders display emotion: How followers respond to negative emotional expression of male and female leaders. *Journal of Organizational Behavior, 21*(2), 221–234. doi:10.1002/(SICI)1099-1379(200003)21:2<221::AID-JOB36>3.0.CO;2-0

Madera, J. M., & Smith, B. D. (2009). The effects of leader negative emotions on evaluations of leadership in a crisis situation: The role of anger and sadness. *The Leadership Quarterly, 20*(2), 103–114. doi:10.1016/j.leaqua.2009.01.007

Marsh, A., & Ambady, N. (2007). The influence of the fear facial expression on prosocial responding. *Cognition and Emotion, 21*(2), 225–247. doi:10.1080/02699930600652234

Marzano, R. J., & Marzano, J. S. (2003). The key to classroom management. *Educational Leadership, 61,* 6–13.

Masters, R. D., & Sullivan, D. G. (1989). Nonverbal Displays and Political Leadership in France and the United States. *Political Behavior, 11*(2), 123–156. doi:10.1007/BF00992491

Matsumoto, D., & Hee Yoo, S. (2005). Culture and Applied Nonverbal Communication. In R. E. Riggio & R. S. Feldman (Eds.), *Applications of Nonverbal Communication* (pp. 255–276). Mahwah, NJ: Lawrence Erlbaum.

Matsumoto, D., & Hwang, H. (2011). Evidence for training the ability to read microexpressions of emotion. *Motivation and Emotion, 35*(2), 181–191. doi:10.1007/s11031-011-9212-2

McArthur, L. Z., & Baron, R. M. (1983). Toward an ecological theory of social perception. *Psychological Review, 90*(3), 215–238. doi:10.1037/0033-295X.90.3.215

Medvedeff, M. E. (2008). *Leader affective displays during a negative work event: influences on subordinate appraisals, affect, and coping strategies.* (Doctoral dissertation). University of Akron. Retrieved from http://etd.ohiolink.edu/send-pdf.cgi/Medvedeff%20Megan.pdf?akron1207753447

Meindl, J. R. (1995). The romance of leadership as a follower-centric theory: A social constructionist approach. *The Leadership Quarterly, 6*(3), 329–341. doi:10.1016/1048-9843(95)90012-8

Monahan, J. L. (1998). I Don't Know It But I Like You The Influence of Nonconscious Affect on Person Perception. *Human Communication Research, 24*(4), 480–500. doi:10.1111/j.1468-2958.1998.tb00428.x

Monahan, J. L., & Zuckerman, C. E. (1999). Intensifying the dominant response: Participant-observer differences and nonconscious effects. *Communication Research, 26*(1), 81–110. doi:10.1177/009365099026001005

Montepare, J. M., & Dobish, H. (2003). The Contribution of Emotion Perceptions and Their Overgeneralizations to Trait Impressions. *Journal of Nonverbal Behavior, 27*(4), 237–254. doi:10.1023/A:1027332800296

Nye, J., & Forsyth, D. R. (1991). The effects of prototype biases on leadership appraisals: A test of leadership categorization theory. *Small Group Research, 22*(3), 360–379. doi:10.1177/1046496491223005

Porter, S., Juodis, M., ten Brinke, L., Klein, R., & Wilson, K. (2009). Evaluation of the effectiveness of a brief deception detection training program. *Journal of Forensic Psychiatry & Psychology, 21*(1), 66–76. doi:10.1080/14789940903174246

Rafaeli, A., & Sutton, R. I. (1987). Expression of emotion as part of the work role. *Academy of Management Review, 12*, 23–37.

Rosenberg, E. (2005). The study of spontaneous facial expressions in psychology. In P. Ekman & E. Rosenberg (Eds.), *What the face reveals: basic and applied studies of spontaneous expression using the facial action coding system* (2nd ed., pp. 3–17). New York: Oxford University press.

Sayette, M. A., Cohn, J. F., Wertz, J. M., Perrott, M. A., & Parrot, D. J. (2004). A Psychometric Evaluation of the Facial Action Coding System for Assessing Spontaneous Expression. *Journal of Nonverbal Behavior, 25*(3), 167–185. doi:10.1023/A:1010671109788

Scherer, K. R. (1992). What does facial expression express? In K. T. Strongman (Ed.), *International review of studies on emotion* (Vol. 2, pp. 139–165). Chichester, UK: Wiley.

Schyns, B., Felfe, J., & Blank, H. (2007). Is Charisma Hyper-Romanticism? Empirical Evidence from New Data and a Meta-Analysis. *Applied Psychology, 56*(4), 505–527. doi:10.1111/j.1464-0597.2007.00302.x

Schyns, B., & Meindl, J. R. (2005). An overview of implicit leadership theories and their application in organizational practice. In B. Schyns & J. R. Meindl (Eds.), *Implicit leadership theories: essays and explorations* (pp. 15–36). Greenwich, CT: Information Age Publishing.

Smith, C. A., & Scott, H. H. (1997). A componential approach to the meaning of facial expressions. In *J. A. Russell, & J. M. Fernández-Dols, The psychology of facial expression* (pp. 229–254). Cambridge, UK: Cambridge University Press. doi:10.1017/CBO9780511659911.012

Smith, J. A., & Foti, R. J. (1998). A pattern approach to the study of leadership emergence. *The Leadership Quarterly, 9*(2), 147–160. doi:10.1016/S1048-9843(98)90002-9

Snodgrass, J. (1992). *Judgment of feeling states from facial behavior: A bottom-up approach.* (Unpublished doctoral dissertation). University of British Columbia.

Stewart, P. (2010). Presidential laugh lines: Candidate display behavior and audience laughter in the 2008. *Politics and the Life Sciences, 29*(2), 55–72. doi:10.2990/29_2_55 PMID:21761981

Stewart, P., & Dowe, P. (2013). Interpreting President Barack Obama's Facial Displays of Emotion: Revisiting the Dartmouth Group. *Political Psychology, 34*(3), 369–385. doi:10.1111/pops.12004

Stewart, P., Waller, B., & Schubert, J. (2009). Presidential speech making style: Emotional response to micro-expressions of facial affect. *Motivation and Emotion, 33*(2), 125–135. doi:10.1007/s11031-009-9129-1

Sullivan, D. G., & Masters, R. D. (1988). "Happy Warriors": Leaders' Facial Displays, Viewers' Emotions, and Political Support. *American Journal of Political Science, 32*(2), 345–368. doi:10.2307/2111127

Surakka, V., & Hietanen, J. K. (1998). Facial and emotional reactions to Duchenne and non Duchenne smiles. *International Journal of Psychophysiology, 29*(1), 23–33. doi:10.1016/S0167-8760(97)00088-3 PMID:9641245

Sutton, R. I., & Rafaeli, A. (1988). Untangling the relationship between displayed emotions and organizational sales: The case of convenience stores. *Academy of Management Journal, 31*(3), 461–487. doi:10.2307/256456

Tassinary, L. G., & Cacioppo, J. T. (1992). Unobservable Facial Actions and Emotion. *Psychological Science, 3*(1), 28–33. doi:10.1111/j.1467-9280.1992.tb00252.x

Todorov, A., Said, C. P., Engell, A. D., & Oosterhof, N. N. (2008). Understanding evaluation of faces on social dimensions. *Trends in Cognitive Sciences, 12*(12), 455–460. doi:10.1016/j.tics.2008.10.001 PMID:18951830

Trichas, S. (2011). *The face of leadership: Perceiving leaders from facial expression.* (Unpublished doctoral dissertation). University of Portsmouth, Portsmouth, UK.

Trichas, S., & Schyns, B. (2012). The face of leadership: Perceiving leaders from facial expression. *The Leadership Quarterly, 23*(3), 545–566. doi:10.1016/j.leaqua.2011.12.007

Tronick, E. Z. (1989). Emotions and emotional communication in infants. *The American Psychologist, 44*(2), 112–119. doi:10.1037/0003-066X.44.2.112 PMID:2653124

Van Kleef, G. (2009). How emotions regulate social life: The emotions as social information (EASI) model. *Current Directions in Psychological Science, 18*(3), 184–188. doi:10.1111/j.1467-8721.2009.01633.x

Wild, B., Erb, M., & Bartels, M. (2001). Are emotions contagious? Evoked emotions while viewing emotionally expressive faces: Quality, quantity, time course and gender differences. *Psychiatry Research, 102*(2), 109–124. doi:10.1016/S0165-1781(01)00225-6 PMID:11408051

Winkielman, P., & Berridge, K. (2003). Irrational wanting and subrational liking: How rudimentary motivational and affective processes shape preferences and choices. *Political Psychology, 24*(4), 657–680. doi:10.1046/j.1467-9221.2003.00346.x

Winkielman, P., & Berridge, K. (2004). Unconscious Emotion. *Current Directions in Psychological Science, 13*, 120–123. doi:10.1111/j.0963-7214.2004.00288.x

Winkielman, P., Berridge, K. C., & Wilbarger, J. L. (2005). Unconscious Affective Reactions to Masked Happy Versus Angry Faces Influence Consumption Behavior and Judgments of Value. *Personality and Social Psychology Bulletin, 31*(1), 121–135. doi:10.1177/0146167204271309 PMID:15574667

Wood, J. L., Schmidtke, J. M., & Decker, D. L. (2007). Lying on Job Applications: The Effects of Job Relevance, Commission, and Human Resource Management Experience. *Journal of Business and Psychology, 22*(1), 1–9. doi:10.1007/s10869-007-9048-7

Woodger, M. J. (2003). Recollections of David o. MclZay's 'The Religious Educator'. *Educational Practices, 4*, 25–39.

Zebrowitz, L. A., & Montepare, J. M. (2008). Social Psychological Face Perception: Why Appearance Matters. *Social and Personality Psychology Compass, 2*(3), 1497–1517. doi:10.1111/j.1751-9004.2008.00109.x PMID:20107613

ADDITIONAL READING

Adams, R., Ambadi, N., Macrae, C., & Kleck, R. (2006). Emotional expressions forecast approach-avoidance behavior. *Motivation and Emotion*, *30*(2), 179–188. doi:10.1007/s11031-006-9020-2

Adelmann, P. K., & Zajonc, R. B. (1989). Facial efference and the experience of emotion. *Annual Review of Psychology*, *40*(1), 249–280. doi:10.1146/annurev.ps.40.020189.001341 PMID:2648977

Ambadar, Z., Schooler, J., & Cohn, J. (2005). Deciphering the enigmatic face: The importance of facial dynamics in interpreting subtle facial expressions. *Psychological Science*, *16*(5), 403–410. doi:10.1111/j.0956-7976.2005.01548.x PMID:15869701

Ansfield, M. E. (2007). Smiling When Distressed: When a Smile Is a Frown Turned Upside Down. *Personality and Social Psychology Bulletin*, *33*(6), 763–775. doi:10.1177/0146167206297398 PMID:17483396

Antonakis, J., & Dalgas, O. (2009). Predicting Elections: Child's Play! *Science*, *323*(5918), 1183. doi:10.1126/science.1167748 PMID:19251621

Arya, A., Jefferies, L., Enns, J. T., & DiPaola, S. (2006). Facial actions as visual cues for personality. *Computer Animation and Virtual Worlds*, *17*, 371–382.

Ashforth, B. E., & Humphrey, R. H. (1993). Emotional labor in service roles: The influence of identity. *Academy of Management Review*, *18*, 88–115.

Back, E., Jordan, T. R., & Thomas, S. M. (2009). The recognition of mental states from dynamic and static facial expressions. *Visual Cognition*, *17*(8), 1271–1286. doi:10.1080/13506280802479998

Banaji, M. R., Hardin, C., & Rothman, A. J. (1993). Implicit Stereotyping in Person Judgment. *Journal of Personality and Social Psychology*, *65*(2), 272–281. doi:10.1037/0022-3514.65.2.272

Bono, J. E., & Ilies, R. (2006). Charisma, positive emotions and mood contagion. *The Leadership Quarterly*, *17*(4), 317–334. doi:10.1016/j.leaqua.2006.04.008

Bould, E., Morris, N., & Wink, B. (2008). Recognising subtle emotional expressions: The role of facial movements. *Cognition and Emotion*, *22*(8), 1569–1587. doi:10.1080/02699930801921156

Burgoon, J. K., Birk, T., & Pfau, M. (1990). Nonverbal Behaviors, Persuasion, and Credibility. *Human Communication Research*, *17*(1), 140–169. doi:10.1111/j.1468-2958.1990.tb00229.x

Carroll, J. M., & Russell, J. A. (1996). Do facial expressions signal specific emotions? Judging emotion from the face in context. *Journal of Personality and Social Psychology*, *70*(2), 205–218. doi:10.1037/0022-3514.70.2.205 PMID:8636880

Cohn, J. F., Zlochoher, A. J., Lien, J., & Kanade, T. (1999). Automated face analysis by feature point tracking has high concurrent validity with manual FACS coding. *Psychophysiology*, *36*(1), 35–43. doi:10.1017/S0048577299971184 PMID:10098378

Dijksterhuis, A., & Bargh, J. (2001). In M. Zanna (Ed.), *The perception-behavior expressway: Automatic effects of social perception on social behavior* (Vol. 33, pp. 1–40). Advances in experimental social psychology San Diego, CA: Academic Press.

Dimberg, U., & Thunberg, M. (1998). Rapid facial reactions to emotional facial expressions. *Scandinavian Journal of Psychology*, *39*(1), 39–45. doi:10.1111/1467-9450.00054 PMID:9619131

Duchenne, G. (1990). *The mechanism of human facial expression*. Cambridge: Cambridge University Press. (Original work published 1859) doi:10.1017/CBO9780511752841

Frank, M. G., Ekman, P., & Friesen, W. V. (2005). Behavioral markers and recognizability of the smile of enjoyment. In P. Ekman & E. Rosenberg (Eds.), *What the face reveals: basic and applied studies of spontaneous expression using the facial action coding system* (2nd ed., pp. 217–238). New York: Oxford University Press. doi:10.1093/acprof:oso/9780195179644.003.0011

Fridlund, A. J. (1994). *Human Facial Expression: An Evolutionary View*. San Diego, CA: Academic.

Gardner, W. L., Fischer, D., & Hunt, J. G. (2009). Emotional labor and leadership: A threat to authenticity? *The Leadership Quarterly*, *20*(3), 466–482. doi:10.1016/j.leaqua.2009.03.011

Hassin, R. R., Bargh, J. A., & Uleman, J. S. (2002). Spontaneous causal inferences. *Journal of Experimental Social Psychology*, *38*(5), 515–522. doi:10.1016/S0022-1031(02)00016-1

Humphrey, R. H. (2012). How do leaders use emotional labor? *Journal of Organizational Behavior*, *33*(5), 740–744. doi:10.1002/job.1791

Kamachi, M., Bruce, V., Mukaida, S., Gyoba, J., Yoshikawa, S., & Akamatsu, S. (2001). Dynamic properties influence the perception of facial expressions. *Perception*, *30*(7), 875–887. doi:10.1068/p3131 PMID:11515959

Keating, C. F., Mazur, A., & Segall, M. H. (1981). Culture and the perception of social dominance from facial expression. *Journal of Personality and Social Psychology*, *40*(4), 615–626. doi:10.1037/0022-3514.40.4.615

Keltner, D., & Ekman, P. (2000). Facial expression of emotion. In M. Lewis & J. Haviland-Jones (Eds.), *Handbook of emotion* (pp. 236–249). New York: Guilford Press.

Knutson, B. (1996). Facial expressions of emotion influence interpersonal trait inferences. *Journal of Nonverbal Behavior*, *20*(3), 165–182. doi:10.1007/BF02281954

Krull, D. S., & Dill, J. C. (1998). Do smiles elicit more inferences than do frowns? The effect of emotional valence on the production of spontaneous inferences. *Personality and Social Psychology Bulletin*, *24*(3), 289–300. doi:10.1177/0146167298243006

Krumhuber, E., & Kappas, A. (2005). Moving smiles: The role of dynamic components for the perception of the genuineness of smiles. *Journal of Nonverbal Behavior*, *29*(1), 3–24. doi:10.1007/s10919-004-0887-x

Krumhuber, E., Manstead, A. S., Cosker, D., Marshall, D., Rosin, P. L., & Kappas, A. (2007). Facial dynamics as indicators of trustworthiness and cooperative behavior. *Emotion (Washington, D.C.)*, *7*(4), 730–735. doi:10.1037/1528-3542.7.4.730 PMID:18039040

Marsh, A. A., Adams, R. B., & Kleck, R. E. (2005). Why do fear and anger look the way they do? Form and social function in facial expressions. *Personality and Social Psychology Bulletin*, *31*(1), 1–14. doi:10.1177/0146167204271306 PMID:15574663

Masters, R. D., & Sullivan, D. G. (1989). Nonverbal displays and political leadership in France and the United States. *Political Behavior*, *11*(2), 123–156. doi:10.1007/BF00992491

Matsumoto, D., & Ekman, P. (1989). American-Japanese cultural differences in intensity ratings of facial expressions of emotion. *Motivation and Emotion, 13*(2), 143–157. doi:10.1007/BF00992959

Mc Culloch, K., Ferguson, M., Kawada, C., & Bargh, J. (2007). Taking a closer look: On the operation of nonconscious impression formation. *Journal of Experimental Social Psychology, 44*(3), 614–623. doi:10.1016/j.jesp.2007.02.001 PMID:18552986

Naidoo, L. J., Kohari, N., Lord, R. G., & Dubois, D. A. (2010). "Seeing" is retrieving: Recovering emotional content in leadership ratings through visualization. *The Leadership Quarterly, 21*(5), 886–900. doi:10.1016/j.leaqua.2010.07.014

Naidoo, L. J., & Lord, R. G. (2008). Speech imagery and perceptions of charisma: The mediating role of positive affect. *The Leadership Quarterly, 19*(3), 283–296. doi:10.1016/j.leaqua.2008.03.010

Niedenthal, P. M. (2007). Embodying Emotion. *Science, 316*(5827), 1002–1005. doi:10.1126/science.1136930 PMID:17510358

Niedenthal, P. M., Winkielman, P., Mondillon, L., & Vermeulen, N. (2009). Embodiment of emotion concepts. *Journal of Personality and Social Psychology, 96*(6), 1120–1136. doi:10.1037/a0015574 PMID:19469591

Parkinson, B. (2005). Do Facial Movements Express Emotions or Communicate Motives? *Personality and Social Psychology Review, 9*(4), 278–311. doi:10.1207/s15327957pspr0904_1 PMID:16223353

Pescosolido, A. T. (2002). Emergent leaders as managers of group emotion. *The Leadership Quarterly, 13*(5), 583–599. doi:10.1016/S1048-9843(02)00145-5

Pugh, S. D. (2001). Service with a smile: Emotional contagion in the service encounter. *Academy of Management Journal, 44*(5), 1018–1027. doi:10.2307/3069445

Roberts, L. M. (2005). Changing faces: Professional image construction in diverse organizational settings. *Academy of Management Review, 30*(4), 685–711. doi:10.5465/AMR.2005.18378873

Schmid, M. M., & Hall, J. A. (2004). Who is the boss and who is not? Accuracy of judging status. *Journal of Nonverbal Behavior, 28*(3), 145–165. doi:10.1023/B:JONB.0000039647.94190.21

Schyns, B., & Meindl, J. R. (2005). An overview of implicit leadership theories and their application in organizational practice. In B. Schyns & J. R. Meindl (Eds.), *Implicit Leadership Theories: Essays and Explorations* (pp. 15–36). Greenwich, Connecticut: Information Age Publishing.

Schyns, B., & Mohr, G. (2004). Nonverbal Elements of Leadership Behaviour. *German journal of human recource research, 18*, 289-305.

Schyns, P., & Oliva, A. (1999). Dr. Angry and Mr. Smile: When categorization flexibly modifies the perception of faces in rapid visual presentations. *Cognition, 69*(3), 243–265. doi:10.1016/S0010-0277(98)00069-9 PMID:10193048

Secord, P. F. (1958). Facial features and inference processes in interpersonal perception. In R. Taguiri & L. Petrullo (Eds.), *Person Perception and Interpersonal Behavior* (pp. 300–315). Stanford, CA: Stanford University Press.

Sy, T., Cote´, S., & Saavedra, R. (2005). The Contagious Leader: Impact of the Leader's Mood on the Mood of Group Members, Group Affective Tone, and Group Processes. *The Journal of Applied Psychology, 90*(2), 295–305. doi:10.1037/0021-9010.90.2.295 PMID:15769239

Wehrle, T., Kaiser, S., Schmidt, S., & Scherer, K. R. (2000). Studying the dynamics of emotional expression via synthesized facial muscle movements. *Journal of Personality and Social Psychology*, 78(1), 105–119. doi:10.1037/0022-3514.78.1.105 PMID:10653509

Wild, B., Erb, M., & Bartels, M. (2001). Are emotions contagious? Evoked emotions while viewing emotionally expressive faces: Quality, quantity, time course and gender differences. *Psychiatry Research*, 102(2), 109–124. doi:10.1016/S0165-1781(01)00225-6 PMID:11408051

Zebrowitz, L. A., Fellous, J., Mignault, A., & Andreoletti, C. (2003). Trait Impressions as Overgeneralized Responses to Adaptively Significant Facial Qualities: Evidence from Connectionist Modeling. *Personality and Social Psychology Review*, 7(3), 194–215. doi:10.1207/S15327957PSPR0703_01 PMID:12788687

KEY TERMS AND DEFINITIONS

Facial Action Coding System (FACS): A highly valid, widely used tool that photo or video analysis observation of 44 anatomically separate facial action units to define exact facial muscle movement and intensity also considering the temporal development of the expression (Ekman et al., 2002; Harker & Keltne, 2001).

Facial Expressions: The visible changes that facial-muscle activity causes to the face. The above definition emanates from the principles set by the facial action coding system (FACS; Ekman, Friesen, & Hager, 2002). Note: The method of electromyography (EMG, Tassinary & Cacioppo, 1992) can also be used for measuring facial muscle movement. EMG can detect facial muscle changes which are not visible with a naked eye. The above definition regards only visible facial expressions.

Implicit Leadership Theories (ILTs): Context-specific cognitive schemas people have about leaders (e.g., Epitropaki & Martin, 2004). Research indicates that when perceivers observe behaviors, they use ILTs as a comparison criterion to classify people into leaders and non-leaders (Gray & Densten, 2007; Nye & Forsyth, 1991; Schyns, Felfe, & Blank, 2007).

Leadership Perception: Analogically with person perception, leadership perception is defined as the judgements a person makes about a leader (Kenny, 1994).

Micro-Expressions: Facial expressions that appear for only a very brief amount of time (e.g., Ekman & Friesen 2003).

Sophisticated Facial Expression Coding Analysis: Facial action coding systems that emphasise in parameters such as exact facial muscle movement, intensity, and temporal aspects (Ekman & Friesen, 1978; Krumhuber, Manstead, & Kappas, 2006).

Subtle Facial Actions: Facial muscle movement or intensity that do not dramatically alter the appearance of a facial expression. For example, an anger expression compared with the exact same anger expression with more widening of the eye aperture, the subtle facial action will be the widening of the eye aperture.

Chapter 11
Emotional Intelligence and Political Skill Really Matter in Educational Leadership

Nikoletta Taliadorou
Open University of Cyprus, Cyprus

Petros Pashiardis
Open University of Cyprus, Cyprus

ABSTRACT

In this chapter, the authors investigate the social skills that school principals ought to exhibit in order to be more effective in the complex environment that characterizes modern schools. Thus, the main aim of this chapter is to provide an in-depth exploration of those social skills that are needed in order for school principals to become more flexible to external and internal requirements and to balance the need for change with stability. Therefore, an attempt is made to investigate the linkages between school leadership, emotional intelligence, political skill, and teachers' job satisfaction, as well as to examine the correlation of emotional and political skills of principals with the job satisfaction of their teachers.

1. INTRODUCTION

Today's schools operate in competitive and complex environments that require educational leaders to possess social effectiveness skills in order to energize their schools towards the achievement of their core purpose. Within this context it is necessary to investigate the social competences of school principals that will equip them to effectively cope with multiple and complex changes. According to Pashiardis (2009), "Leaders need to be cognizant of the power of how one publicly presents oneself

but at the same time realize the dangers involved for their public image" (p. 1).This is necessary in order to be more socially adept and competent when exercising their duties as school leaders. After all it is the principal who binds together the various threads of "values, leadership, vision and culture" (Campbell-Evans, 1993:110).

Based on this assumption, Taliadorou and Pashiardis (2014) investigated whether emotional intelligence and political capacity of school principals influence the way they exercise leadership and in which ways they influence their teachers'

DOI: 10.4018/978-1-4666-6591-0.ch011

job satisfaction. It should be noted from the outset that in the context of this study, leadership behaviors of the principal are perceived, through the adoption of leadership styles. We will base our suggestions on the research results of Taliadorou and Pashiardis (2014), which support the need for an expansion of the theories about what constitutes effective leadership. Specifically, the above researchers developed a dynamic model in an effort to couple and co-examine these areas (Figure 1), after a thorough literature review. Thus, the theoretical model guiding this piece of

Figure 1. Research theoretical model (Taliadorou & Pashiardis, 2014)

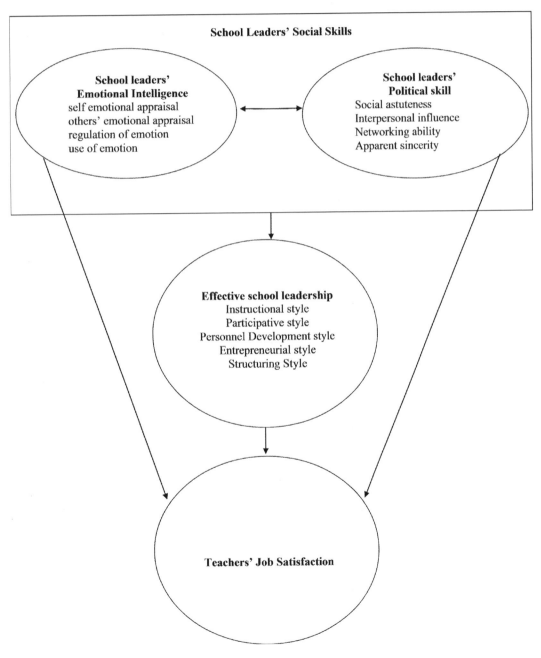

research combines the main research variables that (supposedly) affect the exercise of educational leadership and are analyzed below. In order to find out whether any relations exist between the variables examined, the results are presented in section two of this chapter.

In their study, Taliadorou and Pashiardis (2014) followed the ability model of *Emotional Intelligence (EI)* which defines EI as the ability "to monitor one's own and others' emotions, to discriminate among them and to use the information to guide one's thinking and actions" (Salovey & Mayer, 1990, p. 189). *Political Skill (PS)* is "the ability to effectively understand others at work and to use such knowledge to influence others to act in ways that enhance one's personal and/or organizational objectives" (Ahearn, Ferris, Hochwarter, Douglas, & Ammeter, 2004, p. 311). As for job satisfaction, there is no unique definition of *teacher job satis-*

faction. Therefore, some researchers (Dinham & Scott, 2002; Van Den Berg, 2002) concluded that students' results and positive relationships in the workplace are some of the features that are related with teachers' satisfaction. Finally, as regards to *leadership,* we perceive it as a combination of social influence through which a leader affects employees' feelings, perceptions, and behavior (Humphrey, 2002; Pirola-Merlo, Hartel, Mann, & Hirst, 2002). Furthermore, leadership is treated as a normative, collective, and relational social practice (Blackmore, 1999). Finally, this piece of research is based on the heuristic theoretical framework of educational leadership (Figure 2) as developed by Pashiardis and Brauckmann (2008).

The field research of Taliadorou and Pashiardis was conducted during the school year 2010-2011 in public schools of Primary Education in Cyprus (student ages 6 to 12). A purposive sample was

Figure 2. The Pashiardis-Brauckmann holistic leadership framework (2008)

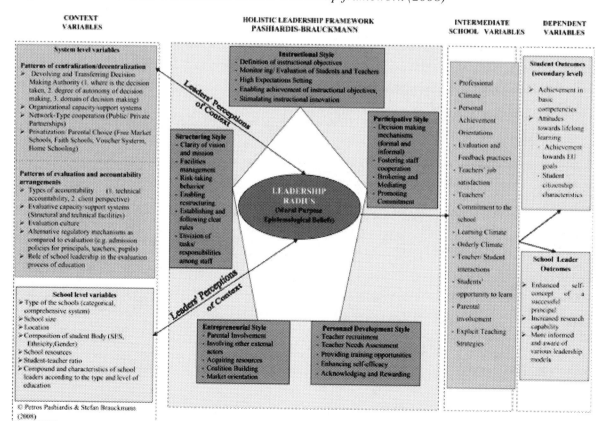

chosen with the selection of principals employed in elementary schools staffed with more than six teachers. The final sample consisted of 182 principals of elementary schools and 910 teachers. For each principal, there was a representation of five teachers working in the particular school year with him/her.

As regards to the methodology, quantitative research methods were used to conduct the research. Specifically, the data analyses were performed using the statistical program SPSS and the EQS program (Bentler & Wu, 1995) for the development of both structural equation models and analysis. The use of this kind of analysis aimed at identifying the effects of emotional intelligence and policy capacity, within the leadership radius of the principal and the job satisfaction of his/her teachers.

The first section of this chapter attempts to answer whether emotional intelligence and political skill really matter in educational leadership and notes the need for further research on these areas. Indeed firstly, we investigate the extent to which the emotional and political skills of principals correlate to their leadership styles and secondly the correlation of emotional and political skills of principals to the job satisfaction of their teachers. In addition, we examine whether emotional intelligence and political skill are two distinct constructs. The second section of this chapter refers to suggestions for educational policy and practice in dealing with the issues arising. The third section deals with the main study conclusions.

2. DO EMOTIONAL INTELLIGENCE AND POLITICAL SKILL REALLY MATTER IN EDUCATIONAL LEADERSHIP?

Investigating the extent to which the emotional and political skills of principals relate to leadership styles

Effective School Leadership Styles

The role and responsibilities of school leaders have changed over the past years. Educational leaders need to think globally, but, at the same time, they need to act locally in an ever increasing tension between these two tendencies which exist in a continuum. According to Pashiardis (2009, p. 1) "Educational leaders around the globe will need to work in a context where the only stable factor is constant change and lead the way in the educational arena for the decades to come". Also, school leadership is highly contextualized both at the system level as well as at the school level. An effective school leader would be wise to identify what his or her particular school context calls for and use a variety of leadership behaviors, in order to reach high educational quality. Also, the quality of leadership matters in determining the motivation of teachers and the quality of teaching that takes place in the classroom (Fullan, 2001; Segiovanni, 1999).

Researchers (Leithwood, 1992; 1993; 1994; Silins, 1992; 1994a; 1994b) have identified the leadership behaviors and practices that lead to a general school reformation. Indeed according to Fullan (2007) "Reform is not just putting into place the latest policy. It means changing the culture of the classrooms, the schools, the districts, the universities and so on." Changing culture is ascendant to introducing, developing and growing reform. The outmost important variable that contributes to school reformation is the relationships between the people working together. This kind of bonding reflects how work is done or not done. Thus, in order for school reform to occur it is necessary to create a culture that supports inquiry, reflection, trust and innovation. Those leadership practices are included in the transformational leadership style, such as empowering and supporting employees (Blase & Blase, 2000), caring about local community aspects (Limerick & Nielsen, 1995), creating and involving all in creating the school vision (Mulford, 1994) and emphasize the importance of building a positive collaborative school climate (Deal & Peterson, 1994). Transformational Leadership conceptualizes the role of using socialized or resourceful power to motivate people toward the service of collective interests. The concept of that kind of leadership is focused on the development and empowerment of others and it has emotional intelligence as its driving force (Power, 2004). Overall, Bass (1985) argued that Transformational leadership has four components: idealized influence, inspirational motivation, intellectual stimulation, and individualized consideration. He maintains that a true leader encourages followers to go beyond self-interest for the good of the organization and influences subordinates by motivating and inspiring them to achieve organizational goals (Bass & Avolio, 1995). As a result, according to Day et al. (2000), through effective school leadership practices, schools are becoming caring, focused, and inquiring communities.

School leaders contribute towards the creation of professional learning communities by bringing stakeholders together to engage in a four-step process: creating a mission statement, developing a vision, developing value statements, and establishing goals. The principal's modeling and reinforcing vision-related behaviors appear critical to the success of the professional learning community (DuFour & Eaker, 2006). Therefore, it is more important that each group articulates what they are prepared to do than what they believe (DuFour & Eaker, 2006). Additionally, active participation in collaborative teams broadens the opportunity for teachers and others to become involved as leaders (Barth, 1990; Fullan, 2005; Sergiovanni, 2004).

The research of Taliadorou and Pashiardis (2014) is based on the heuristic theoretical framework of educational leadership (Figure 2) as developed by Pashiardis and Brauckmann (Pashiardis, 2014). After a thorough literature review over the last few decades on school leadership,

educational governance and school effectiveness, the above researchers extracted and labeled five leadership styles, through their own research on school leaders in various European contexts. Every leadership style consists of specific behaviors and practices which are likely to be exhibited by school principals. One of the worthy conclusions that their research (Pashiardis & Brauckmann, 2008; 2009; Pashiardis, 2014) culminated on was that the theoretical framework is mainly a leadership cocktail mix which contains only the basic ingredients and not the quantities needed of each. Recently, Pashiardis (2012) argued in another book that school principals should have the knowledge to identify and use a variety of leadership styles, after evaluating the circumstances they find themselves in. The five leadership styles that are included in the theoretical leadership framework of Pashiardis and Brauckmann (2008; Brauckmann & Pashiardis, 2011; Pashiardis, 2014) are:

1. **Instructional Style:** Leadership practices and behaviors that enable achievement of instructional objectives and high expectations.
2. **Participative Style:** Leadership practices and behaviors that promote cooperation and commitment.
3. **Personnel Development Style:** Leadership practices and behaviors that promote professional growth and development of teachers.
4. **Entrepreneurial Style:** Leadership practices and behaviors that promote the involvement of external actors and coalition building.
5. **Structuring Style:** Leadership practices and behaviors that promote the establishment and implementation of clear rules, roles and vision.

As we can see from Figure 2, school leaders believe that various external contextual variables influence their leadership radius and, at the same time, they can have an influence on their own context. At the system level there are two categories of context variables that affect their leadership style. First, there are the variables that include patterns of centralization/decentralization: at what level is the decision taken, the degree of autonomy of decision making, organizational capacity/support systems and network-type cooperation. The other category includes patterns of evaluation and accountability arrangements at the national level: technical accountability, client perspective, structural and technical facilities, the evaluation culture, the alternative regulatory mechanisms as compared to evaluation and the role of school leadership in the evaluation process of education.

As for school level the variables that affect leadership styles, these concern the type, the location, and the size of the school. Also very important is the socio-economic composition of the student body, the school resources, the student-teacher ratio and the characteristics of school leaders according to the type and level of their education.

Continuously we are going to refer to the leadership practices and behaviors that are included in every single leadership style. We agree that most day-to-day activities in the school need to be specifically designed to connect teachers, principals, and district administrators with one another and with outside experts in regard to school improvement (Fullan, 2010). All these practices are included in every single leadership style.

First school principals who make use of the *Instructional style*, provide instructional resources, encourage higher order forms of teaching and learning, promote the implementation and use of knowledge in a variety of forms, monitor standards of teaching and learning, provide concrete feedback to staff and utilize evaluation data in order to improve their personnel.

As for the *Participative style*, principals who use this style promote open communication with the staff, leave instructional autonomy to teachers, create a common vision for school improvement, actively involve staff in planning and implementing this vision, solve problems in cooperation with the

teachers, implement participative decision making processes, facilitate decision making by consensus and discuss school affairs with the teachers.

The *Personnel Development style* includes leadership practices and behaviors such as providing recognition for excellence and achievement, rewarding teachers for their special contributions, encouraging the professional development of teachers, registering outstanding performance of teachers, making informed recommendations to personnel placement, transfer, retention and dismissal, complimenting teachers who contribute exceptionally to school activities and informing teachers about possibilities for updating their knowledge and skills.

Principals who use the *Entrepreneurial style* encourage relations between the school and the community and parents, promote cooperation with other organizations and businesses, discuss school goals with relevant stakeholders, utilize appropriate and effective techniques for community and parental involvement, promote two-way communication between the school and the community, project a positive image to the community, build trust within the local community and communicate the school vision to the external community.

Finally, the *Structuring Style* includes practices and behaviors such as ensuring clarity about the roles and activities of staff, ensuring clarity about work priorities, providing clarity in relation to student and staff behavior rules, ensuring that school rules and consequences of misconduct are uniformly applied to all students, working on the creation of an orderly atmosphere, and providing clarity regarding policies and procedures to be implemented.

The question that arises is, how can a principal know which leadership style is the most appropriate under the circumstances? We argue that a school principal who uses emotional intelligence and political skill is more capable of acting in the right direction. Luthans (2002) stated that leader performance and career success are determined less by intelligence and more by social astuteness and savvy. These findings lead us to the conclusion that the organizational behavior of the elementary school principal plays an important role in the effectiveness of the school organization; therefore an appropriate training should be given to those who will be placed to this position.

School leadership styles are significant factors that contribute to teachers' job satisfaction (Glisson & Durick, 1988). Scheerens (2000) further suggests that leadership styles are true indicators of leader effectiveness. Teacher dissatisfaction is also associated with decreased productivity (Zembylas & Papanastasiou, 2004), and thus we need school leaders who can promote teachers' job satisfaction in order to achieve high academic results.

Indeed according to the Pashiardis-Brauckmann Holistic Leadership Framework (2008), besides teachers' job satisfaction, school leadership styles affect also the various intermediate school variables such as school climate, evaluation and feedback practices, teachers' commitment to the school, the learning climate, the parental involvement, students' opportunity to learn and many others. Then, through the usage of effective leadership styles/ practices (as we can see from Figure 2) we have improved student outcomes and the enhancement of self-concept of a successful principal.

As discussed above, school principals' leadership style is a crucial factor in achieving the school mission. Their every day practices and behaviors are decisive factors in creating the impression others have about them, therefore they need to be well-equipped with social skills in order to be effective. Indeed leadership concerns the interaction of leaders with other individuals, so once social interactions are involved, emotional awareness and emotional regulation become important factors affecting the quality of these interactions. In the next section, we discuss whether and to what extent emotional and political skills of principals relate to leadership styles.

Emotional Intelligence

The current flow of research in organizational leadership suggests that social skills are becoming increasingly essential. Further, researchers indicate that organizations should rely less on bureaucratic and hierarchical structures. Thus, we consider that the emotional and political skills of the leader play an important role in the effectiveness of the school organization, and that this importance will continue to grow. Little seems to have been written about the person of the leader and the emotions that person experiences while leading. There are times when principals do want the fairy godmother to come and save them. (Loader 1997, p. 3).

Within the various frameworks of educational reform, there have been calls for educational change with heart and mind (Hargreaves, 1997). Also, according to Zembylas (2009), educational leaders are controlled every day with a diversity of emotions that are associated with personal, professional, relational, political, and cultural issues. Additionally, research results have indicated that emotions play a crucial role in school leaders' lives (Beatty, 2007a, 2007b; Leithwood & Beatty, 2008), because leadership is a social practice dependent on relationships that are both teeming and accomplishing, requiring, particularly for principals, emotional regulation of themselves and of others (Blackmore, 1999). Based on the above, we can deduce that some scholars (Hargreaves, 2001; Leithwood, 2006) recognized the important role of emotions and emotional intelligence both in leadership and professional development early on.

First, according to some researchers (Boler & Zembylas 2003; Fortier 2005; Harding & Pribram 2002; 2004;) emotions need to be conceptualized as public and collaborative constructs, instead of autonomous psychological traits and states. A well accepted definition of emotions is: "*An emotion is usually caused by a person consciously or unconsciously evaluating an event as relevant to a concern (a goal) that is important. An emotion is usually experienced as a distinctive type of mental state, sometimes accompanied or followed by bodily changes, expressions, and actions."* (Oatley & Jenkins 1996, p. 96).

Oatley and Jenkins (1996) maintain that emotions and moods affect perception, attention, memory and judgment. Furthermore, George (2000) supported that emotions influence many actions that are involved with leadership such as creativity, attributions for success and failure, decision making and deductive and inductive reasoning. Understanding our emotions and the emotions of others provides us with the opportunity to develop positive relations with others and have better cooperation. Having in mind the above conceptualization, the balanced regulation of emotions contributes once more to decision making and is correlated with the management of human resources (Hargreaves, 2004).

Understanding the impact of emotions in school leaders' lives, Taliadorou and Pashiardis (2014) focused their research interests on the Emotional Intelligence (EI) of school principals and adopted the ability model of Mayer and Salovey (2007) which conceptualizes EI as a multifaceted construct that comprises several different abilities and skills and it is thought as a promising view from many researchers (Antonakis, Ashkanasy, & Dasborough, 2009; Zeidner, Roberts, & Matthews, 2008). Mayer and Salovey (1997) define EI as a set of interrelated skills concerning "the ability to perceive accurately, appraise, and express emotion; the ability to access and/or generate feelings when they facilitate thought; the ability to understand emotion and emotional knowledge; and the ability to regulate emotions to promote emotional and intellectual growth" (p. 10). Salovey and Mayer (1990) conceptualized EI as composed of four distinct dimensions:

1. Appraisal and expression of emotion in the self (self emotional appraisal [SEA]).

2. Appraisal and recognition of emotion in others (others' emotional appraisal [OEA]).
3. Regulation of emotion in the self (regulation of emotion [ROE]).
4. Use of emotion to facilitate performance (use of emotion [UOE]).

Taliadorou and Pashiardis (2014) chose the above ability model of emotional intelligence because the definition offered by Salovey and Mayer asserts that EI is an ability of sorts that is distinct from personality (though related somewhat to IQ, Ashkanasy & Daus, 2005). Thus, they became convinced that this model might be the way to go despite the low meta-analytic correlation (.19) between the Salovey–Mayer MEIS ability scale of EI and performance outcomes (Van Rooy & Viswesvaran, 2004).

A considerably different approach has been adopted by trait EI models such as Goleman's (1995) who transformed the original ability model of Salovey and Mayer (1990) into a trait definition of emotional intelligence, including many motivational concepts (e.g. zeal and persistence), and finally, equated emotional intelligence with character (Goleman, 1995). Goleman (1995) developed five domains that characterize emotional intelligence: knowing one's emotions, managing emotions, motivating oneself, recognizing emotions in others and handling relationships (1995, p. 43-44). As a result Mayer and his colleagues criticize Goleman for making "extraordinary claims for the concept [of emotional intelligence], and loose description [that] created an explosion of activity in a new, and now increasingly fuzzily defined area" (Mayer, 2001, p. 8). The above researchers were not the only ones that disagreed with the Goleman conception of EI. Also Sternberg (2001) argued that "Much of what is being done under the banner of *emotional intelligence* appears to be conceptually weak and oriented more toward commercial exploitation than toward increasing psychological understanding" (p. 193). As though, Jordan, Ashton James and Ashkanasy

(2006) questioned the hyperbolic claims made by some (e.g., Goleman, Boyatzis, & McKee, 2002), who seem to care more about selling books than advancing science.

As a result of the "cacophony of conceptualizations" of emotional intelligence there has been an abundance of claims about the effect of EI (Antonakis, 2003; Goleman, Boyatzis, & McKee, 2002; Matthews, Zaccaro, & Horn, 2002; Zeidner, Matthews, & Roberts, 2004) at the workplace. Although there are very promising positive research findings of the relationship of emotional intelligence and leadership, many studies have ended in contradictions regarding the necessity of emotional intelligence for leadership behavior; therefore, researchers must be very careful about the methodology that they use in order to prove the validity of the EI/leadership link (Antonakis, 2003; Antonakis et al., 2009; Locke, 2005). Despite all the negative assertions about EI, research in this area needs to continue in order to develop and to further study emotions and, in particular their role in the area of leadership.

Nevertheless, research on the effects of leaders' emotional skills on employees' emotions and work attitudes is limited (Bono, Foldes, Vinson, & Muros, 2007). However, there are some studies which concluded in positive research results such as that leaders' overall EI is positively related to both leaders' and employees' well-being and performance at work (Sy, Tram, & O'Hara, 2006; Wong & Law, 2002). Furthermore, Ashkanasy and Tse (2000) argued that leaders' EI influences the impressions that employees have for their leader. Research findings showed that EI can predict the success of leaders and their effectiveness (Cherniss, 2003; Sivanathan & Fekken, 2002; Van Rooy & Viswesvaran, 2004). Furthermore Beaver's research, (2005) demonstrated a positive correlation between high levels of principals' EI and high-performing schools. Indeed many researchers

(Beavers, 2005; Buntrock, 2008; Moore, 2009) argued that high emotional intelligence leaders are more likely to lead the way to change and achieve their follower's commitment. Moore (2007) after a mixed method research concluded that emotional intelligence programs are very useful for school principals' working life. In another mixed method research, Williams (2008) found that coworkers rated the emotionally intelligent school principals as more effective than those principals who were perceived as less emotionally intelligent. In 2005, Stone, Parker and Wood conducted a piece of research at Ontario public schools with a research sample of 464 school principals and concluded that more capable principals scored higher at emotional intelligence scales.

Concluding on the same theme, Beatty (2000, p. 354) investigated how EI could be involved in the school leadership process as a productive tool in order to achieve organizational goals and increase influence. We believe that school principals with high EI and emotional maturity are more likely to use supportive behavior and treat their teachers with psychological benefits, as they are more sensitive to feelings and emotions of themselves and their teachers.

The research of Taliadorou and Pashiardis (2014) is based on the assumption that EI is mainly related with school leadership styles, through the emotions' political dimension. This assertion is based on Layder's argument (2004) that emotions are related with social power. As Layder (1997) argued power is ever omnipresent because it is a mottled construct, multi-faceted in character and capable of commutation. When a leader is characterized by prestige and power, he/she is capable of controlling the rhythmic flow of social interactions. Finally, according to Turner and Stets (2005, p. 830) "When they talk, others listen and give off positive emotional signals, thus enhancing the powerful or prestigious person's cultural capital and emotional energy". Thus, focusing on the assumption that emotions are political, the next variable that is going to be analyzed is the principal's political skill.

Political Skill

New theories and constructs are nowadays a necessity to the continuously evolving organizational design which tends to rely less on bureaucratic or hierarchical structures (Daft & Lewin, 1993; Stewart & Carson, 1997). As a result, probably more emphasis needs to be given to political skills, as organizations are inherently political arenas (Mintzberg, 1983, 1985). Based on this assumption, a leader needs a combination of multiple skills (social astuteness, positioning, and savvy) beyond intelligence in order to be effective and productive (e.g., Luthans, Hodgetts, & Rosenkrantz, 1988; Mintzberg, 1983). One of the leaders' social skills which is very promising for organizational effectiveness is *political skill*. As stated by Ferris, Perrewe, Anthony, and Gilmore (2000), political skill must be conceived as a characteristic manner of expression, execution, and construction in the work environment and rather not as a single trait or skill. Indeed, political skill is defined as 'the ability to effectively understand others at work, and to use such knowledge in order to influence others to act in ways that enhance one's personal and/or organizational objectives' (Ahearn et al., 2004, p. 311). Ferris, Kolodinsky, Hochwarter, and Frink (2001) contended that political skill combines four dimensions as follows:

1. **Self and Social Astuteness:** Individuals possessing political skill are astute observers of others and keenly attuned to diverse social situations.
2. **Interpersonal Influence/Control:** Politically skilled individuals have a strong and convincing personal style that tends to exert a powerful influence on those around them.

3. **Network Building/Social Capital:** Individuals with strong political skills are adept at using diverse networks of people by easily developing friendships and building strong and beneficial alliances and coalitions.
4. **Genuineness/Sincerity:** Tactics of politically skilled individuals are seen as subtle and their motives do not appear self-serving. They appear to others to be congruent, sincere, and genuine.

Mintzberg (1983) argued that politically skilled individuals are artists in influencing others through persuasion, manipulation, and negotiation. Additionally, politically skilled individuals have the ability to act in a right way according to situational demands and make use of a wide-range of appropriate managerial behaviors that make them appear sincere, inspire support and trust, and effectively influence and control the responses of others. Therefore, politically skilled persons possess social skills that help them to understand and influence others at work, in order to enhance their personal and/or organizational goals. All these assertions about political skill are confirmed by research findings that enhance its importance in the work environment. This argument recently has been supported by a great deal of research evidences which reveal a relationship between political skill and job performance (e.g., Ahearn et al., 2004; Ferris, Treadway et al., 2005; Ferris, Witt, & Hochwarter, 2001; Higgnis, Judge, & Ferris, 2003; Perrewe´, Zellars, Ferris, Rossi, Kacmar, & Ralston, 2004).

One of the worthy results is that, political skill increases performance in team settings (Ahearn et al., 2004) and has been found to be a modulator of job tension (Perrewe´ et al., 2004) and of emotional labor (Treadway et al., 2005) because the political skills make them good negotiators and adept at using diverse networks of people. We believe that a leader's political skill represents a form of goal-directed socialized political behavior that leaders use to exert influence and control others in a way to be seen as genuine and sincere. Furthermore, politically skilled persons possess social competencies that enhance their personal and/or organizational goals through their understanding and influence of others at work, without appearing manipulative.

Meanwhile, there is a significant relationship between employees' ratings of their supervisors' political skill and their evaluations of supervisors' leadership effectiveness (Ferris, Treadway et al., 2005). Also, other research (Treadway et al., 2004) suggests that politically skilled leaders influence their employees' impressions of caring and trust and that leads in improvement of leader-follower relations. Another study found positive political behaviors to be significantly correlated with employee satisfaction with the supervisor ($r = .29$) and satisfaction with work group ($r = .34$) (Fedor et al., 2003). Summarizing all these results, we conclude that political skill has been an important determinant of administration (Semadar et al., 2006) and employee performance (Kolodinsky et al., 2007; Treadway et al., 2007).

Certainly, besides organizations being perceived as fundamentally political arenas (e.g., Fairholm, 1993; Kanter, 1979; Mintzberg, 1985; Pfeffer, 1981; 1992), schools have become complex working environments that require successful players to posses heightened levels of political skill in order to succeed towards the achievement of organizational goals. Based on the above conceptual rationale, it is expected that school principals' political skill accounts for a portion of the variance in their leadership style and their teachers' job satisfaction. Indeed, Pashiardis (2009) argued that educational leaders should be cognizant of the power of how one publicly presents oneself but at the same time, realize the dangers involved for their public image, thus they need to be characterized by political skill. He further stressed that "leaders should become artists in the three 'f's: forming, facing and feeling public opinion" (p. 5). Although, scholars and practitioners alike have acknowledged the existence and importance of politics in school organizations, there has been little effort to investigate the effect of political skill in educational settings.

We think that it is very important for school principals to demonstrate a positive public image because their image is strongly associated with their school's image. In effect, the school principal mirrors the school. As so, wider social forces (teacher status and the portrayal of teachers in the media) are some of the factors that are related with low teachers' job satisfaction (e.g., Dinham & Scott, 1998, 2000; Scott et al., 2001; Van den Berg, 2002; Van den Berg & Huberman, 1999). Therefore, in order for school principals to preserve a positive public image, they have to make use of their political skills. By using their political skills, they may succeed in creating positive relations between the school and the community and parents, promote cooperation with other organizations and businesses, promote two-way communication between the school and the community, project a positive image to the community, build trust within the local community and communicate the school vision to the external community.

Our conviction is that if school principals leverage their emotional and political skills then they may use the right leadership style according to the situation in order to create positive relations with their teachers. Additionally, according to Fineman (1993, p. 31) work organizations are "emotional arenas" and if you lead that kind of organizations it is inevitably an "emotionally charged" process (George, 2000, p. 1046). Moreover, Stater (2005) argued that many leadership behaviors (e.g. building trust) are integrally emotionally connected.

Concluding, through the research overview on emotional intelligence and political skill that we referred to before, it seems questionable whether the above constructs have an overlap on each other or, in other words, if they are interrelated. Thus, in the next section we will try to resolve this assertion through the critical presentation of some research findings.

Are Emotional Intelligence and Political Skill, Two Distinct Constructs?

Ferris's (2005) research findings revealed that the political skill composite score was related to emotional intelligence at a modest level ($r = .53$, $p < .01$) and specifically the dimensions of political skill demonstrated correlations with emotional intelligence that ranged from .38 to .43. Indeed, Ferris et al. (2007, p. 294) argued that there is no overlap of the two constructs because "The nature of emotional intelligence appears to predominantly focus on the emotion-based aspects of interpersonal effectiveness, influence, and control. Conversely, political skill is conceptualized as incorporating knowledge and skill that go beyond emotions".

However, Taliadorou and Pashiardis' (2014) research showed a strong relationship between emotional intelligence and political capacity of the school principal (.78, p< .05). The above researchers argued that a possible explanation of the strong relationship of emotional intelligence and political skill of principals may lie in the approach that leadership skills are perceived as emotional and communication abilities that influence leader-follower interaction (Riggio & Reichard, 2008) and therefore, there is difficulty to discriminate between them. Moreover, leadership is conceptualized as a process of social influence through which a leader affects employees' feelings, perceptions, and behavior (Humphrey, 2002), thus emotional regulation is inevitable in order to construct positive social interactions that are expressed through political skills.

Additionally, this result may have occurred because principals find it difficult to separate emotional skills from political skills as political skills are related to the political dimension of emotions. Therefore, the political dimension of emotions is connected to the way someone regulates both his/her emotions and others in order to use the right behaviors that contribute to maintaining a positive public image. Stets and Turner (2008) pointed out that individuals are strategists, motivated to augment their positive emotional energy within the constraints of the social setting. Indeed, an essential part of leadership for maintaining control and power by principals and to protect oneself from emotional hurt is to manage emotions internally and in display, to detach oneself emotionally from a situation on demand and to depersonalize (Ginsberg & Davies, 2003).

As a result of the strong relation between emotional intelligence and political skill, Taliadorou and Pashiardis (2014) created a new concept the "Emotional-Political Capacity", which is the combination of emotional and political skills that best describe the social skills that a principal should have in order to act effectively and be able to achieve greater job satisfaction of their teachers. This important research finding leads to the assertion that those principals characterized by high emotional and political skills are more likely to lead the organization for change and to achieve the right balance of commitment from their employees. We reached this conclusion because principals who demonstrated not only the desire to utilize emotional and political skills, but they use these skills effectively, they can become more effective; the relevant finding that has emerged from their research is that these skills directly influence the scope of action (leadership radius) of the principal and are directly related with the entrepreneurial leadership style that pays particular emphasis in a principal's positive public image.

Emotional and Political Skills of Principals Relate to Leadership Styles

The second important research evidence produced by Taliadorou and Pashiardis (2014) is that both the emotional intelligence and the political skill of the principal have a positive correlation to his/

her radius of action. As can be seen from Figure 3 (p. 20), the political skill of the principals has a stronger correlation with their leadership radius than their emotional intelligence.

This result occurred possibly because of the strong relationship between emotional intelligence and political capacity of the school principal (.78, p< .05) that we discussed earlier. This finding confirms some previous research results (Semadar et al., 2006) which indicated that political skill was the strongest predictor of managerial job performance and that it had significant incremental validity in the prediction of performance over the prediction provided by the other three social effectiveness constructs (self-monitoring, leadership self-efficacy, emotional intelligence) taken as a whole set.

This result, that "Emotional-Political Capacity" of principals is correlated with their leadership radius, provides the impetus for further study of those emotional and political skills that a school principal should have in order to choose effective behaviors depending on the situation he/she is faced with. This finding has some educational value because we can deduce that through the use of emotional intelligence and political ability, principals may skillfully handle the social interactions in such ways that can help teachers to achieve the collective goals of the school quicker and more efficiently. As mentioned previously, effective leaders are skilled in three f's: forming, facing, and feeling public opinion (Pashiardis, 2009). This means that educational leaders should be characterized by the skill to transform, to respond and to become aware of the public opinion in order to lead and not to be led by the mass. All these skills are encompassed in emotional intelligence and political skill. The result of these abilities is that the principal becomes a role model for teachers and creates social networks of cooperation that promote the effectiveness of his/her employees. According to Taliadorou and Pashiardis (2014), principals characterized by their "Emotional-Political Capacity" tend to get higher scores with

regards to their effective leadership style from their teachers, as revealed by their research. Indeed, when teachers are satisfied by their leaders' behavior, this contributes to their job satisfaction as we are going to further analyze in the next section.

School principals' work behavior is in accordance to their situational role and their "Emotional-Political Capacity", as confirmed by research results (Taliadorou & Pashiardis, 2014). Specifically, the school leadership styles of Pashiardis and Brauckmann (2009) are correlated with emotional intelligence and political skill.

The Correlation of Emotional and Political Skills of Principals with the Job Satisfaction of Their Teachers

For many decades, several research attempts have been aiming to identify sources of teacher satisfaction and dissatisfaction for elementary and secondary school teachers (e.g., Dinham & Scott 2000, 2002; Garrett 1999; Grassie & Carss 1973; Kyriacou, 1987). Research findings concluded that teachers' job satisfaction is associated with certain individual and school characteristics (Spear, Gould, & Lee 2000). On the one hand, job satisfaction is a well-studied organizational variable and on the other, there is no generally agreed definition about what constitutes teachers' job satisfaction. Isen and Baron (1991, p. 35) surmise: "As an attitude, job satisfaction involves several basic components: specific beliefs about one's job, behavior tendencies (intentions) with respect to it, and feelings about it." Simply put, "job satisfaction is an attitude people have about their jobs" (Chelladurai, 1999, p. 230).

Despite the difficulty in defining job satisfaction, researchers (Dinham & Scott, 1998, 2000; Van den Berg, 2002; Scott et al., 2001,2003) have identified a variety of worldwide features that correlate with teachers' job satisfaction. Teachers' job satisfaction levels depend both on individual and school characteristics (Spear, Gould, & Lee 2000). Specifically, teachers' satisfaction or

Figure 3. Structural equation model identifying the extent to which the emotional skills of the principal have an impact on his/her political skills and vice versa. Also, indicated is the extent to which the emotional and political skills of principals correlate to their leadership styles.

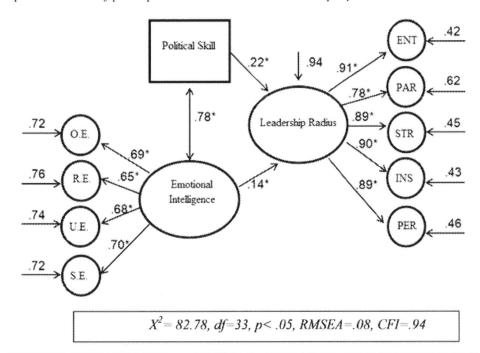

$$X^2 = 82.78, df = 33, p < .05, RMSEA = .08, CFI = .94$$

S.E.: Self Emotional Appraisal
O.E.: Others' Emotional Appraisal
R.E.: Regulation of Emotion
U.E.: Use of Emotion

INS: Instructional style
PAR: Participative style
PER: Personnel Development style
ENT: Entrepreneurial style
STR: Structuring Style

dissatisfaction may be affected by the degree of centralization of the educational system, the lack of professional autonomy, school changes and educational reform, the public image of teachers, the lack of resources, and the unsatisfactory salaries and remuneration practices.

In addition to the above trends that affect the level of satisfaction of teachers, leadership style is one of the major factors that influence both teachers' job satisfaction and their perception of their profession (Bogler, 2002). Teachers argued that decisive factors of their satisfaction are the school working conditions (Xiaofeng & Ramsey, 2008) and the supporting care of their principal (Nir & Bogler, 2008). According to Papanastasiou

and Zembylas (2005), low levels of teachers' job satisfaction occur when teachers feel burnout because of workload, poor payment, and lower appreciation by society.

As a result, Taliadorou and Pashiardis (2014) bearing in mind all of the above, investigated whether the social skills of school principals affect the job satisfaction of their teachers. Their research was intended to build on this domain because previous research findings support the social importance of this syndrome and characterize the job satisfaction of teachers as a key factor, which is linked to the effectiveness of schools (Zigarreli, 1996).

As can be seen above from Figure 4, the findings from their research are very promising as they indicated that there is positive correlation of the emotional intelligence and the political skill of the principal to the job satisfaction of their teachers. This finding confirms the results of other research, such as that of Wong and Law (2002) who found that managers' EI was positively related to employees' job satisfaction. Furthermore Sy et al. (2006) found that managers' self-perceived EI was positively related to employees' job satisfaction and performance and also they found an interaction between employees' and managers'

overall EI such that employees with lower overall EI profited more from leaders' EI. In general, emotional intelligence is a very important factor that provides principals with an understanding on how to achieve the school's goals alongside with their personal goals. Emotionally intelligent school principals inspire their personnel towards self-evaluation practices and promote positive interrelations in order to influence the positive image that employees have for their leader. This is very important because, according to Smith and Ross (2001), the working conditions of teachers are the learning conditions of students. Therefore,

Figure 4. Structural equation model identifying the extent to which the emotional-political capacity of principals correlates to the job satisfaction of their teachers

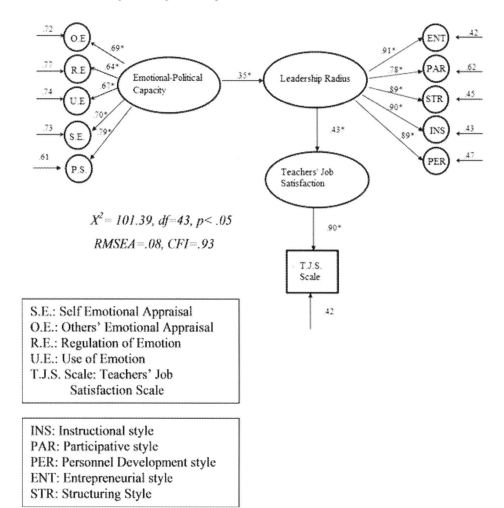

$X^2 = 101.39, df = 43, p < .05$

$RMSEA = .08, CFI = .93$

S.E.: Self Emotional Appraisal
O.E.: Others' Emotional Appraisal
R.E.: Regulation of Emotion
U.E.: Use of Emotion
T.J.S. Scale: Teachers' Job
Satisfaction Scale

INS: Instructional style
PAR: Participative style
PER: Personnel Development style
ENT: Entrepreneurial style
STR: Structuring Style

if the school system does not leverage the job satisfaction of teachers then, as a consequence, they will probably not create positive emotions towards their students.

As for the positive correlation of principals' political skill to the teachers' job satisfaction, this is associated to the research results of Ahearn, (2004) and Treadway (2004) which indicated that the political skill of the leaders impact the reliability and support that followers have for them and are included to the main factors that contribute to the job satisfaction of employees, their cooperation, and minimization of the possibility for resignation. In Taliadorou and Pashiardis' research, school principals' political skill was found to have a stronger correlation with teachers' job satisfaction, than emotional intelligence. This may be explained by the fact that leaders' political skill can be conceptualized as a construct that is expressed through their leadership style which they use in order to shape the impressions formed by their target persons and, therefore be viewed as trustworthy, credible, accountable, and likable.

Furthermore, according to Alexander and Knight (1971), individuals who possess a high degree of political skill, utilize their social astuteness to strategically select methods of influence and self-presentation that present the most situationally appropriate behavior. It is thus reasonable to suggest that, politically skilled school principals may create positive working emotions to their teachers through their leadership behavior, and this is very important because it is connected to their working attitude. Frost (2003) further argued that negative working emotions disorient workers from their job goal. When principals use their interpersonal influence and their capacity for apparent sincerity they appear more genuine and authentic in their behavior, with no ulterior motive. Also, their networking ability allows them to build social capital and leverage it when needed to be even more influential.

All of the above are very important in creating a positive public image for the school principals.

School principals create positive interrelations with parents through their political skills, they promote two-way communication between the school and the community, and they project a positive image to the community and build trust within the local community. The positive public image of the principal contributes to teachers' job satisfaction as revealed by the research of Taliadorou and Pashiardis (2014) and is confirmed by the "third domain" which encompasses factors at the system level, as well as wider social forces, such as teacher status, imposed educational change, and the portrayal of teachers in the media (Dinham & Scott, 1998, 2000).

Concluding, another worthy research result is that when the leadership radius of the principal serves as an intermediate variable, the positive correlation of "Emotional-Political Capacity" of principals on the job satisfaction of teachers increases, as can be seen from Figure 4. The significance of these results is that the principal, in accordance to Norton and Kelly (1997) and Shann (1998), is an important source of satisfaction or dissatisfaction, thus the need arises for school principals to have developed and use both emotional intelligence and political skill. Since the behavior of principals is an important source of job satisfaction or dissatisfaction for their teachers, their emotional intelligence and political skill should be taken into account. Following, bearing in mind all of the above research results, we will make some suggestions for educational research, policy and practice.

3. SUGGESTIONS FOR EDUCATIONAL POLICY AND PRACTICE

Leaders are carrying the burden of emotional labor in greedy organizations that demand excessive physical and emotional work and commitment in order to reduce the costs of production (Fineman, 1993). These conditions typically lead to burnout and early retirement (Gronn, 2003; Hargreaves, 2003). A partial solution to the above may lie in the development of principals' emotional and political skills. The research of Taliadorou and Pashiardis suggests that in order for principals to be more effective, they may need to apply, and interpret differently, assessment and training practices and methods that target specific components of emotional intelligence and political skills, as a function of the disciplinary context too.

As revealed through Taliadorou and Pashiardis' research, the emotional and political skills of principals are related to educational leadership styles. It is therefore possible to suggest that emotional and political skills can be included in the range of characteristics of effective Cypriot principals of primary schools. Such a relationship highlights the social skills of principals as an important area for further research and in the future it would be possible to design experimental or interventional procedures for further examination of this field. Also, the relationship of emotional and political skills of principals with effective leadership styles, as it is presented by multiple methods of data collection, reveals the needs and potential weaknesses of principals in the social skills sector. Therefore, the need arises to develop appropriate training and development programs for principals. This would enhance the effectiveness of schools, because when people are aware of their emotions, they are more able to manage and use them in order to influence the desired reactions of teachers towards the achievement of the school's goals. Similarly, emotional intelligence favors the positive interpersonal interactions (Argyle & Lu, 1990; Herkenhoff, 2004). The handling of emotions may promote or facilitate the adoption of positive social interaction strategies (Cunningham, 1988; Furr & Funder, 1998), such as flexibility in thinking, positive decision making under stressful situations and (generally) effective social behaviors that are necessary in an educational institution.

Leadership preparation programs, then, could take into consideration the importance of the "Emotional-Political Capacity" in leadership and thus give future leaders the tools to navigate effectively through both the personal and the structural/political challenges of leadership. Unfortunately, the preparation programs for school leaders in Cyprus often focus their attention primarily and almost exclusively on the effectiveness and efficiency of schools. Also, they fail to prepare school leaders to engage in the difficult social work that requires a shift in practices, attitudes, and values and limits their ability to address fundamental emotional and political issues. The difficulty of focusing on emotional and political issues becomes even more obvious in a time when school systems want to focus primarily on the achievement of basic skills. However, we do know that educational processes are probably just as important as educational outcomes.

Thus, it would be desirable if future principals attended preparation seminars that help them to leverage their social skills (emotional intelligence and political skill). As mentioned previously, these skills can keenly attune principals to diverse social settings and help them create high self-awareness, adapting their behavior to different targets of influence in different contextual settings in order to achieve their goals and are well positioned to both create and take advantage of opportunities. Leadership training programs should include specific types of activities and leading strategies that can be integrated into training programs such as effective leaders' autobiographies, life histories, workshops focused on emotions and political skills, reflective emotion and political journals, critical incidents, controversial readings, and structured group activities.

Leadership preparation programs are, more than ever before, key factors in preparing leaders of today, not only by including discussions about the nature of social skills as researched in the literature, but also by providing safe venues in which to discuss ways to face the changing landscape in education and, in particular, by preparing administrators to manage a complex role that has the potential of being emotionally-politically effective. Thus, school principals might be trained at using the entrepreneurial leadership style thus, becoming better at managing and leveraging their "Emotional-Political Capacity" in order to achieve their school's increased effectiveness. Specifically, it is desired for principals to use their political skills because this construct refers to the exercise of influence through persuasion and negotiation. As a result, they may achieve their school goals, through their capacity to adjust their behavior to different and changing situational demands in a manner that appears (and probably is) to be sincere, inspires support and trust, and effectively influences and controls the responses of others. Effective school leaders are considered those who recognize the individual needs of all of their teachers and help them in self-development. Also, an effective school leader creates a supportive school environment where teachers are not afraid of making mistakes. If one, therefore, wants to be called an effective school principal, then he/she should be effective not only in administration and leadership but also be characterized by emotional and political skills.

As a result of some of the aforementioned analyses, recruitment and selection methods of school principals could be enriched. For instance, Pashiardis (1993) suggested the creation of Assessment Centers for principal selection, as the interview process is not the most suitable method for principal selection and recruitment, as it has often been reported. For some years now, some school districts in the USA operate Assessment Centers in Education. Each centre is conducted by well-trained assessors whose charge is to observe measure and evaluate the candidates as they complete various exercises and simulations (Pashiardis, 1993). All the participants are evaluated in twelve skills/dimensions: (1) Problem analysis, (2) Judgment, (3) Organizational ability, (4) Decisiveness, (5) Leadership, (6) Sensitivity, (7) Stress tolerance, (8) Oral communication, (9) Written communication, (10) Range of interests,

(11) Personal motivation, (12) Educational values. We believe that future school principals should be evaluated also for their emotional and political skills, as revealed by the research of Taliadorou and Pashiardis (2014) that those constructs have a positive correlation with leadership styles/practices and teachers' job satisfaction. Concluding, one of the most important advantages of Assessment Centers in Education is the feedback that candidates receive from their examiners about their strengths and weakness in the various areas covered.

Another suggestion is that future school principals should be engaged in a mentoring program, because emotional intelligence and political skill involve contextually specific knowledge acquisition, acquired through work experience, mentoring relationships, and other developmental experiences etc. Such contextually specific knowledge is reflected in the types of personal learning which is transmitted through mentoring relationships. The new leaders should have a mentor relationship with more experienced principals or vice-principals in the early stages of their careers. The guidance provided by experienced mentors can target and make salient particularly important pieces of contextual information and provide the experiential development that will build political and emotional skill in individuals. Therefore, we would expect those skills to increase somewhat over time as one gains additional experience and contextual knowledge.

The mentor may be a retired principal who serves as a full-time "coach" working alongside with mentee. In general, mentors could be current or former administrators who work closely with their protégés, often in confidence, and are available to answer just about any kind of question, be it personal or professional. Through this experience it is expected that principals will build a holistic relationship characterized by trust, confidentiality, honesty, sensitivity, shared expertise, and personal and professional growth. Mentoring relationships must be authentic, meaning that the mentor is credible and qualified to comment on performance and the protégé is willing and able to accept the mentor's feedback and incorporate it into his or her practice.

The mentor's role is critical in helping school principals develop emotional intelligence and political skill. Those kind of social skills do not improve overnight. Developing one's emotional intelligence and political skill is truly a lifetime journey and must also commit to a long-term effort. A good mentor will also get to know the mentee principals' strengths, weaknesses, and areas of emotional intelligence and political skill that need the most work. In addition, growth will be well seeded if the school principal is given ample feedback, reinforcement, and reminders to practice new behaviors on the job.

Moreover, a mentor may help school principals reflect on their current philosophies/belief systems and behaviors. Indeed, they should help them identify which belief systems and behaviors are helping them and which may be interfering with their effectiveness. Continuously, a good mentor may challenge the principal to create new belief systems and philosophies that will serve both the school principal and his/her teachers in a better way. Then, the principal may convert his or her belief system or philosophies to productive behaviors and the mentor should mirror the behavioral results of changed belief systems and behaviors that improve followers' reactions.

Concluding, the training programs should provide useful ways to increase and build political skill and emotional intelligence of school principals. Through these programs it is expected that school principals will become more capable in political and emotional skills. Meaning that the school principals may now have a better and more convincing personal style that tends to exert a powerful influence on those around them. Also, they may be adept at using diverse networks of people by easily developing friendships and building strong and beneficial alliances and coalitions and in the end they may appear to others to be congruent, sincere, and genuine. Having

in mind the importance of social skills in school principals' working life, a priority for research should be to learn much more about the political skill and emotional intelligent construct. The present conceptualization of Emotional-Political capacity of school principals that Taliadorou and Pashiardis (2014) suggest, sheds some light on these constructs, and presents a model to guide future research in this important area.

4. SUGGESTIONS FOR FUTURE RESEARCH

There are several suggestions for future research that are worth noting. First, it would be interesting to develop and validate an investigating tool which rates school principals' Emotional-Political Capacity because as revealed from the research of Taliadorou and Pashiardis (2014), this new construct directly affects the leadership radius and teachers' job satisfaction.

Therefore, future research might investigate if emotional intelligence and political skill are really two distinct constructs, because Taliadorou and Pashiardis (2014) found that these two variables have strong correlation. If future research reveals that emotional intelligence and political skill are not distinct constructs, then the new construct, *Emotional-Political Capacity* (Taliadorou & Pashiardis, 2014) may be a better conceptual component to describe the social skills that affect school leadership practices and behaviors.

We assert that the concept of school principal emotional intelligence and political skill is inherently multilevel. As such, future research should attempt to refine the political skill and emotional intelligence constructs in terms of their multilevel antecedents and consequences. We suggest intermediate school variables such as professional climate, personal achievement orientations, parental involvement and explicit teaching strategies are variables that are affected by school principals' leadership radius (Pashiardis & Brauckmann, 2009), and as such future research may investigate the affect of political skill and emotional intelligence of school principals on intermediate school variables.

At the contextual level, future research may benefit from evaluating the effect of emotional intelligence and political skill on dependent variables of school leadership radius such as student outcomes and principal's self-concept. The results of the Taliadorou and Pashiardis study point to the potential interrelationship of social skills on leadership effectiveness. This investigation could further our understanding of the nature of social effectiveness and future research would benefit from evaluating whether emotional intelligence and political skill differentially predict affective and performance-related outcomes in organizations.

Another direction for future research is the examination of gender and values. It may be that political skill and emotional intelligence equip principals who have different values with the ability to influence the relationship with others in a positive manner. As for having gender as an independent variable, a future study should expand our understanding of emotional intelligence and political skill to incorporate the important role that gender and age may play in the possession and development of leadership effectiveness. Also, it would be interesting to examine if emotional intelligence and political skill assist in differentiated ways men and women to overcome difficulties in their relationships with teachers, parents and educational stakeholders.

One more avenue for future research is that researchers might address the extent to which the pervasiveness of political and emotional activity within a school moderates the relationship between principal political and emotional skill and organizational or teachers' outcomes. We consider that future research may benefit from evaluating the eaffect of political emotional climate on the performance of politically and emotionally skilled school principals. Future research would benefit from establishing the dimensions and saliency of

the informal organizational demands for political display and further distinguishing these display demands from the explicit emotional feeling rules. Concluding, further delineation of emotional intelligence and political skill and their interactive relationship with school leadership effectiveness prediction seems to be a promising avenue for future investigation.

5. CONCLUSION

What we have tried to offer is a productive discussion of how emotional intelligence and political skill of school principals affect their leadership behavior/practices and their teachers' job satisfaction. These social skills of the principal could be placed more centrally in the foreground of research into the area of educational leadership. Within educational organizations, as in the wider work organizations, emotions are a site of control with political dimensions. The importance of Taliadorou and Pashiardis' research and its contribution to science, is illustrated by the fact that this is one of the first research efforts undertaken, which indicates that the emotional and political skills may be factors shaping effective educational leadership styles. We would like to suggest that the importance of this research is that, through the exploration of the above topics and its methodology, it provides us with an in-depth analysis of the social skills that Cypriot principals should possess.

Emotional-Political capacity matters in educational leadership as leaders enact their roles of administration and management increasingly through learned emotional and political skills. One of the primary challenges we are faced with as we develop new conceptual frameworks for understanding the dynamics of emotional intelligence and political skill in an educational setting is that those skills are correlated with the school principals' leadership radius and with teachers' job satisfaction. Thus, it is within this context that leadership courses, other supports and training need to be examined. Leadership development needs to combine emotional and political skills, facilitating principals to reflect on the regulation of emotions of self and others, engage in emotional understanding and understand the strengths and limitations of the emotional climate within their schools. Additionally, through political skills, principals influence and control people and situations with relatively little effort, build with effective manner the networks and all these behaviors elevate their status within the organization, and provide scarce resources to their followers. Taken together, these elements provide the politically and emotionally skilled leaders the ability to cast their actions in a genuine and sincere manner and cultivating an open, caring, connected and supportive climate that is committed to authentic relationships.

This chapter provides important feedback to those organizations interested in educational leadership and reform, as it further illuminates (unknown until now) abilities that an effective principal must have. Such knowledge is important because it is expected that in the near future the role of principals will become more demanding and they will be assigned with more responsibilities and duties. The continuous changes in organizations suggest that social skills are increasingly essential. Researchers believe that organizations should rely less on bureaucratic and hierarchical structures. Thus, we consider that emotional and political skills of the leader play an important role in the effectiveness of the school organization, as schools in today's era are competitive and complex environments that require the educational leader to be flexible in external and internal requirements and to balance the need for change with stability (Dougherty, 1996; Lewis, Welsh, Dehler, & Green, 2002).

The development of emotional and political skills coupled with reason in order to enable school principals to select and use appropriate strategies that enhance principals' chances to succeed in their collective goals and "sell their school" to the public and parents, should be a central focus of professional learning provided for principals. Social skills not only influence the decisions being made and actions undertaken but also the collegial interrelationships created at the school place. It is also recommended that those skills should be incorporated as part of further training for future principals in order to improve their efficiency.

In conclusion, the results of this study indicate that two relatively new concepts in school leadership, the emotional intelligence and the political skill of the principal should be subjects of further study, as they have emerged as two very important variables that have direct impact on the leadership radius of the principal and on the job satisfaction of teachers. Therefore, the theories of effective school leadership perhaps should be revised and enriched, taking into account both of the above skills of leaders.

REFERENCES

Ahearn, K. K., Ferris, G. R., Hochwarter, W. A., Douglas, C., & Ammeter, A. P. (2004). Leader political skill and team performance. *Journal of Management*, *30*(3), 309–327. doi:10.1016/j.jm.2003.01.004

Alexander, C. N. Jr, & Knight, G. W. (1971). Situational identities and social psychological experimentation. *Sociometry*, *34*(1), 65–82. doi:10.2307/2786351

Antonakis, J. (2003). Why Emotional Intelligence Does Not Predict Leadership Effectiveness: A Comment On Prati, Douglas, Ferris, Ammater, And Buckley (2003). *The International Journal of Organizational Analysis*, *11*(4), 355–361. doi:10.1108/eb028980

Antonakis, J., Ashkanasy, N. M., & Dasborough, M. T. (2009). Does leadership need emotional intelligence? *The Leadership Quarterly*, *20*(2), 247–261. doi:10.1016/j.leaqua.2009.01.006

Argyle, M., & Lu, L. (1990). Happiness and social skills. *Personality and Individual* 199. *Differences: A Journal of Feminist Cultural Studies, 11*, 1255–1261.

Ashkanasy, N. M., & Tse, B. (2000). Transformational leadership as management of emotion: A conceptual review. In N. Ashkanasy, C. E. J. Härtel, & W. J. Zerbe (Eds.), *Emotions in the Workplace: Research, Theory, and Practice* (pp. 221–235). Westport, CT: Quorum Books.

Barth, R. (1990). *Improving schools from within.* San Francisco, CA: Jossey Bass.

Bass, B. M. (1985). *Leadership and performance beyond expectations.* New York: The Free Press.

Bass, B. M., & Avolio, B. J. (1995). *The multifactor leadership questionnaire – 5x short form.* Redwood: Mind Garden.

Beatty, B. (2007a). Feeling the future of school leadership: Learning to lead with the emotions in mind. *Leading and Managing, 13*(2), 44–65.

Beatty, B. (2007b). Going through the emotions: Leadership that gets to the heart of school renewal. *Australian Journal of Education, 51*(3), 328–340. doi:10.1177/000494410705100309

Beatty, B. R. (2000). The emotions of educational leadership: Breaking the silence. *International Journal of Leadership in Education, 3*(4), 331–357. doi:10.1080/136031200750035969

Bentler, P. M., & Wu, E. J. C. (1995). *EQS for Windows user's guide* [Computer software manual]. Encino, CA: Multivariate Software.

Blackmore, J. (1999). *Troubling Women: Feminism, Leadership and Educational Change.* Buckingham: Open University Press.

Blase, J., & Blase, J. (2000). Implementation of shared governance for instructional improvement: Principals 'Perspectives. *Journal of Educational Administration, 37*(5), 476–500. doi:10.1108/09578239910288450

Bogler, R. (2002). Two profiles of schoolteachers: A discriminant analysis of job satisfaction. *Teaching and Teacher Education, 18*(6), 665–673. doi:10.1016/S0742-051X(02)00026-4

Boler, M., & Zembylas, M. (2003). Discomforting truths: the emotional terrain of understanding difference. In P. Trifonas (Ed.), *Pedagogies of Difference: Rethinking Education for Social Change.* New York: Routledge Falmer.

Bono, E. J., Foldes, H. J., Vinson, G., & Muros, P. J. (2007). Workplace emotions: The role of supervision and leadership. *The Journal of Applied Psychology, 92*(5), 1357–1367. doi:10.1037/0021-9010.92.5.1357 PMID:17845090

Brauckmann, S., & Pashiardis, P. (2011). A validation study of the leadership styles of a holistic leadership theoretical framework. *International Journal of Educational Management, 25*(2), 11–32. doi:10.1108/09513541111100099

Brown, K. M. (2004). Leadership for social justice and equity: Weaving a transformative framework and pedagogy. *Educational Administration Quarterly, 40*(1), 79–110. doi:10.1177/0013161X03259147

Campbell-Evans, G. (1993). *A Values Perspective on School-based Management: School Based Management and School Effectiveness.* London: Routledge.

Chelladurai, P. (1999). *Human Resource Management in Sport and Recreation.* Champagne, IL: Human Kinetics.

Cherniss, C. (2003). *The Business Case for Emotional Intelligence*. Retrieved June 20, 2004, from http://www.eiconsortium.org/research/business_case_for_ei.pdf

Cunningham, M. R. (1988). What do you do when you're happy or blue? Mood, expectancies, and behavioral interest. *Motivation and Emotion, 12*(4), 309–331. doi:10.1007/BF00992357

Daft, R. L., & Lewin, A. Y. (1993). Where are the theories for the new organizational forms? An editorial essay. *Organization Science, 4*, i–vi.

Day, C., Harris, A., Hadfield, M., Tolley, H., & Beresford, J. (2000). *Leading schools in times of change*. Buckingham, UK: Open University Press.

Deal, T., & Peterson, K. (1994). *The leadership paradox: Balancing logic and artistry in schools*. San Francisco, CA: Jossey Bass.

Dinham, S., & Scott, C. (1998). *An international comparative Study of teacher Satisfaction: Motivation and health: Australia, England, and New Zealand*. Paper presented at the Annual Meeting of the American Educational Research Association. New York, NY.

Dinham, S., & Scott, C. (2000). Moving into the third, outer domain of teacher satisfaction. *Journal of Educational Administration, 38*(4), 379–396. doi:10.1108/09578230010373633

Dinham, S., & Scott, C. (2002). *The international Teacher 2000 Project: An International Study of Teacher and School Executive Satisfaction, Motivation and Health in Australia, England, USA, Malta and New Zealand*. Paper presented at the Challenging Futures Conference. Armidale, Australia.

Dougherty, D. (1996). Organizing for innovation. In S. R. Clegg, C. Hardy, & W. R. Nord (Eds.), *Handbook of organization studies* (pp. 424–439). Thousand Oaks, CA: Sage Publications.

DuFour, R., Eaker, R., & DuFour, R. (2006). *On common ground: The power of professional learning communities*. Bloomington, IN: Solution Tree.

Fairholm, G. W. (1993). *Organizational power and politics: Tactics in organizational leadership*. Westport, CT: Praeger.

Fedor, D., Maslyn, J., Farmer, S., & Bettenhausen, K. L. (2003). *Perceptions of positive politics and their impact on organizational outcomes*. Paper presented at the Academy of Management Annual National Conference. Seattle, WA.

Ferris, G. R., Davidson, S. L., & Perrewé, P. L. (2005). *Political skill at work: Impact on work effectiveness*. Mountain View, CA: Davies-Black.

Ferris, G. R., Kolodinsky, R. W., Hochwarter, W. A., & Frink, D. D. (2001). *Conceptualization, measurement, and validation of the political skill construct*. Paper presented at the Annual Meeting of the Academy of Management. Washington, DC.

Ferris, G. R., Perrewé, P. L., Anthony, W. P., & Gilmore, D. C. (2000). Political skill at work. *Organizational Dynamics, 28*(4), 25–37. doi:10.1016/S0090-2616(00)00007-3

Ferris, G. R., Treadway, D. C., Kolodinsky, R. W., Hochwarter, W. A., Kacmar, C. J., Douglas, C., & Frink, D. D. (2005). Development and validation of the political skill inventory. *Journal of Management, 31*(1), 126–152. doi:10.1177/0149206304271386

Ferris, G. R., Treadway, D. C., Perrewe', P. L., Brouer, R. L., Douglas, C., & Lux, S. (2007). Political skill in organizations. *Journal of Management, 33*(3), 290–320. doi:10.1177/0149206307300813

Fineman, S. (1993). Organizations as emotional arenas. In S. Fineman (Ed.), *Emotion in organizations*. London: Sage.

Fortier, A. (2005). Pride politics and multiculturalist citizenship. *Ethnic and Racial Studies, 28*(3), 559–578. doi:10.1080/0141987042000337885

Frost, P. (2003). *Toxic emotions at work: How compassionate managers handle pain and conflict.* Boston: HBS Press.

Fullan, M. (2001). *Leading in a Culture of Change.* San Francisco: Jossey Bass.

Fullan, M. (2005). Leadership and sustainability: System thinkers in action. Thousand Oaks, CA: Corwin Press.

Fullan, M. (2007). *The new meaning of educational change.* New York: Teachers College Press.

Fullan, M. (2010). *All Systems Go: The Change Imperative for Whole System Reform.* Corwin Press.

Furr, R. M., & Funder, D. C. (1998). A multimodal analysis of personal Negativity. *Journal of Personality and Social Psychology, 74*(6), 1580–1591. doi:10.1037/0022-3514.74.6.1580 PMID:9654761

Garrett, R.M. (1999). *Teacher Job Satisfaction in Developing Countries.* ERIC Document Reproduction Service No. ED 459 150.

George, J. M. (2000). Emotions and leadership: The role of emotional intelligence. *Human Relations, 53*(8), 1027–1055. doi:10.1177/0018726700538001

Ginsberg, R., & Davies, T. (2003). The emotional side of leadership. In N. Bennett, M. Crawford, & M. Cartwright (Eds.), *Effective Leadership* (pp. 267–280). London: Sage/Paul Chapman.

Glisson, C., & Durick, M. (1988). Predictors of Job Satisfaction and Organizational Commitment in Human Service Organizations. *American Quarterly, 33*, 61–81.

Goleman, D., Boyatzis, R., & McKee, A. (2002). *Primal leadership.* Boston: HBS Press.

Grassie, M. C., & Carss, B. W. (1973). School Structure, Leadership Quality, Teacher Satisfaction. *Educational Administration Quarterly, 9*(1), 15–26. doi:10.1177/0013161X7300900103

Gronn, P. (2003). *The New Work of Educational Leaders.* London: Paul Chapman.

Harding, J., & Pribram, E. D. (2002). The power of feeling: Locating emotions in culture. *European Journal of Cultural Studies, 5*(4), 407–426. doi:10.1177/1364942002005004294

Harding, J., & Pribram, E. D. (2004). Losing our cool? Following Williams and Grossberg on emotions. *Cultural Studies, 18*(6), 863–883. doi:10.1080/0950238042000306909

Hargreaves, A. (1997). *Positive Change for School Success: The 1997 ASCD Yearbook.* Alexandria, VA: Association for Supervision and Curriculum Development.

Hargreaves, A. (2001). Emotional geographies of teaching. *Teachers College Record, 103*(6), 1056–1080. doi:10.1111/0161-4681.00142

Hargreaves, A. (2003). *Teaching in the Knowledge Society: Education in the Age of Insecurity.* New York, NY: Teachers College Press.

Hargreaves, A. (2004). Inclusive and exclusive educational change: Emotional responses of teachers and implications for leadership. *School Leadership & Management, 24*(2), 287–309. doi:10.1080/1363243042000266936

Herkenhoff, L. (2004). Culturally tuned emotional intelligence: An effective change management tool? *Strategic Change, 13*(2), 73–81. doi:10.1002/jsc.666

Higgnis, C. A., Judge, T. A., & Ferris, G. R. (2003). Influence tactics and work outcomes: A meta-analysis. *Journal of Organizational Behavior, 24*(1), 89–106. doi:10.1002/job.181

Humphrey, R. H. (2002). The many faces of emotional leadership. *The Leadership Quarterly, 13*(5), 493–504. doi:10.1016/S1048-9843(02)00140-6

Isen, A. M., & Baron, R. A. (1991). Positive affect as a factor in organizational behavior. In B. M. Staw & L. L. Cummings (Eds.), *Research in organizational behavior* (Vol. 13, pp. 1–53). Greenwich, CT: JAI Press.

Kanter, R. (1979). Power failure in management circuits. *Harvard Business Review, 57*, 65–75. PMID:10244631

Kolodinsky, R. W., Treadway, D. C., & Ferris, G. R. (2007). Political skill and influence effectiveness: Testing portions of an expanded Ferris and Judge (1991) model. *Human Relations, 60*(12), 1747–1777. doi:10.1177/0018726707084913

Kyriacou, C. (1987). Teacher Stress and Burnout: An International Review. *Educational Research, 29*(2), 146–152. doi:10.1080/0013188870290207

Layder, D. (1997). *Modern Social Theory: Key Debates and New Directions*. London: UCL Press.

Layder, D. (2004). *Emotion in Social Life: The Lost Heart of Society*. London: Sage.

Leithwood, K. (1992). The move toward transformational leadership. *Educational Leadership, 49*(5), 8–12.

Leithwood, K. (1993). *Contributions of transformational leadership to school restructuring*. Paper presented at the Annual Conference of the University Council for Educational Administration. Houston, TX.

Leithwood, K. (1994). Leadership for school restructuring. *Educational Administration Quarterly, 30*(4), 498–518. doi:10.1177/0013161X94030004006

Leithwood, K. (2006). *The Emotional Side of School Improvement: A Leadership Perspective*. Toronto, Canada: Ontario Institute of Education.

Leithwood, K., & Beatty, B. (2008). *Leading with Teacher Emotions in Mind*. Thousand Oaks, CA: Corwin Press.

Lewis, M. W., Welsh, M. A., Dehler, G. E., & Green, S. G. (2002). Product 223 development tensions: Exploring contrasting styles of product management. *Academy of Management Journal, 45*(3), 546–564. doi:10.2307/3069380

Limerick, B., & Nielsen, H. (Eds.). (1995). *School and community relations*. Sydney: Harcourt Brace.

Loader, D. (1997). *The Inner Principal*. London: Falmer Press.

Locke, E. A. (2005). Why emotional intelligence is an invalid concept. *Journal of Organizational Behavior, 26*(4), 425–431. doi:10.1002/job.318

Luthans, F., Hodgetts, R. M., & Rosenkrantz, S. A. (1988). *Real managers*. Cambridge, MA: Ballinger.

Matthews, G., Zeidner, M., & Roberts, R. D. (2002). *Emotional Intelligence: Science and Myth*. Cambridge, MA: MIT Press.

Mayer, J. D., & Salovey, P. (1997). What is emotional intelligence? In D. J. Sluyter (Ed.), *Emotional development and emotional intelligence: Educational implications*. New York: Basic Books, Inc.

Mintzberg, H. (1983). *Power in and around organizations*. Englewood Cliffs, NJ: Prentice Hall.

Mintzberg, H. (1985). The organization as a political arena. *Journal of Management Studies, 22*(2), 133–154. doi:10.1111/j.1467-6486.1985.tb00069.x

Mulford, B. (1994). *Shaping tomorrow's schools (Monograph No. 15)*. Melbourne: Australian Council for Educational Administration.

Nir, A. E., & Bogler, R. (2008). The antecedents of teacher satisfaction with professional development programs. *Teaching and Teacher Education, 24*(2), 377–386. doi:10.1016/j.tate.2007.03.002

Norton, M. S., & Kelly, L. K. (1997). Resource Allocation: Managing Money and Peoples Eye on Education. New York: Larchmont.

Oatley, K., & Jenkins, J. (1996). *Understanding emotion*. Cambridge, MA: Blackwell.

Papanastasiou, E. C., & Zembylas, M. (2005). Job satisfaction variance among public and private kindergarten school teachers in Cyprus. *International Journal of Educational Research, 43*(3), 147–167. doi:10.1016/j.ijer.2006.06.009

Pashiardis, P. (1993). Selection Methods for Educational Administrators in the USA. *International Journal of Educational Management, 7*(1), 27–35. doi:10.1108/09513549310023294

Pashiardis, P. (2009). Educational leadership and management: Blending Greek philosophy, myth and current Thinking. *International Journal of Leadership in Education, 12*(1), 1–12. doi:10.1080/13603120802357269

Pashiardis, P. (2012). *Successful School Principals: International Research and Greek Reality*. Athens: Ion Publishing House.

Pashiardis, P. (Ed.). (2014). Modeling School Leadership Across Europe: In Search of New Frontiers. London: Springer.

Pashiardis, P., & Brauckmann, S. (2008). Evaluation of School Principals. In G. Crow, J. Lumby, & P. Pashiardis (Eds.), *International handbook on the preparation and development of school leaders* (pp. 263–279). New York: Routledge.

Pashiardis, P., & Brauckmann, S. (2009, April). *New Educational Governance and School Leadership – Exploring the foundation of a new relationship in an international context*. Paper presented at the American Educational Research Association Annual Meeting. San Diego, CA.

Perrewé, P. L., Zellars, K. L., Ferris, G. R., Rossi, A. M., Kacmar, C. J., & Ralston, D. A. (2004). Neutralizing job stressors: Political skill as an antidote to the dysfunctional consequences of role conflict stressors. *Academy of Management Journal, 47*(1), 141–152. doi:10.2307/20159566

Pfeffer, J. (1981). *Power in organizations*. Boston: Pitman.

Pfeffer, J. (1992). *Managing with power: Politics and influence in organizations*. Boston: Harvard Business School Press.

Pirola-Merlo, A., Hartel, C., Mann, L., & Hirst, G. (2002). How leaders influence the impact of affective events on team climate and performance in R&D teams. *The Leadership Quarterly, 13*(5), 561–581. doi:10.1016/S1048-9843(02)00144-3

Power, P. G. (2004). Leadership for Tomorrow: Once More, with Feeling, Mt Eliza. *Business Review (Federal Reserve Bank of Philadelphia)*, (Summer/Autumn), 2003–2004.

Riggio, R. E. (1986). The assessment of basic social skills. *Journal of Personality and Social Psychology, 51*(3), 649–660. doi:10.1037/0022-3514.51.3.649

Salovey, P., & Mayer, J. D. (1990). Emotional intelligence. *Imagination, Cognition and Personality, 9*(3), 185–211. doi:10.2190/DUGG-P24E-52WK-6CDG

Scheerens, J. (2000). *Improving School Effectiveness.* Paris: UNESCO.

Scott, C., Dinham, S., & Brooks, R. (2003). The development of scales to measure teacher and school executive occupational satisfaction. *Journal of Educational Administration, 41*(1), 74–86. doi:10.1108/09578230310457448

Scott, C., Stone, B., & Dinham, S. (2001). I love teaching but. . . International patterns of discontent. *Education Policy Analysis Archives, 9*(28).

Semadar, A., Robins, G., & Ferris, G. R. (2006). Comparing the effects of multiple social effectiveness constructs in the prediction of managerial performance. *Journal of Organizational Behavior, 27*(4), 443–461. doi:10.1002/job.385

Sergiovanni, T. (2004). Building a community of hope. *Educational Leadership, 61*(8), 33–37.

Sergiovanni, T. J. (1999, September). Refocusing Leadership to Build Community. *The High School Magazine*, 12-15.

Shann, M. (1998). Professional commitment and satisfaction among teachers in urban middle schools. *The Journal of Educational Research, 92*(2), 67–73. doi:10.1080/00220679809597578

Silins, H. (1994). Leadership characteristics and school improvement. *Australian Journal of Education, 38*(3), 266–281. doi:10.1177/000494419403800306

Silins, H. C. (1992). Effective leadership for school reform. *The Alberta Journal of Educational Research, 38*(4), 317–334.

Silins, H. C. (1994). The relationship between transformational and transactional leadership and school improvement outcomes. *School Effectiveness and School Improvement, 5*(3), 272–298. doi:10.1080/0924345940050305

Sivanathan, N., & Fekken, G. C. (2002). Emotional intelligence, moral reasoning and transformational leadership. *Leadership and Organization Development Journal, 23*(3/4), 198–205. doi:10.1108/01437730210429061

Smith, J., & Ross, C. (2001). *Brief to the Minister of Education's Task Force on effective schools.* Toronto: OECTA.

Spear, M., Gould, K., & Lee, B. (2000). *Who Would be a Teacher? A Review of Factors Motivating and Demotivating Prospective and Practicing Teachers.* Slough: NFER.

Stets, J. E., & Turner, J. H. (2008). The sociology of emotions. In M. Lewis, J. M. Haviland-Jones, & L. Feldman Barret (Eds.), *Handbook of Emotions* (3rd ed., pp. 32–46). New York: Guilford Press.

Stewart, G. L., & Carson, K. P. (1997). Moving beyond the mechanistic model: An alternative approach to staffing for contemporary organizations. *Human Resource Management Review, 7*(2), 157–184. doi:10.1016/S1053-4822(97)90021-8

Sy, T., Tram, S., & O'Hara, A. L. (2006). Relation of employee and manager emotional intelligence to job satisfaction and performance. *Journal of Vocational Behavior, 68*(3), 461–473. doi:10.1016/j.jvb.2005.10.003

Taliadorou, N., & Pashiardis, P. (2014). *Leadership Radius and Teachers' Job Satisfaction: The role of Emotional Intelligence and Political Skill of Elementary School Principals.* (Unpublished doctoral dissertation). Open University of Cyprus, Cyprus.

Treadway, D. C., Duke, A. B., Ferris, G. R., Adams, G. L., & Thatcher, J. B. (2007). The moderating role of subordinate political skill on supervisors' impressions of subordinate ingratiation and ratings of subordinate interpersonal facilitation. *The Journal of Applied Psychology*, *92*(3), 848–855. doi:10.1037/0021-9010.92.3.848 PMID:17484564

Treadway, D. C., Hochwarter, W. A., Kacmar, C. J., & Ferris, G. R. (2005). Political will, political skill, and political behavior. *Journal of Organizational Behavior*, *26*(3), 229–245. doi:10.1002/job.310

Treadway, D. C., Hochwater, W. A., Ferris, G. R., Kacmar, C. J., Douglas, C., Ammeter, A. P., & Buckley, M. R. (2004). Leader political skill and employee reactions. *The Leadership Quarterly*, *15*(4), 493–513. doi:10.1016/j.leaqua.2004.05.004

Turner, J. H., & Stets, J. E. (2005). *The Sociology of Emotions.* New York: Cambridge University Press. doi:10.1017/CBO9780511819612

Van den Berg, R. (2002). Teachers' meanings regarding educational practice. *Review of Educational Research*, *72*(4), 577–625. doi:10.3102/00346543072004577

Van den Berg, R., & Huberman, A. M. (1999). *Understanding and Preventing Teacher Burnout.* Cambridge, UK: Cambridge University Press. doi:10.1017/CBO9780511527784

Van Rooy, D. L., & Viswesvaran, C. (2004). Emotion intelligence: A meta-analytic investigation of predictive validity and nomological net. *Journal of Vocational Behavior*, *65*(1), 71–95. doi:10.1016/S0001-8791(03)00076-9

Wong, C. S., & Law, K. S. (2002). The effects of leader and follower emotional intelligence on performance and attitude: An exploratory study. *The Leadership Quarterly*, *13*(3), 243–274. doi:10.1016/S1048-9843(02)00099-1

Xiaofeng, S. L. (2008). Teachers' job satisfaction: Analyses of the Teacher Follow-up Survey in the United States for 2000–2001. *Teaching and Teacher Education*, *24*(5), 1173–1184. doi:10.1016/j.tate.2006.11.010

Zeidner, M., Matthews, G., & Roberts, R. D. (2004). Emotional Intelligence in the workplace: A critical review. *Applied Psychology*, *53*(3), 371–399. doi:10.1111/j.1464-0597.2004.00176.x

Zeidner, M., Roberts, R. D., & Matthews, G. (2008). The science of emotional intelligence: Current consensus and controversies. *European Psychologist*, *13*(1), 64–78. doi:10.1027/1016-9040.13.1.64

Zembylas, M. (2009). The politics of emotions in education: affective economies, ambivalence and transformation. In E. Samier & M. Schmidt (Eds.), *Emotional Dimensions of Educational Administration and Leadership* (pp. 97–108). New York, NY: Routledge.

Zembylas, M., & Papanastasiou, E. (2004). Job Satisfaction among School Teachers in Cyprus. *Journal of Educational Administration*, *42*(3), 357–374. doi:10.1108/09578230410534676

Zigarelli, M. A. (1996). An empirical test of conclusions from effective schools Research. *The Journal of Educational Research*, *90*(2), 103–109. doi:10.1080/00220671.1996.9944451

KEY TERMS AND DEFINITIONS

Emotional Intelligence: EI is the skill to monitor one's own and others' emotions, to discriminate among them and to use the information to guide one's thinking and actions.

Emotional-Political Capacity: Emotional-Political Capacity is the combination of emotional and political skills. Include self and others' emotional appraisal, regulation and use of emotion, interpersonal influence/control, network building/social capital, genuineness/sincerity and self and social astuteness.

Job Satisfaction: Job Satisfaction is an employee's attitude to his or her job.

Leadership: Leadership is the social influence through which a leader affects followers' feelings, perceptions, and behavior.

Political Skill: Political Skill is the skill to effectively understand others at work, and to use such knowledge to influence others to act in ways that achieve one's personal and/or organizational goals.

Chapter 12
Teacher Leadership:
A Conceptual Analysis

Servet Özdemir
Gazi University, Turkey

Ali Çağatay Kılınç
Karabuk University, Turkey

ABSTRACT

This chapter focuses on teacher leadership, an important variable in the classroom and school improvement literature. The concept of teacher leadership has attracted increased attention in the past two decades. Teachers are assuming more responsibility for leadership roles and functions within schools. Despite the considerable amount of scholarly effort and time spent on investigating the teacher leadership concept, less is known about how it flourishes in the school context and how it relates to classroom and school improvement. Therefore, this chapter tries to shed some light on the teacher leadership concept and discusses its meaning, teacher leadership roles, factors influencing teacher leadership, the relationship between teacher leadership and classroom and school improvement, and future research areas on teacher leadership. Offering a framework for teacher leadership, this chapter is expected to contribute well to the guidance of further research on teacher leadership.

INTRODUCTION

The pressures on schools to improve and sustain the standards of student achievement and engagement have forced them to change the ways they operate and also find alternative perspectives for conventional leadership notions. Schools need to encourage all members to assume leadership roles and to build an understanding of leadership which focuses primarily on improving classroom instruction (Harris & Muijs, 2003a) as educational improvement at the instruction level includes leadership by teachers within and beyond the classroom (York-Barr & Duke, 2004).

A line of researchers have argued that traditional leadership approaches which place the responsibility of leading a school on solely the school principal are far from meeting the needs of students and society as a whole (Barth, 1990; Beachum & Dentith, 2004; Harris & Lambert, 2003; Harris, 2002a, 2003, 2005; Harris & Muijs, 2003a, 2003b; Lambert, 1998, 2003;

DOI: 10.4018/978-1-4666-6591-0.ch012

Leithwood, 2003; Murphy, 2005; Sergiovanni, 2007; York-Barr & Duke, 2004). Gronn (2000) makes it clear that school principals and teachers have reciprocal roles in the school leadership process and that leadership comes from these relationships among school members. This may refer that effective school leadership practices come together with the collaboration of school principals and teachers. Beachum and Dentith (2004) suggest that new approaches and practices of school leadership are required in order to build a more collaborative, democratic and instructionally-driven school environment and to respond well to the diverse needs of students. In line with this argument, Muijs and Harris (2003, 2007) claim that teachers' knowledge, skills and dispositions are regarded as crucial factors in the school improvement journey. Harris and Lambert (2003) further emphasize that encouraging all members of school to assume the responsibility of leadership roles may be one of the reasonable ways to increase the internal capacity of a school by which school may improve the quality of its learning and teaching environment. It is therefore possible to argue that teacher leadership is based on the assumption that teachers as leaders within and beyond their classrooms can contribute well to the quality of instruction and school improvement.

Recent years have witnessed a great deal of research effort on teacher leadership (e.g. Aslan, 2011; Beycioğlu, 2009; Beycioğlu & Aslan, 2010, 2012; Can, 2006, 2009a; Anderson, 2004; Angelle & DeHart, 2011; Ault, 2009; Burgess, 2012; Cosenza, 2010; Fraser, 2008; Frost & Durant, 2003; Frost & Harris, 2003; Harris & Mujis, 2003a; Kendall, 2011; Kenyon, 2008; Kölükçü, 2011; Muijs & Harris, 2003; Nolan & Palazzolo, 2011; Özçetin, 2013; Pounder, 2006; Rutledge, 2009; Scribner & Bradley-Levine, 2010; Whitaker, 1997). Katzenmeyer and Moller (2009) argue that the notion of teacher leadership claiming the idea that teachers must assume leadership roles to contribute to the school improvement has become a prominent issue among scholars in the field of educational administration. York-Barr and Duke (2004) further assert that principals are no longer likely to manage schools on their own because of the pressures of higher quality of teaching and of meeting student needs. Similarly, Harris and Lambert (2003) suggest that teachers as potential leaders have begun to be accepted as key factors in achieving a higher level of student achievement. It is therefore possible to state that teacher leadership may strengthen school capacity for change and improvement by enhancing an environment of collaboration and collegiality.

The purpose of this paper is to examine the concept of teacher leadership in detail. In this regard, the present review aims at addressing following issues: (1) presenting and arguing various definitions of teacher leadership, (2) clarifying teacher leadership roles, (3) investigating the factors that influence teacher leadership, (4) examining the relationship between teacher leadership and classroom and school improvement, (5) discussing future research areas on teacher leadership and (6) conclusion.

DEFINING TEACHER LEADERSHIP

Teacher leadership refers to a context where teachers display leadership behaviors inside and outside the classroom and participate in the process of creating a learning-oriented culture in school, best instructional practices are developed, implemented, and evaluated, and colleagues motivate one another (Katzenmeyer & Moller, 2009). Harris and Muijs (2003a) define teacher leadership under three topics (p. 40):

1. The leadership of other teachers through coaching, mentoring, leading working groups;
2. The leadership of developmental tasks that are central to improved learning and teaching; and

3.   The leadership of pedagogy through the development and modeling of effective forms of teaching.

The concept of teacher leadership covers mainly three improvement areas concerning teachers: (1) personal improvement, (2) collaboration among colleagues, (3) organizational improvement. In this regard, it is clear that teacher leaders primarily improve themselves personally and professionally, collaborate with their colleagues, and contribute to school improvement (Taylor, Goeke, Klein, Onore, & Geist, 2011). The essence of teacher leadership is that all teachers have leadership skills and can use them when they are given opportunities (Barth, 1990). Beycioğlu and Aslan (2012) state that the primary goal of teacher leadership is to transform schools into learning organizations, and that teachers should continue their professional improvement to achieve this goal. According to York-Barr and Duke (2004), the concept of teacher leadership suggests that teachers have a central position in the management of school and school-related processes, and teachers take important roles in the arrangement of learning and teaching processes in school.

Highlighting the informal aspect of teacher leadership, Can (2009a) associates the leadership roles taken by teachers in school with teachers' playing more effective roles in the improvement of learning and teaching processes, improving relationships among colleagues in school, continuing their professional improvement, supporting one another, and producing school-based projects. Muijs and Harris (2006) report that teacher leadership is based on collaboration among teachers, collective responsibility, and professional activities conducted for pedagogical purposes. Murphy (2005) puts forward that teacher leaders mainly take active roles to improve teaching processes and student learning in school, help their colleagues improve themselves, and contribute to the creation of a positive learning environment in school. In this respect, it may be argued that the concept of teacher leadership is based on the idea that maximum use of the knowledge and skills of teachers should be made in the process of creating a more effective learning and teaching environment in school.

TEACHER LEADERSHIP ROLES

The literature about teacher leadership includes intense debates regarding the roles and responsibilities of teacher leaders. For example, Harris and Muijs (2005) address the roles of teacher leaders under four titles: brokering, participative leadership, mediating, and forging close relationships. *Brokering role* is about teachers' transferring the principles for school improvement to classroom and implementing these principles at classroom level. *Participative leadership* refers to teachers' supporting and participating in school change and improvement processes effectively. *Mediating role* is about the perception of teachers as professionals who can provide school with resources when required. Finally, the *forging close relationships role* is the role of teacher leaders concerning the creation of a school climate where colleagues learn from one another, share with one another, and establish positive relationships. Teacher Leadership Exploratory Consortium (TLEC) (2008) carried out quite a detailed study concerning the role and responsibility areas of teacher leaders. Such role and responsibility areas are as follows (pp. 12-14):

1.   **Fostering a Collaborative Culture to Support Educator Development and Student Learning:** Teacher leaders have a theoretical accumulation in regard to student learning, and exert an effort to create a culture based on collective responsibility aimed at improving student learning in school.

2.   **Accessing and Using Research to Improve Practice and Student Learning:** Teacher

leaders know that empirical research guides practice and provides teachers with data for improving teaching. Thus, they lead research teams in school.

3. **Promoting Professional Learning for Continuous Improvement:** Teacher leaders are knowledgeable about learning and teaching processes as well as the school community, and they use such knowledge both to continue their professional improvement and to contribute to the professional improvement of their colleagues.

4. **Facilitating Improvements in Instruction and Student Learning:** Teacher leaders are effective learners, and serve as an example for their colleagues in this matter. Apart from that, they cooperate with their colleagues, and enable the teaching practices performed in school to be congruent with the common vision, mission, and values of school.

5. **Promoting the Use of Assessments and Data for School and District Improvement:** Teacher leaders follow the academic research about class and school and know the methods developed for assessing student success. Teacher leaders collaborate and exchange information with their colleagues in order to make sounder decisions and a more effective assessment.

6. **Improving Outreach and Collaboration with Families and Community:** Teacher leaders know that family, cultures, and community have important impacts on the educational process. Thus, they make an attempt to create a more positive learning environment in school through collaborating with families.

7. **Advocating for Student Learning and the Profession:** Teacher leaders know how local and national educational policies are made and what kinds of roles school leaders, policy-makers, and other stakeholders play in this process. They use this knowledge in order to meet the student needs at maximum

level, develop the most effective teaching practices, and improve student achievement.

Another detailed classification concerning the roles of teacher leaders was provided by Harrison and Killon (2007). According to them, teacher leaders supporting school improvement formally or informally have the following roles:

1. **Resource Provider:** Teacher leaders share all kinds of materials, those about teaching being in the first place, with their colleagues, thereby contributing to their professional improvement.

2. **Instructional Specialist:** Teacher leaders support other teachers in the processes of designing, implementing, and evaluating effective teaching practices.

3. **Curriculum Specialist:** Teacher leaders understand the content of the curriculum, solve the links between the pieces making up the curriculum, and guide teachers in the process of planning and evaluating teaching in regard to how to use the curriculum.

4. **Classroom Supporter:** Teacher leaders try to help other teachers in regard to putting new ideas into practice in the classroom.

5. **Learning Facilitator:** Teacher leaders spend time and exert effort to create a school environment where teachers learn from one another, develop effective teaching practices for student learning, question the teaching conducted, and have positive relationships with their colleagues.

6. **Mentor:** Teacher leaders, serving also as a mentor, help the teachers who are new in profession to gain experience in teaching and to continue their professional improvement.

7. **School Leader:** Teacher leaders, serving also as a school leader, contribute to the improvement of school as a whole by taking different roles including school improvement team member, group leader, school representative, etc.

8. **Data Coach:** Teacher leaders collect, analyze, and use data in order to improve the teaching conducted in school along with their colleagues.
9. **Catalyst for Change:** Teacher leaders initiate, implement, and support the change process in school.
10. **Learner:** Teacher leaders know that they need to learn and continue their improvement effectively in the first place in order to contribute to student learning.

The related literature contains various studies discussing what roles teacher leaders should have in regard to school and classroom (e.g. Can, 2009a; Grant, 2006; Harris, 2002b; Harris & Muijs, 2003a; Helterbran, 2010; Katzenmeyer & Moller, 2009; Lambert, 2003; Lashway, 1998; Leithwood, 2003; Lieberman & Miller, 2005; Murphy, 2005). For instance, Can (2009a) states that teacher leaders firstly prepare an effective learning environment for their students in the classroom and increase the learning motivations of their students. In parallel with that, Harris (2002b) argues that teacher leaders lead the student learning process in the classroom and aim to accomplish learning goals by applying school improvement principles in the classroom. In addition, according to Harris, teachers have a wide range of roles including affecting and motivating other teachers in the school improvement process, guiding them, providing them with specialization and information support, and contributing to the creation of an effective communication and collaboration environment in school. There are some other studies reporting that teacher leaders contribute to the professional improvement of their colleagues [Institute for Educational Leadership (IEL, 2008)], make sure that the strategic objectives of school are adopted by all school members (Lambert, 2003), exert effort to ensure that school maintains its integrity and resists against the pressures and threats coming from the society and focuses on

its objectives (Leithwood, 2003), support effective collaboration and communication processes among colleagues (Grant, 2006; Katzenmeyer & Moller, 2009), and take pedagogical leadership roles for ensuring an effective teaching in school. Harris and Muijs (2003b) summarized the roles of teacher leaders as follows:

The important point is that teacher leaders are, in the first place, expert teachers, who spend at the majority of their time in the classroom but take on leadership roles at times when development and innovation is needed. Their role is primarily one of assisting colleagues to explore and try out new ideas, then offering critical but constructive feedback to ensure improvements in teaching and learning are achieved. (p. 40)

In consideration of the foregoing, it is clear that teacher leaders firstly meet the learning needs of students in their own classrooms at maximum level, design good teaching practices, conduct such practices, and assess the effectiveness of such practices. In addition, teachers may take roles in activities aimed at school improvement, participate in the processes of doing research, data collection, and assessment and evaluation, guide the teachers who are new in profession, and exert effort to create an effective learning and teaching environment in school.

INFLUENTIAL FACTORS ON TEACHER LEADERSHIP

The exhibition of leadership behaviors focusing on improving teaching by teachers refers to a new role pattern for them beyond their boundaries of duty. There are a series of variables influencing the exhibition of leadership behaviors by teachers. This section covers the variables influential on teacher leadership in the light of the related literature.

Organizational Structure

The primary factor influential on teachers' taking responsibility for leadership behaviors in school is school structure. It is stated that the exhibition of leadership behaviors by teachers in schools is associated with the suitableness of school structure for collaboration to take place among school members, the existence of a common decision-making mechanism in school, and the production and sharing of knowledge (Katzenmeyer & Moller, 2009). Harris (2002a) highlights the importance of an organizational structure that can help all school members to collaborate and to follow and assess the works of one another for teacher leadership. It is reported that the school structures where teachers and school members can collaborate as a whole pave the way for teachers to share the teaching practices which they conduct with one another, to contribute to the professional improvement of one another, to develop teaching plans together, to prepare action plans in order to improve student achievement, and to facilitate change processes (College, 2011).

Frost and Harris (2003) state that role structure, responsibilities, accountability, and opportunities for participating in decision-making processes in school, which are all about the organizational structure, are closely associated with the leadership behaviors of teachers. Hart (1995) argues that teacher leaders may have a wider sphere of influence in the schools with a looser organizational structure. Darling-Hammond, Bullmaster and Cobb (1995) claim that schools as professional learning communities are more appropriate for teacher leadership, and that the leadership behaviors of teachers are supported more in such schools. In parallel with that, DuFour, Eaker and DuFour (2005) state that leadership is not perceived as the responsibility and task of a single person in schools as professional learning communities, and that the primary goal in such schools is to uncover the potential of all school members to lead and make

maximum use of it. Therefore, it may be argued that the school structures where school members may collaborate and organizational roles are not divided by strict boundaries are more appropriate for the development of teacher leadership.

The review of the related literature shows that bureaucratic school structures are intensely addressed as an obstacle for the development of teacher leadership. Stating that bureaucratic school structures are still mostly based on single-man leadership, Sergiovanni (1996) says that organizational structures enabling teachers and other school members to use their personal capacities for school purposes are needed to make schools more effective and improve student learning. According to Murphy (2007), the bureaucratic school structures adopting individual accountability rather than a collective approach based on collective responsibility put away teachers from one another and make it difficult for them to collaborate, and thus it is difficult to create an environment suitable for the development of teacher leadership in these kinds of structures.

Teacher leadership brings along the formation of new role patterns among colleagues in school. As a matter of fact, teacher leaders are responsible not only for the teaching performed in the classroom and the learning of the students in their own classrooms, but also for the improvement of school as a whole and the satisfaction of the learning needs of all students at the highest level (Katzenmeyer & Moller, 2009). Ash and Persall (2000) report that teacher leadership cannot be improved in any school structure that prevents teachers from solving problems together, sharing with one another, supporting the professional improvement of one another, and making plans aimed at improving teaching. From this perspective, it seems difficult to say that any school structure which involves the distribution of roles among members in school in an obvious manner and separates administration and teaching processes from one another completely is congruent with the basic assumptions of teacher leadership which puts teachers in a central position in the school administration and improvement process (Murphy, 2005).

The roles of school members are separated obviously in the schools having a bureaucratic school structure and coercive features. That may cause teachers not to go beyond the responsibilities which they are expected to take as per the related laws (Ash & Persall, 2000). In parallel with that, Dee, Henkin and Duemer (2002) argue that bureaucratic school structures generally force teachers to work in a lonely manner and put away them from other employees, thereby providing teachers only with a limited number of opportunities for doing something new. According to Katzenmeyer and Moller (2009), teacher leadership cannot be effective in schools where teachers are not provided with a professional working environment, facilities for collaboration to improve teaching are not presented, and thus teachers perform teaching independently from one another.

Teacher leadership involves that each school member learns and improves his/her professional knowledge and skills, and school improvement mostly depends on school members' improving their capacities (Gronn, 2000). In other words, there is quite a close relationship between teacher leadership and teachers' continuing their professional improvement, learning, and communicating and collaborating with one another effectively. Thus, structure, which is an important factor influential on all processes in school, has an important impact on teacher leadership. For example, a hierarchical school structure implies an organization where the entire power is held by the administration, leadership behaviors are expected from administrators alone, administration and teaching processes are independent from one another, and teachers are not autonomous enough to improve teaching (Harris, 2003). Thus, it can be said that the organizational structure of a school is quite an important factor influential on the development of teacher leadership, and that it is necessary to transform hierarchical and strictly

bureaucratic school structures and the behavior patterns supporting such structures in order to ensure the development of teacher leadership.

Time

Another factor influential on the development of teacher leadership is time (Barth, 2001; Harris & Muijs, 2003a; Zinn, 1997). Curci (2012) found out that school principals and teachers thought that time was one of the factors influential on the development of teacher leadership in school. College (2011) claims that teachers need extra time apart from the time allocated for teaching in order to establish a balance between their teaching behaviors and leadership behaviors, otherwise they may give up leadership behaviors. According to Harris and Muijs (2003a), there is a need for collaborative activities, collective planning by school members, networks for increasing communication and interaction among teachers, and an effective time planning for classroom walkthrough in order to ensure professional improvement and improve student success and engagement in school.

An effective time planning is quite important for teachers both to perform an effective teaching and to contribute to school improvement by displaying leadership behaviors (Can, 2009a). As a matter of fact, teachers, whose primary tasks are to conduct an effective teaching and to satisfy the learning needs of students, have quite a limited time for other roles such as displaying leadership behaviors aimed at contributing to school improvement, participating in decision-making processes actively, collecting data, doing research, and contributing to the professional improvement of their colleagues (Katzenmeyer & Moller, 2009). Claiming that there is a close relationship between teacher leadership and the professional improvement of teachers, Mulford (2003) states that teachers need to continue their professional improvement in order to take the responsibility for leadership behaviors, and enough time should be allocated for professional improvement in school. Another study emphasizes that the most critical factor influential on the development of teacher leadership is collaboration, and that teachers should have enough time for collaboration to improve teaching (TLEC, 2008). Harris and Muijs (2003b) state that teacher leaders need planned time to continue their professional improvement, help their colleagues perform an effective teaching, work in a collaborative manner, establish effective professional networks among teachers, and make classroom walkthrough.

Teacher leadership basically requires teachers to make an extra effort for school improvement and student learning and to try to improve the success of both their own students and all other students in school. Thus, a professional teacher should do more than lecturing. In other words, teacher leaders displaying professional behaviors are expected to construct the time remaining from lessons well, participate in school-related processes actively, conduct research, collect data, and guide other teachers in such free time. In this regard, it is clear that time is one of the most important factors influential on the development of teacher leadership, and teacher leaders need to construct their time in school very well and use it effectively.

School Culture

Another factor influential on teacher leadership is school culture. School culture is an important variable affecting teacher behaviors and shaping leadership processes in school (Danielson, 2006). Teachers' exhibiting leadership behaviors besides their traditional roles means a change in the relationships between teachers and school administrators (Anderson, 2004). According to Harris (2002a), the development of teacher leadership is based on the idea that the active participation of school members in the leadership process may improve student learning, and the democratic

relationships to be established between teachers and school administrators are quite important for the realization of this idea.

Arguing that school culture and climate need to change for teacher leadership to develop in the school environment, Hook (2006) states that any culture supporting collaboration and participation in decision-making processes in school may contribute to the leadership behaviors of teachers, too. Addressing the development of teacher leadership within the context of school culture, Reeves (2008) gives importance to such aspects of school culture as collaboration, open communication, and trust-oriented nature for the development of teacher leadership, and claims that it is quite difficult for teacher leadership to develop in any school environment where school members cannot communicate with one another soundly and they do not trust in one another. Suggesting that school culture can be considered an important factor influential on the development of teacher leadership, Muijs and Harris (2007) say that any culture where teachers and school administrators do not trust in one another and school members act independently of one another may prevent teachers from displaying leadership behaviors and contributing to the school leadership process. Stressing that the unique culture of a school is important for developing teacher leadership and making a positive contribution to student learning, Katzenmeyer and Moller (2009) state that it is very likely for teacher leadership to develop in a school culture that allows close and sharing-based relationships among teachers, supports collaboration, incorporates teachers adopting collective working and strictly committed to school objectives, encourages teachers to acquire new knowledge and skills, includes teachers in decision-making processes, and appreciates leadership behaviors.

Relationships between classifications about organizational culture and the basic assumptions of teacher leadership need to be examined in order to make a sound analysis concerning the relationship between teacher leadership and organizational culture. Thus, the present study dealt with the culture classifications frequently referenced in the studies about organizational culture and the relationship between such classifications and teacher leadership. One of these classifications is the one made by Hofstede (1997). Hofstede classified organizational culture as follows: power distance, individualism/collectivism, masculinity/femininity, and uncertainty avoidance. *Power distance* refers to the level of non-equal distribution of power among individuals in the organization. *Uncertainty avoidance* is about the perceptions of the members of the organization concerning what to do in uncertain situations. *Individualism/collectivism* is about the preferences of the organization members regarding acting independently or in group. Finally, *masculinity/femininity* refers to the explanation of the dominant values in the organization through masculine or feminine characteristics (Hofstede, 1997; Hofstede, Hofstede, & Minkov, 2010; Hofstede, Neuijen, Ohayv, & Sanders, 1990).

Teacher leadership is based on the idea that all teachers in the school have leadership skills, and an effective school improvement and student learning cannot be ensured through an only administrator-focused leadership mentality (Barth, 1990, Harris & Muijs, 2003a, 2003b; Katzenmeyer & Moller, 2009). In other words, teacher leadership requires teachers to play active roles in the school management processes, participate in decision-making processes, and lead school-related processes (York-Barr & Duke, 2004). Authoritarian management is replaced by a more democratic management based on collaboration and communication between administrators and teachers in the schools where there is an improved teacher leadership (Camburn, Rowan, & Taylor, 2003; Frost, 2008; Katzenmeyer & Moller, 2009; Lieberman & Miller, 2005; Spillane, Halverson, & Diamond, 2005; Whitaker, 1997). Thus, it is difficult for teacher leadership to develop in the organizational cultures where power distance is big and distinction between those who manage and those who are managed is obvious. Likewise, Murphy (2007) argues that any big power distance between teachers and school administrators that is based on the mentality that the only task of a teacher is to teach and the task of managing and leading belongs to school administrators alone is one of the important obstacles preventing teachers from taking responsibility for leadership behaviors. According to Harris (2003), the development of teacher leadership is directly proportional to a more democratic school culture. Harris and Lambert (2003) state that teacher leadership is aimed at improving the human capacity of school, and that it is not likely for teachers to take responsibility for leadership behaviors in any organizational culture where the entire organizational power is held by administrators.

The examination of the relationships between individualist/collectivist organizational cultures and teacher leadership implies that teacher leadership is more congruent for a collectivist organizational culture. As a matter of fact, teacher leadership is associated with teachers' taking responsibility for leadership behaviors as a whole, participating in decision-making processes in the organization, collaborating for the improvement of teaching, questioning the teaching conducted, and communicating with their colleagues effectively (Katzenmeyer & Moller, 2009; Harris, 2003; Little, 2000; York-Barr & Duke, 2004). Muijs and Harris (2007) emphasize that teacher leadership is associated with collective behaviors rather than individual efforts. Apart from that, many other studies on teacher leadership put an emphasis on teachers' collectively working, conducting research, taking responsibility for student learning, and trying and evaluating new practices (e.g. Frost & Harris, 2003; Helterbran, 2010; Lambert, 2003; Muijs & Harris, 2003, 2007). Thus, it may be considered that teacher leadership may have a wider sphere of influence in collectivist school cultures.

Relying on the femininity-masculinity distinction of Hofstede (1997), any organizational culture having feminine characteristics can be associated with a role distribution not taking sex as a basis, more tolerance for mistakes, sound communication and collaboration among colleagues, and a more democratic management. Masculine cultures, on the other hand, can be regarded as more competitive and goal-oriented. Teacher leadership is possible only through close and intimate relationships and sharing among teachers and an environment of mutual respect (Harris & Muijs, 2003a). Those teachers who trust in one another, can work together, and are capable of communicating with one another effectively take more responsibility for the improvement of teaching (Barth, 1990). According to Lambert (2002), one should search leadership in the relationships and interactions taking place among individuals in an organization. In consideration of the foregoing, femininity seems to be more congruent for the basic assumptions of teacher leadership.

Uncertainty avoidance, included in the organizational culture classification by Hofstede (1997), refers to the attitudes of organization members towards uncertainties. When there are uncertainties, individuals may differ in the ways of understanding such uncertainties and coping with complicated situations (Sığrı & Tığlı, 2006). That can be explained with the formal and informal aspects of teacher leadership. As a matter of fact, from a formal perspective, teacher leadership is generally associated with such tasks as group leader, specialized teacher or counselor which are included in relevant official regulations (Leithwood & Jantzi, 2000). The informal aspect of teacher leadership can be regarded as a qualification attributed to teachers who take leadership responsibilities, support the multifaceted improvement of their colleagues, and guide their colleagues (Danielson, 2006). However, the roles of informal leaders have not been determined by specific regulations. Being people trusted in and respected by their colleagues, informal leaders lead the generation of new ideas in school, share their knowledge and specialization with other teachers, and guide them (Danielson, 2006; Leithwood & Jantzi, 2000). In this sense, it is not very likely that those teachers who have a negative perception regarding uncertainties, cannot go beyond official rules, procedures, and principles, and do not take risk to take the lead in school. In parallel with that, Helterbran (2010) states that the informal aspect of teacher leadership is much deeper than its formal aspect, and informal leaders are the teachers who take risk, exert effort for the continuous improvement of organizational members, and lead innovations in school. Therefore, it seems difficult for teacher leadership to develop, at least in its informal aspect, in the organizational cultures where there is a strong tendency for uncertainty avoidance.

The related literature contains different classifications regarding organizational culture (Handy, 1981; Harrison, 1972; Şişman, 2002; Terzi, 2000). These classifications generally address organizational culture under various names such as power, role, task, individual, support, success, bureaucracy and task culture. Since each culture has some unique characteristics, it may be expected for teacher leadership to have different reflections within the context of culture's unique characteristics. For example, it is possible to see domination conflicts and conflicts of interest in power-centered cultures (Şişman, 2002). It is known that individuals have a tendency to hold the power and dominate in these kinds of cultures (Harrison, 1972). From this perspective, it does not seem possible for a leadership approach which claims that every teacher has a right and skill to lead to manifest itself in a power-centered organizational culture. According to Frost and Harris (2003), teacher leadership has a wide acceptance in the organizational cultures based on collective responsibility and collaboration.

Official principles, rules, and procedures are primarily regarded in organizational management in role cultures and bureaucratic cultures where change faces anxiety and resistance in general (Harrison, 1972; Terzi, 2000). However, as stated before, teacher leaders have informal tasks, besides their formal tasks, which they undertake by going beyond their role definitions (Can, 2009a; Danielson, 2006; Helterbran, 2010; Leithwood & Jantzi, 2000; Muijs & Harris, 2006; Murphy, 2005). Therefore, it is not likely that the organizational cultures where teachers fulfill their tasks within the limits of official rules alone and do not go beyond their role definitions can contribute to teacher leadership. On the other hand, success and support-oriented cultures attach importance to performing works successfully, accomplishing individual and organizational goals, and appreciating and supporting the efforts of teachers (Sezgin, 2010; Terzi, 2000). The technical essence of school is student learning (Hoy & Miskel, 2004/2010). Teachers contribute to student learning with their professional behaviors and leadership skills (Hoy, 2003). It may be argued that the school cultures which support teachers' efforts for student learning, innovative behaviors, and participation in decision-making processes and help them display leadership behaviors in school are important for the development of teacher leadership (Katzenmeyer & Moller, 2009). Thus, it may be expected for teacher leadership to have a higher possibility of development in supportive and success-oriented school cultures. According to Harris (2003), if there is no supportive school culture based on collaboration and collective responsibility, teacher leadership will only be a marginal activity.

Another noteworthy issue in regard to the relationship between teacher leadership and school culture is about norms – part of organizational culture. As a matter of fact, egalitarian norms which do exist in school cultures and assume that every teacher has equal knowledge, skills, and competency may cause those teachers who have leadership skills, but do not want to get reaction from other teachers to have an abstaining attitude (Katzenmeyer & Moller, 2009). According to Teddlie and Stringfield (2007), norms such as

autonomy, equality, intimacy, and privacy, which do exist in school culture, may prevent the development of teacher leadership. In their study on 17 teacher leaders, Lieberman, Saxl and Miles (2000) proved that egalitarian norms among teachers were one of the most important obstacles preventing teacher leadership. Hook (2006) emphasizes that some teachers have negative perceptions regarding the exhibition of leadership behaviors by their colleagues because they think that their colleagues taking responsibility for leadership behaviors break egalitarian norms.

Principal Support

The review of the related literature shows that one of the mostly examined factors influential on teacher leadership is the perspectives of school principals concerning teacher leadership. Harris and Lambert (2003) emphasized the importance of school principal's roles in developing teacher leadership as follows:

Even though teacher leadership is at the heart of building leadership capacity, the leadership of the headteacher is still the most vital and urgent form of intervention. This is because heads set the climate for improvement, they can empower others to lead and they can provide the much needed energy for change and development. Heads are the catalysts for change and development, they may not implement the changes but they enthuse others to take responsibility for change and development. They engage others in the emotional work of building collaborative, trusting relationships. Without his 'emotional climate' for change, even the most well conceived and received innovation is unlikely to succeed. (p. 38)

According to Mangin (2005), teacher leadership cannot be adopted in the existing school structures automatically, thus the support and positive perceptions of school principals concerning teacher leadership are critical for this matter. A considerable number of the theoretical and empirical studies on teacher leadership emphasize that the perspectives of school principals regarding teacher leadership are one of the primary factors influential on the development of teacher leadership (Anderson, 2004; Beycioğlu, 2009; Can, 2009a; College, 2011; Curci, 2012; Estes, 2009; Katzenmeyer & Moller, 2009; Kenyon, 2008; Mangin, 2005, 2007; Reid, 2011; York-Barr & Duke, 2004; Wilson, 2011; Zinn, 1997). For example, the research findings provided by Mangin (2005) demonstrate that school principals may affect the development of teacher leadership positively by supporting the innovations introduced by teachers to the teaching process and guiding them. Mangin (2007) revealed that the school principals knowing the roles of teacher leaders and communicating with them effectively supported the development of teacher leadership more.

According to Katzenmeyer and Moller (2009), school principals have quite important roles in the exhibition of leadership behaviors by teachers, and they may support the leadership behaviors of teachers with the leadership behaviors they display. Stating that effective school leaders should make use of the leadership skills of teachers in order to accomplish school objectives, Childs-Bowen, Moller and Scrivner (2000) argue that school principals who take into consideration the improvement needs of teachers having a potential to lead have a crucial role in the establishment of a sustainable and effective leadership mentality in school.

Buckner and McDowelle (2000) say that school principals have quite important roles for the development of teacher leadership. According to these authors, schools principals need to do the following in order to enable teachers to display more leadership behaviors and make more contribution to the school improvement process:

1. **Defining Teacher Leadership:** School principals should define teacher leadership, and know what formal teacher leadership and informal teacher leadership mean, which roles teacher leaders may play in school, and how they can contribute to school processes.

2. **Establishing Healthy Relationships with Teacher Leaders:** School principals should regard teacher leaders as a source for school improvement, and encourage them to take responsibility for leadership roles.

3. **Motivating Teacher Leaders:** The quality of the relationships between school environment and teachers may affect the motivation of teachers for playing leadership roles. Thus, any school principal who wants to make use of the leadership potentials of teachers should create a positive working environment in school.

4. **Helping Teachers Improve their Leadership Skills:** The professional improvement and competency areas of teachers have an important influence on teachers' assuming formal and informal leadership roles. Thus, the professional improvement support to be provided by school principals for teachers may have a positive effect on the development of teacher leadership by improving the leadership qualifications of teachers.

5. **Providing feedback:** Feedbacks to be provided by school principals in regard to the improvement processes of relevant teachers are important for the professional development of teacher leaders. It is very likely that teachers who are supported and informed by school principals concerning the effectiveness of the teaching conducted will make more contribution to the school improvement process and focus on student learning more.

Katzenmeyer and Moller (2009) argue that the perspectives of school principals concerning teacher leadership are one of the main factors influential on the development of teacher leadership and improvement of student success. Deal and Peterson (1999) stated that the source of leadership in schools was school principals, but teachers needed to be strengthened in order to sustain leadership, and that the support of school principal underlay teacher leadership. Similarly, Fullan (2005) said that school principals should encourage the potential leaders of schools. In consideration of the fact that teacher leadership is mostly an informal role, the most important factor supporting teacher leadership is all school members, school principal being in the first place (Zinn, 1997). In other words, the exhibition of leadership behaviors by school principals is an important factor for teacher leadership. School principals should remove the possible obstacles to be encountered by teacher leaders in the school environment besides supporting teacher leadership (Rutledge, 2009). Finally, school principals' understanding teacher leadership and finding new ways to support leadership behaviors can be critical for the accomplishment of school objectives (Akert & Martin, 2012).

Other Factors Affecting Teacher Leadership

An attempt was made to explain, in detail, the factors influential on the development of teacher leadership above. The number of these factors can be increased. For example, Zinn (1997) found out that the quality of the relationships among colleagues in school, the support of colleagues for the professional improvement of one another, and psychological and social characteristics of individuals were influential on the development of teacher leadership. Likewise, the research findings provided by Little (2000) revealed the existence of positive relationships between collaboration among teachers and effective teacher leadership. According to Katzenmeyer and Moller (2009), professional improvement plays an important role in the development of teacher leadership, and activities about leadership should be embedded in professional improvement practices in order

to ensure the development of teacher leadership. Harris and Muijs (2003a) report that an effective professional improvement process involving leadership practices may make teachers more ready for leadership roles. Cranston (2000) argues that teachers may improve their leadership skills by establishing professional networks or participating in such networks actively.

THE RELATIONSHIP BETWEEN TEACHER LEADERSHIP AND CLASSROOM AND SCHOOL IMPROVEMENT

Teacher leadership is based on the idea that power and authority in organization should be redefined and be distributed among organization members (Harris & Lambert, 2003). Teacher leadership refers to a leadership mentality where school members work and learn collectively, determine the objectives and vision of school within the framework of a collective responsibility perception, question the teaching conducted in school together, look for ways of improving such teaching, and participate in decision-making processes in school actively (Grant, 2006; Leithwood & Jantzi, 1999, 2000). In fact, it can be said that issues such as improving the quality of the teaching conducted in school and in classroom, determining and meeting the learning needs of students more effectively, developing sounder policies and strategies in accordance with the school objectives with the participation and professional support of teachers, teachers' exerting more efforts for student learning, school members' continuing their professional improvement effectively, and the transformation of school into a learning organization underlie the discussion of the idea that teachers may take the lead within the context of school (Harris, 2002a, 2003, 2005; Harris & Muijs, 2003a; Frost, 2008; Grant, 2006; Katzenmeyer & Moller, 2009; Camburn et al., 2003; York-Barr & Duke, 2004; Whitaker, 1997).

Teacher Leadership and Classroom Improvement

Many researchers emphasize that the center of efforts aimed at school improvement is classroom, and school improvement depends heavily on increasing the quality of the teaching conducted in the classroom (Ash & Persall, 2000; Harris & Lambert, 2003; Harris, 2002a, 2002b; Ovando, 1996; Spillane & Louis, 2002). Some researchers have investigated the effectiveness of school-based reform and change attempts on student learning, and have argued that the unit of analysis should be classroom for a sustainable school improvement (Fullan, 1991, 1992; Hopkins & Harris, 1997). The roles of teacher leaders are intensely discussed in the related literature within the scope of the reflections of change and reform efforts at school level in classroom and the positive effects of such efforts on student learning (Harris & Lambert, 2003; Harris, 2002a, 2002b, Katzenmeyer & Moller, 2009).

The primary expectation from teacher leaders is to share with their colleagues in order to improve classroom teaching, and to make evaluations concerning student learning over cases (Beachum & Dentith, 2004; Little, 2003). Harris (2002a) lists the roles of teacher leaders, being an expert and a practitioner, for classroom improvement as follows:

1. Ensuring the participation of students in activities where they may undergo learning experiences individually or in group in the classroom
2. Creating a supportive learning environment where students share their learning experiences with one another, and their self-esteems are improved
3. Allowing students to evaluate the effectiveness of classroom teaching practices and teaching environment, and attaching importance to such evaluations

4. Providing students with an opportunity to evaluate their own learning experiences

Stating that investment in teacher leadership refers to any investment in the professional improvement and training of teacher leaders, Harris (2002a) thinks that the prerequisite for classroom teaching is teacher's having the skill to develop and implement the most effective teaching practices. From this perspective, it may be argued that teacher leaders firstly exert effort to meet the learning needs of students in their classes. According to Katzenmeyer and Moller (2009), school reform efforts should firstly focus on teacher, the person having the most influence on student learning. That may be considered important in that it shows the relationship between teacher leadership and classroom improvement.

Teacher leaders, being an expert, are firstly responsible for the learning of students in their classrooms. They spend much of their time in their classrooms, make an attempt to determine the learning needs of students and develop effective learning practices for satisfying such needs, and provide students with positive learning experiences (Harris & Muijs, 2003a). Some other studies suggest that the primary tasks of teacher leaders are to prepare an environment increasing learning motivation in the classroom (Can, 2009a) and to transfer school improvement principles to the classroom (Harris, 2002b). Therefore, it may be argued that teacher leaders play an important role in the classroom improvement process.

Teacher Leadership and School Improvement

In its broadest sense, school improvement is a process focusing on improving student learning (Harris & Hopkins, 2000). It is firstly the teacher who is responsible for student learning and the effective realization of reform initiatives in education (Day, 2002). Thus, it can be said that there is a close relationship between school improvement process and teachers' improving their professional knowledge and skills and developing effective teaching practices regarding student learning.

As stated above, teacher leaders play important formal and informal roles in school. Especially the roles played by teacher leaders outside their classes are closely related to school improvement process (Danielson, 2006). For instance, Katzenmeyer and Moller (2009) state that teacher leaders have important tasks outside their classes including helping their colleagues develop effective teaching practices and evaluate the teaching practices they conduct and coaching other teachers. Harris and Muijs (2003a) list the roles played by teacher roles in regard to school improvement as follows:

1. Encouraging colleagues to develop effective teaching practices
2. Participating in activities for developing curriculum
3. Enabling sounder and more effective decisions to be made by participating in the decision-making processes at school level, those about teaching-related processes being in the first place
4. Planning, conducting, and evaluating in-service trainings
5. Supporting the creation of a culture where the teaching conducted in school is questioned

Hallinger and Heck (2010) emphasize that a school improvement process focusing on the improvement of student learning can achieve its goals with a collaborative leadership, and in this process, teachers should participate in decision-making processes in school with their skills and knowledge, employ school resources effectively in order to enable school members to continue their professional improvement in particular, and take responsibility for student learning. Schaffer, Devlin-Scherer and Stringfield (2007) argue that effective teacher leaders develop different teaching practices especially for those students in

their classes who have learning difficulties and contribute to the improvement of teaching in the entire school by sharing such practices with their colleagues.

School improvement is associated with school change, too. Fullan (1991, 1992) reports that change is managed effectively, effective teaching practices having positive impacts on student learning are conducted by teachers effectively, new teaching methods, techniques, and procedure are put into practice, and new solutions are introduced in regard to the learning needs of students in any effective school improvement process. Harris (2002a) claims that teacher leaders, who work as the catalyst of change in school, motivate other teachers to be part of change and adopt it, thereby laying the ground for the establishment of a collective responsibility perception for the accomplishment of school objectives. According to this author, those teacher leaders who collaborate with their colleagues, contribute to their professional improvement, and help them gain experiences in teaching and learn from their mistakes contribute to the effectiveness of the change process in school, too.

The contributions of teacher leaders to school improvement process can be seen when one looks at the relationship between teacher leadership and teacher professionalism. Murphy (2005) reports that teacher leaders display more professional behaviors, produce more effective solutions for improving student success, are motivated more and motivate their colleagues more, have a tendency to improve their professional knowledge and skills continuously and to participate in decision-making processes more, and thus make more contribution to school improvement as a whole. According to Barth (2001), there is a positive relationship between teacher leadership and teacher professionalism, and teacher leaders, being experts, are firstly responsible for student learning and student improvement. In addition, teacher leaders, being professional people, play important roles in the process of developing a professional school culture to enable other teachers to change the teaching methods they employ for a more effective teaching (Doyle, 2000; Smylie, Conley, & Marks, 2002).

Professionalism, emerging in parallel with the exhibition of leadership behaviors by teachers, enables to develop classroom and school-based practices for student learning, and lays the ground necessary for the creation of a learning-focused culture in school (Murphy, 2005). Some other researchers have focused on the parallelism between teacher leadership and teaching as a professional job, too. According to Grant (2006), those teachers who display leadership behaviors have higher professionalism perceptions and focus on student learning more. Similarly, Harris and Muijs (2003a) claim that there is a positive relationship between teacher leadership and professional teacher behaviors, and that teacher leaders contribute to school improvement process with their professional behaviors.

All in all, it can be said that teacher leaders, playing formal and informal roles in school, help to improve student learning, which is the main objective of school improvement, and to create a more effective learning and teaching environment in school.

FUTURE RESEARCH AREAS ON TEACHER LEADERSHIP

The detailed literature review on teacher leadership shows that it is an important factor influential on student learning and school improvement. However, there is quite a limited number of empirical studies on this subject both in Turkey and in other countries. Some empirical studies on teacher leadership conducted in Turkey deal with the perceptions of school administrators and teachers regarding teacher leadership behaviors (Beycioğlu, 2009; Beycioğlu & Aslan, 2012; Kılınç, 2013; Kılınç & Recepoğlu, 2013; Kölükçü, 2011; Yiğit, Doğan, & Uğurlu, 2013), the leadership roles displayed by teacher leaders in the classroom and in

school (Can, 2007; Can, 2009a; 2009b), the roles and strategies of school principals for the improvement of teacher leadership (Can, 2006), the impact of teacher leadership on the development of school leadership capacity (Özçetin, 2013), and relationships between teacher leadership behaviors and classroom climate (Aslan, 2011). Apart from that, a scale for measuring the perceptions and expectations of teachers and administrators concerning teacher leadership was developed in another study (Beycioğlu & Aslan, 2010).

The review of the international literature concerning teacher leadership demonstrates that there are many studies focusing on the relationship between school improvement and student learning (Frost & Harris, 2003; Harris, 2002a; Harris & Muijs, 2003a, 2003b, 2005; Muijs & Harris, 2003, 2006, 2007; Murphy, 2005; 2007; Rutledge, 2009). Apart from that, some other studies examine the perceptions of teachers regarding leadership behaviors (Angelle & DeHart, 2011; Nolan & Palazzolo, 2011), how teachers make sense of teacher leadership (Scribner & Bradley-Levine, 2010), the leadership characteristics of teacher leaders (Ault, 2009), factors supporting and preventing teacher leadership (Beachum & Dentith, 2004; Fraser, 2008; Mangin, 2005, 2007; Zinn, 1997), relationships between teacher leadership and school climate (Muijs & Harris, 2007; Xie, 2008), relationships between teacher leadership and student engagement (Leithwood & Jantzi, 2000), relationships between teacher leadership and school effectiveness (Hook, 2006), and relationships between teacher leadership and teacher efficacy (Burgess, 2012).

Despite the above-mentioned studies on teacher leadership, the common opinion of the important authors of the field is that the existing research is not enough for teacher leadership to be understood and made more effective within the context of school (Frost & Harris, 2003; Katzenmeyer & Moller, 2009; Muijs & Harris, 2007; York-Barr & Duke, 2004). Frost and Harris (2003) list the factors influential on teachers' taking responsibility for leadership behaviors in school, and state that research to be conducted on these factors may play a critical role in the development of teacher leadership (pp. 493-494):

1. **The construction of the professional role of teachers:**
   a. Teachers' Beliefs and Expectations.
   b. Societal Constructions.
2. **The organizational structures:**
   a. Organizational structures.
   b. Organizational Culture.
   c. Social Capital.
3. **Personal capacity:**
   a. Authority.
   b. Knowledge (Pedagogical, Organizational, Community).
   c. Situational Understanding.
   d. Interpersonal Skills.

According to York-Barr and Duke (2004), future research on teacher leadership should provide findings in regard to what contributions teacher leaders may make to classroom and school improvement processes with the formal and informal roles they play, what characteristics teachers should bear in order to play more effective leadership roles, how the egalitarian norms which do exist in school culture can be transformed into norms that support and appreciate teacher professionalism and teacher leadership, how teachers can be made to participate in decision-making processes more actively, how school-based practices can enable teachers to be prepared for leadership roles and continue their professional improvement, how the support of school principals for school teacher leadership can be increased, how school administration can make a better use of teacher leadership, and how the time needed by teachers for their professional improvement can be provided for them. Harris and Muijs (2003b) emphasize that a school culture which is goal-oriented and suitable for student learning and where student needs are met at optimal level is important for the development of teacher leadership, and thus the improvement of student learning. In this respect, the school cultures and structures encouraging teachers to take leadership roles or preventing them from playing such roles should be examined. In addition, future research on teacher leadership may deal with the emotional support provided for teacher leaders by their colleagues, the financial support provided for teacher leaders by school administrations, or other supports provided for contributing to the development of teacher leadership (Mangin, 2007).

CONCLUSION

The present study aimed at examining the concept of teacher leadership through a detailed review of the national and the international literature. Therefore, the study provided explanations and analyses concerning different definitions of teacher leadership, the formal and the informal roles played by teacher leaders within the context of school, the factors influential on the development of teacher leadership, the relationship between teacher leadership and classroom and school improvement, and the tendency of future research on teacher leadership.

Although there are many different definitions concerning teacher leadership, it can be said that the concept is built upon the idea that teachers have knowledge and skills to lead and teachers playing leadership roles in school may make important contributions to student learning. Teachers playing many formal and informal roles in school firstly lead their classrooms, continue their professional improvement effectively, determine the learning needs of their students correctly, design effective teaching practices, help their colleagues improve themselves professionally, and contribute to the creation of a culture based on sharing, learning, producing, questioning, and an environment of positive communication and collaboration among colleagues.

In the light of the literature review conducted in the present study, it can be said that various factors such as organizational culture, time, and the support of school principal are influential on the development of teacher leadership besides the structural characteristics of school. In addition, horizontal organizational constructions, more constructed time, a participative, democratic, and positive organizational culture, and school principals appreciating and supporting teacher leadership are needed for teacher leadership to have a wider acceptance and for teacher leaders to make more contribution to classroom improvement and school improvement.

Teachers spending large part of their time in their classes are firstly responsible for creating an effective learning environment and improving student learning in their classes. In addition, they improve the quality of the decisions made by participating in decision-making processes in school actively, evaluate the data related to school, help their colleagues to plan and conduct effective teaching practices, and guide them outside their classes. In other words, teacher leaders put the leadership behaviors which they display in their classrooms into the service of the school improvement.

There is quite a limited number of studies on teacher leadership both in Turkey and in other countries. A considerable number of the existing studies deal with the definition of the concept, the explanation of its aspects, and the discussion of its theoretical bases. Thus, future research may make important contributions to the theoretical background of the concept through investigating within and out-of-school factors influential on the development of teacher leadership, the contribution of teacher leadership to classroom and school improvement, the perspectives of school principals regarding teacher leadership, and relationships between teacher leadership and organizational structure, school culture, school climate, organizational commitment, organizational citizenship, and organizational learning. Moreover, empirical research may be conducted with different sample groups, at different educational levels, and by using qualitative, quantitative or mixed research methods, or various theoretical studies may be carried out for providing a more effective analysis of the concept.

REFERENCES

Akert, N., & Martin, B. N. (2012). The role of teacher leaders in school improvement through the perceptions of principals and teachers. *International Journal of Education*, *4*(4), 284–299. doi:10.5296/ije.v4i4.2290

Anderson, K. D. (2004). The nature of teacher leadership in schools as reciprocal influences between teacher leaders and principals. *School Effectiveness and School Improvement*, *15*(1), 97–113. doi:10.1076/sesi.15.1.97.27489

Angelle, P. S., & DeHart, C. A. (2011). Teacher perceptions of teacher leadership: Examining differences by experience, degree, and position. *NASSP Bulletin*, *95*(2), 141–160. doi:10.1177/0192636511415397

Ash, R. C., & Persall, J. M. (2000). The principal as chief learning officer: Developing teacher leaders. *NASSP Bulletin*, *84*(616), 15–22. doi:10.1177/019263650008461604

Aslan, M. (2011). *Öğretmen liderliği davranışları ve sınıf iklimi: Öğretmen ve öğrenci görüşleri bağlamında bir araştırma* [Teacher leadership and classroom climate: A study regarding the opinions of teachers and students]. (Unpublished master's thesis). Eskişehir Osmangazi University, Eskişehir, Turkey.

Ault, C. R. (2009). *A case study of leadership characteristics of teacher leaders in an urban literacy program* (Doctoral dissertation). Retrieved from ProQuest Dissertations and Thesis database. (UMI No. 3346278)

Barth, R. S. (1990). *Improving schools from within. Teachers, parents, and principals can make the difference*. San Francisco, CA: Jossey-Bass.

Barth, R. S. (2001). Teacher leader. *Phi Delta Kappan, 82*(6), 443–449. doi:10.1177/003172170108200607

Beachum, F., & Dentith, A. M. (2004). Teacher leaders creating cultures of school renewal and transformation. *The Educational Forum, 68*(3), 276–286. doi:10.1080/00131720408984639

Beycioğlu, K. (2009). *İlköğretim okullarında öğretmenlerin sergiledikleri liderlik rollerine ilişkin bir değerlendirme (Hatay ili örneği)* [An analysis of teacher leadership roles in elementary schools. The case of Hatay province]. (Unpublished doctoral dissertation). İnönü University, Malatya, Turkey.

Beycioğlu, K., & Aslan, B. (2010). Öğretmen liderliği ölçeği: Geçerlik ve güvenirlik çalışması [Teacher leadership scale: A validity and reliability study]. *Elementary Education Online, 9*(2), 764–775.

Beycioğlu, K., & Aslan, B. (2012). Öğretmen ve yöneticilerin öğretmen liderliğine ilişkin görüşleri: Bir karma yöntem çalışması [Teachers and administrators' views on teacher leadership: A mixed methods study]. *Educational Administration: Theory and Practice, 18*(2), 191–223.

Buckner, K. G., & McDowelle, J. O. (2000). Developing teacher leaders: Providing encouragement, opportunities, and support. *NASSP Bulletin, 84*(616), 35–41. doi:10.1177/019263650008461607

Burgess, C. A. (2012). *Teachers' perceptions of teacher leadership and teacher efficacy* (Doctoral dissertation). Retrieved from ProQuest Dissertations and Thesis database. (UMI No. 3493784)

Camburn, E., Rowan, B., & Taylor, J. E. (2003). Distributed leadership in schools: The case of elementary schools adopting comprehensive school reform models. *Educational Evaluation and Policy Analysis, 25*(4), 347–373. doi:10.3102/01623737025004347

Can, N. (2006). Öğretmen liderliğinin geliştirilmesinde müdürün rol ve stratejileri [The roles and the strategies of the principal in improving teacher leadership]. *Erciyes University Journal of the Institute Social Sciences, 21*, 349–363.

Can, N. (2007). Öğretmen liderliği becerileri ve bu becerilerin gerçekleştirilme düzeyi [Teacher leadership skills and its level of realization]. *Erciyes University Journal of the Institute Social Sciences, 22*(1), 263–288.

Can, N. (2009a). *Öğretmen liderliği* [Teacher leadership]. Ankara: Pegem Akademi.

Can, N. (2009b). Öğretmenlerin sınıfta ve okulda liderlik davranışları [Leadership behaviors of teachers in classroom and school]. *University of Gaziantep Journal of Social Sciences, 2*, 385–399.

Childs-Bowen, D., Moller, G., & Scrivner, J. (2000). Principals: Leaders of leaders. *NASSP Bulletin, 84*(616), 27–34. doi:10.1177/019263650008461606

College, M. (2011). *Who's leading now: A case study of teacher leadership* (Doctoral dissertation). Retrieved from ProQuest Dissertations and Thesis database. (UMI No. 3509123)

Cosenza, M. N. (2010). *The impact of professional development schools on teacher leadership* (Doctoral dissertation). Retrieved from ProQuest Dissertations and Thesis database. (UMI No. 3426693)

Cranston, N. C. (2000). Teachers as leaders: A critical agenda for the new millennium. *Asia-Pacific Journal of Teacher Education, 28*(2), 123–131. doi:10.1080/713650688

Curci, M. E. (2012). *An examination of teacher leadership perceptions of teachers and building administrators using a comparative case study approach* (Doctoral dissertation). Retrieved from ProQuest Dissertations and Thesis database. (UMI No. 3499392)

Danielson, C. (2006). *Teacher leadership that strengthens professional practice.* Alexandria, VA: Association for Supervision and Curriculum Development.

Darling-Hammond, L., Bullmaster, M., L., & Cobb, V. (1995). Rethinking teacher leadership through professional development schools. *The Elementary School Journal, 96*(1), 87-106.

Day, C. (2002). School reform and transitions in teacher professionalism and identity. *International Journal of Education and Research, 37*(8), 677–692. doi:10.1016/S0883-0355(03)00065-X

Deal, T., & Peterson, K. (1999). *Shaping school culture: The heart of leadership.* San Francisco: Jossey-Bass.

Dee, R. D., Henkin, A. B., & Duemer, L. (2002). Structural antecedents and psychological correlates of teacher empowerment. *Journal of Educational Administration, 41*(3), 257–277. doi:10.1108/09578230310474412

Doyle, M. (2000, April). *Making meaning of teacher leadership in the implementation of a standards-based mathematics curriculum.* Paper presented at the Annual Meeting of the American Educational Research Association. New Orleans, LA.

DuFour, R., Eaker, R., & DuFour, R. (2005). Recurring themes of professional learning communities and the assumptions they challenge. In R. DuFour, R. Eaker, & R. DuFour (Eds.), *On common ground: The power of professional learning communities* (pp. 1–6). Bloomington, IN: Solution Tree.

Estes, K. R. (2009). *An analysis of the relationship between high school principals' perception of teacher leadership behaviors and school performance* (Doctoral dissertation). Retrieved from ProQuest Dissertations and Thesis database. (UMI No. 3358168)

Fraser, R. J. (2008). *Demystifying teacher leadership in comprehensive high schools* (Doctoral dissertation). Retrieved from ProQuest Dissertations and Thesis database. (UMI No. 3311546)

Frost, D. (2008). Teacher leadership: Values and voice. *School Leadership & Management: Formerly School Organisation, 28*(4), 337–352. doi:10.1080/13632430802292258

Frost, D., & Durant, J. (2003). Teacher leadership: Rationale, strategy and impact. *School Leadership & Management, 23*(2), 173–186. doi:10.1080/1363243032000091940

Frost, D., & Harris, A. (2003). Teacher leadership: Towards a research agenda. *Cambridge Journal of Education, 33*(3), 479–498. doi:10.1080/0305764032000122078

Fullan, M. (1991). *The new meaning of educational change.* London: Cassell.

Fullan, M. (1992). *Successful school improvement.* Buckingham, UK: Open University.

Fullan, M. (2005). *Leadership and sustainability: System thinkers in action.* Thousand Oaks, CA: Corwin.

Grant, C. (2006). Emerging voices on teacher leadership: Some South African view. *Educational Management Administration & Leadership*, *34*(4), 511–532. doi:10.1177/1741143206068215

Gronn, P. (2000). Distributed properties: A new architecture for leadership. *Educational Management and Administration*, *28*(3), 317–338. doi:10.1177/0263211X000283006

Hallinger, P., & Heck, R. H. (2010). Collaborative leadership and school improvement: Understanding the impact on school capacity and student learning. *School Leadership & Management: Formerly School Organisation*, *30*(2), 95–110. doi:10.1080/13632431003663214

Handy, C. B. (1981). *Understanding organizations* (2nd ed.). London: Hazell Watson & Viney.

Harris, A. (2002a). *School improvement: What's in it for schools?* London: Falmer. doi:10.4324/9780203471968

Harris, A. (2002b). Distributed leadership in schools: Leading or misleading? *Management in Education*, *16*(5), 10–13. doi:10.1177/089202060301600504

Harris, A. (2003). Teacher leadership as distributed leadership: Heresy, fantasy or possibility? *School Leadership & Management*, *23*(3), 313–324. doi:10.1080/1363243032000112801

Harris, A. (2005). Teacher leadership: More than just a feel-good factor? *Leadership and Policy in Schools*, *4*(3), 201–219. doi:10.1080/15700760500244777

Harris, A., & Hopkins, D. (2000). Introduction to special feature: Alternative perspective on school improvement. *School Leadership & Management*, *20*(1), 9–14. doi:10.1080/13632430068842

Harris, A., & Lambert, L. (2003). *Building leadership capacity for school improvement*. Maidenhead, UK: Open University.

Harris, A., & Muijs, B. (2003b). Teacher leadership and school improvement. *Educational Review*, *16*(2), 39–42.

Harris, A., & Muijs, B. (2005). *Improving schools through teacher leadership*. Maidenhead, UK: Open University.

Harris, A., & Muijs, D. (2003a). *Teacher leadership: Principles and practice*. London: National College for School Leadership. Retrieved from http://www.nationalcollege.orguk/index./docinfo.htm?id=17417

Harrison, C., & Killion, J. (2007). Ten roles for teacher leaders. *Educational Leadership*, *65*(1), 74–77.

Harrison, R. (1972). Understanding your organization's character. *Harvard Business Review*, *50*(23), 119–128.

Hart, A. W. (1995). Reconceiving school leadership: Emergent views. *The Elementary School Journal*, *96*(1), 9–28. doi:10.1086/461812

Helterbran, V. R. (2010). Teacher leadership. Overcoming "I'm just a teacher" syndrome. *Education*, *131*(2), 363–371.

Hofstede, G. (1997). *Cultures and organizations* (2nd ed.). USA: McGraw-Hill.

Hofstede, G., Hofstede, G. J., & Minkov, M. (2010). *Cultures and organizations: Software of the Mind* (3rd ed.). New York: McGraw-Hill.

Hofstede, G., Neuijen, B., Ohayv, D. D., & Sanders, G. (1990). Measuring organizational cultures: A qualitative and quantitative study across twenty cases. *Administrative Science Quarterly*, *35*(2), 286–316. doi:10.2307/2393392

Hook, D. P. (2006). *The impact of teacher leadership on school effectiveness in selected exemplary secondary schools* (Doctoral dissertation). Retrieved from ProQuest Dissertations and Thesis database. (UMI No. 3219160)

Hopkins, D., & Harris, A. (1997). Improving the quality of education for all. *Support for Learning, 12*(4), 147–151. doi:10.1111/1467-9604.00035

Hoy, W. K. (2003). An analysis of enabling and mindful school structures: Some theoretical, research, and practical consideration. *Journal of Educational Administration, 41*(1), 87–108. doi:10.1108/09578230310457457

Hoy, W. K., & Miskel, C. G. (2010). Eğitim yönetimi: Teori, araştırma ve uygulama [Educational administration: Theory, research, and practice]. (S. Turan, Trans. Ed.). Ankara: Nobel. (Orijinal Edition. 2004).

Institute for Educational Leadership (IEL). (2008). *Teacher leadership in high schools: How principals encourage it-How teachers practice it.* Institute for Educational Leadership. Retrieved February 9, 2014, from http://www.iel.org/pubs/metlife_t eacher_ report.pdf

Katzenmeyer, M., & Moller, G. (2009). *Awakening the sleeping giant. Helping teachers develop as leaders* (3rd ed.). Thousand Oaks, CA: Corwin.

Kendall, L. T. (2011). *The effect of teacher leadership on retention plans and teacher attitudes among New North Carolina teachers* (Master thesis). Retrieved from ProQuest Dissertations and Thesis database. (UMI No. 1500767)

Kenyon, C. L. (2008). *Reframed teacher leadership: A narrative inquiry* (Doctoral dissertation). Retrieved from ProQuest Dissertations and Thesis database. (UMI No. 3321001)

Kılınç, A. Ç. (2013). *İlköğretim okullarında liderlik kapasitesinin belirlenmesi* [Determining the leadership capacity in primary schools]. (Unpublished doctoral dissertation). Gazi University, Ankara, Turkey.

Kılınç, A. Ç., & Recepoğlu, E. (2013). Ortaöğretim okulu öğretmenlerinin öğretmen liderliğine ilişkin algı ve beklentileri [High school teachers' perceptions on and expectations from teacher leadership]. *Kalem International Journal of Educational and Human Sciences, 3*(2), 175–215.

Kölükçü, D. (2011). *İlköğretim okulu öğretmenlerinin öğretmen liderliğini gösteren davranışlarının gereklilik ve sergilenme derecesine ilişkin görüşleri* [Neccessity of demonstrating leadership for elementary school teachers and their views relating to the level of demonstrating leadership] (Unpublished master thesis). Başkent University, Ankara, Turkey.

Lambert, L. (1998). How to build leadership capacity. *Educational Leadership, 55*(7), 17–19.

Lambert, L. (2002). Toward a deepened theory of constructivist leadership. In L. Lambert, D. Walker, D. Zimmerman, J. Cooper, M. Lambert, M. Gardner, & P. Slack (Eds.), *The constructivist leader* (pp. 34–62). New York: Teachers College.

Lambert, L. (2003). *Leadership capacity for lasting school improvement.* Alexandria, VA: Association for Supervision and Curriculum Development.

Lashway, L. (1998). Teacher leadership. *Research Roundup, 14*(3), 2–5.

Leithwood, K. (2003). Teacher leadership: Its nature, development, and impact on schools and students. In M. Brundrett, N. Burton, & R. Smith (Eds.), *Leadership in education* (pp. 103–117). Thousand Oaks, CA: Sage Publications. doi:10.4135/9781446215036.n7

Leithwood, K., & Jantzi, D. (1999). The relative effects of principal and teacher sources of leadership on student engagement with school. *Educational Administration Quarterly, 35*(5), 679–706. doi:10.1177/0013161X99355002

Leithwood, K., & Jantzi, D. (2000). Principal and teacher leadership effects: A replication. *School Leadership & Management, 20*(4), 415–434. doi:10.1080/713696963

Lieberman, A., & Miller, L. (2005). Teachers as leaders. *The Educational Forum, 69*(2), 151–162. doi:10.1080/00131720508984679

Lieberman, A., Saxl, E. R., & Miles, M. B. (2000). Teacher leadership: Ideology and practice. In M. Fullan (Ed.), *The Jossey-Bass reader on educational leadership* (pp. 339–345). Chicago: Jossey-Bass.

Little, J. W. (2000). Assessing the prospects for teacher leadership. In M. Fullan (Ed.), *Educational leadership*. San Francisco, CA: Jossey-Bass.

Little, J. W. (2003). Constructions of teacher leadership in three periods of policy and reform activism. *School Leadership & Management, 23*(4), 401–419. doi:10.1080/1363243032000150944

Mangin, M. M. (2005). Distributed leadership and the culture of schools: Teacher leaders' strategies for gaining access to classrooms. *Journal of School Leadership, 15*(4), 456–484.

Mangin, M. M. (2007). Facilitating elementary principals' support for instructional teacher leadership. *Educational Administration Quarterly, 43*(3), 319–357. doi:10.1177/0013161X07299438

Muijs, D., & Harris, A. (2003). Teacher leadership-Improvement through empowerment?: An overview of the literature. *Educational Management & Administration, 31*(4), 437–448. doi:10.1177/0263211X030314007

Muijs, D., & Harris, A. (2006). Teacher led school improvement: Teacher leadership in the UK. *Teaching and Teacher Education, 22*(8), 961–972. doi:10.1016/j.tate.2006.04.010

Muijs, D., & Harris, A. (2007). Teacher leadership in (in)action. Three case studies of contrasting schools. *Educational Management Administration & Leadership, 35*(1), 111–134. doi:10.1177/1741143207071387

Mulford, B. (2003). *School Leaders: Changing role and impact on teacher and school effectiveness*. Paris: Education and Training Policy Division, OECD. Retrieved January 26, 2014 from http://www.oecd.org/education/school/2635399.pdf

Murphy, J. (2005). *Connecting teacher leadership and school improvement*. Thousand Oaks, CA: Corwin.

Murphy, J. (2007). A history of school effectiveness and improvement research in the USA focusing on the past quarter century. In, T. Townsend (Ed.), International handbook of school effectiveness and improvement (pp. 681-705). Dordrecht, The Netherlands: Springer.

Nolan, B., & Palazzolo, L. (2011). New teacher perceptions of the "teacher leader" movement. *NASSP Bulletin, 95*(4), 302–318. doi:10.1177/0192636511428372

Ovando, M. (1996). Teacher leadership: Opportunities and challenges. *Planning and Changing, 27*(1/2), 30–44.

Özçetin, S. (2013). *Öğretmen liderliğinin okulun liderlik kapasitesinin gelişimine etkisi: Bir durum çalışması* [The effect of teacher leadership on the development of the leadership capacity of the school: A case study]. (Unpublished master's thesis). Akdeniz University, Antalya, Turkey.

Pounder, J. S. (2006). Transformational classroom leadership: The fourth wave of teacher leadership? *Educational Management Administration & Leadership, 34*(4), 533–545. doi:10.1177/1741143206068216

Reeves, D. (2008). *Reframing teacher leadership to improve your school*. Alexandria, VA: Association for Supervision and Curriculum Development.

Reid, M. M. (2011). *Teacher leadership: One case study application* (Doctoral dissertation). Retrieved from ProQuest Dissertations and Thesis database. (UMI No. 3494743)

Rutledge, L. (2009). *Teacher leadership and school improvement: A case study of teachers participating in the teacher leadership network with a regional education service center* (Doctoral dissertation). Retrieved from ProQuest Dissertations and Thesis database. (UMI No. 3439841)

Schaffer, E., Devlin-Scherer, R., & Stringfield, S. (2007). The evolving role of teachers in effective schools. In, T. Townsend (Ed.), International handbook of school effectiveness and improvement (pp. 727-750). Dordrecht, The Netherlands: Springer. doi:10.1007/978-1-4020-5747-2_39

Scribner, S. M. P., & Bradley-Levine, J. (2010). The meaning(s) of teacher leadership in an urban high school reform. *Educational Administration Quarterly, 46*(4), 491–522. doi:10.1177/0013161X10383831

Sergiovanni, T. J. (1996). *Leadership for the school house. How is it different? Why is it important?* San Francisco: Jossey-Bass.

Sergiovanni, T. J. (2007). *Rethinking leadership. A collection of articles* (2nd ed.). Thousand Oaks, CA: Corwin.

Sezgin, F. (2010). Öğretmenlerin örgütsel bağlılığının bir yordayıcısı olarak okul kültürü [School culture as a predictor of teachers' organizational commitment]. *Education and Science, 35*(156), 142–159.

Sığrı, Ü., & Tığlı, M. (2006). *Hofstede'nin "belirsizlikten kaçınma" kültürel boyutunun yönetsel-örgütsel süreçlere ve pazarlama açısından tüketici davranışlarına etkisi* [The effect of "uncertainty avoidance" cultural dimension of Hofstede on managerial-organizational processes and on consumer behaviors in terms of marketing]. *Marmara University Journal of E.A.S, 21*(1), 29–42.

Şişman, M. (2002). *Örgütler ve kültürler* [Organizations and cultures]. Ankara: Pegem A.

Smylie, M. A., Conley, S., & Marks, H. M. (2002). Exploring new approaches to teacher leadership for school improvement. In J. Murphy (Ed.), *The educational leadership challenge: Redefining leadership for the 21st century* (pp. 162–188). Chicago: University of Chicago. doi:10.1111/j.1744-7984.2002.tb00008.x

Spillane, J. P., Halverson, R., & Diamond, J. B. (2001). Investigating school leadership practice: A distributed perspective. *Educational Researcher, 30*(3), 23–28. doi:10.3102/0013189X030003023

Spillane, J. P., & Louis, K. S. (2002). School improvement processes and practices: Professional learning for building instructional capacity. *Yearbook of the National Society for the Study of Education, 101*(1), 83–104. doi:10.1111/j.1744-7984.2002.tb00005.x

Taylor, M., Goeke, J., Klein, E., Onore, C., & Geist, K. (2011). Changing leadership: Teachers lead the way for schools that learn. *Teaching and Teacher Education, 27*(5), 920–929. doi:10.1016/j.tate.2011.03.003

Teacher Leadership Exploratory Consortium (TLEC). (2008). *Teacher leader model standards*. Retrieved January 27 from https://www.ets.org/s/education_topics/teaching_quality/pdf/teacher_leader_model_sta dards.pdf

Teddlie, C., & Stringfield, S. (2007). A history of school effectiveness and improvement research in the USA focusing on the past quarter century. In T. Townsend (Ed.), International handbook of school effectiveness and improvement (pp. 131-166). Dordrecht, The Netherlands: Springer. doi:10.1007/978-1-4020-5747-2_8

Terzi, A. R. (2000). *Örgüt kültürü* [Organizational culture]. Ankara: Nobel.

Whitaker, K. S. (1997). Developing teacher leadership and the management team concept: A case study. *Teacher Educator, 33*(1), 1–16. doi:10.1080/08878739709555154

Wilson, A. G. (2011). *Understanding the cultivation of teacher leadership in professional learning communities* (Doctoral dissertation). Retrieved from ProQuest Dissertations and Thesis database. (UMI No. 3465657)

Yiğit, Y., Doğan, S., & Uğurlu, C. T. (2013). Öğretmenlerin öğretmen liderliği davranışlarına ilişkin görüşleri [Teachers' views on teacher leadership behavior]. *Cumhuriyet International Journal of Education, 2*(2), 93–105.

York-Barr, J., & Duke, K. (2004). What do we know about teacher leadership? Findings from two decades of scholarship. *Review of Educational Research, 74*(3), 255–316. doi:10.3102/00346543074003255

Zinn, L. F. (1997). *Supports and barriers to teacher leadership. Reports of teacher leaders.* Paper presented in the Annual Meeting of American Educational Research Association. Chicago, IL.

ADDITIONAL READING

Ault, C. R. (2009). *A case study of leadership characteristics of teacher leaders in an urban literacy program* (Doctoral dissertation). Retrieved from ProQuest Dissertations and Thesis database. (UMI No. 3346278)

Boles, K., & Troen, V. (1994). *Teacher leadership in a professional development school.* Paper presented at the Annual Meeting of the American Educational Research Association, New Orleans, LA, April.

Darling-Hammond, L. (1990). Teacher professionalism: Why and how? In A. Lieberman (Ed.), *Schools as collaborative cultures: Creating the future now. London*: Falmer.

Day, C., Harris, A., Hadfield, M., Tolley, H., & Beresford, J. (2000). *Leading schools in times of change.* Milton Keynes: Open University.

Gabriel, J. G. (2005). *How to thrive as a teacher leader.* Alexandria, VA: Association for Supervision and Curriculum. *Development.*

Gronn, P. (2000). Distributed properties: A new architecture for leadership. *Educational Management and Administration, 28*(3), 371–338. doi:10.1177/0263211X000283006

Gronn, P. (2003). *The new work of educational leaders: Changing leadership practice in an era of school reform.* London: Paul Chapman.

Hargreaves, A. (1994). *Changing teachers: Changing times.* London: Cassell.

Harris, A. (1999). *Teaching and learning in the effective school.* London: Arena.

Harris, A. (1999). *Effective subject leadership: A handbook of staff development activities.* London: David Fulton.

Hopkins, D., Harris, A., & Jackson, D. (1997). Understanding the school's capacity for development: Growth states and strategies. *School Leadership & Management, 17*(3), 401–411. doi:10.1080/13632439769944

Lieberman, A. (1988). *Building a professional culture in schools.* New York: Teachers College.

Lieberman, A., & Miller, L. (2004). *Teacher leadership.* San Francisco, CA: Jossey-Bass.

Lieberman, A., & Miller, L. (2008). *Teachers in professional communities: Improving teaching and learning.* New York: Teachers College.

Little, J. W. (1995). Contested ground: The basis of teacher leadership in high schools that restructure. *The Elementary School Journal, 96*(1), 47–63. doi:10.1086/461814

Murphy, J. (1991). *Restructuring schools: Capturing and assessing the phenomenon.* New York: Teachers College.

Ogawa, R. T., & Bossert, S. T. (1995). Leadership as an organizational quality. *Educational Administration Quarterly, 31*(2), 224–243. doi: 10.1177/0013161X95031002004

Özdemir, S. (2013). *Eğitimde örgütsel yenileşme* [Organizational innovation in education]. 7th ed.). Ankara: Pegem Akademi.

Reeves, D. B. (2008). *Reframing teacher leadership to improve your school.* Alexandria, VA: Association for Supervision and Curriculum. *Development.*

Rosenholtz, S. J. (1989). *Teachers' workplace: The social organization of schools.* White Plains, NY: Longman.

Schlechty, P. C. (1990). *Schools for the 21st century: Leadership imperatives for educational reform.* San Francisco: Jossey-Bass.

Senge, P. (1990). *The fifth discipline: The art and practice of the learning organisation.* New York: Doubleday.

Sergiovanni, T. J. (1994). *Building community in schools.* San Francisco, CA: Jossey-Bass.

Sergiovanni, T. J. (2001). *Leadership: What's in it for schools?* London: Routledge-Falmer.

Smylie, M. A. (1995). New perspectives on teacher leadership. *The Elementary School Journal, 96*(1), 3–7. doi:10.1086/461811

Stoll, L., & Fink, D. (1996). *Changing our schools: Linking school effectiveness and school improvement.* Buckingham: Open University.

Stoops, B. (2011). *Teacher leadership as meaningful school reform: A snapshot of contemporary teacher leadership.* (Doctoral dissertation). Retrieved from ProQuest Dissertations and Thesis database. (UMI No. 3479675)

Wilmore, E. L. (2007). *Teacher leadership: School improvement from within classrooms.* Thousand Oaks, CA: Corwin.

Xie, D. (2008). *A study of teacher leadership and its relationship with school climate in American public schools: Findings from SASS 2003-2004* (Doctoral dissertation). Retrieved from ProQuest Dissertations and Thesis database. (UMI No. 3303476)

KEY TERMS AND DEFINITIONS

Classroom Improvement: Building a healthy classroom environment appropriate for student learning.

Organizational Structure: How an organization arrange people, jobs, roles, and responsibilities to achieve its purposes.

School Culture: Shared values, norms, and beliefs of school community members.

School Improvement: A long journey of increasing the quality of student learning within school borders.

Teacher Leader: Those teachers who exert effort and time to increase the overall capacity of their school to learn and teach.

Teacher Leadership: Meant to teachers' assuming leadership roles through leading within and beyond classroom and helping colleagues develop their professional knowledge and skills to contribute well to the overall effectiveness of schools.

Chapter 13
Exploring Distributive Leadership in South African Public Primary Schools in the Soweto Region

Raj Mestry
University of Johannesburg, South Africa

Suraiya R Naicker
University of Johannesburg, South Africa

ABSTRACT

The increasing expectations of the principalship and the intensification of the challenges facing schools today have resulted in the emergence of distributive forms of leadership in schools worldwide. These developments prompted research in schools in South Africa, more specifically in the Soweto region, to inquire if distributed leadership had manifested. Soweto is a township in the Gauteng province of South Africa that is associated with the historic struggle against the apartheid government (pre-1994). A qualitative approach executed by means of focus group interviews was employed at three schools to explore the views of teachers who did not hold formal leadership positions. It was found that distributive leadership had not transpired in the schools that are largely rooted in classical leadership practices. This chapter provides an account of the study while elucidating the concept of distributive leadership and examines the role of formal leaders within a distributive leadership framework.

INTRODUCTION

It is widely accepted that effective leadership is paramount to successful schooling (Bush, Kiggundu & Moorosi, 2011; Harris & Muijs, 2005; Huber & Pashiardis, 2008). However, the relevance of traditional leadership models for schools in the twenty-first century are being challenged by theorists, reformers and practitioners, who advocate a fundamental re-conceptualisation of leadership in the twenty-first century (Grant & Singh, 2009; Grenda, 2006; Spillane, 2009). The accepted view of leadership as located in a position or person has been rejected (Gronn, 2003; Senge, 2006; Spillane,

DOI: 10.4018/978-1-4666-6591-0.ch013

2009; Spillane, 2005) in favour of more collective forms of leadership. Leadership is increasingly being viewed as a practice rather than a role (Harris & Spillane, 2008; Sergiovanni, 2005). This raises questions as to where the sources of leadership are located in the contemporary school.

Economic, social, technological and political changes have contributed to the changing role of educational leaders. Globalisation drives the need for high educational standards and for meeting competitive economic demands (Harris & Muijs, 2005:1). Traditional command and control leadership approaches fall short of addressing changes in the current educational environment such as the nature of work in a knowledge society, educational reforms and the accelerated pace of change. Traditional models hindered the practice of more flexible leadership styles and restricted teachers from taking on informal leadership roles (Moloi, 2005; Neuman & Simmons, 2000). In the post-heroic approach, command and control approaches to leadership give way to collaborative approaches that favour human relations, thus encouraging teamwork, participation, capacity building and risk-taking (Oduro, 2004). A shift from the hierarchy to flatter lateral structures is supported by post-modernism, which encourages more fluid organisations and a democratic approach to leadership, featuring inclusivity, participation and consultation (Bush, 2007). Such an approach resonates with the South African context, which strives to uphold democratic principles since the abolishment of apartheid in 1994. Bush (2007) notes the relevance of the participative leadership model for a democratic South Africa where the voices of all stakeholders, such as parents, learners, teachers and the broader community are important. In South Africa, a participative approach to leadership was facilitated by the implementation of site-based management which shifted the locus of control from the principal to all stakeholders in the school community (Van der Mescht &

Tyala, 2008). Site-based management was operationalised in South African schools through the introduction of School Governing Bodies (SGBs) and School Management Teams (SMTs).

The contemporary school has become complex in structure and purpose and therefore organisational change and development will require more fluid and distributed forms of leadership (Crawford, 2005). Dimmock (2003, p.4) argues that in turbulent educational environments "coherent" and "synergistic" approaches to leadership have come about in response to radical change. One of these emerging leadership approaches in schools today that is receiving prominence is distributive leadership. Theorists maintain that distributive leadership captures and reflects the evolving model of leadership in schools today (Harris, 2005a; Hartley, 2007). Schools can no longer be described in terms of traditional leader-follower dualisms (Gronn, 2003; Woods & Gronn, 2009). Spillane (2005, p.143) refers to distributive leadership as an "antidote" to the heroic leadership model. This perspective is shared by Hartley (2007) who strongly asserts that distributive leadership will replace the flawed heroic leadership phase.

We take the stance that the distributive approach, where all members are enabled to act as agents for change, is essential to the success of a school in the twenty-first century. MacBeath and Cheng (2008, p.270) concur with this perspective in the ensuing quote:

Developing leadership is not just about honing the skills of those in the most senior positions, important though that undoubtedly is. It is also about releasing the energies of every member of staff and every learner and about giving each of them a sense that their contributions are valued.

The distributive approach holds promise as theorists call for an alternate paradigm in school leadership. In this chapter we focus on the experiences and perceptions of teachers regarding the phenomenon of distributive leadership in their schools.

The objectives of this chapter are to:

- Explore how leadership is enacted at three public primary schools in Soweto from the point of view of teachers;
- Investigate the consequences of the leadership that is enacted at schools; and
- Determine teachers' views and experiences towards distributive leadership.

We will first examine various traditional models of leadership in a school context to establish whether a new form of leadership in the twenty-first century is necessary for school improvement.

TRADITIONAL MODELS OF LEADERSHIP

Traditional models of leadership referred to such as 'great man' theories or heroic leaders, associate leadership with persons who have authority based on their position in the hierarchy and specific qualities which they utilise to influence their followers (Thornton, 2010). This notion of the heroic leader and leadership as traits and behaviours has dominated the leadership literature entrenching the assumption that leadership is synonymous with the position of the principal (Hargreaves & Fink, 2008; Spillane, 2005). Heroic leadership models emphasised formality and limited leadership opportunities to hierarchical and structural positions.

While traditional models were relevant to the stable and predictable nature of school environments in past eras, their relevance to addressing the complexities in schools today have been challenged (Bush, 2003; Harris & Muijs, 2005). Gronn (2003) contends that work environments are now being reconceptualised as "communities of practice" giving opportunities for multiple leaders and forms of leadership. Furthermore, heroic leadership is

not practical due to the work intensification in schools (Gronn, 2003). Senge (2006) advances the argument that the heroic model is flawed since it denotes that other members of the organisation cannot take on leadership roles nor do they have power to bring about change. Moreover, the heroic leadership approach masks the diverse roles that leaders at different levels in the organisation can play (Senge, 2006). Thornton (2010) agrees that the heroic model keeps the leadership ability of others obscured but also supresses others from taking on leadership roles.

Trait theories, which focus on the characteristics and personality of the leader, are also deemed insufficient in the current school context. These theories neglect the situation as well as environmental factors that contribute to a leader's effectiveness (Hopkins & Jackson, 2003; Horner, 2003). Hence, school leadership can no longer be viewed in terms of the personal attributes of those in formal positions but rather as the product of social interaction and meaningful collaboration (Harris & Muijs, 2005; Spillane, 2005).

Transactional and transformational leadership models have also been considered as being inadequate in the current context of school leadership. Transactional leadership occurs when the leader creates an exchange process with the follower for desired things, while in transformational leadership the leader engages followers in a way that elevates each other to higher levels of motivation and morality (Burns, 1978 cited in Sorenson & Goethals, 2004). Some negative criticisms against transactional and transformational models are that they enable leaders to manipulate their followers, they do not emphasise the growth of leadership in others and, like heroic models, they are individualistic in nature assuming a leader-follower divide (Thornton, 2010). The long-term sustainability of the transformational leadership approach and the scarcity of principals who adopt a transformational approach are problematic (Harris, 2003a). It also appears that transactional and transformational approaches are conceptually flawed and superficial, bearing little relevance to reality (Fink, 2005 cited in Thornton, 2010). A view posited by Fink (2005) is that sustained leadership depends on ordinary and committed individuals rather than charismatic or superhuman heroes. This view is supported by Fullan (2001, p.1-2), who contends that charismatic leaders encourage dependency and are unrealistic role models, and who asserts that "deep and sustained reform depends on many of us, not just on the very few who are destined to be extraordinary". Mulford (2003) further advances the argument that successful principals are not superhuman by virtue of their characteristics or their visions, but are ordinary people who can engage collaboratively with others, who are committed towards achieving school goals and who have a high regard for the teaching profession.

The inadequacies of traditional leadership models give credence to the call for alternate leadership approaches. A focus on leadership styles and personal methods of leaders rather than leadership practice limits our understanding of school leadership (Spillane, 2009). A broader understanding of school leadership that moves beyond traditional models is thus warranted and appears to be emerging in post-heroic approaches.

BACKGROUND AND RATIONALE FOR THE CURRENT TREND TOWARDS DISTRIBUTIVE LEADERSHIP

In contemporary times, tremendous demands have been placed on school principals. Principals are required to take on more roles, perform an increasing number of school leadership practices, demonstrate a vast array of competencies and comply with school leader standards (Mulford, 2003). Principals are not only faced with a range of responsibilities but also an overwhelming workload (Crawford, 2005; Grenda, 2006). The extreme pressure placed on principals have led Gronn (2003, p.147) to describe school leadership as "greedy work" and educational leadership as a "greedy occupation".

There is evidence in the South African literature of the increasing expectations of South African principals as has been experienced by their international counterparts. Principals in South African primary schools are encountering an increasingly unmanageable workload (Botha, 2004). Diverse expectations are required of principals which have shifted from "management and control to the demands for an educational leader who can foster staff development, parent involvement, community support, and student growth and succeed with major changes and expectations" (Mestry & Singh, 2007, p.478). In addition, the principalship is further compounded by demands from both the teacher unions and the Department of Education (Mestry & Grobler, 2003).

The current context in which educational leaders perform their work is fraught with complexities. Complexities arise from school reforms such as those pertaining to curriculum, teaching and learning, assessment, diversity in schools, legislation and policy, educational standards and accountability pressures. Knapp, Copland, Honig, Plecki & Portin (2010) list numerous difficulties that confront educational leaders today such as diverse learner populations, historically disadvantaged learners, limited resources, staff retention, staff morale and special learner needs, which often result in continuous low achievement. In developing countries such as South Africa, there are even greater contextual challenges encountered by principals. These include extreme poverty, unemployment, child-headed families, granny-headed families, drug and alcohol abuse, a high rate of teenage pregnancy in high schools (Bush *et al.*, 2011) and widespread HIV/AIDs (Mouton,

Louw & Strydom, 2012). Principals are expected to ensure successful learner achievement for all children despite these constraints.

The trend towards self-managing schools created new challenges for school leaders such as the devolution of authority and participation with stakeholders (Earley & Weindling, 2004). Principals also find themselves trapped between "external drivers" and "internal drivers" (Harris, 2003b, p.14). External drivers result from new policies which require principals to motivate the staff towards the change and implement the change internally within a relatively short space of time (Harris, 2003b).

Continuous and radical change has affected educational systems worldwide (Botha, 2012), but perhaps to a greater extent in South Africa as the country lurched from forty years of apartheid governance to become a democratic state, after 1994. The post-apartheid South African educational landscape has been described as "volatile" and "changing by the day" (Botha, 2012, p.45). Changes in South Africa included technological and demographic shifts, decentralisation, issues of accountability, societal violence, economic changes and new legislation which have all contributed to the complexities in which principals now find themselves (Mestry, 2009).

Certainly the role of the twenty-first century principal is based on leading and managing change and coping with complexity in an era of delivery. Gronn (2003) asserts that it is in this current context of the expansion and intensification of the work of the principal that distributive forms of leadership have flourished. In a knowledge-intensive enterprise such as teaching and learning it is practically impossible for principals to complete complex tasks without distributing leadership responsibility (Hartley, 2007; Grenda, 2006). Leadership and management can no longer remain the exclusive domain of those in formal leadership positions but has to be extended to other levels in the school (Harris & Muijs, 2005). Furthermore, diverse expertise and flexible forms of leadership

are required to address the complex challenges in the educational landscape (Harris & Spillane, 2008). Maximising the capacity of staff, parents and even learners in order to harness their talents, and develop their skills and knowledge can be considered as a strategic ploy to address change and complexity in organisations. This view of utilising distributive leadership intentionally as a strategic tactic to realign and redesign leadership structures, tasks and procedures towards organisational improvement is strongly advanced by Harris (2013). Distributive leadership is no doubt timely and relevant, an idea whose "time has come" (Hartley, 2007, p.202), a pragmatic response to changing times (Harris, 2007) and "the preferred candidate" of alternative approaches to post-heroic leadership models (Woods & Gronn, 2009, p.430).

CONCEPTUALISING DISTRIBUTIVE LEADERSHIP

Historical Background

Distributive leadership is not an entirely new concept. An early notion of distributive patterns can be traced to Gibb (1954) cited in Gronn (2003, p.27) and is recorded in the "Handbook of Social Psychology". Follet (1973) cited in Gronn (2004) contended that the instruction given by an authority figure was part of a process that was influenced by others. Chester Barnard was of the view that leadership could be exercised by any member of an organisation, while James Thompson was one of the first theorists to point out that leadership does not only flow in a top-down direction but can flow across an organisation as well as up and down the hierarchy (Hargreaves & Fink, 2006). Theorists, who have endorsed distributive leadership historically, appear to have based their preference on ideological beliefs (Hargreaves & Fink, 2006) and the empirical base supporting distributive leadership is rather limited. The idea of distributive leadership has come to the fore in the last two decades (Timperley, 2005) and is gaining momentum. The empirical work of Spillane, Halverson & Diamond (2001) appears to have raised global interest in the concept. The National College of School Leadership (NCSL) in the United Kingdom has endorsed distributive leadership (Hartley, 2009; Woods & Gronn, 2009). South African research into the distributive approach is in its formative stages.

Defining Distributive Leadership

Conceptual ambiguity arises from the close resemblance of distributive leadership to other terms such as dispersed, devolved, shared, collaborative, participative and democratic leadership which are often used interchangeably with distributive leadership. The overlapping idea of all these terms is that leadership is not the domain of any particular person which is the basic premise of distributed leadership (Oduro, 2004). The ambiguity, contends Harris (2005a:164), stems from the collective nature of all these leadership practices. Bennett, Wise, Woods & Harvey (2003) maintain that a conceptualisation of distributive leadership as emergent and resulting from conjoint activity underpins distributive leadership as distinctive from other concepts of leadership. While the appeal of distributive leadership is partly due to its flexible nature (Spillane & Sherer, 2004; Harris, 2007), there is a danger of distributive leadership becoming a "catch-all phrase" for any type of devolved, shared or dispersed type of leadership practice in schools (Harris & Spillane, 2008, p.32).

The literature reveals that there are different conceptualisations of distributive leadership. In its simplest form distributive leadership connotes that "every single organisational member may be influential and display leadership" in various ways and at least some of the time (Gronn, 2004, p.353). In this perspective leadership is not restricted to the principal or other members of the school management team who are formally appointed but extended to teachers who can take on informal leadership roles. For instance teachers can take the lead in shared lesson planning, mentor their colleagues or work in teams and committees. The task or the situation at hand dictates who leads and who follows and not necessarily a person's position in the hierarchy (Copland, 2003 cited in Timperley, 2005:396). Leadership is thus viewed as agency and teachers have the agency to lead change (Harris, 2003c).

Gronn (2003) draws upon the Activity Theory of Engestrom (1999), which emphasizes leadership as a collective phenomenon, the centrality of the division of labour, the interdependency of relationships and the notion of emergent activities. Thus, distributive leadership is seen as an "emergent property of a group or a network of interacting individuals" where leadership is the product of "concerted action" or "conjoint agency" arising from people working together (Gronn, 2000 cited in Leithwood, Day, Sammons, Harris & Hopkins, 2006, p.46). As leaders and followers collaborate in order to accomplish group tasks a blurring of the roles between leaders and followers occurs (Harris & Day, 2003). Leadership is fluid and emergent rather than fixed and is related to collective problem solving and working collaboratively (Harris, 2003a). We decided to ground this study in Activity Theory where "the potential for leadership is present in the flow of activities in which a set of organisation members find themselves enmeshed" (Gronn, 2000 cited in Harris, 2005b, p.163). Principals perform their duties in tandem with others creating activity systems dependent on the division of labour (Gronn, 2003). Activity theory therefore refutes the argument that leadership is the domain of one person such as the principal and provides a framework for the distribution of leadership.

In conceptualising distributive leadership, Spillane (2005) highlights that leadership practice is the focal point rather than leaders themselves or their knowledge, skills, roles, functions and structures. From this perspective the unit of analysis in the study of leadership is leadership practice rather than the individual leader (Spillane *et al.*, 2001). A distributive view frames leadership practice as "a product of the interactions of school leaders, followers, and their situation" (Spillane, 2005, p.144) or "stretched over" the social and situational aspects of school context (Spillane, Halverson & Diamond, 2004, p.5; Spillane *et al.*, 2001, p.23). Situation refers to the "socio-cultural context" which includes artefacts, tools and organisational structures (Spillane & Sherer, 2004, p.6-7). Research undertaken by the Hay Group Education (2004) reported in Arrowsmith (2005) complemented Spillane's conception of the distributive approach. This study found that the organisational and cultural conditions and the relationships between people were viewed as being important in fostering leadership at every level and should therefore be aligned with the strategy and purpose of the school (Arrowsmith, 2005).

Further to the practice aspect of distributive leadership, Spillane (2009) identifies the leader-plus aspect. The leader-plus aspect encourages a view of who is involved in the tasks pertaining to school leadership. It argues, with supporting empirical evidence, that besides the principal and formally appointed school leaders, other members of the school staff take responsibility for leadership activities themselves or co-perform activities with the principal (Spillane, 2009).

A theoretical approach to distributive leadership is that it should be viewed as a tool, analytical framework or a way of thinking about leadership practice rather than as another technique, blueprint or practice (Bennett *et al.*, 2003; Harris, 2005a:11; Spillane, 2009). This is the stance that we adopted in conducting the ensuing research as we sought to understand how leadership practice was enacted in schools in Soweto.

Woods and Gronn (2009) note that distributive leadership is not a type of leadership, like charismatic or transformational leadership, but can be understood as a description of patterns of leadership, which encompasses multiple sources

of influence at schools, different ways in which activities are co-ordinated and interdependent relationships.

In conceptualising distributive leadership it is necessary to make a distinction between delegation and distribution. Delegation, which is associated with the hero-paradigm, is when responsibilities are issued solely in a top-down manner usually from the principal (Oduro, 2004). Distributed leadership by contrast does not rely on the initiative of the principal (Oduro, 2004). Furthermore, distributive leadership incorporates both formal and informal roles of leadership practice in the co-performance of leadership (Harris, 2013). Distribution, unlike delegation, involves reciprocal trust (Harris, 2013; MacBeath, 2005). Relational trust can be developed by principals who engage in lateral learning, interactions among equals, peer mentoring and appraisal as well as mutual criticism and challenge (Macbeath, 2005). Theorists further take the view that distributive leadership is different from dividing task responsibilities among individuals in a compartmentalised manner but involves dynamic interactions between multiple leaders and followers (Timperley, 2005; Harris, 2013). Research conducted by The Hay Group Education (2004) and cited in Arrowsmith (2005:31) found that distributive leadership is not another word for delegation, that it required more control rather than less, that it was entrenched in clarity and accountability and required role definition.

Woods and Gronn (2009) argue that the concept of distributive leadership needs to be extended from a mere descriptive lens of the division of labour in a school to the institutionalisation of democratic principles in the daily operation of schools. In this regard the pragmatic view of distributive leadership in taking on tasks to alleviate the principal's workload can be extended to power sharing and the inclusion of members of the school community in decision making (Woods & Gronn, 2009). Distributive leadership has much to offer in facilitating "employee voice" providing access to "decision-making agenda framing, information input and argumentative deliberation" such that the working environment is transformed into one where participation is expected and institutionalised (Woods & Gronn, 2009, p.442). Such a view of distributive leadership is pertinent to building a democratic society such as South Africa.

By reconceptualising leadership as a practice open to any member of the school community, distributive leadership has extended the boundaries of leadership to teachers, facilitating the concept of teacher leadership.

Teacher Leadership

By rejecting a view of leadership as being confined to formal positions in the hierarchy, leadership opportunity is open to all teachers. Distributive leadership in practice therefore pertains to engaging teachers in leadership so that they can assume responsibility for driving change that will benefit the school (Harris & Muijs, 2005). Extending leadership opportunities to teachers is powerful in acknowledging the important role that they play in improving instruction (Harris & Lambert, 2003). The teacher leadership perspective draws attention to the new and evolving role of teachers in schools. Whereas, traditional notions of leadership restricted South African teachers towards passivity and dependence (Moloi, 2005), distributive leadership provides a shift to a liberating culture characterised by "collective action, empowerment and shared agency" (Harris, 2003b. p.317).

If teachers are expected to play a greater role in leadership tasks and functions then numerous challenges arise. Harris (2003c) even goes to the extent of describing the involvement of teachers in leadership as desirable but unachievable. Teachers have a demanding workload and they may not welcome additional leadership tasks (Oduro, 2004). The selection of teachers for leadership tasks is problematic and could lead to the harassment of teachers or dissatisfaction among their

peers. Furthermore, opportunities for professional development as well as a building of teachers' self-confidence to act as leaders need to be provided (Harris, 2003c). The job descriptions of teachers may also need to be reviewed in place of the new informal leadership expectations required of them.

A distributive leadership environment where teachers take on greater leadership responsibility raises the question of the role of the school principal within distributive leadership.

The Principal as a Facilitator of Distributive Leadership

Distributive leadership does not refute the importance of the formal leader. On account of their symbolic and positional authority (Harris, 2007), principals can play a significant role in facilitating distributive leadership in schools. As gatekeepers to change (Fullan, 2007) principals can either promote or impede the distributive approach from flourishing in schools. There is now empirical evidence that points to the vital role that principals play in promoting distributive leadership (Harris, 2013). However, in order to endorse and facilitate the distributive approach to leadership, principals require an in-depth understanding of leadership practice in the context of the contemporary school. Principals need to be aware that a relationship exists "between vertical and lateral leadership processes" and that the focus of leadership is on interaction between these processes (Leithwood *et al.*, 2006).

The literature indicates that the structural and the cultural conditions in a school influence distributive leadership. Principals are in a position to attend to these aspects. Principals should set up structures to involve teachers and others in leadership practice. In so doing principals are able "to maximise the capacity to lead innovation and improvement" (Harris, 2013, p. 551). Creating leadership opportunities can be done by means of establishing structures such as teams and committees. A collaborative school culture can be encouraged by means of fostering professional learning communities or communities of practice. Communities of practice' can be understood as a collaborative way of working where "individuals are drawn into the community by the process of learning" (Wenger, 1998 cited in Harris & Muijs, 2005, p.17).

Principals can enhance distributive leadership by creating a suitable school climate and promoting the organisational conditions that are necessary for distributive leadership to flourish (Harris & Lambert, 2003). Such conditions include the redistribution of power and authority as well as the building of trust relationships (Harris, 2013; Hopkins & Jackson, 2003; MacBeath, 2005). According to Hopkins and Jackson (2003, p 101), by promoting trust relationships, leaders can "unite the school around shared values and higher-order purposes". Principals are the glue holding the organisation together in order for it to be productive and are responsible for creating a shared culture of expectations through the use of individual expertise (Grenda, 2006; Harris, 2013; Harris & Muijs, 2005).

By adopting a distributive leadership approach, principals can institutionalise a leadership-centred school culture and can play a role in enhancing and sustaining leadership. Harris (2013) conveys that the 'so what' of distributive leadership is that the main role of the principal is to be able to harness the expertise of those in the organisation, to know when this expertise is required and to provide support to these leaders. Principals can play a role not only by distributing leadership but also in developing leadership (Elmore, 2008). An example cited by Elmore (2008) is that if formal leaders in a school are seen to be the ones that always chair meetings then school leadership is based on roles and lacks a developmental view of leadership. Fullan (2001) contends that good leaders are those who develop leaders at other levels for the future of the system as a whole. In this context the principal is seen to be a 'leader of leaders' (Harris & Lambert, 2003).

RESEARCH INTO DISTRIBUTIVE LEADERSHIP

In their seminal work, Spillane *et al.* (2001) investigated distributive leadership practice in thirteen schools in the American state of Chicago. Their study confirmed that leadership is indeed distributed among many individuals in a school and that leadership tasks are co-enacted by two or more leaders. By working as a collective, leadership practice is considered greater than the sum of the practice of each person. The study further revealed that leaders may not have a direct influence in schools since their actions are mediated by artefacts, tools and structures. It was concluded that leadership practice is a product of the interaction of leaders and their particular situation, which included aspects such as tools, material artefacts and language (Spillane *et al.*, 2001). In another study (Spillane, 2009) it was found that leadership activities are co-performed by teachers and formally appointed leaders. A study by Spillane, Camburn and Pareja (2007) further indicated that some principals co-performed over 60% of the activities that they were responsible for while others co-performed less than 10%.

Research was conducted by MacBeath (2005) in eleven schools in the United Kingdom. It was found that in distributing leadership senior leaders were concerned about trusting others to perform tasks for which they were held accountable. They were uncertain about when to 'hold on' to tasks and when to 'let go'. Furthermore, heads needed more clarity about the difference between the concepts of consultation, command and consensus so that they could appropriately use these strategies in decision making. MacBeath's (2005) research further resulted in the development of a taxonomy of distribution where leadership is viewed as a developmental process. The six dimensions of distributive leadership that were identified are listed in a progressive sequence: formal, pragmatic, strategic, incremental, opportunistic and cultural. Formal distribution occurs through roles or a person's job description, pragmatic distribution according to the current need, strategic distribution according to a planned appointment, incremental distribution refers to increasing responsibilities as people demonstrate their capabilities, opportunistic distribution means that teachers take the initiative in leading and cultural distribution occurs when distributive leadership is institutionalised into the school culture (MacBeath, 2005).

There is evidence that distributive leadership has a positive effect on learner outcomes (Hallinger & Heck, 2009), learner growth rates in Maths (Heck & Hallinger, 2010) and on organisational outcomes (Leithwood & Mascall, 2008). Research by Day, Sammons, Leithwood, Harris and Hopkins (2009) revealed that when teachers are involved in leadership their self-efficacy and motivation increases.

In a South African study, Grant (2006) found that hierarchical school organisations, autocratic principals, leadership conceptualised as a formal position and teacher resistance all impede teacher leadership. Another South African study undertaken by Grant, Gardner, Kajee, Moodley and Somaroo (2010) found that teacher leadership was absent in schools and communities. In the study by Grant *et al.* (2010) two main problems were found to hinder teacher leadership. The first was that decision-making had not devolved to team structures and the second was that the leadership styles of formally appointed leaders were autocratic. Bush (2007) points out that the Ministerial Committee's Review of School Governance (2004) revealed that participative decision-making has not taken root in South African schools and that the managerial-leadership framework in schools is bureaucratic and hierarchical in nature. The findings of both Bush (2007) and Grant *et al.* (2010) indicate that educational leadership in South Africa is stuck in the traditional paradigm which is of concern in the light of the preceding discussion which highlights the need for a changing leadership approach in the twenty-first century.

RESEARCH METHODOLOGY

We used a generic qualitative approach to explore the phenomenon of distributive leadership. Generic qualitative research studies seek "to discover and understand a phenomenon, a process, or the perspectives and worldviews of the people involved" (Merriam, 1998). In this study, we sought to understand the perspectives and worldviews of teachers regarding distributive leadership in selected public primary schools. We specifically focused on teachers who were not formally appointed in leadership positions as we wanted to give 'a voice' to this particular group of teachers.

Data collection took place by means of an in-depth focus group interview in each of three primary schools, and document analysis. A feature of focus group interviews is the group interaction that leads to the generation of data which cannot be achieved in individual interviews (Nieuwenhuis, 2007).

All public schools in the Gauteng province [1] are subjected to whole school evaluation by the Gauteng Department of Education (GDE). Based on their evaluation rating, schools are categorised as follows: category one (schools needing urgent attention), category two (schools needing support), category three (schools performing at an acceptable level), category four (good schools) and category five (outstanding schools). From the most recent list that we received from the GDE, there were no schools ranked in categories four and five in the region of investigation. We used purposive sampling to select the three schools, one from each of the remaining categories: School one is a category three school, school two a category one school and school three a category two school. These schools were located within the Johannesburg Central [2] school district.

There were fifteen participants in total of whom twelve were females and three males. Seven of the participants were aged between 30 and 39 years, four between 40 and 49 years and four were older than 49 years. All participants were post level one teachers who did not hold formal leadership positions at the time of the research. We selected teachers who possessed a minimum of five years of teaching experience.

Open-ended questions were used to explore the concept of leadership from the participants' perspective and thereafter semi-structured questions allowed for probing and extended responses on aspects pertaining to distributive leadership. Document analysis was also undertaken in order to complement the interview findings. Documents, such as those relating to the distribution of responsibilities and committee or team structures, were analysed. We piloted our interview approach to ensure that it gave us entrance to the kind of data we were looking for. The interviews were recorded in order to reproduce the participants' original words. Member checks were conducted so that the research participants in each focus group could verify their particular contributions. Validity was also promoted by having colleagues peer review our research procedures and the congruency of the findings with the raw data (Merriam, 2002). This study is limited to only three public primary schools situated within the Johannesburg Central district of the Gauteng Province.

The data were analysed using Tesch's method (Creswell, 2009) which involves the identification and coding of topics, the development of conceptual categories and the formulation of themes and sub-themes.

The interviewees' informed consent to participate in the study was obtained and participants' anonymity and the confidentiality of sources assured.

Discussion of Themes

The main finding is that there is little evidence of distributive leadership in the three primary schools. Four themes emerged and these are presented, together with their respective sub-themes, in Table 1.

A discussion of the themes, together with their respective sub-themes, follows. Codes are used to identify the three schools and the participants in the focus groups at each school as follows: S1 refers to school one in the methodology section, and so on. T1 refers to teacher one in a particular school's focus group, and so on. So, for example, S2,T5 refers to school two and teacher five in that school.

Table 1. Themes and sub-themes of distributive leadership in schools in Soweto

Theme	Sub-Themes
1. Leadership styles	Autocratic leadership style Participative leadership style Power
2. School climate	Staff relationships Teacher morale and motivation Job dissatisfaction Teaching and learning
3. Communication	Meetings Closed communication Transparency
4. Barriers to teacher leadership	Opportunities for teacher leadership Teacher isolation in lesson planning Teacher workload Power relations Professional development

Leadership Styles

There was evidence in all three schools of classical leadership practices, including a strong hierarchy and principals who use autocratic leadership styles. According to a teacher:

Most of the times he's [the principal] the one who dominate[s]. He use[d] to tell us that we need to do one, two, three. And then hierarchy, yes, it is still there...Normally we are being told what we must do... (S1,T5).

In an entrenched hierarchy, power and decision-making remains the domain of the principal and the School Management Team (SMT). Another teacher explained:

I think if maybe we can be given a chance of viewing our understanding and saying whatever we think, especially when coming to the developments in a school, to say I think if we can do one, two, three we'll see the progress. But then you are not being given that chance to say that. Because you are not the leader you can't say that. It must pass through me [the principal] before you can do whatever you do, it must pass through me and if I take it I take it, if I don't take it I'm not taking it (S3,T2).

It appears from the data that a transition to democratic leadership styles has not transpired in these schools. Democratic leadership is consultative, participative and inclusionary (Starratt, cited in Bush, 2007). This is in contrast to the type of leadership described by the participants in their schools which appears to be managerial-leadership and can be described as "authoritarian, hierarchical and inaccessible management styles" where the authority of the principal is conceived as "God-given" and "juridical" (McLennan & Thurlow, cited in Bush, 2007, p.395). The models of schooling that are emerging in the twenty-first century are based on collaboration and networking which require lateral rather than vertical leadership practices (Harris, 2005b). This view is supported by Hargreaves and Fink (2008, p.232) who propose that leaders move away from hierarchical structures to communities, networks or webs premised on shared collaboration, where their function is to "connect and contribute" rather than to "command and control".

Teachers at all three schools were unanimous that principals used positional power to overturn decisions made by school committees: A teacher stated:

... as a team we agreed, we trusted each other. We contributed our views on those eh policies [policies drawn up by teachers for their subject departments], but at the end they were rejected... I think even if you are working in committees somewhere somehow we are still being oppressed because when we agree on something at the end it is being rejected (S1,T5).

The views expressed by participants at this school concurred with those at another school as is evident in the following quote:

... You've got limited say because at the same time being a chairperson of that committee you cannot expose yourself to some of the things which you need to be exposed to or come with suggestions. Then when taken there, top level then they being crushed, crushed, crushed [rejected] and then at the end that opportunity that you, you cannot even make it [the opportunity is lost] (S3,T3).

The examples cited above illustrate that principals do not respect the decisions made by school committees. Distribution involves "relinquishing one's role as ultimate decision-maker, trusting others to make the right decisions" (MacBeath, 2005, p.355). Principals appear to be practicing "contrived collegiality" where committees are formed but the principal has decision-making authority to overrule or ignore committee decisions (Glanz, 2006). Thus, while on the surface there appears to be teamwork in the schools, beneath the surface decision-making is not distributed and power remains largely in the domain of the SMT. Grant *et al.* (2010, p.414) confirm that an indicator of "authentic teamwork" is the participation of teachers in decision-making processes. According to Walker (1994) cited in Van der Mescht & Tyala, 2008, p.223), "it is easy to form so-called teams and then claim that the school is structured collaboratively, but unless there are major shifts in thinking…little real change will result". Perhaps the cultural and structural conditions essential to teamwork have not been established in these schools in Soweto; structural conditions referring to the "logistical arrangements" in schools and cultural conditions referring to the climate, culture and ethos that exists (Van der Mescht & Tyala, 2008, p.223).

There was evidence that collaborative and participative styles of leadership where teachers have an opportunity to express their views were not adequately practised. A teacher commented:

As I said, communication breakdown in the school, because we don't have, you know, when you are a leader you involve, as I said, you involve everybody being the stakeholders of the school. Everybody must take part so but if there is a certain group of people who are doing things on their own then there won't be smooth running of a school (S3,T2).

It appears from the data that teachers do not have a 'voice' in decision-making. A teacher posited that: "We don't have [a voice]. Sometimes when you say things you want to say that comes from your heart then they [the leaders] don't even take it" (S2,T4).

Sackney and Mitchell (2001) cited in Bush (2007) emphasise the significance of 'voice' in post-modern leadership. Participative decision-making fulfils the need of teachers to contribute to matters which affect them and can play a role in the effective functioning of the school (Ibtesam, 2005; Van Deventer, 2003). Furthermore, the involvement of stakeholders in decision-making is essential in dealing with the complex challenges that schools face (Van Deventer, 2003). A participative approach is important in the current school context since it builds staff relations and reduces the workload of the principal through the distribution of leadership functions and roles (Bush, 2007).

The importance of power sharing at schools is articulated by a teacher who remarked:

I think power sharing is very, very vital because if you share responsibilities you won't encounter any problem at any time because people are there to attend to different activities within the school, concerning the school curriculum (S1,T2).

Power sharing enables a movement away from hierarchical control to peer control (Harris & Muijs, 2005) and is therefore essential to distributive leadership and teacher leadership. Alternate power relationships are therefore needed "where the distinctions between followers and leaders tend to blur" (Harris, 2003a:77). This is problematic since schools are hierarchical structures with legitimate power accrued to the principal as the positional leader (Bush, 2003). Hence, principals are accorded rights in decision-making and policy formulation (Bush, 2003). Distributive leadership presents a threat to the status quo (Harris & Muijs, 2005). In the new paradigm principals are required to share decision-making power with staff and distribute both responsibility and power for leadership widely throughout the school (Harris, 2005b).

Activity Theory posits leadership as a collective phenomenon. In order for activities to become units of analysis, a decentring of the individual leader must occur (Gronn, 2003). This can be facilitated by principals who adopt collaborative and participative leadership styles where power is shared with other key players in the school community and where participative decision-making is a reality. Distributive leadership calls for principals who employ participative leadership approaches. Participative leadership places emphasis on group decision-making, democratic principles and the leadership contributions of all stakeholders in the context of site-based management (SBM) (Bush, 2007).

School Climate

The data points to negative school climates which are detrimental to staff relationships, teacher morale, job satisfaction levels and teaching and learning. A teacher commented: "The atmosphere creates hatred amongst us staff… there will be conflict because of one, two, three…There is no trust" (S1,T1).

In an activity system such as a school, poor human relations between teachers will hinder the distribution of leadership. Building trust relationships is an important focus area for the principal because by promoting trust relationships, leaders can "unite the school around shared values and higher-order purposes" (Hopkins & Jackson, 2003). Trust is an important condition that enhances distributive leadership (MacBeath, 2005).

From the data we get a picture of low teacher morale in the three schools. The participants used words such as "disturbed", "not happy", "not satisfied", "discouraging", "demotivating" and "disillusioned" to describe the way they felt at school. If teachers perceive that their needs are not being met, this affects their morale negatively (Steyn, 2002a). By empowering teachers and giving them a voice in decisions that affect them, principals may raise their morale (Kruger & Steinmann, 2003). The morale of teachers may also be raised by granting them more autonomy, by according them professional respect and by giving them recognition and praise for their efforts (Steyn, 2002b).

The low teacher morale appears to impact negatively on the participants' job satisfaction. A teacher expressed: "You even think of staying at home, resigning, forget about everything" (S3,T2), while another teacher asserted that due to the teachers' lack of 'voice' in matters pertaining to the school, "it makes people including myself sometimes even to hate this profession itself" (S1,T5). The unhappy atmosphere has resulted in stress and absenteeism as the following statement shows: "You'll be stressed and you become sick. There's no week where you can find us 100% in the school" (S1,T3).

The data indicates that the respondents cannot perform to their full potential in the current school climate. This has serious consequences for learner achievement. One of the most influential factors on school effectiveness is the enthusiasm and motivation of teachers which enables their total commitment to teaching (Steyn, 2002b). Teachers play an important role in "sustaining, enhancing or even decreasing learner motivation" (Steyn, 2002b, p.84). The principal can play a role as an instructional leader who increases student achievement by influencing the school climate in a positive manner (Ibtesam, 2005).

Communication

Teachers at all three schools offered many examples of ineffective communication at their respective schools. One teacher expressed that there was a lack of formal staff meetings (S3,T3). This claim is supported by the document analysis which reveals an absence of staff meeting records. In addition, there were very few records of School Governing Body Meetings, subject department meetings and school committee meetings. This is disconcerting since meetings are an important horizontal channel of communication which serve to co-ordinate activities and planning, foster collegial relationships and promote teamwork (Prinsloo, 2003).

There was also evidence of closed-communication:

Then, now as we are closed out, our views are not allowed, are not accepted, is a problem because even when we work we don't perform to the maximum. I think it would benefit a lot if maybe we were allowed to contribute our views on the running of the school (S1,T5).

A teacher expressed the fear of victimisation: "So you keep quiet. You can even see this is wrong but you keep quiet because you know if I say this... that person is going to get back at me" (S2,T1). Teachers at S1 and S2 also raised the issue of a lack of transparency at their schools. A participant claimed: "...there's no transparency. Some things are hidden"..."Our leaders must tell us everything on time and mustn't hide some things from us. They must be honest with us" (S2,T4). At S3, the unavailability of the minutes of meetings is not in the interest of enhancing transparency and accountability (Denscombe, 2007). Establishing a collaborative school environment and open communication is considered the single most important factor for school improvement (Ibtesam, 2005). However, open communication requires a climate of trust and understanding between people in the work environment (Fielding, 2005), which the data shows is absent at these schools.

Barriers to Teacher Leadership

Five barriers that impede teacher leadership were identified. One of these barriers was inadequate opportunities for teacher leadership. This was evident at S2 and S3. Teachers at S2 experienced difficulty in stating what leadership opportunities they had and there was evidence of only one school committee, namely, a sports committee. Regarding leadership opportunities for teachers, a teacher

was straightforward: "So far we don't have any opportunities (laughs)" (S3,T3). Another teacher in the same school conveyed that opportunities for leadership were limited and that there was role confusion in committees. Empowering teachers and providing them with leadership opportunities is premised upon the notion that if schools want to improve on the way learners are taught, then they, schools, should provide teachers with opportunities to innovate, grow professionally and collaborate (Harris & Muijs, 2005).

A further barrier to distributive leadership appears to be teacher isolation in lesson planning. It appeared from the following that teachers work individually in the planning of lessons:

When we do preparations we don't do it in a group. We do that individually. So your expertise is yours only, because you cannot impart the knowledge to other teachers .... being just an ordinary post level one teacher you are not given a chance for exposure (S3,T2).

When teachers work individually, an "isolated professional culture" is created, which is a common barrier to the establishment of teacher leadership in schools (Leithwood, et al., 2003, p.198). In a culture of individual work practices there are fewer opportunities for teachers to provide leadership to their peers and teachers are not motivated to develop their own leadership capacities (Leithwood, Jantzi & Steinbach, 2003).

The heavy workload of teachers might hinder their ability to take on leadership tasks and responsibilities. A teacher commented: "At the moment because of our large workload some of the things that even we want to take the leadership there will be somehow too much..." (S3,T3).

Another barrier to teacher leadership that came to the fore was the power relations between teachers and members of the SMT. A teacher remarked: "I think the manager will be a problem because he will not accept and welcome everyone, everyone, except those who maybe feel they are very close to him" (S1,T3). Feelings of insecurity that principals experience due to teachers taking on leadership roles may be reduced if principals are encouraged to view themselves as a 'leader of leaders' (Harris & Lambert, 2003:43).

Finally, a lack of leadership skills development among teachers was cited as an impediment to teacher leadership. A respondent suggested:

Even it could be possible if each and every one of us is trained on the leadership and management because sometimes we might have a conflict of ideas, which might end up resulting in us, maybe some of us, having a conflict amongst ourselves (S1,T5).

The professional development of teachers in leadership is widely supported in the literature (Grant, 2008; Hopkins & Jackson, 2003).

CONCLUSION AND RECOMMENDATIONS

This study indicates that leadership in the three primary schools is rooted in classical leadership practices and that a shift from autocratic styles of leadership, hierarchical structures and non-participative decision-making is needed if distributive leadership is to develop. In order to facilitate this shift towards more collegial and collaborative leadership styles, it is recommended that the Department of Education provide professional development training programmes and workshops for principals and teachers. Such programmes should focus on distributive leadership which promotes teacher leadership and their role in school transformation. In addition, principals need to learn that they can, and how to, share power and decision-making with others. Furthermore, principals should be made aware of the vital role that they can play in establishing both a collaborative and leadership-centred school culture.

Based on the distributive leadership approach, a principal alone cannot be held accountable for the leadership and management of a school. It is recommended that accountability be shared with those role players whose joint endeavours determine school outcomes. The principals in this study avoided power-sharing, the devolution of decision-making and the granting of autonomy to teachers and teams. This reluctance may be influenced by current demands for accountability being placed exclusively on principals' shoulders by higher authorities. This practice needs to be reviewed in the interest of furthering distributive leadership.

The literature suggests that distributive leadership can provide a beneficial approach to educational change in schools (Harris, 2013; Harris, 2006). If distributive forms of leadership are integrated into the complementary vertical leadership structure of schools, and structures such as networks or webs can be introduced, the principal's role can more easily become that of a facilitator, mediator, coach and supporter, thereby encouraging a more collegial school atmosphere (Naicker & Mestry, 2011).

We concur with Hargreaves and Fink (2008) that distributive leadership can be extended to include democratic public and professional involvement in education. Ultimately, democratic nations like South Africa can employ distributive leadership towards the attainment of democratic citizenship and the social vision to address issues of "economic creativity and sustainability, ecological survival and fundamental human rights" (Hargreaves & Fink, 2008, p.239). For us, this is the 'so what' about distributive leadership, that it is not only timely and relevant but that it is futuristic. Woods and Gronn (2009), like Hargreaves and Fink (2008), believe that distributive leadership can be extended to achieve democratic principles. Theorists are now positing that system leadership, which refers to the stretching of leadership across schools (Boylan, 2013), as well as system transformation are dependent on a distributive approach in schools (Huber, Moorman & Pont, 2007; Harris, 2013).

Distributive leadership is a new and emerging field of study in educational leadership and management in South Africa. Further research can be undertaken to explore the views of principals regarding the distribution of leadership. In supporting the need for a re-conceptualisation of leadership practice in the twenty-first century and a search for alternate and relevant models of leadership, this research suggests that distributive leadership has much to offer schools.

REFERENCES

Arrowsmith, T. (2005). Distributed leadership: Three questions, two answers. *Management in Education, 19*(2), 30–33. doi:10.1177/0892020 6050190020701

Bennett, N., Wise, C., Woods, P., & Harvey, J. A. (2003). *Distributed leadership*. Nottingham, UK: National College for School Leadership.

Botha, R. J. (2004). Excellence in leadership: Demands on the professional school principal. *South African Journal of Education, 24*(3), 239–243.

Botha, R. J. (2012). Evolving leadership required in South African schools. *Research in Education, 88*(-1), 40–49. doi:10.7227/RIE.88.1.4

Boylan, M. (2013). Deepening system leadership: Teachers leading from below. *Educational Management Administration & Leadership, 28*(October), 1–16.

Bush, T. (2003). *Theories of educational leadership and management* (3rd ed.). London: Sage.

Bush, T. (2007). Educational leadership and management: Theory, policy, and practice. *South African Journal of Education, 27*, 391–406.

Bush, T., Kiggundu, E., & Moorosi, P. (2011). Preparing new principals in South Africa: The ACE School Leadership Programme. *South African Journal of Education, 31*(1), 31–43.

Crawford, M. (2005). Distributed leadership and headship: A paradoxical relationship? *School Leadership & Management, 25*(3), 213–215. doi:10.1080/13634230500116306

Creswell, J. W. (2009). *Research design: Qualitative, quantitative, and mixed method approaches.* Los Angeles: Sage.

Day, C., Sammons, P., Leithwood, K., Harris, A., & Hopkins, D. (2009). *The impact of leadership on pupil outcomes. Final Report.* London: DCSF.

Denscombe, M. (2007). *The good research guide for small-scale social research projects.* Maidenhead, UK: Open University Press.

Dimmock, C. (2003). Leadership in learning-centred schools: Cultural context, functions and qualities. In M. Brundrett, N. Burton, & R. Smith (Eds.), Leadership in education. London: Sage.

Earley, P., & Weindling, D. (2004). *Understanding school leadership.* London: Paul Chapman Publishing.

Elmore, R. F. (2008). Leadership as the practice of improvement. In D. Hopkins (Ed.), *B. Pont., D. Nusche.* Paris: OECD.

Engeström, Y. (1999). Expansive visibilization of work: An activity-theoretical perspective. *Computer Supported Cooperative Work, 8*(1), 63–93. doi:10.1023/A:1008648532192

Fielding, M. (2005). *Effective communication in organisations: Preparing messages that communicate.* Cape Town, South Africa: Juta.

Fink, D. (2005). *Leadership for mortals.* London: Paul Chapman Publishing.

Fullan, M. (2001). *Leading in a culture of change.* San Francisco: Jossey-Bass.

Fullan, M. (2007). *The new meaning of educational change* (4th ed.). New York: Teachers College Press.

Glanz, J. (2006). *What every principal should know about collaborative leadership.* Thousand Oaks, CA: Corwin Press.

Grant, C. (2006). Emerging voices on teacher leadership. *Educational Management Administration & Leadership, 34*(4), 511–532. doi:10.1177/1741143206068215

Grant, C., Gardner, K., Kajee, F., Moodley, R., & Somaroo, S. (2010). Teacher leadership: A survey analysis of KwaZulu-Natal teachers' perceptions. *South African Journal of Education, 30*, 401–419.

Grant, C., & Singh, H. (2009). Passing the buck: This is not teacher leadership. *Perspectives in Education, 27*(3), 289–301.

Grenda, J. P. (2006). Leadership, distributed. In *Encyclopedia of Educational Leadership and Administration* (Vol. 2, pp. 566–567). London: Sage. doi:10.4135/9781412939584.n323

Gronn, P. (2003). *The new work of educational leaders: Changing leadership practice in an era of school reform.* London: Paul Chapman Publishing.

Gronn, P. (2004). Distributing leadership. In *Encyclopedia of leadership* (Vol. 1, pp. 352–354). London: Sage. doi:10.4135/9781412952392.n81

Hallinger, P., & Heck, R. (2009). Distributed leadership in schools: Does system policy make a difference? In A. Harris (Ed.), *Distributed Leadership: Different perspectives.* Springer Press. doi:10.1007/978-1-4020-9737-9_6

Hargreaves, A., & Fink, D. (2006). *Sustainable leadership.* San Francisco: Jossey-Bass.

Hargreaves, A., & Fink, D. (2008). Distributed leadership: Democracy or delivery? *Journal of Educational Administration, 46*(2), 229–240. doi:10.1108/09578230810863280

Harris, A. 2003a. Teacher leadership and school improvement. In A. Harris, C. Day, C. Hopkins, M. Hadfield, A. Hargreaves, & C. Chapman (Eds.), Effective leadership for school improvement. New York: Routledge Falmer.

Harris, A. (2003b). The changing context of leadership. In A. Harris, C. Day, C. Hopkins, M. Hadfield, A. Hargreaves, & C. Chapman (Eds.), Effective leadership for school improvement. New York: Routledge Falmer.

Harris, A. (2003c). Teacher leadership as distributed leadership: Heresy, fantasy or possibility? *School Leadership & Management, 23*(3), 313–324. doi:10.1080/1363243032000112801

Harris, A. (2005a). Reflections on distributed leadership. *Management in Education, 19*(2), 10–12. doi:10.1177/08920206050190020301

Harris, A. (2005b). Distributed leadership. In B. Davies (Ed.), *The essentials of school leadership.* London: Paul Chapman Publishing.

Harris, A. (2006). Opening up the 'black box' of leadership practice: Taking a distributed leadership perspective. *International Studies in Educational Administration, 34*(2), 37–45.

Harris, A. (2007). Distributed leadership: Conceptual confusion and empirical reticence. *International Journal of Leadership in Education, 10*(3), 315–325. doi:10.1080/13603120701257313

Harris, A. (2013). Distributed Leadership: Friend or Foe? *Educational Management Administration & Leadership, 41*(5), 545–554. doi:10.1177/1741143213497635

Harris, A., & Day, C. (2003). From singular to plural? Challenging the orthodoxy of school leadership. In N. Bennett & L. Anderson (Eds.), Rethinking educational leadership. London: Sage. doi:10.4135/9781446216811.n7

Harris, A., & Lambert, L. (2003). *Building leadership capacity for school improvement.* Maidenhead, UK: Open University Press.

Harris, A., & Muijs, D. (2005). *Improving schools through teacher leadership.* Maidenhead, UK: Open University Press.

Harris, A., & Spillane, J. (2008). Distributed leadership through the looking glass. *Management in Education, 22*(1), 31–34. doi:10.1177/0892020607085623

Hartley, D. (2007). The emergence of distributive leadership in education: Why now? *British Journal of Educational Studies, 55*(2), 202–214. doi:10.1111/j.1467-8527.2007.00371.x

Heck, R., & Hallinger, P. (2010). Testing a longitudinal model of distributed leadership effects on school improvement. *The Leadership Quarterly, 21*(5), 867–885. doi:10.1016/j.leaqua.2010.07.013

Hopkins, D., & Jackson, D. (2003). Building the capacity for leading and learning. In A. Harris, C. Day, C. Hopkins, M. Hadfield, A. Hargreaves, & C. Chapman (Eds.), Effective leadership for school improvement. New York: Routledge Falmer.

Horner, M. 2003. Leadership theory reviewed. In N. Bennett, M. Crawford, & M. Cartwright (Eds.), Effective educational leadership. London: Paul Chapman Publishing.

Huber, S. G., Moorman, H., & Pont, B. (2007). *School leadership for systemic improvement in England.* Retrieved June 10, 2013 from http://www.oecd.org/edu/school/40673692.pdf

Huber, S. G., & Pashiardis, P. (2008). The recruitment and selection of school leaders. In J. Lumby, G. Crow, & P. Pashiardis (Eds.), The development of school leaders. New York: Routledge.

Ibtesam, H. (2005). The relationship between effective communication of high school principals and school climate. *Education, 126*, 334–345.

Knapp, M. S., Copland, M. A., Honig, M. I., Plecki, M. L., & Portin, B. S. (2010). Urban renewal: The urban school leader takes on a new role. *Journal of Staff Development, 31*(2), 25–29.

Kruger, A. G., & Steinmann, F. C. (2003). The organisational climate and culture of schools. In I. Van Deventer & A. G. Kruger (Eds.), *An educator's guide to school management skills.* Pretoria: Van Schaik.

Leithwood, K., Day, C., Sammons, P., Harris, A., & Hopkins, D. (2006). *Successful school leadership: What it is and how it influences pupil learning.* Nottingham, UK: National College for School Leadership.

Leithwood, K., Jantzi, D., & Steinbach, R. (2003). Fostering teacher leadership. In N. Bennett, M. Crawford, & M. Cartwright (Eds.), Effective educational leadership. London: Paul Chapman Publishing.

Leithwood, K., & Mascall, B. (2008). Collective leadership effects on student achievement. *Educational Administration Quarterly, 44*(4), 529–561. doi:10.1177/0013161X08321221

MacBeath, J. (2005). Leadership as distributed: A matter of practice. *School Leadership & Management, 25*(4), 349–366. doi:10.1080/13634230500197165

MacBeath, J., & Cheng, Y. C. (Eds.). (2008). *Leadership for learning: International perspectives.* Rotterdam: Sense Publishers.

Merriam, S. B. (1998). *Qualitative research and case study applications in education*. San Francisco: Jossey-Bass.

Merriam, S. B. (2002). *Qualitative research in practice: Examples for discussion and analysis*. San Francisco: Jossey-Bass.

Mestry, R. (2009). *Continuing professional development and professional learning for principals in South Africa*. Keynote presentation at the conference on The Professional Development of Principals. Mafikeng, North-West Province.

Mestry, R., & Grobler, B. R. (2003). The training and development of principals in managing schools effectively. *Education as Change*, 7, 126–146.

Mestry, R., & Singh, P. (2007). Continuing professional development for principals: A South African perspective. *South African Journal of Education*, 27(3), 477–490.

Moloi, K. C. (2005). *The school as a learning organisation: Reconceptualising school practices in South Africa*. Pretoria: Van Schaik.

Mouton, N., Louw, G. P., & Strydom, G. L. (2012). A historical analysis of the post-apartheid dispensation in South Africa (1994-2011). *International Business and Economics Research Journal*, 11(11), 1211–1222.

Mulford, B. (2003). *School Leaders: Changing roles and impact on teacher and school effectiveness*. Retrieved March 23, 2009 from http://www.oecd.org/dataoecd/61/61/2635399.pdf

Naicker, S. R., & Mestry, R. (2011). Distributive leadership in public schools: Experiences and perceptions of teachers in the Soweto region. *Perspectives in Education*, 29(4), 99–108.

Neuman, M., & Simmons, W. (2000). Leadership for student learning. *Phi Delta Kappan*, 82(1), 9–12. doi:10.1177/003172170008200105

Nieuwenhuis, J. (2007). Qualitative research designs and data gathering techniques. In K. Maree (Ed.), *First steps in research*. Pretoria: Van Schaik.

Oduro, G. K. T. (2004). Distributed leadership in schools. *Education Journal*, 80, 23–25.

Prinsloo, I. J. (2003). Communication skills. In I. Van Deventer & A. G. Kruger (Eds.), *An educator's guide to school management skills*. Pretoria: Van Schaik.

Senge, P. M. (2006). *The Fifth Discipline: The art and practice of the learning organisation* (Revised edition). London: Random House Business Books.

Sergiovanni, T. J. (2005). *Strengthening the heartbeat: Leading and learning together in schools*. San Francisco: Jossey-Bass.

Sorenson, G. J., & Goethals, G. R. (2004). Leadership theories: Overview. In *Encyclopedia of Leadership* (Vol. 2, pp. 867–873). London: Sage. doi:10.4135/9781412952392.n201

Spillane, J. P. (2005). Distributed Leadership. *The Educational Forum*, 69(2), 143–15. doi:10.1080/00131720508984678

Spillane, J. P. (2009). Managing to lead: Reframing school leadership and management. *Phi Delta Kappan*, 91(3), 70–73. doi:10.1177/003172170909100315

Spillane, J. P., Camburn, E. M., & Pareja, A. S. (2007). Taking a distributed perspective to the school principal's workday. *Leadership and Policy in Schools*, 6(1), 103–125. doi:10.1080/15700760601091200

Spillane, J. P., Halverson, R., & Diamond, J. B. (2001). Investigating school leadership practice. *Educational Researcher*, 30(3), 23–28. doi:10.3102/0013189X030003023

Spillane, J. P., & Sherer, J. Z. (2004). *A distributed perspective on school leadership: Leadership practice as stretched over people and place.* Paper presented at the Meeting of the American Education Association. San Diego, CA.

Steyn, G. M. (2002a). The changing principalship in South African schools. *Educare, 31,* 251–274.

Steyn, G. M. (2002b). A theoretical analysis of teacher motivation and morale. *Educare, 31,* 82–101.

Thornton, K. (2010). *The nature of distributed leadership and its development in online environments.* Retrieved September 24, 2010 from http://www.igionline.com/downloads/excerpts/34599.pdf

Timperley, H. S. (2005). Distributed leadership: Developing theory from practice. *Journal of Curriculum Studies, 37*(4), 395–420. doi:10.1080/00220270500038545

Van der Mescht, H., & Tyala, Z. (2008). School principals' perceptions of team management: A multiple case-study of secondary schools. *South African Journal of Education, 28*(2), 221–239.

Van Deventer, I. (2003). Problem solving and decision-making skills. In I. Van Deventer & A.G. Kruger (Eds.), An educator's guide to school management skills. Pretoria: Van Schaik.

Woods, P. A., & Gronn, P. (2009). Nurturing Democracy: The contribution of distributed leadership to a democratic organisational landscape. *Educational Management Administration & Leadership, 37*(4), 430–451. doi:10.1177/1741143209334597

ADDITIONAL READING

Barry, D. (1991). Managing the bossless team: Lessons in distributive leadership. *Organizational Dynamics, 20*(1), 31–47. doi:10.1016/0090-2616(91)90081-J

Bloch, G. (2009). *The toxic mix: What's wrong with South Africa's schools and how to fix it.* Cape Town: Tafelberg.

Chrispeels, J. H. (2004). *Learning to lead together: The promise and challenge of sharing leadership.* Thousand Oaks: Sage.

Christie, P. (1998). Schools as (dis)organisations: The breakdown of culture of learning and teaching in South African schools. *Cambridge Journal of Education, 28*(3), 283–300. doi:10.1080/0305764980280303

Dentith, A. M., Beachum, F. D., & Frattura, E. M. (2006). Leadership, teacher. In *Encyclopedia of Educational Leadership and Administration* (Vol. 2, pp. 583–585). London: Sage. doi:10.4135/9781412939584.n331

Gill, R. (2006). *Theory and practice of leadership.* London: Sage.

Hartle, F., & Thomas, K. (2003). *Growing tomorrow's school leaders: The challenge.* Nottingham, UK: National College for School Leadership.

Kochan, F. K., & Reed, C. J. (2005). Collaborative leadership, community building, and democracy in public education. In F. W. English (Ed.), *The SAGE handbook of educational leadership: Advance in theory, research and practice.* Thousand Oaks: Sage. doi:10.4135/9781412976091.n4

Lumsden, G., Lumsden, D., & Wiethoff, C. (2010). *Communicating in groups and teams: Sharing leadership.* Australia: Wadsworth Cengage Learning.

National College for School Leadership. (2004). *Distributed leadership* [Action Pack]. Nottingham, UK: National College for School Leadership.

Nieuwenhuis, J. (2007). Introducing qualitative research. In K. Maree (Ed.), *First steps in research.* Pretoria: Van Schaik.

Pearsall, J. (Ed.). (2002). *South African Concise Oxford Dictionary* (10th ed.). Cape Town: Oxford University Press.

Presthus, A. M. (2006). A successful school and its principal – Enabling leadership within the organisation. *International Studies in Educational Administration, 34*(2), 82–99.

Ritchie, R., & Woods, P. A. (2007). Degrees of distribution: Towards an understanding of variations in the nature of distributed leadership in schools. *School Leadership & Management, 27*(4), 363–381. doi:10.1080/13632430701563130

KEY TERMS AND DEFINITIONS

Activity Theory: Activity Theory of Engestrom (1999) defines leadership as a collective phenomenon, the centrality of the division of labour, the interdependency of relationships and the notion of emergent activities.

Collective Leadership: Collective practice encourages that all role-players take on a leadership role to attain the school goals. It rejects the focus on individuals or even management teams to take on leadership roles. Instead, it represents a shift to a liberating culture characterised by "collective action, empowerment and shared agency" (Harris, 2003c:317).

Distributive Leadership: This type of leadership is primarily concerned with mobilizing leadership at all levels in the organisation and not relying on leadership from the top.

Hierarchy: A system in which members of an organization or society are ranked according to relative status or authority.

Leadership Styles: It is a leader's style of providing direction, implementing plans, and motivating people with the aim of realizing the institution's goals.

Participative Decision-Making: The extent to which the employer allows or encourages employees to participate in all organisational decisions.

Power: Power is the ability to influence the behavior of people.

School Climate: School Climate refers to the factors that contribute to the tone and attitudes of staff and students in school. It is based on patterns of school life experiences and reflects norms, goals and values.

Teacher Leadership: Teacher leaders assume a wide range of roles to support school and student success.

ENDNOTES

[1]   South Africa comprises of nine provinces, of which Gauteng is one province. The Gauteng Department of Education is responsible for administering schools in the province.

[2]   There are eighteen school districts located within the Gauteng Province. Johannesburg Central is one of the school districts.

Chapter 14
Continuous Change in Educational Organizations

Yasar Kondakci
Middle East Technical University, Turkey

Merve Zayim
Middle East Technical University, Turkey

Kadir Beycioglu
Dokuz Eylul University, Turkey

ABSTRACT

This chapter elaborates on the conceptual and empirical bases of continuous change, a newly developing perspective of organizational change, and brings this new perspective of organizational change to the attention of change scholars and practitioners in educational organizations. Rather than conceptualizing change as a macro-level discrete set of actions, continuous change suggests that change is a micro-level process embedded in daily practices of organizational members. However, continuous change and planned change should not be considered as alternatives to each other in the practice of change, since the former represents the informal, unstructured, and emergent side, and the latter represents the formal, structured, and intentional side of change in organizational context. This chapter argues that the success of change largely depends on the artful interplay between continuous change and planned change rather than focusing on the superiority of one perspective over another.

INTRODUCTION

Organizational change (OC) scholars have developed a rich theoretical background (Langley, Smallman, Tsoukas, & Van de Ven, 2013; Oreg, Vakola, & Armenakis, 2011; Porras & Robertson, 1992; Van de Ven & Poole 1995) and identified content, context, and process factors impacting the effectiveness of change interventions (Armenakis & Bedian, 1999). Nevertheless, conceptualizing and practicing change in organizations is still a controversial topic mainly because of the high failure rate of change interventions and the high human and financial cost that comes along with the failure of change (Beer & Nohria, 2000). Indeed, various scholars agreed that although

DOI: 10.4018/978-1-4666-6591-0.ch014

change interventions are common, the majority of these interventions end up with limited or no success (e.g., Cheng & Walker, 2008; Clegg & Walsh, 2004; Payne, 2008). Ineffective change interventions result in a variety of organizational pathologies such as customer dissatisfaction, low morale, loss of motivation, job dissatisfaction, lack of organizational commitment, cynicism, high turnover, interrupted operations, increased stress, and wasted resources (Dahl, 2011; Jansson, 2013; Lewis, 2000; Mohrman, Tenkasi, & Mohrman, 2003; Reichers, Wanous, & Austin, 1997) and harm organizational capacity for future change attempts. These problems suggest that there exists an important gap in the current conceptualization and practice of OC.

Different scholars identified different reasons behind the high failure rate of change attempts. In addition to the commonly criticized aspects of traditional change approaches such as the gap between theory and practice (Beer & Nohria, 2000), fragmented change approach rather than a holistic one, and overlooking the human side (George & Jones, 2001), several proponents of continuous change went further to suggest a new ontology of organization and change (Langley et al., 2013; Tsoukas & Chia, 2002). That is, continuous change is based on *process* ontology rather than the ontology of *things*. The reality of an organization is that the organization is in a constant state of changing and modifying structural and functional aspects. Hence, an organization is not a given object but "a temporary instantiations of ongoing processes" (Langley et al., 2013, p. 5). In this understanding the context is not surrounded by rigid boundaries but it is a process which is constantly changing. From this perspective the organization is an experiential arena rather than a concrete, fixed, and segregated entity in time and space. Therefore, change is an ordinary practice, not an exceptional period to the stable life of the organization (Tsoukas & Chia, 2002; Orlikowski, 1996). Besides, continuous change alters the origin of change understanding as well. Rather

than conceiving change as a product of managerial plan or program, as in the case of planned change, continuous change suggests that change is a micro-level and small scale process that unfolds in organizational members' daily work practices (Brown & Eisenhardt, 1997). Traditional change interventions are characterized by top-down, large-scale, planned, elitist, and discontinuous change practices. Hence, bottom-up, emergent, and unplanned nature for the process of change were suggested as a remedy for the problems that we encounter in the practice of change (Orlikowski, 1996; Weick & Quinn, 1999). Although the continuous change perspective has been an increasingly intriguing scholarly concern in the last years, the literature still indicated paucity of studies to gain insight on the significance of this new perspective to make sense of the complexity of the change process (Sleegers, van den Berg, & Geijsel, 2000). Another issue in relation to continuous change discussion is related with whether continuous change approach refers to a total theoretical separation from the discontinuous change approach. Based on this brief introduction, the aim of this paper is to (1) trace conceptual and empirical bases of continuous change, identify its dynamics in the organizations, and depict event flow of continuous change, (2) elaborate on the relevance of continuous change in educational settings, and (3) discuss the conceptual ways of fusing continuous and discontinuous changes in schools to respond today's calls for change in school systems.

CONCEPTUAL BASES OF CONTINUOUS CHANGE

Basic Premises of Continuous Change

Weick and Quinn (1999) in their distinction between episodic change (the dominant thinking about change) and continuous change (the emerging thinking about change) suggest that the origin of change is the basic point of distinction between these two change approaches. Since the discontinuous change perspective conceptualizes change as a reaction to an environmental development, as in the case of population ecology (Hannan & Freeman, 1977), or a malfunction in the organization, as in the case of punctuated equilibrium (Gersick, 1991), change is conceived by a group of people at the top. This group is responsible for crafting a plan/program of change and implementing this plan/program. In most cases, the designers of the plan/program function as change agents. As a result, change originates from the top of the organization and is implemented using a top-down approach.

In contrast, continuous change is embedded in the daily practices of organizational members; it is not extraordinary, special, and unusual set of programmed actions within the organizations which suggests that it is a bottom-up process as opposed to a top-down one. March (1981, p. 564) supported this idea with this argument, "in its fundamental structure a theory of organizational change should not be remarkably different from a theory of ordinary action". Change is inherent in everyday conducts and inseparable from the ongoing and situated actions of organizational members. One of the fundamental novelty comes along with this understanding of the origin of change is related to a fundamental shift in change agency. In the dominant perspective, change is a preoccupation of selected few agents at the top, whereas in the new perspective, change is the preoccupation of every member in the organization (Weick, 2000).

Another dimension that distinguishes continuous change is its unintentional nature. That is, every ordinary action reproduces, broadens, or alters the existing work categories or practices (Orlikowski, 1996). Structured organizational dimensions are constantly modified, or even ignored in daily conduct of organizational tasks (Boden, 1994). There is always room for deviations from the intended course (Orlikowski & Hofman, 1997),

which makes this form of change improvisational (Orlikowski, 1996), experimental (Brown & Eisenhardt, 1997), or trial-and-error process (Rerup & Feldman, 2011). Even if organizations carefully craft plans in order to accomplish change, they need to continuously modify these plans in the face of unexpected and unanticipated developments (Barley, 1990). As a result, change agents need to pay attention to the emergent side of the organization (Weick, 2000).

Although the scholars in the field have clarified basic principles of continuous change, there is a need for further conceptualization on two more aspects. Firstly, the unfolding nature of continuous change process needs additional clarification. If change does not necessarily originate from an external imperative and planned action then what are the dynamics of change process and how is the event flow accomplished in this process? Secondly, there is a need for further description on the relationship between continuous change and discontinuous change approaches. Explicating the relationship between continuous and discontinuous change approaches is necessary to make sense of whether continuous change will potentially lead to further fragmentation or unification in organizational change theory or alternatively, whether scholars will reach into a unified theory of organizational change without advocating the supremacy of one perspective (either continuous change or discontinuous change) over the other. The next two sub sections handle these concerns.

Dynamics of Continuous Change

In relation to the first concern, concepts such as individual sensemaking, translation, learning, and improvisation provide deep insights into the dynamics of continuous change (Weick & Quinn, 1999). First, sensemaking suggests that individual interpretation and reframing of organizational reality based on this interpretation are basics to broaden organizational category (Weick, 1995). Sensemaking is a cognitive process through which organizational members interpret and assign meaning whereby people elucidate phenomena and produce inter-subjective accounts (Brown & Humphreys, 2003). Some scholars use sensemaking as a conceptual tool to explicate the cognitive aspect of intentional change interventions. According to continuous change perspective, sensemaking is the process of continuous interpretation of ongoing organizational processes. Every organizational process, including intentional change practices, is interpreted and signified by individual members and new meanings are attributed to organizational processes, which forms one basis of continuous adjustment and adaptation in organizational processes (Weick & Quinn, 1999). Several scholars brought further evidence on how change is embedded in micro processes undertaken by organizational members in their daily conducts. Organizations are sites of human action through which structured and institutional categories are constantly modified, extended or altered in order to fit social reality. In most cases this is not a choice but an obligation in the effort of fulfilling their ordinary work tasks. Hence, institutional innovators are those in peripheral positions, new entrants, cross field agents, or interdepartmental workers (Zietsma & Lawrence, 2010).

Second, several continuous change scholars suggested improvisation as another metaphor for understanding continuous change in organizations (e.g. Brown & Eisenhardt, 1997; Orlikowski & Hofman, 1997; Orlikowski 1996). Improvisation suggests that human beings possess a natural inclination to create meaningful products even in the inexistence of a plan or program. Different scholars indicated the potential of improvisation for strategic renewal (Crossan, 1998), for simultaneous performance of composition and execution (Moorman & Miner, 1998) for exploring, continual experimenting, and tinkering with possibilities (Barrett, 1998) and for contributions in the systems' flexibility to produce more adaptive responses (Bigley & Roberts, 2001; Child & Mc-

Grath, 2001). Likewise, Weick (1998) suggested that in the era in which time creates competitive advantage, people gain speed by doing more things spontaneously without lengthy prior planning exercises and time intervals between planning and implementing. Improvisation gives the ability of spontaneously reacting to fast developments in the environment in a creative and novel way. That is, planning and implementation are not significantly different from each other (Orlikowski, 1996). Unlike change efforts that implement plans, guidelines, or directives, improvisation highlights simultaneous planning and implementation.

Third, relying on the social cognitive perspective, several scholars indicated learning as a conceptual tool for explaining the sources of continuous change. Taking place at different levels, indicating knowledge acquisition, requiring information sharing and entailing interpretation, enabling knowledge retention, and leading to continuity are the characteristics making learning a powerful tool for understanding continuous change (Kondakci, 2005). Learning shows that continuous change entails range of skills and knowledge rather than a specific action and change is not a simple substitution but includes strengthening existing skills and enriching the response repertoire of organizational members (Weick & Quinn, 1999). Several concepts originating from social cognitive theory makes learning an essential tool of understanding continuous change not only in business organizations but also in educational organizations as well. First, productive reasoning, being a cognitive process of reconsidering an individual's own assumptions on a continuous basis, enables discovering errors, which is basic for learning and change (Argyris, 1997). Secondly, Senge's (1990) *learning organizations* also highlights the role of learning in continuous change (Honig, 2008). Learning organizations indicates that individuals continually expand their capacity as part of a team, facilitates change in the minds of people, which is believed to be a fundamental precursor of continuous change. Third, communities of practice is one of the most extensively used learning concepts to understand continuous change (Orr, 1996). The communities of practice perspective reflects practice-based learning and innovation (Lave and Wenger 1991) and indicates that practice and learning are not separate (Brown & Duguid, 1991). This perspective alternates transfer models of learning which isolate knowledge from practice. It suggests a social construction view of learning and puts knowledge back into the context in which it has meaning (Lave & Wenger, 1991). Organizational members construct their own meaning out of interaction with the physical and social world. As a result learning is a contextual issue and it is connected to the conditions in which it is learned (Brown & Duguid, 1991).

Sensemaking, improvisation, and learning elucidate two basic characteristics of continuous change. First, these concepts suggest that continuous change is embedded in organizational process at *micro level*. There are no sudden big jumps but rather the changes are typically in the form of situated accommodations and adaptations. Members share these variations and amplify and sustain these new aspects. Focusing on performative actions, ongoing experimentation, and improvisation rather than structured characteristics of the organization, this perspective suggested that inertial forces have less central role in determination of change (Weick, 2000). As suggested in the communities of practice, each reactivation of organizational work categories (i.e., routines, processes, or rules) ends up with modifications, alterations, and extensions of these categories. Each modification of work practices should not be interpreted as a sign of pathology. Rather these modifications contribute to a better fit of these activities in the face of internal and external demands. As a result, the organization is able to accomplish change just as rapidly as its environment without being exposed to discontinuous, large scale, and frame-breaking change (Weick, 2000).

Secondly sensemaking, improvisation, and learning explain the socially contaminating nature of continuous change. Ongoing social interaction at different levels have been proposed as a source of continuous change (Bruns, 2013; Wright & Zammuto, 2013; Monin, Noorderhaven, Vaara, & Kroon, 2013). Although continuous change focuses on micro level dynamics, social practices are basic to how organizational members experience past practices and relate them to today's practices (Sandberg & Tsoukas, 2011). In their study on routines and organizational schema Rerup and Feldman (2011) proved that different people from different organizations and units contributed to adapting a specific schema. Leclercq-Vandelannoitte (2013, p. 556) also indicated that social interaction in the context of change evokes "dialectics, contradictions, paradox, and tensions to designate the contradictory forces, conflicting interests, opposing demands, and dialectical perspectives". According to Zietsman and Lawrence (2010) organizational members' crossing boundaries are able to translate exogenous practices into field level practices and they produce and institutionalize alternate sets of practices to the organization. According to the authors, the issue is how strong the boundaries are, if too strong they become isolated from the changes in external environment; create contradictions between norms and practices accepted in the fields and those legitimate in the broader society.

Leadership in Continuous Change

Advocacy of bottom-up, unintentional, and emergent change process does not eradicate the role of leadership in continuous change. Nevertheless, the conceptualization of leadership role in continuous change is different. In continuous change, the role of leadership is defined in the broader organizing activity in relation to daily practices rather than to specific interventional change process. The change agent's role is to capture what is emerging from the bottom, rather than imposing a plan, which is basic for innovative organizations. Since change is constant, the key managerial issue is to support the emergence of a new order rather than maintaining control (Lichtenstein, 2000). The understanding of agency is parallel to the communities-of-practice approach (Brown & Duguid, 1991, p. 45)

The basic task of change agents is to author interpretations and label them, and assure dissemination of these interpretations. In other words, the basic task of change agent is noticing, labeling and legitimizing emergent change. This doesn't mean that the members can and should work without assistance and cooperation of the trainers.

Locating the role of the change agent in a broader context (daily practices) rather than a narrow perspective (change process) suggests that change agents go beyond simple reactivation of the routines and sheer repetitiveness of organizing practice. The recent critique of Jansson (2013) on the taken-for-granted practices of organizational change contributes to the understanding of continuous change leadership. The author called for ruling out the common conception of grouping under the organizational hierarchy such as board, top management, middle management, change agent, and even change promoters because such groupings directly cause creation of two parties in the organizations, those who promote change and those who passively receive change. However, human behavior in the complex organizational terrain cannot be confined to organizational hierarchy because practitioners' actions, roles and motivations are conceived and practiced in multiple ways. Parallel to this understanding Davis and Eisenhardt (2011) showed how successful innovation is related to following dynamic organizational processes and rotating leadership rather than simply following appropriate structural configurations and linear conduct. Dynamic organizational processes associated with alternating decision control and rotating leadership process contributes to innovative capacity of successful firms (Davis & Eisenhardt, 2011).

CONTINUOUS CHANGE IN EDUCATIONAL ORGANIZATIONS

What do these ideas of continuous change mean for educational organizations? It is important to note that parallel to the scholars in the broader field of organization sciences, educational researchers indicated the same dissatisfaction with the effectiveness of top-down, planned and mandated change interventions (e.g., Fullan, 1992, 2001; Hallinger, 2003; Levin, 2010). Payne (2008) indicated that change initiative does not result in significant progress in school systems. Similarly Harris (2011, pp. 224-225) stated that "the history of educational change is littered with borrowed or duplicated reform strategies that simply have made little or lasting difference to school or system performance". Although the predominant part of educational change literature adopted managed change perspective in their search for the whats and hows of educational change (Louis, 1994), scholars commonly agree that a strategic, planned, and top-down understanding of change does not fully explain change phenomena in educational organizations (e.g., Gallucci, 2008; Honig, 2008; Louis, 2008; Stein & Coburn, 2008). One criticism raised by Honig (2008) focused on uncertainties and ambiguities during the change process which potentially result in planned and strategic change attempts to go out of their trajectories. Kezar (2005, p. 662) also supported the view of continuous change in higher education and stated that "radical change has many negative consequences; gradual change and innovation appears to be a more promising route to enhance governance in higher education". In a similar vein, Fullan (2001, pp. 50-51) criticized the frequent dominant change understanding and practice due to its fragmented and top-down approach with the following statement:

In schools, for example, the main problem is not the absence of innovations but the presence of too many disconnected, episodic, piecemeal, super-ficially adorned projects. The situation is worse for schools than for businesses. Both are facing turbulent, uncertain environments, but schools are suffering the additional burden of having a torrent of unwanted, uncoordinated policies and innovations raining down on them from hierarchical bureaucracies.

Fullan (1993) also highlighted the inseparability of uncertainty from the change process through his famous quote on the complexity of educational change: "change is a Journey, Not a Blueprint" (p. 24). That is to say, schools are under the pressure of various different new changes and policies concurrently implemented and majorly negative individual responses accompanied with these changes and this would be hardly-managed, frequently wrong, and demanding process if matched with implementation plans. Therefore, limiting educational change to the pre-planned, top-down approaches obviously masks the complex nature of the change and undermines the bottom-up change enactments of organizational members. Evaluating the issue from a planned change perspective, Harris (2011) identified political pressure, over-reliance on 'wrong drivers' of change and failing to undertake a rigorous implementation process as the three sources of disruption in educational change. These arguments inspired the search for another understanding and practice of change in educational organizations.

Ways of Achieving Continuous Change in Educational Organizations

Louis (2008) articulated that change occurs in the form of increments and as a response to stimuli which cause organizational members to reflect and make adjustments on a continuous basis. Hence, tolerance of ambiguities and the ability to respond to emergent local needs in the change process are key change management practices to exploit learning opportunities and bring success-ful change to educational organizations (Gallucci, 2008). Using learning theories, Stein and Coburn (2008) argued that one dynamic behind ongoing improvements in educational organizations is related to networks and practice communities. According to the authors, intentionally built structural characteristics and emerging opportunities shape communities, which influence formal structural-functional characteristics in schools. In a similar understanding, Boyce (2003) suggested that sustaining change in higher education organizations depends on sustaining collective learning, which is possible through rigorous inquiry, skillful dialogue, and examination of the organization in the context of its environment. Gilstrap (2007) utilized the dissipative structures theory to explain the human centered self-organization in schools, which suggests human experience and interaction at individual level as the ways of bringing significant change to educational organizations. These arguments mean that the major shift in assumptions about how change occurs in organizations is equally valid for education as well. Alteration in routines is regarded as another useful way of achieving continuous change in school settings. The application of Feldman's (2000) theory on routinized action in high school settings revealed that as well as the external factors, internal factors also trigger schools for change in their routines (Enomoto & Conley, 2008). That is, apart from the top-down and mandated changes, recurring patterns of behaviors (i.e., tardy monitoring and attendance procedure) can be changed through the ways of repair, expanding, and striving at school level (Conley & Enomoto, 2009).

Organizational learning, in addition, is another way suggested to achieve continuous change in educational organizations (Miller, 1996). Indeed, from the perspective of organizational learning, continuous improvement entails the alteration in individuals' perspectives from the one expecting external sources to solve the problems encountered every day to the one having the responsibility to solve their own problems (Weller & Weller, 1997).

However, Louis (1994) argued that organizational learning fails in creating change and development unless an appropriate interactive environment is created in the school. Specifically, the current schooling model is criticized due to lack of communication network and time for the teachers and principals to work together in a collaborative manner and access to the external ideas so learning cannot be fully accomplished. Similar arguments were also raised by Fullan (2000) on the essence of reculturing in creating improvement at schools. That is, through reculturing, school organizational members shift from limited to regular engagement in the assessment and pedagogy and make necessary improvements accordingly. Therefore, professional learning community can be created and deeper changes can be achieved.

Finally, several scholars applied self-organizing to explain ongoing and continuous change and development in academic and administrative processes of schools (e.g., Davis & Sumara, 2006; Bain, 2007; Pascale, Milleman, & Gioja, 2000). According to Bain, Walker and Chan (2011) simple rules, embedded designs, self-similarity, and dispersed control facilitate a shared cognitive schema, which pushes formal and informal actions of all constituencies (e.g., teachers, principal, and students) into common grounds. Prevalent dynamics in each school led to a unique schema, which guides the practices. This is the one reason of why we cannot achieve a uniform implementation of academic and administrative practices in every school, even in a highly centralized school system. Self-organizing is a bottom up and voluntary process, initiated without external force, which constantly contributes to shaping and reshaping the organization.

Continuous Change Leadership in School

Empowering organizational learning is mostly an issue of culture creation and school leaders' has a vital role in creating and sustaining learning culture to achieve continuous change. Some scholars stressed that transformational leadership has merit in the bottom-up change perspective (van den Berg, Vandenberghe, & Sleegers, 1999). Specifically, transformational leaders are argued to be proactive rather than reactive and welcoming potential problems encountered in the process in a cooperative environment with the followers. According to Hallinger (2003), transformational leadership depends on recognizing the needs of individuals rather than direct control and coordination; thus, the role of a leader in the educational change process is creating an appropriate learning culture in which individuals are self-motivated and committed to make improvements in their schools without an external channeling. Moolenaar, Daly, and Sleegers (2010) substantiated the relationship between transformational leadership and innovative school climate and concluded that when a school principal engages in transformational leadership behaviors, teachers are more willing to take risks and challenge the status quo through developing advanced solutions to the problems. Transformational leadership is regarded as a coping mechanism for both business and educational organizations in the era of continuous change through its effect to create employee commitment, self-regard, and self-confidence to deal with the negative and unexpected impediments of change (Bottery, 2001).

Although creating a climate conducive for continuous change is important, transformational leadership understanding is not totally parallel to the arguments of continuous change developed in the broader field of organization science. However, distributed leadership in educational organizations provides further insights on leadership in continuous change. As Day, Harris, Hadfield, Tolley, and Beresford (2000) have argued in times of rapid changes, there is the need for radical alternatives to the traditional model of leadership. It is more than trying to understand leadership through single/heroic leaders (Harris, 2008). According to Spillane, Halverson, and Diamond (2001, p.

20) distributed leadership, a concept aiming to explain leadership for organizational learning, implies "a social distribution where the leadership function is stretched over the work of a number of individuals and task is accomplished through the interaction of multiple leaders". Distributed leadership alters the traditional understanding of power and influence. Rather than conceiving organizational members as passive recipients of order, distributed leadership indicates that organizational members have the capacity to recognize the need for altering work categories, accomplish small scale changes and share such small scale changes in social settings. Hence, ordinary organizational members contribute to reshaping organizational categories.

Teacher leadership is the most issued reflection of distributed leadership in schools, and it has been debated that teacher leadership has some significant effects on organizational and student learning (Harris, 2008; Leithwood, Mascall, & Strauss, 2009). Therefore, the capacity building in self-organizing schools largely owes to leadership, which is distributed into different parts of the school (Bain et al., 2011).

The arguments on transformational and distributed leadership suggest some practical guidelines to facilitate continuous change in schools. First, leadership is expected to clear what is really unfolding in the organization and formulate what is going on in concrete terms. Being attentive to discursive templates for capturing the difference in any organizational practice is necessary to recognize and take up modifications or alterations in organizations. As a part of this task, leadership is expected to understand and manage how organizational members understand, receive, signify, and enact change because enactment will be totally different from the conceived version of change. The fact that continuous change is closely related to the construction of schema and cognitive frames, school administrators must try first to understand cognitive schema. The principal may try to change the meaning that attributed to the current archetype

and meaning attributed to the proposed archetype. Still another function of leadership is facilitating travel of new practices and extensions in the already existing practices or structures. Simple measures of giving autonomy to experiment with structured organizational categories, embracing modifications and, facilitating knowledge sharing may potentially facilitate travel of ideas. Finally, leadership may take a role in elucidating and retaining adapted/modified/altered practices. For example, school leaders may act as agency and make use of emerging opportunities in schools for refinement of the curriculum, student assessment, leading instructional processes etc.

FUTURE RESEARCH DIRECTIONS

These ideas on continuous change have been worked out in conceptual and empirical studies in the broader field of organization science. Although educational researchers articulate the same dissatisfaction with change interventions, they have not proved eagerness to carry similar conceptual alternatives as guides for practice. There are promising understandings built around self-organizing systems (Bain et al., 2011; Gilstrap, 2007) and learning organizations (Louis, 2008; Gallucci, 2008; Honig, 2008) but there is still a need for more investigations on how things and processes change over time in schools. However, the continuous change perspective potentially provides an important empirical area for educational leadership and administration researchers. Therefore, the call of Langley et al. (2013) to carry out more process research and organizational ethnographists works as well as development and application of quantitative methods for event and sequence analysis in elaborating process understandings are equally valid for change researchers in education as well. Qualitative studies and qualitative data collection techniques served complementary purposes in order to develop a holistic understanding continuous change. On the other hand, holding synoptical acocunts in the study of continuous change is also necessary to document the role of process, content, context and outcomes factors that facilitate continuous change in organizations. Research on continuous change is in its infancy and research on the process of change and the factors predicting continuous change will add breadth not only to the field of educational change but also to the broader field of organization science.

CONCLUSION

This paper suggests several different insights on the way we conceptualize and practice change in educational organizations. First of all, parallel with the arguments of Weick (1979) and March (1981) that referred organizational change as a non-pathological and normal practice, continuous change conceptualizes change as a phenomenon of ordinary times in the lives of organizations. Being a theory of normalcy, continuous change enables to develop a different perspective toward several issues in change and development practices including attitudes of organizational members and role of leadership.

Secondly, continuous change proposes a reversed understanding of resistance toward change. Being embedded in daily practices of organizational members is in the best interest of organizational members if to successfully accomplish tasks. With this character continuous change contributes to democratization of the workplace with its bottom up character. Therefore, change is not a threat but an opportunity of satisfying achievement need and professional growth for organizational members. The real challenge in this understanding is that change is not related to individual attitudes but to accomplish a collective action in organizations. Process variables such as social interaction, cooperation and informal knowledge sharing are highly valued in continuous change because they facilitate crossing boundar-

ies (Zietsma & Lawrence, 2010) and distributing available knowledge among members (Brown & Duguid, 1991). Besides, creating a harmony among group members, as we have seen in the image of improvisation, is necessary because each member operates within an overall framework, conforms to a shared set of values and norms, and has access to a known repertoire of rules and resources (Barrett, 1998; Crossan, 1998; Orlikowski & Hofman, 1997; Weick, 1998). As Jansson (2013) stated this is the one reasons of high failure rate in change interventions because the more we go for 'universalistic' practice of change the more we lose the power 'sociality' in shaping change in a particular organizational context. For example, in and out of change context, trying to understand dominant emotions and responding to these emotions again will increase chances of success of the organizations.

If the understanding change is the property of normal times, then it becomes rather easier to address the issue of whether continuous change and discontinuous change are distinct. It is important to note that the distinction between continuous and discontinuous change is another version of pervasive mode of thinking in organizational change. Change is a conceptual area of bipolar mode of thinking (Pettigrew, 2000). Several scholars have carried out bipolar mode of thinking to differentiate between continuous and discontinuous change. This mode of thinking was also conveyed in educational change discussion as well. Fullan (1993; 1996; 2000) noted that rather than focusing on the superiority of top-down or bottom-up approaches over another, educational changes require the coalescence of both perspectives for sustainability. van den Berg et al. (1999) made a distinction between structural-functional perspective and cultural-individual perspectives to change. The authors contended that structural-functional perspective alone is not enough for the execution of innovation at schools. Cultural-individual perspective facilitates learning in a cooperative manner, allows experimentation, and deals with teachers' ambiguities accompanied with the change; therefore, should be used in an integrated way with the former approach. Louis (2006) in her distinction between anarchic organizations (characterized with random alterations) or goal-directed and rational ones (characterized with planned and goal-oriented change), noted that any of these perspectives alone is not enough to deal with the changes school organizations encounter today; thus, synthesis of both perspectives is needed.

In the broader field of organization science Jansson's (2013) arguments on universality versus practicality, Zietsma and Lawrence's (2010) arguments on recursive relationship between boundary work and practice work, and Tsoukas and Chia's (2002) arguments on radially structured work categories are important in depicting how small scale breakdowns occur in structured organizational categories. Common to these distinctions is that formally structured and informally emergent work categories breed each other in a productive co-existence. Like any defined or structured work category, planned change is signified, shaped and reshaped by organizational members. As soon as they experience the planned change, they start to change it, and share their understanding of planned change social settings. No matter how strong the organization attempt to implement the change plan as it was conceived, organizational members locally interpret, modify, and elaborate on change in their own subjective world. The success of the organization largely related to facilitating the experimentation of organizational members with the structured work categories.

In short, the perspective proposed in this study advocates the grasp of formal (structured, planned) and informal (unstructured, emergent) sides of change. Several authors in their conceptual discussions have indicated the two-folded nature of organizational change. There is always an informal, emerging side in organizations. Yet, as long as the informal structure is not incorporated into the formal process it will not become a part of the organization's repertoire. Management is

expected to artfully keep the balance between formal and informal processes. Following rigid formal policy and loose informal policy may not result in successful change. As Brown and Eisenhardt (1997) stated, constant managerial vigilance is necessary to avoid slipping into pure chaos or pure order. The task of management is to support and nurture the expectations, norms, and resources that guide the ongoing change process. As a result, rather than over relying on plans, managers are suggested to build vision (Smith, 2004). For all of these reasons, the basic task of the change agent is noticing, labeling, and legitimizing emergent change. In most cases what management supplies is not what organizational members need and a gap may emerge in between. Therefore, it is the responsibility of skillful management to supply the real needs rather than communicating abstract expectations and codes of operation (Brown & Duguid, 1991).

Parallel to the call of different authors for exploring to the relations between structured, planned and defined work categories and unstructured and emergent work categories, decoding the interplay between formal and informal dimensions of any organizational reality facilitates continuous change which permeate any organizational reality beyond its boundaries. This understanding helps to change our basic guiding assumptions in the practices of change; that the top of organizational hierarchy lead or orchestrate change; that change must be implemented as planned; that planned change is the only way to accomplish progress in organizations; that resistance is negative and originates from the marginal groups/members. The ideas that planned change (formal action) constantly evolves into different forms in the hands of practitioners facilitate replacing the traditional assumptions with the assumptions; that change originate from typical practitioners; that resistance can be useful to see traps and solicit opportunities and suggests organizations to focus on the practice, discourse, and emotions in the conduct of change. Hence, in this context formal and informal agents' acts alter the content, premises, and structures of proposed changes, which increase the chances of realizing change, but not the proposed form.

REFERENCES

Argyris, C. (1997). Initiating change that preserves. *The American Behavioral Scientist, 40*(3), 299–310. doi:10.1177/0002764297040003006

Armenakis, A. A., & Bedeian, A. G. (1999). Organizational change: A review of theory and research in the 1990s. *Journal of Management, 25*(3), 293–315. doi:10.1177/014920639902500303

Bain, A. (2007). *The self-organizing school: Next generation comprehensive school reforms.* Lanham, MD: Rowman and Littlefield.

Bain, A., Walker, A., & Chan, A. (2011). Self-organization and capacity building: Sustaining change. *Journal of Educational Administration, 49*(6), 701–719. doi:10.1108/09578231111174839

Barley, S. R. (1990). The alignment of technology and structure through roles and networks. *Administrative Science Quarterly, 35*(1), 61–103. doi:10.2307/2393551 PMID:10106582

Barrett, F. J. (1998). Creativity and improvisation in jazz and organizations: Implications for organizational learning. *Organization Science, 9*(5), 605-622. doi:1047-7039/98/0905/0605/$05.00

Beer, M., & Nohria, N. (2000). Resolving the tension between theories E and O of change. In M. Beer & N. Nohria (Eds.), *Breaking the code of change* (pp. 1–35). Boston, MA: Harvard Business School Press.

Bigley, G. A., & Roberts, K. H. (2001). The incident command system: High-reliability organizing for complex and volatile task environments. *Academy of Management Journal, 44*(6), 1281–1299. doi:10.2307/3069401

Boden, D. (1994). *The business of talk.* Cambridge, MA: Polity Press.

Bottery, M. (2001). Globalisation and the UK competition state: No room for transformational leadership in education? *School Leadership & Management, 21*(2), 199–218. doi:10.1080/13632430120054772

Boyce, M. E. (2003). Organizational learning is essential to achieving and sustaining change in higher education. *Innovative Higher Education, 28*(2), 119–136. doi:10.1023/B:IHIE.0000006287.69207.00

Brown, A. D., & Humphreys, M. (2003). Epic and tragic tales: Making sense of change. *The Journal of Applied Behavioral Science, 39*(2), 121–144. doi:10.1177/0021886303255557

Brown, J. S., & Duguid, P. (1991). Organizational learning and communities-of-practice: Toward a unified view of working, learning, and innovation. *Organization Science, 2*(1), 40-57. doi:1047-7039/91/0201/0040/$01.25

Brown, S. L., & Eisenhardt, K. M. (1997). The art of continuous change: Linking complexity theory and time-paced evolution in relentlessly shifting organizations. *Administrative Science Quarterly, 42*(1), 1–34. doi:10.2307/2393807

Bruns, H. C. (2013). Working alone together: Coordination changes expert practice in cross-domain collaboration. *Academy of Management Journal, 56,* 62–83. doi:10.5465/amj.2010.0756

Cheng, Y. C., & Walker, A. (2008). When reform hits reality: The bottleneck effect in Hong Kong primary schools. *School Leadership & Management, 28*(5), 505–521. doi:10.1080/13632430802499994

Child, J., & McGrath, R. G. (2001). Organizations unfettered: Organizational form in an information-intensive economy. *Academy of Management Journal, 44*(6), 1135–1148. doi:10.2307/3069393

Clegg, C., & Walsh, S. (2004). Change management: Time for change! *European Journal of Work and Organizational Psychology, 13*(2), 217–239. doi:10.1080/13594320444000074

Conley, S., & Enomoto, E. K. (2009). Organizational routines in flux: A case study of change in recording and monitoring student attendance. *Education and Urban Society, 41*(3), 364–386. doi:10.1177/0013124508327581

Crossan, M. M. (1998). Improvisation in action. *Organization Science, 9*(5), 593-599. doi:1047-7039/98/0905/0593/$05.00

Dahl, M. S. (2011). Organizational change and employee stress. *Management Science, 57*(2), 240–256. doi:10.1287/mnsc.1100.1273

Davis, B., & Sumara, D. (2006). *Complexity and education: Inquiries into learning, teaching, and research*. Mahwah, NJ: Erlbaum.

Davis, J. P., & Eisenhardt, K. (2011). Rotating leadership and collaborative innovation: Recombination processes in symbiotic relationships. *Administrative Science Quarterly, 56*(2), 159–201. doi:10.1177/0001839211428131

Day, C., Harris, A., Hadfield, M., Tolley, H., & Beresford, J. (2000). *Leading schools in times of change*. Berkshire, UK: Open University Press.

Enomoto, E. K., & Conley, S. (2008). Changing of the guard: How different school leaders change organizational routines. *Journal of School Leadership, 18*, 278–301.

Feldman, M. (2000). Organizational routines as a source of continuous change. *Organization Science, 11*(6), 611-629. doi:1047-7039/00/1106/0611/$05.00

Fullan, M. (1992). *Successful school improvement: The implementation perspective and beyond*. Buckingham, UK: Open University Press.

Fullan, M. (1993). *Change forces: Probing the depths of educational reform*. London: Falmer Press.

Fullan, M. (2000). The three stories of education reform. *Phi Delta Kappan, 81*(8), 581–584.

Fullan, M. (2001). *Leading in a culture of change*. San Francisco: Jossey-Bass.

Fullan, M. G. (1996). Turning systemic thinking on its head. *Phi Delta Kappan, 77*(6), 420–423.

Gallucci, C. (2008). Districtwide instructional reform: using sociocultural theory to link professional learning to organizational support. *American Journal of Education, 114*, 541-581. doi: 0195-6744/2008/11404-0002$10.00

George, J. M., & Jones, G. R. (2001). Towards a process model of individual change in organizations. *Human Relations, 54*(4), 419–444. doi:10.1177/0018726701544002

Gersick, C. J. G. (1991). Revolutionary change theories: A multilevel exploration of the punctuated equilibrium paradigm. *Academy of Management Review, 16*(1), 10–36.

Gilstrap, D. L. (2007). Dissipative structures in educational change: Prigogine and the academy. *International Journal of Leadership in Education, 10*(1), 49–69. doi:10.1080/13603120600933758

Hallinger, P. (2003). Leading educational change: Reflections on the practice of instructional and transformational leadership. *Cambridge Journal of Education, 33*(3), 329–351. doi:10.1080/0305764032000122005

Hannan, M. T., & Freeman, J. (1977). The population ecology of organizations. *American Journal of Sociology, 82*(5), 929–964. doi:10.1086/226424

Harris, A. (2008). *Distributed school leadership: Developing tomorrow's leaders*. London: Routledge.

Harris, A. (2011). System improvement through collective capacity building. *Journal of Educational Administration, 49*(6), 624–636. doi:10.1108/09578231111174785

Honig, M. I. (2008). District central offices as learning organizations: How sociocultural and organizational learning theories elaborate district central office administrators' participation in teaching and learning improvement efforts. *American Journal of Education, 114*(4), 627–664. doi:10.1086/589317

Jansson, N. (2013). Organizational change as a practice: A critical analysis. *Journal of Organizational Change Management, 26*(6), 1003–1019. doi:10.1108/JOCM-09-2012-0152

Kezar, A. (2005). Consequences of radical change in governance: A grounded theory approach. *The Journal of Higher Education, 76*(6), 634–668. doi:10.1353/jhe.2005.0043

Kondakci, Y. (2005). *Practice-based continuous change: A longitudinal investigation of an organizational change process in a higher education organization.* (Unpublished doctoral dissertation). Ghent University, Ghent, Belgium.

Langley, A., Smallman, C., Tsoukas, H., & Van de Ven, A. (2013). Process studies of change in organization and management: Unveiling temporality, activity, and flow. *Academy of Management Journal, 56*(1), 1–13. doi:10.5465/amj.2013.4001

Lave, J., & Wenger, E. (1991). *Situated learning: Legitimate peripheral participation.* Cambridge, UK: Cambridge University Press. doi:10.1017/CBO9780511815355

Leclercq-Vandelannoitte, A. (2013). Contradiction as a medium and outcome of organizational change: A Foucauldian reading. *Journal of Organizational Change Management, 26*(3), 556–572. doi:10.1108/09534811311328579

Leithwood, K., Mascall, B., & Strauss, T. (2009). What we have learned and where we go from here. In K. Leithwood, B. Mascall, & T. Strauss (Eds.), *Distributed leadership according to the evidence* (pp. 269–281). New York: Routledge.

Levin, B. (2010). The challenge of large scale literacy improvement. *School Effectiveness and School Improvement, 21*(4), 359–376. doi:10.1080/09243453.2010.486589

Lewis, L. K. (2000). Communicating change: Four cases of quality programs. *Journal of Business Communication, 37*(2), 128–155. doi:10.1177/002194360003700201

Lichtenstein, B. M. B. (2000). Emergence as a process of self-organizing: New assumptions and insights from the study of non-linear dynamic systems. *Journal of Organizational Change Management, 13*(6), 526–544. doi:10.1108/09534810010378560

Louis, K. S. (1994). Beyond 'managed change': Rethinking how schools improve. *School Effectiveness and School Improvement, 5*(1), 2–24. doi:10.1080/0924345940050102

Louis, K. S. (2006). *Organizing for school change.* London: Taylor and Francis.

Louis, K. S. (2008). Learning to support improvement-next steps for research on district practice. *American Journal of Education, 114*(4), 681–689. doi:10.1086/589320

March, J. G. (1981). Footnotes to organizational change. *Administrative Science Quarterly, 26*(4), 563–577. doi:10.2307/2392340

Miller, D. (1996). A preliminary typology of organizational learning: Synthesizing the literature. *Journal of Management, 22*(3), 485–505. doi:10.1177/014920639602200305

Mohrman, S. A., Tenkasi, R. V., & Mohrman, A. M. Jr. (2003). The role of networks in fundamental organizational change: A grounded analysis. *The Journal of Applied Behavioral Science*, *39*(3), 301–323. doi:10.1177/0021886303258072

Monin, P., Noorderhaven, N., Vaara, E., & Kroon, D. (2013). Giving sense to and making sense of justice in postmerger integration. *Academy of Management Journal*, *56*(1), 256–284. doi:10.5465/amj.2010.0727

Moolenaar, N. M., Daly, A. J., & Sleegers, P. J. C. (2010). Occupying the principal position: Examining relationship between transformational leadership, social network position, and schools' innovative climate. *Educational Administration Quarterly*, *46*(5), 623–670. doi:10.1177/0013161X10378689

Moorman, C., & Miner, A. S. (1998). Organizational improvisation and organizational memory. *Academy of Management Review*, *23*(4), 698–723.

Oreg, S., Vakola, M., & Armenakis, A. (2011). Change recipients' reactions to organizational change: A 60-year review of quantitative studies. *The Journal of Applied Behavioral Science*, *47*(4), 461–524. doi:10.1177/0021886310396550

Orlikowski, W. J., & Hofman, J. D. (1997). An improvisational model for change management: The case of groupware technologies. *Sloan Management Review*, *38*(2), 11–21.

Orlikowski, W. J. (1996). Improvising organizational transformation over time: A situated change perspective. *Information Systems Research*, *7*(1), 63–92. doi:10.1287/isre.7.1.63

Orr, J. (1996). *Talking about machines*. Ithaca, NY: Cornell University Press.

Pascale, R., Milleman, M., & Gioja, L. (2000). *Surfing the edge of chaos: The laws of nature and the new laws of business*. New York, NY: Three Rivers Press.

Payne, C. (2008). *So much reform, so little change: The persistence of failure in urban schools*. Cambridge, MA: Harvard Education Press.

Pettigrew, A. M. (2000). Linking change process to outcomes: A commentary on Ghoshal, Bartlett, and Weick. In M. Beer & N. Nohria (Eds.), *Breaking the code of change* (pp. 243–265). Boston, MA: Harvard Business School Press.

Porras, J. I., & Robertson, P. J. (1992). Organizational development: Theory, practice, and research. In M. D. Dunnette & L. M. Hough (Eds.), *Handbook of industrial and organizational psychology* (pp. 719–822). Palo Alto, CA: Consulting Psychologist Press.

Reichers, A. E., Wanous, J. P., & Austin, J. T. (1997). Understanding and managing cynicism about organizational change. *The Academy of Management Executive*, *11*(1), 48–59.

Rerup, C., & Feldman, M. (2011). Routines as a source of change in organizational schemata: The role of trial-and-error learning. *Academy of Management Journal*, *54*(3), 577–610. doi:10.5465/AMJ.2011.61968107

Sandberg, J., & Tsoukas, H. (2011). Grasping the logic of practice: Theorizing through practical activity. *Academy of Management Review*, *36*(2), 338–360. doi:10.5465/AMR.2011.59330942

Senge, P. (1990). *The fifth discipline: The art and practice of the learning organization*. New York: Doubleday Currency.

Sleegers, P., van den Berg, R., & Geijsel, F. (2000). Building innovative schools: The need for new approaches. *Teaching and Teacher Education*, *16*(7), 801–808. doi:10.1016/S0742-051X(00)00026-3

Smith, A. C. T. (2004). Complexity theory and change management in sport organizations. *Emergence: Complexity & Organization*, *6*(1-2), 70–79.

Spillane, J., Halverson, R., & Diamond, J. (2001). Investigating school leadership practice: A distributed perspective. *Educational Researcher, 30*(3), 23–28. doi:10.3102/0013189X030003023

Stein, M. K., & Coburn, C. E. (2008). Architectures of learning: A comparative analysis of two urban school districts. *American Journal of Education, 114*(4), 583–626. doi:10.1086/589315

Tsoukas, H., & Chia, R. (2002). On organizational becoming: Rethinking organizational change. *Organization Science, 13*(5), 567-582. doi:0195-6744/2008/11404-0003$10.00

Van de Ven, A. H., & Poole, M. S. (1995). Explaining development and change in organizations. *Academy of Management Review, 20*(3), 510–540. doi:10.2307/258786

van den Berg, R., Vandenberghe, R., & Sleegers, P. (1999). Management of innovations from a cultural-individual perspective. *School Effectiveness and School Improvement, 10*(3), 321–351. doi:10.1076/sesi.10.3.321.3500

Weick, K. E. (1979). *The social psychology of organizing*. Reading, MA: Addison-Wesley.

Weick, K. E. (1995). *Sensemaking in organizations*. Thousand Oaks, CA: Sage.

Weick, K. E. (1998). Improvisation as a mindset for organizational analysis. *Organization Science, 9*(5), 543-555. doi:1047-7039/98/0905/0543/$05.00

Weick, K. E. (2000). Emergent change as a universal in organizations. In M. Beer & N. Nohria (Eds.), *Breaking the code of change* (pp. 223–241). Boston, MA: Harvard Business School Press.

Weick, K. E., & Quinn, R. E. (1999). Organizational change and development. *Annual Review of Psychology, 50*(1), 361-386. doi:0084-6570/99/0201-0361$08.00

Weller, L. D., & Weller, S. J. (1997). Quality learning organizations and continuous improvement: Implementing the concept. *NASSP Bulletin, 81*(591), 62–70. doi:10.1177/019263659708159111

Wright, A. L., & Zammuto, R. F. (2013). Wielding the willow: Processes of institutional change in English county cricket. *Academy of Management Journal, 56*(1), 308–330. doi:10.5465/amj.2010.0656

Zietsma, C., & Lawrence, T. B. (2010). Institutional work in the transformation of an organizational field: The interplay of boundary work and practice work. *Administrative Science Quarterly, 55*(2), 189–221. doi:10.2189/asqu.2010.55.2.189

ADDITIONAL READING

Aldrich, H. (1999). *Organizations Evolving*. Thousand Oaks, CA: Sage.

Amburgey, T. L., Kelly, D., & Barnett, W. (1993). Resetting the clock: The dynamics of organizational change and failure. *Administrative Science Quarterly, 38*(1), 51–73. doi:10.2307/2393254

Amis, J., Slack, T., & Hinings, C. R. (2004a). The pace, sequence, and linearity of radical change. *Academy of Management Journal, 47*(1), 15–39.

Argyris, C., & Schön, D. (1978). *Organizational learning: A theory of action perspective*. Reading, MA: Addison-Wesley.

Armenakis, A. A., Harris, S. G., & Feild, H. (1999). Paradigms in organizational change: Change agent and change target perspectives. In R. Golembiewski (Ed.), *Handbook of organizational behavior* (pp. 631–658). New York: Marcel Dekker.

Armenakis, A. A., Harris, S. G., & Mossholder, K. W. (1993). Creating readiness for organizational change. *Human Relations, 46*(6), 681–703. doi:10.1177/001872679304600601

Boonstra, J. J., & Bennebroek Gravenhorst, K. M. (1998). Power dynamics and organizational change: A comparison of perspectives. *European Journal of Work and Organizational Psychology, 7*(2), 97–120. doi:10.1080/135943298398826

Bourdieu, P. (1990). *The logic of practice.* Stanford, CA: Stanford University Press.

Burke, W. W. (2002). *Organization change* (1st ed.). London: Sage.

Capra, F. (1996). *The web of life.* New York: Anchor.

Coleman, J. H. J. Jr. (1999). What enables self-organizing behavior in business. *Emergence, 1*(1), 33–48. doi:10.1207/s15327000em0101_3

Collins, D. (1998). *Organizational change: Sociological perspective.* London: Routledge.

Coveney, P., & Highfield, R. (1995). *Frontiers of complexity.* London: Faber & Faber.

Czarniawska, B., & Joerges, B. (1996). Travels of ideas. In B. Czarniawska & G. Sevon (Eds.), *Translating organizational change* (pp. 13–48). New York: Walter de Gruyter. doi:10.1515/9783110879735.13

DiMaggio, P. J., & Powell, W. W. (1983). The iron cage revisited: Institutional isomorphism and collective rationality in organizational fields. *American Sociological Review, 48*(2), 147–160. doi:10.2307/2095101

Ford, J. D., & Ford, L. W. (1995). The role of conversations in producing intentional change in organizations. *Academy of Management Review, 20*(3), 541–570.

Galpin, T. (1996). *The human side of change: A practical guide to organization redesign.* San Francisco, CA: Jossey-Bass.

Heracleous, L. (2001). An ethnographic study of culture in the context of organizational change. *The Journal of Applied Behavioral Science, 37*(4), 426–446. doi:10.1177/0021886301374003

Heracleous, L., & Barrett, M. (2001). Organizational change as discourse: Communicative actions and deep structures in the context of information technology implementation. *Academy of Management Journal, 44*(4), 755–778. doi:10.2307/3069414

Langley, A., & Tsoukas, H. (2010). Introducing perspectives on process organization studies. In T. Hernes & S. Maitlis (Eds.), *Process, sensemaking and organizing* (pp. 1–26). Oxford, U.K.: Oxford University Press. doi:10.1093/acprof:oso/9780199594566.003.0001

Kotter, J. (1985). *Power and influence: Beyond formal authority.* New York: Free Press.

Kotter, J. P. (1996). *Leading change.* Boston: Harvard Business School.

Mirvis, P. H. (1996). Historical foundations of organization learning. *Journal of Organizational Change Management, 9*(1), 13–31. doi:10.1108/09534819610107295

Orr, J. (1996). *Talking about machines.* Ithaca, NY: Cornell University Press.

Prigogine, I., & Stengers, I. (1984). *Order out of chaos.* New York: Bantam Books.

Pfeffer, J., & Sutton, R. I. (2006). *Hard facts, dangerous half-truths and total nonsense: Profiting from evidence-based management.* Cambridge, MA: Harvard Business School Press.

KEY TERMS AND DEFINITIONS

Continuous Change: Micro level, ongoing, emergent and bottom-up process, which is embedded in daily practices of organizational members rather than being a product of planned interventions (Tsoukas & Chia, 2002). It is ongoing, evolving, and cumulative change (Weick & Quinn, 1999).

Distributed Leadership: "A social distribution where the leadership function is stretched over the work of a number of individuals and task is accomplished through the interaction of multiple leaders" (Spillane, Halverson & Diamond, 2001, p. 20).

Organizational Change: "One type of event, is an empirical observation of difference in form, quality, or state over time in an organizational entity. The entity may be an individual's job, a work group, an organizational strategy, a program, a product, or the overall organization" (Van de Ven & Poole, 1995: 512).

Organizational Learning: "The acquisition of new knowledge by actors who are able to and willing to apply that knowledge in making decisions or influencing others in the organization" Miller (1996: 486).

Planned Change: Deliberate change intervention which originate from a managerial decision to improve system functioning (Porras & Robertson, 1992).

Sensemaking: A cognitive process through which organizational members interpret and assign meaning whereby people elucidate phenomena and produce inter-subjective accounts (Brown & Humphreys, 2003).

Section 3
School Leadership Effects and Student Achievement

Chapter 15
Transformational Leadership and Principals' Innovativeness:
Are They the "Keys" for the Research and Innovation Oriented School?

Jasmin-Olga Sarafidou
University of Thessaly, Greece

Efstathios Xafakos
University of Thessaly, Greece

ABSTRACT

This chapter presents an empirical investigation on aspects of leadership that may predict a school climate promoting research and innovativeness in Greek primary schools. Specifically, the authors examine principals' innovativeness and dimensions of transformational leadership as possible predictors of innovative school climate and teachers' attitudes towards research. Self-administered questionnaires were completed by 190 primary school teachers. The questionnaire included inventories measuring a) principals' innovativeness, b) three dimensions of transformational leadership style (vision building, individual consideration, intellectual stimulation), c) innovative school climate, and d) different aspects of teachers' attitudes towards educational research. Results demonstrate that principals' innovativeness tends to coexist with a leadership style that is transformational. Moreover, an innovative school climate is very likely to be established if the school principal not only provides stimulation and personalized care for teachers but also s/he acts as a model of innovativeness in school. Nevertheless, principals' innovativeness and a transformative leadership does not also ensure a research orientation in school.

INTRODUCTION

School improvement in a rapidly and radically changing societal and educational context is undoubtedly linked with school changes. Such changes require reforming leadership styles and staff roles so that schools turn into learning organizations, that is organizations that function as learning communities where both teachers and students learn together (Voulalas & Sharpe,

DOI: 10.4018/978-1-4666-6591-0.ch015

2005; MacBeath & Mortimore 2001). Learning schools are organizations which improve their quality consistently with social changes, that is, they enhance their effectiveness by continually and collectively reflecting on and enquiring their practice. On the other hand any attempt of school change should be based on evidence; therefore it is important that research is incorporated into plans for school development (Wikeley, 1998; Hewitt & Little, 2005). As a result, current discussions on education put research and innovation at the heart of school change as key characteristics of a school climate promoting educational changes that lead to school improvement (Fullan, 2002; OECD, 2008b; Ferrari, Cachia & Punie, 2009; Fleith, 2000). School climate refers to the observable patterns of behavior, attitudes and feelings that characterize school life while school culture concerns the deeper and more enduring norms and shared values (Isaksen & Lawer, 2002). Schools are, more and more, called to have a research orientation embedded in their culture so that a) the development of learning communities can be effectively promoted and b) decision making can be evidence based. Despite the rich bibliography describing the characteristics of learning schools (Fullan, 1995; Isaacson and Bamburg, 1992; Geijsel, Van den Berg & Sleegers, 1999; Sergiovanni, 1994; Silins, Zarins, Mulford, 2002), there is little empirical evidence on how this can be realized.

There is a growing body of research showing that a research culture is more easily developed within an innovative environment (Carpenter, 2007; Ebbutt, 2002; Worall, 2004), while innovations should be introduced on the basis of research evidence and should also be scientifically evaluated. Therefore, both school innovativeness and a research culture are required in order to ensure effectiveness of school changes. Unless schools value educational research it is not likely that they can make use of it for evidence based

changes. However, several empirical studies still point to the gap between educational research and school practice (Vanderlinde & Van Braak, 2010; Broekkamp & Van – Hout Walters, 2007), despite the fact that the use of research for school improvement is considered fundamental.

To this end, the role of school leadership is crucial. Many authors have stressed the link between transformational leadership and the cultivation of a climate facilitating change and innovation (Geijsel, Van den Berg & Sleegers, 1999; Geijsel, Sleegers, Leithwood & Jantzi, 2003; Moolenaar et al, 2010). According to Jung & Avolio (2000) as cited by Moolenaar et al. (2010, p. 628) "Transformational leaders aim to motivate followers to accomplish and even exceed their initial achievement expectations". Despite the fact that transformational leadership has been found to be positively correlated with an innovative school climate (Moolenaar et al, 2010; Geijsel, Van den Berg & Sleegers, 1999; Tajasom & Ahmad, 2011; Geijsel et al., 2001; Geijsel et al., 2003; Van den Berg & Sleegers, 1996), it is not known whether such a leadership also promotes a school climate where teachers see themselves as learners and make use of research to evaluate their novel practices. Even if a school has a transformative and innovative leader, helping in establishing a school culture that values openness to new ideas thus promoting an innovative school climate, this does not necessarily mean that research engagement is also encouraged, so that innovations are evidence based. Whether innovative schools are characterized by transformational leadership and a school climate promoting teachers' engagement with research is still an underexplored issue. This chapter presents results of an empirical study investigating aspects of school leadership as possible predictors of a school climate promoting research and innovativeness.

BACKGROUND

The Learning School and the Importance of Research and Innovation

During the last years, scientific discourse on school change and improvement is focused on the idea of learning schools. It is argued that schools should function in a way that enhances knowledge for all its members and turn into learning organizations (MacGilchrist, Myers & Reed, 1997). The idea of the school as a learning organization was proposed by educational researchers (Fullan, 1995; Silins, Zarins & Mulford, 2002), as the modern way of school structure, where teachers share ideas and practices in order to bring up necessary changes. The learning organization refers to 'the conditions and procedures that support the ability of an organization to value, acquire, and use information and tacit knowledge acquired from employees and stakeholders to successfully plan, implement, and evaluate strategies to achieve performance goals (Bowen, Rose & Ware, 2006, p.98-99). It was defined by Senge (1990, p.3) as an organization cultivating new ways of thinking and a place where people expand their capability to produce desired results, by continuously trying to learn and learn how to do it collectively. Therefore, the learning organization creates a culture supporting continuous learning for all its members by adopting leadership strategies that promote learning as a participative procedure (Watkins and Marsick, 1993, 1996). The idea of a learning organization stems from the organisational learning theory, as 'organizations learn only through people who learn' (Senge, 1990, p.139). Schools where learning, rather than teaching, is the fundamental value are better prepared to succeed, since if 'the performance of individuals go up, the power of the institution will go up too' (Can, 2011, p.6257).

The idea of a learning school is closely connected to that of professional learning communities, as the term 'learning organization' refers to schools where professional learning communities function (Dufour & Eaker, 1998). A similar definition is given by Stoll et al (2006), as a group of people driven by a common vision for collaboration, who seek ways to enhance both teachers' and students' learning. All members of learning communities are committed to acquire new ideas and accept responsibility for making their organization work (Hiatt-Michael, 2001, p. 113), thus providing an effective way of teachers' professional training. The development of learning communities is found to be associated with teachers professional development (Sargent & Hannum, 2009), one of the main concerns of school leaders. Research findings indicate that teachers' learning communities have a positive impact on student achievement while, at the same time provide a powerful way of teachers' attitudinal and behavioural change towards improvement in school practice (Bolam et al, 2005; Bullough, 2007; Hollins et al., 2004; Sargent & Hannum, 2009; Vescio, Ross & Adams, 2008). Professional learning communities can play an important role in school change (Hord, 1997, p.5), since they support learning through exploration, thus fostering an innovative climate (Bryk et al, 1999).

As literature on the advantages of schools functioning as learning organizations was accumulating (Diggins, 1997; Mulford, 1997; O'Sullivan, 1997; Stoll and Fink, 1996 in Silins, Zarins, Mulford, 2002), researchers attempted to identify the characteristics of learning schools and empirically define the construct. Among the dimensions proposed for the the structure of a learning organization were: promoting inquiry and dialogue, create systems to capture and share learning, connect the organization to its environment, provide strategic leadership for learning, information flow, innovation, tolerance for error, (Marsick & Watkins, 2003, p.139; Bowen et al, 2006, p.100). Therefore, research and innovation are key issues for such schools. At the heart of the learning school is the orientation to the production of new knowledge and its diffusion, that is, engaging with research. The learning school provides a working model for organizational learning comprising learning from research activities. In fact, schools which are more innovative have more characteristics of a learning organization (Geijsel, Van den Berg & Sleegers, 1999).

The learning school is a very important step towards the development of education, through adopting changes needed in school classrooms and the learning process. To this end, the following quote gives the tone: 'the rate of learning within the organization should be equal to or greater than the rate of change in the external environment' (Garratt, 1987, cited in Silins, Zarins & Mulford, 2002). However, systematic investigations on how schools might turn into learning organizations incorporating research and innovation are still scarce (Silins, Zarins & Mulford, 2002; Silins & Mulford, 2002).

Innovative School Climate and Research Culture

Scholars agree that the experience of implementing innovative programs is one of the most important elements of an effective organization and for this reason it is necessary to cultivate an innovative climate (Nonaka, 1994). The innovative school climate can be defined as the shared perceptions of all members of the school community regarding practices, procedures, and behaviors that promote the generation of new knowledge and practices (Moolenaar et al., 2010, p.627). All innovations begin with the creation of new ideas. New ideas are goals that have not yet transformed into products, while innovations refer to creative ideas which can be implemented (Ekvall, 1997; Rank et al., 2004). Creativity is the process of producing new ideas, while innovation is the selection, processing and refining of these ideas and their implementation into practice (Amabile, 1996; Gurteen, 1998). The concepts of creativity and innovation go hand-in-hand: creativity without at least some form of development, refinement, realization or

implementation is almost worthless (Boeddrich, 2004). Apart from the traditional psychological approach on creativity as a trait, organizational psychologists argue that the work environment can affect the creativity of individuals (Amabile et al., 1996; Isaksen & Lauer, 2002). Such an environment is directly related to the creative/innovative climate, established in an organization, so that the individuals' creativity has opportunities to bring results (Groth & Peters, 1999). The construct of a creative climate in a workplace and its dimensions were studied primarily in the context of business administration but later on, it was transferred to the field of education, as creativity and innovation seem to be the keys to school improvement and educational change (Abernathy & Utterback; 1978; McRoy & Gibbs, 2009).

School change and innovation, as a deliberate and planned action, ought to rely on previous research, its implementation must be accompanied by systematic data collection and these data must be used for the assessment of the procedure and the results of innovation. Therefore, the introduction of innovation is in itself a research procedure aiming to improve school effectiveness. The need for evidence-based practice has been noted by many scholars (Hemsley - Brown & Sharp, 2003; Davies, 1999; Hammersley, 2007) and is directly linked to a functional relationship between educational research and practice. Evidence based practice should be understood as a set of principles and a series of activities that can change the way people think about education (Davies, 1999).

A school that values learning for both students and teachers and is committed to evidence based improvement needs to efficiently implement existing research findings and also engage in research in order to support school change and innovation.

During the 80s Stenhouse (1981), argued that it is imperative to replace the view that knowledge in education is generated by experts and suggested the teachers' active role in educational research. He added that 'every class is a laboratory and every teacher is a member of the scientific community'

(Stenhouse, 1981, p.109). Other authors adopted this view and advocated the involvement of teachers in research (Elliott, 1991), since integrating research in the daily work of teachers is very likely to have positive effects on the learning process (Pepper, 1995). School teachers, who are actively involved in research activities, can become more reflective, obtain a better understanding of the climate of their class and decide on the actions to be taken (Oja & Pine, 1989), can reach scientific conclusions about their teaching practices and proceed to modifications or innovations in order to be more effective (Bagakis, 2002). Research should be the "food" for practice, as it feeds the cycle of reflection and the improvement of teaching and learning. Moreover, research activity for new interpretations of the educational process gives teachers new skills and promotes an innovative climate within the school. Carpenter (2007), advocates the necessity of establishing a research culture in schools by providing opportunities to the teachers for research. Through a case study, he showed that this can be achieved by teachers' training on research methods, access to educational research literature, diffusion of new knowledge and creation of research groups within the school.

Despite the numerous efforts attempting to establish links between research and practice, it is well known that little research actually makes its way into teachers' everyday practices. Many teachers are not convinced about the important role of research for their professional identity, perceive published educational research as irrelevant, and do not engage in conducting research themselves (Shkedi, 1998). But changing beliefs, attitudes and practices about using research in schools is difficult because of teachers' lack of familiarization with research aims and procedures (Burkhardt & Schoenfeld, 2003; Broekkamp & Van – Hout Walters, 2007). Factors that may contribute to the development of a strong research culture in schools include teachers' support by the school leader by providing motivation for conducting research within the school and caring for teachers' professional empowerment regarding this area (Worrall, 2004; Carpenter, 2007).

Transformational Leadership and Innovative Learning Schools

Research findings support the association of school leadership with the school culture and particularly with the research culture in schools (Hallinger & Heck, 1998). A strong, positive school leadership can develop a sense of security and confidence in teachers so that they can take risks to explore and try new ideas. School principals can create a climate of encouragement and support by appreciating the achievements of staff with formal and informal ways, so that new ideas can be implemented (Shalley & Gilson, 2004). Because of their important position, they can encourage teachers to engage in research and develop a culture of inquiry and reflection, thus fostering an innovative school climate (Edgerson & Kritsonis, 2006).

The current challenge is the leadership style that meets the needs of modern schools in creating appropriate conditions for effective teaching and learning processes (Deal & Peterson 1990; Leithwood & Jantzi, 1997; Oluremi, 2008). Transformational leadership is considered suitable for implementing new ideas and improving school effectiveness (Bass & Avolio, 1997). According to Bass (1999, p.11) "Transformational leadership refers to the leader moving the follower beyond immediate self-interest through idealized influence (charisma), inspiration, intellectual stimulation, or individualized consideration. It elevates the follower's level of maturity and ideals as well as concerns for achievement, self-actualization, and the well-being of others, the organization, and society." Cultivating an environment that promotes creativity and increasing the confidence of teachers, helps the diffusion of new knowledge and the motivation for more efforts for changes towards the common goal. Transformational leadership aims at increasing the organizational capacity of people in a community and pushes the organization to operate beyond the expected performance levels (Leithwood & Jantzi, 1990). The construct of transformational leadership has four dimensions, "the four I's": a) Intellectual stimulation, b) Individualized consideration, c) Inspirational motivation and d) Idealized influence (Bass & Avolio, 1993), but Geijsel et al. (2009) and Geijsel, Van den Berg & Sleegers (1999) suggested three dimensions in educational context: a) vision building, b) individualized consideration for the needs of members of the organization and c) intellectual stimulation.

Vision building inspires people to work for an important mission, pledging to commit to an environment that has shared values (Bass & Avolio, 1993). Teachers, who work in schools with a shared vision have a common mission and foster common values, thus promoting collegiality. Providing individualized consideration means trying to meet teachers' needs by assigning responsibilities according to their capabilities and talents, linking personal interests for professional development with the objectives of the team and the school. It plays a very important role because it offers recognition and encouragement, just like payment, so that teachers feel that they work in a safe, rewarding environment. The intellectual stimulation, the third dimension of transformational leadership, refers to principals encouraging exploratory thinking, innovation and teacher autonomy. Such stimulation helps the awareness about problems in school and enhances motivation to find solutions. Providing intellectual stimulation increases individual creativity and promotes collective innovativeness (Bain, Mann & Pirola-Merlo, 2001). Leaders facilitate change by encouraging teachers to take risks and try new ideas.

The transformational school leader is interested in teachers' professional development, fosters their need for self-realization and increases their interest for higher achievements. Members of such organizations shape their attitudes beyond the self –interest in order to serve the common vision and cultivate higher expectations. Transformational school leaders inspire teachers, suggest ways to empower school members to collaborate and increase teachers' capacity to develop new and more effective learning and teaching approaches (Hallinger, 2003, p.330). Transformational leadership improves the organizations through changes incorporating research and innovation (Sarros et al., 2008; Moolenaar et al., 2010).

The creative/innovative climate of an organization seems to be associated with all the dimensions of transformational leadership. This association had initially been studied within the field of Business Administration. Transformational leaders create working environments in which all members interact and set goals, face problems and find solutions and implement innovations which ensure the sustainability of the organization (Amabile, 1998; Ancona & Caldwell, 1987; Sarros et al, 2008; Gumusluoglou & Ilsev, 2009). Transformational leadership empowers people in an organization to create a participatory culture that encourages professional development and problem solving thus facilitating the development of professional learning communities (Hargreaves & Fink, 2006; Huffman & Jacobson, 2003; Vera & Crossan, 2004). Therefore, transformational leadership is the leadership style that is more likely to enable learning organizations. Indeed, studies have shown that there is a positive correlation between transformational leadership and organizational innovation (Jung et al., 2003; Gumusluoglu & Ilsev, 2009) while Sarros and his colleagues (2008) found an association with only two of the dimensions of transformational leadership: vision and individualized consideration. In the educational context, research showed that transformational leadership enhances innovative capacity and contributes to the fostering of an innovative school climate (Geijzel, Van den Berg & Sleegers, 1999; Moolenaar et al., 2010). Teachers who work in schools with a clear vision and mission, seem to have higher levels of creativity, tend to experiment with new ideas and implement them (Shamir et al., 1993).

Principals' Innovativeness

A necessary condition for schools functioning as learning organizations are school leaders that are themselves learning models (Bush & Middlewood, 2005). School leaders who are innovative, empower others in the school environment to challenge existing practices and find novel solutions to problems, while stimulating an ongoing discourse necessary for reflection (Coleman, 2007). School principals who are constantly updated on new research results and current educational trends are able to support with arguments their vision and implement innovative changes for school improvement. Innovative schools have principals who discover new ways of doing things and are creative with resources and professional development. Rogers (2003, p.22) described innovativeness as 'the degree to which an individual is relatively earlier in adopting new ideas than the other members of a system'. Therefore, the principal's innovativeness inspires and motivates others to work together to generate new ideas and master new skills, thus creating an innovative school climate. The question arises whether the principal's creativity affects the school climate and research culture only through his/her leadership style or s/he has an additional impact because of her/his role as a model for the profession.

FOCUS OF THE STUDY

As the Greek educational system is centralized and bureaucratic, changes and reforms are usually introduced top-down and schools have low levels of autonomy, there are many limitations regarding the promotion of research, change and innovation in schools (Sarafidou & Nikolaides, 2009). The Greek educational system has the characteristics of a centralized system with some degree of administrative only decentralization (Lainas, 1993, p.257). Despite the efforts for decentralization, the Ministry of Education and Religion keeps control of the national curriculum as well as educational policy and planning, making all decisions on educational issues. Regional and local educational authorities do not have substantial duties. Schools are obliged to follow the detailed syllabi and textbooks produced and provided by the Ministry. The result is that the Greek educational system is one of the most centralized educational systems (Andreou & Papakonstantinou, 1999, p.137; Saitis, 2007, p.56-57). However, guidelines issued by the Ministry in the form of law refer to teachers' duties to use modern and appropriate teaching methods based on students' needs and the characteristics of each subject. They also have to renew and enrich their knowledge on various school subjects and educational fields, not only through the in-service pedagogical guidance provided, but also through their own initiatives for further training. Furthermore, the Flexible Zone of Innovative Actions (FZIA) introduced in 2001 as part of the new Cross-Curricular Integrated Frame of Programs of Study (CCIFPS), allows teachers to use project-based learning for a few hours weekly (Kaldi, Filippatou & Govaris, 2011, p.37). Regarding principals, the same law refers to their duty to guide the school community to set high goals and ensure the conditions for their achievement, to establish a democratic and open to the society school, to guide and assist school teachers in their work and encourage them to take initiatives. Moreover, they have to be themselves a model for such actions.

The present study focuses on aspects of school leadership which are likely to predict a school climate promoting research and innovativeness in Greek primary education. Specifically, we examined the extent to which school principals, as perceived by teachers, are innovative and practicing transformational leadership and whether these characteristics of leadership are associated with a) a school climate facilitating creativity and innovation and b) positive attitudes of teachers towards educational research

Methodology

The research followed the quantitative approach in order to investigate associations between characteristics of school leadership promoting transformations and innovations with innovative school climate and teacher's attitudes towards research. For data collection, questionnaires were administered to participating teachers. Data were analyzed by using the SPSSv.20 software. Factor analysis (PCA method) was employed to provide the structure of teacher's attitudes towards research. After calculating scores for all scales and subscales, the normality of their distribution was examined. Innovative school climate and attitudes towards research were normally distributed (Kolmogorov-Smirnov test) while the leadership variables were nearly normal, as indicated by low skewness and kurtosis. Correlation and regression was used to explore associations and identify significant predictors. The significance level was set at .05 and is noted by * while significance at the level of .01 is noted by **.

Sample

Participants were 190 teachers (125 women and 65 men) of primary education in Greece. Most of them (85%) were working in primary schools and 17 were preschool teachers. Half of the teachers were between 30 and 50 years old (16% in the 31-40 age group and 34% in the 41-50 age group), only 6% were above 50 years old, while 44% were up to 30 years old. More than half of the teachers were working in schools situated in villages (39%) or towns (16%) and the remaining were working in cities (24%) or big urban centers (21%). On the average, they were working in the same school

for the last 3.4 years. Principals had at least two years of service in the same school. Although teachers participating in the study comprised a convenience sample, they came from different schools situated in various geographical areas of Greece. The basic characteristics of teachers in the sample were similar to those in the population. Specifically, the percentage of women in primary schools is 69%, 41% of primary schools is located in urban areas, the 14.0% in semi-urban areas, and the rest in rural areas (National Statistical Service of Greece, 2010). Due to the fact that the years just before the economic crisis in Greece, there have been a lot of recruits and more retirements, the majority of teachers is under 40 years old. In the sample, a percentage of 13% had a postgraduate degree. Involvement in research activities was recorded by 40% of the teachers, either as participants in a research project or conducting their own research, usually as part of the requirements for their postgraduate degree.

Measurements

Teachers' Attitudes Towards Educational Research

The scale was based on a scale by Williams & Coles (2003) and consists of 29 items concerning the value of educational research and its importance for teachers as well as their familiarity with it. Exploratory factor analysis of the responses, by the method of principal components, suggested four attitudinal components. After varimax rotation, the first component comprised 9 items concerning lack of knowledge and interest in educational research (Cronbach's α=.828), the second component comprised 6 items referring to usefulness of educational research (Cronbach's α=.812), the third component comprised 7 items referring to lack of reliability and applicability of educational research (Cronbach's α=.764) and the fourth component comprised 7 items regarding difficulties in accessing educational research (Cronbach's α=.769)

Transformational Leadership

Seventeen out of the 18 items of a scale measuring teachers' perceptions of Transformational Leadership in their school *(*Moolenaar et al, 2010) were used. One item was excluded as not applicable to the Greek context. The scale involved three subscales concerning a) vision building (Cronbach's α=.922, 4 items), b) individualized consideration for teachers' needs (Cronbach's α=.944, 5 items) and c) providing intellectual stimulation (Cronbach's α = .947, 8 items)

Principal's Creativity and Innovativeness

A 18 items scale, measuring teachers' perceptions about the innovative characteristics and creativity aspects of their principal was used, based on a broader inventory developed by Kousoulas (2006). The internal consistency of the scale was very high (Cronbach's α=.975).

Creative/Innovative School Climate

A 28 items scale measuring teachers' perceptions of creativity and innovativeness characteristics in their school climate. The items selected were based on similar inventories developed by (Kousoulas (2006) and Amabile et al. (1996). The internal consistency of the present scale was very high (Cronbach's α = .954).

The items in each scale are presented in the appendix. All measurements were Likert-type on a 5 point scale from 1=disagree to 5=agree. Scores for all scales and subscales were calculated as means of the corresponding item responses.

The questionnaire included a first part recording demographics and other factual data regarding studies and experience with research.

Results

Transformational Leadership and Principal's Innovativeness

On the average, teachers assign transformational characteristics to their principals to some extent, although a small percentage (18%) clearly sees them as transformational (score > 4.5). This is also the case with all three dimensions of transformational leadership style, with individualized consideration showing higher levels than vision building or intellectual stimulation (table 1).

Percentages of clear agreement (score>4.5) are 13% for vision building, 27% for individualized consideration and 18% for intellectual stimulation.

Table 1. Transformational leadership and correlations with principal's innovativeness

	Transformational Leadership[1]		Correlation with Principal's Innovativeness	
	Mean	**SD**	**Pearson's r**	**P**
Transformational Leadership total score	3.50	1.03	.877**	<.001
Vision building	3.38	1.10	.832**	<.001
Individualized consideration	3.66	1.10	.836**	<.001
Intellectual stimulation	3.46	1.03	.847**	<.001

[1]scale from 1=disagree to 5=agree

Principal's innovativeness, on the average, was also just above the neutral position (Mean=3.43, SD=.99), with only 12% of the teachers characterizing their leader as clearly innovative.

Correlations of transformational leadership and all its subscales with the principal's innovativeness were very high (table 1), indicating that principal's innovativeness tends to coexist with a leadership style that is transformational.

Innovative School Climate and the Role of Leader and Leadership

Both the principal's innovativeness and all the subscales of transformational style of leadership were highly associated with an innovative school climate (Table 2).

Multiple regression of innovative school climate scores on a) transformational leadership total scores and b) principal's innovativeness showed that both predictors were significant [beta=.628, P<.001 for transformational leadership and beta=.240, P=.004 for principal's innovativeness], jointly accounting for 71.5% of the variability of school climate. Results emphasize the overwhelming role of the school leader for the school climate. Specifically, the transformational leadership style as well as the principal's innovativeness (to a smaller degree) can powerfully predict the innovativeness of the school climate.

Teachers' Attitudes Towards Research

The structure of teachers' attitudes, following factor analysis consisted of four factors. The first factor (explaining 14.1%) involved 9 items with high loadings (>0,40), expressing lack of interest, knowledge and skills about educational research. The corresponding subscale had a mean=2.43 (SD=.76), that is, on the average teachers rather disagree with this attitudinal dimension, which means that they rather hold positive attitudes regarding interest in and knowledge about research. The second factor (explaining 12.3%) involved 4 items referring to the usefulness of research for the improvement of teaching. The corresponding subscale had a mean=3.84 (SD=.65), that is, on the average, teachers are quite positive regarding this component. The third factor (explaining 11.9%) involved 7 items showing reluctance about the reliability and applicability of research findings in practice. The corresponding subscale had a mean=3.35 (SD=.70), that is, on the average, teachers rather agree expressing a rather negative attitude regarding this component. Finally the fourth factor (10.5%) concerns teachers' difficulties in accessing research products. It includes 7 items regarding prohibiting factors like lack of time or technical support. The corresponding subscale had a mean=3.02 (SD=.80), that is, on the average, teachers neither agree nor disagree with this attitudinal component (Table 3). In summary teachers take some interest in research and think it is rather useful but they also think it is of limited applicability.

Teachers' perceptions about school innovativeness were not associated with their attitudes towards educational research regarding its usefulness or reliability. The other two attitudinal dimensions, namely knowledge/interest in research and

Table 2. Correlations of leadership with innovative school climate

Leadership	Pearson's r	P
Vision building	.790**	<.001
Individualized consideration	.816**	<.001
Intellectual Stimulation	.807**	<.001
Transformational leadership (total)	.840**	<.001
Principal's innovativeness	.789**	<.001

Table 3. Teachers' attitudes towards educational research and correlations with innovative school climate

Teachers' Attitudes Towards Educational Research	Mean	SD	Innovative School Climate Pearson's r
Lack of knowledge and interest	2.43	.76	-.178*
usefulness	3.84	.65	.110
Lack of reliability and applicability	3.35	.70	.035
Difficulty in accessing research	3.02	.80	-.175*

easy access to research findings had very weak correlations with innovative school climate. Therefore, results indicated that the innovative school climate did not imply more positive teacher's attitudes towards research.

Principal's innovativeness was not related to teachers' attitudes towards research, while the transformational characteristics of her/is leadership style were only weakly associated with certain positive aspects of teachers' attitudes towards educational research. Specifically, the less the teachers considered their principal as transformational the more difficulties they reported regarding access to research and the less knowledgeable and interested in research. The pattern was similar for all three dimensions of transformative leadership style. Teachers' attitudes concerning reliability and applicability of research findings and usefulness of educational research were not associated with leadership (Table 4).

Predicting Innovative School Climate

Identifying the combination of variables that significantly predict innovative school climate was attempted by employing stepwise multiple regression. Two of the subscales for transformative leadership style, principal's innovativeness as well as one of the teachers' attitudinal dimensions entered the model, accounting for a total of 72% of the variability in the dependent. The most influential predictors were: provision of individualized consideration by the school principal (beta=.323, P<.001) and principal's innovativeness (beta=.322, P<.001), followed by provision of intellectual stimulation by the principal (beta=.230, P=.010), while teachers' lack of knowledge and interest in research had a small negative impact (beta=-.096, P=.023). It should be noted that building a school vision as one of the components of transformative leadership

Table 4. Correlations of transformational Leadership with teachers' attitudes towards research

	Attitudes Towards Educational Research			
	Lack of Knowledge and Interest	Usefulness	Lack of Reliability and Applicability	Difficulty IN Accessing of Research
	r	r	r	r
Transformational leadership (Total)	-0,177*	0,122	0,018	-0,183*
Vision building	-0,121	0,120	0,061	-0,145*
Individualized consideration	- 0,202**	0,140	-0,007	-0,202**
Stimulation	-0,185*	0,087	-0,004	-0,178*
Principal's innovativeness	-0,032	0,066	0,101	-0,114

style did not have any additional effect, once the other two components as well as the principal's innovativeness were included.

FUTURE RESEARCH DIRECTIONS

Future research should expand the present study including more outcome measures pertaining to school's research culture as well as research and innovation activities. Moreover, both principals' and teachers' perceptions could be recorded in a nested design allowing for the treatment of data by multilevel analysis to examine interactions between the leader and teachers. In such a study measures of the principal's knowledge about and attitudes towards educational research could be included as well as relevant activities. Further research could also focus on the reconceptualization of schools as learning organizations, using appropriate measures of its immergence, and investigate the role of leadership style or the extent to which research is incorporated in this process.

CONCLUSION

Despite the limitations of the Greek educational system, most teachers in the present study found their principals displaying at least some characteristics of both innovativeness and transformational leadership, although few acknowledge them as being really transformational or innovative. It is interesting though that principal's creativity and innovativeness seemed to be a necessary condition for practicing transformational leadership. Such a conclusion is supported by the strong associations between all dimensions of transformational leadership and the principal's innovativeness found in this study. This is not surprising, since attitudes towards change depend on such individual characteristics reflecting one's natural predispositions when faced with innovations. As transformational leaders set goals and have strategies towards

accomplishing them, they have to find ways to overcome arising obstacles. It calls for both exploratory and combinational creativity to find solutions to new problems. Moreover, they have to encourage exploratory thinking and inquiry and motivate the generation and sharing of new ideas. But this may only be accomplished by principals who are themselves creative and innovative. This is why transformational leadership is considered suitable for implementing new ideas in order to improve school effectiveness (Bass & Avolio, 1997). Providing inspiration for changes towards a vision for the school and discover strategies to motivate others, needs somebody who has the ability to imagine the future school and invent the ways to make it true. So, one cannot expect a leadership style that is transformational unless the leader is a model of creativity and innovation.

Regarding the role of leadership in developing a creative/innovative school climate results indicated that principal's innovativeness as well as all three dimensions of transformational leadership were highly correlated with such a school climate. These findings are in accordance with previous research establishing the association between transformational leadership and innovative school climate (Moolenaar et al, 2010; Geijzel, Van den Berg & Sleegers, 1999). But what was additionally found in this study is that both transformational leadership style and principal's innovativeness were jointly strong predictors of an innovative school climate with an additive impact. That is, the association of principal's innovativeness with the innovative school climate is not mediated by transformational leadership style but has also a direct effect. This can be explained by the fact that the leader not only affects the community through her/his leadership practices but also functions as a model. To this end, it should be noted that a school environment characterized by innovativeness may enhance such traits as creativity for all school members including the principal.

Regarding educational research, results indicated that, despite most Greek teachers declare educational research as being generally useful, almost half are not sure about its reliability and applicability for them. Moreover, a substantial percentage clearly accepts they are not knowledgeable of or interested in research, and have difficulties in accessing research findings. This is in accordance with the literature stating that most teachers tend to value research only if it provides answers to questions of the 'what works' type and conforms to their beliefs and values (Pajares, 1992) instead of seeing research activities as 'knowledge mobilization', which intend to build capacity to apply research findings (Cooper, Levin & Campbell, 2009). It seems that there is still a long way to go before a culture that promotes research and inquiry in schools is established (Broekkamp & Van – Hout Walters, 2007) despite the need for evidence based practice (Hemsley - Brown & Sharp, 2003; Hammersley, 2007).

The next question addressed was whether transformational leadership and principal's innovativeness have any effect on the research culture of the school and particularly whether they enhance teachers' positive attitudes or eliminate doubts about the reliability and applicability of research. Results indicated that there is no such association, apart from a weak effect showing that transformational leadership facilitates access to research sources and raises teachers' interest in research, to a very small extend. That is, principal's innovativeness is not related to teachers' attitudes towards research, while the transformational characteristics of her/is leadership style are only weakly associated with certain positive aspects of teachers' attitudes towards educational research. Such findings are alarming, since school changes and innovations should be informed by research rather than make use of tacit knowledge gained from experience. Transformational leadership is supposed to improve organizations through changes incorporating both research and innovation (Sarros et al., 2008; Moolenaar et al., 2010), but this seems to be only partially true. If the school innovations, guided by transformational leaders,

were evidence based and systematically evaluated, one would expect teachers in such schools to have more positive attitudes regarding the usefulness and applicability of educational research. In fact empirical findings indicate that teachers' research literacy is associated with their attitudes towards research (Sarafidou, 2010). We conclude that a research culture is far from being established in schools even if they have a transformative and innovative leader.

SOLUTIONS AND RECOMMENDATIONS

The present study supports previous results indicating that school principals hold a unique position to influence the school members and school climate ensuring implementation of evidence based changes and innovations. If school leadership is to be more effective towards the goal of school development as a learning organization which is innovative, it has to be transformational and also oriented to incorporating the value of educational inquiry and research into the school culture. School leadership postgraduate programs as well as pre-service and in-service training programs should put more emphasis in all aspects of transformational leadership. Moreover, principals should be both innovative and research knowledgeable as well as capable of doing research. Creativity is not limited to natural ability or talent but has to do with a process of developing thinking and cognitive skills to make unforeseen connections and to generate new and appropriate ideas. Therefore it is imperative that the development of such skills should be a goal for programs preparing school leaders for innovative schools. However, the crucial point is that leaders should have adequate competence regarding educational research and be familiar with ways to promote it among teachers. This point has to be taken into account both in leadership training programs and also in the guidelines regarding criteria of suitability for school principals' positions. Teachers' training on research methods combined with their engagement in conducting research has the potential to change their attitudes towards educational research, by increasing their confidence in using research tools (Coleman, 2007; Rust & Meyers, 2006). This, in turn, helps them build habits of inquiry which encourage them to be innovative (Zeichner, 2003) and ultimately create a school culture of inquiry that is prone to initiate and sustain changes informed by research. Therefore, apart from teachers' pre-service and in-service training, it is the leader's responsibility to persuade teachers that research findings cannot indicate unambiguously what educators should do and that the impact of research on practice is complex and indirect (Bates, 2002), aiming at deepening their understanding of the field and this is how educational practice will ultimately improve. Therefore, school leaders should empower teachers regarding the research process in addition to motivate sharing of new ideas, thus promoting an environment receptive to evidence based change and innovation, in a supporting and friendly environment.

REFERENCES

Abernathy, W. J., & Utterback, J. M. (1978). Patterns of industrial innovation. *Technology Review*, *80*(7), 40–47.

Amabile, T., Conti, R., Coon, H., Lazenby, J., & Herron, M. (1996). Assessing the work environment for creativity. *Academy of Management Journal*, *39*(5), 1154–1184. doi:10.2307/256995

Amabile, T. M. (1996). *Creativity in context: Update to the social psychology of creativity*. Boulder, CO: Westview.

Amabile, T. M. (1998). How to kill creativity. *Harvard Business Review*, *76*(5), 77–87. PMID:10185433

Ancona, D., & Caldwell, D. (1987). Management issues facing new product teams in high technology companies. In D. Lewin, D. Lipsky, & D. Sokel (Eds.), *Advances in industrial and labor relations* (Vol. 4, pp. 191–221). Greenwich, CT: JAI Press.

Andreou, A., & Papaconstantinou, C. (1999). *Power and organization - administration of the educational system*. Athens: Nea Shinora. (in Greek)

Bagakis, G. (Ed.). (2002). *The school teacher as a researcher*. Athens: Metechmio. (in Greek)

Bain, P. G., Mann, L., & Pirola-Merlo, A. (2001). The innovation imperative: The relationships between team climate, innovation, and performance in research and development teams. *Small Group Research*, *32*(1), 55–73. doi:10.1177/104649640103200103

Bass, B. M. (1999). Two decades of research and development in transformational leadership. *European Journal of Work and Organizational Psychology*, *8*(1), 9–33. doi:10.1080/135943299398410

Bass, B. M., & Avolio, B. J. (1993). Transformational leadership and organizational culture. *Public Administration Quarterly*, *17*(1), 112–121.

Bass, B. M., & Avolio, B. J. (1997). *The full range leadership development manual for the multifactor leadership questionnaire*. Redwood City, CA: Mindgarden Inc.

Bates, R. (2002). The impact of educational research: Alternative methodologies and conclusions. *Research Papers in Education*, *17*(4), 403–408. doi:10.1080/0267152022000031379

Boeddrich, H.-J. (2004). Ideas in the workplace: A new approach towards organizing the fuzzy front end of the innovation process. *Creativity and Innovation Management*, *13*(4), 274–185. doi:10.1111/j.0963-1690.2004.00316.x

Bolam, R., McMahon, A., Stoll, L., Thomas, S., Wallace, M., … Smith, M. (2005). *Creating and Sustaining Effective Professional Learning Communities* (Research Report no. 637). London: DfES and University of Bristol.

Bowen, G. L., Rose, R. A., & Ware, W. B. (2006). The reliability and validity of the School Success Profile Learning Organization Measure. *Evaluation and Program Planning, 29*(1), 97–104. doi:10.1016/j.evalprogplan.2005.08.005

Broekkamp, H., & van Hout-Wolters, B. (2007). The Gap Between Educational Research and Practice: A literature review, symposium, and questionnaire. *Educational Research and Evaluation, 13*(3), 203–220. doi:10.1080/13803610701626127

Bryk, A., Camburn, E., & Louis, K. S. (1999). Professional community in Chicago elementary schools: Facilitating factors and organizational consequences. *Educational Administration Quarterly, 35*(5Supplement), 751–781. doi:10.1177/0013161X99355004

Bullough, R. V. (2007). Professional learning communities and the Eight-Year Study. *Educational Horizons, 85*(3), 168–180.

Burkhardt, H., & Schoenfeld, A. H. (2003). Improving educational research: Toward a more useful, more influential, and better – funded enterprise. *Educational Researcher, 32*(9), 3–14. doi:10.3102/0013189X032009003

Bush, T., & Middlewood, B. (2005). *Leading and Managing People in Education*. London: Sage Publication.

Can, N. (2011). Developing activities of learning organizations in primary schools. *African Journal of Business Management, 5*(15), 6256–6260.

Carpenter, B. (2007). Developing the role of schools as research organisations: The Sunfield experience. *British Journal of Special Education, 34*(2), 67–76. doi:10.1111/j.1467-8578.2007.00458.x

Coleman, A. (2007). Leaders as Researchers: Supporting Practitioner Enquiry through the NCSL Research Associate Programme. *Educational Management Administration & Leadership, 35*(4), 479–497. doi:10.1177/1741143207002429

Cooper, A., Levin, B., & Campbell, C. (2009). The growing (but still limited) importance of evidence in education policy and practice. *Journal of Educational Change, 10*(2-3), 159–171. doi:10.1007/s10833-009-9107-0

Davies, P. (1999). What is evidence-based education? *British Journal of Educational Studies, 47*(2), 108–121. doi:10.1111/1467-8527.00106

Deal, T., & Peterson, K. (1990). *The Principal's role in shaping school culture*. Washington, DC: Office of Educational Research & Improvement.

DuFour, R., & Eaker, R. (1998). *Professional learning communities at work: Best practices for enhancing student achievement*. Bloomington, IN: National Educational Service.

Ebbutt, D. (2002). The Development of a Research Culture in Secondary Schools. *Educational Action Research, 10*(1), 123–140. doi:10.1080/09650790200200171

Edgerson, D., & Kritsonis, W. A. (2006). Analysis of the Influence of Principal –Teacher Relationships on Student Academic Achievement: A National Focus. *National Journal for Publishing and Mentoring Doctoral Student Research, 1*(1), 1–5.

Ekvall, G. (1997). Organizational conditions and levels of creativity. *Creativity and Innovation Management, 6*(4), 195–205. doi:10.1111/1467-8691.00070

Elliott, J. (1991). *Action Research for Educational Change*. Buckingham, UK: Open University Press.

Fullan, M. (1995). The school as a learning organization: Distant dreams. *Theory into Practice, 4*(34), 230–235. doi:10.1080/00405849509543685

Fullan, M. (2002). The Change Leader. *Educational Leadership, 59*(8), 16–20.

Geijsel, F. P., Sleegers, P. J. C., Leithwood, K., & Jantzi, D. (2003). Transformational leadership effects on teachers' commitment and effort toward school re-form. *Journal of Educational Administration, 41*(3), 229–256. doi:10.1108/09578230310474403

Geijsel, F. P., Sleegers, P. J. C., Stoel, R. D., & Kruger, M. L. (2009). The effect of teacher psychological, school organizational and leadership factors on teachers' professional learning in Dutch schools. *The Elementary School Journal, 109*(4), 406–427. doi:10.1086/593940

Geijsel, F. P., Sleegers, P. J. C., van den Berg, R. M., & Kelchtermans, G. (2001). Conditions fostering the implementation of large-scale innovations in schools: Teachers' perspectives. *Educational Administration Quarterly, 37*(1), 130–166. doi:10.1177/00131610121969262

Geijsel, F. P., Van den Berg, R., & Sleegers, P. J. C. (1999). The innovative capacity of schools in primary education: A qualitative study. *International Journal of Qualitative Studies in Education, 12*(2), 175–191. doi:10.1080/095183999236240

Groth, J. C., & Peters, J. (1999). What blocks creativity? A managerial perspective. *Creativity and Innovation Management, 8*(3), 179–187. doi:10.1111/1467-8691.00135

Gumusluoglu, L., & Ilsev, A. (2009). Transformational leadership, creativity, and organizational innovation. *Journal of Business Research, 62*(4), 461–473. doi:10.1016/j.jbusres.2007.07.032

Gurteen, D. (1998). Knowledge, creativity and innovation. *Journal of Knowledge Management, 2*(1), 5–13. doi:10.1108/13673279810800744

Hallinger, P. (2003). Leading educational change: Reflections on the practice of instructional and transformational leadership. *Cambridge Journal of Education, 33*(3), 329–351. doi:10.1080/0305764032000122005

Hallinger, P., & Heck, R. (1998). Exploring the Principal's Contribution to School Effectiveness: 1980 – 1995. *School Effectiveness and School Improvement, 9*(2), 157–191. doi:10.1080/0924345980090203

Hammersley, M. (Ed.). (2007). *Educational research and evidence-based practice*. Thousand Oaks, CA: Sage.

Hargreaves, A., & Fink, D. (2006). *Sustainable leadership*. Jossey – Bass.

Hemsley-Brown, J., & Sharp, C.Hemsley – Brown. (2003). The use of research to Improve Professional Practice: A systematic review of the literature. *Oxford Review of Education, 29*(4), 449–471. doi:10.1080/0305498032000153025

Hewitt, M. A., & Little, M. (2005). Leading action research in schools. *State of Florida, Department of Education*, 1-30. Retrieved from www.myfloridaeducation.com/commhome

Hiatt-Michael, D. B. (2001). Schools as learning communities: A vision for organic school reform. *School Community Journal, 11*, 113–127.

Hollins, E. R. I, McIntyre, L. R., DeBose, C., Hollins, K. S., & Towner, A. (2004). Promoting a self-sustaining learning community: Investigating an internal model for teacher development. *International Journal of Qualitative Studies in Education, 17*(2), 247–264. doi:10.1080/09518 390310001653899

Hord, S. M. (1997). *Professional learning communities: Communities of continuous inquiry and improvement.* Austin, TX: Southwest Educational Development Laboratory.

Huffman, J., & Jacobson, A. (2003). Perceptions of professional learning communities. *International Journal of Leadership in Education, 6*(3), 239–250. doi:10.1080/1360312022000017480

Isaacson, N., & Bamburg, J. (1992). Can Schools Become Learning Organizations? *Educational Leadership, 50*(3), 42–44.

Isaksen, S., & Lauer, K. (2002). The Climate for Creativity and Change in Teams. *Creativity and Innovation Management, 11*(1), 74–86. doi:10.1111/1467-8691.00238

Jung, D. I., Chow, C., & Wu, A. (2003). The role of transformational leadership in enhancing organizational innovation: Hypotheses and some preliminary findings. *The Leadership Quarterly, 14*(4-5), 525–544. doi:10.1016/S1048-9843(03)00050-X

Kaldi, S. Filippatou, D., & Govaris, C. (2011): Project-based learning in primary schools: effects on pupils' learning and attitudes. *Education, 39*(1), 35-47.

Kousoulas, F. (2006, November). *Assessment of creativity within the school climate as a workplace: Results of a pilot research for the construction of a research instrument.* Paper presented at the 5th National Conference of the Hellenic Educational Society on "Greek Pedagogy and Educational Research". Thessaloniki, Greece. (in Greek).

Lainas, A. (1993). Educational management and curricula: The institutionalization of decentralization and wider participation [in Greek]. *Paidagogiki Epitheorisi, 19*, 254–294.

Leithwood, K., & Jantzi, D. (1990). Transformational Leadership: How Principals Can Help Reform School Cultures. *School Effectiveness and School Improvement, 1*(4), 249–280. doi:10.1080/0924345900010402

Leithwood, K., & Jantzi, D. (1997). Explaining variation in teachers' perceptions of principals' leadership: A replication. *Journal of Educational Administration, 35*(4), 312–331. doi:10.1108/09578239710171910

Leithwood, K., & Jantzi, D. (2003). Transformational leadership effects on student engagement with school. In M. Wallace & L. Poulson (Eds.), *Educational leadership and management* (pp. 194–212). London, UK: Sage. doi:10.4135/9781446216576.n9

MacBeath, J., & Mortimore, P. (2001). *Improving School Effectiveness.* Buckingham, UK: Open University Press.

MacGilchrist, B., Myers, K., & Reed, J. (1997). *The Intelligent School.* London: Paul Chapman.

Marsick, V. J., & Watkins, K. E. (2003). Demonstrating the value of an organization's learning culture: The Dimensions of Learning Organizations Questionnaire. *Advances in Developing Human Resources, 5*(2), 132–151. doi:10.1177/1523422303005002002

McRoy, I., & Gibbs, P. (2009). Leading Change in Higher Education. *Educational Management Administration & Leadership, 37*(5), 687–704. doi:10.1177/1741143209339655

Moolenaar, N., Daly, A., & Sleegers, P. (2010). Occupying the Principal Position: Examining Relationships Between Transformational Leadership, Social Network Position, and Schools' Innovative Climate. *Educational Administration Quarterly, 46*(5), 623–670. doi:10.1177/0013161X10378689

Nonaka, I. (1994). A dynamic theory of organizational knowledge creation. *Organization Science, 5*(1), 14–37. doi:10.1287/orsc.5.1.14

OECD. (2008b). *Innovating to Learn, Learning to Innovate.* Paris: OECD Publishing.

Oja, S. N., & Pine, G. J. (1989). Collaborative Action Research: Teachers' Stages of Development and School Contexts. *Peabody Journal of Education, 64*(2), 96–115. doi:10.1080/01619568709538553

Oluremi, O. F. (2008). Principals' Leadership Behaviour and School Learning Culture in Ekiti State Secondary Schools. *The Journal of International Social Research, 1*(3), 301–311.

Pajares, M. F. (1992). Teachers' beliefs and educational research: Cleaning up a messy construct. *Review of Educational Research, 62*(3), 307–333. doi:10.3102/00346543062003307

Pepper, G. L. (1995). *Communicating in Organizations: A Culture Approach.* New York: McGraw-Hill.

Rank, J., Pace, V. L., & Frese, M. (2004). Three avenues for future research on creativity, innovation, and initiative. *Applied Psychology, 53*(4), 518–528. doi:10.1111/j.1464-0597.2004.00185.x

Rogers, E. M. (2003). *Diffusion of innovations* (5th ed.). New York: Free Press.

Rust, F., & Meyers, E. (2006). The bright side: Teacher research in the context of educational reform and policy-making. *Teachers and Teaching: Theory and Practice, 12*(1), 69–86. doi:10.1080/13450600500365452

Saitis, C. (2007). The principal in the modern school: From theory to practice (3rd ed.). Athens: Self-Publication. (in Greek).

Sarafidou, J.-O. (2010, September). *Teachers' perceptions of educational research, research literacy and individual innovativeness as determinants of their attitudes towards school change.* Paper presented at the British Educational Research Association Annual Conference. Warwick, UK.

Sargent, T. C., & Hannum, E. (2009). Doing more with less: Teacher professional learning communities in resource-constrained primary schools in rural China. *Journal of Teacher Education, 60*(3), 258–276. doi:10.1177/0022487109337279 PMID:21191452

Sarros, J., Cooper, B., & Santora, J. (2008). Building a Climate for Innovation Through Transformational Leadership and Organizational Culture. *Journal of Leadership & Organizational Studies, 15*(2), 145–158. doi:10.1177/1548051808324100

Senge, M. P. (1990). *The Fifth Discipline: The Art and Practice of the Learning Organization.* New York: Doubleday Currency.

Sergiovanni, T. (1994). *Building Community in Schools.* San Francisco, CA: Jossey-Bass Publishers.

Shalley, C. E., & Gilson, L. L. (2004). What leaders need to know: A review of social and contextual factors that can foster or hinder creativity. *The Leadership Quarterly, 15*(1), 33–53. doi:10.1016/j.leaqua.2003.12.004

Shamir, B., House, R. J., & Arthur, M. B. (1993). The motivational effects of charismatic leadership: A self concept based theory. *Organization Science, 4*(4), 577–593. doi:10.1287/orsc.4.4.577

Shkedi, A. (1998). Teachers' attitudes towards research: A challenge for qualitative researchers. *International Journal of Qualitative Studies in Education, 11*(4), 559–577. doi:10.1080/095183998236467

Silins, H., & Mulford, B. (2002). Schools as learning organisations: The case for system, teacher and student learning. *Journal of Educational Administration, 40*(5), 425–446. doi:10.1108/09578230210440285

Silins, H., Zarins, S., & Mulford, B. (2002). What characteristics and processes define a school as a learning organisation? Is this a useful concept to apply to schools? *International Education Journal, 3*(1), 24–32.

Stenhouse, L. (1981). What counts as research? *British Journal of Educational Studies, 29*(2), 103–114. doi:10.1080/00071005.1981.9973589

Stoll, L., Bolam, R., McMahon, A., Wallace, M., & Thomas, S. (2006). Professional learning communities: A review of the literature. *Journal of Educational Change, 7*(4), 221–258. doi:10.1007/s10833-006-0001-8

Tajasom, A., & Ahmad, Z. (2011). Principals' leadership style and school climate: Teachers' perspective. *The International Journal of Leadership in Public Services, 7*(4), 314–333. doi:10.1108/17479881111194198

Van den Berg, R., & Sleegers, P. J. C. (1996). Building innovative capacity and leadership. In K. Leithwood, J. Chapman, D. Corson, P. Hallinger, & A. Hart (Eds.), *International handbook of educational leadership and administration* (pp. 653–699). London, UK: Kluwer Academic. doi:10.1007/978-94-009-1573-2_20

Vanderlinde, R., & Van Braak, J. (2010). The gap between educational research and practice: Views of teachers, school leaders, intermediaries and researchers. *British Educational Research Journal, 36*(2), 299–316. doi:10.1080/01411920902919257

Vera, D., & Crossan, M. (2004). Strategic leadership and organizational learning. *Academy of Management Review, 29*(2), 222–240.

Vescio, V., Ross, D., & Adams, A. (2008). A review of research on the impact of professional learning communities on teaching practice and student learning. *Teaching and Teacher Education, 24*(1), 80–91. doi:10.1016/j.tate.2007.01.004

Voulalas, Z., & Sharpe, F. (2005). Creating schools as learning communities: Obstacles and processes. *Journal of Educational Administration, 43*(2/3), 187–208. doi:10.1108/09578230510586588

Watkins, K., & Marsick, V. (Eds.). (1993). *Sculpting the Learning Organization: Lessons in the art and science of systematic change*. Jossey-Bass.

Watkins, K. E., & Marsick, V. J. (1996). *In action: Creating the learning organization*. Alexandria, VA: American Society for Training and Development.

Wikeley, F. (1998). Dissemination of Research as a Tool for School Improvement? *School Leadership & Management, 18*(1), 59–73. doi:10.1080/13632439869772

Williams, D. A., & Coles, L. (2003, June). *The Use of Research Information by Teachers: information literacy, access and attitudes.* A report for the Economic and Social Research Council.

Worrall, N. (2004). Trying to Build a Research Culture in a School: Trying to find the right questions to ask. *Teacher Development, 8*(2-3), 137–148. doi:10.1080/13664530400200020241

Zeichner, K. (2003). Teacher research as professional development for p-12 educators in the U.S. *Educational Action Research, 11*(2), 301–325. doi:10.1080/09650790300200211

ADDITIONAL READING

Avolio, B. J., & Yammarino, F. J. (2002). *Transformational and charismatic leadership: The Road Ahead.* Oxford, UK: Elsevier Science.

Avolio, B. J., Zhu, W., Koh, W., & Bhatia, P. (2004). Transformational leadership and organizational commitment: Mediating role of psychological empowerment and moderating role of structural distance. *Journal of Organizational Behavior, 25*(8), 951–968. doi:10.1002/job.283

Bass, B. M. (1998). *Transformational Leadership: Industrial, Military, and Educational Impact.* Mahwah, NJ: Lawrence Erlbaum Associates.

Day, C., Harris, A., Hadfield, M., Tolly, H., & Beresford, J. (2000). *Leading schools in times of change.* Buckingham, UK: Open University Press.

DuFour, R., & Fullan, M. (2013). *Cultures built to last: Making PLCs systemic.* Bloomington, IN: Solution Tree.

Earl, L., & Katz, S. (2007). Leadership in networked learning communities: Defining the terrain. *School Leadership & Management, 27*(3), 239–258. doi:10.1080/13632430701379503

Feldhusen, J. F., & Goh, B. E. (1995). Assessing and accessing creativity: An integrative review of theory, research, and development. *Creativity Research Journal, 8*(3), 231–247. doi:10.1207/s15326934crj0803_3

Fullan, M. (2005). *Leadership & sustainability: System thinkers in action.* Thousand Oaks, CA: Corwin Press.

Fullan, M. (2010). *All systems go: The change imperative for whole system reform.* Thousand Oaks, CA: Corwin Press.

Fullan, M. (2013). The new pedagogy: Students and teachers as learning partners. *LEARNing Landscapes, 6*(2), 23–28.

Geijsel, F. P. (2001). *Schools and innovations. Conditions fostering the implementation of educational innovations.* Nijmegen, The Netherlands: Nijmegen University Press.

Giles, C., & Hargreaves, A. (2006). The sustainability of innovative schools as learning organizations and professional learning communities during standardized reform. *Educational Administration Quarterly, 43*(1), 124–156. doi:10.1177/0013161X05278189

Hord, S. M., & Sommers, W. A. (2008). *Leading professional learning communities: Voices from research and practice.* Thousands Oaks, CA: Corwin Press.

Kilicer, K., & Odabasi, H. F. (2010). Individual innovativeness scale (is): The study of adaptation to Turkish, validity and reliability. *Hacettepe University Journal of Education, 38*, 150–164.

Kirtman, L. (2013). *Leadership and teams: The missing piece of the education reform puzzle.* Upper Saddle River, NJ: Pearson Education.

Könings, K., Gruwel, S., & Merrienboer, J. (2007). Teachers' perspectives on innovations: Implications for educational design. *Teaching and Teacher Education, 23*(6), 985–997. doi:10.1016/j.tate.2006.06.004

Lieberman, A. (2000). Networks as learning communities: Shaping the future of teacher development. *Journal of Teacher Education, 51*(3), 221–229. doi:10.1177/0022487100051003010

Northouse, P. G. (2013). *Leadership Theory and Practice* (6th ed.). Thousand Oaks, CA: SAGE.

Printy, S. M. (2008). Leadership for teacher learning: A community of practice perspective. *Educational Administration Quarterly, 44*(2), 187–226. doi:10.1177/0013161X07312958

Reid, J. A., Singh, M., Santoro, N., & Mayer, D. (2011). What does good teacher education research look like? *Asia-Pacific Journal of Teacher Education, 39*(3), 177–182. doi:10.1080/1359866X.2011.588592

Sleegers, P. J. C., Bolhuis, S., & Geijsel, F. P. (2005). School improvement within a knowledge economy: fostering professional learning from a multidimensional perspective. In N. Bascia, A. Cumming, A. Datnow, K. Leithwood, & D. Livingstone (Eds.), *International handbook of educational policy* (Vol. 2, pp. 528–539). Dordrecht, The Netherlands: Springer. doi:10.1007/1-4020-3201-3_26

Smylie, M. A., & Hart, A. W. (1999). School leadership for teacher learning and change: A human and social capital development perspective. In J. Murphy & K. S. Louis (Eds.), *Handbook of educational administration* (pp. 421–442). New York, NY: Longman.

Sparks, D. (2013). Strong teams, strong schools. *Journal of Staff Development, 34*(2), 28–30.

Spillane, J. P. (2005). Primary school leadership practice: How the subject matters. *School Leadership & Management, 25*(4), 383–397. doi:10.1080/13634230500197231

Van den Berg, R., & Sleegers, P. J. C. (1996b). The innovative capacity of schools in secondary education: A qualitative study. *International Journal of Qualitative Studies in Education, 9*(2), 201–223. doi:10.1080/0951839960090207

KEY TERMS AND DEFINITIONS

Innovative School Climate: Concerns attitudes, behaviors, practices and procedures that encourage the generation of new ideas and implementation of novel practices in school.

Learning School: The school which promotes individual and collective learning for students and teachers by expanding their capabilities to value, use, and produce research and innovations.

Principal's Innovativeness: The ability of the school principal to be creative, have new ideas and discover new ways of doing things.

Research Culture: The shared values and perceptions of members of an organization concerning the knowledge, practices, and procedures that promote research activity.

Transformational Leadership: Refers to the leader who urges the organization's members to operate beyond the originally expected levels of performance. The transformational leader develops a shared vision for the organization, promotes changes attending to the needs and professional development of its members and stimulates innovation.

APPENDIX

Transformational Leadership

The Principal of my school....

Vision Building

1. Refers explicitly at our schools goals during decision-making processes
2. Discusses the consequences of the school's vision for everyday practice
3. Uses all possible moments to share the school's vision with the team, the students, parents and others
4. Incorporates the school's vision and goals for the future to talk about the current issues and problems facing the school

Individualized Consideration

5. Takes opinions of individual teachers seriously
6. Listens carefully to team member's ideas and suggestions
7. Is attentive to problems that teachers encounter when implementing innovations
8. Shows appreciation when a teacher takes initiatives to improve the education
9. Helps teachers talk about their feelings

Intellectual Stimulation

10. Encourages teachers to experiment with new didactic strategies
11. Involves teachers in a constant discussion about their own professional personal goals
12. Encourages teachers to try new strategies that match their personal interests
13. Helps teachers to reflect on new experiences
14. Motivates teachers to look for and discuss new information and ideas that are relevant to the school's development
15. Stimulates teachers to constantly think about how to improve the school
16. Offers enough possibilities for teachers; professional development
17. Helps teachers talk about and explain their personal views on education

Principal's Creativity and Innovativeness

The Principal of my school....

1. Appreciates teachers' initiatives and invests in them
2. Acts as a model of creative work
3. Supports and promotes new ideas
4. Emphasizes the evaluation of the implementation of new ideas

5. Sets clear objectives and implementation plans
6. Cares to inform teachers about everything new in education
7. Inspires optimism about the school's future
8. Does not resort to scratchy solutions to emerging problems
9. Identifies issues calling for investigation
10. Tries to ensure access to information resources regarding educational research
11. Is a source of inspiration for teachers
12. Tries to explore and thoroughly analyze causes of emerging problems
13. Emphasizes the flow and sharing of materials and sources
14. Encourages teachers to apply new methods of teaching
15. Tries to clarify the objectives for addressing problems
16. Avoids negative critique of new ideas
17. Supports teachers' collaborative efforts for changes
18. Encourages teachers to engage with research

Creative/Innovative School Climate

1. The climate in this school has a focus on innovative activities
2. There is a climate of innovation and change
3. There is a clear orientation towards creative work in this school
4. There is a real interest in the implementation of innovative ideas
5. This school is open to new ideas
6. Teachers feel free to try innovative teaching approaches
7. Teachers are encouraged to propose original ways of addressing school issues and needs
8. Before a decision is being made many possible alternatives are discussed
9. Teachers' innovative efforts are recognized and rewarded
10. Teachers feel creative through their job
11. The climate regarding teachers' relations is negative
12. There are quite a few organizational problems in this school
13. The exchange of opinions regarding work in this school is facilitated
14. In this school the detailed exploration of problems is emphasized
15. Something new is being attempted in this school bringing optimism and satisfaction to most
16. The climate in this school facilitates free expression of every idea
17. Cooperation among teachers encourages the implementation of original ideas
18. Teachers feel free to choose learning activities
19. Working in this school helps the professional development of teachers
20. There is not enough time for exchange of opinions and ideas between teachers
21. Teachers avoid taking the risk of trying something new
22. Teachers are willing to freely contribute with their opinions
23. Teachers can choose their own ways to accomplish their aims
24. Teachers see problems as challenges for the production of new ideas
25. In this school it is impossible to find the necessary sources to introduce something new
26. New ideas are analytically discussed based on relevant evidence

27. Time is given to search for alternative solutions in school problems
28. New ideas are confronted by criticism in a defensive way

Teachers' Attitudes towards Educational Research

Lack of Knowledge and Interest in Educational Research

1. I don't have the skills to make use of research
2. I am not confident in my ability to interpret the findings of research correctly
3. I believe I am not able to contribute to research
4. I do not see how reading research could be of benefit to me
5. I find it hard to understand the statistical results of scientific articles
6. I find it difficult to find research information on the internet
7. I do not have the opportunity to discuss research with my colleagues
8. Research is not a teacher's job
9. The benefits of changing practice to reflect research findings would be minimal

Usefulness of Educational Research

10. Research is valuable in improving teaching quality
11. Teachers become more effective through their involvement in research
12. Keeping up-to-date with current research is an essential part of professional development
13. Research is valuable in improving teaching quality
14. I would like to make more use of research
15. A lot of research is relevant to my teaching

Lack of Reliability and Applicability of Educational Research

16. Much of the research I hear of/read bears no relation to practice
17. Research conclusions are not always justified
18. Often educational research is not reliable and accurate
19. Implications for practice are not made clear
20. Research is conducted by academics with no grounding in the real issues of teaching
21. Research findings are rarely generalizable to my own setting
22. I feel alienated by the language of research literature

Difficulties in Accessing Educational Research

23. Research reports/articles are not easily available
24. I do not read research because my school does not have a school library
25. I do not have enough time in my work to deal with the new ideas which are proposed by research

26. I cannot find research articles because my school does not have internet access
27. Nobody is ready to consult me on research matters
28. Finding research articles which are related to practice is difficult
29. I do not have time to find and read research

Chapter 16
Exploring the Impact of School Leadership on Student Learning Outcomes:
Constraints and Perspectives

Andreas Kythreotis
Cyprus International Institute of Management, Cyprus

Panayiotis Antoniou
University of Cambridge, UK

ABSTRACT

The chapter aims to explore the various models proposed in the literature related with the impact of school leadership on student academic achievement. In doing so, and drawing mainly from the mediate and indirect models, the chapter also discusses the role of various intermediate/moderate variables that facilitate the impact of principal leadership on student-learning outcomes. Results from a qualitative exploratory study that took place in Cyprus are also presented. This study developed a framework of school principals' actions and strategies that teachers considered as effective in relation to improving their quality of teaching and student outcomes. Some of the problems related with measuring the impact of school leadership on student achievement, such as issues of conceptual and operational definitions of school leadership and methodological issues in research design are also elaborated. Finally, implications for policy and practice on school leadership are discussed and suggestions for future research are provided.

INTRODUCTION

School leadership is internationally recognized as being a key factor for improving quality in education (Hargreaves & Fink, 2006). The concept has been narrowly defined, focusing on leadership functions directly related to teaching and learning (Leiberman, 1995; Kruger & Scheerens, 2012), and broadly defined, referring to all functions, actions and strategies that contribute to student learning (Sheppard, 1996; Marks & Printy, 2003; Leithwood & Jantzi, 2006). In trying to define

DOI: 10.4018/978-1-4666-6591-0.ch016

school leadership, others referred to the concept as direct or indirect. School principals who implement direct leadership are actively involved in the instructional enterprise of the school. Kleine-Kracht (1993) found that the direct leadership activities are the immediate interactions of principals with teachers and others about the classroom, teaching, student performance and curricula. On the other hand, principals who exercise indirect leadership, support efforts focusing on improving academic attainment through non-instructional approaches. Glasman and Heck (1992) support that indirect school leadership may focus on "such activities as decision-making, developing a vision and school purpose, setting goals, communicating expectations for performance, "gatekeeping" with parents and other community interests, and monitoring the work activities at the school site (p. 11).

Nevertheless, across all definitions and frameworks school leadership is directly or indirectly related to the processes of instruction and learning where school principals, teachers, learners, and the curriculum interact. In order to better understand the relationship between leadership and student achievement, during the last three decades, researchers have developed various models, referring to direct, indirect and reciprocal effects (Bossert, Dwyer, Rowan, & Lee, 1982; Hallinger & Heck, 1996, 1998; Leithwood & Levin, 2005; Pounder, Ogawa, & Adams, 1995).

Researchers in the earlier studies were using models in which the relationship between leadership in schools and outcomes at the student level was measured as a direct causal link. More recently, researchers started to use mediated-effects models, which hypothesize that leaders achieve their effect on school outcomes through indirect paths. Throughout the years, various potential mediating variables have come to light, including the mission of the school, educational vision and goals, staff motivation, teacher classroom practice, and student engagement (e.g., Kruger, Witziers, & Sleegers, 2007; Hallinger, Bickman, & Davis,

1996; Hallinger & Heck, 1998; Leithwood, Day, Sammons, Harris, & Hopkins, 2006; Leithwood & Levin, 2005; Mulford & Silins, 2003; Pounder et al., 1995).

Although considerable conceptual and methodological progress has been made, little is known about the paths through which school leaders can enhance organizational structures, the interplay with contextual factors and ultimately improvement of student outcomes (Kruger, Witziers, & Sleegers, 2007; Hallinger, 2003; Hallinger & Heck, 1996). From this perspective, in order to enhance further our understanding of the nature and impact of school leadership, this chapter aims to:

1. Describe the various theoretical models of the way school leadership impacts on student outcomes.
2. Discuss the contradictory results of previous studies and meta-analyses exploring the impact of school leadership on student outcomes.
3. Explore the main conceptual and methodological issues that could explain the contradictory research findings. Issues of definition, research design, instrumentation, data analysis and identifying and measuring appropriately intermediate / moderate variables, under the indirect effects model, are discussed.
4. Present the findings of a qualitative exploratory study searching for effective school principals' actions and strategies.
5. Elaborate on the implications of the existing knowledge-base and research findings for educational policy and provide suggestions for future research.

Based on these objectives, the following sections elaborate more closely on the role of school leaders and the nature of their impact upon student outcomes. In the first section, the classification of the various models describing the impact of school leadership on student outcomes is described. Then, the contradictory findings of research meta-analyses exploring the impact of school leadership on student outcomes are elaborated. The following sections aim to explain those contradictory findings drawing on conceptual and methodological differences among the various studies. In the next section, results from a qualitative exploratory study that took place in Cyprus are also presented. This study developed a framework of school principals' actions and strategies that teachers considered as effective in relation to improving their quality of teaching and student outcomes. Finally, implications for the development of policy on school leadership are discussed and suggestions for future studies that could enhance our understanding on the relation between school leadership and student outcomes are provided.

ISSUES, CONTROVERSIES, PROBLEMS

1. Modelling the Impact of School Leadership on Student Outcomes

In the past three decades, researchers have developed various models to understand the relationship between leadership and student achievement (Bossert, Dwyer, Rowan, & Lee, 1982; Hallinger & Heck, 1996, 1998; Leithwood & Levin, 2005). One of the first to develop a framework to classify the studies examining the effects of school leadership on student outcomes was Pitner (1988). Her framework referred to five theoretical approaches that could be used in studying school leadership effects through non-experimental research designs: (a) *the direct-effects model*, (b) *the moderated-effects model*, (c) the *antecedent-effects model*, *(d) the mediated-effects model and (e) the reciprocal-effects model.*

Earlier studies utilized models in which the relationship between leadership in schools and outcomes at the student level was measured as a direct causal link. *Thus*, the *direct-effects model* proposes that principal's leadership affects students irrespective of other variables within or outside school. While direct-effects studies are common in the literature, they have been criticized for making untenable assumptions about the nature of leadership in organizations. In addition, the process by which the school leader impact on students is rather hidden in a "black box" (Halllinger & Heck, 1996). As a result, these studies do not contribute significantly in our theoretical or practical understanding of the critical school processes through which school principals achieve an impact on school effectiveness (Leithwood et al. 1990).

The second model was based on the acknowledgement that the presence of a third, intermediate variable between principals' leadership and student achievement, could lead to different results (Hallinger and Heck, 1996, 1998; Witziers et al., 2003). For this reason, the *moderated-effect model* proposes that a third variable (in the school or in the environment) moderates the relationship between leadership and school outcomes through its presence or absence. Most of these studies used community socioeconomic and background factors (e.g. high or low school socioeconomic status). Such contextual variables were found to specify, to some extent, the type of leadership principals' exercise in their efforts to improve school outcomes (Halllinger & Heck, 1996).

The antecedent-effects model is more complex than the previous model. Unlike the moderated-effects model where the school leader is considered as the independent variable, in research based on the *antecedent-effects* model "the administration variable stands as both a dependent and an independent variable" (Pitner, 1988, p. 106). As a dependent variable, school principal behavior is subject to influence of other variables within the school and its environment. At the same time, as an independent variable school principal is an agent who acts to influence the actions of teachers, the nature of the school organization and the learning of students (Hallinger & Heck, 1996).

The fourth model, the *mediated-effects model,* assumes that some or all of the impact attained by administrators on school outcomes occurs through manipulation of, or interaction with, features of the school organization. In other words, managers achieve their results through influencing other people behavior and/or attitudes (Bridges', 1977). For this reason, these studies are more useful for theory building than direct-effects studies. As Hallinger and Heck (1996) argue, they are also of potentially significant for revealing paths by which administrators achieve practical results.

Finally, the *reciprocal-effects model* proposes that the relationship between school principals and characteristics of their schools are interactive. In other words, the principal adjusts his or her leadership behavior to processes and characteristics of the particular school. Interestingly, however, no studies had been explicitly designed to test the reciprocal-effects model, as elaborated in the following sections of this chapter.

Reviewing the use of those theoretical models in the literature, one could argue that the older or early studies were mainly based on the direct-effects model, whereas, most of the more recent studies adopt an indirect-effects model. For example, according to a meta-analysis of 40 studies published between 1980 and 1995 conducted by Hallinger and Heck (1996, p. 738), "the studies reviewed most frequently incorporated features of the antecedent-effects, direct effects, and mediated effects models. Less frequently were studies that used the moderated – or reciprocal-effects models in studying the relationship between principal leadership and school effectiveness." Likewise, Scheerens (2012) in presenting the results of several meta-analyses examining the impact of school leadership on student achievement found that research on school leadership effects moves from more simple, direct-effects models to more comprehensive indirect models, such as the moderated-effects model, the *mediated-effects model and* the *reciprocal- effects model.* Stud-

ies based on such indirect models are important since they could identify promising intermediary factors which, when stimulated by specific leadership behaviors, could have an impact on student achievement. Based either on the direct or indirect effects models described above, several studies tried to measure the magnitude of the impact of school principals on student achievement. However, research results vary considerably or have even produced contradictory findings. This issue is elaborated further in the following section of this chapter.

2. Measuring the Impact of School Leadership on Student Learning Outcomes

In order to enhance further our understanding of the impact of leadership on student achievement, researchers have examined more closely the role of school leaders and the nature of their impact upon student outcomes. Findings from school effectiveness and school improvement literature of the past 35 years indicate the important role of school leaders in student learning (Scheerens & Bosker, 1997, Teddlie & Reynolds, 2000, Leithwood *et al.,* 2006; Townsend, 2007; Scheerens, 2012). The general pattern found in such studies supports that principals exercise a measurable, though small, indirect effect on student achievement, whereas the direct effects of principals' leadership on student achievement seem to be very rare (Kythreotis, Pashiardis & Kyriakides, 2010). Likewise, as Kruger and Scheerens (2012) argue, direct effects of leadership on student achievement in basic studies are either not found or are present only in certain national contexts. Thus, studies thereafter (e.g. Hallinger & Murphy, 1985; Krug, 1990, 1992) explored leadership from the perspective of the mediated effects model. However, at the same time the literature demonstrates that both the nature and the degree of principal impact continue to be a subject of debate (Van de Grift, 1999) and research on the effects of school leadership on students' academic achievement has even produced contradictory findings (Antoniou, 2013a).

Particularly, a large number of studies found some effects (Fuller, 1987; Rutter et al., 1979; Andrews and Soder, 1987; Mortimore et al., 1988; Lezotte, 1989; Levine and Lezotte, 1990; Heck, 1992; Reynolds and Cuttance, 1992; Pashiardis, 1995, 1998, 2004), whereas other studies found that the effects are indirect, if not difficult to measure (Hallinger & Heck, 1996, 1998; Leithwood & Jantzi, 1990; Witziers et al., 2003; Edmonds, 1979; Fuller, 1987; Rutter et al., 1979; Andrews and Soder, 1987; Mortimore et al., 1988; Andrews and Bamberg, 1989; Lezotte, 1989; Levine and Lezotte, 1990; Heck, 1992; Reynolds and Cuttance, 1992; Cheng, 1994; Pashiardis, 1995, 1998, 2004). As Scheerens (2012) argues, within the context of empirical school effectiveness research, direct effects of leadership on student achievement in basic studies are either not found or are present only in certain national contexts; when they are present, they are relatively small (cf. Hallinger and Heck 1996a, b). Concerning the Netherlands, Van de Grift and Houtveen (1999) established that, school leadership in primary schools, as measured according to teacher perceptions, had no effect in 1989, while significant positive effects were found in 1993 and 1998. Witziers and Bosker (in Scheerens and Bosker 1997) reported positive effects for the USA, but not for other countries. An overall meta-analysis by Witziers et al. (2003) reveals a small positive effect, which essentially amounts to a weak correlation between school leadership and student achievement.

At the same time, studies utilizing indirect effects models yielded some more positive results. Particularly, Hallinger and Heck (1998) conclude that studies that consider context factors and school characteristics in investigating the effectiveness of the leadership in a school have more positive results regarding the influence of the principal on learning outcomes. Witziers et al. (2003) only found five studies investigating the indirect effects of instructional leadership on student achievement.

Chin (2007) presents a meta-analysis based on 28 studies from Taiwan and the United States. Of the 28 studies only 11 have student achievement as the dependent variable. Teachers' job satisfaction and teachers' perception of effectiveness are also used as dependent variables. Effect sizes are expressed in terms of correlations (Fisher's Z). The average effect size for the 11 studies that have included student achievement is 0.49. Effect sizes vary from 0.010 to 0.89. Median effect sizes are about 0.45. Robinson et al. (2008) conducted a meta-analyses on 22 published studies. Of these 22 studies 12 addressed instructional leadership, five transformational leadership and another five other kind of school leadership concepts. The average effect size, found for instructional leadership was 0.42, expressed in terms of a correlation this would be 0.21. For transformational leadership the effect size was 0.11 ($r = 0.055$), and for the other types of leadership 0.30 ($r = 0.15$). On the other hand, Creemers and Kyriakides (2008) computed the average effect size of leadership on the basis of 29 studies, both primary and secondary schools. The dependent variable was student achievement and their average effect size (Fisher's Z) was 0.068. This low effect size is in line with the effect size found in Scheerens and Bosker (1997), Witziers et al. (2003) and Scheerens et al. (2007). A very recent study based on 20,000 students enrolled in 250 American schools has found that "organic management," including supportive leadership and staff collaboration, had no effect on "achievement growth" (Miller & Rowan, 2006, p. 242).

Based on the above contradictory research findings we could argue that there is no consistent evidence to support the existence and the magnitude of the effects of school leadership on student achievement. Although a strong consensus has developed amongst policy-makers (e.g.,

Barber, 2000), inspectors (e.g., OfSTED, 1993), and academics (e.g., Fullan, 2003; Reynolds et al., 1996) that well-trained leaders have the ability to transform the organizational effectiveness of their schools, there is insufficient evidence to fully justify such arguments. Thus, in the following section we attempt to elaborate on the conceptual and methodological constraints that could explain to some extent the contradictory research findings and could, most importantly, guide future developments in the field.

3. Conceptual and Methodological Constraints

As has been elaborated in the previous section, previous research does not reveal similar and consistent findings in relation to the extent to which school leadership contributes to student achievement. This is important as such inconsistencies lead to a troubling gap between a widespread belief in leadership and the absence of hard evidence of leaders producing substantial improvements in school and pupil outcomes (Bush, 2004). Aware of this inconclusive evidence, the Department for Education and Skills (DfES), in the UK has commissioned research to further investigate the links between leadership and student outcomes (DfES, 2006). In this context, this section aims to identify some of the conceptual and methodological issues, explaining to a certain extent the differences in research findings. These points are not only important for understanding the inconsistencies in research findings, but they could also guide future developments and improvements in our efforts to identify the net impact of school leadership on student achievement.

Conceptual Constraints

The first issue is the problem of definition. There is no unique definition of the concept of principal's leadership, which is broadly accepted

(Hallinger and Heck, 1996, 1998; Witziers et al., 2003; Scheerens, 2012). Moreover, there is no universal paradigm or theory for examining organizational behavior that is valid in all social or organizational contexts (Hallinger and Heck, 1996, 1998; Brauckmann and Pashiardis, 2009). As Hallinger and Heck (1996) mention predominant notions of the principal's role have evolved from manager, to street level bureaucrat, to change agent, to instructional manager, to instructional leader, to transformational leader. A retrospective view of school leadership offered by Hallinger (2007) stresses the three key leadership models which have been identified by empirical research:

1. **1980's Instructional Leadership:** Forces from policy and practice converged with findings from research to create a policy on the instructional leadership role of school principals.
2. **1990's Transformational Leadership:** School leaders continued to be viewed as key players in school improvement but with greater interest in transformational leadership.
3. **2000+ Shared Instructional Leadership:** Both distributed leadership and instructional leadership have gained leverage.

Recent studies have adopted different definitions and different models of school leadership in examining the impact of leadership on student achievement. For example, effects of instructional leadership on student achievement were examined in studies such as those of Anderson (2008), Horng et al. (2010), Louis et al. (2010), O' Donnell and White (2005) and Shin et al. (2010). Likewise, effects of instructional leadership on student achievement were examined in studies such as those of Leithwood and Jantzi (2006), Louis et al. (2010) and Miller and Rowan (2006). Effects of distributed/shared/collective leadership on student achievement were examined in studies such as those of Heck and Hallinger (2009; 2010), Heck and Moriyama (2010), Leithwood and Mascall (2008).

The utilization of different models of school leadership, as described above, that focus on specific sets of leadership activities is problematic not only for defining leadership conceptually, but especially for the consequent development of operational definitions and the methodological decisions based on which the concept of leadership could be measured and observed. As Bruggencate et al., (2012) argues, because of this conceptual diversity, research on the impact of school leadership has failed to give conclusive answers. Recently, researchers have suggested using a more integrated model, which focuses on a broader set of leadership activities than those covered by the specific models applied in earlier research (Hallinger, 2003; Leithwood & Levin, 2005; Robinson, Lloyd, & Rowe, 2008; Thoonen, Sleegers, Oort, Peetsma, & Geijsel, 2011). From this perspective, for example, Kruger and Scheerens (2012) stress the role of all leadership frameworks such as instructional leadership, transformational leadership and distributed, in conceptualizing school leadership, and they move forward presenting an integrated model. Focusing on more generic functions of school leadership that might affect student and organizational outcomes is seen as promising to increase our understanding of the crucial role of school leadership for school effectiveness and school improvement.

Methodological Constraints

In addition to the conceptual issues of framing and defining school leadership, methodological issues of research design and measurement have also contributed to the inconsistencies of research findings in relation to the extent to which school leadership impacts on student achievement.

The first issue is related with the research design. Research on the relationship between school leadership and student achievement is mainly based on two types of research strategies: case study and large-scale quantitative studies (Leithwood & Richl, 2003; Scheerens, 2012). Evidence from qualitative case study - from a wide range of countries and school contexts - shows that successful schools have leaders who make significant contribution to the performance of their schools (Leithwood et al, 2004; Pont et al. 2008). Most of those leadership case studies start by identifying schools that are successful based on their outcome (unusually effective schools), including student academic learning and social goals and then move to analyze the characteristics of successful leadership in these schools. However, the results of such studies are difficult to generalize (Pont et al, 2008) due to issues related with sampling and statistical power. As Leithwood et al., (2004) support external validity and generalizability are missing from such leadership case studies.

On the other hand, the empirical evidence emerging from large-scale quantitative studies aiming to measure the impact of principals on student learning outcomes appears to be more ambiguous and inconsistent, with effect sizes ranging from non-existing to very significant, as already discussed in the previous section of this chapter. Although several reviews (i.e., Hallinger & Heck, 1996, 1998; Leithwood & Jantzi, 1990; Witziers et al, 2003; Scheerens, 2012) conclude that indirect effects of school leadership on pupil learning are small but statistically significant, leadership was found to explain only three to five percent of the variation in student learning across schools (Leithwood et al, 2004). We, therefore, argue that improvements in the research design, measures, instrumentation and statistical analysis could develop significantly our understanding of the leadership impact on student achievement and could reduce the inconsistencies found in the literature.

In relation to the research design, it is important to stress that most of the empirical studies on leadership impact are cross-sectional, based on survey data (Scheerens, 2012). These studies have inherent weaknesses to support casual inference, among other things due to the threat or reversed causality. Acknowledging this limitation, more recent studies have succeeded in addressing achievement gain over time by implementing longitudinal designs. The use of longitudinal data permits the examination of the progress of student achievement and of other school level variables over time, and thus could reveal interesting patterns in relation to the impact of school leadership (Teddlie and Reynolds, 2000; Antoniou, 2012b). Moreover, although different scholars have stressed the need to use more complex causal models, systematic empirical validation of mediated-effects models is scarce (Bruggencate et al., 2012).

In relation to the measures, most studies seem to ignore or not be able to capture important intermediary variables. The overall conclusion emerging from many studies and meta-analyses show that school leaders have a measurable, mostly indirect influence on learning outcomes. This means that the impact of school leaders on student learning is generally mediated by other people, events and organizational factors such as teachers, classroom practices and school climate (Hallinger & Heck, 1998). This finding underscores the powerful role of the school leader in helping to create the conditions for effective teaching and learning. School leaders influence the motivations, capacities and working conditions of teachers who in turn shape classroom practice and student learning (Pont et al, 2008). Thus, it is important to identify and collect data on appropriate measures (variables), which was not always the case for several studies. According to Leithwood and Jantzi (2008) there are four main categories of intermediary variables:

1.   Connection between setting direction (leadership emphasis) and academic climate (intermediary condition).

2.   Developing people (leadership emphasis) and professional capacity of the staff, cooperation and commitment of staff (intermediary condition).
3.   Redesigning the organization (leadership emphasis) and organizational capacity (intermediary condition).
4.   Managing the teaching and learning program (leadership emphasis) and instructional conditions (intermediary condition).

In a similar way Scheerens (2012) in reviewing several meta-analyses describes the intermediary variables that were found to "work". Those variables can be broadly categorized into: (a) Organizational capacity (improvement focus, standard setting, quality of student support, professional capacity of the staff, systematic evaluation), (b) teachers commitment and cooperation, (c) academic climate and (d) instructional conditions. It is important to note that both categorizations of mediator variables described above include quality of teaching. Under indirect effect models, quality of teaching could explain much of the variation in student achievement both within and between schools (Antoniou & Kyriakides, 2011; 2013b; Antoniou, 2012b; Kyriakides et al., 2009). In future studies, particularly when instructional conditions at classroom level would be added, use of multi-level structural equation modeling could be considered in a more effective manner.

In relation to instrumentation and means of data collection, leadership characteristics and intermediate variables are usually measured by questionnaires to principals, teachers and sometimes to students. Student outcomes are mostly achievement in basic subjects such as mathematics and reading. However, an important issue has to do with the validity of the instruments used. Particularly, not all research have utilized Structure Equation Modeling and Confirmatory

Factor Analysis to explore the content, construct, discriminant and convergent validity of the instruments employed to measure the research variables. At the same time issues of reliability and internal consistency need to be addressed. Especially issues of construct validity or explicit measures of school performance as a dependent variable may lead to different findings (Hallinger and Heck, 1998). Likewise, as Scheerens (2012) argues, questionnaires are often of a high inference and judgmental rather than of a factual nature. Particularly in the case of self-reports from school leaders social desirable answering patterns are hard to rule out. In addition, in some cases doubts might be raised about the independence of measures of leadership dimensions and intermediary variables. It may be the case of multi co linearity (Creemers, Kyriakides & Sammons, 2010), i.e., a positive correlation because they measure merely the same underlying dimensions. This occurs frequently when variables are composed from Likert scales and are then entered into a regression model, without checking the inter-correlation coefficients.

In relation to the data analyses, there is a huge variance of techniques used in several studies, some of which are not capable of capturing the net effect of school leadership on student achievement. Depending on the way research models the leadership impact on student achievement, direct effect models could be tested by multi-level analyses, whereas indirect effect models could make use of structural equation modeling, in which the data are usually defined or aggregated to the school level. Nevertheless, given the theoretical models of school leadership that we discussed and the long casual chain between leadership actions and student achievement results, small effect sizes should not really come as a surprise with the kind of research designs that were used. According to Cohen's standards for interpreting effect sizes, the results of several studies on leadership effects should be interpreted as negligible to small. Particularly, according to Cohen (1988) small effects are in order of r=0.10, medium effects r=.30 and large effects r=.50. However, several authors argue that Cohen's standards are to be considered as too conservative. And do not match the practical significance of malleable school variables (Richard et al., 2003; Baumert et al, 2006), this is why it could argue that an r of 0.40 should be seen as remarkable.

Summing up, the best that could be done in terms of improving the design of empirical leadership studies would be to try and to do justice to the complexity of indirect effect models by using longitudinal data, taking in consideration the multi-level structure of data, while possibly addressing reciprocal effects and non-linear relationships. Additionally, the use of appropriate statistical techniques such as multilevel structural equation modeling (multilevel SEM) could permit a more precise examination of the complex relationships between principals' leadership and student achievement. Having described the conceptual and methodological constraints that could explain some of the inconsistencies and contradictions in research findings, the next section presents the findings of an empirical study aiming to identify important mediator variables, based on teachers' responses. As has been elaborated, school leaders have mostly an indirect impact on learning outcomes. Thus, understanding those variables and developing a framework of effective actions and strategies is important, as this could guide our methods to measure more precisely the impact of leadership on student achievement. Since the study reported in the following section was conducted in Cyprus, information about the context of the educational system of Cyprus is provided below in order to enable an international readership to interpret the findings of the study.

The Cyprus Educational System

Cyprus is an island in the northeastern part of Mediterranean with a surface of 9,251 km² and a population of about 800,000, consisting of Greek Cypriots (84%), Turkish Cypriots (12%) and other minorities (4%). The economy of Cyprus mainly depends on tourism, trade, services and agriculture. One of the main characteristics of the educational system in Cyprus is that its administration is centralized and both primary and secondary schools are considered as government, and not as community, institutions (Pashiardis, 2004). Major policy and administrative decisions concerning curricula, staffing, textbook selection, adoption and/or production, and teacher training are made by the Ministry of Education and Culture (MOEC). In Cyprus education is provided through pre-primary and primary schools, secondary general, and secondary technical/vocational schools, public and private universities, and other non-formal institutions and centers. Primary education is provided free of charge and with no entrance requirements in public primary schools available throughout the country for all students aged 6 to 12. Primary schools are co-educational and provide mixed-ability teaching. A university degree in primary school educational studies makes a teacher eligible for inclusion in the official register of candidates for appointment. A teacher's appointment is based on a system where primary priority is determined by the year of submitting the application (on the principle "first come first served"). In relation to their teaching duties, primary school classes are not subject- specific but generic. Thus, the vast majority of primary school teachers is assigned at the beginning of the school year a new class–cohort of students and is responsible for teaching to the students of their class several subjects included in the national curriculum.

Teachers who have completed 12 years of service can apply for promotion to a senior post. Promotion to headship is a result and combination of a credit system which take into account the years of experience, external inspector's evaluations of teaching and academic qualifications. The application is supplemented with a personal interview with the Education Service Commission. Successful teacher applicants are first promoted to vice-principals, and after serving a minimum of 3 years as vice-principals they can apply for school principals. No leadership preparation programs are provided to the teachers wishing to be promoted (Michaelidou & Pashiardis, 2009). In addition, until recently, no provision was made in the system for the induction of newly promoted school principals, who were expected to rely on their university training and the informal support of colleagues to cope with the demands of their job. During the last years, the Cyprus Pedagogical Institute put forward a compulsory National In-service Training Programs for School Leaders. The program is compulsory for all newly promoted head teachers and deputy head teachers (for secondary education) and last for one academic year.

5. Results of a Study Developing a Framework of Effective School Principal Actions and Strategies Based on Teacher Responses

Research Aims

The study was conducted in Cyprus during the school year 2010 – 2011. It aims to explore the principal-teacher relationship as it relates to instructional leadership, by closely examining teachers' perspectives of formal and informal instructionally oriented situations. From this perspective, the actions, behaviors and strategies of school principals practicing exemplary instructional leadership are described and elaborated by the main actors of the teaching and learning process: teachers' themselves (Antoniou, 2012b).

In trying to investigate further the potential paths and the mediator variables by which school principals could maximize their impact on student outcomes the importance of exploring teacher perspectives has been emphasized (Blasé & Blasé, 1999). Exploring teacher perspectives of effective school principal action and strategies is justified not only with reference to the indirect or reciprocal effect models, but also by reference to the results of effectiveness studies over the last years. More particular, over the last two decades studies conducted in different countries revealed that the teacher effect is an important component of the school effect in explaining variation on student achievement in both cognitive and affective outcomes (Teddlie & Reynolds, 2000; Scheerens & Bosker, 1997; Creemers & Kyriakides, 2008; Antoniou & Kyriakides, 2011). The underlying rationale is that while organizational aspects of schools provide the necessary preconditions for effective teaching, it is the quality of teacher – student interactions that principally determines student progress. Thus, it is important to investigate teachers' perceptions of what they perceived to constitute effective instructional leadership approaches.

However, despite the importance of instructional leadership and of the central role of teachers in the teaching-learning process, few studies have directly examined teachers' perspectives on principals' everyday instructional leadership characteristics and the impact of those characteristics on teachers (Blasé & Blasé, 1999; Blasé, 1993; Short, 1995). Most of what we know empirically about leaders' effects on student learning concerns school leaders (Leithwood et al, 2004). This has made uncertain exactly what types of role behavior constitute effective instructional leadership. Indeed, a number of researchers have recognized that although some progress has been made in understanding the relationships among instructional leadership, teaching, and student achievement, most aspects of this complex phenomenon have not been adequately studied (Leithwood, Begley, & Cousins, 1990). Likewise, Short (1995) has called for more research into the effects of school principal actions and strategies on teacher behavior and the relationship of instructional leadership to teaching. As Leithwood et al., (2004, p.7) argue, "displacing the sloganistic uses of the term instructional leadership with the more precise leadership practices specified by well-developed leadership models is much to be desired".

For the purposes of the study a broad definition of instructional leadership has been adopted, consisting of all direct or indirect behaviors and actions of school principals that significantly encourage a focus on improving teacher classroom practices and affecting student outcomes (Leiberman, 1995). Exploring teachers' perspective of effective instructional leadership actions and strategies will enable us to develop a grounded instructional leadership comprehensive framework, describing the actions and strategies of school principals which are perceived as having a positive impact on teachers, on quality of teaching and ultimately on student achievement. The development of such framework could provide important information related to the extent to which teachers in Cyprus experienced effective instructional leadership in the same way as described by previous models reported in the literature (e.g., Duke, 1987; Andrews & Sodder, 1987). In addition, the results of this study and the conceptual framework emerged from the data could be utilized as the 'reconnaissance' stage of future studies aiming to introduce interventions towards the improvement of instructional leadership practices.

Research Methods

The methodology for the data collection and analysis was based on the Symbolic Interaction Theory (Blumer, 1969; Mead, 1934). Under this theory, human beings are viewed as social agents who are influenced by external factors (e.g., school policies, principal leadership) but who are also capable of maintaining distance and able to initiate individual action and meaning through interpretive processes. The basic premise is that human behavior is largely a function of how situations are perceived and interpreted. Symbolic Interaction Theory has also been used in previous studies in the field of educational leadership to address principal-teacher interactions (Blase & Blase, 1999) and student-teacher interactions

(Yogan, 2000). Consistent with symbolic interaction theory, no concepts from the literature were employed a priori to direct data collection.

Data were gathered from primary school teachers (n=90). The teachers participated in the study worked at primary schools from all over Cyprus, thus, data were collected from a variety of locations, in part to reduce the possibility that teachers would be describing the same principal, although this might have occurred to some extent. Involvement in the study was voluntary. Our teacher sample was predominately female, since the vast majority (about 85%) of primary education teachers are female. Particularly, our study sample consisted of nine male and eighty one female primary school teachers. Twenty-three worked in rural and sixty-seven in urban school locations. The average age of teachers was thirty-four and the average number of years in teaching was twelve. The educational level of study participants ranged from bachelor to doctoral degrees. Thirty eight teachers had Bachelor of Arts in Education, fifty-one teachers had master's degrees and one teacher had a doctoral degree.

The data were gathered using semi-structured interviews. Semi-structured interviews are particularly powerful primary sources of data collection since they have the potential to elaborate on a single topic in-depth and increase the probability of gathering a broad range of relevant data about the phenomenon under investigation (Cohen, Manion & Morrison, 2007). The interviews were based on several issues. In the first part, teachers were asked to provide detailed descriptions of the characteristics (e.g. actions, strategies, behaviors, attitudes) of a principal with whom they worked that had a positive impact on their classroom teaching. The teachers were also asked to give detailed examples of positive characteristics and particular actions and strategies that their school principal uses or has been using frequently. From this perspective, they were asked to describe specific "leadership events" or "leadership incidents" to refer to the principal – teacher - pupil interac-

tions. In addition, they were asked to explain how effective were these "incidents" and actions and in which aspects they have had an impact. In addition, they were requested to describe and give a real-life example of the effects (impacts) that the characteristics have on their perceptions and quality of teaching, to describe and illustrate their instructional school principal's objectives associated with the characteristics they identified above and to comment on how effective they perceived that the characteristic is in getting them to think or do what the school principal intends and why. The questions used in the interview were pilot tested in four teacher interviews taking place before the main data collection phase. The results from the pilot interviews led to a better clarification of the concepts mentioned in some questions.

Four postgraduate students, appointed as research assistants, conducted the interviews. All of them had experience in conducting face-to-face interviews and they were also offered additional training by a senior member of the research team. They were also observed and received formative comments during the pilot interviews. The interviews were recorded and transcribed for analysis. In cases where clarifications were required, the respondents were contacted through the telephone. This also ensured that the views of respondents had been accurately recorded by the interviewer. The data were analyzed using the constant comparative method, while two external researchers were also consulted on a regular basis when questions arose. Particularly, the data were coded according to guidelines for inductive-exploratory research and comparative analysis (Glaser, 1978, 1992; Glaser & Strauss, 1967; Strauss & Corbin, 1990). This form of analysis requires a comparison of each new element coded previously with emergent categories and subcategories. Thus, the development of the conceptual framework of effective instructional leadership actions and strategies was grounded to the data, with the data leading to the development of the theory (Glaser and Strauss, 1967).

Research Findings

The results of the study revealed five key components of principal actions and strategies which teachers considered as effective: (1) develop shared school vision and mission, (2) establish a school policy on teacher continuous professional development, (3) monitor student progress (4) promote school learning environment and (5) take the initiative to develop policies resolving emergent issues. It is also important to stress that the majority of the teachers mentioned the importance of establishing and promoting clear policies on all the above issues which were seen as the conditions for effective teaching and learning. Within these five components a variety of actions has been identified by teachers, such as school principals modelling key values and behavior, providing constructive and positive feedback, providing resources and materials and establishing a school-based monitoring system.

This study has provided an in-depth qualitative investigation of the school principals' interactions with teachers, as reported by teachers themselves. The results of the study indicate five major components (themes) of effective shared instructional leadership interactions. The findings echo research that discusses long-understood fundamental human needs for trust, support, and professional interaction (Herzberg, 1966; Maslow, 1954). Principals who are effective instructional leaders demonstrate fundamental respect for the knowledge and abilities of teachers, conceiving of "teacher as intellectual rather than teacher as technician" (Little, 1993, p. 129). The suggested research approach tries to take a different perspective of what is currently going on in organizations, by studying everyday social interaction in terms of 'leadership'.

6. Implications for Educational Policy on School Leadership and Suggestions for Further Research

This chapter discussed issues related with the impact of school leadership on student learning outcomes and elaborated on the several conceptual and methodological constraints identified in the previous studies and in the relevant literature. In the first section, the classification of the various models describing the impact of school leadership on student outcomes has been described. Reference has been made to direct and indirect models and more precisely to the Pitner's (1988) framework which refer to five theoretical approaches, namely the *direct-effects model, the moderated-effects model, the antecedent-effects model, the mediated-effects model and the reciprocal-effect model*. Researchers in the earlier studies were using models in which the relationship between leadership in schools and outcomes at the student level was measured as a direct causal link. More recently, researchers started to use mediated-effects models, which hypothesize that leaders achieve their effect on school outcomes through indirect paths (e.g., Kruger, Witziers, & Sleegers, 2007; Hallinger, Bickman, & Davis, 1996; Hallinger & Heck, 1998; Leithwood, Day, Sammons, Harris, & Hopkins, 2006; Leithwood & Levin, 2005; Mulford & Silins, 2003; Pounder et al., 1995). Interestingly, however, no studies had been explicitly designed to test the reciprocal-effects model, and this could be taken over by future studies in the field.

Then, the contradictory findings of research meta-analyses exploring the impact of school leadership on student outcomes have been elaborated. The general pattern found in such studies supports that principals exercise a measurable, though small, indirect effect on student achievement, whereas the direct effects of principals' leadership on student achievement seem to be very rare (Kythreotis, Pashiardis & Kyriakides, 2010). However, at the same time the literature demonstrates that both the nature and the degree of principal impact continue to be a subject of debate (Van de Grift, 1999) and research on the effects of school leadership on students' academic achievement has even produced contradictory findings (Antoniou, 2013a). Particularly, a large number of studies found some effects, whereas other studies found that the effects are indirect, if not difficult to measure.

Thus, in the following section we attempted to elaborate on the conceptual and methodological constraints that could explain to some extent the contradictory research findings and could, most importantly, guide future developments in the field. The first issue is the problem of definition, since there is no unique definition of the concept of school leadership (Hallinger and Heck, 1996, 1998; Witziers et al., 2003; Scheerens, 2012; Brauckmann and Pashiardis, 2009). As Hallinger and Heck (1996) mention predominant notions of the principal's role have evolved from manager, to street level bureaucrat, to change agent, to instructional manager, to instructional leader and to transformational leader. The utilization of different models of school leadership that focus on specific sets of leadership activities is problematic not only for defining leadership conceptually, but also for the operational definitions and the methodological decisions based on which the concept of leadership could be measured and observed. As Bruggencate et al., (2012) argues, because of this conceptual diversity, research on the impact of school leadership has failed to give conclusive answers. Thus, future studies should move towards adopting integrated models of leadership, focusing on a broader set of leadership activities than those covered by the specific models applied in earlier research. Focusing on more generic functions of school leadership that might affect student and organizational outcomes is seen as promising to increase our understanding of the crucial role of school leadership for school effectiveness and school improvement. Such an approach is also supported by the study briefly presented in this chapter, aiming to develop a framework of school principals' effective actions and strategies based on teachers' responses.

In addition to the conceptual issues of framing and defining school leadership, methodological issues have also been discussed. In relation to the research design, we could argue that there is a need to conduct mixed-methods approach projects, since in the past qualitative case studies (mainly from the school improvement strand) and quantitative large –sample studies (mainly from the school effectiveness strand) were kept in a kind of isolation and in parallel routes. By combining both strategies in a mixed methods design, future studies could overcome problems of external validity and generalizability, which is the case for case studies, and at the same time problems of interpretation and de-contextualization, which is the case for quantitative large-sample studies. Furthermore, in relation to the research design, it is important to stress that most of the empirical studies on leadership impact are cross-sectional, based on survey data (Scheerens, 2012). These studies have inherent weaknesses to support casual inference, among other things due to the threat of reversed causality. Acknowledging this limitation, future studies need to address achievement gain over time by implementing longitudinal designs. The use of longitudinal data permits the examination of the progress of student achievement and of other school level variables over time, and thus could reveal interesting patterns in relation to the impact of school leadership (Teddlie and Reynolds, 2000; Antoniou, 2012b). Moreover, although different scholars have stressed the need to use more complex causal models, systematic empirical validation of mediated-effects models is scarce (Bruggencate et al., 2012). At the same time, we argue that most studies seem to ignore or not be able to capture important intermediary variables. Since the overall conclusion emerging from many studies and meta-analyses show that school leaders have a measurable, mostly indirect influence on learning outcomes, future studies need to identify and measure appropriately important intermediate variables such as quality of teaching, school vision, teacher collaboration etc.

In the next section, we presented the results of a qualitative exploratory study that took place in Cyprus. This study developed a framework of school principals' actions and strategies that teachers considered as effective in relation to improving their quality of teaching and student outcomes. The results of the study revealed five key components of principal actions and strategies which teachers considered as effective: (1) develop shared school vision and mission, (2) establish a school policy on teacher continuous professional development, (3) monitor student progress (4) promote school learning environment and (5) take the initiative to develop policies resolving emergent issues. It is also important to stress that the majority of the teachers mentioned the importance of establishing and promoting clear policies on all the above issues which were seen as the conditions for effective teaching and learning. Within these five components a variety of actions has been identified by teachers, some of which could be taken into consideration in developing an integrated model of school leadership, in the context of Cyprus, and identifying important intermediate variables for future studies exploring the impact of school leadership on student achievement.

School effectiveness and school improvement literature during the past four decades has stressed the important role of school leaders (Pont et al, 2008). As Leithwood et al., (2004) argue, the role of principal leadership on student learning outcomes is significant and was found to be second only to classroom teaching. Thus, exploring

and understanding better the association between school leadership and student learning outcomes has important implications for educational policy related with the selection, the training and the skills required for effective school leaders. To this end, further studies are needed to strengthen our knowledge base and provide more conclusive answers to the extent to which and how school leader's impact on student achievement.

REFERENCES

Anderson, J. B. (2008). Principals' role and public primary schools' effectiveness in four Latin America cities. *The Elementary School Journal, 109*(1), 36–60. doi:10.1086/592366

Andrews, R. L., & Bamberg, J. D. (1989). *Teacher and supervisor assessment of principal leadership and academic achievement*. University of Washington.

Andrews, R. L., & Soder, R. (1987). Principal instructional leadership and school achievement. *Educational Leadership, 44*(6), 9–11.

Antoniou, P. (2012a). The Short- and Long-term Effects of Secondary Schools upon Students' Academic Success and Development. *Educational Research and Evaluation, 18*(7), 621–640. doi:10.1080/13803611.2012.707826

Antoniou, P. (2012b). *Unfolding Instructional Leadership: Developing a Framework of Effective Actions and Strategies based on Teacher Perspectives. CCEAM*. Commonwealth Council for Educational Administration and Management.

Antoniou, P. (2013). Development of Research on School Leadership Through Evidence-based and Theory-Driven Approaches: A Review of School Leadership Effects Revisited. *School Effectiveness and School Improvement, 24*(1), 122–128.

Antoniou, P., & Kyriakides, L. (2011). The Impact of a Dynamic Approach to Professional Development on Teacher Instruction and Student Learning: Results from an Experimental Study. *School Effectiveness and School Improvement, 22*(3), 291–311. doi:10.1080/09243453.2011.577078

Antoniou, P., & Kyriakides, L. (2013). A Dynamic Integrated Approach to Teacher Professional Development: Impact and Sustainability of the Effects on Improving Teacher Behavior and Student Outcomes. *Teaching and Teacher Education, 29*(1), 1–12. doi:10.1016/j.tate.2012.08.001

Barber, M. (2000). *High expectations and standards for all, no matter what: Creating a world class education service in England.* Keynote speech given at the Smith Richardson Foundation. Washington, DC. Retrieved February 4, 2002, from http://www.ncsl.org.uk/index.cfm?pageidOev_auth_barber

Baumert, J., Ludtke, O., & Trautwein, U. (2006). *Interpreting effect sizes in large-scale educational assessments.* Berlin: Max Planck Institute for Human Development.

Blasé, J. (1993). The micropolitics of effective school-based leadership: Teachers' perspectives. *Educational Administration Quarterly, 29*(2), 142–163. doi:10.1177/0013161X93029002003

Blasé, J., & Blasé, J. (1999). Effective instructional leadership: Teachers' perspectives on how principals promote teaching and learning in schools. *Journal of Educational Administration, 38*(2), 130–141. doi:10.1108/09578230010320082

Blumer, H. (1969). Society as Symbolic Interaction. In M. Arnold (Ed.), *Human Behavior and Social Process: An Interactionist Approach.* Houghton-Mifflin.

Bossert, S. T., Dwyer, D. C., Rowan, B., & Lee, G. V. (1982). The instructional management role of the principal. *Educational Administration Quarterly, 18*(3), 34–64. doi:10.1177/0013161X82018003004

Brauckmann, S., & Pashiardis, P. (2009). *From PISA to LISA: New Educational Governance and school leadership: Exploring the foundations of a new relationship in an international context.* Paper presented at the 90th Annual Meeting of the American Educational Research Association. San Diego, CA.

Bridges, E. (1977). The nature of leadership. In L. Cunningham, W. Hack, & R. Nystrand (Eds.), *Educational administration: the developing decades.* Berkeley, CA: McCutchan.

Bruggencate, G., Luyten, H., Scheerens, J., & Sleegers, P. (2012). Modeling the Influence of School Leaders on Student Achievement: How Can School Leaders Make a Difference? *Educational Administration Quarterly, 84*(4), 699–732. doi:10.1177/0013161X11436272

Bush, T. (2004). *The performance of leaders: Aims, impact and development.* Keynote paper presented at the British Educational Leadership, Management and Administration Society's Annual Conference. Stone, UK. Retrieved January 23, 2006, from http://www.shu.ac.uk/bemas/bush2004.html

Cheng, Y. C. (1994). Principal's leadership as a critical indicator of school performance: Evidence from multi-levels of primary schools. *School Effectiveness and School Improvement, 5*(3), 299–317. doi:10.1080/0924345940050306

Chin, J. M.-C. (2007). Meta-analysis of transformational school leadership effects on school outcomes in Taiwan and the USA. *Asia Pacific Education Review, 8*(2), 166–177. doi:10.1007/BF03029253

Cohen, L., Manion, L., & Morrison, K. (2007). *Research Methods in Education* (7th ed.). London: Routledge Taylor & Francis Group.

Creemers, B., Kyriakides, L., & Sammons, P. (2010). *Methodological advances in educational effectiveness research*. London: Taylor & Francis, Ltd.

Creemers, B. P. M., & Kyriakides, L. (2008). *The Dynamics of Educational Effectiveness: A Contribution to Policy, Practice and Theory in Contemporary Schools*. Abingdon, UK: Routledge.

Department for Education and Skills (DfES). (2006). *Programme of research, 2003080 Research into the impact of school leadership on pupil outcomes, tendered, expected start date 2.01.06*. Retrieved January 28, 2006, from http://www.dfes.gov.uk/research/programmeofresearch/index.cfm?type

Duke, D. (1987). *School Leadership and Instructional Improvement*. New York: Random House.

Edmonds, R. (1979). Effective schools for urban poor. *Educational Leadership, 37*(1), 15–24.

Fullan, M. (2003). *The moral imperative of school leadership*. Thousand Oaks, CA: Corwin Press.

Fuller, B. (1987). School effects in the Third World. *Review of Educational Research, 57*, 255–292. doi:10.3102/00346543057003255

Glasman, N. S., & Heck, R. H. (1992). The changing leadership role of the principal: Implications for principal assessment. *Peabody Journal of Education, 68*(1), 5–24. doi:10.1080/01619569209538708

Hallinger, Ph. (1983). *Assessing the instructional management behavior of principals*. (Unpublished Doctoral Dissertation). Stanford University, Palo Alto, CA.

Hallinger, Ph. (1992). The Evolving Role of American Principals: From Managerial to Instructional to Transformational'. *Journal of Educational Administration, 30*(3), 35–48. doi:10.1108/09578239210014306

Hallinger, P., & Heck. (1996b). The principal's Role in School Effectiveness: An Assessment of Methodological Progress, 1980-1995. In K. Leithwood, J. Chapman, D. Corson, P. Hallinger, & A. Hart (Eds.), *International Handbook of Educational Leadership and Administration, Part 2* (pp. 723-783). Kluwer Academic Publishers.

Hallinger, Ph. (2007). *Leadership for Learning: Reflections on the Practice of Instructional and Transformational Leadership*. Paper presented at Doctoral Seminar East Asia University. Tokyo, Japan.

Hallinger, P., Bickman, L., & Davis, K. (1996). School context, principal leadership and student reading achievement. *The Elementary School Journal, 96*(5), 527–549. doi:10.1086/461843

Hallinger, Ph., & Heck, R. H. (1996a). Reassessing the principals' role in school effectiveness: A review of the empirical research, 1980-1995. *Educational Administration Quarterly, 32*(1), 1, 5–44. doi:10.1177/0013161X96032001002

Hallinger, Ph., & Heck, R. H. (1998). Exploring the principal's contribution to school effectiveness: 1980-1995. *School Effectiveness and School Improvement, 9*(2), 157–191. doi:10.1080/0924345980090203

Hallinger, P., & Murphy, J. (1985). Assessing the instructional management behavior of principals. *The Elementary School Journal, 86*(2), 217–247. doi:10.1086/461445

Hargreaves, A., & Fink, D. (2006). *Sustainable Leadership*. San Francisco, CA: Jossey-Bass.

Heck, R. (1992). Principals' instructional leadership and school performance: Implications for policy development. *Educational Evaluation and Policy Analysis*, *14*(1), 21–34. doi:10.3102/01623737014001021

Heck, R. H., & Moriyama. (2010). Examining relationships among elementary schools' contexts, leadership, instructional practices, and added-year outcomes: A regression discontinuity approach. *School Effectiveness and School Improvement*, *21*(4), 377-408.

Heck, R. H., & Hallinger, Ph. (2009). Assessing the contribution of distributed leadership to school improvement and growth in math achievement. *American Educational Research Journal*, *46*(3), 659–689. doi:10.3102/0002831209340042

Heck, R. H., & Hallinger, Ph. (2010). Testing a longitudinal model of distributed leadership-effects on school improvement. *The Leadership Quarterly*, *21*(5), 867–885. doi:10.1016/j.leaqua.2010.07.013

Heck, R. H., & Marcoulides, G. A. (1990). Examining contextual differences in the development of instructional leadership and school achievement. *The Urban Review*, *22*(4), 247–265. doi:10.1007/BF01108463

Heck, R. H., & Marcoulides, G. A. (1993). Principal leadership behaviors and school achievement. *NASSP Bulletin*, *77*(553), 21–27. doi:10.1177/019263659307755305

Horng, E. L., Klasik, D., & Loeb, S. (2010). Principal's time use and school effectiveness. *American Journal of Education*, *116*(4), 491–523. doi:10.1086/653625

Hulpia, H. (2009). *Distributed leadership and organizational outcomes in secondary schools*. Universiteit can Gent (dissertation). Gent.

Kleine-Kracht, P. (1993). Indirect instructional leadership: An administrator's Choice. *Educational Administration Quarterly*, *29*(2), 187–212. doi:10.1177/0013161X93029002005

Krug, S. E. (1990). *Leadership and learning: A measurement-based approach for analyzing school effectiveness and developing effective school leaders: Project Report (Report No. BBB28334)*. Urbana, IL: National Center for School Leadership. (ERIC Document Reproduction Service No. ED327950)

Krug, S. E. (1992). Instructional Leadership: A constructivist perspective. *Educational Administration Quarterly*, *28*(3), 430–443. doi:10.1177/0013161X92028003012

Kruger, M., & Scheerens, J. (2012). Conceptual Perspectives on School Leadership. In School Leadership Effects Revised: Review and Meta-Analysis of Empirical Studies (pp. 1-30). Dordrecht, The Netherlands: Springer.

Kruger, M. L., Witziers, B., & Sleegers, P. J. C. (2007). The impact of school leadership on school level factors: Validation of a causal model. *School Effectiveness and School Improvement*, *18*(1), 1–20. doi:10.1080/09243450600797638

Kyriakides, L., Creemers, B. P. M., & Antoniou, P. (2009). Teacher behavior and student outcomes: Suggestions for research on teacher training and professional development. *Teaching and Teacher Education*, *25*(1), 12–23. doi:10.1016/j.tate.2008.06.001

Kythreotis, A., Pashiardis, P., & Kyriakides, L. (2010). The influence of school leadership styles and culture on student achievement in Cyprus primary schools. *Journal of Educational Administration, 28*(2), 218–240. doi:10.1108/09578231011027860

Leithwood, K., Begley, P., & Cousins, B. (1990). The nature, causes and consequences of principals' practices: An agenda for future research. *Journal of Educational Administration, 28*(4), 5–31. doi:10.1108/09578239010001014

Leithwood, K., Day, C., Sammons, P., Harris, A., & Hopkins, D. (2006). *Successful school leadership: What it is and how it influences student learning (Research Report 800).* London, UK: Department for Education.

Leithwood, K, Jantzi, D., & Steinbach. (1999). *Changing leadership for changing times.* Philadelphia: Open University Press.

Leithwood, K., & Jantzi, D. (2006). Transformational leadership for large-reform: Effects of students, teachers, and their classroom practices. *School Effectiveness and School Improvement, 17*(2), 201–227. doi:10.1080/09243450600565829

Leithwood, K., & Jantzi, D. (2008). Linking leadership to student learning: The contributions of leader efficacy. *Educational Administration Quarterly, 44*(4), 496–528. doi:10.1177/0013161X08321501

Leithwood, K., & Levin, B. (2005). *Understanding Leadership Effects on Pupil Learning.* Paper prepared for the UK Department for Education and Skills. London, UK.

Leithwood, K., Louis, K., Anderson, S., & Wahistrom, K. (2004). *Review of research: How leadership influence student learning?* Wallance Foundation.

Leithwood, K., & Mascall, B. (2008). Collective leadership effects on student achievement. *Educational Administration Quarterly, 44*(4), 529–561. doi:10.1177/0013161X08321221

Leithwood, K., & Riehl, C. (2003). *What We Know About Successful Leadership, Laboratory for Student Success.* Philadelphia: Temple University.

Levine, D. U., & Lezotte, L. W. (1990). *Unusually effective schools.* Madison, WI: The National Center for Effective Schools Research and Development.

Lezotte, L. W. (1989). *Selected Resources Complied for the 7th Annual Effective School Conference.* Rimrock: National School Conference Institute.

Lieberman, A. (1995). Practices that support teacher development: Transforming conceptions of professional learning. *Phi Delta Kappan, 76,* 591–596.

Louis, K. S., Dretzke, B., & Jantzi, D. (2010). Testing a conception of how school leadership influences student learning. *Educational Administration Quarterly, 46*(5), 671–706. doi:10.1177/0013161X10377347

Mead, G. (1934). *Mind, Self and Society.* Chicago: University of Chicago Press.

Michaelidou, A., & Pashiardis, P. (2009). Professional Development of School Leaders in Cyprus: Is it working? *Professional Development in Education, 35*(3), 399–416. doi:10.1080/19415250903069359

Miller, R. J., & Rowan, B. (2006). Effects of organic management on student achievement. *American Educational Research Journal, 43*(2), 219–253. doi:10.3102/00028312043002219

Mortimore, P., Sammons, P., Ecob, R., & Stoll, L. (1988). *School Matters: The Junior Years.* Salisbury: Open University.

O'Donnell, R. J., & White, G. P. (2005). Within the account era: Principals' instructional leadership behaviors and student achievement. *NASSP Bulletin, 89*(645), 56–71. doi:10.1177/019263650508964505

Office for Standards in Education (OfSTED). (1993). *Handbook for the inspection of schools (May 1994 Amendment).* London: HMSO.

Ogawan, R. T., & Bossert, S. T. (1995). Leadership as an organizational quality. *Educational Administration Quarterly, 31*(2), 224–243. doi: 10.1177/0013161X95031002004

Opdenakker, M., & Van Damme, J. (2006). Differences between secondary schools: A study about school context, group composition, school practice and school effects with special attention to public and catholic schools and types of schools. *School Effectiveness and School Improvement, 17*(1), 87–117. doi:10.1080/09243450500264457

Pashiardis, P. (1995). Cyprus Principals and the Universalities of Effective Leadership. *International Studies in Educational Administration, 23*(1), 16–27.

Pashiardis, P. (1997). Towards Effectiveness: What do secondary school leaders need in Cyprus. *British. Journal of In-service Education, 23*(2), 267–282. doi:10.1080/13674589700200018

Pashiardis, P. (1998). Researching the Characteristics of Effective primary School Principals in Cyprus. *Educational Management & Administration, 26*(2), 117–130. doi:10.1177/0263211X98262002

Pashiardis, P. (2004). Democracy and leadership in the educational system of Cyprus. *Journal of Educational Administration, 42*(6), 656–668. doi:10.1108/09578230410563656

Pitner, N. (1988). The study of administration effects and effectiveness. In N. Boyan (Ed.), *Handbook of Research in Educational Administration* (pp. 99–122). New York: Longman.

Pont, B., Nusche, D., & Moorman, H. (2008). Improving School Leadership: Vol. 1. *Policy and Practice.* Paris: OECD Publications.

Reynolds, D., Bollen, R., Creemers, B., Hopkins, D., Stoll, L., & Lagerweij, N. (1996). *Making good schools: Linking school effectiveness and school improvement.* London: Routledge.

Reynolds, D., & Cuttance, P. (1992). *School Effectiveness: Research Policy and Practice.* London: Cassell.

Richard, F. D., Bond, C. F. Jr, & Stokes-Zoota, J. J. (2003). One hundred years of social psychology quantitatively described. *Review of General Psychology, 7*(4), 331–363. doi:10.1037/1089-2680.7.4.331

Rowan, B., Dwyer, D., & Bossert, S. (1982). *Methodological considerations in the study of effective principals.* Paper presented at the Annual Meeting of the American Educational Research Association. New York, NY.

Rutter, M., Maugham, B., Mortimore, P., Ousten, J., & Smith, A. (1979). *Fifteen Thousand Hours: Secondary Schools and Their Effects on Children.* London: Open Books.

Scheerens, J. (Ed.). (2012). *School Leadership Effects Revisited: Review and Meta-Analysis of Empirical Studies.* New York: Springer. doi:10.1007/978-94-007-2768-7

Scheerens, J., & Bosker, R. (1997). *The Foundations of Educational Effectiveness.* Oxford, UK: Elsevier Science Ltd.

Scheerens, J., Luyten, H., Steen, R., & Luyten-de Thouars, Y. (2007). *Review and meta-analyses of school and teaching effectiveness*. Enschede, The Netherlands: Department of Educational Organisation and Management, University of Twente.

Shin, S.-H., & Slater, Ch. L. (2010). Principal leadership and mathematics achievement: An international comparative study. *School Leadership & Management*, *30*(4), 317–334. doi:10.10 80/13632434.2010.498995

Short, E. C. (1995). A review of studies in the first 10 volumes of the Journal of Curriculum and Supervision. *Journal of Curriculum and Supervision*, *11*(1), 87–105.

Teddlie, C., & Reynolds, D. (2000). *The International Handbook of School Effectiveness and Research*. London: Falmer Press.

Thoonen, E., Sleegers, P., Peetma, T., & Oort, F. (2011). Can teachers motivate students to learn? *Educational Studies*, *37*(3), 345–360. doi:10.10 80/03055698.2010.507008

Townsend, T. (Ed.). (2007). *International Handbook of School Effectiveness and Improvement*. Dordrecht, The Netherlands: Springer. doi:10.1007/978-1-4020-5747-2

Van de Grift, W., & Houtven, A. A. M. (1999). Educational leadership and pupil achievement in primary education. *School Effectiveness and School Improvement*, *10*(4), 373–389. doi:10.1076/sesi.10.4.373.3497

Witziers, B., Bosker, R. J., & Krüger, M. L. (2003). Educational Leadership and Student Achievement: The Elusive Search for Association. *Educational Administration Quarterly*, *39*(3), 398–425. doi:10.1177/0013161X03253411

Yokan, L. (2000). School Tracking and Student Violence. In D. K. Wysocki (Ed.), Readings in Social Research Methods (pp. 23-32). Belmont, CA: Thomson Higher Education.

ADDITIONAL READING

Bamburg, J. D., & Andrews, R. L. (1991). School Goals, Principals and Achievement. *School Effectiveness and School Improvement*, *2*(3), 175–191. doi:10.1080/0924345910020302

Blank, R. K. (1987). The role of principal as leader: Analysis of variation in leadership of urban high schools. *Journal of Educational Administration*, *8*(12), 69–80.

Brewer, D. J. (1993). Principal and student outcomes. *Economics of Education Review*, *12*(4), 281–292. doi:10.1016/0272-7757(93)90062-L

Brown, L. I. (2001). A meta-analysis of research on the influence of leadership on student outcomes. Unpublished Ph.D, Virginia Polytechnic Institute and state University, VA.

Day, C., Sammons, P., Hopkins, D., Harris, A., Leithwood, K., & Gu, Q. et al. (2009). *The Impact of School Leadership on Pupil Outcomes*. Nottingham, UK: The National College for School Leadership.

De Maeyer, S., Rymenans, R., van Petegem, P., van den Bergh, H., & Rijlaarsdam, G. (2007). Instructional leadership and pupil achievement: The choice of valid conceptual model to test effects in school effectiveness research. *School Effectiveness and School Improvement*, *18*(2), 125–145. doi:10.1080/09243450600853415

Eberts, R. W., & Stone, J. A. (1988). Student achievement. *Economics of Education Review*, *7*(3), 291–299. doi:10.1016/0272-7757(88)90002-7

Friedkin, N. E., & Logan, C. S. (1994). (1993). School leadership and performance: A social network approach. *Sociology of Education*, *67*(2), 139–157. doi:10.2307/2112701

Gift, W. (1990). Instructional leadership and academic achievement in elementary education. *School Effectiveness and School Improvement, 1*(3), 26–40. doi:10.1080/0924345900010104

Glasman, N. S., & Heck, R. H. (1996). Role-based evaluation of principals: Developing an appraisal system. In K. Leithwood, J. Chapman, D. Corson, P. Hallinger, & A. Hart (Eds.), *International Handbook of Educational Leadership and Administration, Part 2* (pp. 723–783). Netherlands: Kluwer Academic Publishers. doi:10.1007/978-94-009-1573-2_13

Hallinger, P. (1984). *Principal instructional management rating scale.* New York, NY: Leading Development Associates.

Hallinger, P. (1989). *What makes a difference? School context, principal leadership and student achievement.* Paper presented at the annual meeting of the AERA, San Franscisco.

Hattie, J. (2009). *Visible learning: A synthesis of over 800 meta-analyses relating to achievement.* New York: Routledge.

Heck, R. H., & Hallinger, P. (2009). *Testing a dynamic model of organizational leadership and school improvement effects on growth in learning.* Paper presented at the Annual Meeting of American Educational Research Association: Disciplined Inquiry: Educational Research in the Circle of Knowledge, San Diego, CA.

Heck, R. H., Marcoulides, G. A., & Lang, P. (1991). Principal instructional leadership and school achievement: The application of discriminant techniques. *School Effectiveness and School Improvement, 2*(2), 115–135. doi:10.1080/0924345910020204

Krug, S. E. (1992). Instructional leadership, school instructional climate and student learning outcomes. Washington, DC: Offices of Educational Research and Improvement.

Leithwood, K., & Jantzi, D. (2000). Principal and teacher leadership effects: A replication. *School Leadership & Management, 20*(4), 415–434. doi:10.1080/713696963

Leithwood, K., Patten, S., & Jantzi, D. (2000). Testing a conception of how school leadership influences student learning. *Educational Administration Quarterly, 46*(5), 671–706. doi:10.1177/0013161X10377347

Leitner, D. (1994). Do principals, affect student outcomes: An organizational perspectives. *School Effectiveness and School Improvement, 5*(3), 219–238. doi:10.1080/0924345940050302

Louis, K. S., Dretzke, B., & Wahlstrom, K. (2010). How does leadership affect student achievement? Results from a national US survey. *School Effectiveness and School Improvement, 21*(3), 315–336. doi:10.1080/09243453.2010.486586

Marks, H. M., & Printy, S. M. (2003). Principal leadership and school performance: An Integration of transformational and instructional leadership. *Educational Administration Quarterly, 39*(3), 370–397. doi:10.1177/0013161X03253412

Marzano, R. J., Waters, T., & McNulty, B. A. (2005). *School leadership that works: From research to results.* Alexandria, VA: Association to Supervision and Curriculum Development.

Mulford, B. (2006). Leadership for improving the quality of secondary education: Some international development. *New Zealand Journal of Educational Leadership, 21*(1), 7–27.

Reitzug, U. C. (1989). Principal-teacher interactions in instructionally effective and ordinary elementary schools. *Urban Education, 24*(1), 38–58. doi:10.1177/0042085989024001003

Robinson, V. M. J., Lloyd, C., & Rowe, K. J. (2008). The impact leadership on student achievement: An analysis of the differential effects of leadership type. *Educational Administration Quarterly*, *44*(5), 635–674. doi:10.1177/0013161X08321509

Ross, J. A., & Gray, P. (2006). School leadership and student achievement: The mediating effects on teacher beliefs. *Canadian Journal of Education*, *29*(3), 798–822. doi:10.2307/20054196

Scheerens, J. (2008). *Review of research on school and instructional effectiveness*. Enschede: University of Twente, Department of Education and Organization Management.

Scheerens, J., & Witziers, B. (2005). *Educational leadership and student performance*. Enschede: University of Twente, Department of Education and Organization Management.

Silins, H., & Mulford, B. (2004). School as learning organizations: Effects on teacher leadership and student outcome. *School Effectiveness and School Improvement*, *15*(3-4), 443–446. doi:10.1080/09243450512331383272

Southworh, G. (2002). Instructional leadership in schools: Reflections and empirical evidence. *School Leadership & Management*, *22*(1), 73–92. doi:10.1080/13632430220143042

Stringe, H. C. (1993). Defining the principalship: Instructional leader or middle manager. *NASSP Bulletin*, *77*(553), 1–7. doi:10.1177/019263659307755302

Supovitz, J., Sirinides, Ph., & May, H. (2010). How principals and peers influence teaching and learning. *Educational Administration Quarterly*, *46*(1), 31–56. doi:10.1177/1094670509353043

Ten Bruggencate, G., Luyten, H., & Scheerens, J. (2010). *Qualitative analysis of internal data. Exploring indirect effect models of school leadership*. Enschede: University of Twente.

Waters, T., Marzano, R. J., & McNulty, B. A. (2003). *Balanced leadership: What 30 years of research tell us about of leadership on student achievement. A working paper*. Midcontinent Regional Educational Lab., Aurora, CO (BBB23081). Research for Education and Learning.

Wiseman, A. W. (2002, February). *Principals' instructional management activity and student achievement: A meta-analysis*. Paper presented at the Annual Meeting of the Southwestern Educational Research Association, Austin, TX.

KEY TERMS AND DEFINITIONS

Antecedent-Effects Model of School Leadership on Student Achievement: This model proposes that administration variable stands as both a dependent and an independent variable (Pitner, 1988).

Direct-Effects Model of School Leadership on Student Achievement: This model proposes that principal's leadership affects students irrespective of other variables within or outside school (Pitner, 1988).

Distributed Leadership: Participative, bottom up decision making, collaborative practices of leadership that connect hierarchical leadership to instructional leadership and transformational leadership (Hulpia, 2009).

Extended Instructional Leadership: The strategies which broaden the scope of four leadership practices namely managing the instructional program. Extended instructional leadership includes three types: (a) Defining a mission for the school; (b) Managing the curriculum and instruction (narrow instructional leadership; (c) Promoting a learning climate favourable for student and learning (Hallinger, 1983; Kruger & Scheerens, 2012).

Instructional Leadership: Behaviors or actions that the principal, directly or indirectly, engages into coordinate the instructional program and influence student achievement outcome. These behaviors or actions may include assisting teachers in the delivery of instruction, selecting curricular materials, or monitoring the implementation of instructional goals and objectives (Jordan, 1986; Wright, 1991; Kleine-Kracht, 1993).

Mediated-Effects Model of School Leadership on Student Achievement: This model proposes that some or all of the impact attained by administrators on school outcomes occurs through manipulation of, or interaction with, features of the school organization (Pitner, 1988).

Models of Leadership Effects on Students' Achievement: These models conceptualize the possible theoretical approaches that could be used in studying leadership impacts through non-experimental research designs (Pitner, 1988).

Moderated-Effect Model of School Leadership on Student Achievement: This Model proposes that a third variable (in the school or in the environment) moderates the relationship between leadership and school outcomes through its presence or absence (Pitner, 1988).

Narrow Instructional Leadership: Four leadership practices namely managing the instructional program. These four tasks related to curriculum and instruction are the following: (a) Promoting an orderly and stimulating work climate; (b) Emphasizing basic skills; (c) Performing student monitoring; (d) Co-operating student monitoring) (Hallinger, 1983; Kruger & Scheerens, 2012).

Reciprocal-Effects Model of School Leadership: This model proposes that the relationship between school principals and characteristics of their schools are interactive (Pitner, 1988).

Transformational Leadership: The leader who urges the organization's members to operate beyond the originally expected levels of performance. The transformational leader develops a shared vision for the organization, promotes changes attending to the needs and professional development of its members and stimulates innovation (Bass Avolio, 1993; Leithwood Jantzi & Steinbach, 1999).

Chapter 17

The Relationship between Emotional Competence and Instructional Leadership and Their Association with Learner Achievement

Bennie Grobler
University of Johannesburg, South Africa

ABSTRACT

The mandated approach to school leadership in South Africa has not produced any significant improvement in learner achievement during the last decade. A new approach to leadership with greater emphasis on the ideographic dimension of school leadership is necessary. This chapter investigates how principals' can utilize emotional competence and instructional leadership to influence learner achievement. The structures of emotional competence and instructional leadership are investigated using factor analysis and Structural Equation Modeling. These constructs are linked to learner achievement data. Intrapersonal emotional competence impacted directly on interpersonal emotional competence, which in turn, impacted directly and indirectly on all the components of instructional leadership. The postulated pathways in the model were statistically significant and substantively meaningful. The model suggested by this research indicates that learner achievement can be influenced in a collaborative way by school leaders via utilization of emotional competence and the four components of instructional leadership.

INTRODUCTION

Leadership is a multifaceted phenomenon and as such it has often been metaphorically linked to the many facets of a diamond. Which facets in a diamond sparkle and shine depend on which facets catch and reflect the light? In a similar vein the school principal also has many facets or dimensions involved in his/her leadership activities. In this chapter the light will fall on a facet which all principals have but which some use more effectively than others namely emotional intelligence or competence. The utilization of this often hidden facet in conjunction with a second

DOI: 10.4018/978-1-4666-6591-0.ch017

leadership facet or dimension namely instructional leadership, to influence learner achievement, is the topic of this chapter.

BACKGROUND TO THE RESEARCH PROBLEM

The practice of school leadership in South African public schools is guided by mandates published in Government gazettes. Among other things the school principal is responsible for the professional management of the school, implementing all curricular activities and for implementing policy and legislation (PAM, 2003; SA, 2007). Furthermore the action plan of 2014 for South African Schools (SA, 2010; DoBE, 2010a) states that by 2025 a school principal "must be seen to ensure that teaching in the school takes place as it should, according to the national curriculum (DoBE, 2010b), and understand that his or her role as a leader is to be responsible to promote harmony and a sound work ethic within the school community and beyond". School leadership in South Africa, like many other countries, is thus impacted by State and District policies and procedures as well as many other variables. Learner achievement is typically measured via standardized Annual National Assessments. School principals are held accountable for learner achievements in these standardized national assessments yet they only have an indirect influence on learner achievement. Compliance to the mandated national curriculum with its emphasis on measurement of learner achievements could possibly lead to an over emphasis of the bureaucratic role expectations characterized by a prominence of hierarchical authority, rules and regulations and specialization and a decrease in the ideographic expectations such as the use of emotional competence to influence people towards achieving the set goals. Hence aspects of leadership such as emotional competence in influencing learner achievement could be deemed to be less important. Furthermore it could be inferred that

if the learners' academic achievements in terms of minimum average pass percentages in Literacy and Mathematics, as provided in the action plan (DoBE, 2010b), are achieved then the principal has been successful in ensuring that teaching in the school takes place as it should. This chapter argues that the most effective means towards achieving the learning targets as set out in the National Curriculum and Assessment Policy Statement (CAPS) (SA, 2011) and the action plan for 2014 (DBE, 2010b) is for school principals to be instructional leaders as this involves them directly in the teaching and learning process. However, in order to achieve these mandated targets the principal needs to influence teachers regarding the importance of meeting these mandated learner academic targets. To obtain achievement targets through other people can be both cognitively and emotionally challenging as the leader has to be able to mange his/her own emotions as well as those of others (Cline & Necochea, 2000). Leadership in schools thus needs persons who are both cognitively as well as emotionally competent as discussed in the next paragraph.

Any person who wishes to qualify as teacher first needs to acquire a certain level of cognitive competence and in order to qualify for a leadership position in a school one usually also needs to successfully complete graduate and post-graduate programs dealing with school management and leadership. The academic rigors of such programs together with their credentialing procedures typically serve to ensure that those who are able to pass such hurdles are of above average intelligence (Emmerling & Goleman, 2003). To process the complexity of information that principals face daily requires a high level of cognitive ability and hence cognitive competence would be an important part of a school leaders competencies. However, there is still a perception in South Africa that such a cognitive competence is the most important variable influencing learner achievement as was demonstrated by the request received from a group from the private sector who provide financial support for principals to participate in the Advanced Certificate in School Leadership and Management. They requested an investigation of a relationship between the academic achievement of the principals participating in this programme and their schools' achievement in the National Senior Certificate Examination. This seemed to indicate that there was a belief, among the members in this sponsoring group from the private sector, that the cognitive ability of the principals involved was the most important variable related to the academic achievement of the learners in their schools. On analysing the data involved in this request it was found that only 11% of the common variance present between the principals' cognitive achievements and those of the learners in the school could be explained, leaving 89% of the variance unexplained. In other words the effect of the principals' cognitive performance could not be explained by learners' achievement alone. This finding resonates with that of Schultz (2007,p.2) and Emmerling and Goleman (2003,p.6) that the academic achievement of school principals in academic courses is largely the result of their own individual effort while attaining high learner achievements probably involves competencies that integrate cognitive, emotional and social abilities. Sternberg (1997) and Sternberg, Lautrey and Lubert (2002) indicate that while a leaders' cognitive ability is an important aspect of leadership it is not sufficient on its own in predicting personal effectiveness and adaptation to change. Successful school leadership is also about achieving results through other people and hence it is important to investigate their perceptions of the extent to which school principals as leaders utilize emotional competence towards achieving such success. Davidson (2001) suggests that cognition and emotions are interwoven in mental life (through thick connections between the emotional centers and the neocortex) rather than being discretely independent. He further indicates that this is especially so in complex decision-making, self-

awareness, affective self-regulation, motivation, empathy, and interpersonal functioning, all of which are aspects of emotional intelligence.

The academic achievement of learners' in South African schools, as measured by the Annual National Assessments (ANA) and the National Senior Certificate (NSC), is problematic. The results of the latest Annual National Assessments (DoBE, 2012) indicate that only Grade 3 learners achieved a score of 50% and above in their home language. The target for 2014 is that 60% of learners need to achieve above an acceptable level which is set at 50% of learners achieving this level. In 2012 only 2.3% of learners in mathematics in Grade 9 achieved an acceptable level. At an International level South African learners are also well below the international averages. For example in the Progress in International Reading Literacy Studies (Pirls) South African learners' achieved an average of 460 against an international average of 500 (Howie, van Staden, Tshelie, Dowse & Zimmerman, 2011,p. XV1; Rademeyer, 2012). In the Trends in International Mathematics and Science Study (Timms) South African learners' came second last in Mathematics out of 45 countries that participated with an average of 352 compared to the international midpoint of 500. In Science South African learners came last with an average of 332 compared to a midpoint of 500 (HSRC, 2011, p.4; Rademeyer, 2012). These poor National and International Assessment scores can only mean that school leadership in South Africa is going to come under greater external pressure to improve learner results. It could be argued that such pressure on learner achievements could lead to leadership actions based on compliance to legislative mandates and their concomitant written policies, rules and regulations. The benefits of such actions are the orderliness and efficiency which these procedures bring to schools. Mullis, Martin, Foy and Drucker (2012) reported that principals of the schools who participated in PIRLS 2011 regarded the maintenance of an orderly atmosphere in the school as the activity that they most frequently engaged in. In addition Mullis et al. (id.) indicated that these principals valued such positive learning climates as they foster high academic achievements. However, the orderliness associated with learning climates achieved via bureaucratic mandates is often accompanied by dysfunctional consequences such as an increase in coercive forms of power (Morgan, 1997, p.154) resulting in an over emphasis on reliability, delegation of authority and general and impersonal rules which could negatively influence the interpersonal relationships in schools (Grobler, Mestry & Naidoo, 2012, p.212). Principals of public schools are mandated to implement education legislation and have no choice but to do so. However, it is how they implement such legislation that is the most important factor influencing the commitment of the teachers in the school as emotional skills such as emotional awareness and the use of social leadership skills are vital in obtaining the committed action of the teachers. In bureaucratic organizations implementation of legislation often occurs without considering the democratic principles of responsiveness, accountability and transparency because issues arising from the mandates are not thoroughly deliberated (Smit & Oosthuizen, 2011, p. 65). It is at this level of intense deliberation that the principal needs to use emotional competence as he/she is dependent on others to achieve the set goals.

These poor learner achievements in external examinations in public schools in South Africa also inevitably seems to lead to efforts of exerting greater control over the work of teachers by introducing mandates such as measuring teacher performance. A change in work performance of teachers is not something that can be mandated, for as Senge (1999, p. 43) contends, improved work performance relies on an increase in educators' capacity through the establishment of a culture conducive to work and commitment to the change process. To this one could add "a passion for teaching and learning", for it is also

vital and likewise cannot be forced onto teachers via legislation. In fact Fullan (1993) contends that "one cannot mandate that which matters" because what matters for complex change issues such as improved learner academic achievement are commitment to action. In order to influence teachers towards efforts of improving learner achievement it is contended that principals utilize their intrapersonal and interpersonal emotional intelligence as a catalyst for becoming instructional leaders as this will bring them closer to the actual teaching and learning process.

In this Chapter the concepts of instructional leadership, emotional intelligence and their association with learner achievement will be explored. The researcher will make use of literature to investigate the structure of the constructs involved and then design appropriate items to collect more data to test whether the model is substantively meaningful and statistically well-fitting. Such a model could possibly reveal causal linkages between the utilization of emotional intelligence by the principal and the practice of instructional leadership and their relationship to learner achievement.

THE CONSTRUCT OF EMOTIONAL COMPETENCE

According to Emmerling and Goleman (2003, p.12) the emotional intelligence paradigm is characterized by several theories. However, the three which have generated the most interest are the theories of Mayer and Salovey (1997), Bar-On (1998; 2000), Goleman (1998) and Goleman, Boyatzis and McKee (2002). This particular research concentrated only on Goleman's framework (2001) which is specific to the domain of work performance. This was done because of the great importance that people place on learner performance in schools and the tendency to blame the principal in the case of poor examination results. The principal of any school only has an indirect influence on learner achievements and whilst not disputing the importance of the leader's role in such performance it should be remembered that there are many other variables that play a role in learner academic performance (Leithwood, Louis, Anderson and Wahlstrom, 2004, p.18)

Although Gardner (1983, 1999) did not use the term emotional intelligence his use of the concepts intrapersonal and interpersonal intelligences did provide the basis on which the construct of emotional intelligence was based (Polychronoiu, 2009, p.343). Intrapersonal intelligence is the ability to understand your own emotions whereas interpersonal intelligence is your ability to understand the emotions of others. Emotional competence is also a multidimensional theoretical construct and as such it is likely to consist of numerous components or sub-dimensions (Wallace, 2010, p.602). For example the theoretical model introduced by Goleman (1998) included 18 competencies arranged in four clusters namely self-awareness (understanding yourself), self-management (managing yourself), social awareness (understanding others) and relationship management (managing others) (Law, Wong and Song, 2004; Wong, Law and Wong, 2004; Hopkins, 2007: 684). It can be assumed that the clusters referred to are sub-dimensions or first-order factors and that self-awareness and self-management are related to intrapersonal intelligence and social awareness and relationship management are related to interpersonal intelligence.

In an effort to make emotional intelligence more amenable to measurement Boyatzis (1982, p. 21) introduced the concept of job competency as "an underlying characteristic of a person that may be a motive, skill, aspect of one's self-image or social role, or a body of knowledge which he or she has". In line with this competency definition the Consortium for Research on Emotional Intelligence in Organizations (http://www.eiconsortium.org) developed the emotional competence framework. This framework contains five competences namely self-awareness, self-regulation, self-motivation, social awareness and social skills.

Each competence has numerous factors associated with it. For example self-awareness contains emotional awareness, accurate self-assessment and self-confidence. Each of these factors contains attributes or predictors for example in order to display emotional awareness a person must "know which emotions they are feeling and why" and "recognise how their feelings affect their performance". The five competences referred to can also be seen as sub-dimensions of the dimension of emotional competence and the factors as first-order factors of the sub-dimensions. The attributes could serve as predictors of the latent first-order factors.

Goleman (1996) and Bar-On (1997) identified self-awareness as the most important dimension of emotional intelligence. Self-awareness – "knowing one's emotions, recognizing a feeling as it happens – is the keystone of emotional intelligence" (Goleman (1996, p. 43). If someone knows their internal states of emotion, it allows self-control and leads to empathy in others. Further, according to Goleman (1996), self-control or self-managing of our emotions can keep us away from anger, anxiety and gloom and, in turn, allow us to become active in our work and life. Social awareness is recognising emotions in others, or the ability to know how another feels. Goleman (1996: 43) stated, "empathy, another ability that builds on emotional self-awareness, is the fundamental people skill". Empathy is important in relationship management, the skill of managing emotions in others (Goleman, 1996, p. 96).

Gross (2002) indicates that the regulation of emotions can be categorized into antecedent and response focused regulation. In the former, leaders can employ situation selection by using a more teacher-friendly context, such as the classroom to give feedback where the teacher feels more at ease than in an office. The leader could also use the feedback session and modify the situation by concentrating on the positive teaching aspects observed. Negative emotions are stronger than positive ones (Baumeister, Bratslavsky, Finkenauer & Vohs, 2001) and as Boyatzis (2011) indicates, one would suspect that the contagion of negative emotion would ignite a stronger neural sequence than positive emotions. Leaders thus need to manage the possible contagion of emotions using a heightened sense of self-awareness (Boyatzis, 2011). This suggests that a strategy of antecedent emotional regulation should be utilized when dealing with situations that could result in strong negative emotional responses, such as providing feedback to teachers about their teaching performance. Furthermore the situation can be modified by the leader if they indicate that the performance of individual teachers is a mutual problem inherent in teaching and learning, and as such the leader has a supporting role to play. Antecedent focused regulation thus attempts to regulate any negative emotions before they occur. Gross (2002) identifies two ways that a leader can engage in response-focused emotion regulation, namely through strategies of reappraisal and suppression. An initial emotional response to an angry parent could, for example, be reappraised by attempting to define the situation from the parent's point of view. A regulation strategy probably used by most school leaders is that of suppressing an initial emotional response by hiding it behind a pleasant countenance (Grandey & Brauberger, 2002). Suppression of one's emotions is similar to what Fineman (1993) viewed as emotional work. Because this research is using the perceptions of teachers of the extent to which school leaders make use of emotional competence in the workplace, a consideration of Fineman's (1993: 3) research findings could also be valuable. Fineman (1993) differentiates between emotional work, that is the effort put into ensuring that private feelings are repressed or represented in such a way that they are in touch with the socially accepted norms of the teaching profession and emotional labour, which is the commercial exploitation of this principle; when an employee is in effect paid to smile, laugh and be polite or to be caring (Wallace, 2010: 596). Fineman (2003: 8) furthermore implies that there

is a subjective element of emotions in what one feels. The more observable feature is the one shown, the emotional performance, and this is heavily influenced by social conventions and the impressions one wishes to convey to others. Such impressions are also influenced by self-interest as to be perceived in a positive light in the work one does for a living can benefit one's promotion and communication with others. Teachers as the observers of the principal's public performance of feelings may thus not be aware of the tension present between the performativity issues imposed by external agencies such as the Department of Education and the maintenance of a humanistic climate in the school (Cangemi, Burga, Lazarus, Miller & Fitzgerald, 2008, p. 1027). As such, most school leaders would not wish to be seen as losing control of the emotion of anger as it is not the social norm to 'lose your cool'. It is thus unlikely that school leaders will easily display their anger by allowing it to 'boil over'. Because teachers are more likely to base their perceptions of the emotional competence of school leaders on what they actually see, it is possible that only the emotional performance in the public role of school leader will be observed. As Wallace (2010, p. 602) states 'as the principal mulls over his or her emotional performance options in the face of anger, fear, frustration and concern, his or her ultimate decision is not only personal but also political in that it has immediate and cumulative implications for career aspirations as well as for communicative engagement with teachers'. Thus, what 'you see may not be the whole truth' regarding the principal's emotional competence. Perceptions of the emotional competence of the school principal is possibly best seen as an intertwining of perception, feeling and thinking (Lee, 2010, p. 652). Such an intertwined system is also influenced, by among other things, individual personalities, the ways one learns to use language, to express emotions, to think and establish relationships, and the myriad identities one takes on through participation in varied cultural communities. One could, however, make the assumption that the interpersonal competence of a school leader, being more visible to teachers, would elicit more positive perceptions from teachers than their intrapersonal competence.

Stone, Parker and Wood (2005) used a framework similar to that of the Consortium for Research on Emotional Intelligence in Organizations namely an emotional competence framework to explore the relationship between emotional competence and school leadership of principals and vice-principals from nine school boards in Ontario. Among their findings were that total emotional competence was a significant predictor of successful school leaders but that some dimensions of emotional competence were better predictors than others. Successful school leaders are characterized as having above average levels of emotional intelligence which they utilize to communicate and deal with stressful situations more effectively. They further suggested that professional development programs for school leadership should focus on developing the following abilities namely emotional self-awareness; self-actualization; empathy; interpersonal relationships; flexibility; problem solving and impulse control. In 2011 Grobler (2014) probed the perceptions of a random sample of 300 educators in the three Tshwane districts in Gauteng, South Africa, regarding the utilization of emotional competence by their school principals. Emotional competence was postulated to consist of four sub-dimensions namely self awareness, self-regulation, social awareness and social leadership skills. Each sub-dimension had five indicators (predictors) associated with it which measured teachers' perceptions as to the extent that school leadership utilized these emotional competences. These four sub-dimensions were based on the suggestions made by Wolff (2005) in the Technical Manual for the Emotional Competency Framework (ECI). Using a Principal Component Analysis (PCA) with Varimax rotation, Grobler (2014) concluded that Emotional Competence of school principals in this sample consisted of four first-order factors. A second-order procedure

produced two factors which explained 74.05% of the variance present which were named intrapersonal emotional competence and interpersonal emotional competence. They had Cronbach reliability coefficients of 0.85 and 0.89 respectively.

Emotional competence is, however, not without issues and controversies. Emmerling and Goleman (2003:24) indicate that the measurement of emotional competence is somewhat controversial possibly as emotions are seen as unpredictable, irrational, and something to be suppressed in favor of logic and reason. In addition it is difficult to separate some of the attributes of emotional competence from aspects of personality (Baron, 1997; Saklofske, Austin & Minski, 2003). Indeed cognition, emotion and aspects of the personality are interwoven in mental life, through thick connections between the emotional centers and the neocortex (Davidson, 2001). This seems to be especially so when it comes to complex decision-making, self-awareness, affective self-regulation, motivation, empathy and interpersonal competence which are all aspects of emotional intelligence (Emmerling & Goleman, 2003).

A FRAMEWORK FOR INSTRUCTIONAL LEADERSHIP

Bush (2007, p. 401) writes that instructional leadership focuses on teaching and learning and on the behaviour of teachers in working with students. Leaders' influence is directed at student learning via teachers. Southworth (2002) used qualitative research to indicate that modeling, monitoring and professional dialogue and discussion were three strategies that were effective in improving teaching and learning. This implies that modeling, monitoring and professional dialogue could be used as three sub-dimensions of instructional leadership. Jenkins (2009, p. 34) indicates that instructional principals need to free themselves of bureaucratic tasks and focus their efforts on improving teaching and learning. Jenkins (id.)

writes that instructional leaders need to be instructional resource providers, and possess up-to date knowledge of the curriculum, instruction and assessment practices. Interpersonal skills and planning skills are further aspects of importance. Muijs (2010, p. 52) states that instructional leadership is seen as being concerned with hands-on involvement with teaching and learning processes, and with the principal acting as the leader in terms of pedagogy and instruction rather than taking a more hands-off role concerned more strongly with administration. It has also been described as those actions that a principal takes or delegates to others, to promote growth in student learning and making instructional quality the top priority of the school and brings that vision to realization (Hallinger & Heck, 1998). Instructional leaders have a pedagogical vision, have pedagogical expertise and focus on teaching and learning. Muijs, Harris and Crawford (2004) describe an instructional leader as someone who promotes homogeneous approaches to different areas such as teaching and behaviour management in the school, monitors teaching, and makes sure professional development is focused on teaching and learning. Day, Sammons, Hopkins, Harris, Leithwood, Gu, et al., (2009: 12) write that instructional leadership encourages school leaders to focus their influence directly on teachers' pedagogical practices. This definition is, however, based on the assumption that school principals have the expertise, time and capacity to provide their teaching colleagues with meaningful feedback about their instructional practices. According to Horng and Loeb (2010: 66) this portrait of leaders observing practice, providing pointed feedback and modeling instruction when necessary is idealistic and as such it does not fit into the real world of large schools with large numbers of teachers practicing an assorted variety of subject specialties within limited time parameters. Horng and Loeb (2010:69) thus suggest that school leaders should be strong organizational managers. As such they can influence student learning by staffing their schools with

highly effective teachers and supporting those teachers with effective teaching and learning environments rather than focusing too narrowly on their own contribution to classroom instruction. This view where principals spend more time on organizational management opens the door for distributed leadership practices where practices related to pedagogy are imparted directly by teacher leaders rather than their principals.

Blasé and Blasé (1999) used a qualitative approach to examine teacher's perspectives on effective instructional leadership and found that it was based on two major themes namely talking with teachers to promote reflection and promoting professional growth. The first theme, critical reflection, involved talking strategies such as making suggestions, giving feedback, modeling, using enquiry and soliciting advice and opinions and giving praise. Promoting professional growth involved aspects such as emphasizing the importance of teaching and learning, supporting collaborative efforts, developing coaching relationships among educators, encouraging and supporting redesign of programmes, applying the principles of adult learning to all phases of staff development and implementing action research to inform instruction. The two major themes referred to could be seen as sub-dimensions of instructional leadership and focus on teaching and learning. According to Neumerski (2012, p. 318) early definitions of instructional leadership focused on characteristics of successful school leaders in effective schools by isolating personal traits such as gender and leadership styles. Sammons, Hillman and Mortimore (1995) suggested characteristics such as a strong results orientation motivated by an achievement drive, strength of purpose and a willingness to involve others in decision making, be added to the traits. Neumerski (2012, p. 318) indicates that later research moved beyond the identification of personal traits and indicated that successful principals carefully monitor learner progress and instructional time whilst ensuring high visibility.

One of the most widely accepted instruments that attempts to measure teacher perceptions of the principal as an instructional leader in the United States is the Principal Instructional Management Rating Scale (PIMRS) developed by Hallinger (1982) and refined in 1990. The instrument was grounded in a conceptual framework that proposed three dimensions namely defining the school's mission containing two sub-dimensions, managing the instructional program which had three sub-dimensions and promoting a positive school learning climate which contained five underlying sub-dimensions. The original form of the PIMRS (Hallinger, 1982) contained 11 sub-dimensions and revision of the instrument reduced the instrument to 10 sub-dimensions and 50 items (Hallinger, 1990). Hallinger (2005) reasserted the usefulness of this construct in his meta-analytic review of the literature; the PIMRS has been used in more than 199 studies (Hallinger, 2008). In 1996, the Interstate School Leadership Licensure Consortium created the national Standards for School Leaders, influenced in part by Hallinger's framework. Revised in 2008, these standards have been adopted by at least 43 states (Council of Chief State School Officers (CCSSO), some of which have redesigned their principal training programs and evaluations to align with the standards. Although these standards focus on school administration and not instructional leadership in particular, they do highlight some of the behaviors identified as critical to instructional leadership: (a) developing and facilitating a school vision of learning, (b) advocating and nurturing a school culture conducive to student learning, (c) managing the organization for an effective learning environment, (d) collaborating with families and community members and responding to needs and mobilizing resources, (e) acting with integrity and fairness, and (f) understanding and influencing the larger sociopolitical context (http://www.ccsso.org). Studies in the United States of America which used the perceptions of others provided the most valid data (Hallinger, 2011, p. 279).

Leithwood et al., (2004, p. 8) caution against the use of instructional leadership as a mere slogan as this can mask the more important themes common to successful leadership. Successful school leaders have three basic core leadership practices in common namely setting directions, developing people and redesigning the organization. Specific leadership practices that assist with setting directions are the articulation of a vision, fostering the acceptance of group goals and creating high performance expectations (Leithwood et al., 2004, p. 24). Developing people is closely aligned with a leader's ability to improve the quality of teaching and learning which is often invoked when the term "instructional leadership" is used. However, developing people also involves the use of emotional intelligence as the leader has to be able to obtain improved performance from teachers and learners by using the efforts of people outside of self (McColl-Kennedy & Anderson, 2002). This seems to suggest that there is a causal link between instructional leadership and the interpersonal emotional sub-dimension of emotional competence. Leadership practices associated with redesigning the organization involves practices such as strengthening district and school cultures, modifying organizational structures and building collaboration (Leithwood et al., 2004, p. 25). Strengthening school and district cultures and modifying organizational structures will also require that difficult conversations between schools and higher hierarchical levels occur, requiring the utilisation of social emotional attributes associated with effective communication such as dealing with difficult issues in a straight forward manner (Malgas, 2006: 29).

In research conducted in South Africa there seems to be a wide variety of terms that are used in the construct of instructional leadership. For example, Budhal (2000:15) indicates that a principal's role can be divided into management tasks such as instructional leadership tasks, administrative tasks, school marketing, financial management and community liaison. Kruger (1996) writes about the elements that are involved in instructional leadership using terms such as determination of objectives, curriculum coordination, creating a climate conducive to learning, remedial steps, didactic leadership, enrichment programmes and evaluation and examination. Steyn (2002) and Lemmer (1994) refer to the leadership of a school principal as occurring in a regulated environment and that it consists of three broad areas namely instructional, transformational and facilitative. Hoadley, Christie and Ward (2009, p. 386) determined instructional leadership as consisting of the dimensions of the principals' pedagogical expertise, distributed leadership, linkages between management and instruction, context, organizational factors and social relations within the school. Using multiple regression analysis they found that curriculum coverage, parental valuing and support for education and the willingness of the School Governing Body (SGB) to help were significant predictors of Student Achievement Gains Over Time (SAGOT). A pretest on the possible structure of Instructional leadership using teacher perceptions was conducted in 2011 using a random sample of 300 teachers from the three Tshwane districts of Gauteng (Grobler, 2013). The structured questionnaire was designed using the literature study discussed above and contained 40 items applicable to Instructional Leadership. The content validity of the items was checked by two experts in Education Management and Educational Psychology to see whether the items covered the range of meanings involved in the construct. Grobler (2013) postulated that instructional leadership was composed of 10 sub-dimensions namely: designing school goals; communicating school goals; coordinating the curriculum; monitoring learner progress; protecting instructional time; maintaining high visibility; providing incentives for teachers; promoting professional development; providing incentives for learning and learner care. Each of the sub-dimensions had four items measured on a six-point interval scale

and anchored by strongly disagree at one pole and strongly agree at the other pole. As factor analysis is about achieving parsimony of items it is probable that fewer than 10 dimensions will result. It is, for example, possible to visualize these 10 sub-dimensions in an equilateral triangle (see Figure 1) which involves a reduction of the 10 sub-dimensions to four sub-dimensions namely the mandated curriculum content, the teacher the learner and the principal

The first four sub-dimensions of the 10 described above are concerned with the mandated curriculum, its implementation, coordination and assessment and feature at one base of the triangle. The teacher's role via incentives and professional development features at a different base whilst the sub-dimensions dealing with the learner features at the third base. Situated in the middle of the triangle is the school principal as instructional leader. The central position of the principal should allow for effective coordination of the mandated curriculum via educators and learners. It is the principal who coordinates the mandated curriculum content with the teaching and learning processes whilst attempting to ensure that teaching and learning occurs. The data obtained from the teachers in this pretest for the structure of instructional leadership of the school principal was analysed using factor analysis (PCA and varimax rotation). Four first-order factors with reliabilities above 0.8 emerged, which were named ensuring coherence between teaching and learning, modeling effective teaching, facilitating learner achievements and protecting instructional time (Grobler, 2013).

From the above it can be inferred that instructional leadership is a contested concept and varies from an emphasis of the principal spending most of his/her time in the classroom, to one who is more concerned with administrative matters such as ensuring the selection of effective teachers and then ensuring that their teaching performance is well managed. However, such views could

Figure 1. The triangular structure of Instructional Leadership (Adapted from Berglund and Lister, 2010)

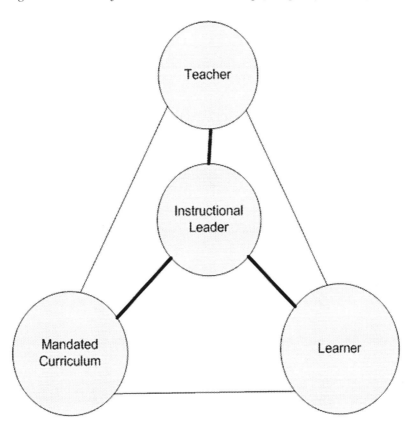

also be due to placing a greater emphasis on the ideographic dimension, where the emphasis is on the development of interpersonal relationships, or an emphasis on the nomothetic dimension by developing the management practices of school leaders. In the South African context a school principal is allocated a relatively small proportion of time to teaching duties and hence the concept of instructional leadership needs to be effective. A school principal could for example, spend more time with the subject heads in the school where the practices involved in the annual national assessments are thoroughly interrogated as a means of facilitating learner achievement. As so much emphasis is placed on learner achievements it could be an effective strategy towards improving learner achievement.

LEARNER ACHIEVEMENT

In this research the results of the Annual National Assessments (ANA) written by Grade 3, 4 and 6 learners' in primary schools and the results of the National Senior Certificate (NSC) for Grade 12 in 2011 were used as a measure of learner achievement (DBE, 2011b). In Grade 3 the results in literacy and numeracy were captured while the results of language and mathematics were used for Grades 4 and 6. Grade 12 learners' write annual examinations in numerous subjects but only home language and mathematics results were utilized. However, not all learners in Grade 12 take mathematics as a subject whilst the standard in home languages varies greatly.

Using the literature discussed above this research investigated the extent that school leadership utilized emotional competence and instructional leadership and its association with learner achievement.

RESEARCH METHODOLOGY

This research is best described as being situated in the positivistic paradigm using a structured questionnaire to elicit the perceptions of teachers regarding the extent to which their principals utilized emotional competence and instructional leadership in their schools. Exploratory Factor analysis (Principal Component Analysis and varimax rotation) was used to investigate the structures of instructional Leadership and Emotional Competence. Confirmatory Factor Analysis (CFA) showed the structure of the latent variables and Structural Equation Modeling (SEM) was then used to investigate the causal influence of the emotional factors on the four sub-dimensions comprising instructional leadership (Byrne, 2001, p. 5) and their association with learner achievement. The Analysis of Moment Structures (AMOS) which produces a path diagram was used to facilitate this process (Arbuckle, 2007). There are two major types of variables in structural equation modeling namely observed (indicator) variables and latent (construct) variables. Latent variables are not directly observable and hence they are inferred constructs based on the observed variables that were selected to define them (Schumacker & Lomax, 2004, p. 196). To operationalise the

various -dimensions involved in the composition of the dependent latent variables, emotional competence and instructional leadership, this research probed the perceptions of teachers by using appropriate items (predictors) from the 2011 research conducted in the three Tshwane districts in Gauteng mentioned earlier in the Chapter. For example, one of the items in the self-awareness sub-dimension of emotional competence asked respondents "to what extent does the leadership in your school show that they are able to remain composed even during trying times?" The scale used to measure their response was anchored by the polar opposites of to no extent (1) at one end and to a very large extent (5) at the other end (see Tables 1 and 2). However, as this questionnaire was used with a different sample of educators it was necessary to test the validity of the constructs and factor analytic procedures were used for this. To determine the construct validity of the postulated emotional competence and instructional leadership constructs, principal component analysis (PCA) as a form of exploratory factor analysis (EFA) was utilized (Norusis, 2007; Field, 2009). The reliability of the various dimensions and sub-dimensions was determined using the Cronbach's Alpha reliability coefficient. A similar six-point scale was used for the 20 items selected from the pretest questionnaire (see Tables 3 to 6) regarding instructional leadership (Grobler, 2013).

Furthermore in structural equation modeling there are two types of latent variables namely latent dependent variables (endogenous latent variables) and latent independent variables (exogenous latent variables). It was postulated that the emotional

Table 1. Items selected for Interpersonal emotional competence (FCT1.1)

Item	Description: To What Extent does the Leadership in yOur School:	Mean	Loading	S.D
C3	Arouse enthusiasm for developing a shared vision and mission	3.61	0.83	1.02
C6	Provide opportunities for you to develop your expertise	3.65	0.806	1.06
C7	Encourage open discussions on contentious issues	3.53	0.802	1.11
C8	Attempt to provide all staff with equal opportunities to develop their talents	3.59	0.802	1.09

Table 2. Items selected for Intrapersonal emotional competence (FCT1.2)

Item	Description: To What Extent does the Leadership in Your School:	Mean	Loading	S.D.
C10	Lead by also doing what they expect from the teachers	3.45	0.725	1.10
C14	Show consistency when dealing with staff	3.32	0.707	1.12
C15	Show that they are able to remain composed even in trying times	3.55	0.705	1.03
C18	Show the ability to take on a tough challenge despite opposition	3.61	0.702	1.04

Table 3. Items in ensuring coherence between teaching and learning (FB1.4)

Item	Description: Indicate Your Extent of Agreement/Disagreement with the Following Statements:	Mean	Loading	S.D
B2	The leadership in this school refers to the school's academic goals when making decisions about the prescribed curricula?	4.49	0.832	1.13
B4	The leadership in this school actively participates with the teachers in reviewing the materials needed for implementing the prescribed curricula?	4.45	0.815	1.22
B3	The school's mission is effectively communicated to the community by the leadership in this school?	4.34	0.814	1.22
B1	The leadership in this school uses staff meetings to discuss the school's academic goals with teachers?	4.89	0.772	1.20

Table 4. Items in modeling effective teaching (FB1.3)

Item	Description: Indicate Your Extent of Agreement/Disagreement with the Following Statements:	Mean	Loading	S.D.
B8	The leadership in this school reinforces superior performance by teachers in staff meetings and school newsletters?	4.19	0.841	1.34
B7	The leadership in this school participates in extra- and co-curricular activities?	4.23	0.826	1.44
B6	The leadership in this school also involve themselves in substituting for teacher who is absent?	4.56	0.806	1.51
B10	The leadership in this school visits classrooms to discuss school issues with teachers and learners?	4.10	0.798	1.41

Table 5. Items in facilitating learner achievement (FB1.1)

Item	Description: Indicate Your Extent of Agreement/Disagreement with the Following Statements:	Mean	Loading	S.D.
B14	In this school the leadership serves as role models for learners regarding a positive attitude towards learning?	4.58	0.846	1.18
B13	The leadership in this school supports teachers actively in their recognition and/or reward of learners' contributions to and accomplishments in class?	4.41	0.834	1.25
B12	The leadership in this school actively supports the use in the classroom of skills acquired during in-service training?	4.52	0.833	1.16
B11	The leadership in this school contacts parents of learners to communicate any improved or exemplary performance on their part?	4.30	0.808	1.24

Table 6. Protecting instructional time (FB1.2)

Item	Description Indicate Your Extent of Agreement/Disagreement with the Following Statements::	Mean	Loading	S.D.
B18	The leadership in this school limits interruptions of instructional time by means of public address announcements during lessons?	4.07	0.811	1.44
B17	The leadership in this school ensures that learners are not called to the office during teaching time?	3.98	0.785	1.42
B19	The leadership in this school ensures that teachers get to their classrooms promptly after school breaks?	4.56	0.752	1.26
B20	The leadership in this school ensures that tardy and truant learners suffer specific consequences for missing lesson time?	4.05	0.732	1.40

competence of school leadership would influence the various dimensions of instructional leadership in a positive way. Furthermore intrapersonal emotional competence was postulated to influence the interpersonal sub-dimension and not vice-versa and hence intrapersonal emotional competence was the exogenous variable in this research. The literature above also suggested one must first understand yourself in order to understand others and hence the intrapersonal sub-dimension is likely to influence the interpersonal sub-dimension. The regression structure between the latent variables of emotional competence and instructional leadership found was also investigated using SEM (Byrne, 2001, p. 6). The structures involved with emotional competence and instructional leadership were tested for possible causal relationships between them and learner achievement. As Intrapersonal Emotional Competence was an exogenous variable present in the model in Figure 6 the possible influence of other independent variables such as school type and home language on it were also investigated but not reported in detail due to limitations of length.

SAMPLE

Following the pretest of 300 educators in the three Tshwane districts of Gauteng in 2011 a stratified sample of 100 schools in the Johannesburg area was obtained in 2012. The sampling frame was a list of public schools obtained from the Gauteng Department of Education (GDE). From this list of 688 public schools in the Johannesburg region of Gauteng (DoBE, 2011a), 100 sample schools were selected according to the probability proportionate to size of the district. Thus 30 schools in Johannesburg Central, 17 schools in Johannesburg East, 21 schools Johannesburg North, 14 schools in Johannesburg South and in 18 schools in Johannesburg West were selected for the sample. On receiving Departmental approval for the research the Institutional Development Officers (IDSOs) from the various districts, who were personally informed about the various ethical procedures involved at a pre-arranged meeting with them, distributed the questionnaires to the schools identified. Each school received between 20 to 30 questionnaires to complete. Thus 2500 questionnaires were distributed. The various ethical procedures such as anonymity and voluntary participation were emphasised. The return rate of questionnaires per district varied with 95.2% of schools in Johannesburg North returning the questionnaires and only 55.6% from Johannesburg Central completed the questionnaires. Of the 2500 distributed by the IDSOs they collected and returned 1758. The return rate was 70.3% which was admirable. Unfortunately questionnaires from two schools had to be omitted due to incomplete data leaving a sample size of 1698 educators which comprises 67.9% of the distributed questionnaires. Section A of the questionnaire asked for certain bio-and demographic information about the respondents'. Gender, age and teaching experience in years, affiliation to a teacher union, type of school and home language were some of the more important demographic variables.

Of the 1698 respondents 64.2% were females and 35.5% were males. Six respondents did not provide their gender. The ratio of female to male respondents in the sample was thus 1.8 females to every male. The Department of Basic Education indicates a gender ratio of 2.5: 1 (DBE, 2011a: 20). The sample in this research was thus slightly over representative of male educators. The mean age of respondents was 42.05 years with a mean of 15.5 years of teaching experience. There were 834 (49.1%) respondents who indicated that they belonged to the South African Teachers Union (Sadtu) while 48.2% belonged to other teacher unions. The sample is not representative of Sadtu membership as about 70% of teachers belong to Sadtu, the largest teacher union in South Africa. With respect to home language there were 26.3% who denoted Nguni as home language, 25.7% who specified Sotho, 29.5% who designated Afrikaans and 12.4% who indicated English. According to the DBE (2011a) there are 43.1% who use Nguni and 14.4% who use Afrikaans as their home languages. The sample was thus over-representative of teachers with Afrikaans as home language and under-representative of Nguni respondents. The sample was also not representative of school type in that 43.1% belonged to Primary schools while 53.3% indicated that they taught at secondary schools. It is possible that the low return rate of the Johannesburg Central district influenced among other demographics the home language statistics. In addition many so called Coloured schools are present in the Johannesburg East and South districts and these educators have Afrikaans as their home language. Hence the data analysis should take this bias introduced in the sample into account.

THE ANALYSIS OF DATA REGARDING EMOTIONAL COMPETENCE

The 20 items devised to test the perceptions of educators about the use of emotional competence in school leadership were subjected to a factor analytic procedure and the resulting Kaiser Meyer Olkin (KMO) as measure of sampling adequacy was 0.978 with a Bartlett's sphericity of $p < 0.05$. The Monte Carlo parallel analysis (Pallant, 2007, p. 191) indicated that two factors could be extracted which explained 61.77% of the variance present. The removal of C2 and C6 (first inverted and then removed because of low reliabilities and communalities) produced two first-order factors explaining resulted which explained 63.54% of the variance present. They were named:

- **FCT1.1:** Interpersonal emotional competence ($\alpha = 0.953$).
- **FCT1.2:** Intrapersonal emotional competence ($\alpha = 0.926$).

The CFA structure of emotional competence is shown in Figure 2.

Haitovsky's significance test (Field, 2009, p. 658) indicated that the observed χ^2 was smaller than the critical value and hence the determinant was not significantly different from zero. Multicollinearity between the latent factors should not be a problem and in addition a PCA was used. A second-order factor analysis on these two first-order factors resulted in only one factor, explaining 91.58% of the variance present which was named *perceptions of the utilisation of emotional competence by school leadership*. It had an alpha Cronbach reliability of 0.966. The eight items shown in Tables 1 and 2 were selected by SPSS 21.0 as having the highest factor loadings and hence they are seen as being the most representative of the latent factors they represent (Field, 2009, p. 631).

Figure 2. The CFA model of intrapersonal emotional competence (FCT1.2) and interpersonal emotional competence (FCT1.1). [Chi-squared(19;n=1696=82.55; mCMIN/DF=4.34;p=0.000; RMR=0.017;SR MR=0.015;GFI=0.988;;CFI=0.994;RMSEA=0.044 (CI 0.035 to 0.054; PCLOSE= 0.812]

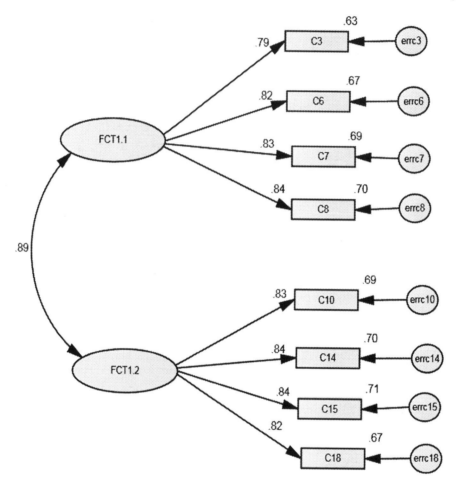

The factor means indicate that the teachers believe that their principals utilize interpersonal emotional competence to a moderate tending to a large extent ($\overline{X}_{FCT1.1.}$ = 3.62) while they believe that principals' utilize intrapersonal emotional competence to a moderate extent only ($\overline{X}_{FCT1.2}$ = 3.50). Furthermore these two factor means differ statistically significantly from one another [t (1693) =11.96; p<0.0005; r=0.3]. This supports the initial postulate that the teachers are more likely to evaluate the principals' interpersonal emotional competence more positively than they would his/her intrapersonal emotional competence.

Another assumption was that intrapersonal emotional competence (FCT1.2) would have a stronger causal influence on interpersonal emotional competence (FCT1.1), rather than the other way around, as this is something that all leaders sense intuitively (see Figure 3). The model fit criteria indicated that there was a good fit between the hypothesised model and the sample data.

The exogenous factor, intrapersonal emotional competence (FCT1.2), had a direct effect on interpersonal emotional competence (FCT1.1). The standardised regression coefficient had a value of 0.89 and an SMC of 0.79 indicating a large direct effect.

The various goodness of fit statistics indicated that the data fitted the model well. The researcher thus used this model together with the instructional leadership model in Figure 5 to postulate a model that could be used to influence learner achievement.

THE ANALYSIS OF DATA REGARDING INSTRUCTIONAL LEADERSHIP

A factor analytic procedure (PCA) using SPSS 21.0 indicated a KMO value of 0.983 and Bartlett's sphericity of p=0.0001 indicating that the process of factor analysis would be feasible. The PCA resulted in six first-order factors explaining 62.15% of the variance present. However, a Monte Carlo PCA for parallel analysis indicated that four factors had random Eigen values that were smaller than the SPSS Eigen values. Hence only four first-order factors were an acceptable solution (Pallant, 2007:191).These sub-dimensions were similar to those found in the pretest and were named ensuring coherence between teaching and learning (FB1.4; α = 0.899), modeling effective teaching (FB1.3; α = 0.911), facilitating learner achievement (FB1.1; α = 0.906) and protecting instructional time (FB1.2; α = 0.922). (See Tables 3 to 6).

Figure 3. A SEM showing the causal impact of intrapersonal on interpersonal emotional competence [Chi-squared (19;n=1696)=82.55; CMIN/DF=4.34;p=0.000; RMR=0.017 SRMR=0.015;GF1=0.988; CFI=0,994;RMSEA=0.044 (CI 0.035 TO 0.054) PCLOSE= 0.812]

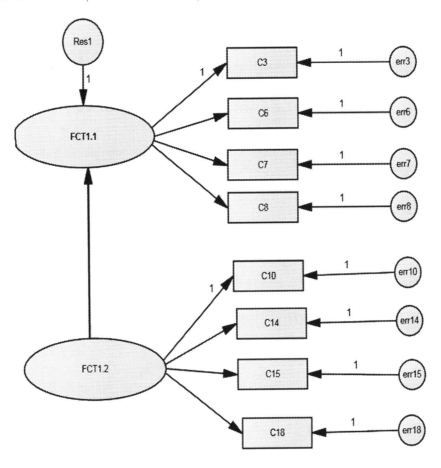

There were five items in each of the four sub-dimensions and the four which displayed the highest factor loadings and which did not load on other items were selected because it informs one about the relative contribution that this item makes to the factor (Field, 2009, p. 631). The variables with the highest correlation coefficients (>0.90) were removed and the model fit tested in order to address the possibility of multicollinearity although when using PCA multicollinearity should not be a problem (Field, 2009: 648). The factor loading can also be thought of as the Pearson correlation between a factor and a variable and it is selected by the SPSS 21.0 programme according to its substantive importance to the factor.

If one considers only the factor means then the teachers agree most strongly with the factor ensuring coherence between teaching and learning ($\overline{X}_{FB1.4} = 4.54$), followed by facilitating learner achievement ($\overline{X}_{FB1.1} = 4.45$). These two factors thus support the research conducted by Hoadley, et al. (2009, p. 386) as they were also concerned with curriculum coverage. Modeling effective teaching ($\overline{X}_{FB1.3} = 4.27$) could be placed third, while protecting instructional time could be seen as the factor that teachers agreed with least strongly ($\overline{X}_{FB1.2} = 4.17$). The teachers in the sample thus partially agreed that their principals were involved in instructional leadership behaviours. The Confirmatory Factor Analytic model (CFA) for instructional leadership is shown in Figure 4. The various fit criteria indicated that the model fitted the data reasonably well.

Structural Equation Modeling (SEM) was then used to investigate possible causal links between the four first-order factors and to determine their direction of influence on one another. According to Schumacker and Lomax (2004: 209) it is best to identify a few good indicators of each latent variable with four indicators being recommended. This researcher identified four indicators from each of the latent first-order factors by using the items

where factor loadings were higher than 0.700 (see Tables 3 to 6). The researcher also reasoned that in order to ensure coherence between teaching and learning (FB1.4) it would be necessary to use the knowledge one had of the various curricula and assessment procedures involved. This could enable the instructional leader to model how effective teaching should occur (FB1.3). In addition modeling such effective teaching was then likely to influence learner achievement (FB1.1). The protection of instructional time (FB1.2) should be something one demonstrates when modeling effective teaching and such protection of instructional time is also likely to influence the learners time on task (see Figure 5). Of the postulated four causal links between the four latent factors only three were found to be statistically significant namely the direct influence of ensuring coherence between teaching and learning (FB1.4) and modeling effective teaching (FB1.3) (R = 0.93; SMC=0.86), the direct influence of modeling effective teaching (FB1.3) on facilitating learner achievement (FB1.1) (R=0.95; SMC=0.90) and the direct influence of modeling effective teaching (FB1.3) on protecting instructional time (FB1.2) (R=0.84; SMC = 0.70) (see Figure 5).

The exogenous variable, namely ensuring coherence between teaching and learning (FB1.4), impacts directly on the endogenous factor of modeling effective teaching (FB1.3) and indirectly on facilitating learner achievement (FB1.1) and protecting instructional time (FB1.2). The influence of ensuring coherence between teaching and learning (FB1.4) on facilitating learner achievement (FB1.1) is mediated by modeling effective teaching (FB1.3) as is the case for protecting instructional time (FB1.). Modeling effective teaching (FB1.3) plays a vital role as it exerts a direct effect on the other two endogenous factors (FB1.1 and FB1.2). The squared multiple correlations (SMCs) which indicates the amount of variance explained by their predictors all had large values (>0.50) and thus the three pathways were

Figure 4. The CFA structure of instructional leadership (FB1.4-Ensuring coherence; FB1.3-Modeling effective teaching; FB1.2-Protecting instructional time; FB1.1-Facilitating learner achievement) [Chi-squared (97;n-1696)=524.55; CMIN/DF=5.41;p=0.000; RMR=0.049; SRMR=0.028;GF1=0.962; CFI=0.971;RMSEA=0.051-CI 0.047 to 0.055) PCLOSE= 0.343]

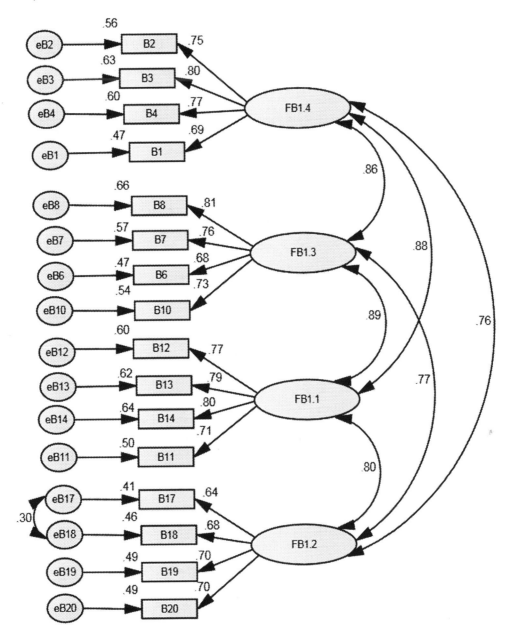

Figure 5. A SEM instructional leadership showing causal linkages (Ensuring coherence between teaching and learning (FB1.4); Modeling effective teaching (FB1.3); Facilitation learner achievement (FB1.1); Protecting instructional time (FB1.2); Chi-squared (99) n=1696=473.48; CMIN/DF=4.78;p=0.000; RMR=0.15; SRMR=0.45;GF1=0.965; CFI=0.974;RMSEA=0.047(CI-0.043 to 0.052); PCLOSE=0.851

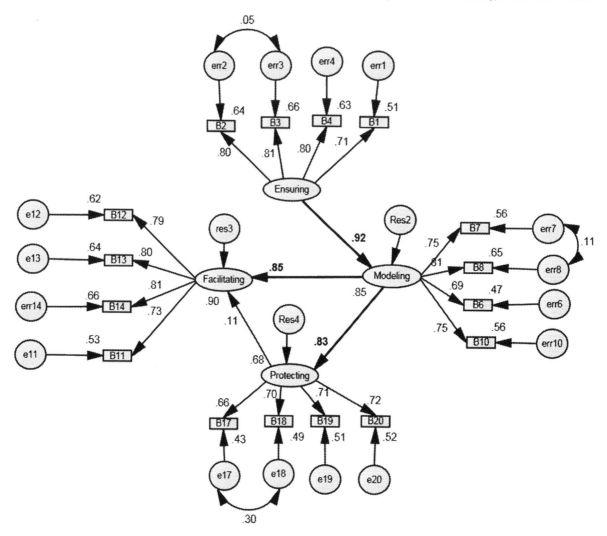

both statistically and substantively significant (see Figure 5). The goodness of fit statistics as provided in Figure 5 indicate a reasonable statistical fit for the postulated model and hence it was deemed appropriate to use this model for investigating its possible links with emotional intelligence and learner achievement.

LEARNER ACHIEVEMENT

The results of the Annual National Assessments (ANA) written by Grade 3, 4 and 6 learners' in primary schools and the results of the National Senior Certificate (NSC) for Grade 12 in 2011 were used as a measure of learner achievement

(DBE, 2011b). In Grade 3 the results in literacy and numeracy were captured while the results of language and mathematics were used for Grades 4 and 6. Grade 12 learners' write annual examinations in numerous subjects but only home language and mathematics results were utilized. However, not all learners in Grade 12 take mathematics as a subject whilst the standard in home languages varies greatly. In addition the results of the home languages were mostly above 90% and indicated little variation among the secondary schools in the sample. A bivariate correlation matrix of the various results obtained by the 78 schools is provided in Table 7.

The data in Table 7 show a high correlation between the utilisation of Emotional Competence and Instructional Leadership in all schools sampled (r= 0.92; R^2=0.85). Instructional leadership showed a significant correlation with the learner achievements in all grades while emotional competence was significantly correlated with all grades with the exception of Grade 12. The correlation coefficients for Instructional Leadership were also higher than they were for Emotional Competence in all Grades involved. This is possibly due to school leaders being more visible when involved with instructional leadership behaviours whilst the intrapersonal aspects of emotional competence are

Table 7. Correlation coefficients between Instructional Leadership, Emotional Competence and learner achievements in Grades 3, 4, 6 and 12 in 2011

		Mean Score of Each School on IL	Mean Score of Each School on EI	G3 Average Score	G4 Average Score	G6 Average Score	G12 Average Score
Mean score of each school on IL	Pearson Correlation	1	.921**	.569**	.488**	.350*	.318*
	Sig. (2-tailed)		.000	.001	.005	.049	.031
	N	78	78	32	31	32	46
Mean score of each school on EI	Pearson Correlation	.921**	1	.428*	.426*	.350*	.265
	Sig. (2-tailed)	.000		.014	.017	.050	.075
	N	78	78	32	31	32	46
G3 Average score	Pearson Correlation	.569**	.428*	1	.657**	.495**	.ᶜ
	Sig. (2-tailed)	.001	.014		.000	.004	.
	N	32	32	32	31	32	0
G4 Average score	Pearson Correlation	.488**	.426*	.657**	1	.823**	.ᶜ
	Sig. (2-tailed)	.005	.017	.000		.000	.
	N	31	31	31	31	31	0
G6 Average score	Pearson Correlation	.350*	.350*	.495**	.823**	1	.ᶜ
	Sig. (2-tailed)	.049	.050	.004	.000		.
	N	32	32	32	31	32	0
G12 Average score	Pearson Correlation	.318*	.265	.ᶜ	.ᶜ	.ᶜ	1
	Sig. (2-tailed)	.031	.075	.	.	.	
	N	46	46	0	0	0	46
**. Correlation is significant at the 0.01 level (2-tailed).							
*. Correlation is significant at the 0.05 level (2-tailed).							
c. Cannot be computed because at least one of the variables is constant.							

not easily visible and hence not easily perceived by teachers. In addition the lower the Grade the higher the correlation between Instructional Leadership and Emotional Competence (see Table 7) indicating that the use of emotional intelligence to influence Instructional Leadership is perceived to be more important in primary schools than in secondary schools. The average scores achieved in the ANAs of the primary school grades were also significantly correlated with one another.

THE STRUCTURAL EQUATION MODEL INVOLVING THE FACTORS FOUND IN EMOTIONAL COMPETENCE, INSTRUCTIONAL LEADERSHIP AND THE LINK WITH LEARNER ACHIEVEMENT

The pathways as obtained in Figures 3 and 5 were retained and a causal link between interpersonal emotional competence and ensuring coherence between teaching and learning (FB1.4) was added (R=0.78; SMC=0.61). This link also makes sense as the principal mostly uses interpersonal emotional competences such as social awareness and social skills to ensure coherence between teaching and the mandated curriculum. In addition the pathways postulated for the linkage to the Primary school average percentage obtained by the sample of schools proved to be statistically significant. The one path added was from facilitating learner achievement (FB1.1 to PS Av.) (R=0.44; SMC = 0.19) and the other was from protecting instructional time (FB1.2 to PS Av) (R=0.48; SMC = 0.23). It could thus be said that their influence on the learner achievement in the primary school was statistically significant with a moderate substantive effect. An additional structural component between interpersonal emotional competence to modeling effective teaching (FB1.3) was added (R=0.26; R^2=0.07). This parameter had a statis-

tically significant but small substantive effect. The appropriate model goodness-of-fit measures were as provided with Figure 6 all indicated that the hypothesized model fits the data well. Haitovsky's χ^2_H also indicated that the determinant was not significantly different from zero and hence multicollinearity should not be a problem (Field, 2009, p. 658).

The model thus involves seven latent factors of which one, namely intrapersonal emotional competence (FCT1.2) can be said to be exogenous and as such it is synonymous to independent variables as they "cause" fluctuations in the values of the other latent factors in the model (Byrne, 2001, p. 5). Changes in the values of exogenous variables are not explained by the model. Rather they are considered to be influenced by other factors external to the model such as gender, age, type of school attended and socioeconomic status of the learners. The endogenous variables in the model such as FCT1.1, FB1.1, FB1.2, FB1.4, FB1.3 and Primary school average (PS Av.) are synonymous with dependent variables and as such are influenced by the exogenous variable in the model, either directly or indirectly (Byrne, id.). Intrapersonal Emotional Competence (FCT1.2) has one arrow representing a structural regression coefficient and thus indicates its direct impact (0.92) on Interpersonal Emotional Competence (FCT1.1). However, Intrapersonal Emotional Competence (FCT1.2) also impacts indirectly on FB1.4, on FB1.3, on FB1.1, on FB1.2 and on PS Av. Thus these instructional leadership variables mediate the effect of intrapersonal emotional competence (FCT1.2) on learner achievement (PS Av) indicating the interconnection of emotional competence with instructional leadership and their impact on learner achievement. The only endogenous factor that impacts directly on two other endogenous variables is modeling effective teaching (FB1.3) as it impacts directly on both facilitating learner achievement (FB1.1) and protecting instructional

Figure 6. A SEM showing the influence of EC on IL and LA [Chi-squared (242; n=1696)=986.84; CMIN/DF=4.08;p=0.000; RMR=0.04; SRMR=0.03;GF1=0.952; CFI=0.971;RMSEA=0,043 9CI0.040 to 0.045) PCLOSE= 1.000]

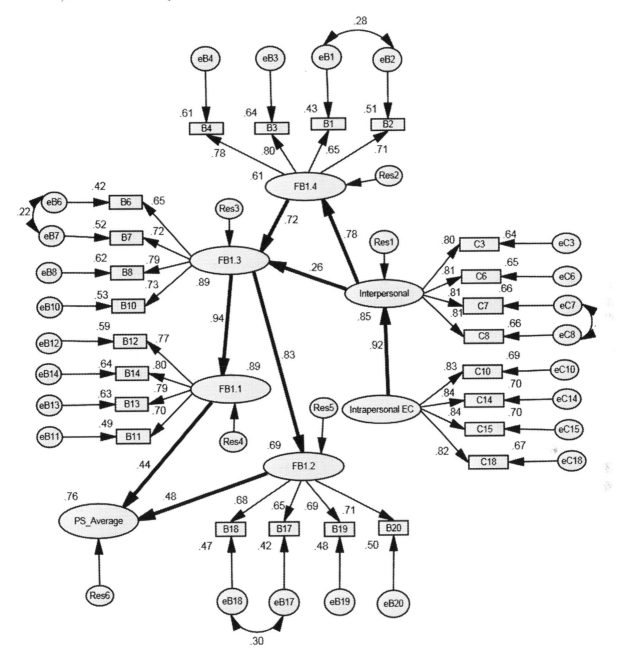

time (FB1.2). The facilitation of learner achievement (FB1.1) in turn impacts directly on learner achievement (PS Av). Protecting instructional time (FB1.2) is influenced in a direct way (0.83) by modeling effective teaching (FB1.2) and in turn

it also impacts indirectly on learner achievement (PS Av). This indicates the importance of modeling effective teaching as a mediating influence on learner achievement.

If one considers the squared multiple correlations (SMCs) of the endogenous variables as provided in the AMOS model, which are independent of all units of measurement, then a comparison of these endogenous factors is possible. Accordingly modeling effective teaching (FB1.3) (R^2 = 0.89) has the largest value, followed by facilitating learner achievement FB1.1 (R^2= 0.88), Interpersonal emotional competence (R^2=0.85), primary school average PS Av (R^2=0.76), protecting instructional time FB1.2 (R^2=0.69), ensuring coherence between teaching and learning FB1.4 (R^2=0.61). These six endogenous factors are thus all substantively meaningful which indicates the interwoveness of emotional competence and instructional leadership.

In general we conclude that the model shown in Figure 6 indicates that the exogenous factor, intrapersonal emotional competence (FCT1.2) influences the six endogenous variables either directly (FCT1.1) or indirectly (FB1.4, FB1.3, FB1.1 and PS Av.). The data in the sample thus indicates that school leadership utilizes both emotional competence and instructional leadership to impact learner achievement. The model in Figure 6 indicates that the larger the intrapersonal emotional competence of school leadership is perceived to be, the larger will be its influence on interpersonal emotional competence and the larger the impact on the various sub-dimensions of instructional leadership and learner achievement

Figure 6 also indicated that Intrapersonal Emotional Competence (FCT1.2) was the only exogenous factor and as such it would be influenced by other independent variables. The influence of gender, school-type, affiliation to teacher unions, socio-economic status of the learners and home language of the respondents were investigated but are not reported in detail owing to length limitations. Significant differences were found in school type with primary school respondents agreeing to a greater extent than secondary school respondents; teacher affiliation to a teacher union with teachers not affiliated to the South African

Democratic Teachers Union (Sadtu) agreeing to a greater extent than Sadtu members; socio-economic context of the majority of the learners in the school with the above average group agreeing to a greater extent than the below average group; home language with Afrikaans and English home language respondents agreeing to a greater extent than the Nguni and Sotho home language groups.

IMPLICATIONS OF THE FINDINGS FOR SCHOOL LEADERSHIP

Emotional competence is something that all leaders intrinsically possess and it is built on the foundations of intrapersonal and interpersonal emotional competence. This research indicated that the intrapersonal sub-dimension influences the interpersonal sub-dimension which agrees with the findings of (Taylor, Bagby, & Parker, 1997) who indicate that the "ability to understand emotions in oneself are linked with one's ability to understand it in others". Furthermore (Boyatzis, 2011, p. 3) confirms the importance of the intrapersonal dimension by suggesting that a heightened sense of self-awareness can promote a more social orientation to others. Techniques to assist a leader with a heightened sense of self-awareness are to know that you are having feelings and become aware of them, to label or understand what they are and then signal yourself that you should do something to change your mood and state. People with high self-assurance are also usually more assertive and are not afraid to stand up for themselves or to let themselves become known to others. Maree and Eiselen (2004:497) also found a low yet significant correlation (r=0.293), in the South African setting, between intrapersonal and interpersonal intelligence among academics in a merger setting. However, the instrument they used was different to the one used in this research. It should also be noted that emotional competence is more latent in some school leaders than in others and hence it is important that all school leaders need to be aware of the emotions they are feeling as these emotions influence what they think, do and say. One is reminded of the African notion of human brotherhood of "a person is a person because of other people which indicates that you can do nothing if you do not get the support of other people" (Sampson, 1999, p. 10). A leader thus also needs to be reflective and open to feedback from his/her followers to enable accurate self-assessment of both strengths and weaknesses. If the principals' position in the hierarchy was based on meritorious learner achievements alone then an obvious strength would probably be teaching ability. These strengths in teaching behaviour should be modeled to others by greater involvement with the various curricular and actual classroom activities.

Regarding emotional competence school leadership also needs to show self-assurance and be assertive when making decisions despite uncertainties and pressures. The research findings suggest a strong positive causal relationship from intrapersonal competence to interpersonal emotional competence and hence a good understanding and regulation of one's own emotions influences understanding and relationships with others. When dealing with situations which could result in strong negative emotional responses such as providing feedback to teachers about their teaching performance, leaders' need to be aware of strategies such as antecedent emotional regulation. Thus being aware of situations which are emotionally loaded enables the leader to anticipate the situation and plan appropriate strategies prior to the situation. The mandated results orientated achievements as stipulated in the schooling for 2025 (SA, 2010) is bound to increase emotional tensions between school principals, teachers and learners and a good understanding of emotional competence is an important precursor in the management of these tensions. This research indicates that a leader with a good understanding of his/her intrapersonal competence will have a larger influence on their social orientation towards oth-

ers. The school principal as leader of the School Management Team (SMT) must be able to remain calm and unflustered as this instills confidence in others and acts as an aid to problem solving.

Interpersonal emotional competence includes aspects such as empathy, a service orientation, political awareness, effective communication, managing conflict and collaboration with others. School leadership thus need to be able to articulate and arouse enthusiasm for the shared vision and mission and guide the performance of others while still holding them accountable for learner achievements. Tense situations needs appropriate diplomacy and tact so that disagreements can be brought to the "surface" so that they can be openly discussed. The causal link between interpersonal emotional competence and ensuring coherence between teaching and learning indicates that leadership should make it clear who is responsible for coordinating the curriculum across the various grade levels whilst ensuring active participation with teachers about curriculum implementation and coverage.

Bush (2007, p. 401) writes that instructional leadership focuses on teaching and learning and on the behaviour of teachers in working with students. Leaders' influence is directed at student learning via teachers. This particular research indicated that Instructional Leadership was composed of four underlying factors namely ensuring coherence between teaching and learning, modeling effective teaching, facilitating learner achievement and protecting instructional time. Ensuring coherence between teaching and learning (FB1.4) was influenced by interpersonal emotional competence (FCT1.1) while it also impacted directly on modeling effective teaching (FB1.3). School leadership should thus ensure that they are familiar with the various curricula as stipulated in the CAPS document (SA, 2011) as this will enable them to model the required stipulations and at the same time such behaviours will impact on the importance of instructional time and also emphasise the importance of learner achievements. This is in agreement with the findings of Hoadley, et al. (2009, p. 386) discussed under Instructional Leadership. School leadership also needs to involve all staff when important decisions regarding teaching and learning are drawn up so that a cooperative climate can be established. School leaders need to maintain a visible presence in school activities and play an active part in actual classroom teaching. In this way school leadership can model the change expected of others. Modeling effective teaching (FB1.3) impacts on facilitating learner achievement (FB1.1) and on protecting instructional time (FB1.2) and school leadership who directly involve themselves in teaching activities demonstrate their own commitment to both learners and staff. It also makes intuitive sense that regular assessment of learner achievements and communication thereof to the school community will facilitate learner achievement.

Any development of school leadership also needs to consider the influence of variables such as school type, socio-economic status of the community in which the school is situated and the prevailing culture of the various ethnic cultures present in the school. The organizational culture (dominated by mandated organizational practices as stipulated in legislative Acts) in which school leadership operates in South Africa is individually orientated and promotion is to a higher post level in the hierarchical structure. However, school leaders also operate in a societal culture, which in South Africa, is dominated by collectivism (Sewlall, 1996) as demonstrated in the teaching profession by Sadtu an affiliate of the Congress of South African Trade Unions (Cosatu). According to Hofstede (1991, p. 63) in a collectivistic culture an employer never hires an individual, but a person who belongs to an ingroup. In some schools the organizational culture can even be replaced by a labour union which serves as an emotional ingroup (Hofstede, 1991, p. 65). In some cases this has even led to violent confrontations. For example, in August 2010 Sadtu members participated in a public servants' strike action where several incidents of assaults, damage to property and intimidation of teachers not supporting the strike action took place (news 24.com.19 August, 2010). School leaders in collectivistic cultures thus find themselves in a difficult position of having to reconcile their mandated role of school leader geared towards the management of individuals with that of a community where personal relationships prevails over the task at hand. A school principal who does not support the emotional ingroup action can easily be condemned to the out-group (Sewlall, 1996).

FUTURE RESEARCH DIRECTIONS

This research did not investigate the possibility of multilevel models as being more appropriate when investigating school level data. Such an investigation is a recommendation for future research. The potential of the emotional intelligence which often lies dormant in school leaders and which constitutes one of the multidimensional facets of leadership is probably the one facet which influences all other leadership dimensions in some direct or indirect way. The role of emotional intelligence in autocratic, bureaucratic, transformational, distributed, primal, charismatic and a host of other leadership styles needs to be investigated. For example is it necessary for school leaders to make use of emotional intelligence to influence people when they already have the power to get them to do what they want them to do? After all school leaders are appointed into positions of authority where they can make use of legislative acts with all their concomitant rules, regulations and procedures to guide any work that needs to be completed. Is it necessary that a school leader uses leadership abilities or will ensuring compliance via the management of legislative acts and regulations also accomplish the same ends?

This researcher contends that leadership is about influencing others towards achieving the aims of the school in an ethically acceptable way.

Being more aware of one's emotions and being able to manage them well can facilitate one's social leadership skills and allow one to influence and inspire other people towards achieving higher performance goals. Research on how to release and develop the vast potential of the emotional intelligence present in all leaders is important.

CONCLUSION

Leadership consists of numerous dimensions and this chapter focused the spotlight on two of those dimensions namely emotional intelligence and instructional leadership and how they can be used to influence learner achievement. The causal pathways present in the model were all substantively and statistically significant. The model furthermore indicated that principals should utilize their intrapersonal emotional competence as a means to influence their interpersonal leadership skills which in turn impact on the four latent factors involved with instructional leadership. Being aware of the causal impacts in the model could assist school principals to make more extensive use of their emotional competence and instructional leadership to impact and improve learner achievements in their schools. This Chapter demonstrated how two of the multidimensional facets of leadership, namely emotional competence and instructional leadership can be utilized towards achieving improved learner achievement.

REFERENCES

Arbuckle, J. L. (2007). *AMOS 16.0: User's guide.* Chicago: SPSS Inc.

Bar-On, R. (1997). *Bar-On Emotional Quotient Inventory. In A Measure of Emotional Intelligence: Technical Manual.* New York, NY: Multi Health Systems.

Bar-On, R. (1998). *The development of an operational concept of psychological well-being.* (Unpublished doctoral dissertation). Rhodes University.

Bar-on, R. (2000). Emotional and social intelligence: Insight from the Emotional Quotient Inventory (EQ-i). In R. Bar-On & J.D.A. Parker (Eds.), Handbook of emotional intelligence (pp. 363-388). San Francisco: Jossey-Bass.

Baumeister, R.F., Bratslavsky, E., Finkenauer, C., & Vohs, K.D. (2001). Bad is stronger than good. *Review of AQ 6 General Psychology, 5*, 323–370.

Berglund, A., & Lister, R. (2010). *Introductory programming and the Didactic triangle.* Paper presented at the 12th Australian Computing Education Conference (ACE 2010). Brisbane, Australia.

Blasé, J., & Blasé, J. (1999). Effective instructional leadership: Teachers' perspectives on how principals promote teaching and learning in schools. *Journal of Educational Administration, 38*(2), 130–141. doi:10.1108/09578230010320082

Boyatzis, R. E. (1982). *The competent manager: A model for Effective Performance.* New York: John Wiley & Sons.

Boyatzis, R. E. (2011). *Neuroscience and Leadership: The Promise of Insights.* Retrieved March 18, 2012, from http://www.iveybusinessjournal.com

Budhal, R. S. (2000). *The impact of the Principal's Instructional leadership on the Culture of Teaching and Learning in the school.* (Unpublished Master's Dissertation). UNISA, Durban, South Africa.

Bush, T. (2007). Educational leadership and management: Theory, policy, and practice. *South African Journal of Education, 27*(3), 391–406.

Byrne, B. M. (2001). *Structural Equation Modeling with AMOS. Basic Concepts, Applications and Programming.* Lawrence Erlbaum.

Cangemi, J. P., Burga, B., Lazarus, H., Miller, R. L., & Fitzgerald, J. (2008). The real work of a leader; a focus on the human side of the equation. *Journal of Management Development, 27*(10), 1026–1036. doi:10.1108/02621710810916286

Cline, Z., & Necochea, J. (2000). Socialisation paradox: A challenge for educational leaders'. *International Journal of Leadership in Education, 3*(2), 151–158. doi:10.1080/136031200292795

Consortium for Research on Emotional Intelligence in Organizations. (n.d.). *The emotional competence framework.* Retrieved March 15, 2011, from http:// www.eiconsortium.org

Council of Chief State School Officers (CCSSO). (2008). *Educational leadership policy standards as adopted by the National Policy Board for Educational Administration* (ISLLC 2008). Retrieved March 17, 2012, from http://www.ccsso.org

Davidson, R. J. (2001). The neural circuitry of emotion and affective style: Prefrontal cortex and amygdala contributions. *Social Sciences Information. Information Sur les Sciences Sociales, 40*(1), 11–37. doi:10.1177/053901801040001002

Day, C., Sammons, P., Hopkins, D., Harris, A., Leithwood, K., & Gu, Q. et al. (2009). *The impact of school leadership on pupil outcomes. Final report. Research report No. DCSF-RR108.* University of Nottingham.

Department of Basic Education. (2010a). Action Plan 2014. *Towards the realization of Schooling 2025.* Retrieved January 28, 2012, from http:// planipolis.iiep.unesco.org

Department of Basic Education. (2010b). Approval of the National Curriculum Statement Grades R -12 as National Education Policy. *Government Gazette.* (No. 34600).

Department of Basic Education. (2011a). *Education Statistics at a glance 2010.* Pretoria: Government Printer.

Department of Basic Education. (2011b). *Report on the Annual National Assessments of 2011.* Pretoria: Government Printer.

Department of Basic Education. (2012). *Annual National Assessments 2012. A guideline for the interpretation and use of ANA results.* Pretoria: Government Printer.

Emmerling, R. J., & Goleman, D. (2003). *Emotional Intelligence: Issues and common misunderstandings.* Retrieved June 16, 2012 from: http:// www.eiconsortium.org

Field, A. (2009). *Discovering Statistics using SPSS* (3rd ed.). London: SAGE.

Fineman, S. (Ed.). (1993). *Emotion in Organizations.* London: Sage.

Fullan, M. (1993). *Change forces: Probing the Depths of Educational Reform.* Bristol, UK: Falmer Press.

Gardner, H. (1983). *Frames of Mind: The Theory of Multiple Intelligences.* New York: Basic Books.

Gardner, H. (1999). *Intelligence Reframed.* New York: Basic Books.

Goleman, D. (1996). *Emotional Intelligence: Why It Can Matter more than IQ.* London: Bloomsbury Publishing.

Goleman, D. (1998). *Working with Emotional Intelligence.* New York: Bantum Books.

Goleman, D. (2001). Emotional intelligence: Issues in paradigm building. In C. Cherniss & D. Goleman (Ed.), The Emotionally Intelligent Workplace (pp. 13–26). San Francisco: Jossey-Bass.

Goleman, D., Boyatzis, R., & McKee, A. (2002). *Primal leadership: Realizing the power of emotional intelligence.* Boston: Harvard Business School Press.

Grandey, A. A., & Brauburger, A. L. (2002). The emotion regulation behind the customer service smile. In Emotions in the workplace. San Francisco, CA: Jossey-Bass

Grobler, B.R. (2013). The school principal as Instructional Leader: A structural Equation Model. *Education as Change, 17*(1), 177-199.

Grobler, B. R. (2014). Teachers' perceptions of the utilisation of emotional competence by their school leaders in Gauteng South Africa. *Educational Management Administration & Leadership,* 1–21. Available at http://ema.sagepub.com/content/early/2014/02/05/1741143213513184

Grobler, B. R., Mestry, R., & Naidoo, S. (2012). The influence of management practices on authentic collaboration with educators. *Journal of Social Sciences, 30*(3), 211–223.

Gross, J. J. (2002). Emotion regulation: Affective, cognitive, and social consequences. *Psychophysiology, 39*(3), 281–291. doi:10.1017/S0048577201393198 PMID:12212647

Hallinger, P. (1990). Principal instructional management rating scale. Version 2.3. Sarasota, FL: Leading Development Associates.

Hallinger, P. (2005). Instructional leadership and the school principal: A passing fancy that refuses to fade away. *Leadership and Policy in Schools, 4*(3), 221–239. doi:10.1080/15700760500244793

Hallinger, P. (2008, March). *Methodologies for studying school leadership: A review of 25 years of research using the Principal Instructional Management Rating Scale.* Paper presented at the Annual Conference of the American Educational Research Association. New York, NY.

Hallinger, P. (2011). Leadership for learning: Lessons from 40 years of empirical research. *Journal of Educational Administration, 49*(2), 125–142. doi:10.1108/09578231111116699

Hallinger, P., & Heck, R. H. (1998). Exploring the principal's contribution to school effectiveness: 1980-1995. *School Effectiveness and School Improvement, 9*(2), 157–191. doi:10.1080/0924345980090203

Hoadley, U., Christie, P., & Ward, L. (2009). Managing to learn: Instructional leadership in South African secondary schools. *School Leadership & Management, 29*(4), 373–389. doi:10.1080/13632430903152054

Hofstede, G. (1991). *Cultures and Organizations: Software of the mind.* Berkshire, UK: McGraw-Hill.

Hopkins, M. M., O'Neil, D. A., & Williams, H. W. (2007). Emotional intelligence and board governance: Leadership lessons from the public sector. *Journal of Managerial Psychology, 23*(7), 683–700. doi:10.1108/02683940710820109

Horng, E., & Loeb, S. (2010). New thinking about instructional leadership. *Kappan, 92*(3), 66–69. doi:10.1177/003172171009200319

Howie, S., van Staden, S., Tsheli, M., Dowse, C., & Zimmerman, L. (2011). *Progress in International Reading Literacy. South African Children's Reading Literacy Achievement.* Pretoria: Centre for Evaluation and Assessment.

Human Science Research Council (HSRC). (2011). *Highlights from TIMMS 2011. The South African perspective.* Pretoria: HSRC.

Jenkins, B. (2009). What it takes to be an instructional leader. *Principal (Reston VA), 88*(3), 34–37.

Kruger, A. G. (1996). *FDEEL 2-9 Study Manual 1: School Management: Internal and external environment, Educational leadership.* Pretoria, South Africa: UNISA.

Law, K. S., Wong, C. S., & Song, L. (2004). Construct Validity of Emotional Intelligence: Its Potential Utility of Management Studies. *The Journal of Applied Psychology*, *89*(3), 483–496. doi:10.1037/0021-9010.89.3.483 PMID:15161407

Lee, C. D. (2010). Soaring above the Clouds, Delving the Ocean's Depths: Understanding the Ecologies of Human Learning and the challenge for Education Science. *Educational Researcher*, *39*(9), 643–655. doi:10.3102/0013189X10392139

Leithwood, K., Louis, K. S., Anderson, S., & Wahlstrom, K. (2004). *How leadership influences student learning. A review of the research*. New York: The Wallace Foundation.

Lemmer, E. M. (1994). *Study Guide ONA 411-Y: Ethnographic research*. Pretoria, South Africa: UNISA.

Malgas, R. W. (2006). *Emotional intelligence in the effective management of the school*. (Unpublished Master's Dissertation). University of Johannesburg, Johannesburg, South Africa.

Maree, J. G., & Eiselen, R. J. (2004). The Emotional Intelligence Profile of Academics in a Merger Setting. *Education and Urban Society*, *36*(4), 482–504. doi:10.1177/0013124504265862

Mayer, J. D., & Salovey, P. (1997). What is emotional intelligence? In P. Salovey & D. Sluyter (Eds.), *Emotional development and emotional intelligence. Implications for educators* (pp. 3–34). New York, NY: Basic books.

McColl-Kennedy, J. R., & Anderson, R. D. (2002). Impact of leadership style and emotions on subordinate performance. *The Leadership Quarterly*, *13*(5), 545–559. doi:10.1016/S1048-9843(02)00143-1

Morgan, G. (1997). *Images of Organization*. London: SAGE.

Muijs, D. (2010). Leadership and Organizational Performance: From research to prescription? *International Journal of Educational Management*, *25*(1), 45–60. doi:10.1108/09513541111100116

Muijs, D., Harris, A., & Crawford, M. (2004). *The role of assistant heads: A review of research*. Paper presented at the International Congress for School Effectiveness and School Improvement. Rotterdam, The Netherlands.

Mullis, I. V. S., Martin, M. C., Foy, P., & Drucker, K. T. (2012). PIRLS 2011: International results in Reading. Chestnut Hill, MA: Boston College.

Neumerski, C. M. (2012). Rethinking instructional leadership, a review: What do we know about Principal, Teacher and Coach instructional leadership, and where should we go from here? *Educational Administration Quarterly*, *49*(2), 310–347. doi:10.1177/0013161X12456700

News 24.com. (n.d.). *Reports of assault in teacher strike*. Retrieved January 4, 2013, from http://www.news24.com/SouthAfrica/News

Norusis, M. J. (2009). *PASW 18. Statistical Procedures Companion*. Chicago: SPSS Inc.

Pallant, J. (2007). *SPSS Survival Manual* (3rd ed.). Berkshire, UK: McGraw-Hill.

Personnel Administrative Measures (PAM). (2003). *Published in Government Gazette 19767*. Pretoria: Government Printer.

Polychroniou, P. V. (2009). Relationship between emotional intelligence and transformational leadership of supervisors. The impact on team effectiveness. *Team Performance Management*, *15*(7/8), 343–356. doi:10.1108/13527590911002122

Rademeyer, A. (2012, December 12). SA leerlinge vaar sleg in dié twee w's (SA learners perform poorly in mathematics and science). *Beeld*, p. 4.

Saklofske, D. H., Austin, E. J., & Minski, P. S. (2003). Factor structure and validity of a trait emotional intelligence measure. *Personality and Individual Differences*, *34*(4), 707–721. doi:10.1016/S0191-8869(02)00056-9

Sammons, P., Hillman, J., & Mortimore, P. (1995). *Key characteristics of effective schools: A review of school effectiveness research*. London, UK: International School Effectiveness and Improvement Centre, Institute of Education.

Sampson, A. (1999). *Mandela: The Authorised Biography*. Johannesburg, South Africa: Jonathon Ball.

Schultz, C. (2007). *Emotional intelligence: An overlooked aspect of effective leadership practices: A review of the literature on desirable traits, behaviours and characteristics for successful leadership promoting transformational change*. Retrieved March 20, 2011, from http://cnx.org/content/m15615/1.2/

Schumacker, R. E., & Lomax, R. G. (2004). *A beginner's guide to Structural Equation Modeling* (2nd ed.). Lawrence Erlbaum.

Senge, R. (1999). *The Dance of Change: The challenges of sustaining momentum in Learning Organizations*. London: Nicholas Brealey.

Sewlall, K. (1996). *Dimensions of culture and their implication for the management in South African schools*. (Unpublished dissertation). Rand Afrikaans University, Johannesburg, South Africa.

Smit, M., & Oosthuizen, I. (2011). Improving school governance through participative democracy and the law. *South African Journal of Education*, *31*(1), 55–73.

South Africa. (2007). *Education Laws Amendment Act, 2007. Government Gazette (No. 30637)*. Pretoria: Government Printer.

South Africa. (2010). *Towards the realization of Schooling 2025. Government Gazette. (No. 33434)*. Pretoria: Government Printer.

South Africa. (2011). *Approval of the National Curriculum Statement Grades R-12 as National Education Policy: Curriculum Assessment Policy (CAPS). Government Gazette (No.34600)*. Pretoria: Government Printer.

Southworth, G. (2002). Instructional leadership in schools: Reflections and empirical evidence. *School Leadership & Management*, *22*(1), 73–92. doi:10.1080/13632430220143042

Sternberg, R., Lautrey, J., & Lubert, T. I. (2002). Where are we in the field of intelligence, how did we get here, and where are we going? In R. J. Sternberg, J. Lautrey, & T. I. Lubart (Eds.), *Models of Intelligence: International Perspectives* (pp. 3–25). Washington, DC: American Psychological Association.

Sternberg, R. J. (1997). *Successful intelligence*. New York: Plume.

Steyn, G. M. (2002). The changing Principalship in South African schools. *Educare*, *32*(1-2), 251–272.

Stone, H., Parker, J. D. A., & Wood, L. A. (2005). *Report on the Ontario Principals' Council leadership study*. Retrieved February 11, 2012, from: www.eiconsrtium.org

Taylor, G. J., Bagby, R. M., & Parker, J. D. A. (1997). *Disorders of affect regulation: Alexithymia in medical and psychiatric illness*. Cambridge, UK: Cambridge University Press. doi:10.1017/CBO9780511526831

Wallace, J. (2010). Facing "reality": The emotional in school leadership programmes. *Journal of Educational Administration, 48*(5), 595–610. doi:10.1108/09578231011067758

Wolff, S.B. (2005). *Emotional Competence Inventory (ECI): Technical Manual.* Hay Group, McClelland Center for research and Innovation.

Wong, C. S., Law, K. S., & Wong, P. M. (2004). Development and validation of a forced choice emotional intelligence measure for Chinese respondents in Hong Kong. *Asia Pacific Journal of Management, 21*(4), 535–559. doi:10.1023/B:APJM.0000048717.31261.d0

ADDITIONAL READING

Bar-On, R (1997). *The Emotional Intelligence Inventory (EQ-I): Technical manual.* Toronto, Canada: Multi-Health systems.

Becker, W. J., Cropanzano, R., & Sanfey, A. G. (2011). Organizational Neuroscience: Taking Organizational Theory inside the neural black box. *Journal of Management, 37*(4), 933–961. doi:10.1177/0149206311398955

Beigi, M., & Shirmohammadi, M. (2010). Training employees of a public Iranian Bank on Emotional Intelligence competencies. *Journal of European Industrial Training, 34*(3), 211–225. doi:10.1108/03090591011031728

Bies, R. J. (2012). The delivery of bad news: A framework for analysis. *Journal of Management, 1*(2), 1–25.

Blunch, N. J. (2008). *Introduction to Structural Equation Modeling using SPSS and AMOS.* London: SAGE.

Boyatzis, R. E. (2001). Developing Emotional Intelligence. In C. Cherniss & D. Goleman (Eds.), *The Emotionally Intelligent Workplace: How to select for, measure and improve Emotional Intelligence in individuals, groups and organizations.* San Francisco: Jossey Bass.

Boyatzis, R. E., & Soler, C. (2012). Vision, leadership and Emotional Intelligence transforming family business. *Journal of Family Business Management, 2*(1), 23–30. doi:10.1108/20436231211216394

Boyne, G., Day, P., & Walker, R. (2002). The evaluation of public service inspection: A theoretical framework. *Urban Studies (Edinburgh, Scotland), 39*(7), 1197–1212. doi:10.1080/00420980220135563

Brauckmann, S., & Pashiardis, P. (2010). A validation study of the leadership styles of a holistic leadership theoretical framework. *International Journal of Educational Management, 25*(1), 11–32. doi:10.1108/09513541111100099

Bridges, E. M. (1992). *The incompetent teacher. Managerial response.* London: Falmer.

Cherniss, C. (2001). Emotional intelligence and organizational effectiveness. In C. Cherniss & D. Goleman (Eds.), *The emotionally intelligent workplace* (pp. 3–26). San Francisco: Jossey-Bass.

Cliffe, J. (2011). Emotional Intelligence: A study of female secondary headteachers. *Educational Management Administration & Leadership, 39*(2), 205–218. doi:10.1177/1741143210390057

Crawford, M. (2007). Emotional coherence in Primary School Headship. *Educational Management Administration & Leadership, 35*(4), 521–534. doi:10.1177/1741143207081061

Elias, M. J. (2009). Social-emotional character development and academics as dual focus of Educational Policy. *Educational Policy, 23*(6), 831–846. doi:10.1177/0895904808330167

Emmerling, R. J., & Boyatzis, R. E. (2012). Emotional and Social intelligence competencies: Cross cultural implications. *Cross-cultural Management. International Journal (Toronto, Ont.), 19*(1), 4–18.

Fineman, S. (2000). Commodifying the Emotionally Intelligent. In S. Fineman (Ed.), *Emotion in Organizations* (2nd ed.). London: SAGE. doi:10.4135/9781446219850.n6

Fineman, S. (2004). Getting the measure of emotion – and the cautionary tale of Emotional Intelligence. *Human Relations, 57*(6), 719–740. doi:10.1177/0018726704044953

Fowlie, J., & Wood, M. (2009). The emotional impact of leaders' behaviours. *Journal of European Industrial Training, 36*(6), 559–572. doi:10.1108/03090590910974428

Gibson, D. E., & Callister, R. R. (2009). Anger in Organizations: Review and integration. *Journal of Management, 36*(1), 66–93. doi:10.1177/0149206309348060

Goleman, D. (1995). *Emotional Intelligence*. New York: Bantam.

Goleman, D. (1998). *Working with Emotional Intelligence*. New York: Bantam.

Goleman, D., Boyatzis, R. E., & McKee, A. (2002). *Primal Leadership: Realising the power of emotional intelligence*. Boston: Harvard Business School Press.

Grobler, B. R. (2012). Changing perceptions of teachers regarding the importance and competence of their principals as leaders. *South African Journal of Education, 32*(1), 40–55.

Hess, J. D., & Bacigalupo, A. C. (2011). Enhancing decisions and decision-making processes through the application of emotional intelligence skills. *Management Decision, 49*(5), 710–721. doi:10.1108/00251741111130805

Hoyt, C. L., Burnette, T. L., & Innella, A. N. (2012). I can do that: The impact of implicit theories of Leadership Role Model Effectiveness. *Personality and Social Psychology Bulletin, 38*(2), 257–268. doi:10.1177/0146167211427922 PMID:22143305

Hughes, J. (2005). Bringing emotion to work: Emotional intelligence, employee resistance and the reinvention of character. *Work, Employment and Society, 19*(3), 603–625. doi:10.1177/0950017005055675

Iszatt-White, M. (2009). Leadership as Emotional Labour: The effortful accomplishment of valuing practices. *Leadership, 5*(4), 447–467. doi:10.1177/1742715009343032

Kilduff, M., Chiaburu, D. S., & Menges, J. L. (2010). Strategic use of Emotional Intelligence in Organizational settings: Exploring the dark side. *Research in Organizational Behavior, 30,* 129–1532. doi:10.1016/j.riob.2010.10.002

Lemmer, E. M. (1994). *Study Guide ONA 411-Y: Ethnographic research*. Pretoria, South Africa: UNISA.

Leung, A. S. M. (2005). Emotional Intelligence or Emotional Blackmail? A study of a Chinese Professional-service firm. *International Journal of Cross Cultural Management, 5*(2), 181–196. doi:10.1177/1470595805054492

London, M., & Beatty, R. W. (1993). 360 degree feedback as a competitive advantage. *Human Resource Management, 32*(2-3), 353–372. doi:10.1002/hrm.3930320211

Love, P., Edwards, D., & Wood, E. (2010). Loosening the Gordian knot: The role of emotional intelligence in construction. *Engineering, Construction, and Architectural Management, 18*(1), 50–66. doi:10.1108/09699981111098685

Nwokah, N. G., & Ahiauzu, A. I. (2010). Marketing in governance: Emotional Intelligence leadership for effective corporate governance. *Corporate Governance, 10*(2), 150–162. doi:10.1108/14720701011035675

Progress in International Reading Literacy Study (PIRLS). (2006). Available from: http://nces.ed.gov. (Accessed 28 January 2012).

Senge, P. (1990). *The fifth discipline*. New York: Doubleday.

South Africa. (2007). *Education Laws Amendment Act. Government Gazette (No. 30637)*. Pretoria: Government Printer.

South Africa. (2010). *Towards the realization of Schooling 2025. Government Gazette. (No. 33434)*. Pretoria: Government Printer.

Southern and Eastern Consortium for Monitoring Educational Quality. (2010). *SACMEQ 111 Project results*. Available from: http://www.sacmeq.org. (Accessed 28 January 2012).

Steyn, G. M. (2002). The changing Principalship in South African schools. *Educare, 32*(1 & 2), 251–272.

Third International Mathematics and Science Study (TIMMS). (1997). *Third International Mathematics and Science Study*. Available from: http://nces.ed.gov. (Accessed on 28 January 2012.

Wong, C. S., Wong, P. M., & Peng, K. Z. (2010). Effect of middle-level leader and teacher emotional intelligence on school teachers' job satisfaction. *Educational Management Administration & Leadership, 38*(1), 59–70. doi:10.1177/1741143209351831

Yariv, E. (2004). Challenging teachers. What difficulties do they pose for their principals? *Educational Management Administration & Leadership, 32*(2), 149–189. doi:10.1177/1741143204041881

KEY TERMS AND DEFINITIONS

Analysis of Moment Structures (AMOS): The analysis of mean and covariance structures or causal modeling and comes in two approaches namely AMOS graphics and AMOS basic. In this research AMOS graphics was used where path diagrams are involved.

Collectivism: Cultural dimension in which people from birth onwards are integrated into strong, cohesive in-groups, which throughout people's lifetime continue to protect them in exchange for unquestioned loyalty.

Emotional Intelligence/Competence: The ability, capacity, skill or self-perceived ability to identify, evaluate and manage your own emotions, of others and of a group.

Individualism: Cultural dimension in which the ties between individuals are loose: everyone is expected to look after himself or herself and his or her immediate family.

Instructional Leadership: The indirect influence of the school principal on the teacher regarding student learning and achievement.

Kaiser-Meyer-Olkin Measure of Sampling Adequacy (KMO): The ratio of the squared correlation between variables to the squared partial correlation between variables. It varies between 0 and 1; a value of 0 indicates that the sum of the partial correlations is large relative to the sum of correlations, indicating diffusion in the pattern of correlations (hence factor analysis is likely to be inappropriate); a value close to 1 indicates that the patterns of correlations are relatively compact and so factor analysis should yield distinct and reliable factors.

Learner Achievement: The academic achievement of learners in standardised national examinations such as the Annual National Assessments (ANA) and the Senior Certificate Examination (SCE).

Structural Equation Modeling (SEM): A statistical methodology that is used to investigate the hypothesised structure of a construct. The relationship between the latent variables of the hypothesised construct is specified and then the data collected are used to determine the goodness of fit with the hypothesised model.

Compilation of References

Abawi, L. (2013a). School meaning systems: The symbiotic nature of culture and 'language-in-use'. *Improving Schools*, *16*(2), 89–106. doi:10.1177/1365480213492407

Abawi, L. (2013b). Metaphor: Powerful imagery bringing learning and teaching to life. *Improving Schools*, *16*(2), 130–147. doi:10.1177/1365480213492409

Abawi, L., & Oliver, M. (2013). Shared pedagogical understandings: Schoolwide inclusion practices supporting learner needs. *Improving Schools*, *16*(2), 159–174. doi:10.1177/1365480213493711

Abernathy, W. J., & Utterback, J. M. (1978). Patterns of industrial innovation. *Technology Review*, *80*(7), 40–47.

Academies Commission. (2013). *Unleashing greatness: Getting the best from an academised system*. London: The Report of the Academies Commission.

ACARA. (2014). *The Australian curriculum*. Canberra, Australia: Australian Curriculum, Assessment and Reporting Authority. Retrieved November 20, 2013, from http://www.australiancurriculum.edu.au

Ackerman, R., Ventimiglia, L., & Juchniewicz, M. (2002). The meaning of mentoring: Notes on a context for learning. In K. Leithwood & P. Hallinger (Eds.), Second International handbook of educational leadership and administration (pp. 1133-1161). Dordrecht, The Netherlands: Kluwer Academic.

Adams, R. (2012). *NAPLAN reporting – Measures and models for reporting gain over time*. Retrieved August 10, 2012, from http://www.coagreformcouncil.gov.au/excellence/docs/improvement/CI_NAPLAN_reporting_2012.pdf

Advance Illinois. (n.d.). *Profile of Illinois' education system*. Retrieved from http://www.advanceillinois.org/profile-of-our-education-system-pages-264.php

Aguinis, H., Simonsen, M. M., & Pierce, C. A. (1998). Effects of Nonverbal Behaviour on Perceptions of Power Bases. *The Journal of Social Psychology*, *138*(4), 455–469. doi:10.1080/00224549809600400 PMID:9664862

Ahearn, K. K., Ferris, G. R., Hochwarter, W. A., Douglas, C., & Ammeter, A. P. (2004). Leader political skill and team performance. *Journal of Management*, *30*(3), 309–327. doi:10.1016/j.jm.2003.01.004

Ahnberg, E., Lundgren, M., Messing, J. and von Schantz Lundgren, I. (2009). Följeforskning som företeelse och följeforskarrollen som konkret praktik. [The Phenomenon 'Research Followers']. *Arbetsmarknad och arbetsliv*, *15*(1).

AITSL. (2011). *National professional standards for teachers, Australian Institute for Teaching and School Leadership (AITSL)*. Carlton South, Australia: Education Services Australia.

Ajzen, I. (1987). Attitudes, traits, and actions: Dispositional prediction of behavior in personality and social psychology. *Advances in Experimental Social Psychology*, *20*(1), 1–63. doi:10.1016/S0065-2601(08)60411-6

Akbaba-Altun, S. (2007). Harmonious texture of cultural values and democracy: Patterns of success. In S. Donahoo & R. C. Hunters (Eds.), *Advances in Educational Administration Teaching Leaders to Lead Teachers: Educational Administration in the Era of Constant Crisis* (pp. 77–97). Amsterdam: Elsevier. doi:10.1016/S1479-3660(07)10005-6

Akert, N., & Martin, B. N. (2012). The role of teacher leaders in school improvement through the perceptions of principals and teachers. *International Journal of Education, 4*(4), 284–299. doi:10.5296/ije.v4i4.2290

Alerby, E., Bergmark, U., Dahlén, G., Rosengren Larsson, I., Vikström, A., & Westman, S. (2010). Ömsesidig samverkan mellan pedagogisk forskning och pedagogisk praktik. [Mutual interaction between educational research and practise]. In Utbildning på veteneskaplig grund. Stockholm: Stiftelsen SAF i samarbete med Lärarförbundet.

Alexander, C. N. Jr, & Knight, G. W. (1971). Situational identities and social psychological experimentation. *Sociometry, 34*(1), 65–82. doi:10.2307/2786351

Allen, C. (2001). What is complexity science? Knowledge of the limits of knowledge. *Emergence: A Journal of Complexity Issues in Organizations and Management, 3*(1), 24-44.

Alsop, S., Gould, G., & Watts, M. (2002). The role of pupils' questions in learning science. In S. Amos & R. Boohan (Ed.), Aspects of teaching secondary science: Perspectives on practice (pp. 39–48). London, UK: Routledge.

Altrichter, H., & Kanape-Willingshofer, A. (2013). Educational standards and external examination of pupils' competencies: Possible contributions of external measurements in attaining quality goals in schools. In B. Herzog-Punzenberger, M. Bruneforth, & L. Lassnigg (Eds.), *National Education Report Austria 2012: Indicators and Topics: An Overview*. Graz: Leykam. Retrieved, 20 February 2014, from https://www.bifie.at/system/files/dl/en_NBB_band3_web.pdf

Altrichter, H., & Heinrich, M. (2007). Kategorien der Governance-Analyse und Transformationen der Systemsteuerung in Österreich. In H. Altrichter, T. Brüsemeister, & J. Wissinger (Eds.), *Educational Governance – Handlungskoordination und Steuerung im Bildungssystem* (pp. 55–103). Wiesbaden: Verlag für Sozialwissenschaften.

Amabile, T. M. (1996). *Creativity in context: Update to the social psychology of creativity*. Boulder, CO: Westview.

Amabile, T. M. (1998). How to kill creativity. *Harvard Business Review, 76*(5), 77–87. PMID:10185433

Amabile, T., Conti, R., Coon, H., Lazenby, J., & Herron, M. (1996). Assessing the work environment for creativity. *Academy of Management Journal, 39*(5), 1154–1184. doi:10.2307/256995

Ancona, D., & Caldwell, D. (1987). Management issues facing new product teams in high technology companies. In D. Lewin, D. Lipsky, & D. Sokel (Eds.), *Advances in industrial and labor relations* (Vol. 4, pp. 191–221). Greenwich, CT: JAI Press.

Anderson, J. B. (2008). Principals' role and public primary schools' effectiveness in four Latin America cities. *The Elementary School Journal, 109*(1), 36–60. doi:10.1086/592366

Anderson, K. D. (2004). The nature of teacher leadership in schools as reciprocal influences between teacher leaders and principals. *School Effectiveness and School Improvement, 15*(1), 97–113. doi:10.1076/sesi.15.1.97.27489

Andreou, A., & Papaconstantinou, C. (1999). *Power and organization - administration of the educational system*. Athens: Nea Shinora. (in Greek)

Andrews, R. L., & Bamberg, J. D. (1989). *Teacher and supervisor assessment of principal leadership and academic achievement*. University of Washington.

Andrews, R., & Soder, R. (1987). Principal instructional leadership and school achievement. *Educational Leadership, 44*(6), 9–11.

Angelle, P. S., & DeHart, C. A. (2011). Teacher perceptions of teacher leadership: Examining differences by experience, degree, and position. *NASSP Bulletin, 95*(2), 141–160. doi:10.1177/0192636511415397

Anstey, M., & Bull, G. (1996). Re-examining pedagogical knowledge and classroom practice. In G. Bull & M. Anstey (Eds.), *The literacy labyrinth* (pp. 89–106). Sydney: Prentice-Hall.

Antonakis, J. (2003). Why Emotional Intelligence Does Not Predict Leadership Effectiveness: A Comment On Prati, Douglas, Ferris, Ammater, And Buckley (2003). *The International Journal of Organizational Analysis, 11*(4), 355–361. doi:10.1108/eb028980

Antonakis, J. (2011). Predictors of leadership: The usual suspects and the suspect traits. In A. Bryman, D. Collinson, K. Grint, B. Jackson, & M. Uhl-Bien (Eds.), *Sage Handbook of Leadership* (pp. 269–285). Thousand Oaks, CA: Sage Publications.

Antonakis, J., Ashkanasy, N. M., & Dasborough, M. (2009). Does leadership need emotional intelligence? *The Leadership Quarterly, 20*(2), 247–261. doi:10.1016/j.leaqua.2009.01.006

Antonakis, J., Day, D. V., & Schyns, B. (2012). Leadership and individual differences: At the cusp of a renaissance. *The Leadership Quarterly, 23*(4), 643–650. doi:10.1016/j.leaqua.2012.05.002

Antoniou, P. (2012a). The Short- and Long- term Effects of Secondary Schools upon Students' Academic Success and Development. *Educational Research and Evaluation, 18*(7), 621–640. doi:10.1080/13803611.2012.707826

Antoniou, P. (2012b). *Unfolding Instructional Leadership: Developing a Framework of Effective Actions and Strategies based on Teacher Perspectives. CCEAM.* Commonwealth Council for Educational Administration and Management.

Antoniou, P. (2013). Development of Research on School Leadership Through Evidence-based and Theory-Driven Approaches: A Review of School Leadership Effects Revisited. *School Effectiveness and School Improvement, 24*(1), 122–128.

Antoniou, P., & Kyriakides, L. (2011). The Impact of a Dynamic Approach to Professional Development on Teacher Instruction and Student Learning: Results from an Experimental Study. *School Effectiveness and School Improvement, 22*(3), 291–311. doi:10.1080/09243453.2011.577078

Antoniou, P., & Kyriakides, L. (2013). A Dynamic Integrated Approach to Teacher Professional Development: Impact and Sustainability of the Effects on Improving Teacher Behavior and Student Outcomes. *Teaching and Teacher Education, 29*(1), 1–12. doi:10.1016/j.tate.2012.08.001

Antúnez, S. (2002). La acción directiva en las instituciones escolares (2nd ed.). Barcelona: ICE-Horsori.

Antúnez, S. (2004). *Organización Escolar y Acción Directiva*. D. F., México: Secretaría de Educación Pública.

Antúnez, S. (2013). *La dirección escolar. Postgrado/Master en dirección de centros para la innovación educativa*. Barcelona: Universitat Autònoma de Barcelona.

APPA. (2014). *APPA submission to the Australian government review of the Australian curriculum*. Australian Primary Principals Association. Retrieved 20 March, 2014, from http://www.appa.asn.au/submissions/Review-of-Australian-curriculum.pdf

Arbuckle, J. L. (2007). *AMOS 16.0: User's guide*. Chicago: SPSS Inc.

Archer, J. (2005). Leadership training seen to fall short. *Education Week, 24*(38), 9.

Argyle, M., & Lu, L. (1990). Happiness and social skills. *Personality and Individual 199. Differences: A Journal of Feminist Cultural Studies, 11*, 1255–1261.

Argyris, C. (1997). Initiating change that preserves. *The American Behavioral Scientist, 40*(3), 299–310. doi:10.1177/0002764297040003006

Armenakis, A. A., & Bedeian, A. G. (1999). Organizational change: A review of theory and research in the 1990s. *Journal of Management, 25*(3), 293–315. doi:10.1177/014920639902500303

Arnold, G., & Civian, J. T. (1997). The ecology of general education reform. *Change, 29*(4), 18–23. doi:10.1080/00091389709602323

Arrowsmith, T. (2005). Distributed leadership: Three questions, two answers. *Management in Education, 19*(2), 30–33. doi:10.1177/08920206050190020701

Ashkanasy, N. M., & Tse, B. (2000). Transformational leadership as management of emotion: A conceptual review. In N. M. Ashkanasy, C. E. Haertel, & W. Zerbe (Eds.), *Emotions in the workplace: Research, theory, and practice* (pp. 221–235). Westport, CT: Quorum Books/Greenwood.

Ash, R. C., & Persall, J. M. (2000). The principal as chief learning officer: Developing teacher leaders. *NASSP Bulletin, 84*(616), 15–22. doi:10.1177/019263650008461604

Aslan, M. (2011). *Öğretmen liderliği davranışları ve sınıf iklimi: Öğretmen ve öğrenci görüşleri bağlamında bir araştırma* [Teacher leadership and classroom climate: A study regarding the opinions of teachers and students]. (Unpublished master's thesis). Eskişehir Osmangazi University, Eskişehir, Turkey.

Aslan, M., Beycioglu, K. & Konan, N. (2008). Principals' openness to change in Malatya, Turkey. *International Electronic Journal for Leadership in Learning, 12*(8).

Ault, C. R. (2009). *A case study of leadership characteristics of teacher leaders in an urban literacy program* (Doctoral dissertation). Retrieved from ProQuest Dissertations and Thesis database. (UMI No. 3346278)

Avolio, B., & Bass, B. (1994). Transformational leadership and organizational culture. International Journal of Public Administration, 17(3-4), 541-554.

Awamleh, R., & Gardner, W. L. (1999). Perceptions of Leader Charisma and Effectiveness: The Effects of Vision Content, Delivery, and Organizational Performance. *The Leadership Quarterly, 10*(3), 345–373. doi:10.1016/S1048-9843(99)00022-3

Aytaç, T. (2004). School-based budgeting. *Milli Eğitim Dergisi, 162.* Available at http://yayim.meb.gov.tr/dergiler/162/aytac.htm

Bagakis, G. (Ed.). (2002). *The school teacher as a researcher.* Athens: Metechmio. (in Greek)

Bain, A. (2007). *The self-organizing school: Next generation comprehensive school reforms.* Lanham, MD: Rowman and Littlefield.

Bain, A., Walker, A., & Chan, A. (2011). Self-organization and capacity building: Sustaining change. *Journal of Educational Administration, 49*(6), 701–719. doi:10.1108/09578231111174839

Bain, P. G., Mann, L., & Pirola-Merlo, A. (2001). The innovation imperative: The relationships between team climate, innovation, and performance in research and development teams. *Small Group Research, 32*(1), 55–73. doi:10.1177/104649640103200103

Barber, M. (2000). *High expectations and standards for all, no matter what: Creating a world class education service in England.* Keynote speech given at the Smith Richardson Foundation. Washington, DC. Retrieved February 4, 2002, from http://www.ncsl.org.uk/index.cfm?pageidOev_auth_barber

Bardach, R. H. (2008). *Leading schools with emotional intelligence: A study of the degree of association between middle school principal emotional intelligence and school success.* (Unpublished Doctoral dissertation). Capella University, Minneapolis, MN.

Barley, S. R. (1990). The alignment of technology and structure through roles and networks. *Administrative Science Quarterly, 35*(1), 61–103. doi:10.2307/2393551 PMID:10106582

Barnett, K., McCormick, J., & Conners, R. (2001). Transformational leadership in schools-panacea, placebo or problem? *Journal of Educational Administration, 39*(1), 24–46. doi:10.1108/09578230110366892

Bar-On, R. (1998). *The development of an operational concept of psychological well-being.* (Unpublished doctoral dissertation). Rhodes University.

Bar-On, R. (2000). Emotional and social intelligence: Insights from the Emotional Quotient Inventory (EQ-i). In R. Bar-On & J. D. A. Parker (Eds.), *Handbook of Emotional Intelligence* (pp. 363–388). San Francisco, CA: Jossey-Bass.

Barrales, A., & Medrano, H. (2011). Realidad y perspectiva de las competencias para el ejercicio directivo en México. In J. Gairín & D. Castro (Eds.), Competencias para el Ejercicio de la Dirección de Instituciones Educativas: Reflexiones y experiencias en Iberoamérica (pp. 98-116). Santiago de Chile: Redage.

Barrett, F. J. (1998). Creativity and improvisation in jazz and organizations: Implications for organizational learning. *Organization Science, 9*(5), 605-622. doi:1047-7039/98/0905/0605/$05.00

Barrick, M., Mount, M., & Judge, T. (2001). Personality and performance at the beginning of the new millennium: What do we know and where do we go next? *International Journal of Selection and Assessment, 9*(1/2), 9–30. doi:10.1111/1468-2389.00160

Barth, R. (1991). *Improving schools from within*. San Francisco: Jossey-Bass.

Barth, R. S. (1990). *Improving schools from within. Teachers, parents, and principals can make the difference*. San Francisco, CA: Jossey-Bass.

Barth, R. S. (2001). Teacher leader. *Phi Delta Kappan, 82*(6), 443–449. doi:10.1177/003172170108200607

Bass, B. (1998). *Transformational leadership: Industrial, military, and educational impact*. Mahwah, NJ: Lawrence Erlbaum Associates.

Bass, B. M. (1985). *Leadership and performance beyond expectations*. New York: The Free Press.

Bass, B. M. (1999). Two decades of research and development in transformational leadership. *European Journal of Work and Organizational Psychology, 8*(1), 9–33. doi:10.1080/135943299398410

Bass, B. M., & Avolio, B. J. (1993). Transformational leadership and organizational culture. *Public Administration Quarterly, 17*(1), 112–121.

Bass, B. M., & Avolio, B. J. (1995). *The multifactor leadership questionnaire – 5x short form*. Redwood: Mind Garden.

Bass, B. M., & Avolio, B. J. (1997). *The full range leadership development manual for the multifactor leadership questionnaire*. Redwood City, CA: Mindgarden Inc.

Bates, R. (2002). The impact of educational research: Alternative methodologies and conclusions. *Research Papers in Education, 17*(4), 403–408. doi:10.1080/0267152022000031379

Bauman, Z. (2007). *Tiempos líquidos*. Barcelona: Tusquets editores.

Baumeister, R.F., Bratslavsky, E., Finkenauer, C., & Vohs, K.D. (2001). Bad is stronger than good. *Review of AQ 6 General Psychology, 5*, 323–370.

Baumert, J., Ludtke, O., & Trautwein, U. (2006). *Interpreting effect sizes in large-scale educational assessments*. Berlin: Max Planck Institute for Human Development.

Beachum, F., & Dentith, A. M. (2004). Teacher leaders creating cultures of school renewal and transformation. *The Educational Forum, 68*(3), 276–286. doi:10.1080/00131720408984639

Beatty, B. (2001). The emotions of educational leadership: Breaking the silence. *International Journal of Leadership in Education, 4*, 331–357.

Beatty, B. (2007a). Feeling the future of school leadership: Learning to lead with the emotions in mind. *Leading and Managing, 13*(2), 44–65.

Beatty, B. (2007b). Going through the emotions: Leadership that gets to the heart of school renewal. *Australian Journal of Education, 51*(3), 328–340. doi:10.1177/000494410705100309

Becker, R. F. (2009). *International branch campuses: Markets and strategies*. London: Observatory for Higher Education.

Beer, M., & Nohria, N. (2000). Resolving the tension between theories E and O of change. In M. Beer & N. Nohria (Eds.), *Breaking the code of change* (pp. 1–35). Boston, MA: Harvard Business School Press.

Begley, P. T. (2006). Self-knowledge, capacity and sensitivity: Prerequisites to authentic leadership by school principals. *Journal of Educational Administration, 44*(6), 570–589. doi:10.1108/09578230610704792

Behn, R. D. (1991). *Leadership counts: Lessons for public managers from the Massachusetts welfare training and employment program*. Harvard University Press.

Belchetz, D., & Leithwood, K. (2007). Successful school leadership: Does context matter and if so, how? In C. Day & K. Leithwood (Eds.), *Successful Principal Leadership in Times of Change* (pp. 117–137). Dordrecht, The Netherlands: Springer. doi:10.1007/1-4020-5516-1_8

Bellamy, G. T., Fulmer, C., Murphy, M., & Muth, R. (2003). A Framework for school leadership accomplishments: Perspectives on knowledge, practice, and preparation for principals. *Leadership and Policy in Schools, 2*(4), 241–261. doi:10.1076/lpos.2.4.241.17892

Bengtsson, J. (1999). *En livsvärldsansats för pedagogisk forskning*. [A Lifeworld Approach for Educational Research]. Paper presented at NERA's Congress. Copenhagen, Denmark.

Bennett deMarrais, K., & LeCompte, M. (1995). *The way schools work: A sociological analysis of education* (2nd ed.). White Plains, NY: Longman Publishers.

Bennett, N., Wise, C., Woods, P., & Harvey, J. A. (2003). *Distributed leadership*. Nottingham, UK: National College for School Leadership.

Benson, M. J., & Campbell, J. P. (2007). To Be, or Not to Be, Linear: An expanded representation of personality and its relationship to leadership performance. *International Journal of Selection and Assessment, 15*(2), 232–249. doi:10.1111/j.1468-2389.2007.00384.x

Bentler, P. M., & Wu, E. J. C. (1995). *EQS for Windows user's guide* [Computer software manual]. Encino, CA: Multivariate Software.

Berglund, A., & Lister, R. (2010). *Introductory programming and the Didactic triangle*. Paper presented at the 12th Australian Computing Education Conference (ACE 2010). Brisbane, Australia.

Bet. (1992/93:UbU3). *Utbildningsutskottets betänkande om ny Högskolelag*. [Committee Report on the New Education Act].

Beycioğlu, K. (2009). *İlköğretim okullarında öğretmenlerin sergiledikleri liderlik rollerine ilişkin bir değerlendirme (Hatay ili örneği)* [An analysis of teacher leadership roles in elementary schools. The case of Hatay province]. (Unpublished doctoral dissertation). İnönü University, Malatya.

Beycioglu, K., & Ozer, N. (2010). *Investigating the aspects of principals' work perceived to be most challenging in the early years: Turkish adaptation of a scale*. Paper presented at EYEDDER. Antalya, Turkey.

Beycioğlu, K., & Aslan, B. (2010). Öğretmen liderliği ölçeği: Geçerlik ve güvenirlik çalışması[Teacher leadership scale: A validity and reliability study]. *Elementary Education Online, 9*(2), 764–775.

Beycioglu, K., & Aslan, B. (2010). Teacher Leadership Scale: A validity and reliability study. *Elementary Education Online, 9*(2), 764–775.

Beycioğlu, K., & Aslan, B. (2012). Öğretmen ve yöneticilerin öğretmen liderliğine ilişkin görüşleri: Bir karma yöntem çalışması[Teachers and administrators' views on teacher leadership: A mixed methods study]. *Educational Administration: Theory and Practice, 18*(2), 191–223.

Beycioglu, K., & Dönmez, B. (2006). Issues in theory development and practice in the field of educational administration. *Educational Administration: Theory and Practice, 12*(47), 317–342.

Biesta, G. (2007). Bridging the Gap between Educational Research and Educational Practice: The Need for Critical Distance. *Educational Research and Evaluation, 13*(3), 295–301. doi:10.1080/13803610701640227

Bigley, G. A., & Roberts, K. H. (2001). The incident command system: High-reliability organizing for complex and volatile task environments. *Academy of Management Journal, 44*(6), 1281–1299. doi:10.2307/3069401

Birkeland, S. A., Manson, T. M., Kisamore, J. L., Brannick, M. T., & Smith, M. A. (2006). A Meta-Analytic Investigation of Job Applicant Faking on Personality Measures. *International Journal of Selection and Assessment, 14*(4), 317–335. doi:10.1111/j.1468-2389.2006.00354.x

Blackmore, J. (1999). *Troubling Women: Feminism, Leadership and Educational Change*. Buckingham: Open University Press.

Blasé, J. (1993). The micropolitics of effective school-based leadership: Teachers' perspectives. *Educational Administration Quarterly, 29*(2), 142–163. doi:10.1177/0013161X93029002003

Blasé, J., & Blasé, J. (1999). Effective instructional leadership: Teachers' perspectives on how principals promote teaching and learning in schools. *Journal of Educational Administration, 38*(2), 130–141. doi:10.1108/09578230010320082

Blase, J., & Blase, J. (2000). Implementation of shared governance for instructional improvement: Principals 'Perspectives. *Journal of Educational Administration, 37*(5), 476–500. doi:10.1108/09578239910288450

Blase, J., & Blase, J. (2004). The dark side of school leadership: Implications for administer preparation. *Leadership and Policy in Schools*, 3(4), 245–273. doi:10.1080/15700760490503733

Blumer, H. (1969). Society as Symbolic Interaction. In M. Arnold (Ed.), *Human Behavior and Social Process: An Interactionist Approach*. Houghton-Mifflin.

Boden, D. (1994). *The business of talk*. Cambridge, MA: Polity Press.

Boeddrich, H.-J. (2004). Ideas in the workplace: A new approach towards organizing the fuzzy front end of the innovation process. *Creativity and Innovation Management*, 13(4), 274–185. doi:10.1111/j.0963-1690.2004.00316.x

Bogdan, R. C., & Biklen, S. K. (2002). *Qualitative research for education: An introduction to theory and methods* (4th ed.). Needham Heights, MA: Allyn and Bacon.

Bogler, R. (2002). Two profiles of schoolteachers: A discriminant analysis of job satisfaction. *Teaching and Teacher Education*, 18(6), 665–673. doi:10.1016/S0742-051X(02)00026-4

Bohlin, I. and Sager, M. (2011). *Evidensens många ansikten*. [The Many Faces of Evidence]. Lund:Arkiv förlag.

Bolam, R., McMahon, A., Stoll, L., Thomas, S., Wallace, M., … Smith, M. (2005). *Creating and Sustaining Effective Professional Learning Communities* (Research Report no. 637). London: DfES and University of Bristol.

Boler, M., & Zembylas, M. (2003). Discomforting truths: the emotional terrain of understanding difference. In P. Trifonas (Ed.), *Pedagogies of Difference: Rethinking Education for Social Change*. New York: Routledge Falmer.

Bolívar, A. (2011). Procesos de mejora basados en datos. La mejora del sistema educativo como proceso derivado de los resultados de la evaluación. In *P. Badía & Mª Vietes (Eds.), Evaluación, resultados -Escolares y sistemas educativos* (pp. 17–30). Madrid: Wolters Kluwer.

Bolívar, A. (2012). *Políticas actuales de mejora y liderazgo educativo*. Málaga: Aljibe.

Bono, E. J., Foldes, H. J., Vinson, G., & Muros, P. J. (2007). Workplace emotions: The role of supervision and leadership. *The Journal of Applied Psychology*, 92(5), 1357–1367. doi:10.1037/0021-9010.92.5.1357 PMID:17845090

Bono, J. E., & Ilies, R. (2006). Charisma, positive emotions and mood contagion. *The Leadership Quarterly*, 17(4), 317–334. doi:10.1016/j.leaqua.2006.04.008

Borkenau, P., & Ostendorf, F. (1990). Comparing exploratory and confirmatory factor analysis: A study on the 5-factor model of personality. *Personality and Individual Differences*, 11(5), 515–524. doi:10.1016/0191-8869(90)90065-Y

Bossert, S. T., Dwyer, D. C., Rowan, B., & Lee, G. V. (1982). The instructional management role of the principal. *Educational Administration Quarterly*, 18(3), 34–64. doi:10.1177/0013161X82018003004

Botha, R. J. (2004). Excellence in leadership: Demands on the professional school principal. *South African Journal of Education*, 24(3), 239–243.

Botha, R. J. (2012). Evolving leadership required in South African schools. *Research in Education*, 88(-1), 40–49. doi:10.7227/RIE.88.1.4

Bottery, M. (2001). Globalisation and the UK competition state: No room for transformational leadership in education? *School Leadership & Management*, 21(2), 199–218. doi:10.1080/13632430120054772

Bowen, G. L., Rose, R. A., & Ware, W. B. (2006). The reliability and validity of the School Success Profile Learning Organization Measure. *Evaluation and Program Planning*, 29(1), 97–104. doi:10.1016/j.evalprogplan.2005.08.005

Boyatzis, R. E. (2011). *Neuroscience and Leadership: The Promise of Insights*. Retrieved March 18, 2012, from http://www.iveybusinessjournal.com

Boyatzis, R. E. (1982). *The Competent Manager: A Model for Effective Performance*. New York, NY: John Wiley & Sons.

Boyatzis, R. E., Goleman, D., & Rhee, K. (2000). Clustering competence in emotional intelligence: Insights from the Emotional Competence Inventory (ECI). In R. Bar-On & J. D. A. Parker (Eds.), *Handbook of emotional intelligence* (pp. 343–362). San Francisco: Jossey-Bass.

Boyce, M. E. (2003). Organizational learning is essential to achieving and sustaining change in higher education. *Innovative Higher Education, 28*(2), 119–136. doi:10.1023/B:IHIE.0000006287.69207.00

Boylan, M. (2013). Deepening system leadership: Teachers leading from below. *Educational Management Administration & Leadership, 28*(October), 1–16.

Brackett, M. A., & Katulak, N. A. (2006). Emotional intelligence in the classroom: Skill-based training for teachers and students. In J. Ciarrochi & J. D. Mayer (Eds.), *Applying emotional intelligence: A practitioner's guide* (pp. 1–27). New York: Psychology Press.

Branch, G. F., Hanushek, E., & Rivkin, S. (2008). *Principal Turnover and Effectiveness*. Paper presented at the annual meeting of the American Economics Association. San Francisco, CA.

Brauckmann, S., & Pashiardis, P. (2009). *From PISA to LISA: New Educational Governance and school leadership: Exploring the foundations of a new relationship in an international context*. Paper presented at the 90th Annual Meeting of the American Educational Research Association. San Diego, CA.

Brauckmann, S., & Pashiardis, P. (2011). A validation study of the leadership styles of a holistic leadership theoretical framework. *International Journal of Educational Management, 25*(1), 11–32. doi:10.1108/09513541111100099

Bravslavsky, C. (2002). *Teacher education and the demands of curricular change*. New York: American Association of Colleges for Teacher Education.

Brewer, D. J., Augustine, C. H., Zellman, G. L., Ryan, G. W., Goldman, C. A., Stasz, C., & Constant, L. (2007). *Education for a new era: Design and implementation of K-12 education reform in Qatar*. Rand Corp. Retrieved December 13, 2013, from http://www.rand.org/pubs/monographs/MG548/

Brewer, D. (1993). Principals and Student Outcomes: Evidence from U.S. High Schools. *Economics of Education Review, 12*(4), 281–292. doi:10.1016/0272-7757(93)90062-L

Bridges, E. (1977). The nature of leadership. In L. Cunningham, W. Hack, & R. Nystrand (Eds.), *Educational administration: the developing decades*. Berkeley, CA: McCutchan.

British Council. (2010). *Secondary education: Opportunities in UK education at secondary level*. Retrieved from http://www.britishcouncil.org/macedonia-education-secondary-education.htm

Broekkamp, H., & van Hout-Wolters, B. (2007). The Gap between Educational Research and Practice: A Literature Review, Symposium, and Questionnaire. *Educational Research and Evaluation, 13*(3), 203–220. doi:10.1080/13803610701626127

Brown, J. S., & Duguid, P. (1991). Organizational learning and communities-of-practice: Toward a unified view of working, learning, and innovation. *Organization Science, 2*(1), 40-57. doi:1047-7039/91/0201/0040/$01.25

Brown, A. D., & Humphreys, M. (2003). Epic and tragic tales: Making sense of change. *The Journal of Applied Behavioral Science, 39*(2), 121–144. doi:10.1177/0021886303255557

Browne-Ferrigno, T., & Muth, R. (2004). Leadership mentoring in clinical practice: Role socialization, professional development, and capacity building. *Educational Administration Quarterly, 40*(4), 468–494. doi:10.1177/0013161X04267113

Brown, K. M. (2004). Leadership for social justice and equity: Weaving a transformative framework and pedagogy. *Educational Administration Quarterly, 40*(1), 79–110. doi:10.1177/0013161X03259147

Brownlee, P. P. (2000). Effecting transformational institutional change. *National Academy Newsletter, 1*(3). Retrieved at http://www.thenationalacademy.org/readings/effecting.html

Brown, S. L., & Eisenhardt, K. M. (1997). The art of continuous change: Linking complexity theory and time-paced evolution in relentlessly shifting organizations. *Administrative Science Quarterly, 42*(1), 1–34. doi:10.2307/2393807

Bruggencate, G., Luyten, H., Scheerens, J., & Sleegers, P. (2012). Modeling the Influence of School Leaders on Student Achievement: How Can School Leaders Make a Difference? *Educational Administration Quarterly, 84*(4), 699–732. doi:10.1177/0013161X11436272

Brunell, A. B., Gentry, W. A., Campbell, W. K., Hoffman, B. J., Kuhnert, K. W., & DeMarree, K. G. (2008). Leader Emergence: The Case of the Narcissistic Leader. *Personality and Social Psychology Bulletin, 34*(12), 1663–1676. doi:10.1177/0146167208324101 PMID:18794326

Bruns, H. C. (2013). Working alone together: Coordination changes expert practice in cross-domain collaboration. *Academy of Management Journal, 56*, 62–83. doi:10.5465/amj.2010.0756

Bryk, A., Camburn, E., & Louis, K. S. (1999). Professional community in Chicago elementary schools: Facilitating factors and organizational consequences. *Educational Administration Quarterly, 35*(5Supplement), 751–781. doi:10.1177/0013161X99355004

Bryk, A., Sebring, P., Allensowrth, E., Luppesco, S., & Easton, J. (2010). *Organizing schools for improvement: Lessons from Chicago.* Chicago: University of Chicago Press.

Bubb, S., & Earley, P. (2008). *From self-evaluation to school improvement: The importance of effective staff development.* Reading, UK: CfBT Education Trust.

Buckner, K. G., & McDowelle, J. O. (2000). Developing teacher leaders: Providing encouragement, opportunities, and support. *NASSP Bulletin, 84*(616), 35–41. doi:10.1177/019263650008461607

Bucy, E. P. (2000). Emotional and evaluative consequences of inappropriate leader displays. *Communication Research, 27*(2), 194–226. doi:10.1177/009365000027002004

Bucy, E. P., & Bradley, S. D. (2004). Presidential expressions and viewer emotion: Counter empathic responses to televised leader displays. *Social Sciences Information. Information Sur les Sciences Sociales, 43*(1), 59–94. doi:10.1177/05390184040689

Bucy, E. P., & Newhagen, J. E. (1999). The Emotional Appropriateness Heuristic: Processing Televised Presidential Reactions to the News. *Journal of Communication, 49*(4), 59–79. doi:10.1111/j.1460-2466.1999.tb02817.x

Budhal, R. S. (2000). *The impact of the Principal's Instructional leadership on the Culture of Teaching and Learning in the school.* (Unpublished Master's Dissertation). UNISA, Durban, South Africa.

Bullock, K. (2009). *The impact of school leadership on pupil outcomes.* Research Report DCSF-RR108. London: Department for Children, Schools and Families (DCSF).

Bullough, R. V. (2007). Professional learning communities and the Eight-Year Study. *Educational Horizons, 85*(3), 168–180.

Burgess, C. A. (2012). *Teachers' perceptions of teacher leadership and teacher efficacy* (Doctoral dissertation). Retrieved from ProQuest Dissertations and Thesis database. (UMI No. 3493784)

Burke, J. R. (1980). *A study of similarities and differences in elementary principals' perceived allocation and ideal allocation of time.* (Doctoral thesis). Florida State University, Tallahassee, FL.

Burkhardt, H., & Schoenfeld, A. H. (2003). Improving educational research: Toward a more useful, more influential, and better – funded enterprise. *Educational Researcher, 32*(9), 3–14. doi:10.3102/0013189X032009003

Bush, T. (2004). *The performance of leaders: Aims, impact and development.* Keynote paper presented at the British Educational Leadership, Management and Administration Society's Annual Conference. Stone, UK. Retrieved January 23, 2006, from http://www.shu.ac.uk/bemas/bush2004.html

Bush, T. (2003). *Theories of educational leadership and management* (3rd ed.). London: Sage.

Bush, T. (2007). Educational leadership and management: Theory, policy, and practice. *South African Journal of Education, 27*, 391–406.

Bush, T. (2010). Leadership development. In T. Bush, L. Bell, & D. Middlewood (Eds.), *The principles of educational leadership and management* (2nd ed., pp. 112–132). London: Sage.

Bush, T., Glover, D., & Sood, K. (2006). Black and minority ethnic leaders in England: A portrait. *School Leadership & Management, 26*(3), 289–305. doi:10.1080/13632430600737140

Bush, T., & Jackson, D. (2002). A preparation for school leadership: International perspectives. *Educational Management Administration & Leadership, 30*(4), 417–429. doi:10.1177/0263211X020304004

Bush, T., Kiggundu, E., & Moorosi, P. (2011). Preparing new principals in South Africa: The ACE School Leadership Programme. *South African Journal of Education, 31*(1), 31–43.

Bush, T., & Middlewood, B. (2005). *Leading and Managing People in Education*. London: Sage Publication.

Bush, T., & Oduro, G. K. T. (2006). New principals in Africa: Preparation, induction and practice. *Journal of Educational Administration, 44*(4), 359–375. doi:10.1108/09578230610676587

Byrne, B. M. (2001). *Structural Equation Modeling with AMOS. Basic Concepts, Applications and Programming*. Lawrence Erlbaum.

Calder, B. (1977). An attribution theory of leadership. In B. Staw & G. Salancik (Eds.), *New directions in organizational behavior* (pp. 179–204). Chicago: St. Claire Press.

Caldwell, B. J. (1994). Leading the transformation of Australia's schools. *Management in Education, 22*(2), 76–84.

Caldwell, B. J., & Spinks, J. M. (2013). *The self-transforming school*. New York, NY: Routledge.

Caldwell, B., Calnin, G., & Cahill, W. (2003). Mission impossible? An international analysis of headteacher/principal training. In N. Bennett, M. Crawford, & M. Cartwright (Eds.), *Effective educational leadership* (pp. 111–130). London: Paul Chapman Publishing.

Caldwell, D. F., & Burger, J. M. (1998). Personality characteristics of job applicants and success in screening interviews. *Personnel Psychology, 51*(1), 119–136. doi:10.1111/j.1744-6570.1998.tb00718.x

Camburn, E., Rowan, B., & Taylor, J. E. (2003). Distributed leadership in schools: The case of elementary schools adopting comprehensive school reform models. *Educational Evaluation and Policy Analysis, 25*(4), 347–373. doi:10.3102/01623737025004347

Campbell, C. (2013). *Whole system change*. Paper presented at the Annual Conference of the British Educational Leadership and Management Association (BELMAS). Edinburgh, UK.

Campbell-Evans, G. (1993). *A Values Perspective on School-based Management: School Based Management and School Effectiveness*. London: Routledge.

Camras, L. A. (2000). Surprise!: Facial expressions can be coordinative motor structures. In M. D. Lewis & I. Granic (Eds.), *Emotion, development, and self-organization* (pp. 100–124). New York: Cambridge University Press. doi:10.1017/CBO9780511527883.006

Canavan, K. (2003). The development of the Catholic Education Office and a system of schools in Sydney since 1965. Sydney, Australia: CEO Sydney.

Canavan, K. (2007). *School review and improvement*. Sydney, Australia: Catholic Education Office.

Canavan, K. (2008). *Building a leadership and learning culture across a school system*. Sydney, Australia: Catholic Education Office.

Cangemi, J. P., Burga, B., Lazarus, H., Miller, R. L., & Fitzgerald, J. (2008). The real work of a leader; a focus on the human side of the equation. *Journal of Management Development, 27*(10), 1026–1036. doi:10.1108/02621710810916286

Can, N. (2006). Öğretmen liderliğinin geliştirilmesinde müdürün rol ve stratejileri[The roles and the strategies of the principal in improving teacher leadership]. *Erciyes University Journal of the Institute Social Sciences, 21*, 349–363.

Can, N. (2007). Öğretmen liderliği becerileri ve bu becerilerin gerçekleştirilme düzeyi[Teacher leadership skills and its level of realization]. *Erciyes University Journal of the Institute Social Sciences, 22*(1), 263–288.

Can, N. (2009a). *Öğretmen liderliği* [Teacher leadership]. Ankara: Pegem Akademi.

Can, N. (2009b). Öğretmenlerin sınıfta ve okulda liderlik davranışları[Leadership behaviors of teachers in classroom and school]. *University of Gaziantep Journal of Social Sciences, 2*, 385–399.

Can, N. (2011). Developing activities of learning organizations in primary schools. *African Journal of Business Management, 5*(15), 6256–6260.

Capra, F. (1997). *The web of life: A new understanding of living systems*. New York: Doubleday.

Cardona, P., & Chinchilla, N. (1999). Evaluación y desarrollo de las competencias directivas. *Harvard Deusto Business Review, 89*, 10–19.

Carpenter, B. (2007). Developing the role of schools as research organisations: The Sunfield experience. *British Journal of Special Education, 34*(2), 67–76. doi:10.1111/j.1467-8578.2007.00458.x

Carr, A. (1994). 'For self or others? The Quest for narcissism and the ego-ideal in work organisations'. *Administrative Theory and Praxis, 16*(2), 208–222.

Carroll, J. M., & Russell, J. A. (1996). Do Facial Expressions Signal Specific Emotions? Judging Emotion From the Face in Context. *Journal of Personality and Social Psychology, 70*(2), 205–218. doi:10.1037/0022-3514.70.2.205 PMID:8636880

Catalan Education Act (LEC). (2009) *Generalitat de Catalunya*. Available at: http://portaldogc.gencat.cat/utilsEADOP/PDF/5422/950599.pdf

Cavazotte, F., Moreno, V., & Hickmann, M. (2012). Effects of leader intelligence, personality and emotional intelligence on transformational leadership and managerial performance. *The Leadership Quarterly, 23*(3), 443–455. doi:10.1016/j.leaqua.2011.10.003

Cemaloglu, N. (2005). The Training of school principals and their employment in Turkey: Current situation, possible developments in the future and problems. *Journal of Gazi Educational Faculty, 25*(2), 249–274.

Chamorro-Premuzic, T. (2007). *Personality and individual differences*. Malden, MA: BPS Blackwell.

Chan, T., & Pool, H. (2002). *Principals' priorities versus their realities: Reducing the gap*. Paper presented at the annual meeting of the American Educational Research Association. New Orleans, LA.

Chandler, D. (2001). *Semiotics: The Basics*. London: Routledge.

Channouf, A. (2000). Subliminal exposure to facial expressions of emotion and evaluative judgments of advertising messages. *European Review of Applied Psychology, 50*, 19–23.

Chelladurai, P. (1999). *Human Resource Management in Sport and Recreation*. Champagne, IL: Human Kinetics.

Cheng, Y. C. (1994). Principal's leadership as a critical indicator of school performance: Evidence from multi-levels of primary schools. *School Effectiveness and School Improvement, 5*(3), 299–317. doi:10.1080/0924345940050306

Cheng, Y. C., & Walker, A. (2008). When reform hits reality: The bottleneck effect in Hong Kong primary schools. *School Leadership & Management, 28*(5), 505–521. doi:10.1080/13632430802499994

Cherniss, C. (2003). *The Business Case for Emotional Intelligence*. Retrieved June 20, 2004, from http://www.eiconsortium.org/research/business_case_for_ei.pdf

Cherulnik, P. D., Donley, K. A., Wiewel, T. S., & Miller, S. R. (2001). Charisma Is Contagious: The Effect of Leaders' Charisma on Observers' Affect. *Journal of Applied Social Psychology, 31*(10), 2149–2159. doi:10.1111/j.1559-1816.2001.tb00167.x

Chesterton, P., & Duignan, P. (2004). *Evaluation of a national trial of IDEAS Project: Report prepared for the Department of Education, Science and Training (DEST)*. Canberra, Australia: DEST.

Cheung, M. F., & Wong, C. S. (2011). Transformational leadership, leader support, and employee creativity. *Leadership and Organization Development Journal*, *32*(7), 656–675. doi:10.1108/01437731111169988

Child, J., & McGrath, R. G. (2001). Organizations unfettered: Organizational form in an information-intensive economy. *Academy of Management Journal*, *44*(6), 1135–1148. doi:10.2307/3069393

Childs-Bowen, D., Moller, G., & Scrivner, J. (2000). Principals: Leaders of leaders. *NASSP Bulletin*, *84*(616), 27–34. doi:10.1177/019263650008461606

Chin, J. M.-C. (2007). Meta-analysis of transformational school leadership effects on school outcomes in Taiwan and the USA. *Asia Pacific Education Review*, *8*(2), 166–177. doi:10.1007/BF03029253

Christenson, S. L., Rounds, T., & Gorney, D. (1992). Family factors and student achievement: An avenue to increase student's success. *School Psychology Quarterly*, *7*(3), 178–206. doi:10.1037/h0088259

Christie, R., & Geis, F. L. (1970). *Studies in Machiavellianism*. New York: Academic Press.

Cilliers, P. (2001). Boundaries, hierarchies, and networks in complex systems. *International Journal of Innovation Management*, *5*(2), 135–147. doi:10.1142/S1363919601000312

Çınkır, Ş. (2010). Problems of primary school headteachers: Problem sources and support strategies. *Elementary Education Online*, *9*(3), 1027–1036.

Clark, B. R. (2004). *Sustaining change in universities: Continuities in case studies and concepts*. New York: Open University Press.

Clark, D., Lotto, L., & Astuto, T. (1984). Effective schools and school improvement: A comparative analysis of two lines of inquiry. *Educational Administration Quarterly*, *20*(3), 41–68. doi:10.1177/0013161X84020003004

Clarke, S., Wildy, H., & Pepper, C. (2007). Connecting preparation with reality: Primary principals' experiences of their first year out in Western Australia. *Leading and Managing*, *13*(1), 81–90.

Clegg, C., & Walsh, S. (2004). Change management: Time for change! *European Journal of Work and Organizational Psychology*, *13*(2), 217–239. doi:10.1080/13594320444000074

Cline, Z., & Necochea, J. (2000). Socialisation paradox: A challenge for educational leaders'. *International Journal of Leadership in Education*, *3*(2), 151–158. doi:10.1080/136031200292795

Cohen, L., Manion, L., & Morrison, K. (2007). *Research Methods in Education* (7th ed.). London: Routledge Taylor & Francis Group.

Cohn, J. F., & Ekman, P. (2008). Measuring Facial Action. In J. A. Harrigan, R. Rosenthal, & K. R. Scherer (Eds.), *The new handbook of Methods in Nonverbal Behavior Research* (pp. 9–64). New York: Oxford University Press. doi:10.1093/acprof:oso/9780198529620.003.0002

Cohn, J. F., Zlochoher, A. J., Lien, J., & Kanade, T. (1999). Automated face analysis by feature point tracking has high concurrent validity with manual FACS coding. *Psychophysiology*, *36*(1), 35–43. doi:10.1017/S0048577299971184 PMID:10098378

Coleman, A. (2007). Leaders as Researchers: Supporting Practitioner Enquiry through the NCSL Research Associate Programme. *Educational Management Administration & Leadership*, *35*(4), 479–497. doi:10.1177/1741143207002429

Coleman, M. (2007). Gender and educational leadership in England: A comparison of Secondary head teachers' views over time. *School Leadership & Management*, *27*(4), 383–399. doi:10.1080/13632430701562991

College, M. (2011). *Who's leading now: A case study of teacher leadership* (Doctoral dissertation). Retrieved from ProQuest Dissertations and Thesis database. (UMI No. 3509123)

Commission on School Leader Preparation in Illinois Colleges and Universities. (2006). School leader preparation: A blueprint for change. *Education*.

Conley, S., & Enomoto, E. K. (2009). Organizational routines in flux: A case study of change in recording and monitoring student attendance. *Education and Urban Society*, *41*(3), 364–386. doi:10.1177/0013124508327581

Connell, R. (2012). Ideology of the marketplace underpins school "reforms". *The Drum: Analysis and opinion on the issues of the day*. Retrieved December 16, 2013, from http://www.abc.net.au/unleashed/3892492.html

Consortium for Research on Emotional Intelligence in Organizations. (n.d.). *The emotional competence framework*. Retrieved March 15, 2011, from http:// www.eiconsortium.org

Conway, J. M., & Abawi, L. (2013). Creating enduring strength through commitment to schoolwide pedagogy. *Improving Schools*, *16*(2), 175–185. doi:10.1177/1365480213493714

Cook, C. R. (2006). *Effects of emotional intelligence on principals' leadership performance*. (Unpublished dissertation). University of Montana. Retrieved, 21 February 2014, from http://scholarworks.montana.edu/xmlui/bitstream/handle/1/1099/CookC0506.pdf?sequence=1

Cooper, A., Levin, B., & Campbell, C. (2009). The growing (but still limited) importance of evidence in education policy and practice. *Journal of Educational Change*, *10*(2-3), 159–171. doi:10.1007/s10833-009-9107-0

Cooper, C. (2010). *Individual Differences and Personality* (3rd ed.). London: Routledge.

Coronel, J. M. (2008). El liderazgo pedagógico: un reto y una posibilidad para la mejora educativa. In A. Villa (Ed.), *Innovación y cambio en las organizaciones educativas* (pp. 337–360). Bilbao: ICE de la Universidad de Deusto.

Cosenza, M. N. (2010). *The impact of professional development schools on teacher leadership* (Doctoral dissertation). Retrieved from ProQuest Dissertations and Thesis database. (UMI No. 3426693)

Costa, A. L., & Kallick, B. (Eds.). (2000). *Discovering and exploring Habits of Mind. Habits of Mind: A developmental series*. Alexandria, VA: Association for Supervision and Curriculum Development.

Costa, P. T. Jr, & McCrae, R. R. (1992). *NEO PI-R professional manual*. Odessa, FL: Psychological Assessment Resources, Inc.

Cotton, K. (2003). *Principals and student achievement: What the research says*. Alexandria, VA: Association for Supervision and Curriculum Development.

Council of Chief State School Officers (CCSSO). (2008). *Educational leadership policy standards as adopted by the National Policy Board for Educational Administration* (ISLLC 2008). Retrieved March 17, 2012, from http://www.ccsso.org

Coveney, P., & Highfield, R. (1995). *Frontiers of complexity*. New York: Fawcett Columbine.

Cowie, M., & Crawford, M. (2007). Principal preparation – still an act of faith? *School Leadership & Management*, *27*(2), 129–146. doi:10.1080/13632430701237198

Cowie, M., & Crawford, M. (2008). Being a new principal in Scotland. *Journal of Educational Administration*, *46*(6), 676–689. doi:10.1108/09578230810908271

Cowley, W. H. (1931). Three distinctions in the study of leaders. *Journal of Abnormal and Social Psychology*, *26*, 304–313. doi:10.1037/h0074766

Cox, E. (2006). What Personality Inventories and Leadership Assessments Say About Aspiring Principals Conceptual Frame. *ERS Spectrum*, *24*(4), 13–20.

Cranston, N. (1996). An investigation of the skills, knowledge and attitudes of principals. *Practising Administrator*, *18*(3), 4–7.

Cranston, N. C. (2000). Teachers as leaders: A critical agenda for the new millennium. *Asia-Pacific Journal of Teacher Education*, *28*(2), 123–131. doi:10.1080/713650688

Crawford, M. (2005). Distributed leadership and headship: A paradoxical relationship? *School Leadership & Management*, *25*(3), 213–215. doi:10.1080/13634230500116306

Creemers, B. P. M., & Kyriakides, L. (2008). *The Dynamics of Educational Effectiveness: A Contribution to Policy, Practice and Theory in Contemporary Schools*. Abingdon, UK: Routledge.

Creemers, B., Kyriakides, L., & Sammons, P. (2010). *Methodological advances in educational effectiveness research*. London: Taylor & Francis, Ltd.

Creighton, T. B., & Jones, G. D. (2001). *Selection or self-selection? How rigorous are our selection criteria for education administration preparation programs?* Paper presented at the annual conference of the National Council of Professors of Educational Administration. Houston, TX.

Creswell, J. W. (2009). *Research design: Qualitative, quantitative, and mixed method approaches.* Los Angeles: Sage.

Cronbach, L. (1949). *Essentials of Psychological Testing.* New York: Harper.

Crossan, M. M. (1998). Improvisation in action. *Organization Science, 9*(5), 593-599. doi:1047-7039/98/0905/0593/$05.00

Crowther, F., Andrews, D., Morgan, A., & O'Neill, S. (2012, Summer). Hitting the bull's eye of school improvement: The IDEAS arrow. *Leading and Managing,* 1-31.

Crowther, F., Ferguson, M., & Hann, L. (2009). Developing teacher leaders: How teacher leadership enhances school success (2nd. ed.). Thousand Oaks, CA: Corwin Press.

Crowther, F. (2011). *From school improvement to sustained capacity.* Thousand Oaks, CA: Corwin Press.

Crowther, F., Andrews, D., & Conway, J. M. (2013). *Schoolwide pedagogy: Vibrant new meaning for teachers and principals.* Melbourne, Australia: Hawker Brownlow Education.

Çukadar, C. (2003). *Managerial problems faced by basic education school principals who are appointed according to regulation No 23472.* (M.A. Thesis). Ankara Unv. YOK document center (No. 126487).

Culican, S. J. (2005). Troubling teacher talk: The challenge of changing classroom discourse patterns. Paper presented at the Annual Conference of the Australian Association for Research in Education. Sydney, Australia. Retrieved June 01, 2014, from http://www.aare.edu.au/data/publications/2005/cul05592.pdf

Cullen, S. (2014). *Teachers warn of 'culture wars' as Christopher Pyne announces back-to-basics curriculum review.* Australian Broadcasting Commission News. Retrieved February 15, 2014 from http://www.abc.net.au/news/2014-01-10/pyne-calls-for-national-curriculum-to-focus-on-benefits-of-west/5193804

Cunningham, M. R. (1988). What do you do when you're happy or blue? Mood, expectancies, and behavioral interest. *Motivation and Emotion, 12*(4), 309–331. doi:10.1007/BF00992357

Curci, M. E. (2012). *An examination of teacher leadership perceptions of teachers and building administrators using a comparative case study approach* (Doctoral dissertation). Retrieved from ProQuest Dissertations and Thesis database. (UMI No. 3499392)

Daft, R. L., & Lewin, A. Y. (1993). Where are the theories for the new organizational forms? An editorial essay. *Organization Science, 4,* i–vi.

Dahl, M. S. (2011). Organizational change and employee stress. *Management Science, 57*(2), 240–256. doi:10.1287/mnsc.1100.1273

Damen, F., VanKnippenberg, D., & VanKnippenberg, B. (2008). Leader Affective Displays and Attributions of Charisma: The Role of Arousal. *Journal of Applied Social Psychology, 38*(10), 2594–2614. doi:10.1111/j.1559-1816.2008.00405.x

Danielson, C. (2006). *Teacher leadership that strengthens professional practice.* Alexandria, VA: Association for Supervision and Curriculum Development.

Daresh, J. C. (2001). *Beginning the principalship* (2nd ed.). Thousand Oaks, CA: Corwin Press.

Daresh, J. C., & Arrowsmith, T. (2003). *A practical guide for new school leaders.* London: Paul Chapman Publishing.

Daresh, J., & Male, T. (2000). Crossing the border into leadership: Experiences of newly appointed British head teachers and American principals. *Educational Management Administration & Leadership, 28*(1), 89–101. doi:10.1177/0263211X000281013

Darling-Hammond, L., Bullmaster, M., L., & Cobb, V. (1995). Rethinking teacher leadership through professional development schools. *The Elementary School Journal, 96*(1), 87-106.

Darling-Hammond, L., LaPointe, M., Meyerson, D., Terry Orr, M., & Cohen, C. (2007). Preparing School Leaders for a Changing World: Lessons from Exemplary Leadership Development Programs. In Stanford Educational Leadership Institute. Stanford University.

Darling-Hammond, L., LaPointe, M., Meyerson, D., Orr, M. T., & Cohen, C. (2007). *Preparing school leaders for a changing world: Lessons from exemplary leadership development programs*. Stanford, CA: Stanford Educational Leadership Institute.

Darling-Hammond, L., Meyerson, D., LaPointe, M. M., & Orr, M. T. (2009). *Preparing principals for a changing world*. San Francisco, CA: Jossey-Bass. doi:10.1002/9781118269329

Darwin, C. (1872/1965). The expression of the emotions in man and animals. Chicago: The University of Chicago Press. (Originally published, 1872.). doi:10.1037/10001-000

Davidson, R. J. (2001). The neural circuitry of emotion and affective style: Prefrontal cortex and amygdala contributions. *Social Sciences Information. Information Sur les Sciences Sociales*, 40(1), 11–37. doi:10.1177/053901801040001002

Davies, P. (1999). What is evidence-based education? *British Journal of Educational Studies*, 47(2), 108–121. doi:10.1111/1467-8527.00106

Davis, B., & Sumara, D. (2006). *Complexity and education: Inquiries into learning, teaching, and research*. Mahwah, NJ: Erlbaum.

Davis, J. P., & Eisenhardt, K. (2011). Rotating leadership and collaborative innovation: Recombination processes in symbiotic relationships. *Administrative Science Quarterly*, 56(2), 159–201. doi:10.1177/0001839211428131

Day, C. (2002). School reform and transitions in teacher professionalism and identity. *International Journal of Education and Research*, 37(8), 677–692. doi:10.1016/S0883-0355(03)00065-X

Day, C., Harris, A., Hadfield, M., Tolley, H., & Beresford, J. (2000). *Leading schools in times of change*. Buckingham, UK: Open University Press.

Day, C., Sammons, P., Hopkins, D., Harris, A., Leithwood, K., & Gu, Q. et al. (2009). *The impact of school leadership on pupil outcomes. Final report. Research report No. DCSF-RR108*. University of Nottingham.

Day, C., Sammons, P., Leithwood, K., Harris, A., & Hopkins, D. (2009). *The impact of leadership on pupil outcomes. Final Report*. London: DCSF.

de Bono, E. (1995). *Mind power: Discover the secrets of creative thinking*. Crows Nest, Australia: Allen & Unwin.

de la Harpe, B., & Radloff, A. (2008). Developing graduate attributes for lifelong learning - How far have we gone? In *Proceedings of the Lifelong Learning Conference*. Central Queensland University.

de la Harpe, B., & Thomas, I. (2009). Curriculum change in universities: Conditions that facilitate education for sustainable development. *Journal of Education for Sustainable Development*, 3(1), 75–85. doi:10.1177/097340820900300115

De Neve, J. E., Mikhaylov, S., Dawes, C. T., Christakis, N. A., & Fowler, J. H. (2013). Born to lead? A twin design and genetic association study of leadership role occupancy. *The Leadership Quarterly*, 24(1), 45–60. doi:10.1016/j.leaqua.2012.08.001 PMID:23459689

Deal, T., & Peterson, K. (1990). *The Principal's role in shaping school culture*. Washington, DC: Office of Educational Research & Improvement.

Deal, T., & Peterson, K. (1994). *The leadership paradox: Balancing logic and artistry in schools*. San Francisco, CA: Jossey Bass.

Deal, T., & Peterson, K. (1999). *Shaping school culture: The heart of leadership*. San Francisco: Jossey-Bass.

Decree 46-2002 (Decreto número 46-2002 - Reglamento de la Ley de Participación Educativa). Retrieved February 16, 2014, from: http://goo.gl/aNFWwM

Dee, R. D., Henkin, A. B., & Duemer, L. (2002). Structural antecedents and psychological correlates of teacher empowerment. *Journal of Educational Administration*, 41(3), 257–277. doi:10.1108/09578230310474412

Denscombe, M. (2007). *The good research guide for small-scale social research projects*. Maidenhead, UK: Open University Press.

Denzin, N. L., & Lincoln, Y. (2007). *The Landscape of Qualitative Research* (3rd ed.). New York: Sage Publications.

Department for Children, Schools and Families. (n.d.). Guidance on Managing staff employment in schools: Guidance for Governors, Headteachers, Local Authorities, London. *DCSF*.

Department for Education (2012). *Governor's Guide to the Law*. Nottingham, UK: DfE.

Department for Education and Skills (DfES). (2006). *Programme of research, 2003080 Research into the impact of school leadership on pupil outcomes, tendered, expected start date 2.01.06*. Retrieved January 28, 2006, from http://www.dfes.gov.uk/research/programmeofresearch/index.cfm?type

Department of Basic Education. (2010a). Action Plan 2014. *Towards the realization of Schooling 2025*. Retrieved January 28, 2012, from http://planipolis.iiep.unesco.org

Department of Basic Education. (2010b). Approval of the National Curriculum Statement Grades R -12 as National Education Policy. *Government Gazette*. (No. 34600).

Department of Basic Education. (2011a). *Education Statistics at a glance 2010*. Pretoria: Government Printer.

Department of Basic Education. (2011b). *Report on the Annual National Assessments of 2011*. Pretoria: Government Printer.

Department of Basic Education. (2012). *Annual National Assessments 2012. A guideline for the interpretation and use of ANA results*. Pretoria: Government Printer.

Departmental Order 03-2012 contains regulations referring to the System of Public Exams for the Selection of School Principals (Orden Departamental No. 03-2012 que reglamenta el Sistema de Concurso de Oposición para seleccionar Directores/as y Sub-Directores/as de los Niveles Básico y Medio, Orientadores/as y Maestras/os de Educación Inicial, Básica y Educación Física de los Centros Educativos públicos en el año 2012). Retrieved February 15, 2014, from: http://goo.gl/zmuRPP

DeRue, D. S., Nahrgang, J. D., Wellman, N., & Humphrey, S. E. (2011). Trait and behavioral theories of leadership: An integration and meta-analytic test of their relative validity. *Personnel Psychology*, *64*(1), 7–52. doi:10.1111/j.1744-6570.2010.01201.x

Dimberg, U., Thunberg, M., & Elmehed, K. (2000). Unconscious facial reactions to emotional facial Expressions. *Psychological Science*, *11*(1), 86–89. doi:10.1111/1467-9280.00221 PMID:11228851

Dimmock, C. (2003). Leadership in learning-centred schools: Cultural context, functions and qualities. In M. Brundrett, N. Burton, & R. Smith (Eds.), Leadership in education. London: Sage.

Dinham, S., & Scott, C. (1998). *An international comparative Study of teacher Satisfaction:Motivation and health: Australia, England, and New Zealand*. Paper presented at the Annual Meeting of the American Educational Research Association. New York, NY.

Dinham, S., & Scott, C. (2002). *The international Teacher 2000 Project: An International Study of Teacher and School Executive Satisfaction, Motivation and Health in Australia, England, USA, Malta and New Zealand*. Paper presented at the Challenging Futures Conference. Armidale, Australia.

Dinham, S., & Scott, C. (2000). Moving into the third, outer domain of teacher satisfaction. *Journal of Educational Administration*, *38*(4), 379–396. doi:10.1108/09578230010373633

Dinh, J. E., Lord, R. G., & Hoffman, E. (in press). Leadership perception and information processing: Influences of symbolic, connectionist, emotion, and embodied architectures. In D. Day (Ed.), *The Oxford Handbook of Leadership and Organizations*. New York: Oxford University Press.

Dinh, J., Lord, R., Gardner, W., Meuser, J., Liden, R., & Hu, J. (in press). Leadership theory and research in the new millennium: Current theoretical trends and changing perspectives. *The Leadership Quarterly*.

DiPaola, M. F. (2003). Conflict and change: Daily challenges for school leaders. In N. Bennett, M. Crawford, & M. Cartwright (Eds.), *Effective Educational Leadership* (pp. 143–158). London: Paul Chapman Publishing.

DISA. (2014). *The Diagnostic Survey of School Alignment (DISA)*. Retrieved January 10, 2014 from http://www.acelleadership.org.au/diagnostic-inventory-school-alignment-disa

DOF. (1982). *Acuerdo número 96, que establece la organización y funcionamiento de las escuelas primarias.* Retrieved February 16, 2014, from: http://goo.gl/JXI4uV

Doha News Staff. (2013, March). *Are Qatar's independent schools broken? An in-depth report.* Retrieved December 13, 2013, from http://dohanews.co/are-qatars-independent-schools-broken-an-in-depth/

Donoso, S., & Arias, O. (2011). Diferencias de escala en los sistemas de educación pública en Chile. *Ensaio Avaliação e Políticas Públicas em Educação, 19*(71), 283–306. doi:10.1590/S0104-40362011000300004

Doud, J., & Keller, E. (1998). *A ten-year study: The K-8 principal in 1998.* Alexandria, VA: National Association of Elementary School Principals.

Dougherty, D. (1996). Organizing for innovation. In S. R. Clegg, C. Hardy, & W. R. Nord (Eds.), *Handbook of organization studies* (pp. 424–439). Thousand Oaks, CA: Sage Publications.

Dovidio, J. F., Heltman, K., Brown, C. E., Ellyson, S. L., & Keating, C. E. (1988). Power Displays Between Women and Men in Discussions of Gender-Linked Tasks: A Multichannel Study. *Journal of Personality and Social Psychology, 55*(4), 580–587. doi:10.1037/0022-3514.55.4.580

Doyle, M. (2000, April). *Making meaning of teacher leadership in the implementation of a standards-based mathematics curriculum.* Paper presented at the Annual Meeting of the American Educational Research Association. New Orleans, LA.

DuFour, R., & Eaker, R. (1998). *Professional learning communities at work: Best practices for enhancing student achievement.* Bloomington, IN: National Educational Service.

DuFour, R., Eaker, R., & DuFour, R. (2005). Recurring themes of professional learning communities and the assumptions they challenge. In R. DuFour, R. Eaker, & R. DuFour (Eds.), *On common ground: The power of professional learning communities* (pp. 1–6). Bloomington, IN: Solution Tree.

DuFour, R., Eaker, R., & DuFour, R. (2006). *On common ground: The power of professional learning communities.* Bloomington, IN: Solution Tree.

Duke, D. (1987). *School Leadership and Instructional Improvement.* New York: Random House.

Earley, P., Evans, J., Collarbone, P., Gold, A., & Halpin, D. (2002). *Establishing the current state of school leadership in England. Department for Education & Skills research report RR336.* London: HMSO.

Earley, P., Higham, R., Allen, R., Allen, T., Howson, J., Nelson, R., & Sims, D. (2012). *Review of the school leadership landscape.* Nottingham, UK: National College for School Leadership.

Earley, P., & Weindling, D. (2004). *Understanding school leadership.* London: Paul Chapman Publishing.

Ebbutt, D. (2002). The Development of a Research Culture in Secondary Schools. *Educational Action Research, 10*(1), 123–140. doi:10.1080/09650790200200171

Eckel, P. D., & Keza, A. J. (2003). *Taking the reins: Transformation in higher education.* Traverse City, MI: American Council on Education and Praeger Publishers.

Eckel, P., Green, M., Hill, B., & Mallon, W. (1999). Taking charge of change: A primer for colleges and universities. *Change,* III.

Edgerson, D., & Kritsonis, W. A. (2006). Analysis of the Influence of Principal–Teacher Relationships on Student Academic Achievement: A National Focus. *National Journal for Publishing and Mentoring Doctoral Student Research, 1*(1), 1–5.

Edmonds, R. (1979). Effective schools for urban poor. *Educational Leadership, 37*(1), 15–24.

Edwards-Groves, C. J., & Hoare, R. L. (2012). "Talking to learn": Focussing teacher education on dialogue as a core practice for teaching and learning. *Australian Journal of Teacher Education, 37*(8), 82–100. doi:10.14221/ajte.2012v37n8.8

Edwards-Groves, C., & Hardy, I. (2013). "Well, that was an intellectual dialogue!" How a whole-school focus on improvement shifts the substantive nature of classroom talk. *English Teaching, 12*(2), 116–136.

Edwards, J. R. (1991). Person-job fit: A conceptual integration, literature review, and methodological critique. In C. L. Cooper & I. T. Robertson (Eds.), *International review of industrial and organizational psychology* (Vol. 6, pp. 283–357). New York: Wiley.

Ekman, P., Friesen, W. V., & Hager, J. C. (2002). *Facial Action Coding System: The Manual*. Research Nexus division of Network Information Research Corporation.

Ekman, P. (1992). Facial expressions of emotion: New findings, new questions. *Psychological Science*, *3*(1), 34–38. doi:10.1111/j.1467-9280.1992.tb00253.x

Ekman, P. (2009). Lie catching and microexpressions. In C. Martin (Ed.), *The philosophy of deception* (pp. 118–142). New York, NY: Oxford University Press. doi:10.1093/acprof:oso/9780195327939.003.0008

Ekman, P., & Friesen, W. (1978). *Facial Action Coding System: A tecnhique for the Measurement of Facial Movement*. Palo Alto, CA: Consulting Psychologists Press.

Ekman, P., & Oster, H. (1979). Facial Expressions of Emotion. *Annual Review of Psychology*, *30*(1), 527–554. doi:10.1146/annurev.ps.30.020179.002523

Ekman, P., & Rosenberg, E. (1997). *What the face reveals: basic and applied studies of spontaneous expression*. New York: Oxford University Press.

Ekvall, G. (1997). Organizational conditions and levels of creativity. *Creativity and Innovation Management*, *6*(4), 195–205. doi:10.1111/1467-8691.00070

El Amouri, S., & O'Neill, S. (in press). Leadership style and culturally competent care: Nurse leaders' views of their practice in the multicultural care settings of the United Arab Emirates. *Contemporary Nurse*. PMID:24950789

Elliott, J. (1991). *Action Research for Educational Change*. Buckingham, UK: Open University Press.

Elmore, R. F. (2000). Building a new structure for school leadership. Washington, DC: The Albert Shanker Institute. Retrieved at http://www.shankerinstitute.org/Downloads/building.pdf

Elmore, R. F. (2008). Leadership as the practice of improvement. In D. Hopkins (Ed.), *B. Pont., D. Nusche*. Paris: OECD.

Emmerling, R. J., & Goleman, D. (2003). *Emotional Intelligence: Issues and common misunderstandings*. Retrieved June 16, 2012 from: http://www.eiconsortium.org

Engeström, Y. (1999). Expansive visibilization of work: An activity-theoretical perspective. *Computer Supported Cooperative Work*, *8*(1), 63–93. doi:10.1023/A:1008648532192

English, F. W. (2003). Cookie-cutter leaders for cookie-cutter schools: The teleology of standardization and the de-legitimization of the university in educational leadership preparation. *Leadership and Policy in Schools*, *2*(1), 27–46. doi:10.1076/lpos.2.1.27.15254

Enomoto, E. K., & Conley, S. (2008). Changing of the guard: How different school leaders change organizational routines. *Journal of School Leadership*, *18*, 278–301.

Epitropaki, O., & Martin, R. (2004). Implicit Leadership Theories in Applied Settings: Factor Structure, Generalizability, and Stability Over Time. *The Journal of Applied Psychology*, *89*(2), 293–310. doi:10.1037/0021-9010.89.2.293 PMID:15065976

Epitropaki, O., & Martin, R. (2005). From Ideal to Real: A Longitudinal Study of the Role of Implicit Leadership Theories on Leader-Member Exchanges and Employee outcomes. *The Journal of Applied Psychology*, *90*(4), 659–676. doi:10.1037/0021-9010.90.4.659 PMID:16060785

Epitropaki, O., Sy, T., Martin, R., Tram-Quon, S., & Topakas, A. (2013). Implicit Leadership and Followership Theories "in the wild": Taking stock of information-processing approaches to leadership and followership in organizational settings. *The Leadership Quarterly*, *24*(6), 858–881. doi:10.1016/j.leaqua.2013.10.005

Estes, K. R. (2009). *An analysis of the relationship between high school principals' perception of teacher leadership behaviors and school performance* (Doctoral dissertation). Retrieved from ProQuest Dissertations and Thesis database. (UMI No. 3358168)

Executive Decree 86 of 4 April 2005 (Decreto Ejecutivo 86 de 4 de abril de 2005, por el cual se establece el perfil para el cargo de Director(a) de Centro Educativo de Educación Media). Retrieved February 15, 2014, from: http://goo.gl/DbYwcb

Eysenck, H. J. (1983). The roots of creativity: Cognitive ability or personality trait? *Roeper Review, 5*(4), 10–12. doi:10.1080/02783198309552714

Facts about Sweden – Education . (n.d.). Retrieved from http://sweden.se/society/education-in-sweden/

Fairholm, G. W. (1993). *Organizational power and politics: Tactics in organizational leadership*. Westport, CT: Praeger.

Farkas, S., Johnson, J., & Duffett, A. (2003). *Rolling up their sleeves: Superintendents and principals talk about what's needed to fix public schools*. New York: Public Agenda.

Farkas, S., Johnson, J., Duffett, A., Foleno, T., & Foley, P. (2001). *Trying to stay ahead of the game: Superintendents and principals talk about school leadership*. Washington, DC: Public Agenda.

Federal Law on Civil Servants. Ordinance number 45 (Ordenanza n° 45 del Estatuto del Funcionario Docente). Retrieved February 15, 2014, from: http://goo.gl/VKyxUl

Fedor, D., Maslyn, J., Farmer, S., & Bettenhausen, K. L. (2003). *Perceptions of positive politics and their impact on organizational outcomes*. Paper presented at the Academy of Management Annual National Conference. Seattle, WA.

Feldman, M. (2000). Organizational routines as a source of continuous change. *Organization Science, 11*(6), 611-629. doi:1047-7039/00/1106/0611/$05.00

Felfe, J., Gatzka, L., Elprana, G., Stiehl, S., & Schyns, B. (2013, May 22). *Further insights into the meaning of motivation to lead*. Paper presented at the European Association of Work and Organizational Psychology Conference 2013. Münster.

Fenwick, L. T. (2000). *The principal shortage: Who will lead?* Cambridge, MA: Harvard Graduate School of Education.

Ferrandino, V. L. (2001). Challenges for 21st century elementary school principals. Phi Delta Kappan, 82(6), 440-442.

Ferris, G. R., Kolodinsky, R. W., Hochwarter, W. A., & Frink, D. D. (2001). *Conceptualization, measurement, and validation of the political skill construct*. Paper presented at the Annual Meeting of the Academy of Management. Washington, DC.

Ferris, G. R., Davidson, S. L., & Perrewé, P. L. (2005). *Political skill at work: Impact on work effectiveness*. Mountain View, CA: Davies-Black.

Ferris, G. R., Perrewé, P. L., Anthony, W. P., & Gilmore, D. C. (2000). Political skill at work. *Organizational Dynamics, 28*(4), 25–37. doi:10.1016/S0090-2616(00)00007-3

Ferris, G. R., Treadway, D. C., Kolodinsky, R. W., Hochwarter, W. A., Kacmar, C. J., Douglas, C., & Frink, D. D. (2005). Development and validation of the political skill inventory. *Journal of Management, 31*(1), 126–152. doi:10.1177/0149206304271386

Ferris, G. R., Treadway, D. C., Perrewe´, P. L., Brouer, R. L., Douglas, C., & Lux, S. (2007). Political skill in organizations. *Journal of Management, 33*(3), 290–320. doi:10.1177/0149206307300813

Fiedler, F. E., & Garcia, J. E. (1987). *New Approaches to Leadership, Cognitive Resources and Organizational Performance*. New York: John Wiley and Sons.

Field, A. (2009). *Discovering Statistics using SPSS* (3rd ed.). London: SAGE.

Fielding, M. (2005). *Effective communication in organisations: Preparing messages that communicate*. Cape Town, South Africa: Juta.

Field, T. M., Woodson, R., Greenberg, R., & Cohen, D. (1982). Discrimination and imitation of facial expressions by neonates. *Science, 218*(4568), 179–181. doi:10.1126/science.7123230 PMID:7123230

Fineman, S. (1993). Organizations as emotional arenas. In S. Fineman (Ed.), *Emotion in organizations*. London: Sage.

Fineman, S. (Ed.). (1993). *Emotion in Organizations*. London: Sage.

Fink, D. (2005). *Leadership for mortals*. London: Paul Chapman Publishing.

Fortier, A. (2005). Pride politics and multiculturalist citizenship. *Ethnic and Racial Studies*, *28*(3), 559–578. doi:10.1080/0141987042000337885

Foskett, N., & Lumby, J. (2003). *Leading and managing education: International dimensions*. London: Sage.

Framework for Good Managerial Performance (Marco de Buen Desempeño del Directivo. Directivos construyendo escuela). Retrieved February 15, 2014, from: http://goo.gl/sXEib4

Frank, M. G., & Ekman, P. (1997). The Ability to Detect Deceit Generalizes Across Different Types of High-Stake Lies. *Journal of Personality and Social Psychology*, *72*(6), 1429–1439. doi:10.1037/0022-3514.72.6.1429 PMID:9177024

Fraser, R. J. (2008). *Demystifying teacher leadership in comprehensive high schools* (Doctoral dissertation). Retrieved from ProQuest Dissertations and Thesis database. (UMI No. 3311546)

Frederick, J. (1992). Ongoing principal development: The route to restructuring urban schools. *Education and Urban Society*, *25*(1), 57–70. doi:10.1177/0013124592025001005

Frijda, N. H., & Tcherkassof, A. (1997). Facial expressions as modes of action readiness. In *J. A. Russell, & J. M. Fernández-Dols (Eds.), The psychology of facial expression* (pp. 78–102). Cambridge, UK: Cambridge University Press. doi:10.1017/CBO9780511659911.006

Frost, D. (2008). Teacher leadership: Values and voice. *School Leadership & Management: Formerly School Organisation*, *28*(4), 337–352. doi:10.1080/13632430802292258

Frost, D., & Durant, J. (2003). Teacher leadership: Rationale, strategy and impact. *School Leadership & Management*, *23*(2), 173–186. doi:10.1080/1363243032000091940

Frost, D., & Harris, A. (2003). Teacher leadership: Towards a research agenda. *Cambridge Journal of Education*, *33*(3), 479–498. doi:10.1080/0305764032000122078

Frost, P. (2003). *Toxic emotions at work: How compassionate managers handle pain and conflict*. Boston: HBS Press.

Fullan, M. (2002). *The change leader*. Retrieved December 13, 2013, from: http://www.cdl.org/resource-library/articles/change_ldr.php

Fullan, M. (2005). Leadership and sustainability: System thinkers in action. Thousand Oaks, CA: Corwin Press.

Fullan, M. (1992). *Successful school improvement*. Buckingham, UK: Open University.

Fullan, M. (1993). *Change forces: Probing the Depths of Educational Reform*. Bristol, UK: Falmer Press.

Fullan, M. (1995). The school as a learning organization: Distant dreams. *Theory into Practice*, *4*(34), 230–235. doi:10.1080/00405849509543685

Fullan, M. (1999). *Change forces*. London: Falmer Press.

Fullan, M. (2000). The three stories of education reform. *Phi Delta Kappan*, *81*(8), 581–584.

Fullan, M. (2001). *Leading in a Culture of Change*. San Francisco: Jossey Bass.

Fullan, M. (2001). *The new meaning of educational change* (3rd ed.). New York: Teachers College Press.

Fullan, M. (2002). The Change Leader. *Educational Leadership*, *59*(8), 16–20.

Fullan, M. (2003). *The moral imperative of school leadership*. Thousand Oaks, CA: Corwin Press.

Fullan, M. (2005). *Leadership and sustainability*. Thousand Oaks, CA: Corwin Press.

Fullan, M. (2006). *Turnaround leadership*. San Francisco: Jossey-Bass.

Fullan, M. (2010). *All Systems Go: The Change Imperative for Whole System Reform*. Corwin Press.

Fullan, M. G. (1996). Turning systemic thinking on its head. *Phi Delta Kappan*, *77*(6), 420–423.

Fuller, B. (1987). School effects in the Third World. *Review of Educational Research*, *57*, 255–292. doi:10.3102/00346543057003255

Fuller, E., Young, M., & Baker, B. D. (2011). Do principal preparation programs influence student achievement through the building of teacher-team qualifications by the principal? An exploratory analysis. *Educational Administration Quarterly*, *47*(1), 173–216. doi:10.1177/0011000010378613

Furnham, A. (1996). The big five versus the big four: The relationship between the Myer-Briggs-Type Indicator (MBTI) and NEO-PI five factor model of personality. *Personality and Individual Differences, 21*(2), 303–307. doi:10.1016/0191-8869(96)00033-5

Furnham, A., & Chamorro-Premuzic, T. (2004). Personality and intelligence as predictors of statistics examination grades. *Personality and Individual Differences, 37*(5), 943–955. doi:10.1016/j.paid.2003.10.016

Furr, R. M., & Funder, D. C. (1998). A multimodal analysis of personal Negativity. *Journal of Personality and Social Psychology, 74*(6), 1580–1591. doi:10.1037/0022-3514.74.6.1580 PMID:9654761

Gaddis, B., Connelly, S., & Mumford, M. D. (2004). Failure feedback as an affective event: Influences of leader affect on subordinate attitudes and performance. *The Leadership Quarterly, 15*(5), 663–686. doi:10.1016/j.leaqua.2004.05.011

Gairín, J. (2011b). Introducción. In J. Gairín, & D. Castro (Eds.), Competencias para el ejercicio de la dirección de instituciones educativas: Reflexiones y experiencias en Iberoamérica (pp. 6-9). Santiago de Chile: FIDECAP.

Gairín, J. (2012). La formación permanente en organización escolar. In D. Lorenzo, & M. López (Eds.), Respuestas emergentes desde la organización de instituciones educativas (pp. 45-81). Granada: Editorial Universidad de Granada.

Gairín, J. (Ed.). (2011a). *La dirección de centros educativos en Iberoamérica: Reflexiones y experiencias.* Santiago de Chile: FIDECAP.

Gairín, J., & Castro, D. (Eds.). (2011). *Competencias para el ejercicio de la dirección de instituciones educativas: Reflexiones y experiencias en Iberoamérica.* Santiago de Chile: FIDECAP.

Gallucci, C. (2008). Districtwide instructional reform: using sociocultural theory to link professional learning to organizational support. *American Journal of Education, 114,* 541-581. doi: 0195-6744/2008/11404-0002$10.00

Gamage, D. T. (1996). Institution of school-based management in New South Wales. In *D.T. Gamage (Ed.), School-based management: Theory, research and practice* (pp. 125–148). Colombo: Karunaratne & Sons.

Garay, S., & Uribe, M. (2006). *Dirección escolar como factor de eficacia y cambio: situación de la dirección escolar en Chile.* Retrieved February 18, 2014, from: http://goo.gl/VHf79e

García San Pedro, M. ª J. (2010). *Diseño y validación de un modelo de evaluación por competencias en la universidad.* (Unpublished doctoral dissertation). Universitat Autònoma de Barcelona, Spain. General Education Act 66-97 (Ley 66-97 Ley General de Educación). Retrieved February 15, 2014, from: http://goo.gl/ErjNU

Garcia-Morales, V. J., Matias-Reche, F., & Hurtado-Torres, N. (2008). Influence of transformational leadership on organizational innovation and performance depending on the level of organizational learning in the pharmaceutical sector. *Journal of Organizational Change Management, 21*(2), 188–212. doi:10.1108/09534810810856435

Gardner, H. (1983). *Frames of Mind: The Theory of Multiple Intelligences.* New York: Basic Books.

Gardner, H. (1999). *Intelligence Reframed.* New York: Basic Books.

Gardner, H. (2006). *Changing minds. The art and science of changing our own and other people's minds.* Boston, MA: Harvard Business School Press.

Gardner, W. L., & Martinko, M. J. (1990). The relationship between psychological type, managerial behavior, and managerial effectiveness: An empirical investigation. *Journal of Psychological Type, 19,* 35–43.

Garrett, R.M. (1999). *Teacher Job Satisfaction in Developing Countries.* ERIC Document Reproduction Service No. ED 459 150.

Geijsel, F. P., Sleegers, P. J. C., Leithwood, K., & Jantzi, D. (2003). Transformational leadership effects on teachers' commitment and effort toward school re-form. *Journal of Educational Administration, 41*(3), 229–256. doi:10.1108/09578230310474403

Geijsel, F. P., Sleegers, P. J. C., Stoel, R. D., & Kruger, M. L. (2009). The effect of teacher psychological, school organizational and leadership factors on teachers' professional learning in Dutch schools. *The Elementary School Journal, 109*(4), 406–427. doi:10.1086/593940

Geijsel, F. P., Sleegers, P. J. C., van den Berg, R. M., & Kelchtermans, G. (2001). Conditions fostering the implementation of large-scale innovations in schools: Teachers' perspectives. *Educational Administration Quarterly*, *37*(1), 130–166. doi:10.1177/00131610121969262

Geijsel, F. P., Van den Berg, R., & Sleegers, P. J. C. (1999). The innovative capacity of schools in primary education: A qualitative study. *International Journal of Qualitative Studies in Education*, *12*(2), 175–191. doi:10.1080/095183999236240

General Assembly of Illinois. (2010). *Public Act 96-0903*. Retrieved at http://www.ilga.gov/legislation/publicacts/fulltext.asp?Name=096-0903

General Education Act 1.264 (Ley 1.264/68 General de Educación). Retrieved February 15, 2014, from: http://goo.gl/bGRa52

General Education Act 28044 (Ley General de Educación N° 28044). Retrieved February 15, 2014, from: http://goo.gl/9mKe9f

Geoghegan, D., O'Neill, S., & Petersen, S. (2013). Metalanguage: The 'teacher talk' of explicit literacy teaching in practice. *Improving Schools*, *12*(2), 119–129. doi:10.1177/1365480213493707

George, J. M. (2000). Emotions and leadership: The role of emotional intelligence. *Human Relations*, *53*(8), 1027–1055. doi:10.1177/0018726700538001

George, J. M., & Jones, G. R. (2001). Towards a process model of individual change in organizations. *Human Relations*, *54*(4), 419–444. doi:10.1177/0018726701544002

Gersick, C. J. G. (1991). Revolutionary change theories: A multilevel exploration of the punctuated equilibrium paradigm. *Academy of Management Review*, *16*(1), 10–36.

Ghiselli, E. E. (1963). Intelligence and managerial success. *Psychological Reports*, *12*(3), 898. doi:10.2466/pr0.1963.12.3.898

Gilstrap, D. L. (2007). Dissipative structures in educational change: Prigogine and the academy. *International Journal of Leadership in Education*, *10*(1), 49–69. doi:10.1080/13603120600933758

Gimeno, J., Beltrán, F., Salinas, B., & San Martín, A. (1995). *La dirección de centros: análisis de tareas*. Madrid: MEC-CIDE.

Ginsberg, R., & Davies, T. (2003). The emotional side of leadership. In N. Bennett, M. Crawford, & M. Cartwright (Eds.), *Effective Leadership* (pp. 267–280). London: Sage/Paul Chapman.

Glanz, J. (2006). *What every principal should know about collaborative leadership*. Thousand Oaks, CA: Corwin Press.

Glaser, J., & Salovey, P. (1998). Affect in Electoral Politics. *Personality and Social Psychology Review*, *2*(3), 156–172. doi:10.1207/s15327957pspr0203_1 PMID:15647152

Glasman, N. S., & Heck, R. H. (1992). The changing leadership role of the principal: Implications for principal assessment. *Peabody Journal of Education*, *68*(1), 5–24. doi:10.1080/01619569209538708

Gleick, J. (1987). *Chaos: Making a new science*. London: Abacus.

Glisson, C., & Durick, M. (1988). Predictors of Job Satisfaction and Organizational Commitment in Human Service Organizations. *American Quarterly*, *33*, 61–81.

Glomb, T. M., & Hulin, C. L. (1997). Anger and gender effects in observed supervisor-subordinate dyadic interactions. *Organizational Behavior and Human Decision Processes*, *72*(3), 281–307. doi:10.1006/obhd.1997.2741 PMID:9606168

Goddard, Y. L., Goddard, R. D., & Tschannen-Moran, M. (2007). A theoretical and empirical investigation of teacher collaboration for school improvement and student achievement in public elementary schools. *Teachers College Record*, *109*(4), 877–896.

Goffee, R., & Jones, G. (2005). Managing authenticity. *Harvard Business Review*, *83*, 86–94. PMID:16334584

Goldberg, L. R. (1990). An alternative „description of personality": The Big-Five factor structure. *Journal of Personality and Social Psychology*, *59*(6), 1216–1229. doi:10.1037/0022-3514.59.6.1216 PMID:2283588

Goldring, E., Jason, H., Henry, M., & Camburn, E. (2008). School Context and Individual Characteristics: What Influences Principal Practice? *Journal of Educational Administration*, *46*(3), 332–352. doi:10.1108/09578230810869275

Goldring, E., Porter, A., Murphy, J., Elliott, S. N., & Cravens, X. (2009). Assessing learning-centered leadership: Connections to research, professional standards, and current practices. *Leadership and Policy in Schools*, *8*(1), 1–36. doi:10.1080/15700760802014951

Goleman, D. (2001). Emotional intelligence: Issues in paradigm building. In C. Cherniss & D. Goleman (Ed.), The Emotionally Intelligent Workplace (pp. 13–26). San Francisco: Jossey-Bass.

Goleman, D. (1996). *Emotional Intelligence: Why It Can Matter more than IQ*. London: Bloomsbury Publishing.

Goleman, D. (1998). What makes a leader? *Harvard Business Review*, (Nov-Dec): 93–102. PMID:10187249

Goleman, D. (1998). *Working with Emotional Intelligence*. New York: Bantum Books.

Goleman, D., Boyatzis, R., & McKee, A. (2002). *Primal leadership: Realizing the power of emotional intelligence*. Boston: Harvard Business School Press.

Gómez-Dacal, G. (2013). *Claves para la excelencia educative: Organizaciones escolares únicas y excepcionales*. Madrid: Wolters Kluwer.

Gonzalez, M., Glassman, N. S., & Glassman, L. D. (2002). Daring to link principal preparation programs to student achievement in schools. *Leadership and Policy in Schools*, *1*(3), 265–283. doi:10.1076/lpos.1.3.265.7889

Gorman, M. R. (1993). *Time management strategies and the implications for instructional leadership of high school principals: A case study analysis*. (PhD thesis). Widener University, Chester, PA.

Government of Jamaica. (1981). *The education act: The regulations 1980*. Kingston, Jamaica: Jamaica Gazette.

Government of Jamaica. (2004). *Task force on education reform Jamaica: A transformed education system*. Kingston, Jamaica: Government of Jamaica.

Grandey, A. A., & Brauburger, A. L. (2002). The emotion regulation behind the customer service smile. In Emotions in the workplace. San Francisco, CA: Jossey-Bass

Grant, C. (2006). Emerging voices on teacher leadership: Some South African view. *Educational Management Administration & Leadership*, *34*(4), 511–532. doi:10.1177/1741143206068215

Grant, C., Gardner, K., Kajee, F., Moodley, R., & Somaroo, S. (2010). Teacher leadership: A survey analysis of KwaZulu-Natal teachers' perceptions. *South African Journal of Education*, *30*, 401–419.

Grant, C., & Singh, H. (2009). Passing the buck: This is not teacher leadership. *Perspectives in Education*, *27*(3), 289–301.

Grassie, M. C., & Carss, B. W. (1973). School Structure, Leadership Quality, Teacher Satisfaction. *Educational Administration Quarterly*, *9*(1), 15–26. doi:10.1177/0013161X7300900103

Gray, J. H., & Densten, I. L. (2007). How Leaders Woo Followers in the Romance of Leadership. *Applied Psychology*, *56*(4), 558–581. doi:10.1111/j.1464-0597.2007.00304.x

Gray, P. B., & Campbell, B. C. (2009). Human male testosterone, pair-bonding, and fatherhood. In P. Gray & P. Ellison (Eds.), *Endocrinology of Social Relationships*. Cambridge, MA: Harvard University Press.

Great Britain Education Act. (2002). *Great Britain education Act: Elizabeth II, sections 35&36*. London: The Stationary Office. Retrieved from http://www.legislation. gov.uk/ukpga/2002/32/contents

Great Britain. (2009). *The school staffing (England) regulations 2009: Elisabeth II, sections 15 & 34*. London: The Stationary Office. Retrieved from http://www.legislation. gov.uk/uksi/2009/2680/contents/made

Grenda, J. P. (2006). Leadership, distributed. In *Encyclopedia of Educational Leadership and Administration* (Vol. 2, pp. 566–567). London: Sage. doi:10.4135/9781412939584.n323

Grobler, B.R. (2013). The school principal as Instructional Leader: A structural Equation Model. *Education as Change*, *17*(1), 177-199.

Grobler, B. R. (2014). Teachers' perceptions of the utilisation of emotional competence by their school leaders in Gauteng South Africa. *Educational Management Administration & Leadership*, 1–21. Available at http://ema.sagepub.com/content/early/2014/02/05/1741143213513184

Grobler, B. R., Mestry, R., & Naidoo, S. (2012). The influence of management practices on authentic collaboration with educators. *Journal of Social Sciences*, *30*(3), 211–223.

Gronn, P. (2000). Distributed properties: A new architecture for leadership. *Educational Management and Administration*, *28*(3), 317–338. doi:10.1177/0263211X000283006

Gronn, P. (2003). *The New Work of Educational Leaders*. London: Paul Chapman.

Gronn, P. (2004). Distributing leadership. In *Encyclopedia of leadership* (Vol. 1, pp. 352–354). London: Sage. doi:10.4135/9781412952392.n81

Gross, J. J. (2002). Emotion regulation: Affective, cognitive, and social consequences. *Psychophysiology*, *39*(3), 281–291. doi:10.1017/S0048577201393198 PMID:12212647

Groth, J. C., & Peters, J. (1999). What blocks creativity? A managerial perspective. *Creativity and Innovation Management*, *8*(3), 179–187. doi:10.1111/1467-8691.00135

Grunes, P., Gudmundsson, A., & Irmer, B. (2014). To what extent is the Mayer & Salovey (1997) model of emotional intelligence a useful predictor of leadership style and perceived leadership outcomes in Australian educational institutions? *Educational Management Administration & Leadership*, *42*(1), 112–135. doi:10.1177/1741143213499255

Gumusluoglu, L., & Ilsev, A. (2009). Transformational leadership, creativity, and organizational innovation. *Journal of Business Research*, *62*(4), 461–473. doi:10.1016/j.jbusres.2007.07.032

Gurteen, D. (1998). Knowledge, creativity and innovation. *Journal of Knowledge Management*, *2*(1), 5–13. doi:10.1108/13673279810800744

Gustavsson, B. (2000). *Kunskapsfilosofi. Tre kunskapsformer i historisk belysning.* [The Philosophy of Knowledge. Three forms of Knowledge in a Historical Perspective]. Stockholm: Wahlström & Widstrand.

Hackman, D. G., Walker, J. M., & Wanat, C. L. (2006). A professional learning community at work: Developing a standards-based principal preparation program. *Journal of Cases in Educational Leadership*, *9*(3), 39–53. doi:10.1177/1555458906289777

Håkansson, J. and Sundberg, D. (2012). *Undervisning på vetenskaplig grund.* [Teaching based on Research]. Stockholm: Natur och Kultur.

Hallinger, P. (1990). Principal instructional management rating scale. Version 2.3. Sarasota, FL: Leading Development Associates.

Hallinger, P. (2005). The emergence of school leadership development in an era of globalization: 1980-2002. In P. Hallinger (Ed.), Reshaping the landscape of school leadership development (pp. 3-22). Lisse: Swets & Zeitlinger.

Hallinger, P. (2008). *Methodologies for Studying School Leadership: A Review of 25 years of Research Using the PIMRS.* Paper prepared for presentation at the annual meeting of the American Educational Research Association. New York, NY. Retrieved, 15 February 2014, from: http://alex.state.al.us/leadership/Principals%20%20Files/RG-5,%20PIMRS_Methods_47.pdf

Hallinger, P., & Heck. (1996b). The principal's Role in School Effectiveness: An Assessment of Methodological Progress, 1980-1995. In K. Leithwood, J. Chapman, D. Corson, P. Hallinger, & A. Hart (Eds.), *International Handbook of Educational Leadership and Administration, Part 2* (pp. 723-783). Kluwer Academic Publishers.

Hallinger, Ph. (1983). *Assessing the instructional management behavior of principals.* (Unpublished Doctoral Dissertation). Stanford University, Palo Alto, CA.

Hallinger, Ph. (2007). *Leadership for Learning: Reflections on the Practice of Instructional and Transformational Leadership.* Paper presented at Doctoral Seminar East Asia University. Tokyo, Japan.

Hallinger, P. (2003). Leading Educational Change: Reflections on the practice of instructional and transformational leadership. *Cambridge Journal of Education, 33*(3), 329–351. doi:10.1080/0305764032000122005

Hallinger, P. (2003). The emergence of school leadership development in an era of globalization: 1980-2002. In P. Hallinger (Ed.), *Reshaping the Landscape of School Leadership Development: A global perspective* (pp. 3–22). Lisse: Swets and Zeitlinger.

Hallinger, P. (2005). Instructional leadership and the school principal: A passing fancy that refuses to fade away. *Leadership and Policy in Schools, 4*(3), 221–239. doi:10.1080/15700760500244793

Hallinger, P. (2011). Leadership for learning: Lessons from 40 years of empirical research. *Journal of Educational Administration, 49*(2), 125–142. doi:10.1108/09578231111116699

Hallinger, P., Bickman, L., & Davis, K. (1996). School context, principal leadership and student reading achievement. *The Elementary School Journal, 96*(5), 527–549. doi:10.1086/461843

Hallinger, P., & Heck, R. (2009). Distributed leadership in schools: Does system policy make a difference? In A. Harris (Ed.), *Distributed Leadership: Different perspectives*. Springer Press. doi:10.1007/978-1-4020-9737-9_6

Hallinger, P., & Heck, R. H. (1998). Exploring the principal's contribution to school effectiveness: 1980-1995. *School Effectiveness and School Improvement, 9*(2), 157–191. doi:10.1080/0924345980090203

Hallinger, P., & Heck, R. H. (2010). Collaborative leadership and school improvement: Understanding the impact on school capacity and student learning. *School Leadership & Management: Formerly School Organisation, 30*(2), 95–110. doi:10.1080/13632431003663214

Hallinger, P., & Murphy, J. (1985). Assessing the instructional management behavior of principals. *The Elementary School Journal, 86*(2), 217–247. doi:10.1086/461445

Hallinger, P., & Snidvongs, K. (2008). Educating leaders: Is there anything to learn from business management. *Educational Management Administration & Leadership, 36*(1), 9–31. doi:10.1177/1741143207084058

Hallinger, Ph. (1992). The Evolving Role of American Principals: From Managerial to Instructional to Transformational'. *Journal of Educational Administration, 30*(3), 35–48. doi:10.1108/09578239210014306

Hallinger, Ph., & Heck, R. H. (1996a). Reassessing the principals' role in school effectiveness: A review of the empirical research, 1980-1995. *Educational Administration Quarterly, 32*(1), 1, 5–44. doi:10.1177/0013161X96032001002

Hammersley, M. (Ed.). (2007). *Educational research and evidence-based practice*. Thousand Oaks, CA: Sage.

Handy, C. B. (1981). *Understanding organizations* (2nd ed.). London: Hazell Watson & Viney.

Hannan, M. T., & Freeman, J. (1977). The population ecology of organizations. *American Journal of Sociology, 82*(5), 929–964. doi:10.1086/226424

Harding, J., & Pribram, E. D. (2002). The power of feeling: Locating emotions in culture. *European Journal of Cultural Studies, 5*(4), 407–426. doi:10.1177/1364942002005004294

Harding, J., & Pribram, E. D. (2004). Losing our cool? Following Williams and Grossberg on emotions. *Cultural Studies, 18*(6), 863–883. doi:10.1080/0950238042000306909

Hare, R. D. (1991). *The Hare Psychopathy Checklist - Revised*. North Tonawanda, NY: Multi-Health Systems.

Hargreaves, A. (1994). *Changing teachers, changing times*. New York: Teachers College Press.

Hargreaves, A. (1997). *Positive Change for School Success: The 1997 ASCD Yearbook*. Alexandria, VA: Association for Supervision and Curriculum Development.

Hargreaves, A. (2001). Emotional geographies of teaching. *Teachers College Record, 103*(6), 1056–1080. doi:10.1111/0161-4681.00142

Hargreaves, A. (2003). *Teaching in the Knowledge Society: Education in the Age of Insecurity*. New York, NY: Teachers College Press.

Hargreaves, A. (2004). Inclusive and exclusive educational change: Emotional responses of teachers and implications for leadership. *School Leadership & Management, 24*(2), 287–309. doi:10.1080/1363243042000266936

Hargreaves, A., & Fink, D. (2006). *Sustainable leadership*. San Francisco: Jossey-Bass.

Hargreaves, A., & Fink, D. (2008). Distributed leadership: Democracy or delivery? *Journal of Educational Administration, 46*(2), 229–240. doi:10.1108/09578230810863280

Hargreaves, A., & Fullan, M. (2012). *Professional capital: Transforming teaching in every school*. New York, NY: Teachers College Press.

Hargreaves, A., & Shirley, D. (2009). *The fourth way: A new vision for education reform*. Thousand Oaks, CA: Corwin Press.

Hargreaves, D. (2001). A capital theory of school effectiveness and improvement. *British Educational Research Journal, 27*(4), 487–503. doi:10.1080/01411920120071489

Harker, L. A., & Keltne, D. (2001). Expressions of Positive Emotion in Women's College Yearbook Pictures and Their Relationship to Personality and Life Outcomes Across Adulthood. *Journal of Personality and Social Psychology, 80*(1), 112–124. doi:10.1037/0022-3514.80.1.112 PMID:11195884

Harris, A. (2003b). The changing context of leadership. In A. Harris, C. Day, C. Hopkins, M. Hadfield, A. Hargreaves, & C. Chapman (Eds.), Effective leadership for school improvement. New York: Routledge Falmer.

Harris, A., & Day, C. (2003). From singular to plural? Challenging the orthodoxy of school leadership. In N. Bennett & L. Anderson (Eds.), Rethinking educational leadership. London: Sage. doi:10.4135/9781446216811.n7

Harris, A., & Muijs, D. (2003a). *Teacher leadership: Principles and practice*. London: National College for School Leadership. Retrieved from http://www.nationalcollege.orguk/index./docinfo.htm?id=17417

Harris, A. (2002a). *School improvement: What's in it for schools?* London: Falmer. doi:10.4324/9780203471968

Harris, A. (2002b). Distributed leadership in schools: Leading or misleading? *Management in Education, 16*(5), 10–13. doi:10.1177/089202060301600504

Harris, A. (2003). Teacher leadership as distributed leadership: Heresy, fantasy or possibility? *School Leadership & Management, 23*(3), 313–324. doi:10.1080/1363243032000112801

Harris, A. (2005a). Reflections on distributed leadership. *Management in Education, 19*(2), 10–12. doi:10.1177/08920206050190020301

Harris, A. (2005b). Distributed leadership. In B. Davies (Ed.), *The essentials of school leadership*. London: Paul Chapman Publishing.

Harris, A. (2006). Opening up the 'black box' of leadership practice: Taking a distributed leadership perspective. *International Studies in Educational Administration, 34*(2), 37–45.

Harris, A. (2007). Distributed leadership: Conceptual confusion and empirical reticence. *International Journal of Leadership in Education, 10*(3), 315–325. doi:10.1080/13603120701257313

Harris, A. (2008). *Distributed school leadership: Developing tomorrow's leaders*. London: Routledge.

Harris, A. (2011). System improvement through collective capacity building. *Journal of Educational Administration, 49*(6), 624–636. doi:10.1108/09578231111174785

Harris, A. (2012). Leading system wide improvement. *International Journal of Leadership in Education, 15*(3), 395–401. doi:10.1080/13603124.2012.661879

Harris, A. (2013). Distributed Leadership: Friend or Foe? *Educational Management Administration & Leadership, 41*(5), 545–554. doi:10.1177/1741143213497635

Harris, A., Day, C., Hadfield, M., Hopkins, D., Hargreaves, A., & Chapman, C. (2003). *Effective leadership for school improvement*. London: Routledge Falmer.

Harris, A., & Hopkins, D. (2000). Introduction to special feature: Alternative perspective on school improvement. *School Leadership & Management, 20*(1), 9–14. doi:10.1080/13632430068842

Harris, A., & Lambert, L. (2003). *Building leadership capacity for school improvement*. Maidenhead, UK: Open University.

Harris, A., & Muijs, B. (2003b). Teacher leadership and school improvement. *Educational Review, 16*(2), 39–42.

Harris, A., & Muijs, B. (2005). *Improving schools through teacher leadership*. Maidenhead, UK: Open University.

Harris, A., Muijs, D., & Crawford, M. (2003). *Deputy and assistant heads: Building leadership potential*. Nottingham, UK: NCSL.

Harris, A., & Spillane, J. (2008). Distributed leadership through the looking glass. *Management in Education*, *22*(1), 31–34. doi:10.1177/0892020607085623

Harris, C., Phillips, R., & Penuel, W. (2011). Examining teachers' instructional moves aimed at developing students' ideas and questions in learner-centered science classrooms. *Journal of Science Teacher Education*. doi:10.1007/s10972-011-9237-0

Harris, D. N., Stacey, R., Ingle, C., & Thompson, C. (2010). Mix and Match: What Principals Really Look for When Hiring Teachers. *Education Finance and Policy*, *5*(2), 228–246. doi:10.1162/edfp.2010.5.2.5205

Harrison, C., & Killion, J. (2007). Ten roles for teacher leaders. *Educational Leadership*, *65*(1), 74–77.

Harrison, R. (1972). Understanding your organization's character. *Harvard Business Review*, *50*(23), 119–128.

Harris, T. B., Li, N., Boswell, W. R., Zhang, X. A., & Xie, Z. (2013). Getting What's New from Newcomers: Empowering Leadership, Creativity, and Adjustment in the Socialization Context. *Personnel Psychology*, n/a. doi:10.1111/peps.12053

Hart, A. W. (1995). Reconceiving school leadership: Emergent views. *The Elementary School Journal*, *96*(1), 9–28. doi:10.1086/461812

Hartley, D. (2007). The emergence of distributive leadership in education: Why now? *British Journal of Educational Studies*, *55*(2), 202–214. doi:10.1111/j.1467-8527.2007.00371.x

Harvey, R. J., Murry, W. D., & Markham, S. E. (1995). *A "Big Five" Scoring System for the Myers-Briggs Type Indicator*. Paper presented at the Annual Conference of the Society for Industrial and Organizational Psychology. Orlando, FL. Retrieved, 3 January 2014, from: http://harvey.psyc.vt.edu/Documents/BIGFIVE.pdf

Hassin, R. R., Bargh, J. A., & Uleman, J. S. (2002). Spontaneous causal inferences. *Journal of Experimental Social Psychology*, *38*(5), 515–522. doi:10.1016/S0022-1031(02)00016-1

Hatch, T., & Gardner, H. (1993). Finding cognition in the classroom: an expanded view of human intelligence. In G. Salomon (Ed.), *Distributed cognitions: Psychological and educational considerations*. Cambridge, UK: Cambridge University Press.

Hattie, J. (2009). *Visible learning*. London: Routledge.

Healy, A. (2008). Expanding student capacities. In A. Healy (Ed.), *Multiliteracies: Pedagogies for diverse learners* (pp. 2–29). Sydney: Oxford University Press.

Heap, J. L. (1985). Discourse in the production of classroom knowledge: Reading lessons. *Curriculum Inquiry*, *15*(3), 245–279. doi:10.2307/1179585

Heck, R. H., & Moriyama. (2010). Examining relationships among elementary schools' contexts, leadership, instructional practices, and added-year outcomes: A regression discontinuity approach. *School Effectiveness and School Improvement*, *21*(4), 377-408.

Heck, R. (1992). Principals' instructional leadership and school performance: Implications for policy development. *Educational Evaluation and Policy Analysis*, *14*(1), 21–34. doi:10.3102/01623737014001021

Heck, R. H., & Hallinger, Ph. (2009). Assessing the contribution of distributed leadership to school improvement and growth in math achievement. *American Educational Research Journal*, *46*(3), 659–689. doi:10.3102/0002831209340042

Heck, R. H., & Marcoulides, G. A. (1990). Examining contextual differences in the development of instructional leadership and school achievement. *The Urban Review*, *22*(4), 247–265. doi:10.1007/BF01108463

Heck, R. H., & Marcoulides, G. A. (1993). Principal leadership behaviors and school achievement. *NASSP Bulletin*, *77*(553), 21–27. doi:10.1177/019263659307755305

Heck, R., & Hallinger, P. (2010). Testing a longitudinal model of distributed leadership effects on school improvement. *The Leadership Quarterly*, *21*(5), 867–885. doi:10.1016/j.leaqua.2010.07.013

Heifetz, R. A., & Linsky, M. L. (2002). *Leadership on the line: Staying alive through the dangers of leading*. Boston, MA: Harvard Business Publishing.

Helps, R. (1994). The allocation of non-contact time to deputy head teachers in primary schools. *School Organization, 14*(3), 243–246. doi:10.1080/0260136940140301

Helterbran, V. R. (2010). Teacher leadership. Overcoming "I'm just a teacher" syndrome. *Education, 131*(2), 363–371.

Hemsley-Brown, J., & Sharp, C. (2003). The Use of Research to Improve Professional Practice: A systematic review of the literature. *Oxford Review of Education, 29*(4), 449–471. doi:10.1080/0305498032000153025

Hendriks, M., & Vingerhoets, A. (2006). Social messages of crying faces: Their influence on anticipated person perception, emotion and behavioral responses. *Cognition and Emotion, 20*(6), 878–886. doi:10.1080/02699930500450218

Herkenhoff, L. (2004). Culturally tuned emotional intelligence: An effective change management tool? *Strategic Change, 13*(2), 73–81. doi:10.1002/jsc.666

Hess, F. M., & Kelly, A. P. (2002). Learning to lead: What gets taught in principal preparation programs? Washington, DC: American Enterprise Institute. Retrieved from http://www.ksg.harvard.edu/pepg/PDF/Papers/Hess_Kelly_Learning_to_Lead_PEPG05.02.pd

Hess, U., Blairy, S., & Kleck, R. E. (2000). The Influence of Facial Emotion Displays, Gender, and Ethnicity on Judgments of Dominance and Affiliation. *Journal of Nonverbal Behavior, 4*(4), 265–283. doi:10.1023/A:1006623213355

Hewitt, M. A., & Little, M. (2005). Leading action research in schools. *State of Florida, Department of Education,* 1-30. Retrieved from www.myfloridaeducation.com/commhome

Hiatt-Michael, D. B. (2001). Schools as learning communities: A vision for organic school reform. *School Community Journal, 11,* 113–127.

Higgnis, C. A., Judge, T. A., & Ferris, G. R. (2003). Influence tactics and work outcomes: A meta-analysis. *Journal of Organizational Behavior, 24*(1), 89–106. doi:10.1002/job.181

Hoadley, U., Christie, P., & Ward, L. (2009). Managing to learn: Instructional leadership in South African secondary schools. *School Leadership & Management, 29*(4), 373–389. doi:10.1080/13632430903152054

Hochschild, A. R. (1983). *The managed heart: Commercialization of human feeling.* Berkeley, CA: University of California Press.

Hoffman, B. J., Woehr, D. J., Maldagen-Youngjohn, R., & Lyons, B. D. (2011). Great man or great myth? A quantitative review of the relationship between individual differences and leader effectiveness. *Journal of Occupational and Organizational Psychology, 84*(2), 347–381. doi:10.1348/096317909X485207

Hofstede, G. (1997). *Cultures and organizations* (2nd ed.). USA: McGraw-Hill.

Hofstede, G., Neuijen, B., Ohayv, D. D., & Sanders, G. (1990). Measuring organizational cultures: A qualitative and quantitative study across twenty cases. *Administrative Science Quarterly, 35*(2), 286–316. doi:10.2307/2393392

Högskolelagen (1992:1434). [The Higher Education Act].

Holder, S. C. (2009). *The relationship between dimensions of Principal Personality type and selected school characteristics.* (Unpublished Dissertation). Mercer University, Atlanta, GA.

Hollins, E. R. I, McIntyre, L. R., DeBose, C., Hollins, K. S., & Towner, A. (2004). Promoting a self-sustaining learning community: Investigating an internal model for teacher development. *International Journal of Qualitative Studies in Education, 17*(2), 247–264. doi:10.1080/0951 8390310001653899

Holmstrand, L., & Härnsten, G. (2003). *Förutsättningar för forskningscirklar i skolan.* [Prerequisites for Research Groups in School]. Stockholm: Skolverket.

Honig, M. I. (2008). District central offices as learning organizations: How sociocultural and organizational learning theories elaborate district central office administrators' participation in teaching and learning improvement efforts. *American Journal of Education, 114*(4), 627–664. doi:10.1086/589317

Hook, D. P. (2006). *The impact of teacher leadership on school effectiveness in selected exemplary secondary schools* (Doctoral dissertation). Retrieved from ProQuest Dissertations and Thesis database. (UMI No. 3219160)

Hopkins, D., & Jackson, D. (2003). Building the capacity for leading and learning. In A. Harris, C. Day, C. Hopkins, M. Hadfield, A. Hargreaves, & C. Chapman (Eds.), Effective leadership for school improvement. New York: Routledge Falmer.

Hopkins, D., & Harris, A. (1997). Improving the quality of education for all. *Support for Learning, 12*(4), 147–151. doi:10.1111/1467-9604.00035

Hopkins, D., Harris, A., Stoll, L., & Mackay, T. (2014). School and system Improvement: State of the art review. *School Effectiveness and School Improvement, 25*(2), 257–281. doi:10.1080/09243453.2014.885452

Hopkins, D., & Jackson, D. (2003). Building the capacity for leading and learning. In A. Harris, C. Day, D. Hopkins, M. Hadfield, A. Hargreaves, & C. Chapman (Eds.), *Effective leadership for school improvement* (pp. 84–104). New York: Routledge Falmer.

Hopkins, M. M., O'Neil, D. A., & Williams, H. W. (2007). Emotional intelligence and board governance: Leadership lessons from the public sector. *Journal of Managerial Psychology, 23*(7), 683–700. doi:10.1108/02683940710820109

Hord, S. M. (1997). *Professional learning communities: Communities of continuous inquiry and improvement.* Austin, TX: Southwest Educational Development Laboratory.

Horner, M. 2003. Leadership theory reviewed. In N. Bennett, M. Crawford, & M. Cartwright (Eds.), Effective educational leadership. London: Paul Chapman Publishing.

Horng, E. L., Klasik, D., & Loeb, S. (2010). Principal's time use and school effectiveness. *American Journal of Education, 116*(4), 491–523. doi:10.1086/653625

Horng, E., & Loeb, S. (2010). New thinking about instructional leadership. *Kappan, 92*(3), 66–69. doi:10.1177/003172171009200319

Hough, L. M. (1992). The "big five" personality variables-construct confusion: Description versus prediction. *Human Performance, 5*, 139–155.

Houston, P. D. (1998, June3). The abc's of administrative shortages. *Education Week.*

Howie, S., van Staden, S., Tsheli, M., Dowse, C., & Zimmerman, L. (2011). *Progress in International Reading Literacy. South African Children's Reading Literacy Achievement.* Pretoria: Centre for Evaluation and Assessment.

Hoy, W. K., & Miskel, C. G. (2010). Eğitim yönetimi: Teori, araştırma ve uygulama [Educational administration: Theory, research, and practice]. (S. Turan, Trans. Ed.). Ankara: Nobel. (Orijinal Edition. 2004).

Hoyle, J., English, F., & Steffy, B. (2002). *Actitudes del directivo de centros docentes.* Madrid: Editorial Centro de Estudios Ramón Areces.

Hoy, W. K. (2003). An analysis of enabling and mindful school structures: Some theoretical, research, and practical consideration. *Journal of Educational Administration, 41*(1), 87–108. doi:10.1108/09578230310457457

Hoy, W. K., & Miskel, C. G. (2013). *Educational administration: Theory, research and practice* (9th ed.). New York: McGraw Hill.

Huber, S. G. (2005). School leader development: Current trends from a global perpective. In P. Hallinger (Ed.), Reshaping the landscape of school leadership development (pp. 273-288). Lisse: Swets & Zeitlinger.

Huber, S. G., & Pashiardis, P. (2008). The recruitment and selection of school leaders. In J. Lumby, G. Crow, & P. Pashiardis (Eds.), The development of school leaders. New York: Routledge.

Huber, S. G., & West, M. (2002). Developing school leaders: A critical review of current practices, approaches and issues, and some directions for the future. In K. Leithwood & P. Hallinger (Eds.), Second International handbook of educational leadership and administration (pp. 1071-1102). Dordrecht, The Netherlands: Kluwer Academic. doi:10.1007/978-94-010-0375-9_37

Huber, S. G., Moorman, H., & Pont, B. (2007). *School leadership for systemic improvement in England.* Retrieved June 10, 2013 from http://www.oecd.org/edu/school/40673692.pdf

Huberman, M. (1989). The professional Life Cicyle of Teachers. *Teachers College Record, 91*(1), 31–57.

Huber, S. G. (2008). Steuerungshandeln schulischer Führungskräfte aus Sicht der Schulleitungsforschung. In R. Langer (Ed.), *Warum tun die das?' Governanceanalysen zum Steuerungshandeln in der Schulentwicklung* (pp. 95–126). Wiesbaden: VS.

Huber, S. G., & Hiltmann, M. (2011). Competence Profile School management (CPSM) – an inventory for the self-assessment of school leadership. *Educational Assessment, Evaluation and Accountability, 23*(1), 65–88. doi:10.1007/s11092-010-9111-1

Huffman, J., & Jacobson, A. (2003). Perceptions of professional learning communities. *International Journal of Leadership in Education, 6*(3), 239–250. doi:10.1080/1360312022000017480

Huinker, D., & Freckmann, J. L. (2004). Focusing conversations to promote teacher thinking. *Teaching Children Mathematics, 10*(7), 352–357.

Huitt, W. (2007). *Success in the conceptual age: Another paradigm shift*. Paper delivered at the 32nd Annual Meeting of the Georgia Educational Research Association. Savannah, GA. Retrieved September 25, 2013, from http://www.edpsycinteractive.org/papers/conceptual-age.pdf

Hulpia, H. (2009). *Distributed leadership and organizational outcomes in secondary schools*. Universiteit can Gent (dissertation). Gent.

Hultman, G. (2012). Ledarskapsforskning – Gamla sanningar och nya ambitioner. [Research on Leadership – Old Truths and New Ambitions]. *Leda & Styra, (2)*, 1-22.

Human Science Research Council (HSRC). (2011). *Highlights from TIMMS 2011. The South African perspective*. Pretoria: HSRC.

Humphrey, R. H. (2002). The many faces of emotional leadership. *The Leadership Quarterly, 13*(5), 493–504. doi:10.1016/S1048-9843(02)00140-6

Humphrey, R. H., Pollack, J. M., & Hawver, T. (2008). Leading with emotional labour. *Journal of Managerial Psychology, 23*(2), 151–168. doi:10.1108/02683940810850790

Hunter, J. E., Schmidt, F. L., & Le, H. (2006). Implications of Direct and Indirect Range Restriction for Meta-Analysis Methods and Findings. *The Journal of Applied Psychology, 91*(3), 594–612. doi:10.1037/0021-9010.91.3.594 PMID:16737357

Hurley, C. (2010). *The Effects of Motivation and Training Format on the Ability to Detect Hidden Emotions*. (Unpublished doctoral dissertation). New York: State University of New York at Buffalo.

Ibtesam, H. (2005). The relationship between effective communication of high school principals and school climate. *Education, 126*, 334–345.

Ibukun, W. O., Oyewole, B. K., & Abe, T. O. (2011). Personality characteristics and principal leadership effectiveness in Ekiti State, Nigeria. *International Journal of Leadership Studies, 6*(2), 246–262.

Illinois School Leader Task Force. (2008). *Illinois School Leader Preparation Task Force recommendations*. Springfield, IL: Author.

Illinois. (n.d.). In *Wikipedia, the free encyclopedia*. Retrieved at http://en.wikipedia.org/wiki/Illinois

Institute for Educational Leadership (IEL). (2008). *Teacher leadership in high schools: How principals encourage it-How teachers practice it*. Institute for Educational Leadership. Retrieved February 9, 2014, from http://www.iel.org/pubs/metlife_t eacher_ report.pdf

Isaacs, W., & Smith, B. (1994). Designing a dialogue session. In P. Senge, A. Kleiner, C. Roberts, R. B. Ross, & B. Smith (Eds.), The fifth discipline fieldbook: Strategies and tools for building a learning organization (pp. 374-381). London: Nicholas Brealey Publishing.

Isaacson, N., & Bamburg, J. (1992). Can Schools Become Learning Organizations? *Educational Leadership, 50*(3), 42–44.

Isaksen, S., & Lauer, K. (2002). The Climate for Creativity and Change in Teams. *Creativity and Innovation Management, 11*(1), 74–86. doi:10.1111/1467-8691.00238

Isen, A. M., & Baron, R. A. (1991). Positive affect as a factor in organizational behavior. In B. M. Staw & L. L. Cummings (Eds.), *Research in organizational behavior* (Vol. 13, pp. 1–53). Greenwich, CT: JAI Press.

Isik, H. (2003a). A new model for training the school administrators. *Hacettepe Üniversitesi Eğitim Fakültesi Dergisi, 24,* 206–211.

Isik, H. (2003b). From policy into practice: The effects of principalship preparation programs on principal behavior. *International Journal of Educational Reform, 12*(4), 260–274.

Izard, C. (1983). *The maximally discriminative facial movement coding system.* Unpublished manuscript. University of Delaware.

Izard, C. E., Dougherty, L. M., & Hembree, E. A. (1983). *A system for identifying affect expressions by holistic judgments.* Unpublished manuscript. University of Delaware.

Jansen, P. G. W., & Vinkenburg, C. J. (2006). Predicting management career success from *assessment* center data: A longitudinal study. *Journal of Vocational Behavior, 68*(2), 253–266. doi:10.1016/j.jvb.2005.07.004

Jansson, N. (2013). Organizational change as a practice: A critical analysis. *Journal of Organizational Change Management, 26*(6), 1003–1019. doi:10.1108/JOCM-09-2012-0152

Jenkins, A. M., & Johnson, R. D. (1977). What The Information Analyst Should Know About Body Language. *Management Information Systems Quarterly, 1*(3), 33–47. doi:10.2307/248711

Jenkins, B. (2009). What it takes to be an instructional leader. *Principal (Reston VA), 88*(3), 34–37.

Jensen, B., & Sonnerman, J. (2014). *Turning around schools: It can be done, Grattan Institute Report No. 2014-1.* Retrieved March 22, 2013, from http://grattan.edu.au/static/files/assets/518f9688/805-turning-around-schools.pdf

Jensen, B., & Reichl, J. (2011). *Better teacher appraisal and feedback: Improving performance.* Melbourne: Grattan Institute.

Jeyaraj, S. (2011). *Organizational cognisance: Introducing a cognitive dimension to the concept of organizational alignment.* (Doctoral dissertation). Faculty of education, University of Southern Queensland. Retrieved March 02, 2014, from http://eprints.usq.edu.au/23412/

John, O. P., Donahue, E. M., & Kentle, R. L. (1991). *The Big Five Inventory--Versions 4a and 54.* Berkeley, CA: University of California, Berkeley, Institute of Personality and Social Research.

Johnson, P. E. (2003). Conflict and the School Leader: Expert or Novice. *Journal of Research for Educational Leaders, 1,* 28–45.

Jowett, B. (Ed.). (1871). *Plato: The Republic.* Project Gutenberg. Retrieved, 15 February 2014, from: http://www.gutenberg.org/files/1497/1497-h/1497-h.htm

Judge, T. A., & Bono, J. E. (2000). Five-factor model of personality and transformational leadership. *The Journal of Applied Psychology, 85*(5), 751–765. doi:10.1037/0021-9010.85.5.751 PMID:11055147

Judge, T. A., Bono, J. E., Ilies, R., & Gerhardt, M. W. (2002). Personality and leadership: A qualitative and quantitative review. *The Journal of Applied Psychology, 87*(4), 765–780. doi:10.1037/0021-9010.87.4.765 PMID:12184579

Judge, T. A., Colbert, A. E., & Ilies, R. (2004). Intelligence and Leadership: A Quantitative Review and Test of Theoretical Propositions. *The Journal of Applied Psychology, 89*(3), 542–552. doi:10.1037/0021-9010.89.3.542 PMID:15161411

Judge, T. A., & Long, D. M. (2012). Individual Differences in Leadership. In D. V. Day & J. Antonakis (Eds.), *The Nature of Leadership* (pp. 179–217). Los Angeles: Sage.

Jung, D. I., Chow, C., & Wu, A. (2003). The role of transformational leadership in enhancing organizational innovation: Hypotheses and some preliminary findings. *The Leadership Quarterly, 14*(4-5), 525–544. doi:10.1016/S1048-9843(03)00050-X

Kaldi, S. Filippatou, D., & Govaris, C. (2011): Project-based learning in primary schools: effects on pupils' learning and attitudes. *Education, 39*(1), 35-47.

Kamler, B., & Comber, B. (2005). Turn-around pedagogies: Improving the education of at-risk students. *Improving Schools, 8*(2), 121–131. doi:10.1177/1365480205057702

Kanter, R. (1979). Power failure in management circuits. *Harvard Business Review, 57,* 65–75. PMID:10244631

Karstanje, P., & Webber, C. F. (2008). Programs for school principal preparation in East Europe. *Journal of Educational Administration*, *46*(6), 739–751. doi:10.1108/09578230810908325

Katzenmeyer, M., & Moller, G. (2009). *Awakening the sleeping giant. Helping teachers develop as leaders* (3rd ed.). Thousand Oaks, CA: Corwin.

Kauffman, S. A. (1995). *At home in the universe: The search for the laws of self-organization and complexity*. New York: Oxford University Press.

Kearney, E., & Gebert, D. (2009). Managing diversity and enhancing team outcomes: The promise of transformational leadership. *The Journal of Applied Psychology*, *94*(1), 77–101. doi:10.1037/a0013077 PMID:19186897

Keating, C. (2003). Messages from Face and Body: Women, Men, and the Silent Expression of Social Status. In D. S. Cobble, B. Hutchison, & A. B. Chaloupka (Eds.), Femininities, masculinities, and the politics of sexual difference(s) (pp. 65-70). Rutgers, the State University.

Keating, C. F., Mazur, A., & Segall, M. H. (1977). Facial Gestures Which Influence the Perception of Status. *Sociometry*, *40*(4), 374–378. doi:10.2307/3033487

Kelley, C., & Peterson, K. D. (2007). The work of principals and their preparation: Addressing critical needs for the twenty-first century. In Jossey-Bass Reader on Educational leadership (pp. 351-402). San Francisco: Wiley and Sons.

Kendall, L. T. (2011). *The effect of teacher leadership on retention plans and teacher attitudes among New North Carolina teachers* (Master thesis). Retrieved from ProQuest Dissertations and Thesis database. (UMI No. 1500767)

Kenny, D. A. (1994). *Interpersonal perception: A social relations analysis*. New York: Guilford.

Kenyon, C. L. (2008). *Reframed teacher leadership: A narrative inquiry* (Doctoral dissertation). Retrieved from ProQuest Dissertations and Thesis database. (UMI No. 3321001)

Keup, J. R., Walker, A. A., Astin, H. S., & Lindholm, J. A. (2001). *Organizational culture and institutional transformation (ERIC Digest ED464521)*. ERIC Clearinghouse on Higher Education.

Kezar, A. (2005). Consequences of radical change in governance: A grounded theory approach. *The Journal of Higher Education*, *76*(6), 634–668. doi:10.1353/jhe.2005.0043

Kidwell, R. E. Jr. (2004). "Small" Lies, Big Trouble: The Unfortunate Consequences of Résumé Padding, from Janet Cooke to George O'Leary. *Journal of Business Ethics*, *51*(2), 175–184. doi:10.1023/B:BUSI.0000033611.50841.55

Kılınç, A. Ç. (2013). *İlköğretim okullarında liderlik kapasitesinin belirlenmesi* [Determining the leadership capacity in primary schools]. (Unpublished doctoral dissertation). Gazi University, Ankara, Turkey.

Kılınç, A. Ç., & Recepoğlu, E. (2013). Ortaöğretim okulu öğretmenlerinin öğretmen liderliğine ilişkin algı ve beklentileri[High school teachers' perceptions on and expectations from teacher leadership]. *Kalem International Journal of Educational and Human Sciences*, *3*(2), 175–215.

Kirk, D. J. & Jones, T. C. (2004). *Effective schools*. Dallas, TX: Pearson Education. Retrieved December 9, 2013 from pearsoneducation.com

Kleine-Kracht, P. (1993). Indirect instructional leadership: An administrator's Choice. *Educational Administration Quarterly*, *29*(2), 187–212. doi:10.1177/0013161X93029002005

Knapp, M. S., Copland, M., Ford, B., Markholt, A., McLaughlin, M., Milliken, M., & Talbert, E. J. (2003). Leading for Learning Sourcebook: Concepts and Examples. Center for the Study of Teaching and Policy, University of Washington.

Knapp, M. S., Copland, M. A., Honig, M. I., Plecki, M. L., & Portin, B. S. (2010). Urban renewal: The urban school leader takes on a new role. *Journal of Staff Development*, *31*(2), 25–29.

Kolodinsky, R. W., Treadway, D. C., & Ferris, G. R. (2007). Political skill and influence effectiveness: Testing portions of an expanded Ferris and Judge (1991) model. *Human Relations, 60*(12), 1747–1777. doi:10.1177/0018726707084913

Kölükçü, D. (2011). *İlköğretim okulu öğretmenlerinin öğretmen liderliğini gösteren davranışlarının gereklilik ve sergilenme derecesine ilişkin görüşleri* [Neccessity of demonstrating leadership for elementary school teachers and their views relating to the level of demonstrating leadership] (Unpublished master thesis). Başkent University, Ankara, Turkey.

Kondakci, Y. (2005). *Practice-based continuous change: A longitudinal investigation of an organizational change process in a higher education organization.* (Unpublished doctoral dissertation). Ghent University, Ghent, Belgium.

Kotter, J. P. (1996). *Leading change.* Boston, MA: Harvard Business School Publishing.

Kousoulas, F. (2006, November). *Assessment of creativity within the school climate as a workplace: Results of a pilot research for the construction of a research instrument.* Paper presented at the 5th National Conference of the Hellenic Educational Society on "Greek Pedagogy and Educational Research". Thessaloniki, Greece. (in Greek).

Kroksmark, T. (2012). *En modellskola på vetenskaplig grund.* [A School Model on a Scientific Basis][online]. Available: http://www.tomaskroksmark.se/modells-kola_vet_grund.pdf

Krug, S. E. (1990). *Leadership and learning: A measurement-based approach for analyzing school effectiveness and developing effective school leaders: Project Report (Report No. BBB28334).* Urbana, IL: National Center for School Leadership. (ERIC Document Reproduction Service No. ED327950)

Kruger, M., & Scheerens, J. (2012). Conceptual Perspectives on School Leadership. In School Leadership Effects Revised: Review and Meta-Analysis of Empirical Studies (pp. 1-30). Dordrecht, The Netherlands: Springer.

Kruger, A. G. (1996). *FDEEL 2-9 Study Manual 1: School Management: Internal and external environment, Educational leadership.* Pretoria, South Africa: UNISA.

Kruger, A. G., & Steinmann, F. C. (2003). The organisational climate and culture of schools. In I. Van Deventer & A. G. Kruger (Eds.), *An educator's guide to school management skills.* Pretoria: Van Schaik.

Kruger, M. L., Witziers, B., & Sleegers, P. J. C. (2007). The impact of school leadership on school level factors: Validation of a causal model. *School Effectiveness and School Improvement, 18*(1), 1–20. doi:10.1080/09243450600797638

Krug, S. E. (1992). Instructional Leadership: A constructivist perspective. *Educational Administration Quarterly, 28*(3), 430–443. doi:10.1177/0013161X92028003012

Krumhuber, E., Manstead, A., & Kappas, A. (2006). Temporal Aspects of Facial Displays in Person and Expression Perception: The Effects of Smile Dynamics, Head-tilt, and Gender. *Journal of Nonverbal Behavior, 31*(1), 39–56. doi:10.1007/s10919-006-0019-x

Kvale, S. (1996). *Interviews: An introduction to qualitative research interviewing.* Newbury Park, CA: Sage Publications.

Kyriacou, C. (1987). Teacher Stress and Burnout: An International Review. *Educational Research, 29*(2), 146–152. doi:10.1080/0013188870290207

Kyriacou, C., & Issitt, J. (2008). What characterises effective teacher-initiated teacher-pupil dialogue to promote conceptual understanding in mathematics lessons in England in Key Stages 2 and 3: A systematic review. Report. In *Research Evidence in Education Library.* London: EPPI-Centre, Social Science Research Unit, Institute of Education, University of London.

Kyriakides, L., Creemers, B. P. M., & Antoniou, P. (2009). Teacher behavior and student outcomes: Suggestions for research on teacher training and professional development. *Teaching and Teacher Education, 25*(1), 12–23. doi:10.1016/j.tate.2008.06.001

Kythreotis, A., Pashiardis, P., & Kyriakides, L. (2010). The influence of school leadership styles and culture on student achievement in Cyprus primary schools. *Journal of Educational Administration, 28*(2), 218–240. doi:10.1108/09578231011027860

Lahdenperä, P. (2011). *Forskningscirkel - Arena för verksamhetsutvecking i mångfald.* [Reseach Circles, Arena for Development in Diversity]. Available: http://www.diva-portal.org/smash/get/diva2:511191/FULL-TEXT01.pdf

Lai Horng, E., Klasik, D., & Loeb, S. (2009). *Principal Time-Use and School Effectiveness.* Institute for Research on Education Policy and Practice, Stanford University.

Lainas, A. (1993). Educational management and curricula: The institutionalization of decentralization and wider participation[in Greek]. *Paidagogiki Epitheorisi, 19*, 254–294.

Läkartidningen. (2007). Svårt att definiera beprövad erfarenhet. [Difficult to define proven experience]. *Läkartidningen, 104*(4), 198-199.

Lambert, L. (2000). *Building leadership capacity in schools.* APC Monographs. Australian Principals Centre (APC). Retrieved November 4, 2013, from http://research.acer.edu.au/apc_monographs/2

Lambert, L. (1998). How to build leadership capacity. *Educational Leadership, 55*(7), 17–19.

Lambert, L. (2002). Toward a deepened theory of constructivist leadership. In L. Lambert, D. Walker, D. Zimmerman, J. Cooper, M. Lambert, M. Gardner, & P. Slack (Eds.), *The constructivist leader* (pp. 34–62). New York: Teachers College.

Lambert, L. (2003). *Leadership capacity for lasting school improvement.* Alexandria, VA: Association for Supervision and Curriculum Development.

Langley, A., Smallman, C., Tsoukas, H., & Van de Ven, A. (2013). Process studies of change in organization and management: Unveiling temporality, activity, and flow. *Academy of Management Journal, 56*(1), 1–13. doi:10.5465/amj.2013.4001

Larry, C. D. (2003). *A study of time management use and preferred time management practices of middle and secondary school principals in selected southern states.* (PhD thesis). University of Alabama, Tuscaloosa, AL.

Lashway, L. (2003). Transforming principal preparation. *ERIC Digest 165.* Retrieved at cepm.uoregon.edu/publications/digests/digest165.html

Lashway, L. (1998). Teacher leadership. *Research Roundup, 14*(3), 2–5.

Lashway, L., Mazzarella, J., & Grundy, T. (1996). Portrait of a Leader. In S. C. Smith & P. K. Piele (Eds.), *School leadership handbook for excellence* (3rd ed., pp. 15–37). Clearinghouse on Educational Management.

Lau, S. (1982). The effect of smiling on person perception. *The Journal of Social Psychology, 117*(1), 63–67. doi:10.1080/00224545.1982.9713408

Lave, J., & Wenger, E. (1991). *Situated learning: Legitimate peripheral participation.* Cambridge, UK: Cambridge University Press. doi:10.1017/CBO9780511815355

Law, K. S., Wong, C. S., & Song, L. (2004). Construct Validity of Emotional Intelligence: Its Potential Utility of Management Studies. *The Journal of Applied Psychology, 89*(3), 483–496. doi:10.1037/0021-9010.89.3.483 PMID:15161407

Lawrimore, B. (2005). From excellence to emergence: The evolution of management thinking and the influence of complexity. In K. A. Richardson (Ed.), *Managing organizational complexity: Philosophy, theory, and application* (pp. 115–132). Greenwich, CT: Information Age Publishing.

Layder, D. (1997). *Modern Social Theory: Key Debates and New Directions.* London: UCL Press.

Layder, D. (2004). *Emotion in Social Life: The Lost Heart of Society.* London: Sage.

Lazaridou, A. (2009). The kinds of knowledge principals use. *International Journal of Education Policy & Leadership, 4*(10).

Le Boterf, G. (2001). *Construire les compétences individuelles et collectives.* Paris: Editions d'Organisation.

Leclercq-Vandelannoitte, A. (2013). Contradiction as a medium and outcome of organizational change: A Foucaldian reading. *Journal of Organizational Change Management, 26*(3), 556–572. doi:10.1108/09534811311328579

Lee, C. D. (2010). Soaring above the Clouds, Delving the Ocean's Depths: Understanding the Ecologies of Human Learning and the challenge for Education Science. *Educational Researcher, 39*(9), 643–655. doi:10.3102/0013189X10392139

Leiberman, A. (1995). Restructuring schools: The dynamics of changing practice, structure and culture. In A. Leiberman (Ed.), *The work of restructuring schools: Building from the ground up* (pp. 1–17). New York: Teachers College Press.

Leithwood, K. (1992). The move toward transformational leadership. *Educational Leadership, 49*(5), 8–12.

Leithwood, K. (1994). Leadership for school restructuring. *Educational Administration Quarterly, 30*(4), 498–518. doi:10.1177/0013161X94030004006

Leithwood, K. (2003). Teacher leadership: Its nature, development, and impact on schools and students. In M. Brundrett, N. Burton, & R. Smith (Eds.), *Leadership in education* (pp. 103–117). Thousand Oaks, CA: Sage Publications. doi:10.4135/9781446215036.n7

Leithwood, K. (2005). *Educational Leadership*. Toronto: Temple University Center for Research in Human Development and Education.

Leithwood, K. (2005). La dimensión emocional del mejoramiento escolar: una perspectiva desde el liderazgo. In Y. Townsend (Ed.), *International handbook of school effectiveness and school improvement* (pp. 615–634). Dordrecht, The Netherlands: Springer.

Leithwood, K. (2006). *The Emotional Side of School Improvement: A Leadership Perspective*. Toronto, Canada: Ontario Institute of Education.

Leithwood, K. A., Jantzi, D., & Steinbach, R. (1999). *Changing leadership for changing times*. Buckingham, UK: Open University Press.

Leithwood, K. A., & Riehl, C. (2005). What we know about successful school leadership. In W. Firestone & C. Riehl (Eds.), *A new agenda for research on educational leadership* (pp. 12–27). New York: Teachers College Press.

Leithwood, K., & Beatty, B. (2008). *Leading with Teacher Emotions in Mind*. Thousand Oaks, CA: Corwin Press.

Leithwood, K., Begley, P., & Cousins, B. (1990). The nature, causes and consequences of principals' practices: An agenda for future research. *Journal of Educational Administration, 28*(4), 5–31. doi:10.1108/09578239010001014

Leithwood, K., Day, C., Sammons, P., Harris, A., & Hopkins, D. (2006). *Successful school leadership: What it is and how it influences student learning (Research Report 800)*. London, UK: Department for Education.

Leithwood, K., & Hallinger, P. (2002). *Second International Handbook of Educational Leadership and Administration* (Vols. 1-2). Boston: Kluwer Academic Publishers. doi:10.1007/978-94-010-0375-9

Leithwood, K., Harris, A., & Hopkins, D. (2008). Seven strong claims about succeeful school leadership. *School Leadership and Management: Formerly School Organization, 28*(1), 27–42. doi:10.1080/13632430701800060

Leithwood, K., & Jantzi, D. (1990). Transformational Leadership: How Principals Can Help Reform School Cultures. *School Effectiveness and School Improvement, 1*(4), 249–280. doi:10.1080/0924345900010402

Leithwood, K., & Jantzi, D. (1997). Explaining variation in teachers' perceptions of principals' leadership: A replication. *Journal of Educational Administration, 35*(4), 312–331. doi:10.1108/09578239710171910

Leithwood, K., & Jantzi, D. (1999). The relative effects of principal and teacher sources of leadership on student engagement with school. *Educational Administration Quarterly, 35*(5), 679–706. doi:10.1177/0013161X99355002

Leithwood, K., & Jantzi, D. (2000). Principal and teacher leadership effects: A replication. *School Leadership & Management, 20*(4), 415–434. doi:10.1080/713696963

Leithwood, K., & Jantzi, D. (2003). Transformational leadership effects on student engagement with school. In M. Wallace & L. Poulson (Eds.), *Educational leadership and management* (pp. 194–212). London, UK: Sage. doi:10.4135/9781446216576.n9

Leithwood, K., & Jantzi, D. (2006). Transformational leadership for large-reform: Effects of students, teachers, and their classroom practices. *School Effectiveness and School Improvement, 17*(2), 201–227. doi:10.1080/09243450600565829

Leithwood, K., & Jantzi, D. (2007). A Review of Transformational School Leadership Research 1996-2005. *Leadership and Policy in Schools, 4*(3), 177–199. doi:10.1080/15700760500244769

Leithwood, K., & Jantzi, D. (2008). Linking leadership to student learning: The contributions of leader efficacy. *Educational Administration Quarterly, 44*(4), 496–528. doi:10.1177/0013161X08321501

Leithwood, K., Louis, K. S., Anderson, S., & Wahlstrom, K. (2004). *How leadership influences student learning. A review of the research.* New York: The Wallace Foundation.

Leithwood, K., Louis, K., Anderson, S., & Wahistrom, K. (2004). *Review of research: How leadership influence student learning?* Wallance Foundation.

Leithwood, K., & Mascall, B. (2008). Collective leadership effects on student achievement. *Educational Administration Quarterly, 44*(4), 529–561. doi:10.1177/0013161X08321221

Leithwood, K., Mascall, B., & Strauss, T. (2009). What we have learned and where we go from here. In K. Leithwood, B. Mascall, & T. Strauss (Eds.), *Distributed leadership according to the evidence* (pp. 269–281). New York: Routledge.

Leithwood, K., & Riehl, C. (2003). *What We Know About Successful Leadership, Laboratory for Student Success.* Philadelphia: Temple University.

Leiva, V. (2014) (Ed.). Asesoramiento educativo. ¿Qué necesitan nuestras escuelas? Viña del Mar: Ediciones Altazor.

Lemmer, E. M. (1994). *Study Guide ONA 411-Y: Ethnographic research.* Pretoria, South Africa: UNISA.

Levacic, R. (2005). Educational leadership as a causal factor. *Educational Management Administration & Leadership, 33*(2), 197–210. doi:10.1177/1741143205051053

Levi, R. (1997). *Vad menas med beprövad erfarenhet?* [What does proven experience mean?] [online]. Available: http://www.sbu.se/sv/Vetenskap--Praxis/Vetenskap-och-praxis/2095/

Levin, B. (2010). Leadership for Evidence-Informed Education. *School Leadership & Management, 30*(4), 303–315. doi:10.1080/13632434.2010.497483

Levin, B. (2010). The challenge of large scale literacy improvement. *School Effectiveness and School Improvement, 21*(4), 359–376. doi:10.1080/09243453.2010.486589

Levin, B. (2013). To know is not enough: Research knowledge and its use. *Review of Education, 1*(1), 2–31. doi:10.1002/rev3.3001

Levin, B., & Fullan, M. (2008). Learning about system renewal. *Educational Management Administration & Leadership, 36*(2), 289–303. doi:10.1177/1741143207087778

Levine, A. (2005). *Educating school leaders.* Washington, DC: The Education School Project.

Levine, D. U., & Lezotte, L. W. (1990). *Unusually effective schools.* Madison, WI: The National Center for Effective Schools Research and Development.

Lewis, K. M. (2000). When leaders display emotion: How followers respond to negative emotional expression of male and female leaders. *Journal of Organizational Behavior, 21*(2), 221–234. doi:10.1002/(SICI)1099-1379(200003)21:2<221::AID-JOB36>3.0.CO;2-0

Lewis, L. K. (2000). Communicating change: Four cases of quality programs. *Journal of Business Communication, 37*(2), 128–155. doi:10.1177/002194360003700201

Lewis, M. W., Welsh, M. A., Dehler, G. E., & Green, S. G. (2002). Product 223 development tensions: Exploring contrasting styles of product management. *Academy of Management Journal, 45*(3), 546–564. doi:10.2307/3069380

Lezotte, L. W. (1989). *Selected Resources Complied for the 7th Annual Effective School Conference.* Rimrock: National School Conference Institute.

Lichtenstein, B. M. B. (2000). Emergence as a process of self-organizing: New assumptions and insights from the study of non-linear dynamic systems. *Journal of Organizational Change Management, 13*(6), 526–544. doi:10.1108/09534810010378560

Lieberman, A. (1995). Practices that support teacher development: Transforming conceptions of professional learning. *Phi Delta Kappan, 76*, 591–596.

Lieberman, A., & Miller, L. (2005). Teachers as leaders. *The Educational Forum, 69*(2), 151–162. doi:10.1080/00131720508984679

Lieberman, A., Saxl, E. R., & Miles, M. B. (2000). Teacher leadership: Ideology and practice. In M. Fullan (Ed.), *The Jossey-Bass reader on educational leadership* (pp. 339–345). Chicago: Jossey-Bass.

Limerick, B., & Nielsen, H. (Eds.). (1995). *School and community relations*. Sydney: Harcourt Brace.

Lingard, R., & Sellar, S. (2013). Looking east: Three national responses to Shanghai's performance in PISA 2009, School improvement. *Professional Voice, 9*(2), 10-19. Retrieved May 31, 2014, from http://www.aeuvic.asn.au/2504_pv_9_2_complete_lr.pdf

Little, J. W. (2000). Assessing the prospects for teacher leadership. In M. Fullan (Ed.), *Educational leadership*. San Francisco, CA: Jossey-Bass.

Little, J. W. (2003). Constructions of teacher leadership in three periods of policy and reform activism. *School Leadership & Management, 23*(4), 401–419. doi:10.1080/1363243032000150944

Loader, D. (1997). *The Inner Principal*. London: Falmer Press.

Locke, E. A. (2005). Why emotional intelligence is an invalid concept. *Journal of Organizational Behavior, 26*(4), 425–431. doi:10.1002/job.318

Locke, E. A., & Kirkpatrick, S. (1991). *The essence of leadership: The four keys to leading successfully*. New York: Lexington Books.

Lord, R. G., de Vader, C. L., & Alliger, G. M. (1986). A meta-analysis of the relation between personality traits and leadership perceptions: An application of validity generalization procedures. *The Journal of Applied Psychology, 71*(3), 402–410. doi:10.1037/0021-9010.71.3.402

Lorenzo, M. (2012). Las comunidades de liderazgo de centros educativos. *Educar, 48*(1), 9-21.

Lorenzo, M. (2004). La función de liderazgo de la dirección escolar: Una competencia transversal. Enseñanza & Teaching. *Revista Interuniversitaria de Didáctica, 22*, 193–211.

Louden, W., et al. (2005). *In teachers' hands: Effective literacy teaching practices in the early years of schooling*. Edith Cowan University. Retrieved July 29, 2013, from http://inteachershands.education.ecu.edu.au/index.php?page=43

Louis, K. S. (1994). Beyond 'managed change': Rethinking how schools improve. *School Effectiveness and School Improvement, 5*(1), 2–24. doi:10.1080/0924345940050102

Louis, K. S. (2006). *Organizing for school change*. London: Taylor and Francis.

Louis, K. S. (2008). Learning to support improvement-next steps for research on district practice. *American Journal of Education, 114*(4), 681–689. doi:10.1086/589320

Louis, K. S., Dretzke, B., & Jantzi, D. (2010). Testing a conception of how school leadership influences student learning. *Educational Administration Quarterly, 46*(5), 671–706. doi:10.1177/0013161X10377347

Louis, K. S., & Marks, H. (1998). Does professional community affect the classroom? Teachers' work and student experience in restructured schools. *American Journal of Education, 106*(4), 532–575. doi:10.1086/444197

Lucas, C. (2000). *Self-organizing systems FAQ*. Retrieved at http://www.calresco.org/sos/sosfaq.htm

Lumby, J., Walker, A., Bryant, M., Bush, T., & Björk, L. G. (2009). Research on leadership preparation in a global context. In M. D. Young, G. M. Crow, J. Murphy & R. T. Ogawa (Eds.), Handbook of research on the education of school leaders (pp. 157-194). New York: Routledge.

Lumby, J., & Coleman, M. (2007). *Leadership and diversity: Challenging theory and practice in Education*. London: Sage.

Luthans, F., Hodgetts, R. M., & Rosenkrantz, S. A. (1988). *Real managers*. Cambridge, MA: Ballinger.

MacBeath, J. (2005). Leadership as distributed: A matter of practice. *School Leadership & Management, 25*(4), 349–366. doi:10.1080/13634230500197165

MacBeath, J., & Cheng, Y. C. (Eds.). (2008). *Leadership for learning: International perspectives*. Rotterdam: Sense Publishers.

MacBeath, J., & Mortimore, P. (2001). *Improving School Effectiveness*. Buckingham, UK: Open University Press.

MacClelland, D. C. (1973). Testing for Competence Rather Than for 'Intelligence'. *The American Psychologist, 28*(1), 1–14. doi:10.1037/h0034092 PMID:4684069

MacGilchrist, B., Myers, K., & Reed, J. (1997). *The Intelligent School*. London: Paul Chapman.

Madera, J. M., & Smith, B. D. (2009). The effects of leader negative emotions on evaluations of leadership in a crisis situation: The role of anger and sadness. *The Leadership Quarterly*, *20*(2), 103–114. doi:10.1016/j.leaqua.2009.01.007

Maleki, M. (2013). Narcissism and Decision-Making Styles Principals. *Asian Journal of Research in Social Sciences and Humanities*, *10*(3), 359–370.

Malgas, R. W. (2006). *Emotional intelligence in the effective management of the school.* (Unpublished Master's Dissertation). University of Johannesburg, Johannesburg, South Africa.

Malpica, F. (2013). *8 ideas clave. Calidad de la práctica educativa. Referentes, indicadores y condiciones para mejorar la enseñanza-aprendizaje.* Barcelona: Graó.

Mangin, M. M. (2005). Distributed leadership and the culture of schools: Teacher leaders' strategies for gaining access to classrooms. *Journal of School Leadership*, *15*(4), 456–484.

Mangin, M. M. (2007). Facilitating elementary principals' support for instructional teacher leadership. *Educational Administration Quarterly*, *43*(3), 319–357. doi:10.1177/0013161X07299438

Mann, R. D. (1959). A review of the relationship between personality and performance in small groups. *Psychological Bulletin*, *56*(4), 241–270. doi:10.1037/h0044587

March, J. G. (1981). Footnotes to organizational change. *Administrative Science Quarterly*, *26*(4), 563–577. doi:10.2307/2392340

Maree, J. G., & Eiselen, R. J. (2004). The Emotional Intelligence Profile of Academics in a Merger Setting. *Education and Urban Society*, *36*(4), 482–504. doi:10.1177/0013124504265862

Marino, P. (2005). Dialogue in mathematics – is it important? *Mathematics in Schools*, *34*(2), 26–28.

Marion, R., & Uhl-Bien, M. (2002). Leadership in complex organizations. *The Leadership Quarterly*, *12*(4), 389–418. doi:10.1016/S1048-9843(01)00092-3

Marks, H. M., & Printy, S. M. (2003). Principal Leadership and School Performance: An Integration of Transformational and Instructional Leadership. *Educational Administration Quarterly*, *39*(3), 370–397. doi:10.1177/0013161X03253412

Marsh, A., & Ambady, N. (2007). The influence of the fear facial expression on prosocial responding. *Cognition and Emotion*, *21*(2), 225–247. doi:10.1080/02699930600652234

Marsick, V. J., & Watkins, K. E. (2003). Demonstrating the value of an organization's learning culture: The Dimensions of Learning Organizations Questionnaire. *Advances in Developing Human Resources*, *5*(2), 132–151. doi:10.1177/1523422303005002002

Martin Korpi, B. (2006). *Förskolan i politiken: om intentioner och beslut bakom den svenska förskolan framväxt.* [Preschool in politics: about intentions and decisions in the emergence of the Swedish preschool]. Stockholm:Utbildnings och kulturdepartementet, Regeringskansliet.

Martínez, M., Badía, J., & Jolonch, A. (2013). *Lideratge per a l'aprenentatge. Estudis de cas a Catalunya.* Barcelona: Fundación Jaume Bofill.

Martinko, M. J., & Gardner, W. L. (1990). Structured Observation of Managerial Work: A Replication and Synthesis. *Journal of Management Studies*, *27*(3), 329–357. doi:10.1111/j.1467-6486.1990.tb00250.x

Marzano, R. J., & Marzano, J. S. (2003). The key to classroom management. *Educational Leadership*, *61*, 6–13.

Masters, R. D., & Sullivan, D. G. (1989). Nonverbal Displays and Political Leadership in France and the United States. *Political Behavior*, *11*(2), 123–156. doi:10.1007/BF00992491

Matsumoto, D., & Hee Yoo, S. (2005). Culture and Applied Nonverbal Communication. In R. E. Riggio & R. S. Feldman (Eds.), *Applications of Nonverbal Communication* (pp. 255–276). Mahwah, NJ: Lawrence Erlbaum.

Matsumoto, D., & Hwang, H. (2011). Evidence for training the ability to read microexpressions of emotion. *Motivation and Emotion*, *35*(2), 181–191. doi:10.1007/s11031-011-9212-2

Matthews, G., Zeidner, M., & Roberts, R. D. (2002). *Emotional Intelligence: Science and Myth*. Cambridge, MA: MIT Press.

Matthews, L. J., & Crow, G. M. (2003). *Being and becoming a principal: Role concepts for contemporary principals and assistant principals*. Boston, MA: Allyn and Bacon.

Mayer, J. D., & Salovey, P. (1997). What is emotional intelligence? In P. Salovey & D. Sluyter (Eds.), *Emotional development and emotional intelligence. Implications for educators* (pp. 3–34). New York, NY: Basic books.

Mayer, J. D., Salovey, P., Caruso, D. R., & Sitarenios, G. (2001). Emotional intelligence as a standard intelligence. *Emotion (Washington, D.C.)*, *1*(3), 232–242. doi:10.1037/1528-3542.1.3.232 PMID:12934682

Mayer, J. D., Salovey, P., Caruso, D. R., & Sitarenios, G. (2003). Measuring emotional intelligence with the MS-CEIT V2.0. *Emotion (Washington, D.C.)*, *3*(1), 97–105. doi:10.1037/1528-3542.3.1.97 PMID:12899321

Mayer, S. J. (2012). *Classroom discourse and democracy: Making meanings together. Critical pedagogical perspectives*. New York: Peter Lang.

Mc Daniel, R. R. Jnr. (2007). Management strategies for complex adaptive systems: Sensemaking, learning, and improvisation. *Performance Improvement Quarterly*, *2*(2), 21–41.

McArthur, L. Z., & Baron, R. M. (1983). Toward an ecological theory of social perception. *Psychological Review*, *90*(3), 215–238. doi:10.1037/0033-295X.90.3.215

McCarthy, M. M. (1999). The evolution of educational leadership preparation programs. In J. Murphy & S.K. Louis (Eds.), Handbook of research on educational administration (pp. 119-140). San Francisco: Jossey-Bass Inc.

McCarthy, M. M. (2002). Educational leadership preparation programs: A glance at the past with an eye toward the future. *Leadership and Policy in Schools*, *1*(3), 201–221. doi:10.1076/lpos.1.3.201.7890

McColl-Kennedy, J. R., & Anderson, R. D. (2002). Impact of leadership style and emotions on subordinate performance. *The Leadership Quarterly*, *13*(5), 545–559. doi:10.1016/S1048-9843(02)00143-1

McCrae, R. R., & Costa, P. T. (1987). Validation of the five-factor model of personality across instruments and observers. *Journal of Personality and Social Psychology*, *52*(1), 81–90. doi:10.1037/0022-3514.52.1.81 PMID:3820081

McEwan, E. K. (2003). *Ten Traits of Highly Effective Principals: From Good to Great Performance*. Thousand Oaks, CA: Corwin.

McKelvey, B. (2002). Microstrategy from microleadership: Distributed intelligence via new science. In A. Y. Lewin & H. Volberda (Eds.), *Mobilizing the self-renewing organization*. Thousand Oaks, CA: Sage.

McKinsey. (2010). *How the world's most improved school systems keep getting better*. McKinsey & Company.

McRoy, I., & Gibbs, P. (2009). Leading Change in Higher Education. *Educational Management Administration & Leadership*, *37*(5), 687–704. doi:10.1177/1741143209339655

Mead, G. (1934). *Mind, Self and Society*. Chicago: University of Chicago Press.

Medd, W. P. (2005). Imagining complex partnerships. In K. A. Richardson (Ed.), Managing organizational complexity: Philosophy, theory, and application (pp. 301-311). Greenwich, CT: Information Ager Publishing.

Medvedeff, M. E. (2008). *Leader affective displays during a negative work event: influences on subordinate appraisals, affect, and coping strategies*. (Doctoral dissertation). University of Akron. Retrieved from http://etd.ohiolink.edu/send-pdf.cgi/Medvedeff%20Megan.pdf?akron1207753447

Meindl, J. R. (1995). The romance of leadership as a follower-centric theory: A social constructionist approach. *The Leadership Quarterly*, *6*(3), 329–341. doi:10.1016/1048-9843(95)90012-8

Meister-Scheytt, C., & Scheytt, T. (2005). The complexity of change in universities. *Higher Education Quarterly*, *59*(1), 76–99. doi:10.1111/j.1468-2273.2005.00282.x

Mendiburu, J. G. (2010). *Personality Typologies as a Predictor of Being a Successful Elementary School Principal*. (Unpublished Dissertation). University La Verne, La Verne, CA.

Merriam, S. B. (1998). *Qualitative research and case study applications in education.* San Francisco: Jossey-Bass.

Merriam, S. B. (2002). *Qualitative research in practice: Examples for discussion and analysis.* San Francisco: Jossey-Bass.

Mestry, R. (2009). *Continuing professional development and professional learning for principals in South Africa.* Keynote presentation at the conference on The Professional Development of Principals. Mafikeng, North-West Province.

Mestry, R., & Grobler, B. R. (2003). The training and development of principals in managing schools effectively. *Education as Change, 7,* 126–146.

Mestry, R., & Singh, P. (2007). Continuing professional development for principals: A South African perspective. *South African Journal of Education, 27*(3), 477–490.

Michaelidou, A., & Pashiardis, P. (2009). Professional Development of School Leaders in Cyprus: Is it working? *Professional Development in Education, 35*(3), 399–416. doi:10.1080/19415250903069359

Middlewood, D. (2010). Managing people and performance. In T. Bush, L. Bell, & D. Middlewood (Eds.), *The principles of educational leadership and management* (2nd ed., pp. 135–150). London: Sage.

Miles, M. B., & Huberman, A. M. (1994). *Qualitative data analysis* (2nd ed.). Newbury Park, CA: Sage.

Miller, D. (1996). A preliminary typology of organizational learning: Synthesizing the literature. *Journal of Management, 22*(3), 485–505. doi:10.1177/014920639602200305

Miller, P. (2013a). *The politics of progression: Primary teachers' perceived barriers to gaining a principalship in Jamaica. Research Report.* Kingston, Jamaica: University of Technology, Jamaica & the Institute for Educational Administration & Leadership – Jamaica.

Miller, P. (2013b). School leadership in the Caribbean: Perceptions, practices, paradigms, London: *Symposium Books*

Miller, P. (2013c). Corruption as redemption? Affiliation as a mark for leadership progression among primary school teachers in Jamaica. *Journal of Education & Practice, 24*(4), 170–180.

Miller, P. (2014). What is a Principal's Quality Mark? Issues and Challenges in Leadership Progression among Primary Teachers in Jamaica. *Research in Comparative International Education, 9*(1), 126–136. doi:10.2304/rcie.2014.9.1.126

Miller, R. J., & Rowan, B. (2006). Effects of organic management on student achievement. *American Educational Research Journal, 43*(2), 219–253. doi:10.3102/00028312043002219

MINEDUC. (2005). *Marco para la Buena Dirección: Criterios para el Desarrollo Profesional y Evaluación de Desempeño.* Santiago de Chile: MINEDUC.

Ministerial Resolution 001/2014 (Resolución Ministerial 001/2014 Normas Generales para la Gestión Educativa 2014). Retrieved Februrary 14, 2014, from: http://goo.gl/Cxyrkb

Ministry of Education and Research. (2008). *Funding of the Swedih school system.* Retrieved from http://www.regeringen.se/content/1/c6/10/15/00/14eaa35c.pdf

Ministry of Education. (2012). *Education statistics 2011-1012: Annual statistical review of the education sector.* Kingston, Jamaica: Planning and Development Division, MoE.

Mintzberg, H. (1983). *Power in and around organizations.* Englewood Cliffs, NJ: Prentice Hall.

Mintzberg, H. (1985). The organization as a political arena. *Journal of Management Studies, 22*(2), 133–154. doi:10.1111/j.1467-6486.1985.tb00069.x

Mischel, W. (1977). The interaction of person and situation. In D. Magnusson & N. S. Endler (Eds.), *Personality at the crossroads: Current issues in interactional psychology* (pp. 333–357). Hillsdale, NJ: Lawrence, Erlbaum.

Mohrman, S. A., Tenkasi, R. V., & Mohrman, A. M. Jr. (2003). The role of networks in fundamental organizational change: A grounded analysis. *The Journal of Applied Behavioral Science, 39*(3), 301–323. doi:10.1177/0021886303258072

Moje, E. B., Ciechanowski, K. M., Kramer, K., Ellis, L., Carrillo, R., & Collazo, T. (2004). Working toward third space in content area literacy: An examination of everyday funds of knowledge and discourse. *Reading Research Quarterly*, *39*(1), 38–70. doi:10.1598/RRQ.39.1.4

Moloi, K. C. (2005). *The school as a learning organisation: Reconceptualising school practices in South Africa*. Pretoria: Van Schaik.

Monahan, J. L. (1998). I Don't Know It But I Like You The Influence of Nonconscious Affect on Person Perception. *Human Communication Research*, *24*(4), 480–500. doi:10.1111/j.1468-2958.1998.tb00428.x

Monahan, J. L., & Zuckerman, C. E. (1999). Intensifying the dominant response: Participant-observer differences and nonconscious effects. *Communication Research*, *26*(1), 81–110. doi:10.1177/009365099026001005

Monin, P., Noorderhaven, N., Vaara, E., & Kroon, D. (2013). Giving sense to and making sense of justice in postmerger integration. *Academy of Management Journal*, *56*(1), 256–284. doi:10.5465/amj.2010.0727

Montepare, J. M., & Dobish, H. (2003). The Contribution of Emotion Perceptions and Their Overgeneralizations to Trait Impressions. *Journal of Nonverbal Behavior*, *27*(4), 237–254. doi:10.1023/A:1027332800296

Moolenaar, N. M., Daly, A. J., & Sleegers, P. J. C. (2010). Occupying the principal position: Examining relationship between transformational leadership, social network position, and schools' innovative climate. *Educational Administration Quarterly*, *46*(5), 623–670. doi:10.1177/0013161X10378689

Moorman, C., & Miner, A. S. (1998). Organizational improvisation and organizational memory. *Academy of Management Review*, *23*(4), 698–723.

Moos, L. (2013). Comparing Educational Leadership Research. *Leadership and Policy in Schools*, *12*(3), 282–299. doi:10.1080/15700763.2013.834060

Moreau, M. P., Osgood, J., & Halsall, A. (2007). Making sense of the glass ceiling in schools: An exploration of women teachers' discourses. *Gender and Education*, *19*(2), 237–253. doi:10.1080/09540250601166092

Morgan, C., Hall, V., & Mackay, H. (1983). *The selection of secondary school headteachers*. Milton Keynes, UK: Open University Press.

Morgan, G. (1997). *Images of Organization*. London: SAGE.

Morris, V. C., Crowson, R., Porter-Gehrie, C., & Hurwitz, E., Jr. (1984). Principals in action: The reality of managing schools. Columbus, OH: Charles E. Merrill Publishing Company.

Morrison, K. R. B. (2002). *School Leadership and Complexity Theory*. London: Routledge-Falmer.

Mortimore, P., Sammons, P., Ecob, R., & Stoll, L. (1988). *School Matters: The Junior Years*. Salisbury: Open University.

Mourshed, M., Chijioke, C., & Barber, M. (2010). *How the world's most improved school systems keep getting better*. McKinsey and Co. Consulting Report.

Mouton, N., Louw, G. P., & Strydom, G. L. (2012). A historical analysis of the post-apartheid dispensation in South Africa (1994-2011). *International Business and Economics Research Journal*, *11*(11), 1211–1222.

Muijs, D., Harris, A., & Crawford, M. (2004). *The role of assistant heads: A review of research*. Paper presented at the International Congress for School Effectiveness and School Improvement. Rotterdam, The Netherlands.

Muijs, D. (2010). Leadership and Organizational Performance: From research to prescription? *International Journal of Educational Management*, *25*(1), 45–60. doi:10.1108/09513541111100116

Muijs, D., & Harris, A. (2003). Teacher leadership-Improvement through empowerment?: An overview of the literature. *Educational Management & Administration*, *31*(4), 437–448. doi:10.1177/0263211X030314007

Muijs, D., & Harris, A. (2006). Teacher led school improvement: Teacher leadership in the UK. *Teaching and Teacher Education*, *22*(8), 961–972. doi:10.1016/j.tate.2006.04.010

Muijs, D., & Harris, A. (2007). Teacher leadership in (in) action. Three case studies of contrasting schools. *Educational Management Administration & Leadership*, *35*(1), 111–134. doi:10.1177/1741143207071387

Mulford, B. (2003). *School Leaders: Changing role and impact on teacher and school effectiveness*. Paris: Education and Training Policy Division, OECD. Retrieved January 26, 2014 from http://www.oecd.org/education/school/2635399.pdf

Mulford, B. (1994). *Shaping tomorrow's schools (Monograph No. 15)*. Melbourne: Australian Council for Educational Administration.

Mullis, I. V. S., Martin, M. C., Foy, P., & Drucker, K. T. (2012). PIRLS 2011: International results in Reading. Chestnut Hill, MA: Boston College.

Mumford, M. D., Hester, K., & Robledo, I. (2012). Methods in Creativity Research: Multiple Approaches, Multiple Levels. In M. D. Mumford (Ed.), Handbook of Organizational Creativity (pp. 39-65). London: Waltham.

Murillo, J., & Román, M. (2013). La distribución del tiempo de los directores y las directoras de escuelas de Educación Primaria en América Latina y su incidencia en el desempeño de los estudiantes. *Revista de Educación, 361*.

Murphy, J. (2001). *Re-Culturing the profession of educational leadership: New blueprints*. Paper commissioned for the first meeting of the National Commission for the Advancement of Educational Leadership Preparation. Racine, WI. Retrieved at ED 464 380.

Murphy, J. (2007). A history of school effectiveness and improvement research in the USA focusing on the past quarter century. In, T. Townsend (Ed.), International handbook of school effectiveness and improvement (pp. 681-705). Dordrecht, The Netherlands: Springer.

Murphy, J. (1994). Transformational change and the evolving role of the principal: Early empirical evidence. In J. Murphy & K. S. Louis (Eds.), *Reshaping the principalship: Insights from transformational reform efforts* (pp. 20–53). Thousand Oaks, CA: Corwin Press.

Murphy, J. (2005). *Connecting teacher leadership and school improvement*. Thousand Oaks, CA: Corwin.

Murphy, J., & Datnow, A. (2003). *Leadership lessons from comprehensive school reform*. Thousand Oaks, CA: Corwin Press.

Murphy, J., & Lewis, K. S. (1999). Introduction: Framing the project. In J. Murphy & K. S. Lewis (Eds.), *Handbook of educational administration* (pp. xxi–xvii). San Francisco: Jossey-Bass.

Myhill, D. (2006). Talk, talk, talk: Teaching and learning in whole class discourse. *Research Papers in Education, 21*(1), 19–41. doi:10.1080/02671520500445425

Naicker, S. R., & Mestry, R. (2011). Distributive leadership in public schools: Experiences and perceptions of teachers in the Soweto region. *Perspectives in Education, 29*(4), 99–108.

NAPLAN. (2011). *The national language conventions and numeracy report*. Canberra: MCEETYA.

National Education Inspectorate. (2010). *Chief Inspector's Report: Inspection Cycle, Round 2, November*. Kingston, Jamaica: Ministry of Education.

Nelson, C. A. (2012). *Building capacity to improve literacy learning*. National Center for Literacy Education/National Council of Teachers of English. Retrieved August 12, 2013, from http://www.ncte.org/library/NCTEFiles/About/NCLE/NCLEshortlitreview.pdf

Nelson, S. W., de la Colina, M. G., & Boone, M. D. (2008). Lifeworld or systems world: WShat guides novice principals? *Journal of Educational Administration, 46*(6), 690–701. doi:10.1108/09578230810908280

Nettles, S. M., & Herrington, C. (2007). Revisiting the importance of the direct effects of school leadership on student achievement: The implications for school improvement policy. *Peabody Journal of Education, 82*(4), 724–736. doi:10.1080/01619560701603239

Neufeld, B. (1995). *Teacher learning in the context of the SDP: What are the opportunities? What is the context?* Paper presented at the annual meeting of the American Educational Research Association. San Francisco, CA.

Neuman, M., & Simmons, W. (2000). Leadership for student learning. *Phi Delta Kappan, 82*(1), 9–12. doi:10.1177/003172170008200105

Neumerski, C. M. (2012). Rethinking instructional leadership, a review: What do we know about Principal, Teacher and Coach instructional leadership, and where should we go from here? *Educational Administration Quarterly, 49*(2), 310–347. doi:10.1177/0013161X12456700

Neuroleadership Institute. (n.d.). *Neuroleadership Institute - Breaking new ground in our capacity to improve thinking and performance.* Retrieved, 21 February 2014, from: www.neuroleadership.org

Nevicka, B., De Hoogh, A. H. B., Van Vianen, A. E. M., Beersma, B., & McIlwain, D. (2011). All I need is a stage to shine: Narcissists' leader emergence and performance. *The Leadership Quarterly, 22*(5), 910–925. doi:10.1016/j.leaqua.2011.07.011

Newmann, F. M., & Associates. (1996). Authentic achievement: Restructuring schools for intellectual quality. San Francisco: Jossey-Bass Publishers.

Newmann, F. M., & Wehlage, G. G. (1995). *Successful school restructuring: A report to the public and educators.* Madison, WI: Wisconsin Center for Education Research.

News 24.com. (n.d.). *Reports of assault in teacher strike.* Retrieved January 4, 2013, from http://www.news24.com/SouthAfrica/News

Ng, D., & Chew, J. (2008). *Innovative designs for enhancing achievement in schools (IDEAS) in Singapore Report No. EP1/04KS.* Singapore: National Institute of Education, Nanyang Technological University.

Ng, K.-Y., Ang, S., & Chan, K. Y. (2008). Personality and Leader Effectiveness: A Moderated Mediation Model of Leadership Self-Efficacy, Job Demands, and Job Autonomy. *The Journal of Applied Psychology, 43*(4), 733–743. doi:10.1037/0021-9010.93.4.733 PMID:18642980

Nieuwenhuis, J. (2007). Qualitative research designs and data gathering techniques. In K. Maree (Ed.), *First steps in research.* Pretoria: Van Schaik.

Nir, A. E., & Bogler, R. (2008). The antecedents of teacher satisfaction with professional development programs. *Teaching and Teacher Education, 24*(2), 377–386. doi:10.1016/j.tate.2007.03.002

Nolan, B., & Palazzolo, L. (2011). New teacher perceptions of the "teacher leader" movement. *NASSP Bulletin, 95*(4), 302–318. doi:10.1177/0192636511428372

Nonaka, I. (1994). A dynamic theory of organizational knowledge creation. *Organization Science, 5*(1), 14–37. doi:10.1287/orsc.5.1.14

Noonan, B., & Renihan, P. (2006). Demystifying assessment leadership. *Canadian Journal of Educational Administration and Policy, 56,* 1–20.

Norcini, J., & Banda, S. (2011). Increasing the quality and capacity of education: The challenge for the 21st century. *Medical Education, 45*(1), 81–86. doi:10.1111/j.1365-2923.2010.03738.x PMID:21155871

Northouse, P. G. (2010). *Leadership: Theory and practice* (5th ed.). Los Angeles, CA: Sage Publications, Inc.

Norton, M. S., & Kelly, L. K. (1997). Resource Allocation: Managing Money and Peoples Eye on Education. New York: Larchmont.

Norusis, M. J. (2009). *PASW 18. Statistical Procedures Companion.* Chicago: SPSS Inc.

Nutley, S., Jung, T., & Walter, I. (2008). The Many Forms of Research-Informed Practice: A Framework for Mapping Diversity. *Cambridge Journal of Education, 38*(1), 53–71. doi:10.1080/03057640801889980

Nye, J., & Forsyth, D. R. (1991). The effects of prototype biases on leadership appraisals: A test of leadership categorization theory. *Small Group Research, 22*(3), 360–379. doi:10.1177/1046496491223005

O'Donnell, R. J., & White, G. P. (2005). Within the account era: Principals' instructional leadership behaviors and student achievement. *NASSP Bulletin, 89*(645), 56–71. doi:10.1177/019263650508964505

O'Neill, S. (2013). Activating the *"language for learning"* through Schoolwide pedagogy: The case of MacKillop school. *Improving Schools, 12*(2), 107–118. doi:10.1177/1365480213492408

O'Neill, S., & Geoghegan, D. (2012). Pre-service teachers' comparative analyses of teacher-/parent-child talk: Making literacy teaching explicit and children's literacy learning visible. *International Journal of Studies in English., 12*(1), 97–128. doi:10.1177/1365480213493709

Oatley, K., & Jenkins, J. (1996). *Understanding emotion.* Cambridge, MA: Blackwell.

Odden, A., & Archibald, S. (2009). *Doubling student performance . . . and finding the resources to do it.* Thousand Oaks, CA: Corwin Press.

Oduro, G. K. T. (2004). Distributed leadership in schools. *Education Journal, 80,* 23–25.

OECD. (2008b). *Innovating to Learn, Learning to Innovate.* Paris: OECD Publishing.

OECD. (2013). *PISA 2012: Results in focus.* Available: http://www.oecd.org/pisa/keyfindings/pisa-2012-results-overview.pdf

OECD. (2014). *Society at a Glance 2014: OECD Social Indicators.* doi:10.1787/soc_glance-2014-en

OEI. (n.d.). *Informe Iberoamericano sobre Formación Continua de Docentes.* Retrieved February 15, 2014, from: http://goo.gl/nZNTLq

Office for Standards in Education (OfSTED). (1993). *Handbook for the inspection of schools (May 1994 Amendment).* London: HMSO.

OfSTED. (2012). *Press release: The importance of leadership - The Annual Report of Her Majesty's Chief Inspector of Education, Children's Services and Skills 2011/12, Ref: NR2012-38.* Manchester, UK: Office for Standards in Education.

Ogawan, R. T., & Bossert, S. T. (1995). Leadership as an organizational quality. *Educational Administration Quarterly, 31*(2), 224–243. doi:10.1177/0013161X95031002004

Oja, S. N., & Pine, G. J. (1989). Collaborative Action Research: Teachers' Stages of Development and School Contexts. *Peabody Journal of Education, 64*(2), 96–115. doi:10.1080/01619568709538553

Oldenburg, R. (1999). *The great good place.* New York: Marlowe & Company.

Oldenburg, R. (2000). *Celebrating the third place: Inspiring stories about the "Great good places" at the heart of our communities.* New York: Marlowe & Company.

Oluremi, O. F. (2008). Principals' Leadership Behaviour and School Learning Culture in Ekiti State Secondary Schools. *The Journal of International Social Research, 1*(3), 301–311.

Ones, D. S., & Viswesvaran, C. (1996). Bandwidth-fidelity dilemma in personality measurement for personnel selection. *Journal of Organizational Behavior, 17*(6), 609–626. doi:10.1002/(SICI)1099-1379(199611)17:6<609::AID-JOB1828>3.0.CO;2-K

Onguko, B. B., Abdalla, M., & Webber, C. F. (2008). Mapping principal preparation in Kenya and Tanzania. *Journal of Educational Administration, 46*(6), 715–726. doi:10.1108/09578230810908307

Opdenakker, M., & Van Damme, J. (2006). Differences between secondary schools: A study about school context, group composition, school practice and school effects with special attention to public and catholic schools and types of schools. *School Effectiveness and School Improvement, 17*(1), 87–117. doi:10.1080/09243450500264457

Oplatka, I., & Waite, D. (2010). The new principal preparation program model in Israel: Ponderings about practice-oriented principal training. In A. H. Mormore (Ed.), Global Perspectives on Educational Leadership Reform: The Development and Preparation of Leaders of Learning and Learners of Leadership (pp. 1071-1102). Bingley, UK: Emerald Group Publishing.

Oreg, S., Vakola, M., & Armenakis, A. (2011). Change recipients' reactions to organizational change: A 60-year review of quantitative studies. *The Journal of Applied Behavioral Science, 47*(4), 461–524. doi:10.1177/0021886310396550

Orlikowski, W. J. (1996). Improvising organizational transformation over time: A situated change perspective. *Information Systems Research, 7*(1), 63–92. doi:10.1287/isre.7.1.63

Orlikowski, W. J., & Hofman, J. D. (1997). An improvisational model for change management: The case of groupware technologies. *Sloan Management Review, 38*(2), 11–21.

Orr, J. (1996). *Talking about machines.* Ithaca, NY: Cornell University Press.

Orr, M. T., & Orphanos, S. (2011). How graduate-level preparation influences the effectiveness of school leaders: A comparison of the outcomes of exemplary and conventional leadership preparation programs for principals. *Educational Administration Quarterly, 47*(1), 18–70. doi:10.1177/0011000010378610

Ovando, M. (1996). Teacher leadership: Opportunities and challenges. *Planning and Changing, 27*(1/2), 30–44.

Özçetin, S. (2013). *Öğretmen liderliğinin okulun liderlik kapasitesinin gelişimine etkisi: Bir durum çalışması* [The effect of teacher leadership on the development of the leadership capacity of the school: A case study]. (Unpublished master's thesis). Akdeniz University, Antalya, Turkey.

Pajares, M. F. (1992). Teachers' beliefs and educational research: Cleaning up a messy construct. *Review of Educational Research, 62*(3), 307–333. doi:10.3102/00346543062003307

Pallant, J. (2007). *SPSS Survival Manual* (3rd ed.). Berkshire, UK: McGraw-Hill.

Papanastasiou, E. C., & Zembylas, M. (2005). Job satisfaction variance among public and private kindergarten school teachers in Cyprus. *International Journal of Educational Research, 43*(3), 147–167. doi:10.1016/j.ijer.2006.06.009

Pascale, R., Milleman, M., & Gioja, L. (2000). *Surfing the edge of chaos: The laws of nature and the new laws of business*. New York, NY: Three Rivers Press.

Pashiardis, P. (Ed.). (2014). *Modeling School Leadership Across Europe - In Search of New Frontiers*. Dordrecht. The Netherlands: Springer.

Pashiardis, P., & Brauckmann, S. (2009, April). *New Educational Governance and School Leadership – Exploring the foundation of a new relationship in an international context*. Paper presented at the American Educational Research Association Annual Meeting. San Diego, CA.

Pashiardis, P. (1993). Selection Methods for Educational Administrators in the USA. *International Journal of Educational Management, 7*(1), 27–35. doi:10.1108/09513549310023294

Pashiardis, P. (1995). Cyprus Principals and the Universalities of Effective Leadership. *International Studies in Educational Administration, 23*(1), 16–27.

Pashiardis, P. (1997). Towards Effectiveness: What do secondary school leaders need in Cyprus. *British. Journal of In-service Education, 23*(2), 267–282. doi:10.1080/13674589700200018

Pashiardis, P. (1998). Researching the Characteristics of Effective Primary School Principals in Cyprus. *Educational Management Administration & Leadership, 26*(2), 117–130. doi:10.1177/0263211X98262002

Pashiardis, P. (2004). Democracy and leadership in the educational system of Cyprus. *Journal of Educational Administration, 42*(6), 656–668. doi:10.1108/09578230410563656

Pashiardis, P. (2009). Educational leadership and management: Blending Greek philosophy, myth and current Thinking. *International Journal of Leadership in Education, 12*(1), 1–12. doi:10.1080/13603120802357269

Pashiardis, P. (2012). *Successful School Principals: International Research and Greek Reality*. Athens: Ion Publishing House. in Greek

Pashiardis, P., & Brauckmann, S. (2008). Evaluation of School Principals. In G. Crow, J. Lumby, & P. Pashiardis (Eds.), *International handbook on the preparation and development of school leaders* (pp. 263–279). New York: Routledge.

Pashiardis, P., Kendeou, P., Michaelidou, A., & Lytra, E. (2014). Exploring a New Cocktail Mix in Cyprus: School Principals' Epistemological Beliefs and Leadership Styles. In P. Pashiardis (Ed.), *Modeling School Leadership across Europe - In Search of New Frontiers*. Dordrecht, The Netherlands: Springer. doi:10.1007/978-94-007-7290-8_8

Patton, M. Q. (1990). *Qualitative Evaluation and Research Methods* (2nd ed.). Newbury Park, CA: Sage.

Paulhus, D. L., & Williams, K. M. (2002). The dark triad of personality: Narcissism, Machiavellianism, and Psychopathy. *Journal of Research in Personality, 36*(6), 556–563. doi:10.1016/S0092-6566(02)00505-6

Payne, C. (2008). *So much reform, so little change: The persistence of failure in urban schools*. Cambridge, MA: Harvard Education Press.

Pearson, S. S., Honeywood, S., & O'Toole, M. (2004). Not learning for sustainability: The challenge of environmental education in a university. *International Research in Geographical and Environmental Education*, *14*(3), 173–186. doi:10.1080/10382040508668349

Pepper, G. L. (1995). *Communicating in Organizations: A Culture Approach*. New York: McGraw-Hill.

Perrewé, P. L., Zellars, K. L., Ferris, G. R., Rossi, A. M., Kacmar, C. J., & Ralston, D. A. (2004). Neutralizing job stressors: Political skill as an antidote to the dysfunctional consequences of role conflict stressors. *Academy of Management Journal*, *47*(1), 141–152. doi:10.2307/20159566

Personnel Administrative Measures (PAM). (2003). *Published in Government Gazette 19767*. Pretoria: Government Printer.

Petrides, K. V. (2011). Ability and trait emotional intelligence. In T. Chamorro-Premuzic, A. Furnham, & S. von Stumm (Eds.), *The Blackwell-Wiley Handbook of Individual Differences*. New York: Wiley.

Pettigrew, A. M. (2000). Linking change process to outcomes: A commentary on Ghoshal, Bartlett, and Weick. In M. Beer & N. Nohria (Eds.), *Breaking the code of change* (pp. 243–265). Boston, MA: Harvard Business School Press.

Pfeffer, J. (1981). *Power in organizations*. Boston: Pitman.

Pfeffer, J. (1992). *Managing with power: Politics and influence in organizations*. Boston: Harvard Business School Press.

Pieterse, A. N., Van Knippenberg, D., Schippers, M., & Stam, D. (2009). Transformational and transactional leadership and innovative behavior: The moderating role of psychological empowerment. *Journal of Organizational Behavior*, *31*(4), 609–623. doi:10.1002/job.650

Pirola-Merlo, A., Hartel, C., Mann, L., & Hirst, G. (2002). How leaders influence the impact of affective events on team climate and performance in R&D teams. *The Leadership Quarterly*, *13*(5), 561–581. doi:10.1016/S1048-9843(02)00144-3

Pitner, N. (1988). The study of administration effects and effectiveness. In N. Boyan (Ed.), *Handbook of Research in Educational Administration* (pp. 99–122). New York: Longman.

Planning Institute of Jamaica. (2010). *Vision 2030 national development plan: Education sector plan 2009-2030*. Kingston, Jamaica: PIOJ.

Polkinghorne, D. E. (1989). Phenomenological research methods. In R. S. Valle & S. Halling (Eds.), *Existential-phenomenological perspectives in psychology* (pp. 41–60). New York: Plenum. doi:10.1007/978-1-4615-6989-3_3

Polychroniou, P. V. (2009). Relationship between emotional intelligence and transformational leadership of supervisors. The impact on team effectiveness. *Team Performance Management*, *15*(7/8), 343–356. doi:10.1108/13527590911002122

Pont, B., Nusche, D., & Moorman, H. (2008). *Mejorar el liderazgo escolar: Política y práctica*. París: OECD. Retrieved May 24, 2014, from: http://goo.gl/aAQZwC

Pont, B., Nusche, D., & Moorman, H. (2008). Improving School Leadership: Vol. 1. *Policy and Practice*. Paris: OECD Publications.

Pont, B., Nushe, D., & Moorman, H. (2008). *Mejorar el liderazgo escolar*. Paris: OECD.

Porras, J. I., & Robertson, P. J. (1992). Organizational development: Theory, practice, and research. In M. D. Dunnette & L. M. Hough (Eds.), *Handbook of industrial and organizational psychology* (pp. 719–822). Palo Alto, CA: Consulting Psychologist Press.

Porter, S., Juodis, M., ten Brinke, L., Klein, R., & Wilson, K. (2009). Evaluation of the effectiveness of a brief deception detection training program. *Journal of Forensic Psychiatry & Psychology*, *21*(1), 66–76. doi:10.1080/14789940903174246

Pounder, J. S. (2006). Transformational classroom leadership: The fourth wave of teacher leadership? *Educational Management Administration & Leadership*, *34*(4), 533–545. doi:10.1177/1741143206068216

Power, P. G. (2004). Leadership for Tomorrow: Once More, with Feeling, Mt Eliza. *Business Review (Federal Reserve Bank of Philadelphia)*, (Summer/Autumn), 2003–2004.

Powney, J., Wilson, V., & Hall, S. (2003). *Teachers' careers: The impact of age, disability, ethnicity, gender and sexual orientation*. London: Department for Education and Skills.

Pozner, P. (2000). *Competencias para la profesionalización de la gestión educativa*. Buenos Aires: IIPE-UNESCO.

Pratt, N. (2006). 'Interactive' teaching in numeracy lessons: What do children have to say? *Cambridge Journal of Education, 36*(2), 221–235. doi:10.1080/03057640600718612

Prinsloo, I. J. (2003). Communication skills. In I. Van Deventer & A. G. Kruger (Eds.), *An educator's guide to school management skills*. Pretoria: Van Schaik.

Quiroga, M. (Ed.). (2013). *Crónica directiva docente: Cambio y liderazgo desde la zona de incomodidad*. Valparaíso: U. Católica de Valparaíso. Regulation on the "Public Exam for the Selection of Educators" (Reglamento "Concurso Público de Oposición para la Selección de Educadores"). Retrieved February 15, 2014, from: http://goo.gl/DYSr8i

Rademeyer, A. (2012, December 12). SA leerlinge vaar sleg in dié twee w's (SA learners perform poorly in mathematics and science). *Beeld*, p. 4.

Rafaeli, A., & Sutton, R. I. (1987). Expression of emotion as part of the work role. *Academy of Management Review, 12*, 23–37.

Rank, J., Pace, V. L., & Frese, M. (2004). Three avenues for future research on creativity, innovation, and initiative. *Applied Psychology, 53*(4), 518–528. doi:10.1111/j.1464-0597.2004.00185.x

Raskin, R., & Terry, H. (1988). A principal-components analysis of the Narcissistic Personality Inventory and further evidence of its construct validity. *Journal of Personality and Social Psychology, 54*(5), 890–902. doi:10.1037/0022-3514.54.5.890 PMID:3379585

Rayfield, R., & Diamantes, T. (2004). Task analysis of the duties performed in Secondary School administration. *Education, 124*(4), 709–713.

Reardon, K. K., Reardon, K. J., & Rowe, A. J. (1998, Spring). Leadership styles for the five stages of radical change. *Acquisition Review Quarterly*, 129-146.

Reeves, D. (2008). *Reframing teacher leadership to improve your school*. Alexandria, VA: Association for Supervision and Curriculum Development.

Rego, A., Sousa, F., Marques, C., & Cunha, M. P. (2012). Authentic leadership promoting employees' psychological capital and creativity. *Journal of Business Research, 65*(3), 429–437. doi:10.1016/j.jbusres.2011.10.003

Regulation 63903 (Reglamento N° 63903 del Estatuto Docente). Retrieved February 15, 2014, from: http://goo.gl/bwFwLQ

Reichers, A. E., Wanous, J. P., & Austin, J. T. (1997). Understanding and managing cynicism about organizational change. *The Academy of Management Executive, 11*(1), 48–59.

Reid, M. M. (2011). *Teacher leadership: One case study application* (Doctoral dissertation). Retrieved from ProQuest Dissertations and Thesis database. (UMI No. 3494743)

Rerup, C., & Feldman, M. (2011). Routines as a source of change in organizational schemata: The role of trial-and-error learning. *Academy of Management Journal, 54*(3), 577–610. doi:10.5465/AMJ.2011.61968107

Reynolds, M. (2011). *An Investigation of the Emotional Intelligence Competencies of National Middle Schools to Watch Principals*. (Unpublished Dissertation). Eastern Kentucky University. Retrieved, 15 February 2014, from: http://encompass.eku.edu/cgi/viewcontent.cgi?article=1041&context=etd

Reynolds, D., Bollen, R., Creemers, B., Hopkins, D., Stoll, L., & Lagerweij, N. (1996). *Making good schools: Linking school effectiveness and school improvement*. London: Routledge.

Reynolds, D., & Cuttance, P. (1992). *School Effectiveness: Research Policy and Practice*. London: Cassell.

Richard, F. D., Bond, C. F. Jr, & Stokes-Zoota, J. J. (2003). One hundred years of social psychology quantitatively described. *Review of General Psychology, 7*(4), 331–363. doi:10.1037/1089-2680.7.4.331

Richardson, K. A. (2005). To be or not to be? That is [not] the question: Complexity theory and the need for critical thinking. In K. A. Richardson (Ed.), Managing organizational complexity: Philosophy, theory, and application, (pp. 21-46). Greenwich, CT: Information Age Publishing.

Riggio, R. E. (1986). The assessment of basic social skills. *Journal of Personality and Social Psychology, 51*(3), 649–660. doi:10.1037/0022-3514.51.3.649

Robinson, V., Lloyd, C., & Rowe, K. (2007). The Impact of Leadership on Student Outcomes: An Analysis of the Differential Effects of Leadership Types. *Educational Administration Quarterly, 44*(5), 635–674. doi:10.1177/0013161X08321509

Rockstuhl, Th., Seiler, S., Ang, S., Van Dyne, L., & Annen, H. (2011). Beyond General Intelligence (IQ) and Emotional Intelligence (EQ): The Role of Cultural Intelligence (CQ) on Cross-Border Leadership Effectiveness in a Globalized World. *The Journal of Social Issues, 67*(4), 825–840. doi:10.1111/j.1540-4560.2011.01730.x

Rogers, E. M. (2003). *Diffusion of innovations* (5th ed.). New York: Free Press.

Rose, D. (2005b). *Learning to read: Reading to learn: Submission to the National Inquiry into the Teaching of Literacy 2005.* Canberra: Department of Education, Science and Training. Retrieved September 12, 2013, from http://www.dest.gov.au/sectors/school_education/policy_initiatives_reviews/key_issues/literacy_numeracy/national_inquiry/documents/pdf2/sub_315_pdf.htm

Rose, D. (2005a). Democratising the classroom: A literacy pedagogy for the new generation. *Journal of Education, 37,* 131–167.

Rosenberg, E. (2005). The study of spontaneous facial expressions in psychology. In P. Ekman & E. Rosenberg (Eds.), *What the face reveals: basic and applied studies of spontaneous expression using the facial action coding system* (2nd ed., pp. 3–17). New York: Oxford University press.

Rosing, K., Frese, M., & Bausch, A. (2011). Explaining the heterogeneity of the leadership-innovation relationship: Ambidextrous leadership. *The Leadership Quarterly, 22*(5), 956–974. doi:10.1016/j.leaqua.2011.07.014

Rowan, B., Dwyer, D., & Bossert, S. (1982). *Methodological considerations in the study of effective principals.* Paper presented at the Annual Meeting of the American Educational Research Association. New York, NY.

Rowe, K. (2005). *Teaching reading: Report of the National Inquiry into the Teaching of Literacy.* Canberra: Department of Education, Science and Training. Retrieved June 16, 2013, from http://www.dest.gov.au/nitl/documents/report_recommendations.pdf

Rule, N. O., Freeman, J. B., Moran, J. M., Gabrieli, J. D. E., Adams, R. B., & Ambady, N. (2010). Voting behavior is reflected in amygdala response across cultures. *Social Cognitive and Affective Neuroscience, 5*(2-3), 349–355. doi:10.1093/scan/nsp046 PMID:19966327

Rust, F., & Meyers, E. (2006). The bright side: Teacher research in the context of educational reform and policy-making. *Teachers and Teaching: Theory and Practice, 12*(1), 69–86. doi:10.1080/13450600500365452

Rutledge, L. (2009). *Teacher leadership and school improvement: A case study of teachers participating in the teacher leadership network with a regional education service center* (Doctoral dissertation). Retrieved from ProQuest Dissertations and Thesis database. (UMI No. 3439841)

Rutter, M., Maugham, B., Mortimore, P., Ousten, J., & Smith, A. (1979). *Fifteen Thousand Hours: Secondary Schools and Their Effects on Children.* London: Open Books.

SAD. (2011), *Asking effective questions: Provoking student thinking/deepening conceptual understanding in the mathematics classroom.* Student Achievement Division (SAD), Ontario Schools, Special Edition 21: 1-8. Retrieved March 01, 2014, from http://www.edu.gov.on.ca/eng/literacynumeracy/inspire/research/CBS_AskingEffectiveQuestions.pdf

Saitis, C. (2007). The principal in the modern school: From theory to practice (3rd ed.). Athens: Self-Publication. (in Greek).

Saklofske, D. H., Austin, E. J., & Minski, P. S. (2003). Factor structure and validity of a trait emotional intelligence measure. *Personality and Individual Differences, 34*(4), 707–721. doi:10.1016/S0191-8869(02)00056-9

Salgado, J. F., Viswesvaran, C., & Ones, D. S. (2001). Predictors Used for Personnel Selection: An Overview of Constructs. In N. Anderson, D. Ones, H. Sinangil & C. Viswesvaran (Eds.), Handbook of Industrial, Work & Organizational Psychology: Personnel Psychology (vol. 1). Academic Press.

Salgado, J. F., Anderson, N., Moscoso, S., Bertua, C., de Fruyt, F., & Rolland, J. P. (2003). A Meta-Analytic Study of General Mental Ability Validity for Different Occupations in the European Community. *The Journal of Applied Psychology*, *88*(6), 1068–1081. doi:10.1037/0021-9010.88.6.1068 PMID:14640817

Salovey, P., & Mayer, J. D. (1990). Emotional intelligence. *Imagination, Cognition and Personality*, *9*(3), 185–211. doi:10.2190/DUGG-P24E-52WK-6CDG

Sammons, P. (1999). *School effectiveness*. The Netherlands: Swetz and Zeitlinger.

Sammons, P., Hillman, J., & Mortimore, P. (1995). *Key characteristics of effective schools: A review of school effectiveness research*. London, UK: International School Effectiveness and Improvement Centre, Institute of Education.

Sampson, A. (1999). *Mandela: The Authorised Biography*. Johannesburg, South Africa: Jonathon Ball.

Sandberg, J., & Tsoukas, H. (2011). Grasping the logic of practice: Theorizing through practical activity. *Academy of Management Review*, *36*(2), 338–360. doi:10.5465/AMR.2011.59330942

Santa Fe Institute. (n.d.). Retrieved at http://en.wikipedia.org/wiki/Santa_Fe_Institute

Santonus, M. (1998). *Simple: Yet complex*. Retrieved at http://www.cio.com/archive/enterprise/041598_qanda_content.html

Sarafidou, J.-O. (2010, September). *Teachers' perceptions of educational research, research literacy and individual innovativeness as determinants of their attitudes towards school change*. Paper presented at the British Educational Research Association Annual Conference. Warwick, UK.

Sargent, T. C., & Hannum, E. (2009). Doing more with less: Teacher professional learning communities in resource-constrained primary schools in rural China. *Journal of Teacher Education*, *60*(3), 258–276. doi:10.1177/0022487109337279 PMID:21191452

Sarros, J., Cooper, B., & Santora, J. (2008). Building a Climate for Innovation Through Transformational Leadership and Organizational Culture. *Journal of Leadership & Organizational Studies*, *15*(2), 145–158. doi:10.1177/1548051808324100

Sayette, M. A., Cohn, J. F., Wertz, J. M., Perrott, M. A., & Parrot, D. J. (2004). A Psychometric Evaluation of the Facial Action Coding System for Assessing Spontaneous Expression. *Journal of Nonverbal Behavior*, *25*(3), 167–185. doi:10.1023/A:1010671109788

Schaffer, E., Devlin-Scherer, R., & Stringfield, S. (2007). The evolving role of teachers in effective schools. In, T. Townsend (Ed.), International handbook of school effectiveness and improvement (pp. 727-750). Dordrecht, The Netherlands: Springer. doi:10.1007/978-1-4020-5747-2_39

Scheerens, J. (2012). Summary and Conclusion: Instructional Leadership in Schools. In J. Scheerens (Ed.), School Leadership Effects Revisited: Review and Meta-Analysis of Empirical Studies (pp. 131-150). Dortrecht: Springer.

Scheerens, J. (2000). *Improving School Effectiveness*. Paris: UNESCO.

Scheerens, J. (Ed.). (2012). *School Leadership Effects Revisited: Review and Meta-Analysis of Empirical Studies*. New York: Springer. doi:10.1007/978-94-007-2768-7

Scheerens, J., & Bosker, R. (1997). *The Foundations of Educational Effectiveness*. Oxford, UK: Elsevier Science Ltd.

Scheerens, J., Luyten, H., Steen, R., & Luyten-de Thouars, Y. (2007). *Review and meta-analyses of school and teaching effectiveness*. Enschede, The Netherlands: Department of Educational Organisation and Management, University of Twente.

Scherer, K. R. (1992). What does facial expression express? In K. T. Strongman (Ed.), *International review of studies on emotion* (Vol. 2, pp. 139–165). Chichester, UK: Wiley.

Schleicher, A. (2014). Attacks on PISA are entirely unjustified. *TES Magazine*. Retrieved April 30, 2014, from http://www.tes.co.uk/article.aspx?storycode=6345213

Schmidt, F. L., & Hunter, J. E. (1998). The validity and utility of selection methods in personnel psychology: Practical and theoretical implications of 85 years of research findings. *Psychological Bulletin, 124*(2), 262–274. doi:10.1037/0033-2909.124.2.262

Schuh, K. L. (2003). Knowledge construction in the learner-centered classroom. *Journal of Educational Psychology, 95*(2), 426–442. doi:10.1037/0022-0663.95.2.426

Schultz, C. (2007). *Emotional intelligence: An overlooked aspect of effective leadership practices: A review of the literature on desirable traits, behaviours and characteristics for successful leadership promoting transformational change.* Retrieved March 20, 2011, from http://cnx.org/content/m15615/1.2/

Schumacker, R. E., & Lomax, R. G. (2004). *A beginner's guide to Structural Equation Modeling* (2nd ed.). Lawrence Erlbaum.

Schwarz, C., & Dussart, F. (2010). Christianity in Aboriginal Australia revisited. *The Australian Journal of Anthropology, 21*(1), 1–13. doi:10.1111/j.1757-6547.2010.00064.x

Schyns, B., Felfe, J., & Blank, H. (2007). Is Charisma Hyper-Romanticism? Empirical Evidence from New Data and a Meta-Analysis. *Applied Psychology, 56*(4), 505–527. doi:10.1111/j.1464-0597.2007.00302.x

Schyns, B., & Meindl, J. R. (2005). An overview of implicit leadership theories and their application in organizational practice. In B. Schyns & J. R. Meindl (Eds.), *Implicit leadership theories: essays and explorations* (pp. 15–36). Greenwich, CT: Information Age Publishing.

Scott, C., Dinham, S., & Brooks, R. (2003). The development of scales to measure teacher and school executive occupational satisfaction. *Journal of Educational Administration, 41*(1), 74–86. doi:10.1108/09578230310457448

Scott, C., Stone, B., & Dinham, S. (2001). I love teaching but. . . International patterns of discontent. *Education Policy Analysis Archives, 9*(28).

Scribner, S. M. P., & Bradley-Levine, J. (2010). The meaning(s) of teacher leadership in an urban high school reform. *Educational Administration Quarterly, 46*(4), 491–522. doi:10.1177/0013161X10383831

Seashore, K., Leithwood, K., Wahlstrom, K., & Anderson, S. (2010). *Learning from leadership: Investigating the links to improved student learning.* New York: WallaceFoundation.

Sellar, S., & Lingard, R. (2013). Looking east: Shanghai, PISA 2009 and the reconstruction of reference societies in the global policy field. *Comparative Education, 49*(4), 464–485. doi:10.1080/03050068.2013.770943

Selman, J. W. (1991). *An analysis of time-on-task perceptions of public and private college administrators.* Unpublished research paper. University of Auburn, Auburn, Alabama.

Semadar, A., Robins, G., & Ferris, G. R. (2006). Comparing the effects of multiple social effectiveness constructs in the prediction of managerial performance. *Journal of Organizational Behavior, 27*(4), 443–461. doi:10.1002/job.385

Senge, M. P. (1990). *The Fifth Discipline: The Art and Practice of the Learning Organization.* New York: Doubleday Currency.

Senge, P. (1990). *The fifth discipline: The art and practice of the learning organization.* New York: Doubleday Currency.

Senge, P. M. (2006). *The Fifth Discipline: The art and practice of the learning organisation* (Revised edition). London: Random House Business Books.

Senge, R. (1999). *The Dance of Change: The challenges of sustaining momentum in Learning Organizations.* London: Nicholas Brealey.

SEP. (2008). *Sistema Nacional de Formación Continua y superación de maestros en servicio.* México: SEP.

Sergiovanni, T. J. (1999, September). Refocusing Leadership to Build Community. *The High School Magazine*, 12-15.

Sergiovanni, T. (1992). *Moral leadership.* San Francisco: Jossey Bass.

Sergiovanni, T. (1994). *Building Community in Schools.* San Francisco, CA: Jossey-Bass Publishers.

Sergiovanni, T. (2004). Building a community of hope. *Educational Leadership, 61*(8), 33–37.

Sergiovanni, T. J. (1991). *The principalship.* Boston: Allyn and Bacon.

Sergiovanni, T. J. (1996). *Leadership for the school house. How is it different? Why is it important?* San Francisco: Jossey-Bass.

Sergiovanni, T. J. (2005). *Strengthening the heartbeat: Leading and learning together in schools.* San Francisco: Jossey-Bass.

Sergiovanni, T. J. (2007). *Rethinking leadership. A collection of articles* (2nd ed.). Thousand Oaks, CA: Corwin.

Sewlall, K. (1996). *Dimensions of culture and their implication for the management in South African schools.* (Unpublished dissertation). Rand Afrikaans University, Johannesburg, South Africa.

Sezgin, F. (2010). Öğretmenlerin örgütsel bağlılığının bir yordayıcısı olarak okul kültürü[School culture as a predictor of teachers' organizational commitment]. *Education and Science, 35*(156), 142–159.

SFS. (2010). *Skollag.* [Swedish Education Act 2010:800].

Shah, S., & Shaikh, J. (2010). Leadership progression of Muslim male teachers: Interplay of ethnicity, faith and visibility. *School Leadership & Management, 30*(1), 19–33. doi:10.1080/13632430903509733

Shalley, C. E., & Gilson, L. L. (2004). What leaders need to know: A review of social and contextual factors that can foster or hinder creativity. *The Leadership Quarterly, 15*(1), 33–53. doi:10.1016/j.leaqua.2003.12.004

Shamir, B., House, R. J., & Arthur, M. B. (1993). The motivational effects of charismatic leadership: A self concept based theory. *Organization Science, 4*(4), 577–593. doi:10.1287/orsc.4.4.577

Shann, M. (1998). Professional commitment and satisfaction among teachers in urban middle schools. *The Journal of Educational Research, 92*(2), 67–73. doi:10.1080/00220679809597578

Shattock, M. (2005). European universities for entrepreneurship: Their role in the Europe of knowledge. The theoretical context. *Higher Educational Management and Policy, 17*(3), 13–26. doi:10.1787/hemp-v17-art16-en

Sherman, A. (2008). Using case studies to visualize success with first year principals. *Journal of Educational Administration, 46*(6), 752–761. doi:10.1108/09578230810908334

Shin, S. J., Kim, T. Y., Lee, J. Y., & Bian, L. (2012). Cognitive team diversity and individual team member creativity: A cross-level interaction. *Academy of Management Journal, 55*(1), 197–212. doi:10.5465/amj.2010.0270

Shin, S.-H., & Slater, Ch. L. (2010). Principal leadership and mathematics achievement: An international comparative study. *School Leadership & Management, 30*(4), 317–334. doi:10.1080/13632434.2010.498995

Shkedi, A. (1998). Teachers' attitudes towards research: A challenge for qualitative researchers. *International Journal of Qualitative Studies in Education, 11*(4), 559–577. doi:10.1080/095183998236467

Short, E. C. (1995). A review of studies in the first 10 volumes of the Journal of Curriculum and Supervision. *Journal of Curriculum and Supervision, 11*(1), 87–105.

Sığrı, Ü., & Tığlı, M. (2006). *Hofstede'nin "belirsizlikten kaçınma" kültürel boyutunun yönetsel-örgütsel süreçlere ve pazarlama açısından tüketici davranışlarına etkisi* [The effect of "uncertainty avoidance" cultural dimension of Hofstede on managerial-organizational processes and on consumer behaviors in terms of marketing]. *Marmara University Journal of E.A.S, 21*(1), 29–42.

Silins, H. (1994). Leadership characteristics and school improvement. *Australian Journal of Education, 38*(3), 266–281. doi:10.1177/000494419403800306

Silins, H. C. (1992). Effective leadership for school reform. *The Alberta Journal of Educational Research, 38*(4), 317–334.

Silins, H. C. (1994). The relationship between transformational and transactional leadership and school improvement outcomes. *School Effectiveness and School Improvement, 5*(3), 272–298. doi:10.1080/0924345940050305

Silins, H., & Mulford, B. (2002). Schools as learning organisations: The case for system, teacher and student learning. *Journal of Educational Administration, 40*(5), 425–446. doi:10.1108/09578230210440285

Silins, H., Zarins, S., & Mulford, B. (2002). What characteristics and processes define a school as a learning organisation? Is this a useful concept to apply to schools? *International Education Journal, 3*(1), 24–32.

Silva, J.M. (2010). *Líderes e lideranças em escolas portuguesas: Protagonistas, prácticas e impactos.* Vila Nova de Gaia: Fundacçao Manuel Leäo.

Silverthorne, C. (2001). Leadership effectiveness and personality: A cross-cultural study. *Personality and Individual Differences, 30*(2), 303–309. doi:10.1016/S0191-8869(00)00047-7

Simonton, D. K. (1985). Intelligence and personal influence in groups: Four nonlinear models. *Psychological Review, 92*(4), 532–547. doi:10.1037/0033-295X.92.4.532

Şimşek, H. (2004). *Training educational administrators: Comparative cases and implications for Turkey.* Available at: http://www.hasansimsek.net/files/EĞİTİM%20YÖNETİCİLERİNİN%20YETİŞTİRİLMESİ.doc

Siskin, L., & Little, J. (1995). The subject department: Continuities and critiques. In L. Siskin & J. Little (Eds.), *The subjects in question* (pp. 1–22). New York: Teachers College Press.

Sisman, M., & Turan, S. (2004). Education and school management. In Y. Özden (Ed.). Handbook of education and school management (pp. 99-146). Ankara: Pegem A.

Şişman, M. (2002). *Örgütler ve kültürler* [Organizations and cultures]. Ankara: Pegem A.

Sivanathan, N., & Fekken, G. C. (2002). Emotional intelligence, moral reasoning and transformational leadership. *Leadership and Organization Development Journal, 23*(3/4), 198–205. doi:10.1108/01437730210429061

Sjøberg, S. (2012). Visible Learning - Ny giv for norsk skole.[Visible Learning – New deal for Norwegian Schools]. *Utdanning, 21,* 44–47.

SKOLFS. (2011:37). *Skolverkets föreskrifter om introduktionsperiod och kompetensprofiler för lärare och förskollärare.* [Regulations on introduction period and competency profiles for teachers and preschool teachers].

Skolinspektionen. (2012). *Rektors ledarskap.* [Principals' leadership]. Stockholm: Skolinspektionen.

Skolverket. (2007). *Skolverkets lägesbedömning 2007.* [Assessment 2007]. Stockholm: Skolverket.

Skolverket. (2008). *Skolverkets lägesbedömning 2008.* [Assessment 2008]. Stockholm: Skolverket.

Skolverket. (2009). *Skolverkets lägesbedömning 2009.* [Assment 2009]. Stockholm: Skolverket.

Skolverket. (2010a). *Curriculum for the Preschool, Lpfö 98 Revised 2010.* Stockholm: Skolverket.

Skolverket. (2010b). *Skolverkets lägesbedömning 2010.* [Assessment 2010]. Stockholm: Skolverket.

Skolverket. (2011a). *Skolverkets lägesbedömning 2011 Del 2 - Bedömningar och slutsatser.* [The Swedish Natonal Agency's assessment of the situation in 2011. Part 2 – Assessments and Conclusions]. Stockholm: Skolverket.

Skolverket. (2011b). *Promemoria om evidens på utbildningsområdet.* [Memorandum on evidence in the field of education]. Stockholm: Skolverket.

Skolverket. (2013a). *An assessment of the situation in the Swedish school system 2013 by the Swedish National Agency for Education.* Stockholm: Skolverket.

Skolverket. (2013b). *Facts and figures 2012.* Stockholm: Skolverket.

Skolverket. (2014). *Research for classrooms: Scientific knowledge and proven experienced in practise.* Stockholm: Skolverket. Retrieved from http://www.skolverket.se/om-skolverket/publikationer/visa-enskild-publikation?_xurl_=http%3A%2F%2Fwww5.skolverket.se%2Fwtpub%2Fws%2Fskolbok%2Fwpubext%2Ftrycksak%2FRecord%3Fk%3D3229

Skolverket. (n.d.). *An overview of the Swedish education system.* Retrieved from http://www.skolverket.se/om-skolverket/andra-sprak-och-lattlast/in-english/the-swedish-education-system/an-overview-of-the-swedish-education-system-1.72184

Slater, C. L., Boone, M., Nelson, S., De La Colina, M., Garcia, E., & Grimaldo, L. et al. (2007). *El Escalafón y el Doble Turno*: An International Perspective on School Director Preparation. *Journal of Educational Research & Policy Studies, 6*(2), 60–90.

Slater, C. L., Garcia, J. M., & Gorosave, G. L. (2008). Challenges of a successful first-year principal in Mexico. *Journal of Educational Administration, 46*(6), 702–714. doi:10.1108/09578230810908299

Sleegers, P., van den Berg, R., & Geijsel, F. (2000). Building innovative schools: The need for new approaches. *Teaching and Teacher Education, 16*(7), 801–808. doi:10.1016/S0742-051X(00)00026-3

Smith, A. C. T. (2004). Complexity theory and change management in sport organizations. *Emergence: Complexity & Organization, 6*(1-2), 70–79.

Smith, C. A., & Scott, H. H. (1997). A componential approach to the meaning of facial expressions. In *J. A. Russell, & J. M. Fernández-Dols, The psychology of facial expression* (pp. 229–254). Cambridge, UK: Cambridge University Press. doi:10.1017/CBO9780511659911.012

Smith, C. R. (Ed.). (2012). *El management del siglo XXI.* Madrid: BrandSmith.

Smith, F., Hardman, F., Wall, K., & Mroz, M. (2004). Interactive whole class teaching in the National Literacy and Numeracy Strategies. *British Educational Research Journal, 30*(3), 395–411. doi:10.1080/0141192041000 1689706

Smith, J. A., & Foti, R. J. (1998). A pattern approach to the study of leadership emergence. *The Leadership Quarterly, 9*(2), 147–160. doi:10.1016/S1048-9843(98)90002-9

Smith, J., & Ross, C. (2001). *Brief to the Minister of Education's Task Force on effective schools.* Toronto: OECTA.

Smit, M., & Oosthuizen, I. (2011). Improving school governance through participative democracy and the law. *South African Journal of Education, 31*(1), 55–73.

Smylie, M. A., & Bennett, A. (2005). What do we know about developing school leaders? A look at existing research and next steps for new study. In W. A. Firestone & C. Riehl (Eds.), *A new agenda for research in educational leadership* (pp. 138–155). New York: Teachers College Press.

Smylie, M. A., Conley, S., & Marks, H. M. (2002). Exploring new approaches to teacher leadership for school improvement. In J. Murphy (Ed.), *The educational leadership challenge: Redefining leadership for the 21st century* (pp. 162–188). Chicago: University of Chicago. doi:10.1111/j.1744-7984.2002.tb00008.x

Snodgrass, J. (1992). *Judgment of feeling states from facial behavior: A bottom-up approach.* (Unpublished doctoral dissertation). University of British Columbia.

Snook, I., O'Neill, J., Clark, J., O'Neill, A.-M., & Openshaw, R. (2009). Invisible Learnings?: A Commentary on John Hattie's Book - Visible Learning: A Synthesis of Over 800 Meta-analyses Relating to Achievement''. *New Zealand Journal of Educational Studies, 44*(1), 93–106.

Sofaer, S. (1999). Qualitative methods: What are they and why use them? *Health Services Research, 34*(5), 1101–1118. PMID:10591275

Sorenson, G. J., & Goethals, G. R. (2004). Leadership theories: Overview. In *Encyclopedia of Leadership* (Vol. 2, pp. 867–873). London: Sage. doi:10.4135/9781412952392.n201

SOU. (1948). *1946 års skolkommissions betänkande med förslag till riktlinjer för det svenska skolväsendets utveckling* [The 1946 Education Commission report with proposed guidelines for the development of the Swedish school system]. Stockholm: Ecklesiastikdepartementet.

SOU. (1997). *Att erövra omvärlden.* [To conquer the external environment].

SOU. (2008) *En hållbar lärarutbildning.* [A sustainable teacher education program].

SOU. (2009). *Att nå ut och nå ända fram. Hur tillgången till policyinriktad utvärdering och forskningsresultat inom utbildningsområdet kan tillgodoses.* [Reaching out and reaching all the way. How the availability of policy-oriented evaluation and research results within the field of education can be met].

South Africa. (2007). *Education Laws Amendment Act, 2007. Government Gazette (No. 30637).* Pretoria: Government Printer.

South Africa. (2010). *Towards the realization of Schooling 2025. Government Gazette. (No. 33434).* Pretoria: Government Printer.

South Africa. (2011). *Approval of the National Curriculum Statement Grades R-12 as National Education Policy: Curriculum Assessment Policy (CAPS). Government Gazette (No.34600)*. Pretoria: Government Printer.

Southworth, G. (2002). Instructional leadership in schools: Reflections and empirical evidence. *School Leadership & Management, 22*(1), 73–92. doi:10.1080/13632430220143042

Spear, M., Gould, K., & Lee, B. (2000). *Who Would be a Teacher? A Review of Factors Motivating and Demotivating Prospective and Practicing Teachers*. Slough: NFER.

Spencer, L. M., & Spencer, S. M. (1993). *Competence at work. Models for superior performance*. New York: John Wiley & Sons.

Spiegelhalter, D. (2013). The problems with PISA statistical methods. *Opinion, Stats Life, Royal Statistical Society*. Retrieved May 10, 2014, from http://www.statslife.org.uk/opinion/1074-the-problems-with-pisa-statistical-methods

Spillane, J. P., & Sherer, J. Z. (2004). *A distributed perspective on school leadership: Leadership practice as stretched over people and place*. Paper presented at the Meeting of the American Education Association. San Diego, CA.

Spillane, J. P. (2005). Distributed Leadership. *The Educational Forum, 69*(2), 143–15. doi:10.1080/00131720508984678

Spillane, J. P. (2009). Managing to lead: Reframing school leadership and management. *Phi Delta Kappan, 91*(3), 70–73. doi:10.1177/003172170909100315

Spillane, J. P., Camburn, E. M., & Pareja, A. S. (2007). Taking a Distributed Perspective to the School Principal's Workday. *Leadership and Policy in Schools, 6*(1), 103–125. doi:10.1080/15700760601091200

Spillane, J. P., Halverson, R., & Diamond, J. B. (2001). Investigating school leadership practice: A distributed perspective. *Educational Researcher, 30*(3), 23–28. doi:10.3102/0013189X030003023

Spillane, J. P., & Louis, K. S. (2002). School improvement processes and practices: Professional learning for building instructional capacity. *Yearbook of the National Society for the Study of Education, 101*(1), 83–104. doi:10.1111/j.1744-7984.2002.tb00005.x

Srivastava, S., John, O. P., Gosling, S. D., & Potter, J. (2003). Development of personality in early and middle adulthood: Set like plaster or persistent change? *Journal of Personality and Social Psychology, 84*(5), 1041–1053. doi:10.1037/0022-3514.84.5.1041 PMID:12757147

Stacey, R. (2000). *Strategic management and organisational dynamics* (3rd ed.). Essex, UK: Pearson Education Ltd.

Stake, R. E. (2000). Case studies. In N. K. Denzin & Y. S. Lincoln (Eds.), *A handbook of qualitative research* (p. 437). Thousand Oaks, CA: Sage.

State Education Office. (1994). *Propuesta para un Manual de Puestos y Funciones para Escuelas del Nivel Básico*. Retrieved February 15, 2014, from: http://goo.gl/mGFipJ

Stein, M. K., & Coburn, C. E. (2008). Architectures of learning: A comparative analysis of two urban school districts. *American Journal of Education, 114*(4), 583–626. doi:10.1086/589315

Stenhouse, L. (1981). What counts as research? *British Journal of Educational Studies, 29*(2), 103–114. doi:10.1080/00071005.1981.9973589

Sternberg, R. J. (2003). Giftedness According to the Theory of Successful Intelligence. In N. Colangelo & G. Davis (Eds.), Handbook of Gifted Education (pp. 88-99). Boston MA: Allyn and Bacon.

Sternberg, R. J. (1997). *Successful intelligence*. New York: Plume.

Sternberg, R. J. (2006). The Nature of Creativity. *Creativity Research Journal, 18*(1), 87–98. doi:10.1207/s15326934crj1801_10

Sternberg, R. J., & Lubart, T. I. (1996). Investing in creativity. *The American Psychologist, 51*(7), 677–688. doi:10.1037/0003-066X.51.7.677

Sternberg, R. J., & O'Hara, L. A. (1999). Creativity and intelligence. In R. J. Sternberg (Ed.), *Handbook of Creativity* (pp. 251–272). Cambridge University Press.

Sternberg, R., Lautrey, J., & Lubert, T. I. (2002). Where are we in the field of intelligence, how did we get here, and where are we going? In R. J. Sternberg, J. Lautrey, & T. I. Lubart (Eds.), *Models of Intelligence: International Perspectives* (pp. 3–25). Washington, DC: American Psychological Association.

Stets, J. E., & Turner, J. H. (2008). The sociology of emotions. In M. Lewis, J. M. Haviland-Jones, & L. Feldman Barret (Eds.), *Handbook of Emotions* (3rd ed., pp. 32–46). New York: Guilford Press.

Stewart, G. L., & Carson, K. P. (1997). Moving beyond the mechanistic model: An alternative approach to staffing for contemporary organizations. *Human Resource Management Review, 7*(2), 157–184. doi:10.1016/S1053-4822(97)90021-8

Stewart, P. (2010). Presidential laugh lines: Candidate display behavior and audience laughter in the 2008. *Politics and the Life Sciences, 29*(2), 55–72. doi:10.2990/29_2_55 PMID:21761981

Stewart, P., & Dowe, P. (2013). Interpreting President Barack Obama's Facial Displays of Emotion: Revisiting the Dartmouth Group. *Political Psychology, 34*(3), 369–385. doi:10.1111/pops.12004

Stewart, P., Waller, B., & Schubert, J. (2009). Presidential speech making style: Emotional response to micro-expressions of facial affect. *Motivation and Emotion, 33*(2), 125–135. doi:10.1007/s11031-009-9129-1

Steyn, G. M. (2002). The changing Principalship in South African schools. *Educare, 32*(1-2), 251–272.

Steyn, G. M. (2002a). The changing principalship in South African schools. *Educare, 31*, 251–274.

Steyn, G. M. (2002b). A theoretical analysis of teacher motivation and morale. *Educare, 31*, 82–101.

Stogdill, R. M. (1948). Personal factors associated with leadership: A survey of the literature. *The Journal of Psychology, 25*(1), 35–71. doi:10.1080/00223980.1948.9917362 PMID:18901913

Stoll, L., Bolam, R., McMahon, A., Wallace, M., & Thomas, S. (2006). Professional learning communities: A review of the literature. *Journal of Educational Change, 7*(4), 221–258. doi:10.1007/s10833-006-0001-8

Stoll, L., & Fink, D. (1999). *Para cambiar nuestras escuelas. Reunir la eficacia y la mejora*. Barcelona: Ed. Octaedro.

Stoll, L., & Temperley, J. (2009). Creative leadership: A challenge of our times. *School Leadership & Management, 29*(1), 65–78. doi:10.1080/13632430802646404

Stone, H., Parker, J. D. A., & Wood, L. A. (2005). *Report on the Ontario Principals' Council leadership study*. Retrieved February 11, 2012, from: www.eiconsrtium.org

Styf, M. (2012). *Pedagogisk leding för en pedagogisk verksamhet - Om den kommunala förskolans ledningsstruktur*. [Pedagogical leadership for educational activities]. Umeå: Umeå University.

Suchan, B., Wallner-Paschon, C., & Bergmüller, S. (2009). Profil der Lehrkräfte und der Schulen in der Sekundarstufe I. In J. Schmich & C. Schreiner (Eds.), *TALIS 2008. Schule als Lernumfeld und Arbeitsplatz. Erste Ergebnisse des internationalen Vergleichs* (pp. 16–30). Graz: Leykam.

Sullivan, D. G., & Masters, R. D. (1988). "Happy Warriors": Leaders' Facial Displays, Viewers' Emotions, and Political Support. *American Journal of Political Science, 32*(2), 345–368. doi:10.2307/2111127

Supreme Decree 0813, of March, 9, 2011 (Decreto Supremo 0813 de 9 de marzo de 2011). Retrieved February 14, 2014, from: http://goo.gl/JPFC17

Supreme Education Council. (2011). *Above 30% teachers not qualified*. Retrieved December 18, 2013 from: http://thepeninsulaqatar.com/index.php/news/qatar/163929/above-30pc-teachers-not-qualified

Supreme Education Council. (2012). *Independent Schools*. Retrieved November 13, 2013, from http://www.sec.gov.qa/En/pages/Glossary.aspx

Supreme Education Council. (2013a). *Education Institute*. Retrieved November 13, 2013, from http://www.sec.gov.qa/En/SECInstitutes/EducationInstitute/Pages/home.aspx

Supreme Education Council. (2013b). *Evaluation Institute*. Retrieved November 13, 2013, from http://www.sec.gov.qa/En/SECInstitutes/EvaluationInstitute/Pages/home.aspx

Surakka, V., & Hietanen, J. K. (1998). Facial and emotional reactions to Duchenne and non Duchenne smiles. *International Journal of Psychophysiology, 29*(1), 23–33. doi:10.1016/S0167-8760(97)00088-3 PMID:9641245

Sutton, R. I., & Rafaeli, A. (1988). Untangling the relationship between displayed emotions and organizational sales: The case of convenience stores. *Academy of Management Journal, 31*(3), 461–487. doi:10.2307/256456

Sweden in brief. (n.d.). Retrieved from http://sweden. se/?s=sweden+in+brief

Sy, T., Tram, S., & O'Hara, A. L. (2006). Relation of employee and manager emotional intelligence to job satisfaction and performance. *Journal of Vocational Behavior,* 68(3), 461–473. doi:10.1016/j.jvb.2005.10.003

Tajasom, A., & Ahmad, Z. (2011). Principals' leadership style and school climate: Teachers' perspective. *The International Journal of Leadership in Public Services,* 7(4), 314–333. doi:10.1108/17479881111194198

Taliadorou, N., & Pashiardis, P. (2014). *Leadership Radius and Teachers' Job Satisfaction: The role of Emotional Intelligence and Political Skill of Elementary School Principals.* (Unpublished doctoral dissertation). Open University of Cyprus, Cyprus.

Tallerico, M. (2000). Gaining access to the superintendency: Headhunting, gender and colour. *Educational Administration Quarterly,* 36(1), 18–43. doi:10.1177/00131610021968886

Tassinary, L. G., & Cacioppo, J. T. (1992). Unobservable Facial Actions and Emotion. *Psychological Science,* 3(1), 28–33. doi:10.1111/j.1467-9280.1992.tb00252.x

Taylor, K. C. (2007). *A study of principal's perceptions regarding time management.* (PhD thesis). Kansas State University, Lawrence, KS.

Taylor, G. J., Bagby, R. M., & Parker, J. D. A. (1997). *Disorders of affect regulation:Alexithymia in medical and psychiatric illness.* Cambridge, UK: Cambridge University Press. doi:10.1017/CBO9780511526831

Taylor, M., Goeke, J., Klein, E., Onore, C., & Geist, K. (2011). Changing leadership: Teachers lead the way for schools that learn. *Teaching and Teacher Education,* 27(5), 920–929. doi:10.1016/j.tate.2011.03.003

Taylor-Powell, E., & Renner, M. (2003). *University of Wisconsin Extension, Program Development and Evaluation: Analyzing qualitative data.* Retrieved December 18, 2013 from website: http://learningstore.uwex.edu/ assets/pdfs/g3658-12.pdf

Teacher Leadership Exploratory Consortium (TLEC). (2008). *Teacher leader model standards.* Retrieved January 27 from https://www.ets.org/s/education_topics/ teaching_quality/pdf/teacher_leader_model_sta dards.pdf

Teachers' Statute. Act number 14.473 (Ley 14.473 de 1958, Estatuto del Docente). Retrieved Februrary 14, 2014, from: http://goo.gl/YGLw2x

Teddlie, C., & Stringfield, S. (2007). A history of school effectiveness and improvement research in the USA focusing on the past quarter century. In T. Townsend (Ed.), International handbook of school effectiveness and improvement (pp. 131-166). Dordrecht, The Netherlands: Springer. doi:10.1007/978-1-4020-5747-2_8

Teddlie, C., & Reynolds, D. (2000). *The International Handbook of School Effectiveness and Research.* London: Falmer Press.

Teixidó, J. (2007). *Competencias para el ejercicio de la dirección escolar: Bases para un modelo de desarrollo profesional de directivos escolares basado en competencias.* Retrieved October 21, 2013, from: http://goo.gl/lwMC5

Teixidó, J. (2010). Hacia un cambio de modelo en la dirección escolar. Luces y sombras de un camino tortuoso. In *A. Manzanares (Ed.), Organizar y dirigir en la complejidad: Instituciones educativas en evolución* (pp. 81–118). Madrid: Wolters Kluwer.

Terzi, A. R. (2000). *Örgüt kültürü* [Organizational culture]. Ankara: Nobel.

The Independent. (2011, September 10). *UK has too many types of school: As PM backs free schools, senior figures complain of 'liquorice allsorts' system.* Retrieved from http://www.independent.co.uk/news/education/ education-news/experts-uk-has-too-many-types-of-school-2352191.html

Thirteen. (2014). *Workshop: Constructivism as a paradigm for teaching and learning.* Retrieved October, 08, 2013, from http://www.thirteen.org/edonline/concept-2class/constructivism/index.html

Thody, A., Papanaoum, Z., Johansson, O., & Pashiardis, P. (2007). School principal preparation in Europe. *International Journal of Educational Management*, *21*(1), 37–53. doi:10.1108/09513540710716812

Thompson, S., Hillman, K., Wernert, N., Schmid, M., Buckley, S., & Munene, A. (2012). *Highlights from TIMMS & PIRLS 2011 from Australia's perspective*. Melbourne, Australia: Australian Council for Education Research (ACER). Retrieved September 22, 2013, from http://www.acer.edu.au/documents/TIMSS-PIRLS_Australian-Highlights.pdf

Thomson, P. (2009). *School leadership: Heads on the block?* London: Routledge.

Thoonen, E., Sleegers, P., Peetma, T., & Oort, F. (2011). Can teachers motivate students to learn? *Educational Studies*, *37*(3), 345–360. doi:10.1080/03055698.2010.507008

Thornton, K. (2010). *The nature of distributed leadership and its development in online environments*. Retrieved September 24, 2010 from http://www.igionline.com/downloads/excerpts/34599.pdf

Timperley, H. (2011). Knowledge and the Leadership of Learning. *Leadership and Policy in Schools*, *10*(2), 145–170. doi:10.1080/15700763.2011.557519

Timperley, H. S. (2005). Distributed leadership: Developing theory from practice. *Journal of Curriculum Studies*, *37*(4), 395–420. doi:10.1080/00220270500038545

Todorov, A., Said, C. P., Engell, A. D., & Oosterhof, N. N. (2008). Understanding evaluation of faces on social dimensions. *Trends in Cognitive Sciences*, *12*(12), 455–460. doi:10.1016/j.tics.2008.10.001 PMID:18951830

Tomás, M. (2013). *El liderazgo educativo. Postgrado/Master en dirección de centros para la innovación educativa*. Barcelona: Universitat Autònoma de Barcelona.

Toumi, H. (2011). *Report: Around one third of teachers in Qatar lack proper qualification*. Doha, Qatar: Gulf. Retrieved November 13, 2013 from http://NewsDetailsTheTeachingProfession07June2006currentsofreformoverturntraditionsonteachertrainingand careers/GulfNews.com

Tovey, J., & Patty, A. (2013). OECD report finds Australian students falling behind. *The Sydney Morning Herald*. Retrieved February 20, 2014, from http://www.smh.com.au/national/education/oecd-report-finds-australian-students-falling-behind-20131203-2you0.html

Townsend, T. (Ed.). (2007). *International Handbook of School Effectiveness and Improvement*. Dordrecht, The Netherlands: Springer. doi:10.1007/978-1-4020-5747-2

Treadway, D. C., Duke, A. B., Ferris, G. R., Adams, G. L., & Thatcher, J. B. (2007). The moderating role of subordinate political skill on supervisors' impressions of subordinate ingratiation and ratings of subordinate interpersonal facilitation. *The Journal of Applied Psychology*, *92*(3), 848–855. doi:10.1037/0021-9010.92.3.848 PMID:17484564

Treadway, D. C., Hochwarter, W. A., Kacmar, C. J., & Ferris, G. R. (2005). Political will, political skill, and political behavior. *Journal of Organizational Behavior*, *26*(3), 229–245. doi:10.1002/job.310

Treadway, D. C., Hochwater, W. A., Ferris, G. R., Kacmar, C. J., Douglas, C., Ammeter, A. P., & Buckley, M. R. (2004). Leader political skill and employee reactions. *The Leadership Quarterly*, *15*(4), 493–513. doi:10.1016/j.leaqua.2004.05.004

Trichas, S. (2011). *The face of leadership: Perceiving leaders from facial expression*. (Unpublished doctoral dissertation). University of Portsmouth, Portsmouth, UK.

Trichas, S., & Schyns, B. (2012). The face of leadership: Perceiving leaders from facial expression. *The Leadership Quarterly*, *23*(3), 545–566. doi:10.1016/j.leaqua.2011.12.007

Tronick, E. Z. (1989). Emotions and emotional communication in infants. *The American Psychologist*, *44*(2), 112–119. doi:10.1037/0003-066X.44.2.112 PMID:2653124

Tsoukas, H., & Chia, R. (2002). On organizational becoming: Rethinking organizational change. *Organization Science*, *13*(5), 567-582. doi:0195-6744/2008/11404-0003$10.00

Turan, S. (2004). Educational administration as a balancing discipline in the human sciences between modernity and post-modernity. *Akdeniz University Journal of Faculty of Education, 1*(1), 1–8.

Turner, J. H., & Stets, J. E. (2005). *The Sociology of Emotions.* New York: Cambridge University Press. doi:10.1017/CBO9780511819612

Twenge, J. M., & Campbell, W. K. (2003). "Isn't It Fun to Get the Respect That We're Going to Deserve?" Narcissism, Social Rejection, and Aggression. *Personality and Social Psychology Bulletin, 29*(2), 261–272. doi:10.1177/0146167202239051 PMID:15272953

Ullman, A. (1997). *Rektorn. En studie av en titel och dess bärare.* (akad. avhandling) [A study of a title and its holders]. Stockholm: HLS förlag.

Vaccaro, I. G., Jansen, J. J., Van Den Bosch, F. A., & Volberda, H. W. (2012). Management innovation and leadership: The moderating role of organizational size. *Journal of Management Studies, 49*(1), 28–51. doi:10.1111/j.1467-6486.2010.00976.x

Van de Grift, W., & Houtven, A. A. M. (1999). Educational leadership and pupil achievement in primary education. *School Effectiveness and School Improvement, 10*(4), 373–389. doi:10.1076/sesi.10.4.373.3497

Van de Ven, A. H., & Poole, M. S. (1995). Explaining development and change in organizations. *Academy of Management Review, 20*(3), 510–540. doi:10.2307/258786

Van den Berg, R. (2002). Teachers' meanings regarding educational practice. *Review of Educational Research, 72*(4), 577–625. doi:10.3102/00346543072004577

Van den Berg, R., & Huberman, A. M. (1999). *Understanding and Preventing Teacher Burnout.* Cambridge, UK: Cambridge University Press. doi:10.1017/CBO9780511527784

Van den Berg, R., & Sleegers, P. J. C. (1996). Building innovative capacity and leadership. In K. Leithwood, J. Chapman, D. Corson, P. Hallinger, & A. Hart (Eds.), *International handbook of educational leadership and administration* (pp. 653–699). London, UK: Kluwer Academic. doi:10.1007/978-94-009-1573-2_20

van den Berg, R., Vandenberghe, R., & Sleegers, P. (1999). Management of innovations from a cultural-individual perspective. *School Effectiveness and School Improvement, 10*(3), 321–351. doi:10.1076/sesi.10.3.321.3500

Van der Mescht, H., & Tyala, Z. (2008). School principals' perceptions of team management: A multiple case-study of secondary schools. *South African Journal of Education, 28*(2), 221–239.

Van Deventer, I. (2003). Problem solving and decision-making skills. In I. Van Deventer & A.G. Kruger (Eds.), An educator's guide to school management skills. Pretoria: Van Schaik.

Van Es, E. A., & Sherin, M. G. (2002). Learning to notice: Scaffolding new teachers' interpretations of classroom interactions. *Journal of Technology and Teacher Education, 10*(4), 571–596.

Van Iddekinge, C. H., Ferris, G. R., & Heffner, T. S. (2009). Test of a multistage model of distal and proximal antecedents of leader performance. *Personnel Psychology, 62*(3), 463–495. doi:10.1111/j.1744-6570.2009.01145.x

Van Kleef, G. (2009). How emotions regulate social life: The emotions as social information (EASI) model. *Current Directions in Psychological Science, 18*(3), 184–188. doi:10.1111/j.1467-8721.2009.01633.x

van Manen, M. (1997). *Researching lived experience* (2nd ed.). London, Canada: Althouse Press.

van Manen, M. (2007). Phenomenology of Practice. *Phenomenology & Practice, 1*(1), 11–30.

Van Rooy, D. L., & Viswesvaran, C. (2004). Emotion intelligence: A meta-analytic investigation of predictive validity and nomological net. *Journal of Vocational Behavior, 65*(1), 71–95. doi:10.1016/S0001-8791(03)00076-9

Vanderlinde, R., & van Braak, J. (2010). The Gap between Educational Research and Practice: Views of Teachers, School Leaders, Intermediaries and Researchers. *British Educational Research Journal, 36*(2), 299–316. doi:10.1080/01411920902919257

Vargas, F. (2004). *40 preguntas sobre competencia laboral.* Montevideo: CINTERFOR/OIT.

Veliyath, R., & Sathian, K. (2005). Dealing with complexity in organizational control processes: Drawing lessons from the human brain. In K. A. Richardson (Ed.), Managing organizational complexity: Philosophy, theory, and application, (pp. 201-216). Greenwich, CT: Information Age Publishing.

Vera, D., & Crossan, M. (2004). Strategic leadership and organizational learning. *Academy of Management Review*, *29*(2), 222–240.

Vescio, V., Ross, D., & Adams, A. (2008). A review of research on the impact of professional learning communities on teaching practice and student learning. *Teaching and Teacher Education*, *24*(1), 80–91. doi:10.1016/j.tate.2007.01.004

Villa, A. (2003). *Elementos significativos de la LOCE con relación a las competencias directivas*. Retrieved October 21, 2013, from: http://goo.gl/Xrm6xC

Villarroel, D. (2014). *Competencias profesionales del Equipo Directivo del sector particular subvencionado chileno en contexto vulnerable*. (Unpublished doctoral dissertation). Universitat Autònoma de Barcelona, Barcelona, Spain.

Viñao, A. (2005). La dirección escolar: un análisis genealógico-cultural. In M. Fernández Enguita & M. Gutiérrez (Eds.), *Organización escolar, profesión docente y entorno comunitario* (pp. 35–81). Madrid: Akal.

Voulalas, Z., & Sharpe, F. (2005). Creating schools as learning communities: Obstacles and processes. *Journal of Educational Administration*, *43*(2/3), 187–208. doi:10.1108/09578230510586588

Walker, J. (2009). *Reorganizing Leaders' Time: Does it Create Better Schools for Students?* Paper presented to the Annual Conference of the National Council of Professors of Educational Administration. San Antonio, TX.

Wallace, M., & Pocklington, F. (1998). *Managing complex change: Large scale reorganisation of schools*. Paper presented at the Annual Meeting of the American Educational Research Association. San Diego, CA.

Wallace, J. (2010). Facing "reality": The emotional in school leadership programmes. *Journal of Educational Administration*, *48*(5), 595–610. doi:10.1108/09578231011067758

Walsh, S. (2006). Talking the talk of the TESOL classroom. *ELT Journal*, *60*(2), 133–141. doi:10.1093/elt/cci100

Waters, T., Marzano, R. J., & McNulty, B. (2003). *Balanced leadership: What 30 years of research tells us about the effect of leadership on student achievement*. Aurora, CO: Mid-Continent Research for Education and Learning.

Watkins, K. E., & Marsick, V. J. (1996). *In action: Creating the learning organization*. Alexandria, VA: American Society for Training and Development.

Watkins, K., & Marsick, V. (Eds.). (1993). *Sculpting the Learning Organization: Lessons in the art and science of systematic change*. Jossey-Bass.

Watson, D. (1989). Strangers' ratings of the five robust personality factors: Evidence of a surprising convergence with self-report. *Journal of Personality and Social Psychology*, *57*(1), 120–128. doi:10.1037/0022-3514.57.1.120

Webber, C. F., & Scott, S. (2010). Mapping principal preparation in Alberta, Canada. *Journal of Education and Humanities: Theory and Practice*, *1*, 75–96.

Webber, C. F., & Sherman, A. (2008). Researching leadership preparation from the inside: A Canadian perspective. In P. Sikes & A. Potts (Eds.), *Researching education from the inside: Investigations from within* (pp. 64–79). Oxon, UK: Routledge.

Weick, K. E. (1998). Improvisation as a mindset for organizational analysis. *Organization Science, 9*(5), 543-555. doi:1047-7039/98/0905/0543/$05.00

Weick, K. E., & Quinn, R. E. (1999). Organizational change and development. *Annual Review of Psychology, 50*(1), 361-386. doi:0084-6570/99/0201-0361$08.00

Weick, K. E. (1979). *The social psychology of organizing*. Reading, MA: Addison-Wesley.

Weick, K. E. (1995). *Sensemaking in organizations*. Thousand Oaks, CA: Sage.

Weick, K. E. (2000). Emergent change as a universal in organizations. In M. Beer & N. Nohria (Eds.), *Breaking the code of change* (pp. 223–241). Boston, MA: Harvard Business School Press.

Weller, L. D., & Weller, S. J. (1997). Quality learning organizations and continuous improvement: Implementing the concept. *NASSP Bulletin, 81*(591), 62–70. doi:10.1177/019263659708159111

Wells, G. (2010). Dialogue, inquiry and the construction of learning communities. In B. Lingard, J. Nixon, & S. Ranson (Eds.), *Transforming learning in schools and communities* (pp. 236–256). London: Continuum.

Westerlaken, K. M., & Woods, P. R. (2013). The relationship between psychopathy and the Full Range Leadership Model. *Personality and Individual Differences, 54*(1), 41–46. doi:10.1016/j.paid.2012.08.026

Whitaker, K. S. (1997). Developing teacher leadership and the management team concept: A case study. *Teacher Educator, 33*(1), 1–16. doi:10.1080/08878739709555154

Wikeley, F. (1998). Dissemination of Research as a Tool for School Improvement? *School Leadership & Management, 18*(1), 59–73. doi:10.1080/13632439869772

Wild, B., Erb, M., & Bartels, M. (2001). Are emotions contagious? Evoked emotions while viewing emotionally expressive faces: Quality, quantity, time course and gender differences. *Psychiatry Research, 102*(2), 109–124. doi:10.1016/S0165-1781(01)00225-6 PMID:11408051

Wildy, H., Clarke, S. R. P., & Slater, C. (2007). International perspectives of principal preparation: How does Australia fare? Leading and Managing Special Edition, 13(2), 1-14.

Wildy, H., & Clarke, S. (2008). Charting an arid landscape: The preparation of novice principals in Western Australia. *School Leadership & Management, 28*(5), 469–487. doi:10.1080/13632430802500106

Wildy, H., & Clarke, S. (2009). Using cognitive interviews to pilot an international survey of principal preparation: A Western Australian perspective. *Educational Assessment, Evaluation and Accountability, 21*(2), 105–117. doi:10.1007/s11092-009-9073-3

Wildy, H., Clarke, S., Styles, I., & Beycioglu, K. (2010). Preparing novice principals in Australia and Turkey: How similar are their needs? *Educational Assessment, Evaluation and Accountability, 22*(4), 307–326. doi:10.1007/s11092-010-9106-y

Wildy, H., & Louden, W. (2000). School restructuring and the dilemmas of principals' work. *Educational Management and Administration, 28*(3), 173–184. doi:10.1177/0263211X000282006

Williams, D.A., & Coles, L. (2003, June). *The Use of Research Information by Teachers: information literacy, access and attitudes.* A report for the Economic and Social Research Council.

Williams, H. W. (2008). Characteristics that distinguish outstanding urban principals: Emotional intelligence, social intelligence and environmental adaptation. *Journal of Management Development, 27*(1), 36–54. doi:10.1108/02621710810840758

Willis, J. (2007). *Foundations of Qualitative Research: Interpretive and Critical Approaches.* Thousand Oaks, CA: Sage Publications.

Wilson, A. G. (2011). *Understanding the cultivation of teacher leadership in professional learning communities* (Doctoral dissertation). Retrieved from ProQuest Dissertations and Thesis database. (UMI No. 3465657)

Winkielman, P., & Berridge, K. (2003). Irrational wanting and subrational liking: How rudimentary motivational and affective processes shape preferences and choices. *Political Psychology, 24*(4), 657–680. doi:10.1046/j.1467-9221.2003.00346.x

Winkielman, P., & Berridge, K. (2004). Unconscious Emotion. *Current Directions in Psychological Science, 13*, 120–123. doi:10.1111/j.0963-7214.2004.00288.x

Winkielman, P., Berridge, K. C., & Wilbarger, J. L. (2005). Unconscious Affective Reactions to Masked Happy Versus Angry Faces Influence Consumption Behavior and Judgments of Value. *Personality and Social Psychology Bulletin, 31*(1), 121–135. doi:10.1177/0146167204271309 PMID:15574667

Wise, C., Bradshaw, P., & Cartwright, M. (2012). *Leading Professional Practice in Education.* New York: Sage.

Witziers, B., Bosker, R. J., & Kruger, M. L. (2003). Educational leadership and student achievement: The elusive search for an association. *Educational Administration Quarterly, 39*(3), 398–425. doi:10.1177/0013161X03253411

Wolff, S.B. (2005). *Emotional Competence Inventory (ECI): Technical Manual*. Hay Group, McClelland Center for research and Innovation.

Wonderlic, E. F. (2003). Wonderlic Personnel Quicktest (WPT-Q) User's Guide. Libertyville, IL: EF Wonderlic.

Wong, C. S., & Law, K. S. (2002). The effects of leader and follower emotional intelligence on performance and attitude: An exploratory study. *The Leadership Quarterly, 13*(3), 243–274. doi:10.1016/S1048-9843(02)00099-1

Wong, C. S., Law, K. S., & Wong, P. M. (2004). Development and validation of a forced choice emotional intelligence measure for Chinese respondents in Hong Kong. *Asia Pacific Journal of Management, 21*(4), 535–559. doi:10.1023/B:APJM.0000048717.31261.d0

Woodger, M. J. (2003). Recollections of David o. MclZay's 'The Religious Educator'. *Educational Practices, 4*, 25–39.

Wood, J. L., Schmidtke, J. M., & Decker, D. L. (2007). Lying on Job Applications: The Effects of Job Relevance, Commission, and Human Resource Management Experience. *Journal of Business and Psychology, 22*(1), 1–9. doi:10.1007/s10869-007-9048-7

Woods, P. A., & Gronn, P. (2009). Nurturing Democracy: The contribution of distributed leadership to a democratic organisational landscape. *Educational Management Administration & Leadership, 37*(4), 430–451. doi:10.1177/1741143209334597

Worrall, N. (2004). Trying to Build a Research Culture in a School: Trying to find the right questions to ask. *Teacher Development, 8*(2-3), 137–148. doi:10.1080/13664530400200020241

Wright, A. L., & Zammuto, R. F. (2013). Wielding the willow: Processes of institutional change in English county cricket. *Academy of Management Journal, 56*(1), 308–330. doi:10.5465/amj.2010.0656

Wright, P., Horn, S., & Sanders, W. (1997). Teacher and classroom context effects on student achievement: Implications for teacher evaluation. *Journal of Personnel Evaluation in Education, 11*(1), 57–67. doi:10.1023/A:1007999204543

Wrigley, T. (2006). *Another school is possible*. New York, NY: Trentham Books.

Wu, M. (2009). *Interpreting NAPLAN results for the layperson*. Retrieved October 10, 2013, from http://www.edmeasurement.com.au/_publications/margaret/NAPLAN_for_lay_person.pdf

Xiaofeng, S. L. (2008). Teachers' job satisfaction: Analyses of the Teacher Follow-up Survey in the United States for 2000–2001. *Teaching and Teacher Education, 24*(5), 1173–1184. doi:10.1016/j.tate.2006.11.010

Yan, W., & Enrich, L. C. (2009). Principal preparation and training: A look at China and its issues. *International Journal of Educational Management, 23*(1), 51–64. doi:10.1108/09513540910926420

Yiğit, Y., Doğan, S., & Uğurlu, C. T. (2013). Öğretmenlerin öğretmen liderliği davranışlarına ilişkin görüşleri[Teachers' views on teacher leadership behavior]. *Cumhuriyet International Journal of Education, 2*(2), 93–105.

Yin, R. K. (2009). *Case study research: Design and methods* (4th ed.). Thousand Oaks, CA: Sage.

Yokan, L. (2000). School Tracking and Student Violence. In D. K. Wysocki (Ed.), Readings in Social Research Methods (pp. 23-32). Belmont, CA: Thomson Higher Education.

York-Barr, J., & Duke, K. (2004). What do we know about teacher leadership? Findings from two decades of scholarship. *Review of Educational Research, 74*(3), 255–316. doi:10.3102/00346543074003255

Youngblood, M. (1997). *Life at the edge of chaos*. Dallas, TX: Perceval Publishing.

Young, M. D., & Brewer, C. (2008). Fear and the preparation of school leaders: The role of ambiguity, anxiety, and power in meaning making. *Educational Policy, 22*(1), 106–129. doi:10.1177/0895904807311299

Yukl, G. (2011). Contingency theories of effective leadership. In A. Bryman, D. Collinson, K. Grint, B. Jackson, & M. Uhl-Bien (Eds.), *Sage Handbook of Leadership* (pp. 286-298). Thousand Oaks, CA: Sage Publications.

Zaccaro, S. J., Foti, R. J., & Kenny, D. A. (1991). Self-monitoring and trait-based variance in leadership: An investigation of leader flexibility across multiple group situations. *The Journal of Applied Psychology*, *76*(2), 308–315. doi:10.1037/0021-9010.76.2.308

Zaccaro, S. J., Kemp, C., & Bader, P. (2004). Leader traits and attributes. In J. Antonakis, A. T. Cianciolo, & R. J. Sternberg (Eds.), *The Nature of Leadership* (pp. 101–124). Thousand Oaks, CA: Sage.

Zebrowitz, L. A., & Montepare, J. M. (2008). Social Psychological Face Perception: Why Appearance Matters. *Social and Personality Psychology Compass*, *2*(3), 1497–1517. doi:10.1111/j.1751-9004.2008.00109.x PMID:20107613

Zeichner, K. (2003). Teacher research as professional development for p-12 educators in the U.S. *Educational Action Research*, *11*(2), 301–325. doi:10.1080/09650790300200211

Zeidner, M., Matthews, G., & Roberts, R. D. (2004). Emotional Intelligence in the workplace: A critical review. *Applied Psychology*, *53*(3), 371–399. doi:10.1111/j.1464-0597.2004.00176.x

Zeidner, M., Roberts, R. D., & Matthews, G. (2008). The science of emotional intelligence: Current consensus and controversies. *European Psychologist*, *13*(1), 64–78. doi:10.1027/1016-9040.13.1.64

Zembylas, M. (2009). The politics of emotions in education: affective economies, ambivalence and transformation. In E. Samier & M. Schmidt (Eds.), *Emotional Dimensions of Educational Administration and Leadership* (pp. 97–108). New York, NY: Routledge.

Zembylas, M., & Papanastasiou, E. (2004). Job Satisfaction among School Teachers in Cyprus. *Journal of Educational Administration*, *42*(3), 357–374. doi:10.1108/09578230410534676

Zhang, A. Y., Tsui, A. S., & Wang, D. X. (2011). Leadership behaviors and group creativity in Chinese organizations: The role of group processes. *The Leadership Quarterly*, *22*(5), 851–862. doi:10.1016/j.leaqua.2011.07.007

Zhang, X., & Bartol, K. M. (2010). Linking empowering leadership and employee creativity: The influence of psychological empowerment, intrinsic motivation, and creative process engagement. *Academy of Management Journal*, *53*(1), 107–128. doi:10.5465/AMJ.2010.48037118

Zietsma, C., & Lawrence, T. B. (2010). Institutional work in the transformation of an organizational field: The interplay of boundary work and practice work. *Administrative Science Quarterly*, *55*(2), 189–221. doi:10.2189/asqu.2010.55.2.189

Zigarelli, M. A. (1996). An empirical test of conclusions from effective schools Research. *The Journal of Educational Research*, *90*(2), 103–109. doi:10.1080/00220671.1996.9944451

Zinn, L. F. (1997). *Supports and barriers to teacher leadership. Reports of teacher leaders.* Paper presented in the Annual Meeting of American Educational Research Association. Chicago, IL.

About the Contributors

Kadir Beycioglu, PhD, is an associate professor of Educational Administration at Dokuz Eylul University Buca Faculty of Education in the Department of Educational Sciences, İzmir, Turkey. His study topics are mainly on educational change, school development, and educational leadership. He is also interested in the ethical use of ICT in education. He is a member of the International Study of Principal Preparation (ISPP) project and International School Leadership Development Network – Social Justice Leadership Strand by BELMAS and UCEA. He has published several articles in leading international journals including *Teaching and Teacher Education, Computers and Education, Educational Assessment, Evaluation and Accountability, Journal of Management Development, Journal of School Public Relations,* and *KEDI Journal of Educational Policy*. He has also acted as guest editor for some international journals and books and has published chapters in books. Dr. Beycioglu is the founding editor of the *International Journal of Cyber Ethics in Education* (IGI) and has been serving as a member of the editorial board or as reviewer for some leading journals such as *Journal of Mixed Methods Research* (SAGE), *Learning and Individual Differences* (Elsevier), *Journal of Research on Technology in Education* (ISTE), *International Journal of Leadership in Education: Theory & Practice* (Taylor & Francis), *Computers & Education* (Elsevier), *International Journal of Educational Development* (Elsevier), *International Journal of Teacher Leadership,* and *the Qualitative Report*. He has been a member of the European Educational Research Association, British Educational Leadership, Management & Administration Society, and the Commonwealth Council for Educational Administration and Management.

Petros Pashiardis is a Professor of Educational Leadership and the Academic Coordinator of the "Educational Studies" Program with the Open University of Cyprus. Petros studied Educational Administration at the University of Texas at Austin as a Fulbright Scholar. He has also worked or lectured in many countries including Great Britain, India, New Zealand, Greece, Germany, South Africa, Switzerland, Australia, Sweden, and the United States. In 2008, he co-edited the *International Handbook on the Preparation and Development of School Leaders*, together with Jacky Lumby and Gary Crow. For the period 2004-2008, Professor Pashiardis was President of the Commonwealth Council for Educational Administration and Management. He is now on the Board of Governors of the Commonwealth Foundation. During his travels, he has collaborated extensively with CSOs from all these countries in the areas of School Leadership and Educational Policy training school leaders and creating school leadership organizations in various countries around the commonwealth in an effort to contribute towards the attainment of MDGs, as they relate to improving equality of opportunity for Education for All. His latest book in English was published by Springer Publications in 2014, under the title *Modeling School Leadership Across Europe: In Search of New Frontiers*.

* * *

Panayiotis Antoniou is a Lecturer in Educational Leadership and Evaluation and the coordinator of the MPhil *Perspectives on Education* at the Faculty of Education, University of Cambridge. He is also a member of the Cambridge Leadership for Learning Network (LfL) and an Official Fellow of Darwin College. His research interests are in school leadership, educational effectiveness and improvement at the teacher, school and system levels. He is also interested in teacher professional development and has been involved in research projects related with human resource management in education and teacher and school evaluation. He is the coordinator and member of the research panel for several research projects funded by international institutions and organizations such as the ICSEI, ESF, European Parliament, etc. He has presented and published his work extensively in international conferences and peer-reviewed journals.

Aleix Barrera-Corominas, BA in Pedagogy (UAB), Diploma in Labour Relations (UAB), BS in Labour Science (Open University of Catalonia), and MA in Human Resource Management (Open University La Salle), since 2007, works as Research Technician in the Department of Applied Pedagogy at UAB, and he is member of EDO (SGR2005-, SGR2009-397), and of RedAGE. At present, he is adjunct professor at the same Department (since 2012) and he is PhD candidate in Quality of Educational Innovation in UAB, studying the impact evaluation of professional communities of practice in organizations. His main research interests emphasize on evaluation of training (transference and impact), communities of practices, and organization development. Likewise, he has been member of researches on knowledge creation and management, educational cooperation, leadership, academic access and success, vulnerable groups, and feedforward, among others.

Sabine Bergner is a research assistant at the Department of Leadership and Entrepreneurship at Graz University (Austria). She specialises in personality, leadership, personnel selection, and the development of psychometric instruments in leadership. More recent research includes the relationship between leadership behaviour and neurophysiological activities. Sabine Bergner studied Psychology at the University of Graz, followed by a PhD in Psychology and a Bachelor in English Literature from the University of Graz. At the Department of Leadership and Entrepreneurship, she is in charge of a wide variety of research projects regarding individual differences in leadership. She is a chartered organisational psychologist, teaches at different universities, and designs psychometric tools for leadership selection and development. Her research is published in international journals and presented in worldwide conferences. Sabine Bergner is a member of the European Association of Work and Organizational Psychology, the Austrian Psychological Society, and the German Psychological Society.

Diego Castro is a Professor in Department of Applied Pedagogy, Science Education Faculty, Universitat Autònoma de Barcelona. Expert in social work and holds a degree in Social Education, a BA in Pedagogy, and a Master's in Human Resource Management, as well as a PhD in Science of Education. He is specialised in leadership and management environments in educational institutions, one of his main research interests besides management and university governance and the process of innovation and improvement. He is also a counsellor and lecturer in various universities and centres in Spain and Latin America.

Miren Fernández-De-Álava, BA in Translation and Interpretation (French/English), Certificate in Pedagogic Aptitude in French Language, and Master in Educational Research from UAB; Scholarship holder of the Department of Education, Universities and Research of the Basque Government; and, at present, pre-doctoral trainee research staff during the period 2011-2015 (432-01-2/2011); has worded in ESADE in the Direction of Educational Innovation and Academic Quality (DIPQA, by its Catalan acronym), and now is member of EDO (SGR2005-, SGR2009-397) and of RedAGE, and PhD candidate in Education in the Department of Applied Pedagogy at UAB. Her main research interests emphasize informal learning in communities of practice of Public Administration, and how to recognize and evaluate it. Likewise, she has been member of researches on knowledge creation and management, educational cooperation, leadership, academic access and success, and vulnerable groups, among others.

Joaquín Gairín, primary school teacher, graduate degree in social work, psychologist and pedagogue from Universitat Autònoma de Barcelona (UAB), Professor of Didactics and of Educational Management at UAB, has wide-ranging teaching and institutional experience. He has been head of an educational center, faculty dean, university department head, and head of the Institute of Education (ICE, by its Spanish and Catalan acronym) and board member of the education and training cluster, at and from UAB. International consultant, he takes part in school reform programs in Spain and Latin America, he runs the Organizational Development Team (EDO, by its Spanish and Catalan acronym)—consolidated by the Autonomous Government of Catalonia (SGR2005-, SGR2009-397)—and the Support Network for Education Management in Ibero-America (RedAGE, by its Spanish and Catalan acronym), and he leads projects on social and educational development. His main research interests emphasize on organisational development, educational change processes, leadership, evaluation of programmes and institutions, ICT in training, and impact evaluation, among others.

Bennie Grobler was a teacher of Physical Science and secondary school principal from 1969 to 1989 when he joined the Rand Afrikaans University as Senior Lecturer in the Department of Educational Management. He became an associate professor in 2000 and a professor in 2003 in the Department of Education Leadership and Management. In 2005 RAU became the University of Johannesburg where he was appointed as professor and Head of the Department of Education Leadership and Management. He specializes in quantitative research and retired from UJ at the end of 2008 but remained in part-time service until the end of 2012. He is still actively involved with quantitative data analysis and serves as promoter and supervisor for postgraduate students.

Maj-Lis Hörnqvist is an associate professor in pedagogy at Centre for Principal Development at Umeå University. She received her PhD in Teaching and Learning from Luleå University of Technology. She has a background as a teacher in secondary school and as a special education teacher in upper secondary school. She has also been head of the Teacher Education Program at Luleå University of Technology and Deputy Rector at Umeå School of Education. She teaches primarily in the Principal Training Program, and is also the supervisor of the Master's degree program in educational leadership. Her research interests are within the area of leadership for learning, with a focus on principals.

Georgeta Ion, degree in Psychology and Educational Sciences, MD in Management and Evaluation in Education by University of Bucharest, and PhD in Educational Sciences by University of Barcelona. Her research topics are, among others: study of higher education institutions, relationship between educational research and educational policy and practices. She has been involved in innovative projects at higher education level and researched about competences-based assessment and research-based education. She has been involved in consultancy activity for the public administration in Romania and for several research and development projects at European level. Currently, she is lecturer in pedagogy and educational organizations at the Universitat Autonoma de Barcelona.

Anna Kanape-Willingshofer works as a research assistant at the Department of Education and Educational Psychology at Linz University (Austria). Her research interests include personality, leadership, educational leadership, as well as leadership motivation and leadership aspirations in educational contexts. Anna Kanape-Willingshofer studied Psychology and English at the University of Graz, where she also worked at the Department of Personality Psychology. Her PhD at Linz University (supervisor: Herbert Altrichter) focuses on the influence of personal and situational factors on teachers' aspirations for school principalship in Austria. At Linz University, she is responsible for psychological courses for students in teaching programs, as well as for the evaluation of a Master's program on School Management and for courses on Research Methods in this Master's program. She has presented her work at various international (educational as well as psychological) conferences.

Ali Çağatay Kılınç received his Bachelor Degree from Gazi University Gazi Faculty of Education Department of English Language Teaching. He earned his MA in 2010 and PhD in 2013 from Gazi University Institute of Educational Sciences. He worked as an English teacher in Tosya Namık Kemal Primary School (2006-2011) and as a research assistant in Gazi University Gazi Faculty of Education Department of Educational Sciences (2011-2013). He is currently employed as an Assistant Professor in Karabuk University, Faculty of Letters, Department of Educational Sciences. His research interests are educational leadership, teacher professionalism, teacher motivation, organizational climate and culture, organizational commitment, and school capacity.

Yasar Kondakci, PhD, is an Associate Professor in Educational Administration and Planning at the Middle East Technical University in the Department of Educational Science. He gained his PhD from Ghent University, Belgium, in the field of management and organization. His research focuses mainly on organizational change, school effectiveness and improvement, and higher education. His research has been published in several internal journals including *Higher Education, Journal of Educational Administration*, and *Educational Management Administration and Leadership*. His teaching focuses on educational administration, organizational change and development in schools, strategic planning in educational organization, and research methods in education. He acted as a council member in European Educational Research Association in 2008-2009.

Andreas Kythreotis is a Visiting Lecturer in Educational Management at the Postgraduate Programme of Educational Leadership and Management, Cyprus International Institute of Management. He also works in primary education in Cyprus. His studies include undergraduate studies at the Pedagogical Academy of Cyprus (Teacher's Diploma, 1986) and at the University of Patra, Greece (BA in Primary

Education, 1996), and graduate studies at the University of Bath, UK (MA in Educational Management, 1997) and at the University of Cyprus (PhD in Educational Management, 2006). His research interests are in principal leadership and school culture and their effects on school effectiveness and teacher job satisfaction. He has presented his work in international conferences and journals.

Angeliki Lazaridou is an Assistant Professor in the area of Organization and Administration of Education in the Department of Primary Education, at the University of Thessaly. She teaches courses in educational administration and leadership, both at the undergraduate and graduate levels. Dr. Lazaridou has studied general pedagogic at the University of Athens, has a diploma in Special Education-Early Intervention from the University of Athens, a Master's degree in Early Childhood/Special Education from the University of Alberta, Canada, and a Doctoral degree in Educational Administration and Leadership from the same university. Her teaching and research interests focus on leadership, with an emphasis on issues of principalship, ethics and values, gender, and complexity theories.

Raj Mestry, BComm (Hons), DEd, is a Professor at the University of Johannesburg, South Africa. He is the former Head of Department in the Department of Education Leadership and Management at the University of Johannesburg and is a rated National Research Foundation (NRF) researcher. He has published numerous articles in various national and international journals and has co-authored four books on financial and human resource management. He lectures in the BEd (Hons) and Master's level in Human Resource Management in Education and School Financial Management, and serves on the executive of the Education Association of South Africa.

Paul Miller, PhD, is Reader in Education at Brunel University. He is formerly Professor of Educational Leadership & Management at the University of Technology, Jamaica. He is well published in the field of Educational/School Leadership and is the editor of the book, *School Leadership in the Caribbean: Perceptions, Practices, Paradigms* (Symposium Books, 2013). Paul founded the Institute for Educational Administration & Leadership-Jamaica (IEAL-J) and is one of its directors. He is also a Board Member of the Commonwealth Council for Educational Administration & Management (CCEAM). Paul has active memberships in the London Centre for Leadership in Learning and the British Educational Leadership, Management, and Administration Society (BELMAS).

Suraiya R. Naicker was a primary school educator in South Africa for 16 years, 9 of which were spent in a school leadership and management position. She was awarded a scholarship from the University of Johannesburg to complete an MEd degree in Educational Leadership and Management and recently completed her PhD after being awarded a further scholarship from the same university. She lectures in educational leadership and management at the University of Johannesburg. Her research areas in educational leadership include distributive leadership and system-wide change.

Taliadorou Nikoletta is a schoolteacher of Public Primary School in Cyprus since 2004. She studied Human and Social Science (BSc) and Educational Administration (MSc) at the University of Theassalia, Greece. Since 2014, she is a holder of a PhD degree on Educational Leadership and Policy of the Open University of Cyprus. Her Doctoral dissertation has the following title, "Exercising Leadership and Teachers' Job Satisfaction: Examine the Role of Emotional Intelligence and Political Skill of Primary School

Principals." She presented her Doctoral proposal at the ICSEI Congress 2011 an International Congress "School Effectiveness and Improvement Linking Research, Policy and Practice to Promote Quality in Education" at Limassol, Cyprus, and the results of her Doctoral research at the CCEAM 2012 Conference "New Trends, New Challenges in Educational Leadership and Governance" at Limassol, Cyprus.

Shirley O'Neill is an Associate Professor in the School of Linguistics, Adult and Specialist Education at the University of Southern Queensland, Australia. She is the Associate Director, Literacy Pedagogies and Learning in the Leadership Research International (LRI) group and School Coordinator of Applied Linguistics. Her research and teaching relates to school improvement and particularly literacy learning and assessment, English as a second/foreign language, and is an advocate for service learning in pre-service teacher education and international language exchange. She has a special interest in reading and writing, and the analysis of classroom dialogue in exploring effective pedagogy and is the co-president of the International Society for Leadership in Pedagogies and Learning (isIPAL).

Servet Özdemir earned his Bachelor Degree from Department of Educational Administration and Planning, College of Educational Sciences, Ankara University in 1983. He received his MA from Department of Educational Administration and Planning, Institute of Social Sciences, Ankara University in 1986 and his PhD from Department of Educational Administration and Planning, Institute of Social Sciences, Selçuk University in 1989. He worked for Ministry of National Education as General Director of Higher Education (2002-2003), General Director of Primary Education (2003-2006), and President of National Education Academy (2005-2006). His research areas are educational change and innovation, organizational development, project management, conflict management, centralized and decentralized management, leadership, teacher training, and motivation. He has presented hundreds of seminars on his research areas. He is still working as a full professor in Gazi University, Gazi Faculty of Education, Department of Educational Sciences.

Michael H. Romanowski is a Professor and the Coordinator of the Master of Educational Leadership Program in the College of Education at Qatar University in Doha, Qatar. He earned his PhD from Miami University and brings to the classroom over 25 years of diverse educational experiences including academic positions in the USA, China, and currently, Qatar. He has presented his research at conferences throughout the world and has authored numerous publications in scholarly book and journals. Professor Romanowski teaches graduate courses in leadership, curriculum, and research methodologies, and continues to research and write in the areas of educational reform, leadership, curriculum, and other educational and cultural issues.

Esther Salat, Pedagogue and Social Educator, has been responsible for the educational policies of the City Council of Sant Cugat del Vallès since 2011. She holds an MA in Local Government, a Degree in Social and Educational Services Management, and a Degree in Management and Local Government. She specializes in policies that affect children and youth, and she has been involved in numerous Catalan educational organizations. She is a professor in the Department of Applied Pedagogy, part of the Science Education Faculty, at the Universitat Autònoma de Barcelona. She is currently leading projects for social and educational development.

Jasmin-Olga Sarafidou is a Professor of Research Methodology at the Department of Primary Education, University of Thessaly, Greece, and Director of the Postgraduate Program on Educational Organization and Management. Previously, she worked at the Research Institute of Child Health, Athens, as head of the Statistics and Documentation Section, from 1980 to 2007. She studied Mathematics at the University of Patras, Greece, and did her MSc on Applied Statistics at the University of Oxford, UK, as a British Council scholar. She holds a PhD from the School of Health Sciences, University of Crete. She has published many articles in scientific journals and is the author of one book and co-author of another, in Greek.

Marina Tomàs is a Primary Teacher, Pedagogue, and Doctor in Philosophy and Education Science at the University of Barcelona (UB). She teaches in the Area of Didactics and School Organisation in the Department of Applied Pedagogy of the Universitat Autònoma de Barcelona. She has led many research projects (I+D) on organisational culture in the university and change processes. She has also led other projects on leadership, participation, decision-making, and gender at the university. She has authored several publications, including over ten books and numerous articles, some of which were published in prestigious international journals. She has worked on several occasions for the Catalan educational administration on school autonomy and management.

Savvas Trichas got his BA in Primary Education from University of Cyprus, his MA in Education: International Management and Policy Studies from University of Birmingham, and his PhD in Human Resources Marketing and Management from University of Portsmouth. His research interests focus on nonverbal communication and leadership. Specifically, in his latest studies, he investigated facial expression in the context of leadership and he is a certified coder of facial expressions. Additionally, he has several publications in scientific journals (e.g., *The Leadership Quarterly*) and has done numerous seminars which include micro-expressions, nonverbal communication in organizations, and deception of detection, for several universities and organizations, such as University of Cyprus, University of Durham, and Marfin Laiki Bank. Dr. Savvas Trichas is currently working as a full time primary education teacher and part-time lecturer at the Open University of Cyprus.

Helen Wildy is Winthrop Professor and Dean of the Faculty of Education at The University of Western Australia. Her background as a student of a very small rural primary school in Western Australia underpins her commitment to education, particularly the leadership of small schools. As a student in the Faculty of Education of UWA, she completed a Master's degree in Education in 1990 and PhD in 1998. She currently conducts research and supervises Doctoral and Master's students in a range of leadership and school improvement topics, particularly related to the use of assessment data by school leaders. She has been chief investigator or co-chief investigator in research projects worth more than $7m since 2000. For the past decade, she has worked with school sectors in Western Australia on projects to present national assessment data in formats that are accessible to school leaders and teachers. She is Director of Performance Indicators for Primary Schools (PIPS) Australia, a literacy and numeracy assessment program for students entering school, used by over 600 schools in all Australian states and territories. Her most recent ARC funded research projects involved the development of instruments to measure performance: one related to the selection of school principals, another to measure the outcomes of treatment for young adolescents in residential rehabilitation programs. She is a founding member of the International Study of Principal Preparation (ISPP) project.

Efstathios Xafakos is a primary school teacher and a PhD student in Organization and Administration of Education at the Department of Primary Education, University of Thessaly, Greece. He studied at the Pedagogical department of the Aristotle University of Thessaloniki, Greece, and did his MSc on Organization and Administration of Education at the University of Thessaly, Greece.

Merve Zayim is a PhD student in Educational Administration and Planning at The Middle East Technical University in the Department of Educational Sciences. She received her MSc degree in 2010 from The Middle East Technical University in the same field. She has been working as a research assistant at METU for five years. She currently works on the projects about school change and assists the Master's-level research methods course. She has published several papers in national and international journals and presented papers at some leading congresses. Her research interests include organizational change, attitudes towards change, emotions toward change, and trust.

Index